AT GETTYSBURG

The Controversial Civil War General Who Committed
Murder, Abandoned Little Round Top, and
Declared Himself the Hero of Gettysburg

James A. Hessler

SB

Savas Beatie
New York and California

Cataloging-in-Publication Data is available from the Library of Congress.

ISBN 978-1-932714-84-5

05 04 03 02 01   5 4 3 2 1
First paperback edition, first printing

SB

Published by
Savas Beatie LLC
521 Fifth Avenue, Suite 1700
New York, NY 10175
Phone: 610-853-9131

Editorial Offices:

Savas Beatie LLC
P.O. Box 4527
El Dorado Hills, CA 95762
Phone: 916-941-6896
(E-mail) editorial@savasbeatie.com

Savas Beatie titles are available at special discounts for bulk purchases in the United States by corporations, institutions, and other organizations. For more details, please contact Special Sales, P.O. Box 4527, El Dorado Hills, CA 95762, or you may e-mail us at sales@savasbeatie.com, or visit our website at www.savasbeatie.com for additional information.

For Michele, Alex, and Aimee

and in memory of my parents, Donald and Kathleen Hessler

Major General Daniel Edgar Sickles

Contents

Contents (continued)

———————————

Photos and Illustrations

Photos and illustrations have been distributed throughout
the book for the convenience of the reader.

Cartography

Preface

It seems to be a cliché for authors to begin Gettysburg books by apologizing for writing yet another. Fortunately, this is not a recent development. As early as 1902, Lieutenant Colonel William A. Fox wrote in the New York Monuments Commission's battle report: "Another history of Gettysburg may seem superfluous and presumptuous."[1] Fox's history of the battle was written under the auspices of Gettysburg's most influential participant: Daniel Edgar Sickles.

Major General Sickles is known to students of the battle for his controversial and unauthorized advance to the Peach Orchard on July 2, 1863, seemingly in defiance of Major General George Meade's orders. Sickles' participation in the battle lasted barely twenty-four hours, yet no single action dictated the flow of the second day's combat (and much of the third day) more than his controversial advance. Common historical place names such as Devil's Den, the Wheatfield, and the Peach Orchard might not exist today were it not for Sickles. One of Gettysburg's most mythical moments, the last-minute defense of Little Round Top, would almost certainly have occurred quite differently were it not for Sickles. Whether the battle's outcome would have been any different we will never know, but the history that occurred surely would have been significantly altered. As a result of his actions, no participant with the possible exception of James Longstreet has generated more controversy and hostility in Gettysburg's "history."

Sickles' importance to Gettysburg transcends his one day of battle. He is reviled by many Gettysburg students for his post-battle participation in attempts to remove George Meade from command of the Army of the Potomac. The feud between Sickles, Meade, and their partisans are as much a part of Gettysburg's history as the battle itself, and they added a considerable quantity of primary material (often inaccurate and self-serving) to the Gettysburg historical record. Sickles would return to Gettysburg many times during his remaining fifty years of life. These visits provided him numerous opportunities to give speeches and talk to news reporters, ensuring that his version of Gettysburg's history would be perpetuated. On a positive note, he was a driving force in placing monuments on the field and in establishing Gettysburg National Military Park, even though he is more often remembered today for the financial misappropriations that led to his expulsion from New York's monument commission.

When one combines his battlefield performance with his post-battle efforts, it is obvious that he stands as one of Gettysburg's most monumental figures. Yet, typical battlefield visitors know virtually nothing about him, and what knowledge they do have is almost universally negative. There are only a handful of Sickles biographies in print, all of which are either dated or (sometimes) poorly researched. Only historian Richard Sauers has produced any significant full-length treatments of Sickles within the context of Gettysburg.

This book is not a traditional Sickles biography. His contribution to Gettysburg is its primary focus. Until now, no full-length work has attempted to provide a comprehensive view of Sickles and Gettysburg: what led him there, his actions on the field, the post-battle controversies, and his role in developing the National Military Park. The second day's battle between Sickles' Third Corps and James Longstreet's Confederate First Corps necessarily slides into the spotlight, as does one of the battlefield's most underrated and influential areas: the Peach Orchard. Sickles abandoned Cemetery Ridge because he preferred the terrain surrounding Joseph Sherfy's peach orchard. Why?

As Lieutenant Colonel Fox predicted more than a century ago, some prospective readers may well believe another Gettysburg book is "superfluous and presumptuous." For a small body of readers, this may be true. But a greater majority of well-meaning Gettysburg students have been trained by the novel *The Killer Angels* and motion picture *Gettysburg* to believe that July 2, 1863, is really the story of Joshua Chamberlain and Little Round Top. Dan Sickles has been relegated to the role of a stereotypical political general conspiring against George Meade to blunder away the battle for the Union cause. Sickles was considerably more three-dimensional than many recent Gettysburg works have influenced readers to believe. From the Federal perspective, for better or worse, Gettysburg's second day was Sickles' battle. Readers don't have to like Dan Sickles, but as with any historical figure, an open-minded appreciation of his full character and actions, both positive and negative, will help them better understand the events that occurred around him.

A final reason for this book is that Dan Sickles remains one of the war's most fascinating characters. He had many influential friends as well as enemies. He rose from Tammany Hall politics in New York City, to defendant in a sensational murder trial, to playing a pivotal role on the war's greatest battlefield. He followed up those accomplishments with another five decades in the public eye as a controversial war hero and politician.

As long as Gettysburg produces such entertaining individuals, there should be no apology for writing and reading about them.

Acknowledgments

Although many Gettysburg historians personally despise Dan Sickles, I was still fortunate enough to receive much support and assistance during the completion of this project. The staffs of several institutions generously provided their time, access, and permission (where necessary) to use their materials: John Heiser at Gettysburg National Military Park, Tim Smith at Adams County Historical Society, Dr. Richard Sommers at United States Army Military History Institute (Carlisle Barracks, PA), John-Michael Muller at Yale University (Beinecke Rare Books and Manuscripts Library), Tammy Kiter at New York Historical Society, RA Friedman and the staff at Historical Society of Pennsylvania, Thomas Lannon and Laura Ruttum at New York Public Library (Manuscripts and Archives Division), Jane Cuccurullo from The Green-Wood Cemetery, Michael Rhode, Brian F. Spatola, and Kathleen Stocker at the National Museum of Health and Medicine, Armed Forces Institute of Pathology, Michael R. Ridderbusch at West Virginia University Libraries, and Laura Clark Brown at Wilson Library, The University of North Carolina at Chapel Hill.

Many thanks to fellow Licensed Battlefield Guide Jack Drummond and his wife Marianne who provided me with much of their own research material and have continuously supported my efforts. Thanks as always to my friend Charlie Householder for (very) critically reading a draft, providing photos, and for constantly challenging me during our years of battlefield hikes together. We don't always agree on everything, but I do find the arguments useful! I am indebted to my friend Bob Gerber for navigating through the New York Public Library and for then suggesting my eventual publisher. Bob is also a member of the Phil Kearny Civil War Round Table and my gratitude to Joe Truglio, Vic Conversano, Norman Dykstra, Sylvia Mogerman, Ivan Kossak, and the entire gang for your support and enthusiasm over the years.

George Newton, who is a Licensed Battlefield Guide and author of *Silent Sentinels: A Reference Guide to the Artillery of Gettysburg* (Savas Beatie, 2005), read an advance version of this book and made several corrections for which I am very grateful. Licensed Battlefield Guide Tim Smith assisted me in his role at the Adams County Historical Society and with his own insight on the attempts to re-bury Sickles at Gettysburg. Sue Boardman, who is a Licensed Battlefield Guide and also is co-owner of the Antique Center of Gettysburg, generously provided access to her large collection of battlefield photographs. Many friends also supplied their own research, photos, encouragement, and advice: Michael

S. Bennett from Daniel E. Sickles Camp 3, Sons of Union Veterans of The Civil War, Jim Bowback, Sickles reenactor Richard "Red" Davis, Licensed Battlefield Guide Truman Eyler, Norm and Linda Gaines, Licensed Battlefield Guide Fred Hawthorne, Licensed Battlefield Guide Bobby Housch (and webmaster for www.gettysburgdaily.com), Emmitsburg-area historian John Miller, Mike Nuss, author and historian J. David Petruzzi, Sickles descendant John Shaud, Licensed Battlefield Guide Ellen Pratt, Licensed Battlefield Guide Phil Lechak, Jim Glessner, Eric Lindblade, Erik Dorr, Mike Noirot, John Hoptak, and Danny Roebuck. I would also like to acknowledge my Guide "mentor" Rich Kohr for helping to shape many of my perceptions of this battle, even if he seldom has a good word to say about General Sickles. (Rich, of course any errors in interpretation are mine alone.)

None of this would be possible without my publisher, Savas Beatie, and managing director Theodore P. Savas, who gave Sickles a home. His designer Ian Hughes gave the book its public persona with its striking jacket design. Marketing director Sarah Keeney, Veronica Kane, and Tammy Hall helped promote the book. I am thankful for all their efforts. Brad Gottfried, author of *The Maps of Gettysburg* (Savas Beatie, 2007) and *The Maps of First Bull Run* (Savas Beatie, 2009), among other works, greatly improved my battle narrative by providing maps. My appreciation to Andy Turner at *Gettysburg Magazine*, which published portions of this work in Issue #34 under the title "Sickles Returns."

Most of all, I am indebted to my family—wife Michele, son Alex, and daughter Aimee—for tolerating the long hours (both at home and away) that went into completing this book and for allowing Dan Sickles to live with us for many years. In addition to moral support, Michele helped me with formatting, editing, indexing, and website development. It's finally done!

James A. Hessler
January 2009

Order of Battle: The Third Corps at Gettysburg

Army of the Potomac
Maj. Gen. George G. Meade

Third Corps
Maj. Gen. Daniel Sickles / Maj. Gen. David Birney

1st Division: Maj. Gen. David Birney / Brig. Gen. J. H. Hobart Ward

1st Brigade: Brig. Gen. Charles Graham / Col. Andrew Tippin
57th, 63rd, 68th, 105th, 114th, 141st Pennsylvania

2nd Brigade: Brig. Gen. J. H. Hobart Ward / Col. Hiram Berdan
20th Indiana, 3rd, 4th Maine, 86th, 124th New York,
99th Pennsylvania, 1st, 2nd U.S. Sharpshooters

3rd Brigade: Col. Regis de Trobriand
17th Maine, 3rd, 5th Michigan, 40th New York, 110th Pennsylvania

2nd Division: Brig. Gen. Andrew Humphreys

1st Brigade: Brig. Gen. Joseph Carr
1st, 11th, 16th Massachusetts, 12th New Hampshire, 11th New Jersey,
26th Pennsylvania

2nd ("Excelsior") *Brigade*: Col. Wm. Brewster
70th, 71st, 72nd, 73rd, 74th, 120th New York

3rd Brigade: Col. George Burling
2nd New Hampshire, 5th, 6th, 7th, 8th New Jersey, 115th Pennsylvania

Artillery Brigade: Capt. George Randolph / Capt. Judson Clark—guns: 30
1st New Jersey, Battery B, 1st New York, Battery D, 1st Rhode Island, Battery E,
4th US, Battery K, New York Light Artillery, 4th Battery

Chapter 1

Murder!

P robably no participant journeyed to Gettysburg on a more colorful road than did Daniel Edgar Sickles. By 1863, he was already known as an attorney of questionable ethics, the product of corrupt New York politics, a former protégé of President James Buchanan, the defendant in a sensational murder trial, a friend of President and Mrs. Lincoln, and the highest ranking non-West Pointer in the Army of the Potomac. By the summer of 1863, Sickles had already experienced more peaks and valleys than most men witness in a lifetime.

Dan was born in New York City, the only child of George Garrett and Susan (Marsh) Sickles. His birth date is of some debate, a fact often unnoticed by Gettysburg scholars. The consensus among biographers is that he was born on October 20, 1819, although varying references (some provided by Sickles himself) range from 1819 to 1825. For example, his 1914 New York *Times* obituary states he lived "to almost 91," implying an 1823 birth date. His military record claims he was thirty-nine in June 1861, suggesting an 1821 birth year. On at least one occasion, Sickles told newspaper reporters he was born in 1825; a posthumously published New York monument history concurred. The 1910 U.S. Federal census lists the date as "about 1826." One theory for the discrepancy is that his parents may not have married until 1820, and that he post-dated his 1819 birth in order to downplay the stigma of being born prior to the wedding. Another, less scandalous, scenario is that other dates are the result of vanity or a failing memory. If we accept a birth year of 1819, Sickles was just shy of his forty-fourth birthday when he fought at Gettysburg.[1]

There is little reliable information about Sickles' early days. In later life, he talked infrequently of his prewar years; the focus was typically on Gettysburg

A pre-Civil War image of Dan Sickles. *Library of Congress*

and the Civil War. One accepted fact is that his father, George Sickles, was a real estate speculator who ended up quite wealthy. Around 1838, in order to prepare him for college, Dan's parents installed him into the household of Lorenzo L. Da Ponte, a New York University professor and attorney, where Dan lived and studied. Professor Da Ponte's colorful father was eighty-nine year old Lorenzo Da Ponte, who had been the librettist for three of Mozart's operas and was the first Professor of Italian Literature at Columbia College. The elder Da Ponte

A woodcut of Teresa Sickles. *Library of Congress*

was the household patriarch until he died in August 1838. Also residing under the same roof was the elder Da Ponte's adopted daughter Maria and her husband, Antonio Bagioli, a successful composer and music teacher. Perhaps it was his exposure to the Da Ponte household that influenced Sickles' lifelong love of theater and particularly opera. Given that Dan and Maria were the same age, there were rumors (as repeated in Frank Haskell's memoir) that Dan and his future mother-in-law had a sexual affair. More important to Dan's future was the fact that the Bagiolis had a child living under the same roof, an infant daughter Teresa who was born around 1836.[2]

When Professor Da Ponte died in 1840, Sickles broke down uncontrollably at the funeral. One witness said that Dan was overcome by a "spasm of grief" and "raved, tore up and down the graveyard shrieking and I might even say yelling, so much so that it was impossible for us who were his friends to mollify him in any measure by words." His grief became so "aggravating" to the other mourners, who feared "his mind would entirely give way," that he was forcibly removed from the cemetery. His remarkable outburst lasted nearly ten minutes. Only a few days later, however, the same friend found him to be excessively "light-hearted." This episode reveals much about Sickles' character. As the friend realized with great understatement, Sickles was "subject to very sudden emotions."[3]

Sickles was no stranger to the law. As early as 1837, he was indicted for obtaining money under false pretenses. But after Lorenzo's death, Sickles dropped out of school to study law under Benjamin F. Butler, a leading Democrat and attorney. Sickles passed the bar in 1843. During these years, he continued to gain a reputation for questionable practices. He was nearly prosecuted for appropriating funds from another man, was accused of pocketing money that had been raised for a political pamphlet, and charged with improperly retaining a mortgage that he had pledged as collateral on a loan. His exposure to Butler's political connections, however, opened the door to a political career.[4]

His status as a lawyer, albeit one of questionable ethics, helped launch Sickles' political career, which began in 1844 when he wrote a campaign paper for James Polk and became involved in New York's Tammany Hall political machine. Sickles later liked to call himself "a tough Democrat; a fighting one; a Tammany Hall Democrat." Not everyone was as impressed. "One might as well try to spoil a rotten egg as to damage Dan's character," scoffed New York diarist George Templeton Strong. Sickles' political career was inextricably linked to stories about ballot tampering, theft, deceptive practices, and even brawls. One night, an angry mob burst into a Tammany meeting and threw him violently down a flight of stairs. (He managed to slow his fall by grabbing a banister and, although stunned and bleeding, was not seriously injured.) Still, his star rose, and in 1847 he was elected to the New York Assembly. He also found time for his only military association prior to the Civil War. As was common with prominent men of the era, Sickles joined the 12th New York State Militia in 1849, retiring from it in 1853 with the rank of major.[5]

Sickles continued to be active within the Democratic Party during the 1850s. He was a member of the Baltimore convention that nominated Franklin Pierce for the Presidency in 1852, and the following year he was appointed a New York City corporation counsel. Still a bachelor, he was gaining a reputation for fast and extravagant living. One contemporary admitted that Sickles "led the life of a very fast young man." Money reportedly "poured through his fingers." He became a "frequenter" of a Mercer Street bordello that was known as "the most select . . . and orderly establishment of a disreputable character in the city." A prostitute named Fanny White ran the house, and according to her biographer, she reportedly "formed an attachment for Sickles and he became her protégé. It is stated that she paid his tailor's bills, gave him jewelry to wear and kept him abundantly supplied with money." While a member of the State Assembly, he was censured by his outraged colleagues for bringing her into the Assembly chamber. There were even rumors that he exchanged her services for campaign favors. If true, Dan Sickles may be Gettysburg's only corps commander with "pimp" on his diverse resume.[6]

White soon learned that Sickles was bringing "his fascinating powers to bear on a certain Italian young lady" and, while in public one evening, White allegedly retaliated by beating him "unsparingly and unreservedly" with a heavy riding whip. White's suspicions were accurate. The "young Italian" was Teresa Bagioli, whom the nearly thirty-three year old Sickles married in September 1852. The same girl Sickles had lived with when she was an infant was now a sixteen-year old student at a Catholic boarding school. Much to the objections of both his and her parents, they were married by New York's mayor in a private civil ceremony. Why had a rising political star married a teenager? An anonymous family acquaintance later told the New York *Times* that "the consequences of this secret wedding soon made concealment impossible." In other words, Teresa may have been pregnant. After eventually reconciling with their parents and the Catholic Church, a second ceremony was performed in March 1853 at the home of the Roman Catholic Archbishop. The exact date of their daughter Laura's birth is unclear, but there is some contemporary suggestion that it occurred later in 1853, which would potentially leave the summer of 1852 (before the marriage) open as a conception date. There were also rumors of other children, which was not surprising given Dan's reputation. One accusation held that Sickles was the natural father of James Gordon Bennett, Jr. In 1913, a New Jersey man named Alfred Molyneux had himself re-baptized as Alfred Sickles, and claimed to be an abandoned offspring of Dan and Teresa. Despite these colorful stories, history has recognized Laura as Dan and Teresa's only child.[7]

Teresa's pictures reveal an attractive dark-haired Italian. Six years into her marriage, as the wife of a congressman in Washington, she was described as "more like a school girl than a polished woman of the world" with a "sweet, amicable manner." Conversely, while preparing Edgcumb Pinchon's biography on Sickles, Pinchon's researcher rejected the schoolgirl image, describing her instead as a "beautiful, voluptuous siren, without brains or shame" with a "lust for men" whom Sickles "loved to madness."[8]

Now a member of Tammany Hall's elite, in May 1853 Dan was offered a post as assistant to James Buchanan, the new American minister in London. Sickles initially declined the offer because the $2,500 annual salary "would hardly pay for my wine and cigars." The initial rejection may have been simple posturing, for he soon reconsidered and won over Buchanan, who was impressed by Sickles' "manners, appearance, & intelligence." Sickles and Buchanan set sail for England in August 1853. Teresa did not initially accompany him (she was either in the late stages of her pregnancy or had a new infant to care for). Sickles did not travel alone, for the prostitute Fanny White apparently accompanied him.[9]

While in London, Sickles enjoyed wearing his New York militia uniform, and Buchanan did refer to him as "Col. Sickles." Dan created an uproar, and embarrassed Buchanan's diplomatic efforts, by refusing to participate in a toast to the Queen's health on July 4, 1854. There were conflicting allegations that Dan brought Fanny to one of the Queen's receptions and introduced the prostitute to Her Majesty. (An 1860 biography of White claimed that Fanny was "near succeeding it is alleged in obtaining an introduction." Antagonistic New York papers, on the other hand, claimed that Sickles did successfully arrange the meeting.) By the time Teresa and new daughter Laura reached London in the spring of 1854, Fanny was back in New York. Teresa quickly became a favorite of Buchanan, a sixty-two year old bachelor, despite the fact that she was barely eighteen. Biographer Pinchon and his researcher were privately convinced that Teresa and Buchanan had an affair and that Sickles "understood it thoroughly, and worked the combination for all it was worth." (Such a liaison would have been doubtful if Buchanan was a homosexual, as some historians believe.) Buchanan also became attached to his new aide, writing, "Sickles possesses qualifications . . . for a much higher place." Although he admired Sickles' abilities, Buchanan criticized Dan's work habits, his handwriting (not a trivial complaint since this burdened Buchanan's staff, who had to recopy Dan's notes), and the fact that Sickles "spends a great deal of money." In what would become one of Sickles' lifelong habits whenever he was in a diplomatic assignment, he quickly grew tired of his role. "It would suit me better to stay away another year on account of the present condition of N.Y. politics," Sickles wrote in June 1854, "but I am tired of London and of this mission." Buchanan likewise was growing tired of Sickles' preference for fast living over professional attentiveness, and they mutually agreed on Sickles' resignation.[10]

Dan and Teresa returned to New York at the end of 1854, where it was evident that politics suited him better than diplomacy. He was elected to the New York State Senate in 1855, and was also named chairman of Tammany's executive committee. Decades before he would help develop Gettysburg National Military Park, he organized a special committee that was instrumental in creating New York's Central Park. Sickles did not create or champion New York City's need for a great public park, but he helped consolidate advocates of the park, obtained consensus on a site, and assisted the governor in signing enabling legislation. His motives were not entirely pure, for he participated in a syndicate to purchase building lots near the park. Sickles freely admitted as much: "I foresaw visions of fortune for myself and associates in the not far distant future, when the park should be established." Ultimately nothing came of the syndicate, but to his credit he continued to pursue the park's development. Sickles enlisted the help of New York friend Charles K. Graham, a surveyor and former navy midshipman who had helped construct the dry docks at the Brooklyn Navy Yard. Sickles had Graham make huge "before and after" drawings of the proposed park, which Sickles used to help steer the bill through the state legislature. Sickles' influence was strictly political; writer Frederick Law Olmsted and architect Calvert Vaux won the park's landscape design contest, and construction was not officially completed until 1873. So it was with perhaps some overstatement that Sickles would later watch thousands enjoy the park and proudly admit, "I have a fatherly feeling for Central Park."[11]

In the spring of 1856, Sickles decided to run for Congress and help promote Buchanan's bid for the presidency. In a speech on Buchanan's behalf, Sickles espoused the Democrats as "the only party that professed and practiced justice to all men . . . [and] offered the only ground for the perpetuity and salvation of the Union." Candidate Sickles was physically described as, "not stout but well knit together, complexion fair, eyes blue and expressive, mouth firm, and his general bearing . . . thoroughly indicative of . . . unflinching determination." He wore a full drooping moustache. His contemporaries noted his "fondness" for women and, despite the fact that he was married and starting a family, was considered "somewhat of a lady-killer." The ever-critical diarist George Templeton Strong thought Sickles belonged "to the filthy sediment of the [law] profession, and lying somewhere in its lower strata. Perhaps better to say that he's one of the bigger bubbles of the scum of the profession, swollen and windy, and puffed out with fetid gas." It is fair to conclude that Sickles did not receive Strong's vote when he was elected to Congress in November by a wide margin, the same election that resulted in Buchanan's elevation to the presidency.[12]

Sickles arrived in Washington for Buchanan's inauguration in March 1857. That spring, before his first Congress even opened, Dan was lobbying to have Charles Graham appointed as civil engineer at the Brooklyn Navy Yard while simultaneously arranging to have the current holder of the position fired. Dan declined the incumbent's challenge to a duel, but one morning the man burst into Sickles' room at the Willard Hotel and began to whip the new Congressman with a cowhide. During the ensuing struggle, Sickles grabbed the whip and the man fled. The attacker published a note in a New York paper, claiming Sickles' "whole career has been a series of unparalleled debaucheries. Graduating from the worst sinks of iniquity in this city, he has led the life of a professional vagabond. In debt to everybody . . . he stands before the public . . . a disgraced and vanquished man." Graham got his job. Sickles' New York enemies kept him in the papers even while he shifted his attention to Washington. In October 1857, he brought a libel action against James Gordon Bennett when the New York *Herald* accused him of stealing from the Post Office—a felony.[13]

Dan and Teresa set up their household on the prestigious Lafayette Square, across the street from the Executive Mansion, and President Buchanan was a frequent guest. The annual rent of the fine home was $3,000, or roughly equal to his congressional salary. In addition to Dan, Teresa, and daughter Laura, the large household included several servants. Washington wives played an important role in their husband's careers, and Teresa had significant social obligations. She was expected to attend or host a party nearly every day and night. It was not uncommon for available bachelors to act as escorts for married women when their politician husbands were unavailable. Dan was frequently focused on his rising career. He would later admit that an active political career "forces a good husband to keep bad hours." Good husband or not, Teresa suspected that his extramarital affairs had never really ceased.[14]

It was during this time that Sickles met Philip Barton Key. He was born in 1818, four years after his father Francis Scott Key penned "The Star Spangled Banner." In 1853, Philip was appointed United States Attorney for the District of Columbia. He married in 1845 and had four children before his wife died in the 1850s. Although he was considered tall and athletic, he claimed that his wife's death shattered his health. He was increasingly unable to attend to his professional duties and committed most of his work to assistant Robert Ould. Key's inattentiveness was openly questioned following his inability to prosecute a California Congressman for murder in 1856. The New York *Times* later criticized Key as being "indolent and unread to a degree almost beyond belief in one filling such a position." But his supposed poor health did not prevent his attendance at Washington parties. One hostess called him "the handsomest man in all Washington . . . he was a prominent figure at all the principal fashionable functions; a graceful dancer, he was a favorite with every hostess of the day." It was also said that "no man in Washington was more popular with the ladies." Key and Sickles were introduced through a mutual friend. The former was worried that Buchanan might replace him, and the latter agreed to intercede on his behalf; Key was reappointed to his position.[15]

Key and Sickles quickly became friends. When Sickles was traveling or attending Congressional sessions, which was often, Key accompanied Teresa to social functions. Gossip, quiet and limited at the outset, began to grow. When Sickles learned that a clerk was spreading rumors that Teresa and Key had spent time together at an inn, Dan confronted Key, who vehemently denied the charge. Key managed to have the terrified clerk retract his story. Calling it "ridiculous and disgusting slander," Key convinced Sickles that, "Here's an end to this nonsense." In fact, Key was a liar, and he and Teresa were having an affair. Sickles would be labeled by future historians as "The Congressman who got away with murder," but Sickles' vantage point was somewhat different. He had given Key, a man who now owed his professional position to Sickles, an opportunity to personally own up to the affair. Key responded by lying and continuing to meet with Teresa. While Sickles was in New York, he asked a friend to "look in on" Teresa while he was away. When the friend and his wife stopped by the Sickles home unexpectedly one afternoon, they discovered Teresa and Key alone in a study with a half-empty bottle of champagne. Sickles' household staff recalled another evening when Teresa and Key had remained locked in the drawing room until the early morning hours. Dan, meanwhile, won a bitter re-election fight that fall among accusations from his opponent of voter fraud and questions of how a Congressional salary supported such a lavish lifestyle.[16]

Key's and Teresa's romantic relationship heated up. The pair began meeting in a rented house on Washington's Fifteenth Street, a poor neighborhood only two blocks north of Lafayette Square. Inquisitive neighbors began to notice an unusually distinguished-looking man and woman using the house. Key also took to signaling Teresa from Lafayette Square by waving a white handkerchief while standing across from the Sickles' residence. He used a pair of opera glasses to detect her signals from inside the house.[17]

Unfortunately for Key, on February 24, 1859, Sickles received a letter signed by "Your Friend R.P.G." The note told Sickles about the house on Fifteenth Street, which Key rented "for no other purpose than to meet your wife Mrs. Sickles. He hangs a string out of the window as a signal to her that he is in and leaves the door unfastened and she walks in and sir I do assure you with these few hints I leave the rest for you to imagine." One can only imagine Sickles' reaction. Unsuccessful in his previous effort at direct confrontation, the aggrieved husband undertook a more discreet course of action this time around. The next day, Sickles went to the House of Representatives, flung himself onto a sofa in a state of emotional pique, and asked clerk George Wooldridge to investigate. Wooldridge questioned Fifteenth Street residents as well as Sickles' household staff. Convinced the rumors were true, he reported his findings to the congressman.[18]

On the evening of February 26, Dan extracted a full confession from Teresa. She admitted, in writing, to meeting with Key in the Fifteenth Street house. "How many times I don't know . . . Usually stayed an hour or more. There was a bed in the second story. I did what is usual for a wicked woman to do." Teresa also did "not deny that we have had connection in this house [the Sickles' residence], last spring, a year ago, in the parlor, on the sofa." To add insult to injury, "Mr. Key has ridden in Mr. Sickles' carriage, and has called at his house without Mr. Sickles' knowledge, and after my being told not to invite him to do so, and against Mr. Sickles' repeated request." Teresa admitted that the confession had been "written by myself, without any inducement held out by Mr. Sickles of forgiveness or reward, and without any menace from him." Historians have speculated on why Dan had the written confession prepared. The most cynical interpretation is that he intended to use the confession as a defense in case of violence. A more reasonable assumption is that the shrewd attorney intended to use it in a divorce proceeding.[19]

The next day, February 27, was a warm Sunday afternoon. Unaware of Teresa's confession, Philip Barton Key approached the Sickles house several times, slowly twirling his white handkerchief as an apparent signal for Teresa. Dan had summoned his friends George Wooldridge and Samuel Butterworth, an old Tammany Hall crony who happened to be in town. Butterworth arrived to find Dan "lying on his face on his pillow, overwhelmed with grief." Suggesting that Dan's first thoughts were for himself, he melodramatically told Butterworth, "I am a dishonored and ruined man. I cannot look you in the face!" Sickles eventually pried himself away from his couch long enough to spot Key. "That villain has just passed my house! My God, this is horrible!"

Butterworth tried to calm Sickles down, but Dan was convinced everything was public knowledge and that "the whole town knew it!" As their story later developed, Sickles supposedly asked Butterworth to go with him to the clubhouse across the square, where Key held membership, and determine if Key had rented any rooms for illicit purposes. It was an odd request, given that Sickles already knew the couple used the house on Fifteenth Street. Butterworth supposedly agreed and walked out of the house, later insisting that he had no idea that Sickles intended to harm Key. Before following Butterworth, Sickles armed himself with a revolver and a pair of derringers.[20]

It was now approximately 2:00 p.m., and Key was on the square's southeast corner near Pennsylvania Avenue, across from the presidential mansion. When Butterworth approached from the Sickles house, Key greeted him with, "What a fine day we have!" After a brief exchange, Butterworth continued toward the club. Sickles rapidly approached along the same route, shouting, "Key, you scoundrel, you have dishonored my house—you must die!" Key thrust his hand into his pocket—did he have a weapon?—and moved toward Sickles. Sickles produced a gun and fired at close range. The first shot grazed Key. When he attempted to fire a second time, Key grabbed him and the two men began to struggle. Sickles' gun was knocked to the ground. He turned and started to pull away when Key grabbed him from behind with both arms. Sickles broke free and pulled another gun out of his pocket.[21]

"Murder! Murder!" shouted Key as he backed away. "Don't shoot!" He removed the object from his pocket—his opera glass—and threw it at Sickles. Just ten feet away, Sickles fired a second bullet. This one hit Key two inches below the groin. Key tried to grab onto a nearby tree, but slumped onto the ground at Sickles' feet. Up to this point, Sickles had no way of knowing that Key was unarmed. Dan might very well have left his house expecting armed combat, and had he stopped now, he might have had a valid self-defense argument. Key's act of reaching into his pocket could have given Sickles reasonable cause to believe that Key carried something more deadly than an opera glass. But the emotional Sickles could not stop. Instead, he pulled the trigger a third time. The gun misfired. He cocked the piece yet again, placed it on Key's chest, and pulled the trigger again. This time the bullet entered below Key's heart. Sickles placed the barrel next to Key's head and squeezed the trigger once more, but once again it misfired.[22]

The numerous eyewitnesses in Lafayette Square surrounded the two men. Towering above the prostrate Key, Sickles demanded, "Is the scoundrel dead?" He repeated that Key had "violated" and "dishonored" the Sickles marriage.

Dramatic newspaper re-creation of the Key murder. *Library of Congress*

Butterworth, who had watched the shooting, led Sickles away while several others carried Key to the clubhouse. He died shortly thereafter from the fatal chest wound. Accompanied by Butterworth, Sickles surrendered himself. Before the congressman was led to jail he was allowed a moment with Teresa (as long as he promised not to hurt her), during which he confessed, "I've killed him!"[23]

The murder of Philip Barton Key, and accompanying trial of Congressman Dan Sickles, had all of the scandalous elements expected to thrill the American reading public: adultery, politics, celebrity, and a handsome corpse. Newspapers across the country provided extensive coverage of the so-called "Sickles Tragedy"; the shocking killing was daily front-page news in large markets such as New York. Even in smaller markets such as Gettysburg, readers of the local *Compiler* were furnished with all details of the case, meaning that Gettysburg's residents would have had the opportunity to know Sickles by reputation before he arrived there in 1863.[24]

An immediate and significant show of public sympathy broke out for the accused. As the New York *Times* reported on March 15, weeks before the trial opened, "there appears to be no second opinion as to the certainty of Mr. Sickles' acquittal" but "national interest" arose from "the general desire to see the whole case fairly put, and the million scandals of mystery laid to rest by the plain facts." Longtime Sickles critic George Templeton Strong recorded that the killer "has attained the dignity of a homicide. . . . Were he not an unmitigated blackguard and profligate, one could pardon any act of violence committed on such provocation." It was readily apparent that, even to his enemies, adultery was a justifiable excuse for the crime. The defense team's strategy was also telegraphed early. The *Times* reported two weeks before the trial opened that the defense would examine whether the "criminal connection" between Key and Teresa "excuses the slaying of the seducer by the husband's hand." The paper cited several recent precedents in Dan's favor, including a Virginia case where a defendant had committed a similar murder and the jury acquitted him "without leaving the box." Perhaps it was because of this support that when Dan was visited by a newsman in his cell on the eve of trial, the reporter was startled to "find him looking so well. His manner was pleasantly natural." The overwrought emotionalism that had brought on the shooting was nowhere in evidence and the accused conversed easily on a variety of topics.[25]

Sickles' many friends, including both his and Teresa's fathers, were in evidence when the trial began on April 4, 1859. In a nineteenth century version of the legal "Dream Team," Sickles had no less than eight high-powered attorneys representing him, led by James T. Brady. At least four of the lawyers, such as John Graham (brother of Charles Graham) and Thomas Francis Meagher, were close friends from New York. Although he was not the lead attorney, the defense team is best remembered for the presence of future Secretary of War Edwin Stanton. Mr. and Mrs. Stanton had been among the circle of dinner guests who had frequented the Sickles home. Of more importance was the fact that Stanton was widely respected for his knowledge of constitutional and civil law. The high-powered defense team was opposed by only one man. Robert Ould, Key's assistant, had been elevated to District Attorney after Key's murder. (Ould would later serve as the Confederacy's Assistant Secretary of War and Commissioner for Exchange of Prisoners.) Key's family and friends realized that Ould was over-powered and soon hired him an assistant. The courtroom was packed with spectators and newsmen from across the country when the doors opened for business.[26]

Prosecutor Ould's indictment read that Sickles, "being moved and seduced by the instigation of the devil" had assaulted and murdered Key with "malicious aforethought." Sickles pleaded "Not guilty" in a clear and firm tone. An observing reporter thought that he was "exhibiting no unusual marks of agitation" and throughout the trial, reporters generally found his demeanor to be unusually calm, even given his most "humiliating" circumstance. The first three days were spent on jury selection, and there was considerable difficulty finding impartial jurors. Several prospective candidates expressed the opinion that they would acquit if selected. By the second day of the trial, at least one reporter wrote, "I will not be at all astonished if Sickles is acquitted with the least trouble." Sickles was said to exhibit "evident satisfaction at the popular expression in his favor. . . ."[27]

Once jury selection was completed, Ould delivered an emotionally charged argument that Sickles, "a walking magazine," had taken deliberate care in arming himself against Key, who had only "a poor and feeble opera-glass." The prosecution called twenty-eight witnesses, many of whom had witnessed the murder. Butterworth was not called to testify, which seemed odd on two accounts: he had been with Sickles immediately prior to the shooting, and because his own story had a number of holes. Another witness who was not called was J. H. W. Bonitz, a young White House page who had been told to leave town by none other than President Buchanan. These exclusions raised questions as to whether political pressure was preventing the prosecution from vigorously pursuing the case. Teresa was also not called to testify; she spent the entire trial in seclusion and was soon sent to New York with Laura.[28]

Sickles' lawyers decided they would throw the prosecutor off-stride by not making an opening argument until after the prosecution called its witnesses. As a result, the defense did not commence until April 9. Beginning with John Graham's lengthy opening, Sickles' team took the offensive and argued that adultery with another man's wife was a crime, making Key a criminal himself, and that Sickles had a right to "protect" Teresa who was, in essence, his property. Sickles' lawyers told the court that Dan's discovery of the affair was tantamount to actually catching Teresa and Key in the act. Graham further argued that the recent discovery of the affair, compounded by seeing Key in front of his own house, had produced "mental unsoundness" sufficient to cause deadly violence. Sickles, Graham argued, became increasingly and intensely "mortified" until "his mind became diseased." It was this final point, believed to have been originated by attorney James Brady, that made the trial noteworthy beyond its scandalous aspects. Although complete insanity was a valid and previously-established defense, the Sickles team argued before an American jury for the first time what would become known as the "temporary insanity" defense.[29]

The strategy required Sickles' attorneys to argue strenuously in favor of admitting Teresa's "habitual adultery" into evidence. Without proof of adultery, there could be no temporary insanity question. The prosecution naturally objected, and the admissibility question was argued for days. The judge finally ruled that Dan's cries that Key had "violated his bed" were facts of the case, and thus the jury had to have the adultery explained. It was a significant victory for the Sickles team. The trial was no longer about simply murder, and in many ways it was no longer an insanity trial. Instead, Key and Teresa were now on trial for adultery. The defense produced forty-three witnesses whose euphemistic testimony described Teresa's affair. Dan's surprisingly calm demeanor cracked at this stage of the proceedings, and he had to be excused three times during testimony. After one particularly grueling session, he was described as "his vision quenched in scalding tears, his limbs paralyzed, his forehead throbbing as though it had been bludgeoned by some ruffian, and his whole frame convulsed." Whether the courtroom histrionics were real or an award-winning performance, the jury witnessed firsthand a husband who was mentally unable to bear his wife with another man.[30]

The prosecution scored a minor victory when the judge refused to admit Teresa's confession into evidence, but it appeared verbatim in newspapers nationwide. The confession was considered a lurid public disclosure for that era, and papers in San Francisco were censured for obscenity. Teresa was disgraced and permanently marked by the country as a ruined woman. "Those who have known her will grieve sorely at the necessity of giving her up as lost," editorialized the New York *Times*. Had Dan approved of the confession's publication? The Associated Press was "requested on the part of Mr. Sickles to state that he deeply regrets for many reasons, but particularly for the sake of his child, who must one day read the record of her mother's shame, that the confession of Mrs. Sickles was published; the publication was contrary to his wishes and if it had been within his power he would have suppressed it." Were his denials sincere? The confession's mysterious publication was consistent with his life-long custom of using the newspapers, sometimes anonymously, to fight his battles. It was a pattern that woud repeat itself after Gettysburg.[31]

Ould attempted to retaliate by introducing Dan's own "personal history" into evidence, including proof that he had also committed adultery throughout his marriage, such as meeting a "Mrs. Sickles" at a hotel in Baltimore. The hotel owner, however, was not allowed to testify. Many writers have commented on the apparent hypocrisy: the wife's infidelity on trial, but not the husband's. However, the defense needed to disprove malice and prove that insanity existed when the murder occurred. Dan may (or may not) have been temporarily insane when he killed Key, but his own adultery had not been the cause. For that reason, it was Teresa's actions, and not his own, which were on trial.[32]

Stanton began the defense's closing arguments on April 23. He described Teresa as a "wretched mother, the ruined wife, [who] has not yet plunged into the horrible filth of prostitution to which she is rapidly hurrying. . . ." Stanton argued that although she was lost as a wife, Dan had actually rescued the mother of his child. Key's death was a "cheap sacrifice" when compared to the fate from which Dan had saved Teresa and Laura. Stanton continued:

> The theory of our case is, that there was a man living in a constant state of adultery with prisoner's wife, a man who was daily by a moral- no, by an immoral power- enormous, monstrous, and altogether unparalleled in the history of American society, or in the history of the family of man, a power over the being of this woman . . . dragging her, day by day, through the streets in order that he might gratify his lust. The husband beholds him in the very act of withdrawing his wife from his roof, from his presence, from his arm, from his wing, from his nest, meets him in that act and slays him, and we say that the right to slay him stands on the firmest principles of self-defense.

Despite the novel concept of temporary insanity, Stanton's "theory of our case" was actually a more mundane self-defense against the adulterer. James Brady continued the theme on April 26. In comparing Key's white handkerchief as a "foul substitute" to "that star-spangled banner" of his "noble father," it became "a solemn duty of the American citizen to protect his home against the invasion of the traitor, who . . . under the pretext of friendship, inflicts a deadly wound upon his happiness, and aims also a blow at his honor." Brady warned the jury that Dan could not be convicted if any evidence had shown the murder to be justifiable.[33]

At the end of closing arguments, Judge Thomas Crawford instructed the jury to be "satisfied, beyond all reasonable doubt" of Sickles' sanity and if there were any doubt then "Mr. Sickles should be acquitted." More significantly, questions of insanity should be considered "at the moment" when the crime was committed. Judge Crawford basically validated the defense's case: American jurors were now allowed to consider a defendant's sanity at the moment a crime was committed, and to give the defendant the benefit of the doubt if any uncertainty existed. This legal landmark drew little public commentary from the press or legal experts. Adultery was the primary issue of the trial. It was the real key to the defense strategy—and it sold more newspapers.[34]

The jury deliberated for only seventy minutes before returning with a verdict of "Not Guilty." Pandemonium and cheers broke out in the courtroom. "The verdict," readers of the Gettysburg *Compiler* were informed, "seems to have been anticipated . . . The scene was a wild one and great enthusiasm prevailed." While those in the courtroom lost control, the "only man apparently unmoved in this eruption" was Sickles himself. An observer noticed that he gathered "his nerves in a strong struggle." So many people swarmed Dan to offer their congratulations that police had to escort him out of the court. Surrounded by his friends and father, he worked through cheering crowds, was placed into a carriage, and driven away. That evening, while Dan sought "repose," James Brady invited the jury to a party at the National Hotel. The foreman expressed his gratitude that he had "lived to render such a verdict." A reporter canvassed the jurors and confirmed that adultery, not insanity, had been the deciding factor: "in the absence of any adequate punishment by law for adultery, the man who violates the honor and desolates the home of his neighbor, does so at the peril of his life, and if he falls by the outraged husband's hands, he deserves his doom." The legal precedent, which everyone was talking about, was not temporary insanity, but rather that "when a man violated the sanctity of his neighbor's home he must do so at his peril." In the end, it was Key's own adulterous actions, and not Dan's mental state, that had ensured Sickles' freedom.[35]

Most newspapers praised the verdict. Some wondered if the prosecution had not pursued the case energetically enough, since Sickles was, after all, "a fast friend of the highest officer in the nation." The judge's conduct was also questioned, with one paper going so far as to claim that "while Mr. Crawford is Judge, no member of Congress can be convicted of a criminal offense." Such doubts were not the prevailing opinion. In general, the moral temperament of the era viewed Key in the wrong and Sickles as the sympathetic avenger. Unremorseful, Dan returned to the crime scene with two friends to graphically recreate the killing. He assured them that he had every intention to kill Key that day. Less dramatically, in later years Sickles was seen revisiting the square alone. He would gaze "earnestly" at Key's old clubhouse window and then look across the square to his old residence. Alone at the spot where he had killed Key, the aging Sickles silently mused over the murder, undisturbed by passersby.[36]

The public's appetite for Sickles news did not end with the verdict. At least one retailer in Baltimore thought that the Sickles name might be good for business. Picking's Clothing company ran advertisements in the Gettysburg *Compiler* under the caption, "The Sickles' Trial." Picking's reminded readers that the shooting of Key "created the greatest excitement. The people talk about it on the streets and in their houses, and look upon these tragedies as being unparalleled in history. So it is with Picking's Clothing. . . ."[37]

Speculation turned toward the presumably scandalous forthcoming divorce. It was reported that Mrs. Sickles "will resist any application of her husband for a divorce, and will furnish proof of infidelity on his part which will prevent any decree in his favor." The New York *Times* wrote that the homicide had been committed due to "terrible provocation," and that the verdict had been reached "in conformity with the best public sentiment of the land." Nevertheless, it was now "expected that a decent regard for the proprieties of life . . . would have induced him to withdraw himself and his sad domestic story at once from the eye of the world." Within only three months of the acquittal, however, shocking rumors began to circulate that the infamous couple had reconciled. In fact, they had corresponded extensively during the trial. The New York *Herald* circulated a story in July that their families had convinced them to salvage their marriage and, "it is said their love is greater than ever." The New York *Tribune* reported "from various sources" that they were "now living . . . in marital relations as before." America's most notorious couple was indeed back together.[38]

The reconciliation turned public opinion resoundingly against Dan, and the verdict of innocence was now openly questioned. A correspondent for the Philadelphia *Press* argued that if Teresa "can be forgiven now [then] Key ought to have been forgiven in February . . . under the circumstances, as now developed, [Key] ought to have been spared." The New York *Sun* editorialized with regret "that Mr. Key is not alive to witness Mr. Sickles' restoration to sanity, and his full condonation of his wife's 'indiscretions.'" The New York *Evening Post* chimed in, "The inquiry everywhere now is, why Key was killed at all, or, having been killed, why such extraordinary efforts were made to screen the slayer." Many of Dan's friends understandably scrambled for cover. The *Tribune* was "assured that in taking this remarkable step, Mr. Sickles has alienated himself from most, if not all, of those personal and political friends who devotedly adhered to him during his recent imprisonment and trial." The New York *Herald* fumed that Dan and Teresa were "representatives of a bad state of society, wherein political success and power are to be had at any sacrifice of personal honor and private morality."[39]

Since every aspect of the story had played in the newspapers, it was probably no surprise when Dan used the press to respond to the relentless criticism. The response was vintage Sickles. Referring to a "recent event in my domestic relations," the unapologetic attorney supposedly took on full responsibility for his actions. Gettysburg residents read Sickles' side of the story in the July 25 edition of the *Compiler*. They could not have imagined that the unrepentant tone of the letter would be remarkably similar to speeches Sickles would make in their own town, on another topic, in the coming decades:

> Referring to the forgiveness which my sense of duty and my feelings impelled me to extend to an erring and repentant wife . . . I did not exchange a word with one of my counsel upon the subject, nor with anyone else. My reconciliation with my wife was my own act, done without consultation with any relative, friend or adviser. Whatever blame, if any belongs to the step, should fall alone upon me.[40]

Sickles knew that his actions were perhaps "fatal to my professional, political, and social standing," but "I have seen enough of the lives of others, to teach me that, if one be patient and resolute, it is the man himself who indicates the place he will occupy." Sickles closed by appealing to America to "aim all their arrows" at him and to spare his wife and child.

Although Dan's manifesto received some support, the overall response remained decidedly negative. Tireless critic George Templeton Strong speculated that Teresa "had a hold on him and knew of matters [that] he did not desire to be revealed." Dan had "sacrificed all his hopes of political advancement and all his political friends and allies. He can hardly shew [sic] himself at Washington again." He was now a political embarrassment rather than a rising star.[41]

The upshot of all this was that Dan Sickles remained uncharacteristically on the sidelines when he reported back to Congress on December 5, 1859. He had little influence, actively participated in few debates, and was ostracized by his colleagues. He remained dressed in "exquisite taste," but he would enter the House "quietly from the side-door, and takes his seat on one of the sofas on the western side of the House, where, resting his head on his gloved hand, he remains seated, taking no part in the discussions- voting, when called upon, in a low voice. . . . He seems conscious that public opinion is greatly against him." Southern diarist Mary Chesnut famously observed Sickles "sitting alone on the benches of the Congress. . . . He was left to himself as if he had smallpox. There he sat—unfriended, melancholy, slow, solitary, sad of visage." When Chesnut asked why he was such an outcast, a friend sniffed that killing Key "was all right . . . It was because he condoned his wife's profligacy, and took her back . . . Unsavory subject." It surprised no one when Sickles declined to run for another term. It was a shockingly swift fall for the husband and wife who had arrived in Washington with so much promise only a few short years before.[42]

The rise and fall of Dan Sickles' first tenure in Congress offers insight into both his character and his later battlefield performance. The Key murder remains his most well-known prewar accomplishment, overshadowing his otherwise lengthy political resume. But, as far as Gettysburg is concerned, the episode demonstrated that when under severe stress (as he would be again on the morning of July 2, 1863), Sickles' reaction would likely be more emotional than thoughtful. The trial also provides an early example of the means Sickles would go to save himself when faced with public censure and potential humiliation. The Key scandal's most lasting impact on Gettysburg was the fact that it drove Sickles out of Congress. The killing, acquittal, and reconciliation with Teresa ensured that Sickles would be looking for a new opportunity when the Civil War started. Such disgrace would have destroyed less durable men. Resiliency and re-invention would become hallmarks of Dan's lengthy career.

Chapter 2

The Making of a First Class Soldier

Tensions had rapidly escalated over the slavery question during Dan Sickles' tenure in Congress. "I saw this Republic drifting without a pilot on the stormy sea of revolution," Sickles would recall of this period decades later. "Now it is plain to all that the day of compromises had passed away . . . Slavery would yield only to the sword." On several occasions, Sickles later declared that Washington's alcohol-fueled social circuit—the same one that had helped destroy his marriage—also played a large part in the growing tensions. During an 1862 recruiting drive, he accused prewar Southern legislators of frequently passing out drunk. "There never was a state that seceded that did not secede on whiskey." Later, he elaborated on his bizarre views to a news reporter when he claimed, "The War of the Rebellion was really a whiskey war. Yes, whiskey caused the Rebellion!" Congress was "whiskey in the morning . . . then whiskey all day; whiskey and gambling all night. . . . The fights—the angry speeches—were whiskey."[1]

As a Democrat in the prewar Congress, Sickles had traditionally voted with the Democratic Southern bloc, and considered it an "illusion" that the Union could be preserved by force. But his conciliatory attitudes changed when open hostilities erupted with the firing on the supply ship *Star of the West* in January 1861. He felt betrayed by the position in which Southern Democrats had placed his party, and he briefly transformed himself from outcast to firebrand. Speaking before the House of Representatives on January 16, 1861, an outraged Sickles called the Southern actions "unmitigated war" and announced that the "loyal" citizens of New York were "unanimous" for the Union. Regis de Trobriand, who would later serve as an officer under Sickles in the Army of the Potomac, wrote that the congressman was "Disgusted with the bad faith of his old allies, and irritated at the false position in which they had put the Democrats of the North; he considered his party as in duty bound, more than any other, to carry on the war . . . unto the complete triumph of the national government."[2]

Because his last session of Congress ended in March, Sickles was back in New York practicing law as a private citizen when Southern artillery ringing Charleston harbor opened fire on Fort Sumter on April 12, 1861. As with so many aspects of Sickles' colorful life, there are multiple versions about how he ended up in the army. The most popular account finds him drinking at Delmonico's when his friend, Captain William Wiley, offered to raise a regiment if Sickles agreed to command it. In a postwar paper, Sickles claimed that he had enlisted fully expecting to serve in the ranks, but as he was getting ready to leave for camp, he was convinced by his friends "that I could better serve the cause by raising a regiment" and "thus rapidly was I advanced from the ranks to the grade of a regimental commander." Sickles also loved to tell the story of how he met up with President Abraham Lincoln, who needed every "Democrat of prominence . . . right up in the front line of the fighting." Lincoln assured Sickles, "I do not want you to serve as a private. I believe in pushing the Democrats who want to fight right up to the head, where everybody can take a lesson from their example. I want you to go out and raise some troops for service." Whether the story is completely true—it seems preposterous to imagine a man like Sickles serving as a common private—there is little doubt that Lincoln needed the support of Democrats like Sickles; indeed, the two men would mutually exploit each other's strengths for the remainder of the war. Sickles' new military career was also aided when a friendly presence ended up within Lincoln's administration. In January 1862, Lincoln named Sickles' former defense attorney, Edwin Stanton, as his secretary of war.[3]

Sickles and Captain Wiley received permission to raise a brigade rather than a regiment, which was fortuitous for Sickles since colonels commanded regiments while brigadier generals commanded brigades. The excitement following the capitulation of Fort Sumter made it relatively easy to gather large numbers of men to a flag. Using speeches and calls to patriotic duty, the pair recruited about 3,000 eager enlistees, which Sickles promptly dubbed the "Excelsior Brigade" after the New York State motto ("Ever Upward"). Often forgotten today is that the original Excelsiors included company contributions from Michigan, Massachusetts, Pennsylvania, and New Jersey. Sickles' notoriety carried with it a fair amount of baggage. One newspaper illustration mocked the brigade's recruiting efforts by depicting an officer (whose pocket is being picked) soliciting lowly candidates in front of a liquor store in the city's

Five Points slums, alongside a sarcastic caption of "The Capitol is in danger[.] Sickles Brigade to the Rescue!!!"[4] The historian of the Excelsior Brigade remembered the ridicule they were subjected to when they joined Dan Sickles' outfit:

> A person belonging to the Excelsior Brigade met with nothing but scorn and contempt from the majority of the people, and to be a member of the Sickles' Brigade, was all that was necessary to exclude you from any society or company, and repeatedly have I felt the sting of such insults myself—no name was too bad for you; one would call you this and another would call you that, and even a person's own relatives would censure him for joining such a Brigade as that of Daniel E. Sickles.[5]

Sickles overcame the bad press "by winning to himself the good will of his men, and so popular did he become, that no inducement, however strong, could have any effect toward turning them against him." His old friend Charles Graham quit his post at the Brooklyn Navy Yard and joined, bringing 400 of his Navy Yard workers with him. What started as a pair of regiments—the Excelsior (or First Excelsior) and Jackson (Second Excelsior)—eventually swelled into three, and then five, regiments. (It would be several months before the regiments received their numeric New York state designations.) Although Sickles acted as the brigade commander, he was officially colonel of the First regiment. Graham eventually received command of the Fifth. A young Yale graduate named Joseph Hopkins Twichell was studying for the clergy when he enlisted in the Second Excelsior Regiment in April 1861. The Excelsior Brigade, Twichell observed, was "composed as it is of rough, wicked men. . . ."[6] Twichell was impressed when Sickles, an Episcopalian whom an acquaintance later remembered as being violently anti-Catholic, introduced his two chaplains (Twichell and First Excelsior chaplain Charles Bulkley) to the new brigade. "Had you heard this address, blindfolded," Twichell wrote his family,

> I am sure you would never have recognized the speaker as Danl. E. Sickles, i.e., if you had formed the opinion of him which the recorded events of his public life seem to [have] induced in most cases. His opening words concerning the power of God and the accountability of men and nations, might well have emanated from any pulpit in the land. His idea of the Christian ministry and its offices indicated that he had thought on the subject. In short, I could see no reason why Gen. Sickles, in theory at least,

was not himself admirably fitted to undertake the Chaplaincy of his own regiments.[7]

After his opening remarks, Sickles "made another speech, better and more pious if possible than the last." Among the spectators in the gallery was Teresa Sickles, but Bulkley warned Twichell not to mention it, "lest it might get into the papers." Afterward, Bulkley asked Twichell to ride with Teresa and her mother to the Sickles home. Twichell refused. "Some how or other I had not the courage. I did not want to look the woman in the face . . . I expect to learn much more from Mr. B. concerning this sadly notorious family."[8]

Problems arose when New York's Governor Edwin Morgan gave in to pressure from state politicians who argued that too many of New York's regiments were being drawn from the city. Morgan told Sickles and Wiley to disband all but eight of their companies, and the state hesitated to officially muster the Excelsiors into service. Sickles blamed it all on "unscrupulous partisans and a few newspapers that [said] troops raised by Sickles or other Democrats would march over to Jeff Davis in the very first battle in which they were engaged." The result of such opposition was that Sickles' brigadier general commission was not issued. Refusing to take no for an answer, Sickles headed for Washington to meet with President Lincoln and request that the Excelsiors be enlisted as United States Volunteers. Lincoln liked Sickles' initiative and still needed fighting Democrats. "Gen. Sickles adopted this course rather than the ordinary one—through the state Gov't," Joe Twichell wrote on May 15, "in order to avoid the delays of red-tapeism to a certain extent, and to thwart some plans supposed to be set on foot by political opponents to hamper his movements."[9]

The delays increased tensions in camp. The captains of at least two Excelsior companies filed grievances against Sickles in the State Supreme Court asking to be released from service. According to The New York *Times*, one captain complained that "his command were induced to join the Brigade by promises which had not been fully realized." Another captain alleged that his men had borne all of their travel expenses from Pittsburgh, only to have Sickles place them under "officers from among his own City friends." When the company tried to desert by ferry to Philadelphia, Sickles led a detachment with fixed bayonets down to the docks to keep them in camp. A lack of patience was not the only problem faced by the men. Sanitation was always an issue, as was alcohol abuse. Chaplain Twichell, however, was "pleased to observe that the General is flat-footed on the matter of temperance among officers—I do not say that he insists on total abstinence, but anything like getting tight he frowns upon."[10]

Sickles was finally issued orders on July 20, 1861, stating that "as many of the regiments under your command as are accepted, mustered into service, armed and ready, be without delay put en route to Harper's Ferry." Lincoln needed troops, and on July 22, the day after the Federal disaster at First Bull Run, the brigade finally broke camp. Sickles and the first three regiments departed immediately, while the newer two regiments left shortly thereafter. In December, the War Department issued orders designating the Excelsiors as New York Volunteer troops and the five regiments were re-christened the 70th through 74th New York. Having raised a brigade, Sickles presumed his brigadier generalship was assured. Officially he was commissioned colonel of the First (Excelsior) Regiment of United States Volunteers on June 29, 1861, but in practice he was functioning as the general of the Excelsior Brigade, and the men treated him as such. He was nominated as brigadier general of volunteers on September 3, but in another political twist, the Senate delayed his confirmation for several months. With Sickles' future rank in doubt, Private Alfred Oates of the Fifth Regiment wrote, "I do not know what they are going to do with Sickles. . . . We would not like to see him removed for he has always done well for us." Ever the opportunist, Sickles used his time in Washington to further ingratiate himself with Lincoln and work on getting the promotion put through.[11]

When Sickles marched off to war, he left his friend William Wiley with the bill for housing, feeding, and supplying the men. The bill that came due, in Wiley's estimate, totaled $283,000. He would later complain bitterly that Sickles had "marched off with three regiments, and paraded them before Lincoln, and said he had done all this out of his own pocket. There were piles of judgments against him in the offices. . . . He left me in the lurch. . . . I left him [Sickles] on account of it; denounced him then, and have done so since." Sickles later admitted that all of his accounts were paid except a "not inconsiderable amount" for which the vouchers were allegedly lost when two of his aides-de-camp were killed during the Peninsula Campaign. Although Wiley seems to have been left primarily on the hook, as late as 1877 Sickles was sued by a potential creditor for repayment. Sickles replied to the suit, not unreasonably, that such advances had been made "as a personal patriotic contribution" to the United States government, and not "for his personal benefit, nor upon his personal promise to repay the same." In any event, he never mastered managing large amounts of money.[12]

Few imagined in late 1861 that Daniel E. Sickles had stepped into a new role that he would play for the remainder of his long life. With no military education or training, he probably gave little serious thought to a career in the army. It is with some irony, then, that his new public persona was that of war hero—an image he would carefully cultivate for the next fifty years.

Sickles has become synonymous with the label of "political general." When applied to the American Civil War, the term characterizes officers who achieved their rank with little or no prior military training. Among many Civil War historians, the phrase has also come to imply military incompetence. Sickles was hardly unique in this regard, for the true test of battlefield competence involved more than a West Point education.

During the Civil War, the president commissioned generals, whose appointment was then subject to Senate confirmation. Political considerations, such as the general's party, state, and ethnicity, were facts of life in the appointment process. Because Lincoln needed to retain and develop the support of Northern war Democrats, he appointed a number of prominent Democrats as generals. Examples include Benjamin Butler, John McClernand, John Logan, and eventually Dan Sickles. Ethnic appointments, which were believed needed to win support among distinct immigrant groups, included the Eleventh Corps' Franz Sigel and Carl Schurz, along with "Irish Brigade" founder Thomas Meagher. Some of these men, like Logan, made excellent corps commanders. Many professional soldiers like Henry Halleck, however, despised the concept of raising a man from civilian life to a prominent position within the army. "It seems but little better than murder to give important commands to such men," grumbled Halleck.[13]

It was often the performance of these men off the battlefield, rather than on it, that earned the disdain of their counterparts. Regis de Trobriand, a French immigrant and non-West Pointer himself, "knew a retired merchant of New York, filled with the vanity of wearing the uniform" who raised a regiment of cavalry and was commissioned a colonel. "His camp was near us; he was never there. On the other hand, he displayed his uniform continually on the sidewalks of Pennsylvania Avenue and in the bar-rooms of the great hotels. He was present at all the receptions at the White House . . . sustained by the double power of money and political influence, he was nominated brigadier-general . . . without ever having drawn his saber from the scabbard, he returned home, to enjoy in peace the delight of being able to write the title of 'General' upon his visiting-cards."[14]

Sickles exhibited some of these characteristics. The Excelsiors spent late 1861 posted in lower Maryland locales, such as Budds Ferry, Piscataway, and Charlotte Hall, where future nemesis General George Sykes accused "a command [First Excelsior] under a Colonel [William] Dwight of Sickles' brigade" of inflaming local anti-Union sentiments by "carrying away of slaves and horses and the destruction of private property. . . . Complaints of this command were universal." Sickles used his proximity to Washington to frequently call upon the Lincolns. Through these visits and a mutual friend, Henry Wikoff, he became friends with another "outcast," Mary Todd Lincoln. In December 1861, excerpts from Lincoln's forthcoming speech to Congress were published in the New York *Herald*. The leak was considered so serious that a House Judiciary Committee opened an investigation. Wikoff eventually admitted to telegraphing portions of the speech to the *Herald*. How he received access to the speech remained unclear. It was widely believed that Mary Todd was somehow responsible. Sickles worked actively as Wikoff's counsel and ultimately pinned the leak on long-time White House gardener John Watt. Watt testified that he had read the speech one day while strolling through the Executive Mansion and then repeated it verbatim to Wikoff. The House Committee was satisfied, Watt was later fired, and Wikoff and Mary Todd were officially cleared. Still, many considered the resolution suspicious and wondered what influence Sickles had exerted on Watt. If Mrs. Lincoln was actually the source of the leak, then Sickles had saved the Lincolns from an embarrassing scandal, and he probably expected that he would be repaid at some point in return. He frequently socialized with Mrs. Lincoln throughout 1862, and although the Lincolns and Stanton appeared to be in his corner, Sickles still needed a benefactor within the army, where there remained a divide between the old-time regular officers and the new political appointments.[15]

The "professional" general who would eventually have a profound effect on Sickles' career was Joseph Hooker. Hooker was slightly older than Sickles, born in 1814, and was an 1837 West Point graduate. When George B. McClellan became General-in-Chief of the Armies of the United States in the fall of 1861, he began re-organizing his command. In the spring of 1862, the army's Third Corps was organized and given to Major General Samuel P. Heintzelman. Hooker became one of Heintzelman's three division commanders, and Sickles' Excelsior Brigade was assigned to Hooker's division. Although Sickles would later relate that he and Hooker became friends at first sight, Hooker was initially suspicious of his new subordinate who flaunted his relationship with Lincoln. In truth, the two large egos butted heads early on. In one instance during March 1862, when runaway slaves were seeking shelter in the army's camps, Hooker issued orders permitting slave hunters to enter and search for their property. When Sickles was shown Hooker's order, he ordered the slave hunters "out of the lines at once!" In 1879, after Hooker and Sickles had been friends for more than sixteen years, Hooker admitted, "When McClellan put him [Sickles] under me I objected, but McClellan said he knew of no one else that could manage him."[16]

In March 1862, Sickles received what appeared to be a fatal blow to his military aspirations when the Senate declined his appointment as brigadier general. Lincoln had no choice but to revoke the submission. Sickles reverted to the rank of colonel. Sickles and his supporters were outraged, especially after Hooker elevated Colonel Nelson Taylor to command the brigade. Calling the order "illegal, unauthorized and unjust," Sickles reminded Hooker that he was still the brigade's senior colonel and should remain in command until replaced by a brigadier general. Hooker disagreed.[17]

Ironically, just as Sickles' military career was floundering, the spring of 1862 offered promise for the Excelsiors' first major combat action. During March, General McClellan transported his Army of the Potomac to the tip of the Virginia peninsula between the York and the James rivers. His plan was to drive northwest up the narrow strip of land and capture Richmond. Before departing the army to plead his case in Washington, however, Sickles experienced his first taste of enemy fire. Leading one of the campaign's numerous reconnaissances, Sickles and a hand-picked detachment of the "huskiest and most reliable [men] that I could find" moved from Liverpool Point, Maryland, toward Stafford Court House, Virginia. Sickles later claimed he collided with two of General James Longstreet's infantry regiments, though a contemporary news account stated the opposition was comprised of 600 enemy cavalrymen. "There was a hot fight," wrote the former Congressman. "This was the first time that I or any of my men had been under fire. I was surprised when it was over and the Confederates had retired, evidently thinking we were the advance of a whole army. I was surprised that I had taken it so coolly. Mind you, I do not say this boastingly; simply as a man reviewing his sensations under certain conditions."[18]

Immediately thereafter on April 6, Sickles pulled away toward Washington on a gunboat and issued his farewell to the Excelsior Brigade. "Protesting that this [Hooker's] order is unlawful and unjust, I obey it because obedience to superior authority is the first duty of a soldier. . . . Whether we are separated for a day or forever, the fervent wishes of my heart will follow you forever on every field." Chaplain Twichell hoped Sickles would be back. The officer, he wrote, "has gone to plead his case with the authorities. I hope sincerely that he will succeed, although the opposition is bitter and powerful." The Excelsiors moved forward without him and on May 5, approximately one year after they first began to organize, Colonel Nelson Taylor led them into their first major combat at Williamsburg. Much of the battle was fought by the Third Corps, with the Excelsiors reporting a staggering 772 casualties in killed, wounded, captured, and missing. The baptismal bloodletting at Williamsburg was why May 5 was selected as the date for the annual Third Army Corps reunions that would be held for more than fifty years.[19]

While his men were fighting and dying on the Virginia peninsula, Sickles was busy in Washington trying to restart his brigadier nomination. He knew he could count on Lincoln and Stanton, and the New York newspapers. The former congressman worked allies in both Houses to build support, openly wondering if Maryland senators opposed him because he refused to allow hunting of runaway slaves in camp. On April 25, Lincoln re-nominated him for brigadier general. On May 13, eight days after Williamsburg, the Senate confirmed his nomination by the razor thin margin of 19-18. (The Excelsior Brigade historian believed the brigade's gallantry at Williamsburg helped influence the vote, and was the "death blow" to Sickles' political enemies.) Orders were officially issued on May 24 for "Brig. Gen. D. E. Sickles" to report to Hooker and once again take command of the Second Brigade of Hooker's division, Third Corps. Dan was enthusiastically greeted by the men and expressed the "deepest sorrow" that he had missed the most recent battle. He somehow saved himself again. Sickles, finally, was a brigadier general.[20]

Within days of returning, General Sickles saw his first major combat at Fair Oaks (or Seven Pines). In Sickles' absence, McClellan had moved the army up the Virginia Peninsula to the outskirts of Richmond. On May 31, Confederate General Joseph E. Johnston attacked Samuel Heintzelman's Third Corps and General Erasmus Keyes' Fourth Corps, both of which appeared isolated from the rest of McClellan's army south of the rain-swollen Chickahominy River. Hooker's division remained unengaged during the heavy fighting of the 31st, but Heintzelman moved it forward as a ready reinforcement when the Confederate attack was renewed on the morning of June 1. While Hooker was moving the division toward Heintzelman's right, Heintzelman detached Sickles' brigade and shifted it to the left (without Hooker's knowledge) and issued orders directly to Dan during the ensuing fight. Sickles deployed the Excelsiors under fire, recalling that Rebel minie balls seemed specifically directed at

Brigadier General Sickles
Author's Collection

mounted officers. By all accounts, including his own, Sickles acquitted himself well both offensively and defensively. "Gen. Sickles was enthusiastically cheered as the regiments passed him," wrote Twichell. George McClellan specifically praised two bayonet charges by the Second Excelsiors in a message to Edwin Stanton. "The dashing charge of the Second and Fourth Regiments," reported Sickles, "the cool and steady advance of the Third, occurred under my

General Joseph Hooker

National Archives

immediate observation, and could not have been surpassed." But most importantly for the newly minted brigadier general, Hooker finally seemed to be warming up to him. Although he griped that Sickles' detachment was "without my knowledge," Hooker referred to Sickles as the brigade's "gallant leader," and "their intrepid chief." Dan was still prone to go over Hooker's head, however, and demonstrated as much when he presented a captured Confederate "omnibus" to corps commander Heintzelman as a gift. The Excelsiors reported seventy-four casualties in what was (with combined casualties exceeding 11,000) the largest Eastern Theater battle up to that point in the war. But the most significant impact of the battle at Fair Oaks took place on the Confederate side, when General Johnston was severely wounded and eventually replaced in command by Robert E. Lee.[21]

While General Lee spent the next several weeks reorganizing his new army, McClellan accommodated his opponent by remaining in place. The Excelsiors spent much of the time on picket duty. On June 19, while riding at the front, Lieutenant Joseph L. Palmer, Sickles' aide-de-camp, took a minie ball through the brain. Although Sickles was now ignoring his wife and daughter in New York, Sickles "mourned as for a son" over Palmer's death, recalled Twichell. On June 25, the Seven Days Battles began when McClellan ordered Hooker and Philip Kearny's Third Corps divisions to move aggressively along the Williamsburg Road in preparation for moving the Federal siege artillery closer to Richmond. Hooker's morning attack faltered in large part because Sickles' brigade, on the right of Hooker's line, encountered difficulties moving through portions of White Oak Swamp, and then met heavy Confederate resistance on the right flank. Sickles and Colonel George Hall of the Second Excelsiors were reconnoitering the right when a heavy volley hit Hall's line and caused part of the regiment (in Sickles' words) to break "to the rear in disgraceful confusion." Sickles called for the remaining men to hold their ground and "used my best exertions," along with the help of nearby officers, to "rally the fugitives." This was all "mortifying" to Sickles because it occurred in Hooker's presence, but Hooker's report noted Sickles' "great gallantry in rallying a part of the Seventy-first New York Regiment and returning it to action after it had given way." Darkness ended the fighting. After Oak Grove, the Excelsiors remained active throughout the Seven Days, reporting 308 casualties from June 25 to July 1 as General Lee took the offensive in an effort to destroy the Army of the Potomac or drive it away from Richmond. Sickles was earning his battlefield experience.[22]

But even while in the field, Dan lost none of his taste for the lavish lifestyle that he had enjoyed in New York and Washington. When a steamboat arrived in camp loaded with supplies intended for the sick and wounded, Sickles was asked to transport the supplies to the hospitals. Ever the negotiator, he dickered, "I gave it on condition that my headquarters should be included in the sick list, entitled to one wagon load." Thus Sickles was able to surprise Hooker, the Comte de Paris, Phil Kearny, and several others with a lavish banquet of chicken, ham, beef, fruits, vegetables, and "purple and . . . amber liquid."[23]

Sickles did not stay long with his brigade. On July 16, orders arrived to "proceed to New York for the purpose of pushing forward recruiting for the regiments of his brigade. . . . The general commanding relies upon General Sickles to use his utmost exertions to hasten the filling up of his regiments and to rejoin his command at the earliest possible moment." Because he spent the late summer of 1862 giving recruiting speeches, Sickles missed both Second Bull Run and Antietam. Perhaps the most amazing example of the rehabilitation of Sickles' reputation occurred when some old backers in Tammany wanted him to run again for Congress. A relieved Twichell notified his family that Sickles "will decline nomination for Congress. . . . He is getting fixed in his new place most successfully and will probably serve himself, as well as the country, better here than in the warfare of words." Hooker's star was also on the ascendant. A press wire that read "Fighting—Joe Hooker" had been erroneously translated and appeared throughout the country as "Fighting Joe

Hooker." Hooker earned fully his nickname as a combat warrior, and was promoted to command the First Corps, which he led capably at Antietam.[24]

The enlisted men were not so kindly disposed to Sickles' prolonged absence. "We began to think it is time Daniel was coming to his Brigade," wrote the previously supportive Private Alfred Oates of the 5th Excelsior Regiment. "Colonel Graham and Daniel Sickles has only been with us in one fight and that was at Fair Oaks. The boys think more of Colonel Taylor than they do of Dan." Sickles did not rejoin his brigade until early November. When McClellan did not organize a strong pursuit of Lee's severely wounded Army of Northern Virginia following the heavy fighting at Antietam, Lincoln replaced him with General Ambrose Burnside. Burnside consolidated his army into three "Grand Divisions" of two infantry corps and attached cavalry. Hooker's growing reputation as an aggressive fighter carried him into command of the Center Grand Division, which included the Third Corps and Fifth Corps. Several notable changes occurred in the resulting shakeup. Among them, New Yorker Dan Butterfield was given command of the Fifth Corps in Hooker's "Grand Division," and George Stoneman replaced Heintzelman as Third Corps commander.[25]

Sickles was given command of Joe Hooker's old Second Division of the Third Corps. The advancement was astonishing given that only a few months ago his brigadier generalship was in serious doubt and he had done little fighting in the interim (although he had performed well when called upon). Ironically, his minimal battle experience did not hurt him. Although he missed Second Bull Run and Antietam, neither campaign showered much credit on the army's participating officers. He had support in high places and his recruiting speeches made good copy in the newspapers, all of which furthered his reputation as a fighting War Democrat. While West Pointers such as McClellan and John Pope were proving disappointments on the battlefield, Sickles was working Washington insiders and the New York papers to create an image as a successful and battle-hardened general. Despite his lack of extensive experience, Excelsiors like Joe Twichell thought "Sickles is brave as a lion and is much admired for his judgment. He has the making of a first class soldier in him. . . ."[26]

This phase of his career, in which he transformed himself from a disgraced ex-Congressman, again highlighted Sickles' ability to rise above adversity. Just as he had maneuvered his way out of a murder indictment, he sidestepped through a potential minefield of opposition to obtain his military aspiration.

Regis de Trobriand, who would rise to the rank of brigadier general in the Union army, considered Sickles "in many ways a typical American":

> He has a quick perception, an energetic will, prompt and supple intelligence, an active temperament. Naturally ambitious, he brings to the service of his ambition a clear view, a practical judgment, and a deep knowledge of political tactics. When he has determined on anything, he prepares the way, assembles his forces, and marches directly to the assault. Obstacles do not discourage him, but he never attempts the impossible, and as he has many strings to his bow, if one breaks, he will replace it by another.
>
> In him, ability does not exclude frankness. He likes, on the contrary, to play with the cards on the table with his friends and against his enemies . . . But let a friend deceive him, or an enemy cease to oppose him, then both become equally indifferent to him, and he goes on his way, troubling himself no further about them. . . . he rarely fails to make a good impression, even upon those who may be the least prepossessed in his favor.[27]

Although he did sometimes benefit from his father's deep pockets, Sickles was still in many ways a self-made success. He made himself a leader, but not everyone believed the role fit him well. "I noticed when I first saw Sickles, I felt he was unnatural," General Oliver Howard later commented. Many contemporaries commented upon, and sometimes ridiculed, his speech patterns. "I can always remember Sickles' voice as he piped up," recalled General Howard. W. H. Bullard remembered, "[an] old Clarion voice the boys knew so well." Mark Twain described Sickles' voice as monotonous, and in "perfectly constructed English . . . and as there is no animation in it, it soon becomes oppressive by its monotony and it makes the listener drowsy."[28]

Sculptor James Kelly, who knew Sickles in the postwar years, was less charitable than Twain. Sickles, he wrote, "had a very bumptious air, and talked in a high falsetto voice with a pursing of the lips, an arching of the eyebrows and a tilting of the chin; with an over-articulation of his words, in an effort vulgarians give when they are trying to make the impression that they are very genteel." Kelly found Sickles "a rather coarse man" and "it is peculiar about a man like that; when they try to appear refined, they become effeminate . . . when he talks, he talks like a sissy. The same as a girl when she puts on men's clothes and tries to act like a man. She is apt to overdue it and talk like a randy man."[29]

Sissy or not, the one inescapable criticism firmly directed against Sickles is that he was being given increasingly higher levels of responsibility without the commensurate experience. In assessing the performance of "amateurs" such as Dan Sickles, many "professionals" complained that these newcomers lacked the theoretical applications necessary to master the art of warfare. At the tactical level this was probably true, at least initially. There was little in civilian life to prepare Sickles for marching and maneuvering large bodies of troops under fire. It is also true that West Point graduates were more likely to be familiar with Antoine Henry Jomini's writings, or had studied under the instruction of Dennis Hart Mahan, or had read Henry Halleck's text *Elements of Military Art and Science*.

At a practical level, however, the professionals were often as ill-prepared as their new counterparts. The West Point curriculum generally favored topics such as engineering, mathematics, fortification, and army administration over actual strategy and tactics. Except for frontier garrison encounters against Indians, most professional generals had also not seen any combat since the Mexican War, and none of them had executed the large scale offensives of a Chancellorsville or of a Gettysburg. George McClellan was second in his West Point class, which prepared him to be an excellent organizer, but that did not translate into battlefield victories. Conversely, men such as future general-in-chief Nelson Miles performed well on the field but had never attended West Point. As a result, both amateurs and professionals had to adjust to the realities of this new war under fire, and a diligent citizen general such as Sickles could make up for the lack of education by studying his manuals on drill and tactics. Sickles certainly had the mental ability and aggressive spirit to excel as a regimental or brigade commander. But each successive promotion required an increased ability to coordinate and maneuver larger bodies of troops and to act more independently, but in cooperation with the army as a whole. As a result, Sickles' rapid promotion to division command, and then again to corps leadership, would become his greatest military shortcoming.[30]

At the battle of Fredericksburg in December 1862, George Stoneman's Third Corps consisted of David Birney's First Division, Sickles' Second Division, and Amiel W. Whipple's Third Division. First Division commander David Bell Birney was born in Alabama on May 29, 1825. His father, James Birney, a prominent anti-slavery leader, was nominated for president in 1844. The well-educated younger Birney moved to Philadelphia to practice law and became a prominent member of the city. He was active in Philadelphia's prewar militia, and although his militia unit never assembled for drill or parade, he

Brigadier General
David Birney

Library of Congress

volunteered its services
when Lincoln called for
troops in April 1861. The
regiment later became
the 23rd Pennsylvania
(Birney's Zouaves), and
he entered service as their
lieutenant colonel. Birney
was elevated to brigadier
general in February 1862
and received command
of a Third Corps brigade
in what later became Phil
Kearny's division. At Fair
Oaks, Sickles' battlefield
baptism,   Heintzelman
complained that Birney's brigade did not advance as directed. After the battle,
Heintzelman brought him up on court-martial for disobeying orders. Kearny
supported Birney against the charges, and Birney was (in Heintzelman's words)
"honorably acquitted." When Kearny was killed in September 1862, Birney
succeeded him to command of the division. He would lead the organization
until the Third Corps was disbanded in 1864.[31]

History has not always been kind to Birney. Theodore Lyman knew Birney
after Gettysburg, and described him as a man "who had many enemies" due
primarily to a "cold, covert manner." Birney was a "pale, Puritanical figure, with
a demeanor of unmovable coldness." Still, Lyman thought Birney's military
advancement well-earned, for "we had few officers who could command
10,000 men as well as he. . . . I always felt safe when he had the division; it was
always well put in and safely handled." One of Birney's men thought he could
"act as a bust for his own tomb, being utterly destitute of color" and "as
expressionless as Dutch cheese." Gouverneur K. Warren, who could be hot-

tempered in his own right, claimed that he and Birney once drew swords in an argument over the right of way for their columns. Regis de Trobriand led a brigade under Birney at Gettysburg and became close with the general. De Trobriand considered Birney "a man of ability and education, a gentleman of excellent manners, as well as a distinguished officer. . . . [He] had inherited the patriotism of his father, but not his political radicalism." Birney was senior to Sickles in division command, and had a longer resume of combat experience associated with the Third Corps than did Sickles. Birney's First Division would see more fighting at Fredericksburg, while Sickles again had little action.[32]

Serving on Sickles' staff at Fredericksburg was a fledgling young New York attorney named Henry Tremain. The well-educated Tremain was a former lieutenant and regimental adjutant in the 73rd New York. At Fair Oaks, Tremain served as the brigade's aide-de-camp and acting assistant adjutant-general. It was upon Tremain, Sickles wrote in his report, "whom I relied for nearly all the staff duty in the field throughout the day." Tremain was captured at Second Bull Run and sent to Libby Prison. Fortunately, he was quickly paroled and returned to service after negotiating a special exchange. He joined Sickles' staff, and by the time of the Fredericksburg campaign had been promoted to captain. He would continue his affiliation with Sickles and the Third Corps for the remainder of his life.[33]

At Fredericksburg, Robert E. Lee's two large corps of infantry under James Longstreet and Thomas "Stonewall" Jackson occupied a range of hills and ridges behind the city and guarded crossings along the Rappahannock River. Despite Lee's strong defensive position, Burnside intended to cross the river and push on toward Richmond. In order to do so, he planned to build bridges across the river at three places—two opposite the city and another about one mile downstream. During the morning of December 12, Sickles was directed to follow George Getty's Ninth Corps division across the center pontoon bridge. Late in the day, Hooker received orders to send two divisions to support Major General William Franklin's left wing south of the city. After waiting all afternoon without crossing, Sickles and Birney's divisions were instead marched downriver shortly before sundown. The night was dark and foggy. As the division bedded down for another cold night, Sickles spent the night walking among the sleeping soldiers. He was "inexpressibly sad," he later claimed, because he knew that so many young men would "hear the last roll call" before another sunset. He finally wrapped himself in a buffalo robe and fell asleep by a camp fire.[34]

The battle that opened on the morning of December 13 was launched by Federal troops who had crossed the river the previous day. Relegated to the role of observer, Sickles watched while Federal forces assaulted Lee's position on the heights and plain beyond the city, which "the enemy occupied in vast force, strengthened by elaborate works and defenses for infantry and artillery." Sickles and Birney were waiting to support the Union left (Franklin) on the plain south of Fredericksburg while the right wing massed in and about the city before assaulting the heights above them. "The field of battle was veiled," recalled Sickles, "as on the day before, by mists, made denser by the heavy fire, both of artillery and musketry, now becoming general along the line; yet it was easy to see that on the left we were gaining ground, and on the right our troops were gallantly moving up the heights against the enemy's works."[35]

Franklin's attack force was arrayed to Sickles' and Birney's left front, and consisted of three divisions from John Reynolds' First Corps under Abner Doubleday, John Gibbon, and George Meade. Early that morning, Reynolds informed Meade that his division would have "the honor of leading" the attack from the Federal left against the southern end of Lee's long line. The objective was a wooded height occupied by Stonewall Jackson's infantry. Between the Confederate-held heights and the plateau on which Franklin's Left Grand Division was posted was a depression or hollow several hundred yards long through which Meade's men would have to pass. "Owing to the wood, nothing could be seen of them," George Meade wrote, "while all our movements on the cleared ground were exposed to their view."[36]

Meade's attack began around noon. His division advanced several hundred yards and exploited a 500-yard gap between two brigades of A. P. Hill's division. The thrust smashed into Jackson's line and caused a rupture that threatened to break the front wide open. Meade's First Brigade met a severe fire in its front and artillery shells enfiladed its right. John Gibbon's division had advanced on Meade's right, but had failed to reach the heights. Meade's other two brigades followed, but were not in a position to exploit the break or support his exposed position. Meade dispatched staff officers requesting support, but before help could arrive the Confederates counterattacked, hammering Meade on the front and flanks. Like so many Civil War offensives, Meade and Gibbon were driven back in confusion and with heavy loss. By about 2:00 p.m., Reynolds' attack had failed.[37]

About 11:30 a.m., before Meade's attack, Franklin ordered Stoneman to send one of his Third Corps divisions to support Reynolds. Stoneman selected Birney's division to cross the river, leaving Sickles' division behind "to hold

Major General
George G. Meade

itself in readiness to cross at a moment's notice." Birney reported to Reynolds, who ordered him to deploy his men "in the field in rear of General Meade's division, as a support to the intended attack." Stonewall Jackson's batteries, which commanded the open field, punished Meade, Gibbon, and Birney's exposed troops. Reynolds ordered Birney to retire, but the move was still underway when Birney received one and perhaps as many as three requests for assistance from Meade. When neither Birney nor Gibbon was able to lend direct assistance to the embattled troops, a furious Meade reportedly rode to the rear, found Birney, and verbally castigated him. Birney, however, was authorized to accept orders from Reynolds, not Meade. Reynolds credited Birney's arrival "at this critical moment" with saving unsupported Federal artillery. When the Confederates counterattacked in force, Birney's regiments hit them with a well-directed fire, took some prisoners, and drove Jackson's infantry back to their starting point.[38]

Shortly after 2:00 p.m., Sickles received orders from Stoneman to also move his division to the front. By the time Sickles arrived, Gibbon's division appeared to have abandoned the field. Sickles formed two lines on Birney's right, where the Confederates briefly threatened Sickles' own right until a combination of sharpshooters and artillery secured the flank. Chaplain Joe Twichell watched a mounted Sickles directing some artillery fire "as unconcernedly as if riding before a plough." The presence of Birney and Sickles strengthened Reynolds' line. With the exception of skirmishing and some artillery fire, little of consequence occurred on the Federal left for the remainder of the battle. Meanwhile, on the Union right, Burnside continued with a series of futile assaults against Lee's strong position atop Marye's Heights.

Sickles' men spent the night at their post in the cold darkness, while he and his staff discussed the day's defeat over a fire. The exhausted Third Corps, like much of the Union army, spent the next two nights lying on the damp field without blankets and exposed to occasional picket fire. Stoneman and Franklin joined Reynolds in praising Birney, whose supporters later pointed out that he was in close proximity to Reynolds, was under Reynolds' supervision, and received praise (and not censure) from Reynolds himself. Unfortunately, Sickles had not enjoyed a similar opportunity for battlefield honors. The casualties told the story: Birney suffered nearly 1,000 from all causes, compared to Sickles' 100. Army-wide, the losses told a similar tale. Fredericksburg was an unmitigated disaster. The fighting claimed nearly 13,000 Federals in killed, wounded, captured, and missing, against only 5,300 Confederates. [39]

In his report, Meade neither censured nor praised Birney, but he did acknowledge that he had requested Birney's support early in the attack. Meade later explained that he had asked Birney three times to come to his assistance. Although Meade admitted that Birney arrived "just in time" to get his men out, Meade still thought Birney's division "might have come up sooner than it did." Writing privately to his wife on December 16, Meade blamed his failure on a lack of support and the enemy's strong "redoubts." Again in private correspondence, this time dated December 30, Meade turned his fire against his friend John Reynolds: "he knows I think he was in some measure responsible for my not being supported on the 13th as he was commanding the corps & had the authority to order up other troops—and it was his business to have seen that I was properly supported. . . . This is all confidential & for you alone." (The passage was later omitted from the publication of Meade's *Life and Letters*.) It was against Birney that Meade seems to have held the longest grudge. Seventeen months later, long after Reynolds had apparently been forgiven, Meade would tell his wife that he and Birney would "always" have Fredericksburg "between us."[40]

This dispute between Meade and Birney may have planted the seeds of animosity between Meade and the Third Corps that blossomed at Gettysburg. Blaming other units for a lack of support was common practice following Civil War battles, but Birney never accepted Meade's criticism. Birney blamed the fiasco on Franklin for "not sending more troops to the attack." Nearby divisions, including Sickles', did not attack "because all of us were under the supervision of officers who [would] not permit it." A division commander "was a small part of the great army and has to act strictly under orders. I did well and thoroughly all that I was ordered to do." Birney also admitted that while under fire, he had told a reporter that Meade's Reserves "might run and be damned." The heart of the dispute can be boiled down to this: Birney believed he had done all that was ordered, and Meade believed Birney could and should have done more.[41]

Birney's law partner later wrote that Birney's Fredericksburg conduct was often criticized "by officers of the army who had only heard one version of the story, and of comment in social circles, where General Birney and his accusers are both known. . . ." (Birney and Meade were both Philadelphians.) Criticism of Birney's Fredericksburg conduct continues to make its unchallenged way into Gettysburg literature today. Regardless of who was in the wrong, the result was that Meade had made an enemy of a prominent general in the Third Corps—and the bitterness may have seeped its way into the ranks. When Meade assumed command of the Army of the Potomac on the eve of Gettysburg, one Third Corps officer wrote that Meade was disliked within the corps, especially by Birney.[42]

Fredericksburg's bloody failure led inauspiciously into 1863 for Sickles and the Army of the Potomac. When Burnside was relieved on January 25, Abraham Lincoln promoted Joe Hooker to command the Army of the Potomac. Lincoln told Hooker that he considered him a "brave and skillful soldier," but the President feared "that the spirit which you have aided to infuse into the Army, of criticising their Commander, and withholding confidence from him, will now turn upon you." Charles Benjamin, who occupied positions within the Army and at the War Department, attributed Hooker's rise to the exertions of influential men "who believed in, and hoped to rise with him." Benjamin ultimately credited Hooker's promotion to a faction that was interested in elevating Secretary of the Treasury Salmon P. Chase, a friend of Dan Butterfield, to the presidency.[43]

One of Hooker's first orders of business was to settle on his staff. Hooker wanted Brigadier General Charles Stone as his chief of staff, but when Edwin Stanton refused Stone's appointment, Hooker settled on Dan Butterfield. Butterfield was born in 1831 at Utica, New York, into a prominent family. His father, John Butterfield, was a pioneer in express transportation and a principal founder in what later became the American Express Company. Like Sickles, Butterfield was not a West Pointer. He graduated from Union College, worked for his father, and studied law. Butterfield had been active in the New York militia and mustered into service in May 1861 as colonel of the 12th New York

Militia (the same unit in which Sickles had served in the early 1850s). More of an administrator than warrior, in 1862 Butterfield devised a special bugle call for directing brigades in battle, and also turned an old cavalry call into "Taps." In early 1863, he published a manual entitled *Camp & Outpost Duty for Infantry.* Appointed a brigadier general of volunteers in September 1861, Butterfield led the Fifth Corps at Fredericksburg. Joshua L. Chamberlain, who had served under him, was once asked if Butterfield was a good soldier. "Yes, he was a fine disciplinarian. In battle he always took his place according to the Army Regulations—300 yards to the rear. I never saw him in at the head of the column or in advance of his line."[44]

In late December 1862, after Fredericksburg but before Hooker assumed command of the army, Burnside replaced Butterfield and raised George Meade as the head of the Fifth Corps. (Both were major generals, but Meade was senior to Butterfield by eight days.) Butterfield resented being superseded, asking his friend Senator Henry Wilson "if anything can be done to save my command." The change created lasting friction between Butterfield and Meade. In all probability, Butterfield's new assignment as Hooker's chief of staff was helped both by his connections with Salmon Chase and his growing friendship with Hooker and Sickles. "Hooker is ambitious & very susceptible of flattery," Meade complained to his wife, and "Butterfield has been playing on the weaknesses." Many of the professionals would learn to hate Butterfield in his new role.[45]

Like Butterfield, citizen soldier Sickles also rose in Hooker's wake. The army was reorganized and General Stoneman was reassigned to command of the cavalry. Although Brigadier General Sickles had led a division during only one campaign—and had seen but little combat during that time—Hooker placed him in command of the Third Corps. The assignment was officially considered only "temporary" because Republicans in the Senate, still questioning his Democrat loyalty and probably his qualifications as well, resisted (again) in appointing him a major general. They refused to confirm him until March 9 (to rank from November 29). By the end of March, the "temporary" designation was removed from Major General Sickles' corps command.[46]

One of the significant problems festering within the Army of the Potomac, passed-over officers such as Regis de Trobriand complained, was that the "list for promotion did not come from military recommendations. . . . The greater part were put there from outside recommendation, and, above all, by political influence." As the highest ranking non-West Pointer in the Army of the

Potomac—a distinction he would carry into Gettysburg—Sickles' promotion to major general and command of the Third Corps was an amazing development even for that politically charged organization. Sickles succeeded by doing what he did best: latching onto prominent stars, in this case both Hooker and Lincoln, and convincing them that his aggressive temperament overcame his actual lack of experience. Not everyone was convinced. "Dan Sickles is a Major Genl. and commands a Corps in this Army," an amazed Frank Haskell wrote. "Was he ever a man? Did he not have criminal intercourse with the mother of his wife [sic] for years before his marriage? Did he not shoot Key many months after the knowledge of the crime of his wife, and then take that wife back to his bed?" According to Haskell, the men would taunt Sickles by singing within Dan's hearing, "Sickles killed a man/Sickles killed a man. . . ."[47]

Hooker initially retained Burnside's "Grand Division" organization. Fifth Corps commander George Meade was given the Center Grand Division, which included Sickles' Third Corps. The upshot was that for a few days in late January and early February, Sickles was under Meade's direct command. What could have been a fascinating command structure (Meade as a middle man between Hooker and Sickles) was terminated on February 5, when Hooker abolished the Grand Division structure. Hooker's immediate lieutenants were now responsible only for their own corps.[48]

If David Birney thought his combat experience, which exceeded Sickles', warranted promotion to major general or command of his own corps, then he was sorely disappointed. Birney remained a brigadier general in command of the First Division. Brigadier General Hiram Berry also received a promotion to major general and was assigned to command Sickles' former Second Division. Berry, thirty-eight years old, was another "amateur," a former member of the Maine legislature and town mayor who was active in Maine's local prewar militia. Berry had made brigadier general in April 1862 and led a brigade at Fredericksburg. Birney was particularly irritated by Berry's promotion, since Berry had previously commanded a brigade in Birney's division, and had now jumped over him to a higher rank. Though he may have been disgusted by the arrangement Birney accepted life under Sickles, who Birney thought "has many qualities to commend him as a soldier. I prefer him to mamby pamby Heintzleman who never had an original idea, a brave impulse, or a friendship in his life." In short order, Sickles and Birney became friends.[49]

The Army of the Potomac marked time, waiting for the spring of 1863 to arrive. Sickles set the tone by throwing a huge New Year's party, complete with a five piece band and a man who "chirruped like a bird." "The programme was to first salute the General," Chaplain Joe Twichell wrote, "then salute his victuals and drink. . . . Father O'Hagan and I . . . observed that rum was flowing freely. . . ." Regis de Trobriand, who had a great time, wrote that Sickles did things in "grand style" and "kept open house at his headquarters . . . The champagne and whiskey ran in streams. I wish I could add that they were used in moderation."[50]

Contemporaries described Sickles as liable to drink to excess on social occasions, but was otherwise a moderate drinker. Hooker, however, was known for hard drinking, among other social vices. But for all his faults, Hooker was too good of a soldier to let drinking interfere with his duties. "Whatever may have been his habits in former times," George Meade wrote, "since I have been associated with him in the army I can bear testimony of the utter falsehood of the charge of drunkenness." Charles Wainwright, who would command the First Corps artillery at Gettysburg, confided to his diary, "I should say that his failing was more in the way of women than whiskey." One brothel-filled section of Washington's Second Ward had famously become known as "Hooker's Division." Sickles had never practiced marital fidelity while at home, and with Teresa exiled in New York, he must have especially enjoyed the winter serving under a man of similar interests.[51]

Sickles, Butterfield, and Hooker were now close friends, and each brought their own reputational baggage to the relationship. Hooker had his women and alcohol, and Sickles added murder (and more women) into the mix. Butterfield's antecedents, however, were the most bizarre of the trio. As Washington Roebling explained, Butterfield in his youth "loved to see houses burn & was charged with having set many buildings on fire in Utica, N.Y." It was this sullied trio that set the army's social and morality standards in the months prior to Gettysburg. "The Army of the Potomac sank to its lowest point," Captain Charles Adams famously complained. "It was commanded by a trio, of each of whom the least said the better. . . . All three were men of blemished character. During that winter (1862-3) when Hooker was in command, I can say from personal knowledge and experience that the headquarters of the Army of the Potomac was a place to which no self-respecting man liked to go, and no decent woman would go. It was a combination of bar-room and brothel."[52]

One general who was decidedly excluded from this social calendar was the new Fifth Corps commander, George Meade. Already unpopular in the Third Corps and resented by the new chief of staff, Meade had no interest in their social vices and held the Regular soldier's healthy dose of disrespect for amateurs like Sickles and Butterfield. Meade's relationship with headquarters during the winter of 1862-63 had a decided impact on how men like Dan Sickles fought and remembered Gettysburg.

The happily married Meade was the professional and personal antithesis of Sickles. Meade graduated from West Point in 1835, and his front-line experience commanding troops under fire, first as a captain and then as a brigadier general of volunteers during the war's early stages, exceeded Robert E. Lee's. Meade's bravery and commitment were never questioned (at least prior to Gettysburg), and he worked his way up through division command at Antietam and Fredericksburg before assuming the leadership of the Fifth Corps. Meade, wrote General Alexander Webb, was "utterly fearless [and] he never sent a man where he had not been himself." When Hooker was promoted to army command, Meade told his wife, "I believe Hooker is a good soldier; the danger he runs is of subjecting himself to bad influences, such as Dan Butterfield and Dan Sickles, who being intellectually more clever than Hooker, and leading him to believe they are very influential, will obtain an injurious ascendancy over him and insensibly affect his conduct."[53]

Another trait that set Meade apart from both Sickles and Butterfield was that he was a self-professed novice at politics. "I am completely fuddled about politics. . . . Either carry on the war as it ought to be, with overwhelming means, both material and personal, or else give it up altogether. I am tired of half-way measures and efforts . . . I am in favor of . . . a vigorous prosecution of the war with all means in our power."[54] Lieutenant Colonel Theodore Lyman, who later served Meade as a volunteer aide-de-camp, described his superior as . . .

> a thorough soldier, and a mighty clear-headed man; and one who does not move unless he knows where and how many his men are; where and how many his enemy's men are, and what sort of country he has to go through. I never saw a man in my life who was so characterized by straight forward truthfulness as he is. He will pitch into himself in a moment, if he thinks he had done wrong; and woe to those, no matter who they are, who do not do right.[55]

While Meade did not share Hooker's, Sickles', and Butterfield's fondness for women and alcohol, his social exclusion was also at least partially due to his personality, which was less magnetic than any of the three men. There is no indication that Meade was the man anyone would turn to when looking for a good time. Assistant Secretary of War Charles Dana claimed Meade "was totally lacking in cordiality toward those with whom he had business, and in consequence was generally disliked by his subordinates." A staff officer compared Meade to "a firecracker, always going bang at somebody near him." General Webb, however, did not think Meade's moniker as the "old snapping turtle" was the result of a bad disposition. Rather, in Webb's view, Meade "thought too quick and expected others to think the same—without his source of information." Meade's correspondence suggests that he deeply felt the pressure of his increasing responsibilities. "I sometimes feel very nervous about my position, they are knocking over generals at such a rate." Meade was also like many of the old Army Regulars who resented finding themselves at professional peer-levels with amateurs like the sullied newcomer Sickles.[56]

In mid-February, when Meade had trouble obtaining a leave of absence from Hooker, the frustrated old soldier complained that "I do not like his entourage. Such gentlemen as Dan Sickles and Dan Butterfield are not the persons I should select as my intimates, however worthy and superior they may be." One month later, Meade was entertaining camp visitors when he decided to visit Hooker. "The General was, however, absent at a grand wedding which took place yesterday in camp, followed last night by a ball, and I understand another ball is given to-night by General Sickles. Not being honored with an invitation to these festivities, I did not go." Even Chaplains Twichell and O'Hagan drank some wine at the event and found Sickles "most familiar and agreeable."[57]

On March 17, the Irish Brigade celebrated St. Patrick's Day. "Most of the general officers of the army," wrote Second Corps staff officer Josiah Favill, "with their many lady friends, were invited. . . . Hooker looked superb, followed by a great crowd of staff officers and retinue of mounted ladies." The Third Corps responded on March 27 with a party of its own. The master of ceremonies was none other than David Birney, the supposed "pale, Puritanical figure, with a demeanor of ummovable coldness." The event received extensive newspaper coverage. According to the New York *Herald*, "Fighting Joe was there in his usual trim. Sickles was there, as suave and courteous as Sickles always is." An attendee recalled that "General Sickles and staff reached the ground, and the platform commenced to fill. Prominent in the foreground were several real live women, be-silked, be-furred, and bonneted like those of a more civilized state." Colonel Wainwright was more direct: "How they managed to scare up such a number of females I cannot imagine."[58]

President and Mrs. Lincoln visited the army in early April. Birney thought the president looked as "gaunt as a spectre." A banquet was held with Hooker and his corps commanders at Sickles' headquarters. For once Meade was invited, and he labeled the affair "a very handsome and pleasant dinner." Also in camp was Princess Salm-Salm, a circus rider and actress whose husband commanded the 8th New York. The princess must have been an impressive woman, for she makes an appearance in numerous Federal memoirs. With uncharacteristic understatement, Sickles admitted only that she was "youthful and attractive." It was due to the princess that Dan nearly ran afoul of Mary Todd Lincoln. When he realized that the president was depressed over the war's mounting casualties, Sickles tried to cheer Lincoln up. "I proposed to several of the ladies that they should kiss Lincoln, but there were serious objections," he later explained. None of the ladies were willing to lead off until Princess Salm-Salm agreed. Once she began, the others quickly followed suit. "Lincoln, it is needless to say, enjoyed the fun." Tad Lincoln, the president's son, was present and relayed every detail to the First Lady. The next day Dan learned that Mrs. Lincoln was "very angry with me." According to Butterfield, everyone at headquarters noted her "freezing coldness whenever Sickles was present." Mary Todd reportedly told her husband, "As for General Sickles, he will hear what I think of him and his lady guests. It was well for him that I was not there at the time." Sickles suffered through a decidedly awkward dinner with the Lincolns the next evening, during which he "saw at once how much I was out of favor." Fortunately for Sickles' social prospects at the Executive Mansion, the president joked his way out of the mess and peace was eventually restored.[59]

In between social events, Hooker succeeded in reorganizing and reinvigorating the demoralized army. One of Hooker's most lasting innovations, visible today on nearly every Gettysburg Union monument, was the adoption of corps badges. During the previous summer, General Phil Kearny designed a distinguishing diamond-shaped patch of red flannel for his division's soldiers to wear on their caps. The division now belonged to David Birney, and the men still wore the diamond to distinguish the "Kearny Division." Dan Butterfield, in one of his administrative inspirations, suggested to Hooker that a similar unique badge be given "for the purpose of ready recognition of corps and divisions." Hooker liked and adopted the idea. Since Birney's division was in the Third Corps, Sickles' entire corps retained the diamond, or "lozenge," as its enduring corps symbol.[60]

As winter turned to spring, and the army prepared to embark on what would evolve into the Chancellorsville campaign, Sickles was optimistic that Hooker had improved "the discipline and morale" so that the army was "for its numbers, more efficient in all respects than it had ever been before." Not everyone was as convinced. "Confidence enough is felt in Hooker, I think," General Marsena Patrick told his diary on April 28, "but not a great deal in some of his Corps Commanders . . . Sickles & the most of his crew, are poor—very poor concerns, in my opinion." Foreshadowing his own use of councils of war during the Gettysburg campaign, George Meade wrote ominously that Hooker "is remarkably reticent of his information and plans; I really know nothing of what he intends to do." The secrecy might result in "important plans" being "frustrated by subordinates, from their ignorance of how much depended on their share of work."[61]

Chapter 3

I Think it is a Retreat

Although the battle of Chancellorsville was fought two months before Gettysburg, what happened in May had a direct impact on the July battle's tactics, personality conflicts, and even the eventual outcome. Unlike earlier battles, Sickles saw significant action at Chancellorsville, and he would carry the lessons he learned there into Pennsylvania later that summer.

The Spring 1863 campaign opened with the armies of Joseph Hooker (130,000) and Robert E. Lee (61,000) locked in an apparent stalemate along the Rappahannock River around Fredericksburg. Lee's Army of Northern Virginia had been significantly reduced by the detachment of much of James Longstreet's First Corps for operations south and east of Richmond around Suffolk, Virginia. For Hooker and the Army of the Potomac, the time to strike had arrived. Rather than repeat General Ambrose Burnside's attempt to attack Lee frontally, Hooker decided on a bold plan to turn Lee's left flank. Hooker combined George Meade's Fifth Corps, Oliver Howard's Eleventh Corps, and Henry Slocum's Twelfth Corps into a strong column that marched on a wide detour northwest upstream to cross the river beyond the Southern flank, turn back east, and strike Lee's rear. John Sedgwick, meanwhile, commanded a diversionary column that remained in and around Fredericksburg. His mission was to keep Lee's army pinned down there while Hooker turned his flank and George Stoneman's Federal cavalry rode into Lee's rear to threaten Confederate supply and communications lines. By stealing a flank march on Lee, Hooker hoped Lee would fall back (and so abandon his powerful river line and the Fredericksburg defenses), or stand and fight at a disadvantage (and be beaten where he stood).[1]

The Federal move began on April 27. By the 30th, Hooker's main column was across both the Rappahannock and Rapidan rivers. Joined by Darius Couch's Second Corps, the powerful flanking force began to concentrate beyond Lee's left around the crossroads at the small hamlet of Chancellorsville about ten miles west of Fredericksburg. This portion of Spotsylvania County was known as the Wilderness because it was covered with dense second-growth woods laced with small streams, gullies, briars, and thick underbrush. Only a handful of large clearings worthy of the name dotted the landscape. Chancellorsville sat at the intersection of several roads, including the Orange Turnpike and the Plank Road, which ran east to Fredericksburg and so was the most direct route leading like a giant arrow toward Lee's lines.

The first stage of the operation worked smoothly for the Federals. Lee became suspicious of Sedgwick's "apparent indisposition to attack," however, and on the 29th his cavalry commander, James Ewell Brown (Jeb) Stuart, confirmed Hooker's river crossings. The pressing dilemma brought out the best in Lee, who reacted with his characteristic aggressiveness. He did not retreat, however, but instead decided to come out of his defenses and offer battle. Instead of doing so with his entire army, he violated one of the cardinal rules of warfare and divided his command in the face of superior numbers. The same night that Stuart brought him the information (April 29), Lee put Thomas "Stonewall" Jackson's corps in motion to confront Hooker at Chancellorsville while the balance of his army remained in its Fredericksburg defenses to confront Sedgwick.[2]

Dan Sickles had originally been assigned to support Sedgwick, but at 1:00 p.m. on April 30, he received orders to report to Hooker at Chancellorsville. Sickles reached the commanding general about 9:00 a.m. on May 1 and was ordered to mass "my forces in the forest, near the junction of the roads leading to Ely's and the United States Fords." Captain Francis Donaldson of the 118th Pennsylvania was introduced to Sickles for the first time. The general was "leisurely sauntering" near Hooker's headquarters. The captain found him "to be an affable, pleasant man, not at all distant or hard to approach, as would have been supposed by reason of his rank." Sickles apologized, "I am sorry gentlemen that I have nothing with which to extend the hospitalities," but a nearby officer produced a bottle of Drake's Plantation Bitters, which the group socially drank ("strangled over the vile stuff" as Donaldson wrote.) Sickles, like most of the army, believed that Hooker's plan had thus far been "conducted with perfect success . . . as to be a complete surprise to the enemy."[3]

Neither army had an overwhelming desire to become entangled in the Wilderness because the thick undergrowth would restrict troop movements, limit the usefulness of artillery, and (in Hooker's case) potentially neutralize his advantages in superior numbers and firepower. On Friday, May 1, with roughly 70,000 men under his direct influence, Hooker set out with three columns to push through the Wilderness and continue east toward Fredericksburg. Confederate detachments under Lafayette McLaws and Jackson intercepted the move. The collision that followed seems to have surprised the Federals. Hooker responded by ordering his men to fall back into the Wilderness toward Chancellorsville. Like many other officers, the withdrawal angered and bewildered George Meade, who later wrote, "[J]ust as we reached the enemy we were *recalled* [emphasis in original]." Not only had Hooker failed to get his army out of the Wilderness, but he had surrendered the initiative to his opponent.

Jackson, meanwhile, continued pressing the Federals, who started digging in for a defensive battle. As the Federal army's new position coalesced, Hooker expressed concerns that Oliver Howard's Eleventh Corps, which held the extreme right flank, was not fully secure. Hooker wanted the flank contracted and swung back to a more secure position, but Howard argued that it would demoralize the Eleventh Corps to fall back even farther. Although he agreed to build field fortifications, Howard declined any assistance.[4]

That evening near dusk, Lee and Jackson met near the intersection of the Orange Plank Road and Catharine Furnace Road, a little more than one mile east of Chancellorsville. After determining that Hooker's left flank was securely fixed on the Rapidan River and well defended, the pair of Southern generals turned their attention to the Federal right. Neither general knew where Hooker's right flank was situated, but cavalry intelligence brought in by Fitz Lee's troopers suggested it was about two miles west of Chancellorsville, and therefore open to the possibility of being turned. Jackson's chaplain, Beverly Tucker Lacy, knew the area well and confirmed that the local road system would allow the Confederates to swing in an arc south, west, and then north to outflank Hooker's right. Lee divided his outnumbered army again, cleaving it into three widely separated pieces. His own direct command consisted of about 15,000 infantry and cavalry intended to hold Hooker's attention in front of Chancellorsville. The force left behind at Fredericksburg under Jubal Early, about 12,400 troops, had orders to prevent John Sedgwick from capturing the heights above the town and opening a direct route into Lee's rear. Jackson, meanwhile, accompanied by Stuart's cavalry to screen the flanking operation, would lead a grand total of 33,000 men (infantry, artillery, and cavalry) to find and turn the enemy flank. Jackson's tradition was to start his marches at first light, but circumstances delayed the column until 7:00 a.m. the following morning.[5]

Joe Hooker's line that Saturday, May 2, extended slightly more than six miles in length. The Federal line fronted generally south and ran roughly east to west. Meade's Fifth Corps held the left (east) side anchored near the Rapidan River. On Meade's right was a slightly protruding salient near Chancellorsville occupied by two Second Corps divisions under Winfield Hancock and William French. Henry Slocum's Twelfth Corps was next in line, forming the army's left center. Sickles threw Brigadier General David Birney's division on Slocum's right, holding Hiram Berry's and Amiel Whipple's divisions in reserve. On Birney's right, holding the army's right (west) flank, was Oliver Howard's Eleventh Corps. Howard's outfit was the smallest corps in the army and his right ended along the Orange Turnpike with no natural feature anchoring the line. In military terms, the army's right flank was "in the air." Howard's men, however, were the farthest Federals from the enemy and so seemed the least likely to see substantial action.[6]

About sunrise, Sickles and engineer Cyrus Comstock accompanied Hooker on an inspection tour of the Federal right flank. Sickles claimed that he accompanied Hooker because his proximity to Howard increased his own interest in the army's right. According to Sickles, the soldiers demonstrated "irrepressible enthusiasm" for Hooker as they rode along the lines. When the party reached Howard's sector they noticed several gaps in his front and reached the conclusion that his line was overextended. Engineer Comstock urged Howard to close the gaps, but he remonstrated. How could an enemy in any serious numbers come crashing through the tangled Wilderness from that direction? Some fortifying along his lines had already been done, but Howard had not yet refused his flank to make it more difficult to turn.[7]

By 8:00 a.m., the head of Jackson's Confederate column had been underway for about an hour. Near the Catharine Furnace, the Furnace Road crossed a stretch of high open ground. Some three-quarters of a mile north was Hazel Grove, an important elevation occupied by David Birney's division of Sickle's Third Corps. Federal observers perched in trees began reporting to Birney that enemy infantry, artillery, and wagons were crossing the open space and moving west in the general direction of the Federal right flank. "About 8 o'clock Saturday morning I first saw the enemy's column moving continuously across our front towards the right," Birney later recalled. "It was in plain sight, with trains, ambulances. . . ." Birney "immediately" passed these messages up

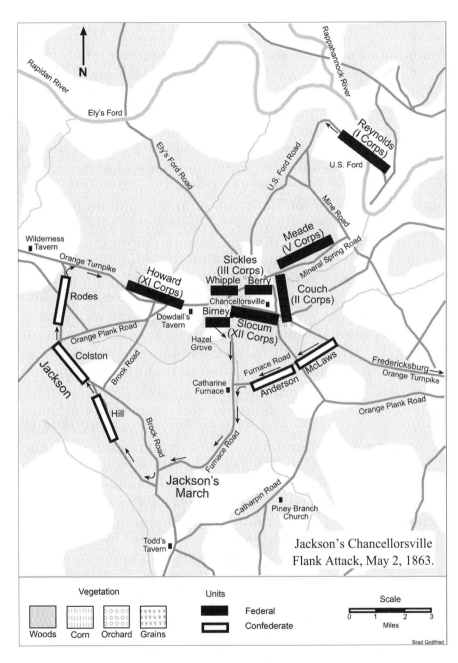

Jackson's Chancellorsville
Flank Attack, May 2, 1863.

Vegetation

Woods Corn Orchard Grains

Units

Federal
Confederate

Scale

0   1   2   3
Miles

Brad Gottfried

the command chain, but both Hooker and Sickles were absent on their inspection tour and so no response was forthcoming for about ninety minutes. Sickles thought it was shortly after 9:00 a.m. when "a movement of the enemy was reported to me by General Birney. I had then returned to headquarters." During that delay, Jackson's men covered nearly another three miles.[8]

Hooker instructed Sickles to personally investigate the report. The Third Corps leader rode to Hazel Grove and "satisfied myself that it was a movement in great force." When he reported as much to the army commander and suggested he bring up some rifled guns to shell the Confederates, Hooker agreed. Between 10:00 a.m. and 11:00 a.m., Judson Clark's battery opened on the enemy, who double-quicked across the opening in the woods. The Southerners, boasted Sickles, were "vainly endeavoring to escape our well-directed and destructive fire." Jackson detached Colonel Emory Best's 23rd Georgia Infantry regiment to remain behind and "guard the flank of the column in motion against a surprise." While the remaining infantry scurried past the gap, orders were also sent for Jackson's heavy corps train to take a more roundabout route to avoid the artillery fire.[9]

Hooker, meanwhile, cautioned Howard to prepare for a possible flank attack, since intelligence offered "good reason to suppose that the enemy is moving to our right." Hooker also ordered Sickles to reconnoiter to the east where Lee had halted on May 1, but not to the south where Jackson's column was spotted. Two regiments from Berry's division advanced and drove back enemy pickets until they ran into solid Confederate defensive lines that triggered a sharp skirmish. Sickles later called the movement a "brilliant reconnaissance" that demonstrated for Hooker that the enemy on his left was still in place and ready for a fight.[10]

Other than warning Howard, Hooker appears to have done little to strengthen his army. Sickles, on the other hand, appeared characteristically aggressive. He reported enemy movements to not only Hooker but to Slocum and Howard, "inviting their cooperation" in case Hooker "should authorize me to follow up the enemy and attack his columns. At noon I received orders to advance cautiously toward the road followed by the enemy, and harass the movement as much as possible." Sickles later claimed it was he who proposed to "strengthen" the reconnaissance, with the intention of gaining possession of the Furnace Road on which Jackson was marching and either cut off the enemy if they were retreating, or cut them in half if they were attacking.[11]

Sickles ordered Birney's division forward, along with the support of Hiram Berdan's U.S. Sharpshooters. Berdan's men, with Birney in the rear, pushed south toward the 23rd Georgia's skirmishers. It was now about 1:00 p.m., and while it may have appeared to Sickles, Berdan, and Birney that they were about to strike the enemy's main flank, they didn't realize that Jackson's infantry column had already crossed the Furnace clearing. It was now about five hours after Jackon's march was first detected. Colonel Best's 23rd Georgia stalled Berdan and Birney long enough for the last of Jackson's trains to turn off, but the Georgians were eventually overwhelmed and at least 276 were captured. The large cache of prisoners, Sickles later claimed, confirmed they were part of Jackson's corps. The Southern captives estimated their fighting strength at approximately 40,000 men. If Sickles indeed gained this intelligence, time was rapidly running out to make good use of it.[12]

Since Jackson's column was actually turning south at the Catharine Furnace (before eventually turning north by west toward Howard's flank), and since only wagons were still visible, Sickles reached a conclusion that would have lasting import on the battle. At 1:30, he reported to Hooker, "I think it is a retreat. Sometimes a regiment then a few wagons. . . ." Later, when the error of this conclusion became apparent, he modified his opinion. In his report dated May 20, he wrote that "the movement indicated a retreat on Gordonsville or an attack upon our right flank—perhaps both, for if the attack failed the retreat could be continued." Still later, he told the Congressional Committee on the Conduct of the War, "The direction which the enemy's column took . . . was susceptible of two interpretations. It was, perhaps, a movement in retreat; for they had a large train with them, a great many wagons, and all arms, except cavalry, were in large force." The other "interpretation," of course, turned out to be the correct one: a flank attack that rolled up part of the Army of the Potomac.[13]

Sickles' report that the Rebels were in retreat probably reached Hooker's headquarters around 2:00 p.m. The report gained easy acceptance among prominent Federal officers. "I was deceived at the time of Jackson's attack," Oliver Howard later admitted, "and did believe, with all the other officers, that he was making for Orange Court House." Sickles' report served to reinforce Hooker's hope that his plans were still proceeding successfully. Another event helped foster the same mistake. General Lee's chief of staff, Colonel Robert Chilton, had earlier misinterpreted an order that started Confederates under Jubal Early and William Pendleton out of their Fredericksburg defenses. Federal observers passed the erroneous intelligence to Butterfield and Hooker that the enemy was abandoning Sedgwick's front. The intelligence seemed sound all the way around and convinced Hooker. At 2:30 p.m., he sent his corps commanders a circular ordering them to be ready to move early the next day. At 4:10 p.m., Hooker telegraphed Sedgwick to seize Fredericksburg, and included this mistaken statement: "We know that the enemy is fleeing, trying to save his trains. Two of Sickles' divisions are among them."[14]

Around 3:00 p.m., Captain Alexander Moore of Hooker's staff appeared at Howard's Eleventh Corps headquarters with a message from Sickles. "I am advancing a strong line of two brigades to ascertain whether the enemy is retreating," he wrote. "General Birney reports that he has reached a brigade of the enemy in rifle-pits, posted, as I think, to cover the retreating column. I will attack if the enemy is not stronger than the reports so far represent him, and occupy the road by which he is retreating. Please support my advance." Howard, however, had received orders from Hooker to keep a strong reserve on hand and so declined Sickles' request. Perhaps an hour later, Moore returned with a direct order from Hooker for Howard to support Sickles' move. Reluctantly, Howard detached Francis Barlow's brigade for the task, and decided to lead the brigadier to the scene himself. Barlow's departure left the Eleventh Corps with fewer than 11,000 men. Federal artillery, which poured fire on what Sickles still referred to as "the retreating column of the enemy," helped Birney gain the Furnace Road.[15]

Sickles had bigger plans than simply advancing Birney. He requested permission to make "a flank attack" on Jackson and asked that three regiments of Alfred Pleasonton's cavalry, along with horse artillery, be sent to his support in order to launch a vigorous pursuit. As Pleasonton later recalled, "Sickles sent word that the Rebels were retreating towards Gordonsville. . . . Hooker sent for me, said he wanted an officer experienced in that part of the field." When Pleasonton arrived near Hazel Grove, "Sickles sent word the enemy were retreating and ordered me to follow." With infantry from the Eleventh and Twelfth corps, both Birney and Whipple's divisions, together with Pleasonton's cavalry, the Federal force gathered near the Catharine Furnace had swelled to nearly 25,000 men. By this time, Hooker was too preoccupied with supporting Sickles' planned assault to give much thought to Howard's Eleventh Corps and the army's exposed right flank.[16]

With his typical self-confidence, Sickles "found every indication that looked to a complete success as soon as my advance could be supported." Confederate resistance on his front had momentarily ceased, "and although our scouts reported a considerable force on the right and in front, it was evident that in a few minutes five or six regiments would be cut off and fall into our hands." Sickles claimed that he was "about to open my attack in full force" when an aide arrived from Howard to warn him that Stuart's cavalry was in his rear, Stonewall Jackson was nearby, and "our troops were retreating." No sounds of a major engagement from the right-rear were audible, so an incredulous Sickles "felt very indignant at this communication; I utterly disbelieved it." A few moments later another aide arrived "begging" Sickles to send a regiment of Pleasonton's cavalry to Howard, adding "that his corps had given way, and that our right flank had been carried by the enemy, and that Jackson was in my rear."

Unfortunately for the Federals, the reports were accurate. Jackson had successfully deployed approximately one-half mile opposite the Eleventh Corps' right flank and attacked in depth across a broad front against Howard's narrow wing. When Jackson's infantry came bouncing out of the Wilderness against Howard's unsuspecting soldiers, the Eleventh Corps broke and fled in wild disorder. Elements stood here and there and did their best to stem the tide, but the weight of the attack was too great to withstand. By the time Sickles learned of the growing debacle, Jackson's brigades were pushing east using the Orange Turnpike as a guide.[17]

Sickles' own attack plan was quickly abandoned. The collapse on the right happened so fast that he had barely sent staff officers to recall Birney and Whipple when hundreds of men from the Eleventh Corps appeared. Jackson's infantry were quick to follow. "The fugitives of the Eleventh Corps swarmed from the woods and swept frantically across the cleared fields in which my artillery was parked," Sickles wrote. "The exulting enemy at their heels mingled yells with their volleys, and in the confusion which followed it seemed as if cannon and caissons, dragoons, cannoneers, and infantry could never be disentangled from the mass in which they were suddenly thrown." Sickles and Pleasonton readied their artillery to stop Jackson's columns. After Howard's "panic-struck hordes" had cleared Sickles' front, Confederates stepped out of the woods and reportedly called out, "We are friends, don't fire!" Pleasonton was not fooled by the ruse and the Union guns opened on the pursuers. Sickles praised Pleasonton's actions in his report, and Captain James Huntington of Battery H, 1st Ohio Artillery, recalled that Sickles "warmly expressed his approbation" for the manner in which Huntington's command held its ground. Birney's division retraced its steps in the growing darkness to Sickles and Pleasonton. Birney found both generals deploying artillery and cavalry "with which they had managed to stay Jackson's corps . . . and, in my opinion, saved the army from a great disaster."[18]

Ignoring his own significant contribution to the presumption that Jackson was in retreat, Sickles later blamed the entire campaign's failure to the "giving way" of the Eleventh Corps. Birney blamed the Eleventh Corps rout on its "disregard of rules of warfare, had its pickets too close to the main body, and was surprised by the sudden massed attack of the enemy on its right flank and rear." Although Birney didn't witness their flight, it was described to him "by officers who saw it, as disgraceful in the extreme." George Meade also blamed the day's misfortunes on the "bad behavior" of Howard's corps. Second Corps staff officer Josiah Favill complained, "Howard's men had stacked arms and were playing cards and loitering about without any thought of danger, when the enemy sailed right into them, driving them like flocks of sheep . . . deaf to all entreaties many of them actually ran right across into the arms of the very men they were trying to avoid. It was really ludicrous."[19]

Most of Howard's fugitives ran east down the Turnpike toward Chancellorsville. The sounds of the attack had not yet reached the Chancellor house. About 6:30 p.m., Hooker and two staff officers were on the porch when one noticed a commotion down the road. After studying it for a moment, the aide shouted, "My God, here they come!" Hooker, his staff, and headquarters cavalry vainly tried to halt the flight. Cavalry was usually effective at stopping stampeding infantry, but most of the army's horsemen had been sent to support Sickles' planned attack. Hooker's only nearby infantry reserve was Hiram Berry's Third Corps division, so he ordered Berry's men to move to the front. The strongest motivation to stop running may have been Hooker's order for the Twelfth Corps soldiers to shoot fleeing Federals. Whatever the reason, Howard's men began to halt. Sickles would later boast that he and Pleasonton had "succeeded in checking Jackson," but by 8:00 p.m., darkness, disorganization, exhaustion, and scattered Union defensive efforts had done more to slow Jackson's attack than anything Sickles and Pleasonton had accomplished. Still, Sickles had held his ground when others had fled. In a stunning turn of events, about 9:00 p.m. Jackson was reconnoitering in front of his lines when he was accidentally shot by his own men. The general was carried from the field and died on May 10.[20]

Hooker patched together a line fronting north and west to block any further attempts by Jackson's troops to drive up the Turnpike and Plank Road. The road was now straddled by both armies, with Jackson's men to the west and Hooker's soldiers to the east. Hazel Grove was still under Third Corps control and anchored by thirty-four guns, but was now a salient sticking out from Hooker's main line. Perhaps still agitated by his lost opportunity at the Catharine Furnace, Sickles obtained permission for one of the boldest and most questionable of Civil War tactics: a nighttime attack. Theodore Dodge wrote that the objective was to recapture some guns, caissons, and portions of Whipple's ammunition trains that had been left in the woods in front of Sickles, and to join his right with Slocum's new line. The tactical aspects of the plan were rather simple: Birney's and Whipple's divisions would advance straight from Hazel Grove to the Orange Plank Road. "The plan was to charge into the woods with the bayonet," wrote Regis de Trobriand, "striking down the enemy where we found him." According to Birney, he received orders from Sickles about midnight "to attack Jackson's corps with my division, driving them from the plank road and the small earthworks."[21]

When the order came to move out, Birney's nervous men fixed bayonets and stepped off. The Confederates were on their left and front. Once in the darkened woods, the Federal formations began to break up. Sporadic firing broke out, but no one was sure who was firing at what. Nerves added to the tension felt in every trigger finger, and before long the firing was wildly out of control, with some of it penetrating the backs of those walking in the front rank. Somehow, Sickles forgot to notify General Henry Slocum of his attack, so when he heard the shooting, the Twelfth Corps commander ordered Federal artillery at Fairview to fire into the moving masses. Some of Birney's men shifted to the right and collided with Alpheus Williams' divisional line (Twelfth Corps), a mistake that triggered the exchange of more friendly fire. So confused was the affair that the 3rd Michigan boldly captured a Twelfth Corps battery, and two regiments from Thomas Ruger's Twelfth Corps brigade fired into one another. According to Abner Doubleday, a division commander in John Reynolds' First Corps, some of Sickles' men thought themselves surrounded and surrendered to Hiram Berry's division. Private John Haley of the 17th Maine recalled that some of the officers were "so frightened that they couldn't have told their names." A rumor spread that Brigadier General J. H. Hobart Ward had been taken prisoner, but had instead ridden down two of his own men while fleeing for the rear.[22]

The attack fiasco came to a fitful end when Sickles' two disorganized divisions made their way back to where they started. It was about 1:00 a.m. when Birney reported to Sickles that "we held the road and works, and had recaptured the artillery and caissons taken from us during the stampede of the 11th corps." Sickles pronounced the exercise a success, but Theodore Dodge wrote that, despite a gallant attack, Sickles "overstated" the benefits, having recovered only part of Whipple's trains and "one or two guns." According to Charles Mattocks of the 17th Maine, "This midnight affair was a bad thing as we fought both Rebs and Federals." In the end, the midnight offensive became just a footnote in a long and bloody day filled with deadly blunders. The attack was a fitting example of Sickles' aggressive temperament overruling sound military judgment.[23]

Hooker decided to contract his lines on Sunday, May 3. Birney, Whipple, and more than thirty artillery pieces were still in the Hazel Grove salient. Although the bulge divided Lee's forces into two separate wings (and so offered the Federals a small glimmer of hope of defeating Lee in detail), Fighting Joe was now thinking defensively. He may have feared that Sickles could be caught in a crossfire delivered by Lee to his rear (south), and Jackson's corps to the front and left. A withdrawal, however, would mean giving up Hazel Grove, an open grassy ridge several hundred yards long. Confederate artillerist E. Porter Alexander described it as "a beautiful position for artillery." If Confederate batteries occupied it, they could strike the Federal lines all the way to the Plank Road as well as the Federal artillery massed at Fairview, a high and open clearing just southwest of Chancellorsville. Almost certainly unaware of the significance of that key terrain feature, before daylight Hooker ordered Sickles to abandon Hazel Grove and march his two divisions and batteries to Fairview. Since Howard's corps had been effectively wrecked as an organized fighting body, Sickles' two divisions could be used to reinforce the main battle line. The decision to abandon Hazel Grove, many historians have argued, would have a profound influence on Sickles and his controversial actions at Gettysburg just two months later.[24]

Charles Graham's Pennsylvania brigade (the same regiments that would occupy the Peach Orchard salient on July 2 at Gettysburg) comprised the rearguard with James Huntington's Ohio battery. During the Federal withdrawal, James Archer's Confederate brigade of A. P. Hill's division attacked near daylight. The Southern infantry climbed over the undefended breastworks and quickly flanked Graham. Three of Huntington's six guns were captured, prompting him to complain about the lack of infantry support. By 6:45 a.m., the Rebels occupied Hazel Grove. Jeb Stuart, who had replaced the wounded Jackson in temporary command of the Second Corps, recognized the terrain for what it was—an outstanding artillery platform—and immediately ordered Alexander to fill it with guns. Within a short time seven Southern batteries comprising twenty-eight pieces were unlimbered. Most of the Federal line, including Hooker's headquarters at the Chancellor house, was within distant view. Alexander added fourteen guns along the Plank Road so that the Fairview position could be hit with converging artillery fire.[25]

When Stuart attacked, his infantry advanced from the west. Most of the assault struck the front of the Third and Twelfth corps. "Then began a desperate battle," Regis de Trobriand remembered, "the brunt of which the Third Corps had still to bear." Sickles thought that the "vigor and tenacity of the enemy's attack seemed to concentrate more and more upon my lines near the Plank road and on my left flank." Four of A.P. Hill's brigades, now under Stuart's command, smashed into Hooker's line near the Plank Road, striking Hiram Berry's division. A bullet struck General Berry while he was delivering orders. "I am dying," he exclaimed to his staff. "Carry me to the rear." The mortally wounded commander was taken to the Chancellor house, where he later died.[26]

After Berry's fall, the Third Corps position experienced a near-crisis when Edward Thomas' Georgians threatened to take Fairview in the flank and rear. At the height of the assault, Brigadier General Joseph J. Revere "shamefully" (in Sickles' words) marched the Excelsior Brigade and a portion of two others off of the field to the rear. Revere claimed that his command was "broken" and "was almost without ammunition and quite out of rations," and that he only intended to move "them down the road for the purpose of reorganizing and bringing them back to the field comparatively fresh." Thomas fought his way within 800 yards of the Chancellor house before being driven back by a successful counterattack from William French's Second Corps division. Sickles reformed the Excelsiors "under my own supervision" behind Fairview and relieved Revere, who was eventually court-martialed. In his report, Sickles emphasized that Revere had subjected "these proud soldiers for the first time to the humiliation of being marched to the rear while their comrades were under fire."[27]

The attack continued. "The bullets ricocheted in our ranks," Regis de Trobriand recalled, "shells burst around us, and the balls which passed over the first line found a mark in the second." By midmorning, Williams' Twelfth Corps brigades south of the Plank Road were out of ammunition and suffering heavy casualties. As Williams led his men to the rear, the Third Corps was ordered to replace them. When a colonel asked Sickles where they should go, Sickles shouted, "Fall in here with no reference to regiments, brigades, or divisions. You are all my men! We must hold this line if every man of us should fall!" Charles Graham's brigade moved into the Twelfth Corps breastworks just in time to bear the brunt of an attack by Robert Rodes' Confederate division. After intense combat, Stephen Ramseur's brigade broke Graham's line and threatened Fairview. Federal artillery in the sector began limbering up and hauling out.[28]

When Confederate gunner E. P. Alexander learned from Union prisoners that the Chancellor house was Hooker's headquarters, he began raining artillery fire against the postion. "A converging fire of the enemy's guns from front, right, and left swept the ground" near the Chancellor house wrote Josiah Favill, "round shot and shell filled the air about us, and confusion reigned supreme." Colonel Henry Madill of the 141st Pennsylvania had his horse killed from under him and counted seven bullet holes in his coat. A lieutenant in the 3rd Maine was cut in two by a shell, his legs thrown to one side and his trunk to the other. Regis de Trobriand saw a caisson explode and an artilleryman burned "black as a negro. He runs shrieking toward the ambulances." Amidst the chaos strolled Sickles, remembered de Trobriand, who "goes by in his turn at a walk, with a smiling air, smoking a cigar. 'Everything is going well,' said he, in a loud voice, intended to be heard." Sickles lowered his voice and promised de Trobriand that he would receive a star for the May 2 midnight fight.[29]

Under attack by "heavy columns," and having thrown in his final reserves, Sickles sent Major Henry Tremain to Hooker for reinforcements. Tremain arrived at the Chancellor house to find Hooker on the porch. Seconds later, a Confederate solid shot struck a nearby pillar. A portion of it smashed into Hooker, who dropped to the floor and, in Henry Tremain's words, was "picked up for dead." Hooker was still very much alive, albeit "senseless." Tremain would eventually return to Sickles without instructions or support. Hooker was carried to a tent in the rear to recuperate. He was slowly regaining his senses when George Meade arrived and proposed an attack by his Fifth Corps on the Confederate left flank. Hooker refused.[30]

Sickles later boasted that with another corps in support, he could have not only counter-attacked but would have "carried the day." He ultimately blamed the Federal debacle on Hooker's wound and his being unable to send support. Sickles was careful not to publicly blame Hooker for forcing him to abandon Hazel Grove. Without support or communication from the commanding general, the enemy pressure forced Sickles to fall back toward the Chancellor house, which was now on fire. The fighting ex-congressman set up an initial line behind the smoking structure until Second Corps commander Darius Couch took temporary command and ordered Sickles to fall back another three-quarters of a mile with the rest of the army. Couch supervised the Federal retreat from Chancellorsville and formed a new 'U' shaped line north of Chancellorsville, enclosing the U.S. Ford crossing of the Rappahannock. The Confederates captured Chancellorsville around 10:00 a.m., bringing the two converging Southern wings of the widely separated army together. To add final insult to injury, Lee countermarched several brigades east toward Fredericksburg and beat back an attempt by Sedgwick to penetrate his rear. The repulse of Sedgwick ended the disastrous Sunday for the Federals, backed against the Rappahannock and beaten on two fronts while their commanding general recovered from his stupor.[31]

Hooker remained committed to a defensive posture on May 4. Sickles lost his second division commander in two days when Amiel Whipple was mortally wounded by a Confederate bullet during a skirmish near Chancellorsville. He was taken to Washington, where he died three days later. Of Sickles' original three division leaders, only David Birney survived. Sickles praised all three in his report for their performance during the disastrous battle: "The gallantry of Whipple was gracefully acknowledged by his promotion before his wound proved to be mortal. The dashing leadership of Birney has already received a like recognition. The chivalrous Berry proved but too soon how well he had deserved the highest rank in our service. . . ."[32]

That night, Hooker assembled his commanders in his tent. Generals Sickles, Meade, Howard, Reynolds, Couch, Butterfield, and Warren were present. (Henry Slocum arrived as the meeting was ending.) The council was unusual because this was the first time Hooker had invited his subordinates to participate in the decision-making process. "Hooker," Darius Couch recalled, "stated that his instructions compelled him to cover Washington, not to jeopardize the army, etc." Hooker essentially proposed two options to the group: a forward movement the next day or a retreat across the Rappahannock and an end to the campaign. "It was seen by the most casual observer that he had made up his mind to retreat," concluded Couch.[33]

Hooker and Butterfield departed to allow the corps commanders the opportunity to discuss the options. According to Couch, "We were left by ourselves to consult, upon which Sickles made an elaborate argument, sustaining the views of the commanding general." According to Warren's recollections, Sickles professed that since he was not a professional soldier his view might carry less weight, but (ever the politician) he considered the matter more political than military. Sickles argued that the uncertainties were "against us," a victory was "doubtful," and that another battlefield defeat could endanger Washington. In the end, Dan did not think that a withdrawal "would be fatal."[34]

Meade, Howard, and Reynolds were in favor of advancing. Meade expressed doubts that "we could get off our guns" in a retreat, and that the protection of Washington was a clichéd excuse and should not be considered.

Couch voted with Sickles against an advance. That placed the corps commanders at three votes in favor of advancing and two votes for retreating. When Hooker returned and polled each general, Sickles raised an additional concern about the army's supply and communication lines should an advance take place. Meade argued that the risk of withdrawing in the face of an aggressive enemy was actually greater than the risk of attacking. Hooker rejected Meade's concerns on the grounds that Lee would be "only too glad to have us go back." Hooker and his allies later claimed that in meeting Meade's objections, Hooker could now count Meade in favor of a retreat. Hooker ended by informing the council that he would "take upon himself the responsibility of retiring the army to the other side of the river."[35]

As the generals left the tent, John Reynolds blurted out, "What was the use of calling us together at this time of night when he intended to retreat anyhow?" On the morning of May 5, Hooker issued orders for the army to prepare to re-cross the Rappahannock. Ironically (given the criticism that would be directed against him after Gettysburg) it was George Meade who concluded that "Lee committed a terrible blunder in allowing us to come back; he might have destroyed us by a vigorous attack while we were retreating."

"No strategic advantage of any importance was gained on either side," was what Sickles later concluded of Chancellorsville. His hindsight was essentially correct. Both armies essentially returned to their former positions along the Rappahannock. Lee had once again befuddled another Union commander, but the victory at Chancellorsville was a costly one for Southern arms. Stonewall Jackson would not survive his wounds, and thousands of irreplaceable casualties had been knocked out of the ranks. Southern losses totaled about 13,000 men from all causes.[36]

Total Federal casualties topped 17,000, marking Chancellorsville as the army's costliest battle up until that time. Despite the huge losses, Sickles correctly noted later that the army "still remained competent to win at Gettysburg, as it did win it." While the corps under Reynolds and Meade had seen little action and suffered few casualties, Sickles' Third Corps lost 4,124 men, second only to Sedgwick's larger Sixth Corps, which suffered higher losses in six days of fitful fighting around Fredericksburg. The Excelsior regiments reported 250 casualties. Although there were some charges that Graham's brigade had abandoned artillery on Sunday, and both Birney and Graham ridiculed Charles Collis of the 114th Pennsylvania for hiding behind a tree and then falsifying his report, in general the corps had fought well. The men knew that they, along with Slocum's Twelfth Corps, had borne the brunt of stopping the Confederate attacks, and unlike Howard's Eleventh Corps, had held their ground. "The quality of the fighting, with the exception of the 11th Corps, was better than ever before," thought Chaplain Twichell. "Our corps fought well," General Birney wrote, "my division as usual suffered terribly. . . . I am proud of them." For as long as the Third Corps veterans lived they were proud of the role they had performed at Chancellorsville.[37]

Some historians have credited Sickles with a solid performance at Chancellorsville. Whatever success he enjoyed was really more of a reflection of the Third Corps' fighting abilities than on Sickles' first true test as a corps commander. His own specific performance was a harbinger of what would follow at Gettysburg. He fought aggressively, but demonstrated questionable military judgment. His misreading of Jackson's "retreat" on May 2 contributed to a general lack of preparedness for Jackson's flank attack (although Sickles' conclusion that Jackson was retreating does not excuse Howard's lack of readiness.) On the other hand, Sickles has been criticized for failing to organize a more "determined" assault against Jackson's flanking column. The Third Corps leader was acting under instructions from Hooker to remain cautious. By the time he organized a potentially large scale assault, which would have included nearby infantry and cavalry, Jackson was already striking Howard.[38]

On the positive side of the ledger, Sickles and Pleasonton helped stop Jackson's tidal wave after Howard had been routed. Even allowing for the usually exaggerated post-battle claims of the episode's significance, of which Pleasonton in particular was accused, the defensive effort demonstrated Sickles' fighting character: he was willing to stand his ground while others fled. The midnight attack on May 2-3 was vintage Sickles. A professional soldier probably would not have seriously considered launching a nighttime offensive in the Wilderness, but Sickles threw caution to the wind and ordered the attack anyway. The result, as we have seen, was a chaotic mess.

Gettysburg scholars routinely point to Sickles' forced withdrawal from Hazel Grove on May 3 as the primary motive for seizing the higher terrain along the Emmitsburg Road at Gettysburg later that summer. His voluminous postwar writing and speeches suggest otherwise. Sickles was deeply influenced by Jackson's flanking attack on May 2. At Chancellorsville, Lee had massed his forces on the Federals' right flank and had almost swept the entire Army of the Potomac out of position. At Gettysburg, Sickles would hold the army's left flank—determined to not reprise Howard's role.

After Chancellorsville, George Meade insisted that he had favored an advance by the army and was particularly disappointed in Hooker's collapse under pressure, "thus proving that a man may talk very big when he has no responsibility, but that is quite a different thing, acting when you are responsible and talking when others are." Meade's "only fear is that Hooker, goaded by the attacks that are now made on him, may be induced to take some desperate step in the hope of retrieving his waning fortunes." Meade's fears proved correct. Trouble began when criticism of Hooker predictably appeared within the press and inside the army's ranks. Meade eventually had to deny a rumor that he saved the army when Hooker was wounded, but he was infuriated to see newspaper reports that Hooker's retreat was due to "to the weak councils of his corps commanders. This is a base calumny," he exclaimed. Pennsylvania Governor Andrew Curtin visited Meade on May 12, and drew the general into expressing "my disappointment at the caution and prudence" exhibited by Hooker "at the critical moment of the battle . . . and at the withdrawal of the army, to which I opposed." Meade naively intended for his views to remain private, and was surprised when Hooker returned from Washington with word that Curtin was spreading stories that both Reynolds and Meade "had lost all confidence" in Hooker. An embarrassed Meade tried to explain that although Curtin had no right to use him in such a manner, Meade did essentially agree with Curtin's story. "To this Hooker assented and expressed himself satisfied with my statement."[39]

In reality, Hooker was far from satisfied. He probably believed that Meade was maneuvering for his job. The army commander confronted Meade on May 18 with the accusation "that Reynolds and myself had determined him to withdraw. I expressed the utmost surprise at this statement. . . ." Hooker admitted that during the May 4 war council Meade had expressed the opinion that it was impracticable to withdraw the army, but since Hooker considered it "perfectly practicable to withdraw," Hooker did not consider Meade in favor of an advance. Meade replied that this "was a very ingenious way of stating what I had said; that my opinion was clear and emphatic for an advance." When Hooker refused to retract his opinion, Meade realized that he was now "at open war with Hooker."[40]

On May 22, Meade asked the other corps commanders to share their recollections of the war council. John Reynolds agreed that "you were decidedly in favor of an advance in the direction of Fredericksburg . . . that you considered this army had already too long been made subservient to the safety of Washington. . . . This drew the remarks from General Sickles." On the other hand, Oliver Howard replied to Meade's inquiry: "I understood you at first to say that you thought it best to attack, for you believed a retreat would be disastrous. After General Hooker returned to the tent . . . and gave his decided opinion that he would withdraw the army in safety, I think you made no further objections, and, from something you said—what, I do not precisely recall—the impression I had was, that your opinion in favor of an attack was contingent upon the practicability of withdrawing the army to this side of the Rappahannock."[41]

Sickles, who according to the *Herald* spent two hours "closeted" with Lincoln on May 16, responded to Meade on May 26. Before answering Meade's question, Sickles peevishly lectured, "it will not be irrelevant to refer to the regret which I expressed, when the consultation began, that written inquiries or propositions were not submitted to the council. . . . If my suggestions, predicated upon the unsatisfactory mode in which the deliberations of the council were to be conducted, had not been disregarded, the issue of which you inform me could not have arisen."[42] Getting to the point, Sickles told Meade:

> You expressed the opinion that General Hooker should attack the enemy; that a retrograde movement in his presence, flushed with the success of his flank attack, the retreat of Sedgwick and the reoccupation of Fredericksburg had become impossible. This opinion afterward yielded somewhat to other considerations; among these were our deficiency in supplies; our imperiled communications, the hazards of a general engagement with an enemy . . . the instructions which required the commanding general to protect Washington; and the consequences to the North which would follow disaster to this army. At the close of the discussion, my impression was that your original preferences appeared to have been surrendered to the clear conviction of the commanding general.[43]

And thus the council at Chancellorsville increased the strain on the already tenuous Meade–Sickles relationship. Events would bear out that Sickles' response was a rare political mistake, for he unwittingly damaged further his relationship with his soon-to-be commanding general. Sickles completely misread Meade's rising star within the army's upper echelons of command, or Meade's potential was unnoticeable. Although neither party knew it at the time, Sickles would return to this portrayal of Meade—indecisive and lacking force of decision—repeatedly for decades to come. Following Gettysburg, allies of both Sickles and Joe Hooker would attempt to convince the country that Meade intended to retreat from Gettysburg. Did the earlier Chancellorsville debate between Meade and Hooker serve as the genesis for this story?[44]

If Meade's star was rising, Hooker's was clearly not. The newspapers insisted that his days at the head of the army were numbered, and that his replacement would be none other than Dan Sickles. James Gordon Bennett of the New York *Herald* called "the attention of President Lincoln to General Sickles as the man" to replace Hooker and that the defeat might have been avoided if Hooker had promptly supported Sickles' attack on Jackson's flank. Although Sickles had never attended a military academy, Bennett reminded readers that neither had Julius Caesar or George Washington. An appalled George Templeton Strong wrote in his diary on May 17 that a "trustworthy piece of information" from Washington indicated that "Sickles (!!!) is to succeed Hooker in command. . . . A very doubtful improvement, but there are judicious men who rate Sickles very high."

There is no evidence to suggest that Lincoln ever gave serious consideration of Sickles for the command of the Army of the Potomac, but the New York politician's ego must have swelled at the thought of not only being presented as a viable candidate for the command, but that he was being compared to other "amateurs" the likes of Caesar and Washington! Sickles' remarkable recovery following the Key murder scandal continued.[45]

Chapter 4

No One Ever Received
a More Important Command

Both armies struggled to reorganize in the wake of Chancellorville's staggering casualties. Many might have shared the opinion of Captain Charles Francis Adams, who observed that "Sickles, Butterfield, and Hooker are the disgrace and bane of this army; they are our three humbugs, intriguers and demagogues. Let them be disposed of and the army would be well satisfied to be led by any of the corps commanders." Joe Hooker, however, still held his job at the top of the army.

The most significant command change occurred when Winfield Scott Hancock was given charge of the Second Corps when Darius Couch resigned. The reorganization of Sickles' Third Corps was made necessary by the death of two of his three divisions commanders, in addition to casualties suffered. The late General Whipple's Third Division was broken up and folded into the other two divisions. David Birney was promoted to major general and retained command of the First Division. Birney considered the promotion bittersweet, for his commission was dated May 20; anyone with an earlier Chancellorsville-dated promotion would supersede him. Command of the Second Division was given to Andrew Humphreys, who replaced the late General Berry.[1]

Andrew A. Humphreys had led the Third Division, Fifth Corps, at Chancellorsville. Born in 1810, Humphreys was a Philadelphia native and an 1831 West Point graduate. His first assignments were in artillery and against Seminole Indians, but like many of the Old Army officers, he had little combat experience prior to the Civil War. Humphreys had briefly resigned from the army in 1836, and like George Meade, worked in civilian life as a lighthouse

Brigadier General
Andrew A. Humphreys

Library of Congress

engineer before returning in 1838 with an appointment to the Corps of Topographical Engineers. Despite expertise in scientific disciplines, Humphreys bristled at the thought that he was anything but a soldier. "Why, anyone who knows me intimately, knows that I had more of the soldier than a man of science in me." Humphreys steadily expressed his deep desire to command troops instead of serving in staff capacities. His first real experience leading large bodies of men under fire came at Fredericksburg. There, he led his Fifth Corps division in the last of six massive but futile assaults against Marye's Heights, where his 5,000-man division suffered more than 1,000 casualties. Like most of the Old Army professionals, Humphreys could be profane and often was a strict disciplinarian. Assistant Secretary of War Charles Dana thought Humphreys was "one of the loudest swearers" he had ever met, a man of "distinguished and brilliant profanity." Although Dana considered Humphreys to be without vanity, Humphreys' personal correspondence suggests otherwise. On the eve of his new assignment to the Third Corps, he wrote of his former command: "It is acknowledged throughout this army that no officer ever did as much with troops of short term of service as I have done with these, and it is acknowledged at the same time that no one else would or could have done as much."[2]

Humphreys apparently welcomed his new Third Corps assignment. He was happy to be getting a more experienced division (which still included the Excelsiors), an outfit he considered "one of the best in the whole army."

Despite the constant profanity, when he was not in action Humphreys offered something of a scholarly appearance and was known to be "continually washing himself and putting on paper dickeys." According to General Birney, Humphreys was "what we call an old granny, a charming, clever gentleman, fussy. . . ." Humphreys, Warren, and Meade belonged to what Birney considered the army's engineer clique. Meade was sorry to lose his friend from Fifth Corps, whom he considered "a most valuable officer, besides being an associate of the most agreeable character."[3]

While the Third Corps reorganized, the Chancellorsville survivors came to grips with the heavy losses they had suffered. The field officers of Charles Graham's brigade met and passed "resolutions conveying a sense of the severe loss they had sustained at Chancellorsville." On May 11, Regis de Trobriand attended a "grand review of the 3rd Corps. . . . The review was a beautiful sight, but in spite of its martial bearing, there was something sad, it was pierced by the ghosts of 4,000 of our men, left on the battlefield, that seemed to float above our decimated regiments. . . . But after all, you can't make an omelette without breaking some eggs, and you can't have a battle without breaking many heads."[4]

Later in the month, a presentation of more than 400 "Kearny Badges of Honor" was given to Birney's non-commissioned officers and privates for meritorious service at Chancellorsville. Sickles gave the presentation speech to a crowd that included Generals Meade, Birney, Humphreys, and Graham, among others. The New York *Herald* covered the ceremony as if it were a social event, pronouncing it "one of the happiest impromptu efforts of the season."[5]

Shortly after the ceremony, Sickles left for New York on what was supposed to be a ten-day leave of absence "rendered necessary by the impaired state of his health," reported the *Herald*. Sickles had, apparently, been wounded. "I received a serious injury at the battle of Chancellorsville," he later testified. "I cannot perhaps call it technically a wound, but I received a contusion from a fragment of a shell, which affected my general health very seriously, and it became necessary for me to avail myself of a leave of absence for the benefit of my health; which leave I applied for about three weeks after we returned."[6]

Dan returned home and spent most of June recuperating with Teresa and daughter Laura. Living quietly in the background, Teresa enjoyed none of the prestige that should have befitted a major-general's wife. Her husband, though, was a celebrity again. The New York Board of Councilmen celebrated his return and the New York *Times* worried that he would be gone from the army too long as he has "proven himself a thoroughly competent and complete master of himself and his position."[7]

The organizational challenges facing Robert E. Lee were heavier than those that fell upon Hooker's shoulders. Filling the hole left by Stonewall Jackson's death was on the minds of everyone associated with the Army of Northern Virginia. Lee eventually decided to restructure his entire army, dividing his two large corps into three. He promoted Richard Ewell to command Jackson's Second Corps and A. P. Hill to command the new Third Corps. James Longstreet retained command of his First Corps, which had rejoined the army just after the Chancellorsville operations came to a close. Whenever and wherever the next battle was fought, Lee would wage it with a radically different command structure. Strategically, the costly Chancellorsville victory had accomplished little for Lee. Hooker's army had escaped, and both sides were left in the same basic positions near Fredericksburg. Food and supplies for Lee's army were running dangerously low in Virginia, while elsewhere, General Ulysses S. Grant was threatening the vital city of Vicksburg in an effort to cut off Confederate control of the Mississippi River. Later in May, Lee met with Jefferson Davis and Secretary of War James Seddon in Richmond to discuss the army's next move. Despite reservations on Davis' part, Lee convinced Davis and Seddon that a move north would pull Hooker away from Virginia, clear Federal troops from the Shenandoah Valley, and disrupt Federal campaigns in Virginia for the summer. Emboldened by the confidence of Chancellorsville, Lee and Davis agreed on a thrust north above the Potomac River. On June 3, Lee began withdrawing his army from its Fredericksburg lines.[8]

Hooker was aware of Lee's movements as early as June 4. Unsure of Lee's intent or final destination, Hooker began squabbling with Washington over his orders and troop dispositions. When the Army of the Potomac finally began moving in pursuit, the Third Corps (still without Sickles) broke camp about June 10. The days were long and sweltering, and the road dust laid several inches thick. One day the corps tramped thirty long miles. "I was completely exhausted when we finally halted," wrote General Humphreys, who enjoyed the luxury of traversing the miles on horseback. While Sickles convalesced in New York, Lee moved north into Pennsylvania. The movement triggered a large cavalry battle on June 9 at Brandy Station, followed by a series of other actions at Winchester, Aldie, Middleburg, and Upperville. The new campaign was underway.[9]

Like every other Federal soldier, Fifth Corps commander George Meade knew nothing of Lee's goals. What he was sure about was that if Lee could "destroy or cripple this army, he will have no opposition to his progress of invasion." Meade was predisposed to fight a defensive battle, believing that if "they assume the offensive and force us into a defensive attitude, our morale will be raised, and with a moderate degree of good luck and good management, we will give them better than they can send." But Meade was still on the outs with Hooker's headquarters, and admitted that he knew "nothing of what is going on."[10]

Even as the army marched and fought, rumors circulated over Hooker's fate. "Meade or Reynolds seems to be the favorite . . . and either is respectable and would be a great improvement on the drunk- murdering- arson dynasty now prevailing of Hooker, Sickles, and Butterfield," concluded Captain Charles Francis Adams. John Reynolds met with Meade during the march. According to Reynolds, he told President Lincoln that he was not interested in Hooker's job. Although Meade considered Reynolds "a very good fellow," there remained a bit of professional rivalry between the men. Both Meade and his wife resented the fact that Reynolds received command of his own corps before Meade (especially since Reynolds had missed several battles after falling asleep and being captured after Gaines' Mill). Meade also harbored some resentment over Reynolds' lack of support at Fredericksburg. Meade was "very glad" for Reynolds' successes, but also resigned himself that Reynolds "is very popular & always impresses those around him with a great idea of his superiority & has had very strong friends." As for his own prospects, Meade thought it unlikely that he would be named, "because I have no friends, political or others, who press or advance my claims or pretensions."[11]

As the days of June passed, Hooker continued arguing with General Halleck about his orders, particularly those that mandated the Army of the Potomac cover Washington and Harpers Ferry. Hooker believed, erroneously, that he was outnumbered and so was unable to keep both locations covered while actively pursuing Lee's army. He wanted Harpers Ferry abandoned, but Halleck refused to approve it unless "absolutely necessary." Hooker, who had never fully accepted Halleck's authority, asked to refer the matter directly to Lincoln and Stanton. Before receiving a reply, Hooker wired Washington on June 27: "My original instructions require me to cover Harpers Ferry and Washington. I have now imposed upon me, in addition, an enemy in my front of more than my number. I beg to be understood, respectfully, but firmly, that I am unable to comply with this condition with the means at my disposal, and earnestly request that I may at once be relieved from the position I occupy."[12]

While Hooker was dueling with his superiors, Sickles was planning a return to the army. As late as June 17, the New York *Times* was reporting that Sickles would "not return, for the present" to the army, and the paper was lobbying instead for him to take command of all New York troops. A few days later in Washington, Captain James E. Smith (who was waiting to return to his own command, the 4th New York Independent Battery) ran into Sickles, "who directed me to be on the lookout, as he intended to start for the front when he could reach the army by rail, and that by so doing I could go with him." On June 27, they departed Washington on a special train bound for the front. Their progress was slow because of a report that "guerillas" were raiding the countryside, but they reached the army at Frederick, Maryland, without incident about 1:00 am on June 28. One of the train's passengers was Colonel James Hardie of Henry Halleck's staff, but neither Sickles nor Smith knew the nature of Hardie's business. "Hardie," Sickles later complained, "who was the bearer of the order putting Meade in command, sat by my side from Washington to Frederick, chatting all the way, without revealing a word of his mission."[13]

"My health was not restored," Sickles claimed upon his return to his Third Corps, "and under the circumstances I should not have returned to the army for perhaps several weeks." Sickles also noted that he would have missed the great battle had it not been for Hooker, who "sent me a message summoning me from New York where I was slowly recovering from a contusion received at Chancellorsville. He announced the coming battle, asking me to join my command instantly." Supposedly against the advice of his doctors, Sickles arrived in Frederick in time to see his friend Hooker "sacrificed, on the eve of battle, by the action of Halleck."[14]

At 3:00 a.m. on June 28, Colonel Hardie woke George Meade from his sleep by telling the Fifth Corps leader that "he had come to give [him] trouble." Never the optimist, Meade's first thought was that he was being relieved or arrested, but Hardie instead handed him an order from General Halleck placing Meade in command of the Army of the Potomac. Halleck's orders included the line that, given "the circumstances, no one ever received a more important command." Meade, assured Halleck, would "not be hampered by any minute instructions" and was "free to act as you may deem proper." All of this was contingent upon Meade remembering "the important fact that the Army of the Potomac is the covering army of Washington. . . . You will, therefore, maneuver and fight in such a manner as to cover the capital and also Baltimore, as far as circumstances will admit. Should General Lee move upon either of these places, it is expected that you will either anticipate him or arrive with him so as to give him battle." Halleck placed Harpers Ferry "under your direct orders" and also authorized him "to remove from command, and to send from your army, any officer or other person you may deem proper, and to appoint to command as you may deem expedient. . . ."[15]

A "confounded" Meade reportedly "became much agitated, protesting against being placed in command of an army that was looking toward Reynolds as the successor." Meade also expressed the "responsibility so heavily placed on him in presence of the enemy and when he was totally ignorant of the positions and dispositions of the army." According to Hardie, Meade said "half playfully, 'Well, I've been tried and condemned without a hearing, and I suppose I shall have to go to execution.'" Meade wired his acceptance to Halleck at 7:00 a.m. "[I]n ignorance of the exact condition of the troops and position of the enemy," Meade determined to "move toward the Susquehanna, keeping Washington and Baltimore well covered, and if the enemy is checked in his attempt to cross the Susquehanna, or if he turns toward Baltimore, to give him battle."[16]

At Chancellorsville, Meade had argued that the protection of Washington had become a cliché, an excuse against aggressive action. Now he had direct orders to "cover" both Washington and Baltimore, a directive that limited his ability to operate freely against Lee. Of more immediate concern was his lack of knowledge of the army's disposition. Hooker had kept Meade "in total ignorance" of his plans. Once Meade accepted, Hardie notified General Hooker—who seems to have "construed favorably the delay in responding to his tender of resignation"— that his bluff had been called. The surprised general "could not wholly mask the

Major General
Dan Butterfield

revulsion of feeling." Hardie, Meade, Hooker, and Chief of Staff Butterfield met to discuss the transfer of command. Although it was apparent to Hardie that "much coldness existed" between Meade and Butterfield, Meade asked the chief of staff to remain and brief him on the army's condition. The information he received "shocked" him: the army was widely scattered. Meade's stunned amazement prompted Hooker to retort "with feeling." The meeting was tense throughout, due mainly to what was later described as "Hooker's chagrin and Meade's overstrung nerves."[17]

Among the first to offer Meade congratulations was First Corps commander John Reynolds. Outside of his own corps or circle of friends, Meade was not as well known as some of the other corps commanders. Frank Haskell, who served on the staff of another Meade friend, John Gibbon, observed that those officers who knew him "all thought highly of him, a man of great modesty, with none of those qualities, which are noisy and assuming, and hankering for cheap newspaper fame—not at all of the 'gallant' Sickles stamp." Conversely, Captain Francis Donaldson of the 118th Pennsylvania wrote, "'Old Four Eye' . . . appears to be a man universally despised in the Fifth Corps. He certainly cares very little for the rank and file. . . ."[18]

When Sickles reported to Hooker sometime that morning, the latter "informed me that he had been relieved from command." Sickles later claimed that the change in command "was no sooner announced" than he began to hear from friends "earnest remonstrances against my serving under Meade. They knew he was hostile, dating from several incidents in the Chancellorsville campaign." Sickles wrote that he consulted with Hooker, who advised that "you cannot ask to be relieved on the eve of battle; wait at least until after the engagement." (If the story is true, one wonders why Hooker did not heed his own advice.) After reporting to Meade, Sickles returned to his Third Corps as it was passing through Frederick.[19]

Unaware of the developments then in progress, General Birney had marched the Third Corps from Middletown, Maryland, to Frederick. Birney commanded the corps in Sickles' absence, to the satisfaction of many officers including Regis de Trobriand. "We cannot desire anything better than to have him [Birney] as our chief in the next battle, probably within two or thee days." However, Sickles' return relieved Birney of corps command and returned him to command of the First Division.[20]

After meeting with Hooker, Meade had to decide upon a chief of staff. Dan Butterfield had made few friends in the position. Colonel Charles Wainwright, commander of the First Corps Artillery Brigade, called Butterfield a "little

Napoleon" and thought he was "most thoroughly hated by all officers at headquarters as a meddling, over-conceited fellow." Provost Marshal Marsena Patrick claimed Butterfield "thinks himself very smart, but is in reality nearly a fool about some things—I am utterly disgusted with him." Sickles, on the other hand, considered his friend more than competent. "Meade's [Gettysburg] campaign was shaped by Hooker's movements and executed by General Butterfield."[21]

There is little doubt that Meade wanted someone else in the job. He approached Andrew Humphreys, Gouverneur K. Warren, and Seth Williams about accepting the post, but each declined. Humphreys spent several hours mulling the offer, "which I desired not to do until after the coming battle, and circumstances admitted of my postponing a decision until then." Humphreys, in his words, "declined or deferred" the offer. Humphreys' response was somewhat disingenuous, for it gave Meade the impression that he was only "deferring" the decision. Humphreys wanted to command troops in the field and was hoping to one day lead a corps. He eventually accepted the offer after the battle, but only with the understanding that it was a temporary assignment.[22]

Rebuffed by his preferred candidates, Meade asked Butterfield to stay on as chief of staff; Butterfield accepted. Some have suggested that Butterfield was selected to retain continuity, but it appears more likely that Meade had few viable options. With hindsight, we know the retention of Butterfield helped guarantee Gettysburg's post-battle controversies between Meade and the Hooker-Sickles-Butterfield axis. Butterfield would claim credit for nearly every significant decision made at headquarters, including the allegation that he obtained Hooker's complete plans, which were in turn adopted wholesale by Meade. Whether or not there was any truth to the claims, months later Congress believed such stories enough to give Joe Hooker primary thanks for the Gettysburg victory.[23]

Meade's first objective as commander was to get the army moving. From the immediate available information, he estimated that Lee's Army of Northern Virginia was more than 100,000 strong. According to his reports, the army had crossed the Potomac and was moving up the Cumberland Valley. Meade decided to march north on a main line from Frederick to Harrisburg with his left and right wings spread as far as possible, keeping Baltimore and Washington covered, halt Lee's advance toward Harrisburg, and bring on a battle "at some point." Further developments would depend on what he could learn of Lee's movements, but by June 29, the army's seven infantry corps were moving north toward Pennsylvania. The weather was hot, some roads were dusty, and rounding up numerous drunken stragglers in Frederick was anything but easy.[24]

The Southern army was also advancing. Richard Ewell's Second Corps led the Confederate advance into Pennsylvania, and by June 28 was preparing to move on the state capital at Harrisburg. General Lee, however, had lost contact with his main cavalry body under Jeb Stuart during the march north, and without reconnaissance reports from his reliable cavalier, Lee found it "impossible to ascertain [Hooker's] intentions." From a spy, Lee and Longstreet learned that the Federal army had crossed the Potomac and was advancing northward. The Federals threatened to reach Lee's communication lines west of South Mountain. Although Lee was initially skeptical of the report, he decided to deter Hooker "from advancing farther west, and intercepting our communication with Virginia" by concentrating his scattered army "east of the mountains." As a result, Lee ordered Ewell to fall back from Harrisburg and "either move directly on Gettysburg or turn down to Cashtown," a small village about ten miles west of Gettysburg and slightly east of a key gap in the mountain range. If all went according to plan, Lee's army would concentrate before waging a major engagement.[25]

By June 29, George Meade was at Middleburg, where he was pressuring the army for more rapid movement. Sickles and the Third Corps were to march to Taneytown. With the exception of Reynolds' First Corps, the other corps were not moving rapidly enough to suit Meade. Hancock's Second Corps was delayed leaving Monocacy Junction. The new Second Corps commander, always unsparing in his criticism, blamed the delay on "an irresponsible person at these headquarters, a clerk, who failed to deliver" orders. Meade suggested that the offending party be "brought to punishment" but did not rebuke his friend Hancock for the delay. That evening, Henry Slocum complained that someone else's trains would prevent his Twelfth Corps from reaching the day's objectives.[26]

The men of the Third Corps gave Sickles what Joe Twichell called "a most complimentary welcome" back on June 29. "Great cheers swelled along the lines as he rode by and all hands feel relieved at his return." Still, the day's frustrations spilled over at headquarters where Seth Williams, the army's adjutant general, issued Sickles a dispatch at 7:00 p.m. "I am directed by the commanding general to inform you that the train of your corps is at a stand-still at Middleburg, and delaying, of course, all movements in the rear. He wishes you to give your immediate and personal attention to keeping your train in motion." No reply from Sickles has been found. In contrast, Winfield Hancock at least attempted to explain his own Second Corps delay and sent Meade follow-up assurances that he would make up for lost time.[27] If Sickles did not send similar assurances to his new commander, it may explain why Meade had Seth Williams dispatch a more prickly follow-up on June 30:

Commanding Officer Third Corps:

The commanding general noticed with regret the very slow movement of your corps yesterday. It is presumed you marched at an early hour, and up to 6 p.m. the rear of your column had not passed Middleburg, distant from your camp of the night before some 12 miles only. This, considering the good condition of the road and the favorable state of the weather, was far from meeting the expectation of the commanding general, and delayed to a very late hour the arrival of troops and trains in your rear. The Second Corps in the same space of time made a march nearly double your own. Situated as this army now is, the commanding general looks for rapid movements of the troops.[28]

The relationship between Meade and Sickles continued to deteriorate. Sickles had enjoyed a close relationship with Hooker's army headquarters. Under Hooker, he could compensate for his relative inexperience through open communications that kept him in tune with the commanding general's objectives. Now he was entering into Pennsylvania on the outside of headquarters, and as the campaign progressed his anxiety and indecision increased. While these dispatches from Meade probably demonstrate some level of personal animosity toward Sickles, a full reading of the June 30 headquarters correspondence reveals a new army commander increasingly cognizant of his mounting responsibilities and the likelihood of a major collision with Lee's army in the very near future. (Meade even authorized the "instant death of any soldier who fails to do his duty at this hour.") Sickles was not in a position to do anything but keep his corps moving. Events were transpiring rapidly on June 30, and Meade had more to worry about than just Dan Sickles.[29]

Lee's scattered army, meanwhile, continued marching toward a concentration near South Mountain. That same morning Henry Heth, who commanded a division in A.P. Hill's Corps, ordered Johnston Pettigrew's brigade to "procure supplies at Gettysburg." General John Buford's Federal cavalry division had also been ordered to scout around Gettysburg. Buford entered the town from the south around 11:00 a.m., just as Pettigrew's infantry was marching leisurely from Cashtown toward Gettysburg from the west. "Found everybody in a terrible state of excitement on account of the enemy's advance upon this place," Buford reported. Without any orders to engage the enemy, Pettigrew withdrew his brigade and retraced his steps to Cashtown. Buford now knew that a Confederate infantry force of unknown size was west of town. That evening, Heth reported the encounter to A.P. Hill. Unsure of the nature of the Union forces Pettigrew reported at Gettysburg, Hill sent word to Lee that "I intended to advance the next morning and discover what [is] in my front."[30]

On June 30, Meade moved his headquarters to Taneytown. He assigned John Reynolds to "assume command of the three corps forming the left wing," a move that gave him oversight of Sickles' Third Corps, Oliver Howard's Eleventh, and his own First Corps. By 9:45 a.m., Reynolds decided to move his corps "to Marsh Creek, about half way to Gettysburg. The enemy are reported moving on Gettysburg from Fairfield and Cashtown." Eventually setting up his headquarters at Moritz Tavern, Reynolds directed Howard to be ready to move in on his left, in case Lee should make an advance from that direction.[31]

As the morning progressed, Meade became convinced that "the enemy are advancing, probably in strong force, on Gettysburg" and believed that he "has relieved Harrisburg and Philadelphia, and now desires to look to his own army, and assume position for offensive or defensive, as occasion requires, or rest to the troops." Meade thought that Buford's presence at Gettysburg should give Reynolds plenty of warning if the Confederates moved either in his direction or on Howard at Emmitsburg. If that happened, Meade promised Reynolds reinforcements from "the corps nearest to you, which are Sickles', at Taneytown, and Slocum's, at Littlestown. . . . If, after occupying your present position, it is your judgment that you would be in better position at Emmitsburg than where you are, you can fall back without waiting for the enemy or further orders. Your present position was given more with a view to an advance on Gettysburg, than a defensive point."[32]

Believing reports from Reynolds that "the enemy has appeared at Fairfield, on the road between Chambersburg and Emmitsburg," Meade decided to bolster his left (Reynolds and Howard) by sending Sickles to Emmitsburg and Hancock to Taneytown. Sedgwick's Sixth Corps was also directed to move to Manchester on the army's right. Meade had done well thus far by placing his army's infantry (with the exception of Sedgwick's Sixth Corps) and artillery all within ten miles of Taneytown and supporting distance of one another. "It is of the utmost importance that you should move with your infantry and artillery to Emmitsburg with all possible dispatch,"[33] Seth Williams wrote Sickles. Meade sent Sickles another order at 12:45 p.m.:

> The major-general commanding directs that you move your corps up to Emmitsburg. You will take three days' rations in haversacks, 60 rounds of ammunition, and your ambulances. Your trains will remain parked here until further orders. General Reynolds' First Corps, and General Howard's Eleventh Corps, are between Emmitsburg and Gettysburg. General Reynolds will command the left wing, consisting of the First, Eleventh, and Third Corps. The enemy are reported to be in force in Gettysburg. You will move without delay. You will report to General Reynolds, and throw out strong pickets on the roads from Emmitsburg to Greencastle and Chambersburg. Mechanicstown, on your left, is occupied by a brigade of cavalry, with whom you will communicate.[34]

Meade still had the authority to issue orders directly to Sickles (rather than going through Reynolds the wing commander), but Sickles had different orders from Reynolds. Issued from Moritz Tavern on June 30, Reynolds directed Sickles to "camp upon Cat Tail Branch with your command, and for you to also send a staff officer to these headquarters . . . [and] to face toward Gettysburg, and cover the roads leading from Gettysburg." Meade's orders superseded Reynolds' instructions, but given Sickles' inexperience and lack of confidence in dealing with Meade, the latest orders simply confused him. He sent a request (written from Third Corps headquarters at Bridgeport) to Williams asking for clarification:

> GENERAL: Inclosed please find communication from Major-General Reynolds. It is in accordance with my written orders, received from headquarters Army of the Potomac at 1 p.m., but in conflict with the verbal order given me by the general commanding while on the march. Shall I move forward? My First Division is about a mile this side of Emmitsburg.[35]

The episode probably did not increase Sickles' confidence in Meade's ability to issue clear and decisive instructions; nor would it have increased Meade's confidence in Sickles' ability to receive them. Not only did Meade bypass the wing commander, but he also gave orders directly to Sickles' newest division commander, Andrew Humphreys, whose Second Division had reached Taneytown on the 29th. Around mid-day on the 30th, Humphreys received orders to march toward Emmitsburg. He also received an order to report to Meade's headquarters before departing. When he reached Emmitsburg, explained Meade, Humphreys was to examine the ground "and see whether it would do to fight a battle there." At this point, Meade was still considering any number of potential contingencies.[36]

Weary from the last forty-eight hours of exertion and the conflicting orders from Meade and Reynolds, Sickles sent a message to Reynolds at 7:45 p.m. indicating that he had gone into camp at Bridgeport along the Monocacy River, about five miles southeast of Emmitsburg and roughly halfway between Emmitsburg and Taneytown. The Third Corps march of June 30 had been a short one. Charles Mattocks in the 17th Maine wrote that the corps departed Taneytown at 1:00 p.m. and halted "near" Emmitsburg at 6:00 p.m. "By direction of the general commanding," Sickles notified Reynolds, "I have gone into camp here [Bridgeport], countermanding a previous order to go to Emmitsburg, and am to await here further orders from headquarters Army of the Potomac." One suspects that Sickles probably longed for Joe Hooker's command as he settled down for the night.[37]

Headquartered that evening at Gettysburg, John Buford sent late word (after 10:30 p.m.) that A.P. Hill's corps "is massed back of Cashtown, 9 miles from this place. His pickets, composed of infantry and artillery, are in sight of mine." Buford also reported the nearby roads "terribly infested with roving detachments of cavalry. Rumor says Ewell is coming over the mountains from Carlisle. . . ." Unsure of what Lee intended, Reynolds decided to advance his First Corps toward Gettysburg in the morning to support Buford and find out. Sickles and the Third Corps, as part of Reynolds' wing, would presumably follow Reynolds to Gettysburg.[38]

Chapter 5

The Third Corps Marches in the Right Direction

In the wake of assuming command of the Army of the Potomac, George Meade had skillfully managed to both advance into Pennsylvania and maneuver his army to cover Baltimore and Washington. By daylight of July 1, 1863, John Buford was in Gettysburg and his cavalry videttes were positioned west of town, having made arrangements for "entertaining" the enemy "until General Reynolds could reach the scene." Oliver Howard's and Dan Sickles' corps were close enough to lend support, if needed. General Henry Heth's Confederate division departed Cashtown for Gettysburg (to "discover" what was out in front) about 5:00 a.m. Sometime after 7:00 a.m., Heth's advance collided with Buford's cavalry outposts near Marsh Creek. A smatter of small arms fire broke the peacefulness of the early summer morning. The battle at Gettysburg was underway.[1]

In Taneytown, meanwhile, Meade instructed his engineers, including Chief Engineer Gouverneur K. Warren and Chief of Artillery Henry Hunt, to "look about and select some general ground . . . by which, in case the enemy should advance on me across the South mountain, I might be able, by rapid movement of concentration, to occupy this position and be prepared to give him battle upon my own terms." His engineers discovered just such a location in Maryland along Pipe Creek between Middleburg and Manchester. Meade issued an order from Taneytown to his corps commanders on July 1 (known as the Pipe Creek Circular) outlining a plan to fall back to this line if the army was attacked.[2]

All things considered, Meade felt "satisfied that the object of the movement of the army in this direction has been accomplished, viz, the relief of

Harrisburg, and the prevention of the enemy's intended invasion of Philadelphia, &c., beyond the Susquehanna." It was no longer Meade's "intention to assume the offensive until the enemy's movements or position should render such an operation certain of success." If Lee assumed the offensive, Meade would "withdraw the army from its present position, and form line of battle with the left resting in the neighborhood of Middleburg, and the right at Manchester, the general direction being that of Pipe Creek." If the move became necessary, Reynolds' wing, which included Sickles' Third Corps, would "deploy toward Middleburg." Henry Slocum was given command of two corps with the intent of deploying in the middle of the line between Reynolds (on the left) and John Sedgwick's Sixth Corps (on the right) at Manchester. Hancock's Second Corps would be "held in reserve in the vicinity of Uniontown and Frizellburg, to be thrown to the point of strongest attack, should the enemy make it." In the event of this action, the army's "trains and impedimenta will all be sent to the rear of Westminster." Significantly, Meade was leaving every option on the table: "The time for falling back can only be developed by circumstances. . . . Developments may cause the commanding general to assume the offensive from his present positions. . . ."[3]

Subsequent events would prevent any of this order from being fully executed. Nevertheless, the existence of the Pipe Creek Circular caused Meade untold consternation. Meade's enemies, including but not limited to Dan Sickles, manipulated the orders to support their premise that Meade never intended to fight at Gettysburg and was unworthy of credit for the victory. "The army was to fall back," Sickles would tell the Joint Committee on the Conduct of the War in 1864, "and not to follow up the enemy any further; the general regarding the objects of the campaign to have been accomplished, and considering Washington, Baltimore, and Pennsylvania to have been relieved. The circular indicated a line of retreat." Meade, however, testified the order was a "mere contingent . . . intended only to be executed under certain circumstances."[4]

The Pipe Creek Circular never reached Reynolds, nor did he receive another message that Meade also dictated that morning. In the latter message, Meade noted that he "cannot decide whether it is his best policy to move to attack until he learns something more definite of the point at which the enemy is concentrating." Asking for Reynolds' view, Meade thought that if "the enemy is concentrating to our right of Gettysburg, that point would not at first glance seem to be a proper strategic point of concentration for this army. If the enemy is concentrating in front of Gettysburg or to the left of it, the general is not

View from old Emmitsburg Road looking toward Emmitsburg.

Emmitsburg Historical Society

sufficiently well informed of the nature of the country to judge of its character for either an offensive or defensive position." Meade gave Reynolds the option to utilize General Humphreys at Emmitsburg to help evaluate the terrain's potential for defensive or offensive operations.[5]

Sometime before daybreak on July 1, Sickles ordered Henry Tremain to locate General Reynolds and obtain the wing commander's orders for the Third Corps. Sickles had moved from Bridgeport to Emmitsburg early that morning. The Excelsior's 72nd New York regimental history notes that the men arrived in Emmitsburg about 8:00 a.m. Sickles was still under the impression that the Third Corps was to remain near Emmitsburg. Tremain left for Gettysburg on horseback to seek out orders. As he approached the town along the Emmitsburg Road, he "heard a gun, then another. It was artillery." Tremain found Reynolds and his staff below the town with James Wadsworth's First Corps division rapidly approaching from the south. In his memoirs, Tremain claimed to have overheard Reynolds involved in some sort of an internal debate about where to form his men. When he met Wadsworth, Reynolds pointed to the west and instructed his division leader, "you had better turn off here." The sounds of gunfire were increasing northwest of town.[6]

Turning his attention to Tremain, Reynolds instructed, "Tell General Sickles *I think* [emphasis in original] he had better come up." There were no further instructions. As Tremain put it, "1,000 scenarios" raced through his mind. Frustrated that Reynolds did not provide more details, Tremain rode back to seek out Sickles near Emmitsburg. What Tremain did not know was that Buford's troopers were fighting a dismounted delaying action against A. P. Hill's advancing infantry and were slowly being pushed back toward Gettysburg. By 10:00 a.m. Reynolds was in process of committing his First Corps into battle on McPherson Ridge, a low ridge line west of the Lutheran Theological Seminary.[7]

Sickles' Third Corps, meanwhile, continued to concentrate near Emmitsburg. Humphreys met up with Sickles to determine whether the corps should remain there. When Humphreys was given the impression that "we should probably remain there some hours," he left to to examine "the ground thoroughly in every direction," as Meade had ordered him to do. His task would take some time, but when he finished, Humphreys was "not satisfied with the ground at all."[8]

Around 11:00 a.m., Hancock's Second Corps arrived at Taneytown, where Hancock reported to Meade's headquarters. Meade explained what little he knew to Hancock, at best a general overview of the unfolding situation. According to Hancock, Meade "had made up his mind to fight a battle on what was known as Pipe creek . . . and that he was then preparing an order for that movement." About thirty minutes later, Meade received his first positive intelligence of the Confederate movement on Gettysburg.[9]

About 11:30 a.m., one of Reynolds' aides rode into Taneytown with an urgent verbal message from Reynolds: "the enemy are advancing in strong force, and that I fear they will get the heights beyond the town before I can." Rather than planning for a withdrawal, Reynolds intended to "fight them inch by inch, and if driven into the town, I will barricade the streets and hold them back as long as possible." Shortly thereafter, Meade received another dispatch from cavalryman John Buford (penned about 10:10 a.m.) indicating that A.P. Hill's forces were driving "my pickets and skirmishers *very* rapidly." Meade implied to Hancock that Reynolds' presence at Gettysburg "was really a mask" to allow the Pipe Creek line to be occupied in the rear. But it turned out that the enemy started to march down . . . a little earlier than anticipated." Buford and Reynolds delayed the enemy, in Hancock's words, "until the commander of the army should come to some decision."[10]

Major General
John Reynolds

National Archives

At 12:30 p.m., Meade had Chief of Staff Butterfield draw up orders for Hancock. Fearing the "possible failure of General Reynolds to receive the order to withdraw his command by the route through Taneytown, thus leaving the center of our position open," Meade directed Hancock to march his corps to Gettysburg and cover Reynolds' withdrawal. That plan changed abruptly about 1:00 p.m. when Meade received news that Reynolds had been killed early in the fighting. Hancock was already briefed on his plans, so Meade directed him to ride to Gettysburg and "assume command of the corps there assembled, viz, the Eleventh, First, and Third, at Emmitsburg. If you think the ground and position there a better one to fight a battle under existing circumstances, you will so advise the general, and he will order all the troops up." It was 1:10 p.m.[11]

As Meade later pointed out, not only was Hancock "fully aware" of Meade's plans, but Gettysburg was "a place which I had never seen in my life." The army commander needed an examination of the ground performed to determine if there was a more advantageous position in the "immediate neighborhood" for the army to concentrate. Since Meade was still unsure where the army would ultimately concentrate, Hancock was given the momentous latitude to determine if Gettysburg was a better position than Pipe Creek.[12]

Launching Hancock toward Gettysburg raised the sticky matter of seniority. At that time, Hancock was junior in rank to every infantry corps commander except George Sykes. Even Dan Sickles, the ultimate amateur, outranked Hancock. When the Second Corps leader reminded Meade that both Howard and Sickles were his seniors, Meade assured him that the situation demanded as much: Hancock was acquainted with Meade's views, and the army commander had the authority to appoint anyone to command as deemed "expedient." Personally, the assignment did not trouble Hancock because he was "an older soldier than either of them [Sickles and Howard]. But I knew that legally it was not proper, and that if they chose to resist it, it might become a very troublesome matter to me." Butterfield, who was also aware of the potential for trouble, instructed Hancock that Henry Slocum would take command when he arrived on the field. Hancock left Taneytown for Gettysburg around 1:30 p.m. He rode in an ambulance for the first two or three miles in order to review maps and acquaint himself with the country and, significantly, the proposed Pipe Creek geography.[13]

Meanwhile, Oliver Howard arrived in Gettysburg ahead of his Eleventh Corps and, when notified of Reynolds' death, assumed command of both the field and the left wing. In one of the battle's pivotal decisions, Howard "came to the conclusion that the only tenable position for my limited force was the ridge to the southeast of Gettysburg, now so well known as Cemetery Ridge. The highest point at the cemetery commanded every eminence within easy range." At 1:00 p.m., Howard sent identical messages to both Sickles and Henry Slocum (whose Twelfth Corps was only five miles distant near Two Taverns) informing them of the engagement with Hill's corps, and that Richard Ewell's Second Corps was advancing toward Gettysburg from the north. Sickles was directed to forward Howard's dispatch to Meade. At 1:30 p.m., about the time Hancock was leaving Taneytown, Howard sent his brother, Major Charles Howard, with another more direct message for Sickles: Reynolds was dead and Sickles should "move up to Gettysburg as rapidly as possible."[14]

After his unsatisfactory meeting with Reynolds, Sickles' aide Henry Tremain probably reached Emmitsburg between 11:30 a.m. and noon. He found Sickles resting his corps. As Sickles later put it, his men "had been severely marched for many days, and a great many of them were barefooted." Tremain relayed Reynolds' earlier order that the Third Corps should move forward. Sickles, however, did not immediately order his corps to move out. The politician- turned-general was still struggling mightily with Reynolds' wing commander assignment, and was torn between seemingly contradictory orders from Meade and Reynolds. Sickles had never been in serious action before without the friendly oversight of Joe Hooker. His lack of independent experience was showing, and he was nearly paralyzed with indecision over what to do next.[15]

Tremain briefly departed to refresh himself. During his absence, Sickles decided to send another staff officer, Captain Alexander Moore, to Gettysburg. According to Moore, he departed Emmitsburg around 2:00 p.m. with orders to "communicate with General Reynolds." Tremain, meanwhile, returned to find Sickles "pacing" and "reticent, having asked few questions." The inactivity troubled the staffer. As Sickles saw it, he had received at least three conflicting orders from Meade and Reynolds. Was Sickles to hold Emmitsburg, be prepared to execute the Pipe Creek Circular, or rush to Reynolds' support? The deadlock was broken shortly after 3:00 p.m. when Major Charles Howard arrived with the news that Reynolds was dead and that General Howard wanted the Third Corps marched to Gettysburg. "I, of course, considered the question very anxiously,"[16] Sickles later told the Congressional Committee on the Conduct of the War:

> My preliminary orders in going to Gettysburg [Emmitsburg] were to go there and hold that position with my corps, as it was regarded as a very important flanking position, to cover our rear and line of communication. Then on the other hand was this order of General Meade which I had received that morning, contemplating another and entirely different line of operations. Then there was this new fact which I assumed was not known to General Meade, who was ten miles or so distant. I therefore determined to take the principal part of my corps and move as promptly as possible to Gettysburg.[17]

According to Sickles' 3:15 p.m. reply, this may have been the *third* communication he had received from General Howard (the record is ambiguous). "I have at this moment received a communication from an officer of your staff, and also two written communications, dated at 1 and 1.30 p.m. I shall move to Gettysburg immediately." Sickles ordered Tremain to ride ahead and notify Howard. In line with Howard's instructions, Sickles notified Meade of his movement.[18] Still conflicted about the proper course of action, Sickles sent the following note to Meade's Assistant Adjutant General, Seth Williams, at 3:15 p.m.:

> A staff officer from Major-General Howard and a communication from him (dated Gettysburg 1.30 p.m.) has just reached me. A large force of the

enemy has engaged him in front of Gettysburg. General Reynolds was killed early in the action. General Howard requests me to support him, and I shall march with my corps toward Gettysburg immediately, moving on two parallel roads. I shall be found on the direct turnpike road from Emmitsburg. I inclose communication from General Howard.[19]

Given the many uncertainties, before leaving for Gettysburg Sickles decided on a more prudent course than simply abandoning Emmitsburg. At 3:25 p.m., he addressed another note to Seth Williams informing him that he was leaving two brigades and two batteries near Emmitsburg. Given his doubts over Meade's preference, this was a wise (and for Dan a surprisingly conservative) decision. Sickles considered the smaller force at Emmitsburg "ample" to protect that position since he now believed the enemy's main body was in his front toward Gettysburg. Holding Emmitsburg were Regis de Trobriand's and George Burling's brigades, accompanied by James Smith and George Winslow's batteries.[20]

At 3:30 p.m., David Birney received orders to report to Howard at Gettysburg. Sickles accompanied Birney, two First Division brigades (Graham and Ward), and two artillery batteries as the column moved toward Gettysburg along the main Emmitsburg Road. Somehow, no one bothered to notify General Humphreys that the majority of his division was also departing. Humphreys, who had been absent fulfilling Meade's request to examine the terrain, returned about 4:00 p.m. and "perceived that some of the troops had left the ground. In my absence orders had been sent to march up to Gettysburg at once. I immediately followed on as rapidly as I could, and when I got to the head of the column I found that orders had been received between three and four o'clock to march at once." Since Birney and Sickles were moving on the main Emmitsburg Road, Humphreys' division (Carr and Brewster's brigades), together with Seeley's artillery, traveled on a parallel road about two miles to the west.[21]

Sickles later told Congress, "I therefore moved to Gettysburg on my own responsibility." Many historians credit Sickles with, if nothing else, "marching to the sounds of the guns." In later decades Sickles himself frequently claimed that he decided on his own hook to march to Gettysburg in defiance of Meade's orders. Dan told an audience in 1890 that his orders from Meade "were to hold Emmitsburg at all hazards . . . based on the supposition that the enemy's point of concentration would be at or near Emmitsburg, but no enemy was near . . . The situation of Howard, so pressed by superior numbers, was hard to resist.

Why stay here in idle security, in formal obedience to orders?" Sickles made his decision and, "It must be said, at least, that the Third Corps marches in the right direction—toward the enemy." Such talk created the image of an aggressive Sickles heading to Howard's rescue, ignoring Meade's orders to hold a position in the rear.[22]

Many Third Corps veterans accepted this aggressive portrayal. Thomas Rafferty of the 71st New York, for example, wrote this:

> Here was a dilemma which might have perplexed a weaker man. In fact, another of our corps commanders, and one of the best of them, too, on receiving the same dispatch, refused to move his corps without an order from General Meade. [An apparent reference to Henry Slocum.] However, it did not trouble Sickles long. He obeyed the dictates of common sense, and at once hurried his corps forward to place it where it would do the most good . . . thus flatly disobeying the orders of his commander.

Sickles partisans admired their man's apparent fighting spirit and most historians have followed suit by praising Sickles for moving toward Gettysburg. Modern historian Stephen Sears, for example, acknowledged that Sickles "was the one nonprofessional soldier in the quartet of Meade, Howard, Slocum, and Sickles who displayed the one spark of soldierly initiative in this situation." It came too late in the day, "but at least he showed the initiative."[23]

But does Sickles deserve such praise? Probably about three hours passed after Sickles received Reynolds' order and before he began marching toward Gettysburg. Both Sickles' and Tremain's accounts were just vague enough to hinder accurate identification of the precise time Tremain delivered Reynolds' order. David Birney's report claims that Sickles ordered him to Gettysburg at 2:00 p.m.—or nearly ninety minutes earlier than he actually received his orders. Was the error an honest one or intentional?[24]

An even more cynical interpretation assumes that the entire portrayal of Sickles' agonizing over the orders was, as another historian termed it, "pure theater." Bill Hyde noted that the rapidly changing situation should have caused Reynolds' orders to supersede any previous instructions, but then weakens his own argument by admitting, "it did not, of course, negate Meade's previous order."[25]

Sickles' confusion was justified by a late afternoon order General Meade sent the Third Corps commander instructing him not to abandon Emmitsburg.

When Meade learned of Howard's order to send Sickles to Gettysburg, Meade had Butterfield fire off a note to Sickles at 4:45 p.m.:

> The major-general commanding has just learned that General Howard has ordered you from Emmitsburg up to Gettysburg. General Hancock has been ordered up to assume command of the three corps—First, Eleventh, and Third. The general does not wish the approaches through Emmitsburg left unguarded, as they cover our left and rear. He desires you to hold on until you shall hear from General Hancock, leaving a division at Emmitsburg, as it is a point not to be abandoned excepting in an extremity. A copy of this will be transmitted to General Hancock. Please put yourself in communication with him.[26]

Unfortunately for Meade, Sickles had already departed for Gettysburg more than one hour earlier. Neither Reynolds nor Howard had suggested leaving a covering force at Emmitsburg. Unsure of Meade's wishes, it was Sickles who had prudently left two brigades behind (which was only slightly less than the full division that Meade ordered.)

While all of this was transpiring, A. P. Hill and Richard Ewell's Confederate corps crushed the Federal First and Eleventh corps and drove them off the fields north and west of Gettysburg. Sometime between 3:30 p.m. and perhaps as late as 4:30 p.m. (estimates of the exact time vary widely) Hancock arrived on Cemetery Hill where, together with Generals Howard, Warren, and Buford, he began rallying the defeated Union infantry and artillery on the high ground south of town. According to Captain Halstead of Abner Doubleday's staff, the consensus was unanimous that Cemetery Hill was a "very strong position." Hancock allegedly announced, rather dramatically if true, "Very well, sir, I select this as the battlefield."[27]

After chasing the Federals through town, the Confederates did not continue on to Cemetery Hill. Nor did they launch an attack that evening on Culp's Hill to the right of Cemetery Hill. Uncertain of the enemy's strength or disposition, General Ewell read his discretionary orders from Lee accordingly and declined to continue the battle that evening. Whether the Confederates could have captured the high ground will never be known, but Hancock and Howard formed a defensive line there of perhaps 7,000 infantry and cavalry, together with forty-three pieces of artillery.[28]

That evening, Lee and General Longstreet, commander of the Confederate First Corps, conferred on Seminary Ridge. According to Longstreet's published postwar accounts, he proposed to "throw our army around by their left, and we shall interpose between the Federal army and Washington" and await an attack. Lee, however, surprised Longstreet when he responded decisively: "No, the enemy is there, and I am going to attack him there." Although the day had been a stunning Confederate tactical victory, Lee found himself in something of a dilemma. The victory notwithstanding, he had allowed himself to be drawn into a major battle about ten miles east of South Mountain, which had successfully screened his army and protected his tenuous supply and communication lines stretching back into Virginia. Maneuvering in the presence of the enemy without most of Jeb Stuart's invaluable cavalry to screen his flanks and front posed considerable dangers. Lee understood this dilemma when he determined that "A battle thus became, in a measure, unavoidable. Encouraged by the successful issue of the engagement of the first day . . . it was thought advisable to renew the attack." It was a calculated risk that, after considering all options, Lee thought best to adopt. The only question was where to "renew the attack."[29]

Meanwhile, General Hancock worked to strengthen the Union position. His immediate concern was the ground to the right of Cemetery Hill (Culp's Hill and what later became known as Stevens Knoll), which he reinforced with artillery and First Corps infantry. Around 4:00 p.m., Hancock dispatched a rider with a verbal message for Meade that Cemetery Hill could be held until nightfall. To Hancock's relief, Henry Slocum and his tardy Twelfth Corps finally began trickling onto the field after 5:00 p.m. Dan Sickles had not been the only Federal corps commander confused over how to react on July 1. Oliver Howard had sent repeated messages to Slocum to bring up his corps, which was only some five miles away near Two Taverns. Only now, after 5:00 p.m., was he reaching the front.[30]

At 5:25 p.m., Hancock sent Meade a written message indicating concern that the line's left could be turned by way of Emmitsburg. "Slocum is now coming on the ground, and is taking position on the right, which will protect the right. But we have, as yet, no troops on the left, the Third Corps not having yet reported; but I suppose that it is marching up. If so, its flank march will in a degree protect our left flank." With Cemetery and Culp's hills relatively secure, Hancock had to deal with the army's nebulous left flank. "[T]he immediate need of a division on the left was imperative," he told Brigadier General John Geary, whose Twelfth Corps division arrived ahead of Slocum. General Geary reported, probably not accurately, that the enemy "was reported to be attempting to flank it, and cavalry were already skirmishing in front of that position." Geary extended his First and Third Brigades "to a range of hills south and west of the town, which I occupied with two regiments of the First Brigade. These hills I regarded as of the utmost importance, since their possession by the enemy would give him an opportunity of enfilading our entire left wing and center with a fire which could not fail to dislodge us from our position."[31]

Meade, meanwhile, sent Hancock a message of his own at 6:00 p.m.. "I thought it prudent to leave a division of the Third Corps at Emmitsburg, to hold in check any force attempting to come through there. It can be ordered up tonight, if required. It seems to me that we have so concentrated, that a battle at Gettysburg is now forced upon us, and that if we can get up our people and attack with our whole force, to-morrow, we ought to defeat the force the enemy has." Meade notified Henry Halleck about the same time that the army was concentrating at Gettysburg.[32]

Within the next ninety minutes, Meade ordered the Fifth Corps, Sixth Corps, and the remainder of the Third Corps forward. A dispatch was sent at 7:30 p.m. to "Commanding Officer at Emmitsburg: The major-general commanding directs that the division of General Sickles' corps ordered to remain at Emmitsburg move up to join their corps at the field in the vicinity of Gettysburg with the greatest dispatch." Meade expected "the division to be up by daylight to-morrow." At the same time, Meade also sent orders to bring up John Sedgwick's large Sixth Corps, which had earlier been redirected toward Taneytown, "Your march will have to be a forced one to reach the scene of action, where we shall probably be largely outnumbered without your presence." Meade's army was not "largely outnumbered," but this misconception would bring on the campaign's most memorable forced march and influence Meade's strategy throughout the battle.[33]

Some time during this period, Sickles' staff officers began to arrive on Cemetery Hill. Captain Alexander Moore had departed Emmitsburg at about 2:00 to open communications with Reynolds. When he reached Gettysburg, he learned that Reynolds was dead, and instead met Howard, who was "anxious" to learn when the Third Corps would be up. Moore then raced back toward Emmitsburg, and met up with Birney leading his division forward, somehow missing both Tremain and Sickles who were ahead of Birney and already looking for Howard.[34]

Having apparently bypassed Captain Moore, Henry Tremain next arrived on Cemetery Hill. Tremain also didn't record his arrival time, but was in advance of the Third Corps to notify Howard of Sickles' approach. Tremain noticed "numerous stragglers" as he relayed Sickles' message to Howard and

Hancock. Tremain then sent an orderly back to conduct Sickles forward. "In due time a group of horsemen appeared with whom I soon recognized the standard indicating Third Corps headquarters." It must have been near 7:00 as Tremain then rode out to guide Sickles in to Generals Howard and Hancock.[35]

"I made a forced march," Sickles later claimed, "and arrived there about the time that General Howard had taken position on Cemetery Hill. I found his troops well posted in a secure position on the ridge. The enemy in the meanwhile had not made any serious attack upon him during my march. The arrival of my force seemed to reassure General Howard in the security of his position." Given that Howard had spent much of the day awaiting both Sickles and Slocum's arrival, Howard was probably relieved to see any help. Nevertheless, Howard's gratitude at this arrival would become just one of the many favorite Gettysburg tales that Sickles would spin in later years; he would often imply (falsely) that his arrival saved the day for the Union cause. Someone was sent back to guide Birney and his two brigades into the lines. When he arrived, Birney massed his men in the rear between Cemetery Ridge and the Taneytown Road, but some straggling regiments (such as the 141st Pennsylvania) did not go into camp until "about dark."[36]

With Slocum finally on the field, Hancock turned over command about 7:00 p.m. and began heading back toward Taneytown. According to Sickles, Slocum ordered the Third Corps to be "massed on the left of Cemetery Ridge." Sickles was still interested in resolving his earlier conflicting orders from Meade, unaware that Meade had ordered the remainder of the Third Corps to come up from Emmitsburg. He was acutely aware that he had come to Gettysburg without Meade's approval and undoubtedly felt some anxiety about his awkward relationship with his new commanding officer.[37] At 9:30 p.m., Sickles decided to justify his actions, and also offer Meade a suggestion or two:

> Before the receipt of your dispatch (dated 4:45 p.m.), four brigades and three batteries of my corps had advanced to the support of General Howard, and reached Gettysburg.
>
> I left two brigades and two batteries at Emmitsburg, assuming that the approaches through Emmitsburg toward our left and rear must not be uncovered.
>
> General Hancock is not in command—General Howard commands. My impression is, if I may be allowed to make a suggestion, that our left and rear are not sufficiently guarded. Nothing less than the earnest and frequent appeals of General Howard, and his supposed danger, could

have induced me to move from the position assigned to me in general orders; but I believed the emergency justified my movement.

Shall I return to my position at Emmitsburg, or shall I remain and report to Howard?

If my corps is to remain in position here, I hope my brigades at Emmitsburg (and batteries) may be relieved and ordered to join me.

This is a good battle-field.[38]

Over the ensuing years, when Sickles was again fighting the battle in various public forums, he repeatedly claimed that the intention of his message was to urge Meade to concentrate at Gettysburg. He also boasted that his march from Emmitsburg had been "against orders."[39] When testifying before the Committee on the Conduct of the War, Sickles claimed that his note had been prompted by a difference in opinion between the assembled corps commanders as to whether they should remain at Gettysburg:

I wrote to General Meade . . . begging him by all means to concentrate his army there and fight a battle, stating in my judgment that it was a good place to fight; that the position of General Howard was an admirably chosen one, and that the enemy would undoubtedly mass there in great force, and that in my judgment it would be most destructive to the morale of the army to fall back, as was apparently contemplated in his order of that morning.[40]

In reality, even a cursory analysis of Sickles' message reveals that his primary goal was to justify his actions. Not only did Sickles not "urge" the concentration of Union forces, he actually offered to return to Emmitsburg if Meade disapproved of his move to Gettysburg. Ironically, even at this hour, Sickles' observation that "our left and rear are not sufficiently guarded" revealed anxiety over the position that Sickles would fatefully occupy on the following day.

Around 11:00 p.m., still unaware that Meade wanted his entire corps at Gettysburg, Sickles and Birney ordered Charles Graham to return to Emmitsburg and assume command of those troops left behind. Graham's instructions were as follows: "The position is of the utmost importance, as it covers the left and rear of this army, and must be held at all hazards." Graham was also reminded to give special care to the corps ammunition and headquarters trains. If unable to hold Emmitsburg, Graham was told to retreat toward Taneytown. Graham departed Gettysburg in the darkness, but when about one mile from Emmitsburg, he was met by one of Meade's aides with new orders to assemble the troops and "march to Gettysburg without delay."[41]

Sickles received a late, and probably unplanned, dinner that night. On Cemetery Hill, the Evergreen Cemetery's caretaker Elizabeth Thorn (her husband Peter was away in the service) was hiding in the gatehouse basement with her elderly parents and children. Sometime around sundown, a soldier entered and asked if she would make supper for General Howard. Thorn prepared the meal, assuming Howard would arrive shortly. Howard didn't arrive until nearly midnight, however, and when he did he had Sickles and Slocum with him. Thorn seemed the most impressed with Howard's presence, but with three generals in her company, she did not speak while they ate. After the meal was finished, Thorn returned to her basement. The family remained there until daylight, when Howard sent orders for them to leave.[42]

General Hancock, meanwhile, rode back to Taneytown and met with Meade about 9:00 p.m. In Hancock's version of events, Meade had determined to fight at Gettysburg based "upon the representations I had made, and the existence of known facts of the case." Hancock had also taken the precaution of ordering John Gibbon to halt the Second Corps "two or three miles behind Gettysburg, in order to protect our rear from any flank movement of the enemy" against Cemetery Ridge's worrisome left flank.[43]

About 10:00 p.m., Meade departed Taneytown for Gettysburg. His party included his son, Captain George Meade, Henry Hunt, and an engineer from Warren's staff, Captain William H. Paine. The group arrived on Cemetery Hill between midnight and 1:00 a.m., where they met a party that included Sickles, Howard, Slocum, and Warren. "Is this the place to fight the battle?" Meade asked Howard. According to Howard, he and Slocum were conferring with Meade near the cemetery gatehouse when Sickles, who had been lying down nearby, "piped up: 'It's a good place to fight from, Sir!'." Meade was pleased that his generals were all in agreement on the position's strength. "I am glad to hear you say so, gentlemen. I have already ordered the other corps commanders to concentrate here and it is too late to change."[44]

When the meeting ended, Meade set out on a nighttime examination of Cemetery Ridge. His reconnaissance party included Howard, Hunt, and engineer Paine. Captain Paine sketched a map in the darkness and while in the saddle (apparently something he was good at), and marked the positions that Meade intended for each corps in the line. Meade ordered Paine to distribute the map to his corps commanders, and also instructed General Hunt to see that the artillery was properly placed. Hunt said that the moonlight inspection covered the Union line "so far as then occupied." Howard recalled, "It was a very beautiful scene, but Gen. Meade did not see it. He was planning— planning." Just north of Little Round Top, the officers turned around and headed toward Culp's Hill.[45]

Robert Carter of the 22nd Massachusetts later pointed out the incredibly difficult situation within which Meade found himself at the close of July 1. He had never seen or been to Gettysburg, and the "very near-sighted" general had made this first examination in dim moonlight. New to command, Meade was "exhausted, mentally and physically, by the terrible strain which he had been under." The reconnaissance was as thorough as one could expect, but it also poses questions as far as the Sickles controversy is concerned. How thorough an examination could have been conducted at approximately 2:00 a.m. by exhausted men in pitch darkness? Since Meade's party did not ascend Little Round Top, how much of Geary's position did they actually see? Did the Paine map physically place Sickles on Little Round Top? A surviving copy in the National Archives (if it is a battlefield copy) places the Sixth Corps on the far left of the Union line in front of the Round Tops, with Sickles' corps to its right.[46]

Thanks to the skillful pre-battle maneuvering of his army, Meade also ended the day with a command that was either on the field or (with the exception of the still-marching Sixth Corps) would be within supporting distance about sunrise. The long and historic day was not yet over, for Andrew Humphreys and his two brigades were still en route from Emmitsburg. As discussed previously, Humphreys was moving from Emmitsburg to Gettysburg on a road that ran about two miles west of the main route Sickles and Birney had used. The division departed Emmitsburg without Humphreys about 4:00 p.m. When Humphreys caught up with the head of his column, he met the corps inspector general, Lieutenant Colonel Julius Hayden, and a local doctor who "acted as a guide for the route that General Sickles wished me to take." The guides were a welcome insurance even though earlier that morning Humphreys had purchased a local map that included all of the surrounding roads.[47]

Sickles had not forgotten Humphreys' division. In addition to Hayden's presence, Humphreys apparently received at least two messengers from Sickles while en route. Sometime "about dusk, a staff officer from General Sickles gave me directions from him to take position on the left of Gettysburg when I got up." Then when "about half way to Gettysburg," Humphreys later testified, "I received a note from General Sickles, which had been written to him by General Howard, telling him to look out for his left as he moved up (on the main road I suppose was meant) from Emmitsburg." This must have imbued Humphreys with extra caution since he was already two miles to the left [west] of the road that Sickles had marched along. "Just after this I met a person who had conducted a portion of the first corps up in the morning, and he told me that there were none of our troops on the west side of the Emmitsburg road." When his vanguard reached a fork in the road that branched off to the right and united with the Emmitsburg Road, Humphreys decided to take it. Colonel Hayden, however, insisted that Sickles wanted Humphreys guided in by the way of the Black Horse Tavern, which was on the road from Fairfield and well west of the Emmitsburg Road.[48]

A skeptical Humphreys directed his brigades to close up and continue marching quietly through the darkness. According to one version, Humphreys rode ahead toward the tavern with a small staff. The innkeeper, Mr. Bream, told the party that thirty-six pieces of Rebel artillery had been seen on a nearby hill just before sundown, and he pointed out Confederate pickets. In his report, General Carr claimed his men marched within 200 yards of the enemy pickets without being discovered. In another more colorful version, Thomas Rafferty of the Excelsior's 71st New York claimed the error was discovered only because "one of the bummers of my own regiment (I must admit we had our share of them) had been straggling from the line of march on a foraging expedition" and captured a "rebel bummer, who was on the same errand."[49]

Humphreys later boasted that the enemy was "not aware of my presence, and I might have attacked them at daylight with the certainty of at least temporary success." Choosing the wiser course of action, the wayward brigades retraced their steps and headed back from whence they had come. The exhausted men trudged along in the hazy moonlight until they could finally see the "extensive smoldering fires of some troops." Humphreys had finally reached Union lines, and Sickles' assistant adjutant general, Lieutenant Colonel Orson Hart, arrived to guide his men into position. When Humphreys informed Sickles of the "circuitous route by which I had come," Sickles assured him that Hayden had been mistaken in guiding the division via Black Horse Tavern. "It shows what can be done by accident," explained the division commander.

It was about 1:00 a.m. when Humphreys' men fell asleep in the shadow of a rocky hill that would one day become known as Little Round Top.[50]

Postwar view of the Sherfy house, taken from the Emmitsburg Road (in the foreground) looking southwest. *Sue Boardman*

Chapter 6

In Some Doubt as to Where He Should Go

T he morning of July 2 started early for the two Third Corps brigades and artillery that had remained at Emmitsburg. The men had settled in for the night with instructions to be prepared for an early morning march to Gettysburg. Around 2:00 a.m., Regis de Trobriand received Meade's orders to move to Gettysburg forthwith. Burling's brigade, however, was well scattered to better protect nearby roads and, given the darkness, could not not be fully assembled until nearly 4:00 a.m. De Trobriand claimed it was "daylight" before they started, and the men hit the road without breakfast, with only ten-minute halts at the end of each hour to make coffee. "It was a weird night march," wrote a member of the 2nd New Hampshire. "The consciousness of impending battle had by some subtle influence taken possession of the minds of the men."[1]

John Buford's cavalry division, along with Lieutenant John Calef's artillery battery, had been posted during the night of July 1 along the Emmitsburg Road on the Union left. Buford's specific location remains unclear, partially because a cavalry line was considerably more fluid and mobile than a static infantry line, but at least a portion of Colonel Devin's brigade occupied the Sherfy Peach Orchard. (The 6th New York Cavalry's battlefield monument says that they bivouacked in the orchard.) The reports of Pleasonton, Buford, and Devin all simply referred to a posting on the extreme "left" of the Union line. Colonel Devin wrote that on the morning of July 2 he "was engaged reconnoitering in rear of the enemy's right," meaning that he moved west of the Emmitsburg Road. A detachment from the 9th New York Cavalry ended up west of Pitzer's Schoolhouse, and later claimed to discover Longstreet's approaching column, but the acquisition of any significant intelligence is not reflected in reports filed by Buford or Devin.[2]

For that portion of the Third Corps already on the battlefield, Henry Tremain wrote that the Third Corps "had simply gone into bivouac, pretty much in the gloom of the evening [of July 1]" and that "neither the batteries nor the infantry were occupying any special posts selected for defense or offence. That awaited the light, and was now to be done." The 141st Pennsylvania's regimental history recorded that Humphreys' division was posted "just north of . . . George Weikert's house." Birney's division was to the left, "Graham's brigade on the right of the division bivouacked in column by regiments, on a knoll in a field south of George Weikert's house. . . . Ward's brigade went into bivouac to the left and a little in front of Graham." The 105th Pennsylvania's historian recorded that when the sun rose on July 2, the left of Birney's division rested "at the foot of Round Top."[3]

The sunlight offered Sickles' men ample opportunity to familiarize themselves with their new surroundings. Pickets were sent forward to the Emmitsburg Road, and Tremain noted that the "enemy's pickets, too, were discovered to be stronger and nearer to us than had been supposed." The 63rd Pennsylvania of Graham's brigade spent the morning on picket duty on line with the Emmitsburg Road. Major John Danks wrote that they were initially placed onto the line at 10:00 p.m. on July 1, along the road with their left flank covering the Wheatfield Road. Danks reported that a concentrated picket firing began early the next morning against the right of his line. Sometime during the morning, the 63rd was pushed forward (west) to a fence that ran in rear of the Sherfy house parallel to the Emmitsburg Road. Between 11:15 a.m. and noon, several companies of the 105th Pennsylvania were also ordered onto the skirmish line in support of the 63rd, "which was keeping up a brisk fire on the skirmishers of the enemy." The 105th also reported that the "fire from the enemy's sharpshooters was severe." Private Alfred Craighead, 68th Pennsylvania, also recalled, "Skirmishing commenced about nine o'clock on the morning of July 2, and gradually increased in severity until the battle opened in earnest."[4]

The Joseph Sherfy farm sat at the intersection of the Emmitsburg and Wheatfield roads. Sherfy built the family's two-story brick farmhouse, still standing today at the intersection's northwest corner, in the early 1840s. Sherfy's farm was considered average size for the area, approximately fifty acres, and had several outbuildings on the property. Sherfy was typical of many local farmers who were required by the hard and rocky Pennsylvania soil to supplement their farming incomes. His occupation in the 1860 census was listed as "Fruit Dealer" rather than "farmer." The fruit resulted from a peach

Postwar view of the Sherfy Peach Orchard looking
toward the Round Tops. *Sue Boardman*

orchard Sherfy owned and operated on his farm. A young peach orchard
directly across the Emmitsburg Road (east) from the farmhouse had been
planted in a six-acre lot the previous year. The trees were not yet producing
fruit, unlike Sherfy's more mature four-acre lot directly at the Emmitsburg and
Wheatfield Roads intersection. It was this mature lot that would forever
become known as the Peach Orchard.[5]

Several properties were in proximity to Sherfy during the summer of 1863.
Roughly west and south of Sherfy were the Warfield and J. Snyder farms.
Warfield was a free black who owned a farm on the south side of the
Millerstown Road, which ran perpendicular to the Emmitsburg Road and cut
through Seminary Ridge just south of Sherfy's land. Snyder was directly across
from Warfield on the north side of the road. North and west of Sherfy were the
farms of Jean Staub and Henry Spangler. Across the Emmitsburg Road,
northeast of Sherfy was the farm of Daniel Klingle. Sherfy's closest neighbor,
directly across (on the east side of) the Emmitsburg Road at the northeast
corner of the Wheatfield Road intersection was the elderly John Wentz. The
original buildings disappeared long ago, but in 1863 the Wentz house stood
approximately seventy-five feet north of the Wheatfield Road. Locals later
remembered the home as being made of logs and weatherboarding. It was
probably a one-and-one-half story structure, similar in size to the existing

Leister or Bryan houses. Two outbuildings sat approximately 120 yards north of the house. The Sherfy's less mature peach orchard ran about 250 yards north and about 150 yards east of the Wentz buildings.[6]

Given Sherfy's location on the Emmitsburg Road, Union troops, including Sickles' Third Corps, had passed by the property in large numbers on July 1. But it was the terrain surrounding the Sherfy and Wentz farms that interested both armies on July 2. The Sherfy farm sits atop an unnamed ridge intersecting the Emmitsburg Road. Sherfy's peach orchard was about 580 feet above sea level, compared to Plum Run (near the base of Little Round Top) which is about 520 feet above sea level. (By way of contrast, Little Round Top is approximately 650 feet above sea level.) The Emmitsburg Road's ridge was roughly halfway between, and somewhat parallel to, the Confederate line of battle on Seminary–Warfield ridges and Meade's intended line on Cemetery Ridge. It was this elevation surrounding the Sherfy farm that would eventually catch Dan Sickles' attention later that morning. He would eventually reach the conclusion that the position would offer the Confederates a potential artillery platform from which they could pummel the Union lines.[7]

In addition to the elevation's potential artillery benefits, the terrain offered another advantage that was not lost on Third Corps officers. The Emmitsburg Road itself was one of only three major roads into Gettysburg that were still under Union control following the fighting of July 1. The other two roads, the Taneytown Road and Baltimore Pike, were of greater importance because they were behind Meade's lines and thus served as potential supply and communication routes leading south. But the Emmitsburg Road had served as a means for the Union's First, Third, and portions of the Eleventh Corps to arrive on the battlefield. The detachment of Sickles' Third Corps left in Emmitsburg would be arriving on this same road later in the morning. Strategically, the road helped to cover Meade's left flank and Union occupation of the Emmitsburg Road could potentially control the Confederates' approach should Lee attempt to turn the Union left. With the exception of the occasional farm buildings and fences, the area leading from the Third Corps positions on Cemetery Ridge up to the road was generally open, allowing room for troops and artillery to maneuver.

Tremain's July 1 role as messenger between Reynolds and Sickles had given him an opportunity to see the ground in daylight. In addition to the elevation along the Emmitsburg Road, Tremain expressed concern to Sickles about the Millerstown Road "that intersected the Emmitsburg highway, near Humphreys left picket; and I was ordered to tell General Birney to picket that road . . . as far toward the enemy as practicable and to keep [Sickles] fully informed." Tremain eventually received a message from Birney that there were, as yet, no enemy forces on his left. Tremain passed the report on to Meade.[8]

While the Third Corps officers and men familiarized themselves with their corner of Pennsylvania, Meade positioned his army. The Second Corps, temporarily under the command of John Gibbon, moved up the Taneytown Road behind the Round Tops and began arriving on the field between 5:30–6:00 a.m. Meade initially ordered Hancock to place these new arrivals behind Cemetery Hill to support the Union right. It wasn't until 7:00 or 8:00 a.m. that he ordered the Second Corps to form a line running approximately one mile south along Cemetery Ridge, with the Taneytown Road behind it. Gibbon was apparently told that, once his men were in position, Sickles would be on his left.[9]

Brigadier General James Barnes' First Division of Fifth Corps had camped during the night only a few miles outside Gettysburg. His men reached Gettysburg about 7:00 a.m. Major General George Sykes, commanding Meade's former Fifth Corps, reported that he "took position on the right of our line" and subsequently massed near a bridge over Rock Creek on the Baltimore Pike, "and within reach of the Twelfth Army Corps." Sykes further reported that "while thus situated" he was "directed to support the Third Corps . . . with a brigade, should it be required." At this time, only two of Sykes' divisions, (Generals Barnes and Ayres) were on the field.[10]

In addition to Graham's Third Corps detachment, which was still on the march from Emmitsburg, other elements of Meade's army were still converging on Gettysburg as the morning hours ticked away. John Sedgwick's large Sixth Corps was on a forced march from Manchester via the Baltimore Pike and would not arrive until later that afternoon. Meade's artillery was also still coming together. According to Captain John Bigelow, commanding the 9th Massachusetts Battery, the Union Artillery Reserve left Taneytown at "early dawn" on July 2 and thought that it was "about eleven in the forenoon" before it arrived at Gettysburg "and was parked in the rear of Cemetery Hill."[11]

While the army was concentrating, Henry Tremain claimed that the "Third Corps troops, except as to their picket lines, were yet unposted. They were in large part reclining where they had spent the night; and their location proved to be on low ground, easily commanded by the land in front, and running off to the left." According to Tremain's postwar memory, the men of the Third Corps "would be at the mercy of the occupants of the 'high ground' at the rear of the extreme left, as well as the possessors of the elevated land at the immediate front of the extreme left, i.e. the Peach Orchard. Indeed, this could easily be perceived when the morning mists had arisen."[12]

In contrast to Tremain's perceived inactivity, Henry Hunt wrote that "the morning was a busy and in some respects an anxious one; it was believed that the whole Confederate army was assembled, that it was equal if not superior to our own in numbers, and that the battle would commence before our troops were up." Some demonstrations on Ewell's front, along with the relatively short distance between Confederates in town and Federals on Cemetery Hill, suggested an attack against the Union right. Meade, in fact, entertained the idea of launching his own offensive from the Union right. "Early in the morning it had been my intention," he later explained, "as soon as the 6th Corps arrived on the ground . . . to make a vigorous attack from our extreme right upon the enemy's left." Slocum would command the attacking column, which would have included his Twelfth Corps, along with the Fifth and Sixth Corps. Slocum and Warren, however, "reported that the character of the ground in front was unfavorable to making an attack," and combined with the fact that the Sixth Corps would not arrive until early afternoon, Meade "abandoned my intention to make an attack from my right." As Henry Hunt later wrote, with the proposed attack abandoned, "Meade postponed all offensive operations until the enemy's intentions should be more clearly developed."[13]

The primary advantages of Meade's Cemetery Ridge position, as it continued to develop that morning, rested in the line's shape and the fact that elevations were available to protect both the left and right flanks. After Hancock and Howard occupied Cemetery Hill the previous afternoon, Hancock wisely ensured that Culp's Hill to the right was also occupied in order to protect against enemy movements in that direction. Since the fledgling Union line was still vulnerable to an attack at that time from the west and south (possibly via either the Emmitsburg or Taneytown roads), Hancock—and later Meade—curved the line south along Cemetery Ridge from Cemetery Hill toward Little Round Top. Chancellorsville was still fresh on everyone's mind. Only two months earlier, Stonewall Jackson had collapsed an exposed Union flank. A successful defense of both Little Round Top on the left and Culp's Hill on the right would be needed to prevent a repeat of that at Gettysburg. Meade's position famously came to take the shape of a giant fishhook (the hook roughly consisting of the line from Culp's Hill to Cemetery Hill and Cemetery Ridge). In addition to geographic anchors on each flank, the fishhook's most redeeming feature was that it allowed Meade the advantage of interior lines. Meade could reinforce, communicate with, or coordinate movements from one end of the line to the other more quickly and easily than could General Lee, whose army would soon occupy a longer exterior line position. General James Wadsworth later explained the Union position's benefits: "Every man in the army was available. The whole army was concentrated on about three miles square; the reserve was within thirty minutes' march of any part of the line." Meade's troop movements further benefitted from use of the Taneytown Road and Baltimore Pike in the rear. Although neither army commander was absolutely confident of his enemy's strength, we know today that Meade ultimately had more men arrayed on a shorter front than Lee. This was a significant, and perhaps the deciding, factor in the battle's outcome.[14]

Although Meade devoted much of his attention to the right flank and right-center portions of his line (Culp's Hill and Cemetery Hill), he did not neglect his left flank. Elements of Brigadier General John Geary's Twelfth Corps division had been posted on the Union left flank, to the left of Sickles' Third Corps, since about 5:00 p.m. the previous evening. Geary reported that he occupied a line "to a range of hills south and west of the town" until he rejoined the remainder of the Twelfth Corps on the Union right "at 5 a.m. on the 2d, having been relieved by the Third Army Corps, in obedience to orders from Major-General Slocum." Colonel John Patrick of the 5th Ohio in Geary's division reported that he had been ordered on July 1 "to the extreme left of our line, and occupied a hill covered with trees." The 147th Pennsylvania was also placed under Patrick's command in order to extend and increase their frontage. Patrick's command remained there "until the following morning, when we received orders at 5 o'clock to return to the brigade."[15]

If Geary and Patrick's reports are accurate, then the Third Corps was ordered to replace them on Little Round Top sometime around 5:00 a.m. Meade didn't yet realize that potential trouble was brewing on his left when he reported, "by 7 a.m . . . The Second and Third Corps were directed to occupy the continuation of the Cemetery Ridge on the left of the Eleventh Corps."[16] Sickles later told the Joint Committee on the Conduct of the War:

> At a very early hour on Thursday morning [July 2] I received a notification that General Meade's headquarters had been established at Gettysburg, and I was directed by him to relieve a division of the Twelfth Corps, General Geary's division I think, which was massed a little to my left, and which had taken position there during the night. I did so, reporting, however, to General Meade that that division was not in position, but was

merely massed in my vicinity; the tenor of his order seemed to indicate a supposition on his part that the division was in position.[17]

David Birney's report supported Sickles' account: "At 7 a.m., under orders from Major-General Sickles, I relieved Geary's division, and formed a line, resting its left on the Sugar Loaf Mountain [Little Round Top] and the right thrown in a direct line toward the cemetery, connecting on the right" with Humphreys' Third Corps division. Birney also placed a picket line "in the Emmitsburg road, with sharpshooters some 300 yards in advance."[18]

"Birney had relieved the troops of Geary's division and formed his line with his left resting near Little Round Top," Captain George Meade later wrote. "The corps, as thus placed, was, with the exception that Little Round Top was not occupied, posted comfortably to General Meade's instructions." The exact details of Meade's orders, the time they were delivered, and whether they were verbal or written, are unclear. Captain Meade was unsure, so he presumably did not deliver the original, and he later wondered if Sickles had received his orders when General Meade arrived on Cemetery Hill the previous night. "I had sent instructions in the morning to General Sickles . . . directing him to form his corps in line of battle on the left of the 2d corps," General Meade explained to the Committee on the Conduct of the War.[19] "I had indicated to him in general terms, that his right was to rest upon General Hancock's left; and his left was to extend to the Round Top mountain, plainly visible, if it was practicable to occupy it."[20]

Sickles, however, claimed that he was unsure of where he was to go because Geary was allegedly "massed" and did not occupy a specific line. Sickles' critics, on the other hand, argue that he must have known Geary's position, and was only inventing the claim that he was unsure of the position. Either Sickles was simply lying (as most parties assume) or there must be an explanation for the variance. The regimental historian for the 141st Pennsylvania compared the differing times reported by Geary (5:00 a.m.) and Birney (7:00 a.m.) and offered a potential explanation for the confusion. "Geary had moved about five o'clock in the morning, and Sickles did not receive his orders until an hour later, when being ignorant of the position Geary had held, and no officer being left to direct him, the order was imperfectly carried out." However, General Meade claimed that Geary had sent a staff officer to Sickles, and that Geary only departed after "his patience was exhausted" by Sickles' failure to relieve him. Private Robert Carter of the 22nd Massachusetts (who did not support Sickles' actions) also believed Geary's departure "misled" Sickles into not understanding Geary's position, but added that one of Geary's staff officers had "pointed it out to him."[21]

With the Third Corps stretched south along Cemetery Ridge, at least to the foot of Little Round Top, Birney's First Division held the left (south) and Humphreys the right (north). Lt. Col. Thomas Rafferty of the Excelsiors' 71st New York thought the terrain in Birney's front "was so faulty that it was impossible to occupy with any prospect of being able to hold it." The low ground "was quite springy and marshy, and was covered thickly with a growth of stunted bushes . . . and masked by the woods and the broken and rocky ground in our front, affording most excellent positions and covers for the rebels to take possession of without risk, and attack us with every advantage in their favor." Rafferty may be added to the list of men concerned that the Emmitsburg Road dominated this low ground, though he also admitted that the road itself "was overlooked and commanded by both the Round Tops." Rafferty did not believe that Meade had personally inspected the position that Sickles was now ordered to occupy. "We were now on the original line which Meade says 'he had designed us to occupy.' How he came to design it I don't know, as neither he nor any of his staff had ever seen it."[22]

There is a possibility that Meade chose Sickles to guard the left flank because he considered it to be the least likely to receive an attack. Hooker had placed Howard on the right flank at Chancellorsville partially because he lacked confidence in the Eleventh Corps and believed that flank immune from an assault. Was Sickles deployed on the left at Gettysburg for the same reason? In later years, Sickles liked to tell the story that he had warned Meade of the left flank's dangers and that Meade had supposedly responded, "Well, Sickles, do you think that the left is a vulnerable and dangerous place? Suppose you go over there and look after it." Sickles' assignment may simply have been "the luck of the draw," a function of corps position at the close of July 1. But Meade certainly believed his right flank was most likely to see heavy combat, either offensively or defensively; he made sure that Slocum's corps was reunited there and that both the Second and Fifth corps were nearby to reinforce Slocum. Meade probably thought the Third Corps was the least likely of his corps to do battle, at least on July 2, and with the exception of the Eleventh Corps, he probably preferred it that way.[23]

Sometime between 8:00 and 9:00 a.m., General Meade spoke with Captain George Meade, his staffer-son, outside army headquarters at the widow Lydia Leister's farmhouse. The general instructed the captain to visit Sickles "to indicate to him where the general head-quarters [sic] were, to inquire of him if his troops were yet in position, and to ask him what he had to report."[24]

Captain Meade rode down the Taneytown Road about one-half mile to Third Corps headquarters "in a small patch of woods on the west side" of the road. There, Captain Meade found only Captain George Randolph, chief of the Third Corps artillery brigade. Randolph told Meade that Sickles was worn down from the prior day's exertions and was resting in a nearby tent. Randolph carried the message to Sickles and returned a few moments later to inform the captain that "the Third Corps was not yet in position, that General Sickles was in some doubt as to where he should go." The staff officer presumed from Sickles' response that the "previous instructions had evidently been sent and received."[25]

At that moment, Captain Meade later wrote, he did not have precise knowledge of his father's orders to Sickles, so he was unable to provide Randolph with any further clarification. Instead, he quickly rode back to the Leister house and reported to his father, who told him "in a sharp, decisive way" to return and tell Sickles to position the Third Corps "on the left of the Second Corps; that his right was to connect with the left of the Second Corps; that he was to prolong with his line the line of [Second] Corps, occupying the position that General Geary had held the night before."[26]

Returning to Sickles a second time, the captain found Sickles' tents "about to be struck, the general just mounted" and surrounded by several of his staff officers. This time, Meade spoke directly to Sickles, who informed him that "his troops were then moving, and would be in position shortly, adding something as to General Geary's not having had any position, but being massed in the vicinity. He then rode off in the direction of the front." As Captain Meade was about to depart, Randolph requested that General Hunt be sent out to review "some positions he had selected for artillery." Meade set spur to horse and returned to army headquarters.[27]

Around 9:00 a.m., the remaining Third Corps brigades began to arrive from Emmitsburg under General Graham's direction. The men left Emmitsburg sometime after 4:00 a.m. It took an unimpressive four or five hours to cover just nine miles. Graham claimed that as they approached Gettysburg, local citizens warned "that the enemy were advancing in heavy force on my flank." As they neared the Sherfy peach orchard, Captain James Smith noticed that nearby fences had been cleared away and "the pickets and skirmishers were uneasy and kept up a desultory fire, little puffs of thin blue smoke dotting the plain before us, indicating quite distinctly the respective lines of the two greatest

Modern view looking south from Birney's morning bivouac. Photo taken near George Weikert farm. Little Round Top is visible on center horizon. *Author*

armies on earth." After passing Sherfy's, they turned off into the fields to the right, "towards the foot of" Cemetery Ridge where they reported to Sickles. According to Colonel Regis de Trobriand, he reported to Birney at 10:00 a.m. and was placed in line between Ward and Graham's brigades. Burling was sent on to Humphreys' division, where his men massed in columns rather than line and rested until nearly noon. Colonel Charles Merrill of the 17th Maine also noted that "already the pickets of both armies were busily engaged," as did Lt. Col. Rafferty of the 71st New York. The skirmishing helped keep the tension high.[28]

Rafferty later remembered that the ground between the western slope of Cemetery Ridge and the Emmitsburg Road was "divided into fields by stone fences, which we immediately proceeded to level all the way down and clear across to the Emmitsburg Road, so that we had a clear declivity all along the front of our division." General Humphreys said that the order to clear the fences originated with Sickles. Humphreys seems to have done a thorough job clearing his front, but some have questioned whether Birney's division was as active. Portions of fence near the Emmitsburg Road were not leveled because they were potentially within range of enemy pickets. Captain A. W. Givin of the 114th Pennsylvania later explained that fences remained near the north end of the Sherfy buildings because "Our pioneers were sent out to remove the fence and had partly chopped it down when they were compelled to desist by the heavy picket firing."[29]

Captain Judson Clark of the First New Jersey Battery B reported that at "about 9.30 a.m." Randolph ordered his battery "placed in line on the rise of ground midway between General Sickles' headquarters [Trostle farm] and the peach orchard, on the Emmitsburg road, where we remained until about 2 p.m." It is unclear why this movement was ordered, but one scenario is that Clark was ordered up to support the skirmishers along the Emmitsburg Road.[30]

Around 11:00 a.m. Sickles rode to army headquarters, where he finally met with Meade personally. "Not having received any orders in reference to my position," Sickles later told Congress, he claimed that "conclusive indications" of an enemy attack on his front necessitated the meeting. "I went in person to headquarters and reported the facts and circumstances which led me to believe that an attack would be made there, and asked for orders." Sickles, however, "did not receive any orders, and I found that my impression as to the intention of the enemy to attack in that direction was not concurred in at headquarters." Even worse, he continued, "I was satisfied, from information which I received, that it was intended to retreat from Gettysburg." Sickles elaborated that

Modern view of the low ground north of Little Round Top that Sickles disliked. This view looks north toward Cemetery Hill (far horizon), with Cemetery Ridge on right. The woods on left block the view toward the west. *Author*

Meade's "demeanor" gave him the impression that "he did not intend to fight the battle at Gettysburg if he could avoid it. General Butterfield . . . told me that orders were being then prepared for a change of position to Pipe Clay Creek."[31]

Sickles' and Meade's versions on these points differ sharply. Meade later claimed he gave Sickles orders at this 11:00 meeting. But Meade's response, as recorded by his own son, raises doubts as to whether Meade actually had firsthand knowledge of Geary's position. Captain Meade wrote that his father told Sickles "that he [Sickles] was to occupy the position in which he [Meade] *understood that General Hancock had the night before placed General Geary*" [emphasis added]. According to Meade, Sickles replied that "Geary had no position," so Meade spelled it out once again: extend Hancock's line and place his left on the hill later known as Little Round Top. After noting there was very good artillery positions "in the vicinity" and requesting assistance in posting his guns, Sickles asked if he had discretion to post his men according to his judgment. Meade replied, "Certainly, within the limits of the general instructions I have given you; any ground within those limits you choose to occupy, I leave to you." According to Sickles, "I asked General Meade to go over the ground on the left and examine it. He said his engagements did not permit him to do that." Sickles then asked for chief engineer Warren, but as he was also busy, it was agreed that General Hunt, the army's chief of artillery, would accompany him. Meade later said that he thought Hunt's role was to "examine and inspect such positions as General Sickles thought good for artillery, and to give General Sickles the benefit of his [Hunt's] judgment."[32]

Henry Hunt had spent much of the morning inspecting Union lines. When he returned to headquarters, "General Meade told me that General Sickles, then with him, wished me to examine a new line, as he [Sickles] thought that assigned to him was not a good one, especially that he could not use his artillery there." Hunt's inspections had covered both the Union left and right flanks. "I had been as far as Round Top that morning, and had noticed the unfavorable character of the ground," recalled the gunnery officer. Hunt noted in his report that Little Round Top itself offered a "natural termination of our lines, [but the] broken character of the ground in front of the southern half of our line was unfavorable to the use of artillery."[33]

According to Meade, Sickles needed assistance in posting his artillery. Contrary to Meade's recollection, Sickles claimed the goal of having an officer from headquarters accompany him was to make "a careful reconnaissance of the whole position on the left, in reference to its topography and the best line for us to occupy." Hunt's account is a hybrid of the two. He wrote that he was

Modern view taken from area north of Little Round Top and looking west toward Houck's Ridge. The ridge and wood line block the view to the west and the Emmitsburg Road beyond. *Author*

to "examine a new line" in particular for artillery use. Hunt's account, combined with Sickles' request to have Warren (the chief engineer) accompany him, would seem to suggest that more was discussed than simply the posting of artillery.[34]

Hunt accompanied Sickles on the ride toward the Third Corps position. Sickles pointed out the proposed line, which he described as running "from Round Top on the left, perpendicular to the Emmitsburg road, but somewhat *en echelon*, with the line of battle established on Cemetery ridge." The new line proposed was actually in *front* of Cemetery Ridge, but it did cover the Emmitsburg Road. Hunt knew that Sickles had marched from Emmitsburg without his artillery train on July 1, and he initially inferred that Sickles wanted to maintain control of the road until his train arrived.[35]

Since Sickles and Hunt were primarily evaluating suitable artillery positions, they must have discussed the portion of Cemetery Ridge that ran between Hancock's left and Little Round Top. As Sickles told Hunt in 1886, it was "a low, marshy swale and a rocky, wooded belt unfit for artillery & bad front for infantry. Hence my anxiety to get out of the hole where I was & move up to the commanding ground." While Sickles and partisans would later give several reasons for their advance off Cemetery Ridge, it is this reason—perhaps more than any other—that is frequently cited by historians. Sickles feared that this low ground would prohibit his artillery dispositions while being dominated by enemy guns along the higher Emmitsburg Road. Such an event allegedly brought forth the specter of a repeat of Chancellorsville's Hazel Grove.[36]

Hunt later wrote that when they rode "direct to the Peach Orchard," Sickles "pointed out" the Emmitsburg Road ridge that included Sherfy's peach orchard "as his proposed line." This proposed front for the Third Corps, as ultimately deployed later in that afternoon, posed problems in both length and shape. The essentially straight line along Cemetery Ridge, which Meade intended Sickles to occupy, was approximately 1,600 yards long. The Third Corps had roughly 10,675 effectives on the morning of July 2. Sickles later claimed that he lacked sufficient strength to man Meade's proposed front. The the new position proposed by Sickles, however, was nearly twice as long (roughly 2,700 yards flank to flank). The Emmitsburg Road offered no topographical anchors on Sickles' left, unlike the anchoring opportunities offered by the Round Tops on Cemetery Ridge. A primary advantage of occupying Little Round Top was that it formed a natural barrier from an attack against the left flank. When he moved forward, Sickles attempted to address this problem by refusing his left (Birney's division) in a rough line running from the Peach Orchard toward the Round Tops. Sickles' refused left lacked the manpower to reach the rocky hill, a distance of some one mile. As a result, it ended on Houck's Ridge (property owned locally by John Houck). The southern end of the ridge is dominated by large boulders and popularly known as "Devil's Den." Devil's Den lies roughly 500 yards west of Little Round Top, and it was here that Sickles was forced to anchor his left flank. By refusing Birney in such a manner, Sickles could effectively prohibit a Confederate attack directly up the Emmitsburg Road, but in doing so he also created an awkward right angle (or salient) at the Peach Orchard. The salient would be dangerously exposed to attack from two directions—the west and the south, simultaneously.[37]

Hunt noted another problem with Sickles' proposal. At its farthest point, portions of the new line would be about three-quarters of a mile in advance of the remainder of Meade's army on Cemetery Ridge. The distance from the Peach Orchard, roughly the center of Sickles' new line, to Cemetery Ridge was approximately 1,500 yards. This would, in Hunt's words, "so greatly lengthen our line—which in any case must rest on Round Top, and connect with the left of the Second Corps—as to require a larger force than the Third Corps alone to hold it." Not only would Sickles need more men to cover a longer line, but the distance between Sickles and Cemetery Ridge would negate the advantages of Meade's interior lines. Any reinforcements sent to Sickles would have to cover this increased distance.[38]

Despite these readily apparent disadvantages, Hunt believed that Sickles' proposal had some merit. The ridges desired by Sickles "commanded all the ground behind, as well as in front of them, and together constituted a favorable position for *the enemy* [emphasis in original] to hold. This was one good reason for our taking possession of it." (Significantly, however, a piece of terrain that clearly could not be dominated by the Emmitsburg Road ridge was Little Round Top.) Hunt also thought that the dangers of the dreaded salient angle could, in fact, be minimized. "It would, it is true, in our hands present a salient angle, which generally exposes both its sides to enfilade fires; but here the ridges were so high that each would serve as a "traverse" for the other, and reduce that evil to a minimum."[39]

If Hunt's postwar writing is any indication, he seems to have been most concerned about the gap between Sickles' proposed right (which petered out along the Emmitsburg Road) and Hancock's left (which remained anchored on Cemetery Ridge). Because of the northeast-to-southwest direction of the Emmitsburg Road, the distance from Sickles' right near the Klingle house to

Cemetery Ridge was just less than 1,100 yards. One potential way to close the gap between the two corps would be to order the Second Corps to throw its left forward. Hunt, however, hesitated to endorse the move, partially because the woods west of the Emmitsburg Road and directly in front of the salient were not under Union control. Hunt knew "it would be difficult to occupy and strengthen the angle if the enemy already held the wood in its front." Hunt told Sickles to reconnoiter the timber before taking any further action.[40]

About this point in the conversation, Hunt discerned artillery fire on the distant Union right. Believing he had performed his duty in accompanying Sickles, Hunt decided to ride back toward Meade's headquarters rather than await the results of a reconnaissance of the woods. "As I was leaving, General Sickles asked me if he should move forward his corps. I answered, 'Not on my authority; I will report to General Meade for his instructions.'" According to Sickles' version, Hunt added that the position "met with the approval of his [Hunt's] own judgment . . . [and] he said that I would undoubtedly receive" Meade's approval.[41]

Rather than return directly to the right flank, Hunt decided to take an indirect route via Little Round Top, and so would see Sickles' entire proposed line. In light of subsequent events, it was unfortunate that Sickles or an aide did not accompany Hunt. Although Hunt had supposedly already inspected the Union left that morning, it is obvious that there were still lingering questions in his mind about the lay of the terrain. "As I rode back a view from that direction showed how much farther Peach Orchard [sic] was to the front of the direct line than it appeared from the orchard itself." Still more troubling was Sickles' proposed left flank, which would be tangled amongst the rocks in front of Little Round Top. When viewing the proposed line from the Peach Orchard, Hunt had misjudged the position of Houck's Ridge and had erroneously thought that it was continuous with Cemetery Ridge. Now examining the ridge more closely, he apparently realized for the first time that Sickles' desired left anchor would be in front of Little Round Top. To make matters worse, the left flank at Devil's Den would also be commanded by the "much higher Peach Orchard crests" if the orchard fell to the enemy, "and was therefore not an eligible line to occupy, although it became of importance during the battle."[42]

Hunt seems not to have entirely favored Meade's proposed line, thought the Peach Orchard had both strengths and weaknesses, and decidedly did not endorse Sickles' proposed left flank anchor point. Which position, then, did Hunt actually prefer? The choice "would depend on circumstances," explained Hunt. He continued:

The direct short line through the woods [Meade's Cemetery Ridge position], and including the Round Tops, could be occupied, intrenched [sic], and made impregnable to a front attack. But, like that of Culp's Hill, it would be a purely defensive one, from which, owing to the nature of the ground and the enemy's commanding position on the ridges at the angle, an advance in force would be impracticable. The salient line proposed by General Sickles, although much longer, afforded excellent positions for our artillery; its occupation would cramp the movements of the enemy, bring us nearer his lines, and afford us facilities for taking the offensive. It was in my judgment tactically the better line of the two, provided it were strongly occupied, for it was the only one on the field from which we could have passed from the defensive to the offensive with a prospect of decisive results.[43]

The proposed lines offered a perfect example of the contrasts between Sickles' aggressive temperament and Meade's more conservative judgment. Sickles, however, did not command the army. That was Meade's job. But with the Sixth Corps not yet on the field, Meade did not have the extra men to risk extending into an advanced position. Hunt later wrote that it would take both the Third Corps and the Fifth Corps to defend the proposed line. The latter organization was primarily acting as a reserve on the Union right until the Sixth Corps arrived, and Meade was unlikely to authorize a movement that would leave him with no reserve. The timing of the Confederate attack was also a factor. "Had he [Meade] known that Lee's attack would be postponed until 4 p.m., he might have occupied this line in the morning," wrote Hunt after the war, "but he did not know this, expected an attack at any moment, and, ordered the occupation of the *safe* [emphasis in original] line." A defensive battle was just as likely, and perhaps more likely, to win a victory than an offensive battle. "The additional risks of an offensive battle were out of all proportion to the prospective gains," concluded Hunt.[44]

Unfortunately, many of Hunt's objections were settled upon after he left Sickles at the Peach Orchard. If Hunt's postwar writing is any indication, he probably gave Sickles mixed signals during their time together. Hunt's objections became more firmly etched only after he had ridden the length of the proposed line, unaccompanied by Sickles. Even if Hunt had left Sickles with a favorable impression, one thing seems clear: he had not authorized Sickles to advance.[45]

Perhaps due to his concern for the artillery fire on the right, or perhaps because he felt his inspection responsibilities had ended, Hunt did not pass these additional objections along to Sickles. Instead, he returned to headquarters. Hunt later wrote that he briefly told General Meade that "the proposed line [by Sickles] was a good one in itself, that it offered favorable positions for artillery, but that its relations to other lines were such that I could not advise it, and suggested that he examine it himself before ordering its occupation." Captain Meade wrote that Hunt advised that "if he [Hunt] were General Meade, he would not order troops out there until he had personally examined the line." Hunt said that General Meade "nodded assent" and Hunt departed for Cemetery Hill. Once again General Meade received an indication that all was not well on his left flank, but he apparently did not act further on Hunt's report. He probably assumed that Sickles would not be so presumptuous as to move an entire corps out of line without orders. Still, Meade had repeatedly been given warnings of Sickles' uncertainty of where to deploy; he would have been wise to have given the matter more attention than he did.[46]

According to staffer Henry Tremain, "when we returned to Third Corps headquarters, the subject of posting the main line became a practical and imminent one. Moreover, a lively skirmish fire opened on Humphrey's pickets, and betokened some activity on the part of the enemy . . . I was sent in that direction for a report." From a picket post Tremain examined the enemy's skirmishers. "It was too thick a line to be without significance to my mind. I did not like it, and reported on my return that the enemy were doing something behind their skirmish line; but what [it was] I did not know." Lt. Col. Clark Baldwin of the 1st Massachusetts had spent much of the morning on the Union picket line. Around noon, he wrote, "from all appearances I was led to believe that the enemy were preparing to advance."[47]

As the morning slipped into the afternoon, the Army of the Potomac's left flank was in the hands of a corps commander who neither liked nor understood his position. Subsequent events would soon convince Sickles that the enemy attack was about to land squarely against him.

Chapter 7

No Relation to the General Line of Battle

Robert E. Lee was initially unsure of his plans that morning. The evening before, Lee considered launching his main offensive from his left flank, against Meade's right opposite Culp's and Cemetery Hills. But Richard Ewell and his division commanders, especially Jubal Early, convinced Lee that the terrain in their front did not favor such an assault. Lee then proposed contracting his extended lines by drawing Ewell's corps around to Longstreet's right. This too was rejected by Early and company, who did not want to abandon their hard fought ground in the town. They argued that the best chance for success was an attack against the Federal left flank on Cemetery Ridge. Later that night, Lee told Ewell again that he wanted to move Ewell to Longstreet's right. Ewell convinced Lee again, erroneously as events turned out, to leave him in position as he could carry Culp's Hill. Lee could not have been happy that none of his subordinates seemed to want to attack the Federal position, but he was now moving toward planning an attack on Meade's left as July 2 dawned.[1]

That morning, Generals Lee, Longstreet, Hill, Hood, and Heth consulted near Lee's headquarters on Seminary Ridge. General Hood remembered Lee as being anxious to attack. "The enemy is here, and if we do not whip him, he will whip us." But Longstreet remained hesitant, because "the enemy was found in position on his formidable heights awaiting us" and because he was missing his third division, George Pickett's, which was still bringing up the army's rear. In studying the visible portions of Cemetery Ridge, Lee and Longstreet had an imprecise knowledge of where the Union left ended. Without Jeb Stuart's mobile cavalry to scout for him, Lee instead sent out several reconnaissance parties that morning. The most significant of these was led by a staff engineer,

Captain Samuel Johnston, who probably departed with a small party between 4:00 a.m. and 5:00 a.m.[2]

Major General Lafayette McLaws, commanding one of Longstreet's two available divisions, arrived at the head of his column on Seminary Ridge. Using a map, Lee told McLaws "to place your division across" or perpendicular to the Emmitsburg Road and "get there if possible without being seen by the enemy." Lee's objective would have placed McLaws just south of what would later be called the Peach Orchard. McLaws suggested that he would like to reconnoiter, but Longstreet, who was pacing nearby, refused to allow McLaws to leave his division. Longstreet pointed to the map and said, "I wish your division placed so," running his finger in a direction parallel, rather than perpendicular, to the Emmitsburg Road. Lee disagreed. "No, General, I wish it placed just perpendicular to that," or "just the opposite." McLaws reiterated his request to scout with Johnston, but Longstreet again forbade it. Longstreet staffer Moxley Sorrel admitted that the First Corps leader did not approve of Lee's plans and "failed to conceal some anger." As McLaws remembered, "General Longstreet appeared as if he was irritated and annoyed, but the cause I did not ask." McLaws "then went back to the head of my column and sat on my horse and saw in the distance the enemy coming, hour after hour, on to the battle ground."[3]

Meanwhile, Captain Johnston was attending to his reconnaissance. Johnston claimed that he moved south along Willoughby Run, crossed the Emmitsburg Road in the vicinity of the Peach Orchard and "got up on the slopes of Round Top, where I had a commanding view." On his return route, he claimed to have seen three or four Union troopers riding on the Emmitsburg Road. Lee was still in conference with Longstreet and Hill when Johnston returned to Seminary Ridge. Lee seemed surprised to hear that Johnston had reached Little Round Top. Lee instructed Johnston to join Longstreet and aid him "in any way I could." Johnston thought it about 8:00 a.m. when his conference with Lee ended, and 9:00 a.m. when he joined Longstreet.[4]

Captain Johnston's morning reconnaissance has confounded historians since 1863. How had he bypassed John Buford's cavalry pickets along the Emmitsburg Road and then reached Little Round Top without seeing any sign of Sickles' Third Corps or any other Federal troops? Whether he reached Little Round Top or mistakenly ended up on another hill is beyond the scope of this study. What is more important is what Lee learned from the mission. While Johnston's scout did not discover the location of the Federal left flank, it did provide Lee with information as to where the flank was not, which may have convinced Lee that Meade's line ended short of the Round Tops. Johnston's mission helped to convince Lee to use Longstreet in a main attack to drive in the Federal left, while Ewell demonstrated against Meade's distant right flank.[5]

Longstreet, however, did not get his troops (two divisions under Lafayette McLaws and John Hood) into motion until about noon. Their objective was to move into a position on the right of A. P. Hill's Third Corps on Seminary Ridge less than three miles to the south. This would have placed them roughly opposite the left of Humphreys' division front and the right of Birney's. But after crossing the Fairfield Road, about 500 yards beyond the Black Horse Tavern, Longstreet's command reached a small knoll that was visible to Union signal stations on Little Round Top. The divisions were forced to turn around and "counter- march" by another route that would eventually take them along Willoughby Run. During the maneuver, Hood's division crowded into McLaws' rear, causing some confusion. The new route was far from ideal and McLaws admitted there was "very considerable difficulty, owing to the rough character of the country in places and the fences and ditches we had to cross."[6]

If Lee intended to repeat Stonewall Jackson's stunning Chancellorsville flank attack, he must have been surely disappointed on July 2 at Gettysburg. Both Jackson (at Chancellorsville) and Longstreet (at Gettysburg) started with an imperfect understanding of where the Federal flank was located; but there were significant differences between maneuvering in Virginia and maneuvering in Pennsylvania. Jackson was aided at Chancellorsville by intelligence gathered from both Stuart's cavalry and friendly locals. Longstreet had neither to help him at Gettysburg. Lee did assign Captain Johnston to assist in guiding Longstreet, but in a comedy of Confederate errors, Johnston claimed to be unaware of any such role and gave Longstreet no help. Unlike at Chancellorsville, Longstreet did not enjoy a dense tangled Wilderness to help screen his march, and he had to burn considerable time trying to avoid being seen by Little Round Top's signal stations as he approached Sickles' front. Also, unlike at Chancellorsville, Sickles insisted the enemy was getting ready to attack and not retreat.

As noted previously, when Henry Hunt visited Sickles at the Peach Orchard shortly after 11:00 a.m. he declined to endorse Sickles' proposed movement. Part of his objection was because the woods west of the Emmitsburg Road were not under Union control. Hunt said it was he who advised Sickles to reconnoiter the woods before making any additional movements. Writing decades later, Henry Tremain suggested that the reconnaissance was ordered because the Third Corps officers feared that the

Confederates would use the Millerstown crossroad to hit the left of any Third Corps troops or trains that might be arriving from Emmitsburg. Tremain wrote that his role as a courier on July 1 had given him ample opportunity to worry about this road, and he suggested that he deserved much of the credit for ordering the reconnaissance. Not surprisingly, both Birney and Colonel Hiram Berdan, whose U.S. Sharpshooters conducted the scout, later claimed the idea as their own. (However, since Berdan's battle report indicates that he received the order from Birney, we can probably rule out Berdan as the source.) Whoever deserved the credit, Berdan received orders to "feel the enemy, and to discover their movements, if possible." Only two months earlier at Chancellorsville, Berdan's sharpshooters had led Birney into the unknown against Jackson's moving column near Catharine Furnace. Now under different conditions, Berdan was called upon again.[7]

Berdan took four companies of his First U. S. Sharpshooters, approximately 100 men, and an additional 210 men of the 3rd Maine Infantry across the Emmitsburg Road to flush out the suspicious woods. Berdan reported, "I moved down the Emmitsburg road some distance beyond our extreme left and deployed the sharpshooters in a line running nearly east and west, and moved forward in a northerly direction parallel with the Emmitsburg road." This description would have initially put them in Biesecker's Woods south of the Millerstown Road, although Birney's report stated that the group used the Millerstown crossroad itself to reach Warfield Ridge. Lieutenant Colonel Casper Trepp, of the First U. S. Sharpshooters, complained that whatever the actual route, their every move was "in plain view of the enemy . . . the enemy must have seen every man from the time we reached the road until we entered the woods."[8]

While Berdan's expedition less than stealthily explored the woods west of Sickles' salient, Henry Tremain rode to General Meade's headquarters with a status report. Tremain found Meade studying county maps in a "little room with a low ceiling in a small, old fashioned farm house." Waiting in the room, Tremain became "embarrassed" as Meade refused to acknowledge his presence. After an indeterminable delay, Meade looked up with an inquisitive "Well, sir." Tremain relayed his brief report to Meade, after which the general silently returned to studying his map. After yet another embarrassingly awkward pause, Tremain offered that "Gen. Sickles requested Gen. Meade's orders about the Emmitsburg Road." General Meade replied that "he would send cavalry to patrol it, and that orders had been sent to the trains." A frustrated Tremain was dismissed and returned to Third Corps headquarters. Perhaps as a result of this meeting, at 12:50 p.m. Butterfield dispatched an order for the Artillery Reserve to "send a battery to report to General Sickles on the left."[9]

Berdan's group probably reached Pitzer's Woods, "a dense wood" on the west side of the Emmitsburg Road, around noon. "We soon came upon the enemy," Berdan reported, "and drove them sufficiently to discover three columns in motion in rear of the woods, changing direction, as it were, by the right flank." Berdan and Trepp's surprised men collided with three Alabama regiments (the 8th, 10th, and 11th) in Brigadier General Cadmus Wilcox's brigade of R. H. Anderson's division. Wilcox's brigade was on the extreme right of the Confederate army, and Wilcox had orders to refuse his right flank against any potential enemy attacks. In bending back his line, Wilcox fronted southeast and south in the direction of the Peach Orchard and Pitzer's Woods. Like his Yankee counterparts, Wilcox had been wary of his position and had ordered the 10th Alabama to occupy Pitzer's Woods, and the 11th to form in line in the open field to the left. He ordered his two regiments to advance behind a line of skirmishers and it was while executing this movement that Berdan and Wilcox collided, giving the Union men the impression that the Confederates were advancing toward the Emmitsburg Road. The spirited firefight lasted for probably twenty minutes until Berdan ordered his men to fall back to the east side of the Emmitsburg Road. The U.S. Sharpshooters suffered some twenty casualties, while the 3rd Maine added another forty-eight.[10]

Most of the action was visible from the Union's Round Top signal station. "Enemy's skirmishers are advancing from the west, 1 mile from here," Signal Officer A. B. Jerome wrote in a message to Butterfield at 11:45 a.m. Another, more ominous message, followed ten minutes later: "The rebels are in force, and our skirmishers give way. One mile west of Round Top signal station, the woods are full of them."[11]

As noted previously, Buford's cavalry and John Calef's artillery had been posted on the extreme Union left, along the Emmitsburg Road, since the previous evening. The reports of both Colonel Thomas Devin and Lieutenant Calef indicate they deployed in Berdan's support, whom Devin said "were engaged in my front." But shortly thereafter, a blunder occurred within the Union command chain that would significantly influence Sickles' eventual actions. Meade had issued orders for Buford to "collect all the trains in the vicinity of Taneytown and take them down to Westminster." Buford's two brigades on the field had performed hard service throughout the campaign, and on July 1 in particular. Although casualties had been relatively slight, as Captain Meade later pointed out, Buford's horses through lack of forage and "loss of

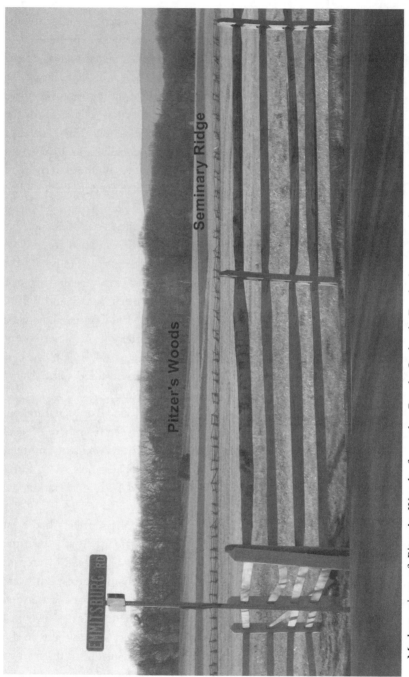

Modern view of Pitzer's Woods from the Peach Orchard. Berdan's reconnaissance stumbled across Wilcox's Confederates in these woods, convincing Sickles that he had to move forward. *Author*

shoes from continuously hard work, were becoming unserviceable." Believing that cavalry commander Alfred Pleasonton would bring in replacements, Buford's cavalry was withdrawn in order to guard the trains and refit. The real error occurred when Pleasonton neglected to bring up any substitutes. The left flank of Meade's army was now unprotected by any cavalry screen, a situation that justifiably alarmed Sickles when he learned of it.[12]

Ironically, the reports of Pleasonton, Buford, and Devin all implied they retired because they were relieved by the Third Corps! Buford reported that "the division became engaged with the enemy's sharpshooters on our left, and held its own until relieved by General Sickles' corps, after which it moved to Taneytown, and bivouacked for the night." An "exceedingly annoyed" Meade learned of the mistake and "emphatically" notified Pleasonton at 12:50 p.m. that he did not intend to withdraw all cavalry support from Sickles' left and that "the patrols and pickets upon the Emmitsburg road must be kept on as long as our troops are in position." But it would not be until 1:45 p.m. that Pleasonton would send an order to Brigadier General David McM. Gregg, commanding the cavalry's Second Division, to bring forward a "regiment" to replace Buford's division. Unfortunately, Gregg was on the right side of Meade's line, and events unfolded so rapidly that he was unable to arrive in time to support Sickles.[13]

At 1:30 p.m., the Union's Round Top signal station spotted a strong Confederate force, much larger than skirmishers, apparently moving toward Meade's right flank. The warning read: "A heavy column of enemy's infantry, about 10,000 strong, is moving from opposite our extreme left toward our right." This seemed to confirm fears that Lee would move against the Union right. However, what the signal officer saw was in reality Longstreet's column counter-marching back from the vicinity of Blackhorse Tavern. The signal officer was unaware that after the column had passed from sight, Longstreet changed direction again and was headed toward the Union left. Although Longstreet has received considerable criticism for his long and slow march, he was inadvertently successful in masking his real intentions from the observing Union signal station.[14]

Meade recorded the arrival of the Sixth Corps at 2:00 p.m. The time of its arrival is significant in that Meade "immediately directed the Fifth Corps to move over to our extreme left, and the Sixth to occupy its place as a reserve for the right." Had Lee and Longstreet been able to launch the attack before 2:00 p.m., the large Sixth Corps would not have been on the field, and the Fifth Corps might not have been as readily available to provide timely support in defense of Meade's left. Meade and the Union commanders incorrectly believed they were outnumbered and that the Sixth Corps presence was a necessity before taking any decisive action. By delaying their attack until about 4:00 p.m., the Confederates allowed Meade every available opportunity to concentrate his army.[15]

Meanwhile, according to Berdan, it was "about 2 o'clock" when he returned to Union lines and reported his "discoveries" to Birney who, in turn, reported to Sickles that "three columns of their forces were found marching to our left." The message was a pivotal culmination of the morning's events. With the removal of Buford's cavalry screen from his left, Berdan's "important information" must have been the final straw for Sickles. He perceived a continued lack of support from headquarters, and he now believed he had proof that the enemy was making a move toward his left flank. Confederates had been reported near the Millerstown Road and approaching the Emmitsburg Road. If Sickles wanted to prevent the enemy from occupying the Peach Orchard ridge, then he had to get there before they did.[16]

Unfortunately the significance of Berdan's firefight and its relevance to Sickles' actions has been historically muddied by inflated postwar claims that Berdan had stumbled upon and delayed Longstreet's main attack. The sharpshooters' regimental history claimed that their 300-man expedition had "stopped the advance of 30,000 foes. No greater display of heroism, no more self-sacrificing spirit of patriotism can be cited in the annals of war . . . surely, it may be fairly said to be a turning point in the Rebellion." Berdan himself made similarly boastful postwar claims that he had stalled the lead elements of "Longstreet's column." Postwar speeches, such as the one James Longstreet gave at Gettysburg's twenty-fifth anniversary reunion only added to the fantastic tales: "The firing in question saved Sickles and the day. It caused me a loss of forty minutes, and could I have saved five of those minutes, the battle would have gone against Meade on the 2nd day." Of course, any claims that Berdan directly delayed Longstreet are patently false. Wilcox's regiments had no affiliation with Longstreet's First Corps and were not leading Longstreet into position. Further, given that Longstreet's main body was moving from the general vicinity of Blackhorse Tavern while the firefight was in progress, there is no way that the sharpshooters could have directly impacted Longstreet's march while fighting in Pitzer's Woods. The sight of three Alabama regiments was surely disconcerting to Berdan's men, but it is unlikely they could have been mistaken for "30,000 foes."[17]

Berdan's intelligence, however, was still significant. Sickles' detractors often argue that since Wilcox was not actually part of Longstreet's main flanking movement, then the firefight in Pitzer's Woods did not discover a potentially significant threat to the Union left. In other words, Berdan's report should have given Sickles no cause for concern. This reasoning ignores the fact that at the time the discovery was made, Sickles, Berdan, and Birney had no way of knowing that Wilcox was not part of the main attack. This information was only known after the war ended, and was not available to Sickles when he made his fateful decision on July 2, 1863. Limited only to what Sickles knew *at the moment he had to make his decision*, all he knew was that his reconnaissance had stumbled into woods filled with Rebels reportedly moving in his direction. He had convinced himself all morning that the enemy would make a move toward his left flank, his officers believed it, and Berdan obliged by reporting large "columns" moving in his direction. Unfortunately, the exaggerated postwar claims, which Sickles regrettably supported fully, intentionally distorted the true significance of Berdan's reconnaissance. Sickles' conclusion, though based upon a misreading of the true situation, was still accurate: Confederates were moving to attack the Union left.[18]

Berdan's report did have a significant psychological impact on Sickles. Sickles alluded to this point in his introduction to Helen Longstreet's 1905 book *Lee and Longstreet at High Tide* when he wrote, "the formation and movements of the attacking column had been discovered by my reconnaissance; this exposure put an end to any chance of surprise." Sickles had not actually "discovered" the "attacking column," but he believed *at that time* that he had. Longstreet's attack had inadvertently lost its element of surprise.[19]

There is the possibility that Berdan's discovery of Wilcox impacted Longstreet's tactical deployment. As we have seen, the initial stages of his march had been attempted in secrecy. When Longstreet was finally ready to place Hood and McLaws' divisions along Warfield Ridge around 3:00 p.m., he abandoned any further attempts at secrecy. Was Longstreet made aware of Wilcox's and Berdan's fight while he moved his divisions into position, and did he conclude that stealth was no longer necessary? As the Confederates burned time looking for an alternate strategy, Sickles wrote, "these circumstances were, of course, known to General Lee; hence he saw no reason to reproach Longstreet for delay." If that is true, then Berdan inadvertently impacted Longstreet's actions, though not to the extent that the exaggerated postwar accounts claimed.[20]

As Birney stated in his report, Sickles ordered him "to change my front to meet the attack. I did this by advancing my left 500 yards, and swinging around the right so as to rest on the Emmitsburg road at the peach orchard." It would take some time to move his three brigades forward, and he probably wasn't fully deployed until as late as 3:30 p.m. Birney reported his division was a "line," but due to the distance he had to cover and his lack of manpower to do so, he never occupied a "line" in the true sense. He anchored Ward's brigade on his left at Devil's Den, and Graham's brigade on the right at the Peach Orchard "with his right on the Emmitsburg road." Birney's smallest brigade, under Regis de Trobriand, was inserted in the middle with an expectation to support the other two.[21]

General Humphreys' Second Division had spent much of the morning "massed" on Cemetery Ridge. Humphreys did not see Sickles during the morning; he specifically stated that Sickles never sent for him, and as a result he stayed with his division. Humphreys admitted that he had "no knowledge" of Birney's position, which was hidden from view by trees on his left. Humphreys later testified that his first line was "in a hollow" and "near the foot of the westerly slope" of Cemetery Ridge. Humphreys' left connected with Birney's right before Birney advanced, but Humphreys' right was approximately 500 yards in front of the left flank of John Caldwell's Second Corps division. At that time of the day, neither Humphreys nor Caldwell were overly concerned by this gap between their divisions.[22]

It was probably while Birney was advancing on his left that Humphreys was directed by Sickles to move Burling's brigade to Birney's right rear "and make it subject to his order for support." Humphreys "was at the same time authorized to draw support, should I need it" from Caldwell's Second Corps division, and "was authorized to draw from the Artillery Reserve should I require more." The detachment of Burling's brigade to support Birney was consistent with the assumption that a Confederate flank attack would hit Birney before Humphreys. Birney directed the brigade to mass in Trostle's Woods, where Burling formed in column of regiments closed in mass, suggesting they would be ready to move elsewhere when called upon.[23]

Humphreys testified that about 4:00 p.m. (this was Humphreys' later estimate, but the actual time must have been earlier) "in compliance with General Sickles's orders, I moved my division forward" so that his line now ran along the Emmitsburg road. A common thread that appears throughout Third Corps accounts is explicit in both Humphreys and Birney's reports. Birney reported that when he moved forward, Sickles "informed me that a division from the Second and one from the Fifth Corps had been ordered to be in readiness to support me." Humphreys said essentially the same in his report, and later told Congress that he was "authorized to call on General Caldwell . . . for such support as I might want." At the same time that he learned that Burling was to support Birney, Humphreys sent to Hancock to inquire whether Caldwell's division "was ready to support me." If both Birney and Humphreys' accounts are accurate, and Humphreys probably had no motivation to fabricate the story, then the question remains open as to exactly how and when Sickles was given the impression that his subordinates could draw upon the other corps for help. This would become a point of contention following the battle.[24]

Despite the fact that their left was supposed to be connected to Sickles' right, the men of John Caldwell's Second Corps division knew little of the Third Corps' intentions. Josiah Favill, an officer on General Zook's staff, recorded that about 2:00 p.m. they observed Sickles' corps make what he described as "several incomprehensible movements." Lieutenant William Wilson, on Caldwell's staff, thought it was closer to 4:20 p.m. when "officers and men curiously watched the formation of Sickles' 3d Corps on the line of the Emmitsburg road. Many were the criticisms made and opinions expressed as to the comparative merits of the line he was directed to take and the one he selected." General Hancock was with his corps at the time (he thought it was about 4:00 p.m.) and admittedly admired "the spectacle" but is famously alleged to have remarked that it was "beautiful to look at, but gentlemen they will not be there long."[25]

Hancock's chief of staff, Lieutenant Colonel Charles H. Morgan, recalled that none of the observers initially thought Sickles was actually taking a new line. "The line he took up was a good one of itself," Morgan wrote, "but bore no relation to the general line of battle. His right flank was nearly a mile in front of the Second Corps, and his left was still more unprotected . . . there can be no valid excuse for precipitating a battle in front of the general line, as was done at Gettysburg. It was very unfortunate that General Sickles moved onto the field by way of the Emmitsburg road for in riding along this Emmitsburg road one gets an exaggerated idea of the importance of the ridge on which the road lies, and underestimates the lesser ridge running from Cemetery Hill towards Round Top." Morgan thought that Sickles' critics ultimately dealt "very tenderly" with him due to his "known bravery, and the terrible wound he received on the field. He committed a great blunder."[26] Along with the remainder of the puzzled Second Corps officers, Lieutenant Frank Haskell wondered:

What his purpose could have been is past conjecture. . . . I suppose the truth probably is that Gen. Sickles supposed he was doing for the best; but he was neither born nor bred a soldier. But one can scarcely tell what may have been the motives of such a man,— a politician, and some other things, exclusive of the Barton Key affair, — a man after show, and notoriety, and newspaper fame, and the adulation of the mob! O, there is a grave responsibility on those in whose hands are the lives of ten thousand men. . . . [27]

On the other hand, many of Sickles' Third Corps contemporaries viewed their commander as a man of action whose requests for support had been rebuffed at army headquarters. Lt. Colonel Rafferty argued that "no attention was paid to" Sickles' concerns and "General Sickles had one sterling quality of a good soldier—he was equal to an emergency; and left as he now was to the exercise of his own judgment, he was prompt to act." Strategically, the new line "would at once compel the enemy to develop his plan of attack, as our position there menaced any attempt he might make at turning our flank, and in fact compelled him to attack us, or suspend his movement and await our attack." Although the verdict of history has demonstrated that Sickles' movement did not "compel" Lee to attack, the new position did cause the Confederates to significantly modify their plans.[28]

Sickles' artillery chief, Captain George Randolph, also approved of the move. He thought that the "low, unprotected" ground of the original position was easily commanded by the Emmitsburg Road ridge. Randolph thought the new position "notwithstanding the sharp angle in our line made necessary by the formation of the ground, to be a much more desirable one."[29] Not surprisingly, Henry Tremain also agreed. He wrote his family on July 10:

We knew where the battle would begin. I felt certain, for I told General Sickles on Wednesday night (as I had been over the ground more and had therefore better opportunities for knowing) that if the enemy attacked the army at all in its present position, it would be in certain localities on the left, which I designated and Thursday morning [July 2] he examined the topography and agreed with me. It was then he pressed on General Meade the necessity for changing his lines to meet such an anticipated attack. It was in that very locality, and by the roads I designated that the enemy did come and hurl upon us their tremendous force.[30]

By mid-afternoon, both Birney and Humphreys were now well in advance of Cemetery Ridge. On the left or southern end of the new Third Corps line was General Ward's brigade of Birney's division, fewer than 1,600 men anchoring the army's left flank in the vicinity of Devil's Den. Ward also had the support of Captain James Smith's 4th New York Independent Battery. Smith wrote in his battery history that Captain Randolph "piloted" Smith's guns to the steep and rocky Houck's Ridge "about 1:00 p.m." Unable to place all six of his guns on the ridge, Smith deployed four pieces there and the other two in Plum Run valley behind him. Although Ward's left was anchored on the large rock formation, there remained the danger that any attacking forces could still move around Devil's Den, flank his left, and penetrate the Plum Run valley in his rear. Aware of this danger, Smith's two rear guns were deployed facing south to cover the entry to the gorge. Across the Plum Run valley, approximately 500 yards behind [east of] Ward rose Little Round Top. Except for Union signalmen, the rocky heights were unoccupied.[31]

Next in line was Regis de Trobriand's brigade, which filed into a large wheatfield on Ward's right. The twenty-six acre wheatfield was part of a larger tract of farmland owned by George Rose and run by his brother John. De Trobriand had fewer than 1,400 men immediately available, and was unable to solidly connect with either Ward on his left or Graham on his right. De Trobriand had the impression that his role was to support Ward and/or Graham, so he placed his regiments in column "ready to support either of the other two brigades according to circumstances." De Trobriand attempted to connect with Graham at the Peach Orchard by placing the 3rd Michigan regiment in advance of his main line as a long skirmish line. The 3rd Michigan's right connected with the left of the 3rd Maine at a right angle. The 3rd Maine had been placed as skirmishers by Graham to cover the southern flank of the Peach Orchard. De Trobriand's position was supported by Captain George Winslow's six-gun 1st New York Light, Battery D. Winslow's position was fronted by Rose's woods, and some of the supporting Union infantry later complained that the timber minimized Winslow's effectiveness.[32]

Charles Graham's brigade occupied the Peach Orchard on de Trobriand's right. Graham was the only one of Birney's brigades touching the Emmitsburg Road, but it did not have sufficient strength to cover his assigned front. The 3rd Maine was deployed as skirmishers to help cover the gap between Graham and de Trobriand. Graham's main line formed a right angle at the intersection of the Wheatfield and Emmitsburg roads, with one wing facing south and the other facing west. Behind the skirmish line and on the north side of the Wheatfield

Road, the 141st and 68th Pennsylvania regiments fronted south. To their right, fronting west along the Emmitsburg Road (moving left to right as the line extended north) were Graham's 114th, 57th, and 105th Pennsylvania regiments. The 63rd Pennsylvania was skirmishing west of the Emmitsburg Road beyond the Sherfy house, and was supported by several companies of the 105th Pennsylvania "Wild Cats." Judson Clark's battery remained in the vicinity of the Peach Orchard, having been posted there earlier that morning.[33]

Graham's right flank, comprised of the the 105th Pennsylvania, ended at the Trostle farm lane [modern United States Avenue]. The lane bisected the Emmitsburg Road between the Wentz and Klingle properties and ran roughly east toward Cemetery Ridge. Sickles set up his headquarters at the Trostle farm, on the north side of the lane roughly halfway between the Emmitsburg Road and Cemetery Ridge. Humphreys continued the Third Corps line along the Emmitsburg Road north of the Trostle lane. Since Burling's brigade had been detached to support Birney, Humphreys had only two brigades remaining (William Brewster and Joseph Carr) totaling about 3,500 men. Humphreys initially placed only Carr's brigade on the front line, and left Brewster (whose command included Sickles' old Excelsior Brigade) in reserve. But Carr, who ran his line along the Emmitsburg Road from just south [left] of the Klingle house to several hundred yards south of the Codori farm on his right, also lacked the manpower to cover his entire front. A gap remained between Carr's left and Graham's right. Humphreys attempted to correct this by inserting Brewster's 72nd and 71st New York regiments into the front line. Even worse was the fact that Carr's right was completely in the air, unconnected with the left flank of Hancock's Second Corps, which remained securely along Cemetery Ridge slightly less than one mile to the rear (east). Humphreys elected to keep four of Brewster's regiments (the 70th, 73rd, 74th, and 120th New York) in reserve, leaving this important issue unresolved.[34]

For all of Dan Sickles' many faults, he was correct on one key point: the primary Confederate attack would occur on his front. At Chancellorsville, he misread intelligence and assumed an enemy retreat. Now, two months later at Gettysburg, he again misread intelligence, misinterpreted Meade's orders, and overestimated the importance of the Emmitsburg Road to convince himself that Lee was massing against the Federal left. This time, Sickles was correct. And by moving forward into the Peach Orchard, he occupied one of the key objectives of the Confederate attack plan.[35]

Sometime around 3:00 p.m., Longstreet's two divisions concluded their long countermarch. As Longstreet's column began approaching Pitzer's Woods and Warfield Ridge, Longstreet informed Lafayette McLaws: "There is nothing in your front; you will be entirely on the flank of the enemy." What neither officer knew was that much had changed since Lee and Longstreet developed their plan of attack earlier that morning. "My head of column soon reached the edge of the woods," McLaws reported, "and the enemy at once opened on it with numerous artillery, and one rapid glance showed them to be in force much greater than I had, and extending considerably beyond my right." As his long column came online, McLaws rode forward to get "a good look at the situation, and the view presented astonished me, as the enemy was massed in my front, and extended to my right and left as far as I could see. . . . Thus was presented a state of affairs which was certainly not contemplated when the original plan or order of battle was given, and certainly was not known to General Longstreet a half hour previous."[36]

Historians have long wondered where Lee presumed the Union left flank ended. The answer is essential to understanding Lee's true plan of attack on July 2, 1863, and also helps appreciate the impact of Sickles' occupation of the Peach Orchard. Unfortunately, Lee and Longstreet provide little guidance on this key question, primarily because their reports contain a murky mixture of information that was known both before and after the fact.

Lee filed three reports on Gettysburg. Each document was more detailed than the last as Lee received additional supporting information from subordinates. Lee's first version was written from "near Gettysburg" on July 4. It simply says that the enemy "took up a strong position in rear of the town, which he immediately began to fortify, and where his re-enforcements joined him." Lee's second report was dated July 31: "The enemy held a high and commanding ridge, along which he had massed a large amount of artillery. . . . In front of General Longstreet the enemy held a position from which, if he could be driven, it was thought our artillery could be used to advantage in assailing the more elevated ground beyond, and thus enable us to reach the crest of the ridge." Longstreet "was directed to endeavor to carry this position."[37]

Lee's final, and most detailed, report was not submitted until January of 1864. It reads, in part:

> The enemy occupied a strong position, with his right upon two commanding elevations adjacent to each other, one southeast and the other, known as Cemetery Hill, immediately south of the town, which lay at its base. His line extended thence upon the high ground along the Emmitsburg road, with a steep ridge in rear, which was also occupied. . . .

It was determined to make the principal attack upon the enemy's left, and endeavor to gain a position from which it was thought that our artillery could be brought to bear with effect. Longstreet was directed to place the divisions of McLaws and Hood on the right of Hill, partially enveloping the enemy's left, which he was to drive in. General Hill was ordered to threaten the enemy's center, to prevent re-enforcements being drawn to either wing, and co-operate with his right division in Longstreet's attack.[38]

Lee's July 31 report can be interpreted two ways. He described two distinct Federal lines, one along the Emmitsburg Road "in front of Longstreet" and another line along Cemetery Ridge, "the more elevated ground beyond." Certainly these two lines existed in the afternoon, after Sickles had moved forward and after Longstreet was finally in position. But except for skirmishers, cavalry, and some artillery, the dual line that Lee described did not exist in the morning, when the attack plan was presumably first formulated. An alternative scenario is that the terrain and poor reconnaissance fooled Lee into thinking that there was one Federal line with the ground "in front of Longstreet" along the Emmitsburg Road being an extension of the "more elevated ground" to the north (i.e. Cemetery Hill). Longstreet's report, that the enemy had "taken a strong position, extending from the hill at the cemetery along the Emmitsburg road" would seem to support this scenario.[39]

Lee's January 1864 report would clearly seem to settle the argument in favor of two Federal lines: "His line extended thence upon the high ground along the Emmitsburg road, with a steep ridge in rear, which was also occupied. This ridge was difficult of ascent, particularly the two hills above mentioned as forming its northern extremity, and a third at the other end, on which the enemy's left rested." But this is clearly a description of Meade's afternoon line after Sickles' unauthorized advance. When Lee presumably developed his plan in the morning, it seems unlikely that the terrain could have fooled him into thinking that *both* the Emmitsburg Road and Little Round Top were occupied. In reality, the Emmitsburg Road was not occupied in force until later, and Captain Johnston's morning reconnaissance had crossed over an undefended Emmitsburg Road (and he supposedly told Lee that Little Round Top was unoccupied). Thus the 1864 report probably can not be used as a window into Lee's morning strategy development since it describes Federal positions that did not, and probably could not have appeared to exist, when Lee developed his morning plans.[40]

Modern view from the Peach Orchard looking toward Cemetery Hill. If Meade's left had ended along the Emmitsburg Road, Longstreet's attack "up the Emmitsburg Road" would have tried to roll up the Union line toward Cemetery Hill.

Author

Longstreet's July 27 report, which was dated prior to Lee's second and third reports, favors a one-line scenario. The enemy "had taken a strong position, extending from the hill at the cemetery *along the Emmitsburg road*" [emphasis added]. This is also inaccurate, for Meade's main line never stretched completely from Cemetery Hill along the road. But it seems reasonable that Longstreet's report represents the best information available to the Confederates at that time (July 27). Viewing the ground today, one can easily see how the terrain might have given the Confederates such a misconception. If one looks east from Seminary Ridge (near the present-day North Carolina monument) toward Cemetery Ridge, the northeast to southwest axis of the Emmitsburg Road angles farther away from Cemetery Ridge as the road runs south. Combined with the rolling terrain, it is difficult to ascertain the distance between the road and Cemetery Ridge as the road passes in front of such landmarks as the Peach Orchard and Little Round Top. Looking from Seminary Ridge, the rolling countryside could have obscured Union troops positioned along southern Cemetery Ridge once the Federal line extended past the Codori farm or the modern Pennsylvania monument. This observation has led many historians to believe that Lee assumed Meade's line ended on Cemetery Ridge somewhere near the site of the Pennsylvania monument, rather than on the road as Longstreet's report indicates.[41]

Neither of Longstreet's two division commanders, McLaws and Hood, filed a report following the battle. Both omissions are unfortunate. McLaws, however, wrote a detailed letter to his wife on July 7 that sheds some light on his activities:

> [On July 2] we moved around Gettysburg towards the Emmitsburg road, to arrive at the Peach orchard, a small settlement with a very large Peach Orchard attached [sic]. The intention was to get in rear of the enemy who were supposed to be stationed principally in rear of Gettysburg or near of it. The report being that the enemy had but two regiments of infantry and one battery at the Peach orchard. On arriving at the vicinity of the Orchard, the enemy were discovered in greater force than was supposed..."[42]

Of McLaws' four brigade commanders—Generals Kershaw, Barksdale, Semmes, and Wofford—only Kershaw filed a report (Semmes and Barksdale were killed.) According to Kershaw, when his brigade reached the Pitzer schoolhouse near the Millerstown crossroad, Longstreet "directed me to advance my brigade and attack the enemy at that point, turn his flank, and extend along the cross-road [Millerstown], with my left resting toward the Emmitsburg road."[43] Sometime about 3:00 p.m., the head of Kershaw's column reached Warfield Ridge, giving Kershaw his first view of Sickles' line:

> I found him [the enemy] to be in superior force in the orchard, supported by artillery, with a main line of battle intrenched in the rear and extending to and upon the rocky mountain to his left *far beyond the point at which his flank had supposed to rest* [emphasis added]. To carry out my instructions, would have been, if successful in driving him from the orchard, to present my own right and rear to a large portion of his line of battle.[44]

McLaws and Kershaw are consistent on two points. They moved to the attack under the misconception that the Federal line did not extend as far south of the town as it in fact did. "The major assumption of this plan was that the Federal line on Cemetery Ridge was short," explained historian Douglas Southall Freeman. (Freeman was partially correct: the Confederates believed the line to be short, but it is arguable whether they thought it was on Cemetery Ridge.) They also believed the orchard would only be lightly defended, but more Union forces were discovered than expected. Significantly, Sickles had refused Birney's division line back toward Devil's Den, rather than ending his line on the Emmitsburg Road, for the very purpose of disrupting a flank attack by Lee up the Emmitsburg Road. Sickles was successful because Kershaw could not execute his orders to turn the Federal flank since it would expose his right and rear to the far left of Sickles' line.[45]

Confederate artillery reports are frustratingly brief. In Porter Alexander's case this brevity is especially surprising given his large volume of postwar analysis.[46] The report of Captain Basil C. Manly, commanding Company A of the First North Carolina Artillery, however, explicitly confirms that the Confederates had miscalculated the location of Meade's left flank and that their desired objective was now held in strong force by Sickles:

> The road on which we moved [Millerstown] was perpendicular to the enemy's line, *but it was supposed that their left did not extend to this point of intersection to which we were moving. My instructions were, if we gained this point, we would be on the enemy's left flank, and that I must form line on the left, and attempt to rake their line.* [emphasis added]

When we arrived within a few hundred yards of the cross-roads mentioned above, we discovered that the enemy held it with a large force of infantry and artillery, [emphasis added] which opened upon us immediately.[47]

History can not record how Longstreet's attack would have developed if Sickles' Third Corps had remained several hundred yards farther east on Cemetery Ridge. But when Sickles refused his line at an angle from the Peach Orchard toward Devil's Den, McLaws' division was not able to drive the Federal line up the Emmitsburg Road (toward Cemetery Hill) from the Peach Orchard vicinity, as he was ordered to do. Had Sickles ended his line on the Emmitsburg Road (as Lee and Longstreet apparently believed), the Confederates would have had an opportunity to drive up the road and sweep him out of position. The unexpected Union deployment around the Peach Orchard forced the Confederate generals to make major on-the-spot modifications to the attack. As Longstreet reported, once it became apparent that Sickles' line stretched well past the orchard, Hood's division was "moved on farther to our right" in order to locate the true end of Meade's line, and to "partially envelope" it.[48]

Not only did Lee and Longstreet erroneously plan on using the Peach Orchard to drive in Meade's left flank, but continued occupation of the orchard itself was also a significant objective in their plan. This second point is often lost in the post-battle criticism directed at Sickles. Both Sickles and his officers had been worried all morning that the Confederates would see the value in using the Emmitsburg Road ridge as an artillery platform to pummel Union positions on Cemetery Ridge. If Lee's reports accurately reflect his strategy, then Sickles accurately out-guessed General Lee.

To reiterate this point, as noted previously, Lee's report of July 31 stated: "In front of General Longstreet the *enemy held a position from which, if he could be driven, it was thought our artillery could be used to advantage in assailing the more elevated ground beyond, and thus enable us to reach the crest of the ridge* [emphasis added]." Lee desired an elevated artillery platform in advance of Cemetery Ridge, and on Longstreet's front, to support an assault on the ridge itself. Lee confirmed that he was describing the Peach Orchard when he further reported: "After a severe struggle, Longstreet succeeded in getting possession of and holding the desired ground." The only position that fits this description is the Peach Orchard. Lee's report of January 1864 confirmed again that Longstreet was directed to obtain an artillery platform on the Emmitsburg Road from which Federal forces were ultimately driven.[49]

Commenting from the Federal perspective, Henry Hunt knew that the Peach Orchard ridge was vital to Lee's plans. Hunt thought that Lee apparently "mistook the few troops on the Peach Orchard ridge in the morning for our main line, and that by taking it and sweeping up the Emmitsburg road under cover of his batteries, he expected to 'roll up' our lines to Cemetery Hill."[50]

Some historians have argued that Sickles exaggerated the importance of the Peach Orchard in Lee's objectives during his post-battle attempts to justify his advance to that point. As historian Richard Sauers wrote, "many historians have fallen into the same trap and have repeated the same error of reasoning." However, the theory that Lee intended to turn the Federal left at or near the Peach Orchard, and then use the orchard as an artillery platform, is supported by several contemporary Confederate accounts. It was not an invention of postwar posturing. The fact that Lee was later unable to convert the Peach Orchard to his benefit does not diminish the fact that Lee (as stated in his own reports) considered it a potentially valuable position at the time he launched his attack. In fact, the Confederates' ultimate inability to use the Peach Orchard to their advantage confirms only that Lee and Longstreet both joined Sickles in overestimating its military value. The Peach Orchard might not have been as strong of a position as expected, but it certainly influenced movements on both sides.[51]

Whether Lee and Longstreet thought that the Federal left rested on the Emmitsburg Road, or that they were now in position to simply roll up the Cemetery Ridge line, or believed they could easily occupy the Peach Orchard, they were wrong on every count. The Confederate attack was being initiated under a misapprehension of the strength, length, shape, and position of Meade's left flank. Sickles' move forward, for better or worse, forced the Confederates to modify their plans. Sickles' advance, more than any individual action, dictated the flow of fighting on Gettysburg's second day and would also significantly impact the third day.[52]

Longstreet's postwar *Battles and Leaders* account, if accurate, essentially acknowledges that he and Lee modified their plan to the best circumstances available:

> . . . as the line was deployed I rode along from left to right, examining the Federal position and putting my troops in the best position we could find. *General Lee at the same time gave orders for the attack to be made by my right—following up the direction of the Emmitsburg road* [emphasis added] toward the Cemetery Ridge, holding Hood's left as well as could be toward the

Emmitsburg road, McLaws to follow the movements of Hood, attacking at the Peach Orchard the Federal Third Corps, with a part of R. H. Anderson's following the movements of McLaws to guard his left flanks.[53]

When he reached Warfield Ridge, McLaws deployed his division with two brigades in front: Joseph Kershaw on the right (south of the Millerstown Road) and William Barksdale on the left (north of the road). His second pair of brigades under Semmes and Wofford were placed in the rear as reserves. When Longstreet sent McLaws a series of impatient messages inquiring why he had not yet charged, the division commander replied that careful preparation was required. Just when McLaws was ready to move out, another courier arrived from Longstreet with orders for him to "wait until Hood got into position."[54]

Longstreet had decided to delay the attack until Hood's division was moved to McLaws' right and placed in position to drive in Sickles' extended Federal left. According to Kershaw, "Hood's division was then moving in our rear toward our right, to gain the enemy's left flank, and I was directed to commence the attack so soon as General Hood became engaged, swinging around toward the peach orchard, and at the same time establishing connection with Hood, on my right, and co-operating with him. It was understood he was to sweep down the enemy's line in a direction perpendicular to our then line of battle." But in yet another Confederate breakdown, Hood's division neither advanced promptly nor up the Emmitsburg Road, "perpendicular" to Kershaw's line. Like Longstreet, McLaws, and Kershaw, when Hood finally got into position, he did not like what he saw in front of him.[55]

Chapter 8

Isn't Your Line Too Much Extended?

At 3:00 p.m., with the Union Sixth Corps having finally arrived, and still unaware that his left flank was moving out of position, Meade called a meeting with his corps commanders. "The commanding general desires to see you at headquarters," Butterfield related to Sickles, Sedgwick, Sykes, Newton, Slocum, Howard, and Hancock.[1] At the same hour, Meade sent the following dispatch to General-in-Chief Henry Halleck in Washington:

> I have concentrated my army at this place today. The Sixth Corps is just coming in, very much worn out, having been marching since 9 p.m. last night. The army is fatigued. I have today, up to this hour, awaited the attack of the enemy, I having a strong position for defensive. I am not determined, as yet, on attacking him till his position is more developed. He has been moving on both my flanks, apparently, but it is difficult to tell exactly his movements. I have delayed attacking, to allow the Sixth Corps and parts of other corps to reach this place and to rest the men. Expecting a battle, I ordered all my trains to the rear. If not attacked, and I can get any positive information of the position of the enemy which will justify me in so doing, I shall attack. If I find it hazardous to do so, or am satisfied the enemy is endeavoring to move to my rear and interpose between me and Washington, I shall fall back to my supplies at Westminster. . . . I feel fully the responsibility resting upon me, but will endeavor to act with caution.[2]

Following the battle, Meade's enemies (specifically Sickles and Dan Butterfield) attempted to prove that Meade was planning to retreat from

Gettysburg. Butterfield later testified before the Congressional Committee that "General Meade [during the morning of July 2] directed me to prepare an order to withdraw the army from that position." Earlier that morning, Meade had asked Butterfield to familiarize himself with the local roads and prepare an order as a contingency in case the army was compelled to fall back. Butterfield interpreted this, or so he said, as proof of Meade's intention to retreat. Butterfield testified that he spent the majority of the morning and early afternoon preparing this draft. "After finishing it, I presented it to General Meade, and it met with his approval." Butterfield also managed to show his draft to John Gibbon, who exclaimed, "Great God! General Meade does not intend to leave his position?" The draft was neither published nor retained by the army, and Meade claimed to not even remember the episode until months later when confronted by Congress' Joint Committee on the Conduct of the War.[3]

The mid-afternoon meeting was also an opportunity for Meade's critics to further portray him as indecisive and befuddled by his new responsibilities. His need to call "councils of war," they said, was proof of his indecisive nature. Sickles and his allies claimed Meade intended to discuss a retreat at this 3:00 p.m. meeting. We will never know what would have been discussed at this meeting, because events intervened to prevent its occurrence. Fortunately for Meade's reputation, the dispatch to Halleck survives as a clear indication of his intentions. Meade knew his position was strong defensively, and he was going to allow the Sixth Corps (which had marched more than thirty miles) to rest before deciding on any offensive operations. But the desire to wait on the Sixth Corps was also based on the inaccurate premise that Lee's army greatly outnumbered his own. Meade's dispatch also allowed for the possibility that he might be forced to fall back toward his supplies at Westminster. This can be interpreted two ways. Meade's supporters argue that it demonstrates his prudent flexibility in planning for every contingency. His enemies, however, argued that it proved Meade was looking for the first opportunity to retire without battle.[4]

Henry Hunt understood the proper necessity of contingency planning. He argued that Meade's actions and dispatches throughout the day proved that a retreat was never seriously considered. Hunt noted that he never received an order to withdraw the army's Artillery Reserve, which surely would have been necessary if Meade intended to abandon Gettysburg. Hunt also argued that Meade exhibited boldness in staying—he had risked an attack in the morning before the entire Union army had concentrated.[5]

At this late hour of the afternoon Meade was also unsure which flank (if any) would be attacked. Sickles and some of his officers had definite opinions of their own. They were convinced the attack would fall on their front. Sickles would be proven correct by events, but as he embellished in one of his many postwar speeches, "at the supreme moment—3 P.M. July 2— when the enemy was advancing to attack, we had no plan of action, no order of battle. For Meade the battle of July 2 is a surprise, like the battle of July 1."[6]

The particulars that led to the proposed 3:00 p.m. meeting are surprisingly muddled. Neither Meade nor supporters such as Warren or James Biddle mentioned it in their reports or later in Congressional testimony. As the Army of the Potomac's corps commanders began arriving at headquarters for Meade's 3:00 p.m. council, Chief Engineer Warren rode up with startling news. "There seemed to be some doubt about whether he [Sickles] should occupy a line in front, or the one on the ridge in the rear," Warren later testified, "and I am not sure but a report had come in from some of our officers that that position was not occupied. I know I had sent an officer there to ascertain and report." The suggestion has also been made that Warren (or another officer) had been sent to check on Little Round Top due to the signal station's reports of advancing Confederates. Warren finally confirmed what had been brewing all morning: Sickles' corps was out of position and there were no infantry on Little Round Top. Meade ordered General Sykes to move his Fifth Corps to the left flank, and told him he would meet him there. Meade was mounting his horse when Sickles arrived at headquarters.[7]

Sickles later testified before the Joint Committee:

> While I was making my disposition on this line I received a communication from headquarters to attend a consultation of corps commanders. I sent word verbally by the officer who brought me the communication, begging, if possible, to be excused, stating that the enemy were in great force in my front, and intimating that I would very soon be engaged, and that I was making my dispositions to meet the attack. I hastened forward the movements of my troops as rapidly as possible, and had got my batteries in position, when I received another and peremptory order to report at once in person at headquarters, to meet the corps commanders. I turned over the command temporarily to General Birney in my absence, feeling assured that before I could return the engagement would open.[8]

"I hastened to headquarters with all speed," Sickles continued, "but before I got there the sound of the cannon announced the battle had opened. However, I was quite near headquarters at the time and pushed on, but found that the consultation had been broken up by the opening of the battle." Sickles later added that Meade greeted him with, "You need not dismount, General. I hear the sound of cannon on your front. Return to your command. I will join you there at once." Captain Meade's version essentially agrees with this account.[9]

As Sickles rode "rapidly" back to his corps, Meade followed a short distance behind. According to Tremain, "the battle was thoroughly opened," likely a reference to artillery (perhaps Judson Clark's battery) rather than large-scale infantry fire. Sickles later told Congress, "On my way [back] I found that the enemy were moving up to the attack in great force, in two lines of battle, supported by three columns. Fortunately, my left had succeeded in getting into position on Round Top and along the commanding ridge to which I have referred; and those positions were firmly held by the Third Corps." This statement, taken under oath, was perhaps Sickles' most blatant lie. The Third Corps never occupied either Big Round Top or Little Round Top at any time during the battle, and at that particular moment neither did any other Union infantry corps.[10]

When Meade passed the left of Winfield Hancock's Second Corps, he was, as he later explained, "wholly unprepared to find it [Sickles' corps] advanced far beyond . . . the line of the Second Corps. Its lines were over half a mile out to the front, to the Emmitsburg Road, entirely disconnected with the rest of the army, and beyond supporting distance." Meade was initially accompanied by Warren. As the pair rode south along Cemetery Ridge and Meade began to turn toward the Peach Orchard, he reportedly pointed toward Little Round Top and told Warren to "ride over and if anything serious is going on, attend to it." Warren departed Meade and galloped toward the hill accompanied by orderlies and two lieutenants.[11]

"I rode out to the extreme left, to await the arrival of the Fifth Corps and to post it, when I found that Major-General Sickles, commanding the Third Corps, not fully apprehending the instructions in regard to the position to be occupied, had advanced, or rather was in the act of advancing, his corps some half a mile or three-quarters of a mile in front of the line of the Second Corps, on the prolongation of which it was designed his corps should rest," Meade later reported. "Having found Major-General Sickles, I was explaining to him that he was too far in advance, and discussing with him the propriety of

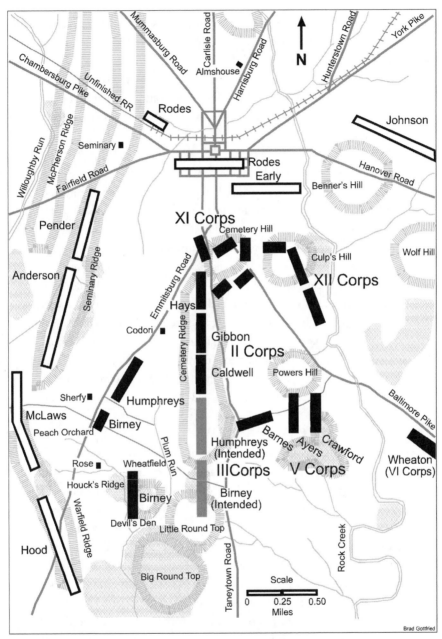

Meade and Lee's positions after Dan Sickles moved forward. The lightly shaded troops on the southern end of Cemetery Ridge represent the line that Meade wanted Sickles to occupy.

withdrawing, when the enemy opened on him with several batteries in his front and on his flank, and immediately brought forward columns of infantry and made a most vigorous assault.[12]

Meade told the Congressional Committee that he arrived on Sickles' front a few minutes before 4:00 p.m. Finding Sickles' "position very much in advance of what it had been my intention that he should take," Meade asked Sickles to indicate his new line:

> When he had done so I told him it was not the position I had expected him to take; that he had advanced his line beyond the support of my army, and that I was very fearful he would be attacked and would lose the artillery, which he had put so far in front, before I could support it, or that if I undertook to support it I would have to abandon all the rest of the line which I had adopted—that is, I would have to fight the battle out there where he was. General Sickles expressed regret that he should have occupied a position which did not meet with my approval, and he very promptly said that he would withdraw his forces to the line which I had intended him to take. . . . But I told him I was fearful that the enemy would not permit him to withdraw, and that there was no time for any further change or movement. And before I had finished that remark, or that sentence, the enemy's batteries opened upon him and the action commenced.[13]

Captain Meade's recollections added that General Meade declared that the new position was beyond supporting distance of the remainder of the army and was also neutral ground—neither side could occupy it to advantage. Meade warned that Sickles would either lose his artillery or be forced to abandon the entire line. Sickles offered to withdraw his troops when, according to Captain Meade, his father responded, "Yes, you may as well, at once. The enemy will not let you withdraw without taking advantage of your position, but you have to come back, and you may as well do it at once as at any other time." Sickles was about to implement the order when "the batteries opened with a terrific cannonade in front and to the left of the Peach Orchard." Meade told Sickles "it was too late to retire, and ordered him to hold on and do the best he could, telling him that he would be supported." Captain Meade's claim that his father initially ordered Sickles to fall back appears a trivial detail at first glance, and is missing from many other accounts. The detail is significant because during the long post-battle controversy, Sickles frequently claimed that Meade did not order him to pull back and therefore must have approved of the new position. Perhaps Captain Meade added this statement to his own version as a defense against Sickles' charge.[14]

Sickles' 1864 testimony before the Joint Committee claimed he admitted to Meade that "I could not, with one corps, hold so extended a line against the rebel army; but that, if supported, the line could be held; and in my judgment, it was a strong one, and the best one." This outlandish claim leads to the obvious question as to why Sickles would have advanced in the first place if he knew he could not hold his new position without additional support.[15] Sickles also told Congress:

> I stated, however, that if he [Meade] disapproved of it was not too late to take any position he might indicate. He said 'No'; that it would be better to hold that line, and he would send up the Fifth Corps to support me. I expressed my belief in my ability to hold that line until supports could arrive. He said he would send up the Fifth Corps on my left, and that on my right I could look to General Hancock for support on my right flank. I added that I should want considerable artillery; that the enemy were developing a strong force of artillery. He authorized me to send to General Hunt who commanded the reserve of the artillery, for as much artillery as I wanted. I then assured him of my entire confidence in my ability to hold the position; which I did.[16]

For a man so talented at stretching the truth, Sickles was at least able to keep one aspect of his story relatively consistent as the years passed. A longstanding postwar contention of Sickles and his partisans was their insistence that Meade agreed to fully support Sickles by placing additional infantry (Meade allegedly telling Sickles: "I'll send up the Fifth Corps, and Hancock will give any other supports you may require") and artillery reserves ("send to Hunt for what you want") under Sickles' command. Given the mutual animosity between Meade and Sickles, and the fact that Sickles had seriously misinterpreted Meade's orders, it seems improbable that Meade would have entrusted Sickles with anything more than the Third Corps infantry. Nevertheless, Tremain wrote to his family on July 10 that "just after the ball opened General Meade agreed with [Sickles] and promised him support." Unfortunately "the supports were not placed under his command and were not handled as intelligently as they would have been by one who knew the surroundings more perfectly."[17]

Later recollections of events make it obvious that partisans of both Sickles and Meade were willing to bend the historical record to suit their own versions of accuracy. Regardless of how the move was spun, Sickles was in the wrong. Still, General Meade and his staff share at least some responsibility for the fiasco. It was assumed that Sickles, Captain Meade later stated,

> . . . fully understood where he was to go. The character of the messages sent by him [Sickles] to the commanding general left no impression on the mind of the latter [Meade], that there was any misunderstanding. Later in the day, when it was discovered that in what an extraordinary position General Sickles had placed his corps, General Meade deemed it barely possible he had misconstrued his orders. Not until nine months after the battle, when the remarkable proceedings before the committee on the conduct of the war had developed themselves did he come to the conclusion that his orders had been willfully disregarded.[18]

That Meade had "no impression" that Sickles harbored any confusion about his intended position challenges credibility. Sickles, for whatever mistakes he was guilty of, had made several attempts to clarify the matter. There had been ample warnings before 3:00 p.m. that Meade's left flank required more personal attention: Sickles had told Captain Meade he did not know where to go; Sickles' 11:00 a.m. visit to headquarters echoed this; the signal station on Little Round Top spotted Confederate activity in Pitzer's Woods; Berdan had collided with the enemy opposite Sickles' new position; and Buford's cavalry had been removed from the left flank. Meade also failed to heed Hunt's suggestion that he inspect the line. Various reasons have been given for Meade's failure to maintain better control over Sickles, including a more urgent focus on his right flank, exhaustion, the unfamiliarity of his new role, poor staff work, and a real belief that Sickles knew where to place his corps. Meade may have simply dismissed Sickles' concerns as those of an amateur. Whatever the reason, while Sickles bears the blame for ultimately acting independent of his orders, the commanding general must share some responsibility for not ensuring that those orders were executed in accordance with his wishes.

Lt. Col. Thomas Rafferty of the 71st New York supported Sickles' decision, but he didn't necessarily blame Meade for the breakdown. "As yet unaccustomed to the handling and disposing of a large army, and diffident of his own powers and capacity to do so," explained Rafferty, "it is no wonder that he did not at that time prove himself as equal to the exigencies of the occasion as he so successfully did at subsequent periods of his command of that army." Rafferty blamed much of the problem on sloppy staff work. "They [Meade's staff] should have known all about our line of battle; have made themselves familiar with its salient points, its capabilities for defense or its facilities for offensive operations. They should have directed and controlled the positions of the various corps; should have been the eyes of General Meade, the brains to plan, and under his direction, the hands to execute. . . . But they did none of these things. They knew absolutely nothing of the position of affairs on the left flank; hardly knew whether there was any left flank."[19]

It was up to Warren to "accidentally stumble" onto the true state of affairs. While Meade and Sickles squabbled, Warren arrived at Little Round Top. "[F]rom that point I could see the enemy's lines of battle," recalled the army's chief engineer. Warren's worst fears were confirmed when he discovered the hill was occupied by only two or three signal corps officers. Standing near the summit, he spotted Longstreet's long battle line stretching far enough south to overlap Sickles' left flank at Devil's Den. Warren sent messages to both Meade and Sickles requesting "that we would at once have to occupy that place very strongly." Meade had already ordered the entire Fifth Corps to the left, but now fearful it would not arrive in time, he also ordered General Humphreys' Third Corps division to move toward Little Round Top.[20]

Meade sent one of his aides, Major Benjamin Ludlow, to locate Humphreys. Ludlow rode from the direction of the Peach Orchard, giving Humphreys the distinct impression that Meade was still personally in the grove. The order Humphreys received was "to move at once toward Round Top and occupy the ground there, which was vacant. Some reference was made at this time also I think, to the intended occupation of that ground by the Fifth Corps." Humphreys promptly began to move his division, but told Ludlow he didn't like the idea of vacating his position because it would increase the gap between Sickles' right and Hancock's left. Once Ludlow departed, Humphreys set off to locate Meade himself. The division leader rode "at full speed" toward the Peach Orchard and quickly met another of Meade's aides along the way "who informed me General Meade recalled his order and that I should occupy the position General Sickles had directed me to take." Meade had by this time received confirmation that the Fifth Corps reinforcements were approaching Little Round Top and so Humphreys' division was no longer needed.[21]

A Sickles aide found a frustrated Humphreys counter-marching his division back toward the Emmitsburg Road and instructed him to resume the position originally ordered by the corps commander. The whole incident probably took no more than five minutes, and despite the accolades that were later showered on the precision of the movements, Humphreys admitted that he did not consider it worth mentioning in his official report. Following the battle, Sickles claimed his Third Corps received no orders from Meade following their Peach Orchard conference. Because aides from both Meade and Sickles had approached Humphreys from the vicinity of the Peach Orchard, however, it is almost certain that Sickles was aware of Meade's orders to Humphreys. In the larger scheme of things, Sickles' advance was causing chaos within the Army of the Potomac's command structure, and it would not be the only time that troops would be marched and counter-marched along Sickles' wing.[22]

The opening of the Confederate artillery bombardment removed any lingering doubts about where the main Confederate attack would land, and provided an excellent opportunity to exploit some of the weaknesses inherent in Sickles' new position. The massive cannonade that ushered in "Pickett's Charge" on July 3 has cast a long shadow over most artillery studies of Gettysburg, with the result that the spectacular duel preceding Longstreet's July 2 assault has been largely overlooked. Colonel Edward Porter Alexander, who was given tactical control of Longstreet's artillery, compared the second day's artillery action to the fighting at Sharpsburg (Antietam), which was referred to by some participants as "Artillery Hell." Despite Sharpsburg's fearsome reputation, "I don't think there was ever in our war a hotter, harder, sharper artillery afternoon" than the second day at Gettysburg, concluded Alexander.[23]

Earlier that morning, Alexander had been ordered by Lee and Longstreet to place his guns in position opposite the Federal left. In addition to his own reserve artillery battalion (temporarily commanded by Major Frank Huger), Alexander had been given tactical control of McLaws' artillery battalion (commanded by Colonel Henry Cabell), and Hood's artillery battalion (commanded by Major Mathias Henry). By Alexander's own estimate, he had fifty-four guns at his disposal. The exact time Alexander opened fire is unclear. He later wrote that the guns opened about 3:45 p.m. Regardless of the precise time, the Confederates enjoyed a distinct advantage over their Union counterparts: their guns were in position when the first shots were fired, while the majority of the Union batteries were not.[24]

Sickles' line was now much closer to Alexander's artillery than it otherwise would have been had it remained on Cemetery Ridge. Two of Henry's batteries, supporting Hood's division on the southern end of the line, could hit Devil's Den and the Wheatfield, while guns near the Emmitsburg Road could fire up the road and hit Third Corps targets in and near the Peach Orchard at distances between 1,100 to 1,400 yards. Henry's other two batteries (eight guns) were not deployed, supposedly because there wasn't enough room on their front. Colonel Cabell's battalion of four batteries dropped trail south of the Millerstown Road. Of these, at least two guns from Captain Edward McCarthy's battery also appear to have not been deployed. Alexander would fail to deploy (or delay deploying) several Confederate guns that afternoon, a mistake that would rob the Confederates of potential numeric superiority when Federal resistance later proved "obstinate." Alexander also initially failed to exploit the advantages of his exterior lines. He did not place any guns directly west of the Peach Orchard until well after the action was underway, depriving his batteries of the ability to converge their fire against Sickles' bulging salient and the weakest part of his extended line.[25]

On the Federal side, Judson Clark's battery had been posted earlier that morning on "the rise of ground midway between Sickles' headquarters and the peach orchard." Clark spotted Hood's division "passing in column across the Emmitsburg road to our left and front, and distant about 1,400 yards, and, by direction of General Sickles, I placed my battery in position, and opened fire upon their position." When Captain George Randolph, Sickles' Third Corps artillery chief, spotted a Confederate battery unlimbering near the intersection of the Millerstown and Emmitsburg roads, he ordered Clark to move his battery forward closer to the Peach Orchard. Graham's brigade was nearby and Colonel Henry Madill, commander of the 141st Pennsylvania, said the infantry was "ordered to lie down. At this point we sustained a severe fire from artillery for some time, the enemy having a good range." Randolph piloted Captain James Smith's 4th New York Independent Battery to Houck's Ridge and placed Captain George Winslow's Battery D, First New York Light Artillery, into an open wheatfield supporting Regis de Trobriand's brigade. The fighting had opened in earnest.[26]

Henry Hunt, meanwhile, had determined that the Confederate artillery fire opposite Cemetery Hill "would lead to nothing serious," and sometime after 3:00 p.m. returned "to the Peach Orchard, knowing that its occupation would require large reinforcements of artillery." Hunt noted that Sickles' infantry was already posted and he was met by Captain Randolph, "who informed me that he had been ordered to place his batteries on the new line." Hunt could see "Generals Meade and Sickles, not far off, in conversation" and erroneously supposed that Meade had consented to Sickles' movement. Hunt immediately requested more guns from General Robert O. Tyler's Artillery Reserve and "authorized other general officers to draw on the same force." Since Randolph had already posted Smith and Winslow's batteries on the far left, Hunt assisted in the posting of additional batteries on the right of Sickles' line.[27]

Near the Peach Orchard, Captain Nelson Ames' First New York Light, Battery G, was the first from Tyler's reserve to arrive on the field. In fact, Ames had received his orders to report to Sickles at 11:00 a.m., before Hunt had sent in the call for more batteries. (Despite Sickles' later claims, this suggests the left flank was not being completely ignored by headquarters.) Captain Randolph ordered Ames to "take position in a thick peach orchard, and engage the enemy's batteries at a distance of 850 yards." Since the opposing Confederates had already unlimbered, Ames was one of several Union batteries that had to run the gauntlet under fire. The pounding he took while heading toward the orchard's rising ground convinced Ames that he was the target of no fewer than three enemy batteries. "I was obliged to halt in plain sight of the enemy," he reported, "to clear away two fences which the supporting infantry had failed to throw down as they had been ordered to do."[28]

Ames placed his six guns in the orchard fronting southwest toward Cabell's battalion and opened with spherical case and shell. The smoke draping over the orchard's foliage quickly reduced visibility. Despite the many problems with Sickles' position, the orchard's elevation offered Ames some advantage. The slight knoll caused many of the Confederate shots to land in front of his guns and rebound overhead. This may explain why Ames' battery reported only seven casualties, all wounded, during the long afternoon. The orchard's elevation also allowed Ames to keep his ammunition caissons closer to the guns than normal and "sheltered in the rear just where the ground began to descend." This close proximity provided for easier re-supply but also increased the danger of an ammunition chest being hit by an enemy projectile.[29]

At Sickles' Trostle farm headquarters, Chaplain Joe Twichell took cover behind the large barn. He recalled the duel as "the most terrific artillery fire I ever witnessed. . . . It was awful. For half an hour it raged incessantly. Grape, canister, solid shot, and shell whizzed and shrieked and tore past us." Twichell watched as nearby trees and animals were torn apart by shell fragments. "Every moment I expected to be struck." Eventually the wounded started to come in. "One of our boys was brought to us with both legs gone."[30]

When General Tyler received Hunt's orders to send artillery to the Third Corps front, he ordered Lieutenant Colonel Freeman McGilvery (commander of the 1st Volunteer Artillery Brigade) to report to Sickles with a pair of batteries. McGilvery chose Captain John Bigelow's 9th Massachusetts and

Captain Charles Phillips' 5th Massachusetts and reported to Sickles, who told him to inspect the ground and place his guns. Accompanied by Bigelow, McGilvery made a brief reconnaissance under fire and decided to deploy the pair of batteries to cover the open ground between the Peach Orchard and the Wheatfield. This gap was the result of Sickles' insufficient manpower to cover his new front. In addition to the gap, Captain Bigelow spotted other defects in Sickles' line. "The angle at the Peach Orchard was most difficult to defend, circled as it was (on both sides) by commanding ridges" that allowed Confederate guns to concentrate "their fire and enfiladed the two lines of the angle, with destructive effect."[31]

Bigelow moved his battery into action via the farm lane that ran past Sickles' headquarters at the Trostle farm. During a brief halt at the farm, Bigelow remembered that "a spirited military spectacle lay before us; General Sickles was standing beneath a tree close by, staff officers and orderlies coming and going in all directions." Approximately 500 yards away, near the Peach Orchard, Bigelow noted "white smoke was curling up from the rapid and crashing volleys" of artillery "while the enemy's shells were flying over or breaking around us." Bigelow ran his battery from the Trostle farm south into position along the Wheatfield Road. Even as he was on the move, Bigelow was already under fire, since Confederate batteries to the southwest probably had a view of his approach. Not only was Bigelow unable to return fire while crossing the field, but the amount of time needed to unlimber and get in position increased his vulnerability. Bigelow started taking casualties "before we could fire a single gun."[32]

Captain Charles Phillips' 5th Massachusetts battery moved into position on Bigelow's right and fronted roughly southwest. Bigelow was already "engaged briskly" when Phillips arrived. Phillips quickly returned fire and silenced the batteries to his front after a short exchange. The Confederate batteries, partially hidden by a stone wall and tree line on Warfield Ridge, were not completely visible to Phillips, but "the smoke of the enemy's guns could be seen over a rolling, open country."[33]

Captain Patrick Hart arrived on the scene with his four-gun 15th New York Independent Battery about the same time as Bigelow and Phillips. McGilvery selected a position for Hart to occupy, and Hart was moving his battery there when he was intercepted by General Hunt, "who ordered me to take a position on the left of the peach orchard." Hunt posted Hart to the right of Clark's battery. Once in place, Hart "directed the fire of my battery on one of the enemy's batteries, which was doing heavy execution on our line of battle."[34]

In 1891, however, Hart told historian John Bachelder something different than what appeared in his official report. In his later version, Hart claimed he had written orders from Hunt to "report without delay to Sickles." Looking all over for Sickles, Hart finally noticed a party of officers under a large tree to his rear. Riding to the tree, Hart inquired of several staff officers where Sickles could be located. The officers refused to cooperate and Hart was about to return to his battery when Sickles stepped forward and identified himself. Sickles "pointed over his shoulder and ordered me to go out there and you will find room enough to fight your Battery." It was only while Hart was riding to place his guns in Sickles' vague and undefined position that Hunt intervened and posted Hart.[35]

The deployment of George Burling's infantry brigade, meanwhile, serves as an illustration of how Sickles' command and control was breaking down. Burling had been previously detached from Humphreys' division and ordered to support Birney, who massed Burling in Trostle's Woods. At roughly 3:45 p.m. Burling received orders to move forward (west) out of the woods at the double quick toward the Emmitsburg Road. Confederate projectiles found the range as the brigade advanced from the woods. After moving no more than one hundred yards, Burling ordered his men to return to the shelter of the timber. When Captain John Poland of Sickles' staff rode forward to demand why Burling had pulled back, the brigade leader countermanded his order and began moving forward a second time until a message from Birney ordered him to shift his brigade to the left. Burling's brigade had just crossed the Wheatfield Road when yet another order arrived detaching the 2nd New Hampshire and 7th New Jersey regiments to report directly to Graham. Similar orders arrived peeling away one regiment after another until his brigade was scattered along Sickles' line. When the general eventually reported back to Humphreys, he did so without a command.[36]

Captain Randolph placed yet another Third Corps battery, Lieutenant John Bucklyn's First Rhode Island, Battery E, along the Emmitsburg Road in the 150-yard gap between the Wentz and Sherfy buildings. Along with Smith's battery at Devil's Den, the combined Union fire temporarily silenced Henry and Cabell's battalions. Being on the left end of the line, Smith's guns were particularly effective in hitting the Confederates with what Cabell complained was "a flanking fire from the enemy's mountain batteries." Porter Alexander was impressed with the Union artillery's obstinacy and the damage it was inflicting upon Cabell's guns. "The Federal artillery was ready for us and in their usual full force and good practice. The ground at Cabell's position gave little protection, and he suffered rapidly in both men and horses." When Longstreet noticed that no Confederate guns were unlimbered immediately west of the Peach Orchard, he pointed to a gap in front of General Lafayette McLaws' lines and asked him, "Why is not a battery placed here?" McLaws protested that a battery would "draw the enemy's artillery [fire] right among my lines . . . [and] be in the way of my charge, and tend to demoralize my men." Unimpressed, Longstreet ordered that guns be placed in the gap. Four of the six batteries from Alexander's own battalion (still temporarily under Huger's command and the only battalion not yet in action) answered the call.[37]

Two of Huger's batteries were placed immediately left of Cabell and just south of the Millerstown Road, while two more batteries were placed immediately north of the road. The deployment proved the wisdom of McLaws' prediction when the guns immediately drew Federal counter battery fire and sent tree limbs and shrapnel into the ranks of his waiting infantry. Although some authors (McLaws among them) have taken Longstreet to task for this, the corps leader was making excellent use of the Confederate exterior line to smother the Union salient. The best way for Longstreet to use Sickles' salient against him was to hit the Union line from two sides. Huger could now fire from the west while Cabell and Henry did the same from the south. Huger's placement was perhaps Alexander's most effective moment during the entire battle; why it took him at least thirty minutes to realize the potential of his position remains unclear.[38]

Union artillery accounts consistently confirm that the new threat from directly west of the orchard was an unwelcome surprise. Ames, who called the action as "sharp an artillery fight" as he had even seen, said a Confederate battery "opened upon my right from a grove 500 yards distant, and at the same time a new battery opened on my front." Phillips reported, "we were most annoyed by a battery on our right, hidden from us by the rising ground and the Peach orchard which enfiladed our line." Hart wrote, "They poured a tremendous cross-fire into me, killing three of my men and wounding five, also killing thirteen horses."[39]

One of the unique aspects of Sickles' position in advance of Cemetery Ridge was the relative proximity of the opposing artillery and infantry. Sharpshooters from the 2nd New Hampshire were posted among the Wentz buildings, close enough to give the Confederates a "wicked reception." Captain Osmund Taylor reported that his Virginia battery was firing with canister, which was typically intended to defend against attacking infantry at relatively short range. Any final analysis of Sickles' performance in the Peach Orchard and along the Emmitsburg Road has to factor in the effect of his infantry being subjected to demoralizing artillery fire from close range prior to the main Confederate attack. The men of the 2nd New Hampshire recalled "closely hugging the ground" for "two hours and more." Colonel Andrew Tippin of Graham's 68th Pennsylvania reported that his men suffered "severely from the destructive fire of the enemy's batteries posted on our left and front." As one member of the 57th Pennsylvania recalled it, "we were exposed to one of the hottest artillery fires we ever encountered."[40]

The regimental historian of the Excelsiors' 72nd New York echoed these comments. The regiment, he reported, spent one hour "lying under the heaviest artillery fire the corps had ever experienced." While terrain and positioning protected some more than others, the Third Corps leaders did little to create their own protection. Thomas Rafferty, of the Excelsiors' 71st New York, claimed that Graham's brigade in particular was "sadly decimated by the fire of Longstreet's artillery on the hill above him. Our men not having yet learned, what they did later in the war, to cover themselves in an hour with a substantial breastwork." Watching the action from farther north on Cemetery Ridge, one soldier in George Willard's unoccupied Second Corps brigade could see the dense smoke that "rose in huge volumes like heavy summer clouds, enveloping the combatants and obscuring the sun."[41]

While Sickle's infantry hugged the earth, Tyler and McGilvery poured in more guns from the Artillery Reserve. McGilvery posted two sections of Captain James Thompson's Independent Pennsylvania Light Artillery between Hart and Ames. The artillery action also spread to Humphreys' front when a Confederate battery from A. P. Hill's Corps under Captain George Patterson unlimbered about 300 yards north of Alexander's battalion, roughly 800 yards west of Humphreys' line. Two Federal batteries under Lt. Francis Seeley and Lt. John Turnbull near the Klingle house, however, "immediately opened fire with solid shot and spherical case, and, after a rapid and well-directed fire, lasting about fifteen minutes, succeeded in silencing this battery [Patterson] and causing it to retire." The artillery on both sides would continue firing after Longstreet's infantry stepped off Warfield Ridge and began their attack.[42]

Sickles' salient at the Peach Orchard offered the Confederates the ability to pound it with converging and enfilade fire. The heavy target density in and around the Peach Orchard should have increased the potential for more Federal guns to be hit by enfilade, ricochet, and overshoots. Despite their advantage in this regard, the Confederates lost at least twelve—and possibly as many as fourteen—guns (including Patterson's seven pieces that were driven off) during the duel; during the same period, the Federals did not report the loss of a single gun. Alexander had at least fifty-four guns (his own estimate) available for use, but he may have ultimately deployed as few as forty-one during the course of the assault. Counting all of the Federal batteries involved (with the exception of Winslow in the Wheatfield, who played a minimal part in this phase) the Federals may have inserted as many as fifty-six guns into action. Alexander allowed himself to be outgunned and permitted Hunt, McGilvery, and Randolph to successfully engage several Southern batteries with a smothering fire. The fact that Sickles and the Third Corps commanders had been tipped off to a pending attack, and had sent orders for reinforcements in advance of the assault also contributed to Alexander's failure. Although Sickles' infantry suffered under the bombardment, and many Federal batteries expended their ammunition, Longstreet's artillery arm did not turn in a good performance that afternoon.[43]

Sickles' unauthorized advance and Meade's last minute discovery would keep Union commanders scrambling all afternoon, but in the early stages the Federal artillery responded successfully by siphoning guns from the Artillery Reserve to supplement Third Corps batteries and bolster Sickles' weaker position. Although Hunt's cannons were ultimately unable to prevent Sickles' line from collapsing, Alexander's inability to destroy or disperse the Federal artillery meant that Longstreet's infantry would have to advance under fire. The long bombardment also removed any final element of surprise, if any still existed, for Longstreet's flank attack. While Sickles was already on the alert, the opening of Longstreet's artillery guaranteed that the Southern infantry would not bound out of the woods against an unsuspecting Federal line, as Jackson had done to Oliver Howard only two months earlier. There was still much to be decided, however, on the afternoon of July 2, 1863, when Hood's division, holding Longstreet's right flank, opened the infantry assault sometime around 4:00 p.m.[44]

A modern view of Devil's Den and Houck's Ridge taken from the foot of the "Slaughter Pen." (Compare to the early postwar view that appears on page 163.) *Author*

The "Key" of the Battleground

History records that Thomas J. "Stonewall" Jackson's flank attack succeeded at Chancellorsville primarily because of the element of surprise, aided substantially by Dan Sickles' reports that Jackson was retreating. William Fox, the New York Monument Commission's postwar historian, thought a repeat of Jackson's attack with a "disguised march was natural, in view of Jackson's success at Chancellorsville." Sickles agreed, arguing that the "conception of the enemy's movement [on July 2] was based upon Jackson's assault on our right flank at Chancellorsville," with one significant difference: "the menacing attitude of my corps, in close proximity to Longstreet's column, threatening its flank, compelled every inch of ground to be disputed from the outset."[1]

William Oates, whose Confederate regiment eventually attacked Little Round Top, believed that "Sickles' apprehension of another flank movement on Lee's part, as at Chancellorsville, was well founded. . . . To guard against a similar surprise, Sickles changed his first formation and placed Birney's fine division, well supported, on his flank and facing to the rear, which thwarted Lee's plan of attack made two hours before, which was a masterly piece of strategy when made." One of Sickles' enlisted men, Private John Haley of the 17th Maine, wrote that although Sickles had formed a "weak line," the difference between Gettysburg and Chancellorsville was that "we suffered no surprise" at Gettysburg.[2]

Although Sickles had left both Round Tops undefended, a signal station atop Little Round Top recorded Longstreet's infantry forming on Warfield Ridge to the west. "[F]rom this point the greater part of the enemy's forces could be seen and their movements reported," wrote Captain Lemuel B.

Norton, the Union Chief Signal Officer. At 3:30 p.m., Norton "discovered the enemy massing upon General Sickles' left, and reported the fact to General Sickles and to the general commanding." The enemy, he continued, finally "opened a terrific fire, but our left was fully prepared for them." The message might have been sent too late to have any real impact on Sickles' troop dispositions, but it was further evidence that Longstreet's flank attack lacked the critical element of surprise that had marked Jackson's successful Chancellorsville maneuver.[3]

General John B. Hood's division moved south past McLaws' line and into position, extending Longstreet's right flank across the Emmitsburg Road. Hood later recalled his instructions as simply, "place my division across the Emmettsburg [sic] road, form line of battle, and attack." When Hood's batteries opened fire during the initial artillery assault, the response from Smith's New York battery at Devil's Den helped develop the Federal lines. And like many other Southern officers that day, Hood did not like what he saw. David Birney's division appeared to angle off to the southeast and end on Little Round Top, with a "line bending back and again forward, forming, as it were, a concave line as approached by the Emmettsburg road. A considerable body of troops was posted in front of their main line, between the Emmettsburg road and Round Top mountain." Hood realized that the extension of Birney's line from the Peach Orchard to the front of Little Round Top (but not on the hill itself as Hood inaccurately believed) prevented an attack "up" the Emmitsburg Road as ordered. Not only would such an attack allow the Federals holding the extreme left flank to rake Hood's exposed right flank and rear, but the immense boulders dotting the landscape would break apart Hood's formations. After several vain attempts to get Longstreet's permission to move around the Round Tops and take the Federals in the rear, Hood began his infantry attack.[4]

General Fitzhugh Lee later admitted that General Robert E. Lee was "deceived by [Sickles' position] and gave orders to attack up the Emmitsburg Road, partially enveloping the enemy's left, which Longstreet 'was to drive in'." Unfortunately for Confederate hopes, "there was much behind Sickles." Unable to attack up the road, Hood knew his only hope of "enveloping the enemy's left" would require him to abandon the Emmitsburg Road in the process. As a result of Sickles' position, Hood moved the axis of his attack east toward Devil's Den and the Round Tops—under the circumstances his only practical option. Hood's "digression" (as he reportedly called it) combined with Sickles' advance to dictate the flow of fighting.[5]

Postwar view of Devil's Den looking west from Plum Run valley
toward the Den and Houck's Ridge. GNMP

There is a common misconception that Longstreet's attack was intended to
be *en echelon* by brigade, a progressive attack that required each brigade to move
only after the brigade on its right had advanced. This interpretation appears
accurate for R. H. Anderson's division of A. P. Hill's Third Corps, which was
supporting on Longstreet's left. Porter Alexander also considered it a
progressive attack, the management of which he described as "conspicuously
bad." Such an attack had been used on previous occasions, he explained, "and
always with poor success." Although Longstreet's attack was essentially
executed as a progressive attack, there is substantial proof that no such attack
was *intended* for Longstreet's brigades. In fact, if Longstreet's attack was
supposed to be *en echelon*, then someone neglected to inform at least two of his
key brigade commanders. General Jerome Robertson, commanding a brigade
in Hood's division, understood that "the attack on our part was to be general,
and that the force of General McLaws was to advance simultaneously with us
on my immediate left." General Joseph Kershaw, a brigadier under McLaws,
also thought that William Barksdale's brigade on his left "would move with me
and conform to my movement." Ultimately, Longstreet's attack was executed *en
echelon by division*, with Hood attacking first, followed by McLaws. Based on the
numerous post-battle complaints of Confederate brigade commanders,

Longstreet's brigades and divisions were apparently launching the attack with an imperfect understanding of how they were to support one another.[6]

A strategy based upon an *en echelon* attack would make more sense if Longstreet had intended to progressively hit different sectors of Sickles' line in order to either break through or force Meade to send reinforcements from other points of his battle line. This does not appear to have been the plan. Longstreet intended Hood's division to drive in the Federal left, not progressively attack it. McLaws' role was either to hammer away at the Peach Orchard front or, as Kershaw believed, connect with Hood as they drove the Federal line toward Gettysburg. In any event the Confederate plan failed, and Sickles would spend decades praising the fighting performance of his Third Corps. While it is true that the common soldier fought admirably while defending a less than admirable position, they were aided by questionable Confederate strategy, disjointed tactics, and poor communication.[7]

When it finally stepped off, Hood's division swept generally eastward toward Sickles' left flank. At this time Birney's Second Brigade, under the command of Brigadier General J. H. Hobart Ward, formed the extreme left of the Union army at Devil's Den. With more than 2,100 men, Ward led the largest brigade in Meade's army. His 3rd Maine and 1st US Sharpshooters, however, were detached and operating near the Peach Orchard, leaving Ward with six regiments of about 1,650 men. Like their counterparts in Graham's brigade near the Peach Orchard, Ward's men had also neglected to build any breastworks prior to the Confederate assault. This was especially surprising since the rocky terrain offered ample protective opportunities. As one veteran remembered it, "we had not yet learned the inestimable value of breastworks, and instead of spending our time rolling the loose stones into a bullet-proof line, we lounged about on the grass and rocks."[8]

The far right of Hood's divisional line was held by Evander Law's Alabama brigade, which pulled away from the Emmitsburg Road as it headed east toward Big Round Top in pursuit of withdrawing U.S. sharpshooters. As Law moved toward the Round Tops, Jerome Robertson's Texas brigade, on Law's left, also abandoned the Emmitsburg Road, heading toward Ward's line on Houck's Ridge. Law's sweep around Devil's Den to the Round Tops demonstrated how easily Sickles' position could be flanked. Captain James Smith had four of the six rifled Parrotts in his 4th New York battery posted directly on Houck's Ridge. (His other two pieces were posted behind the ridge facing south to cover the opening into the Plum Run valley between Devil's Den and Little Round Top.) Smith recalled that his guns "tore gap after gap throughout the ranks of

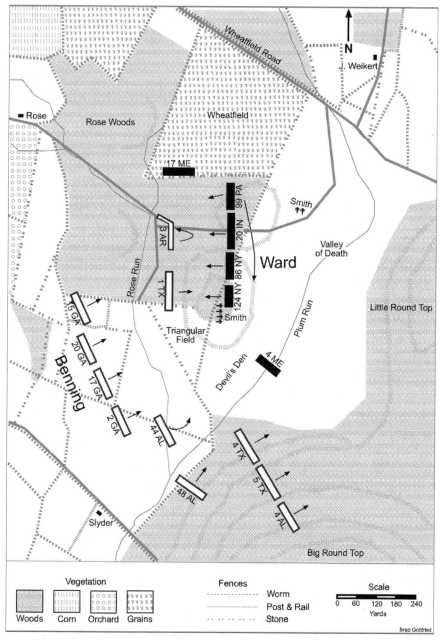

Ward's brigade and Smith's battery defend Devil's Den against Hood's
attack (Law, Robertson, and Benning's brigades.) Several of Law's
and Robertson's regiments outflank Ward and
head toward Little Round Top.

the Confederate foe." Robertson agreed, reporting that as his brigade advanced through the intervening fields, "for half a mile we were exposed to a heavy and destructive fire of canister, grape, and shell." The Confederates also had to deal with fire "from the enemy's sharpshooters . . . behind the numerous rocks, fences, and houses in the field." Fighting on the defensive, Sickles' infantry held an early advantage because Longstreet's men had to cross largely open ground under fire to engage them.[9]

According to General Ward, his men held their fire "until the enemy came within the distance prescribed [200 yards], when the whole command fired a volley. This checked the enemy's advance suddenly, which gave our men an opportunity to reload, when another volley was fired into them." Sickles appears to have played no active role during this critical phase, but it was representative of his entire afternoon's defense as Ward shuffled troops along Houck's Ridge. All but one company of the 4th Maine moved into the gorge between Devil's Den and Big Round Top, while Ward's three right regiments (from right to left: the 99th Pennsylvania, 20th Indiana, and 86th New York) advanced between 50-150 yards to obtain a defensive position along a stone wall on the ridge. On Ward's right, Birney had also ordered the 17th Maine from Regis de Trobriand's brigade to enfilade Robertson's left from behind a low stone wall on the Wheatfield's southern boundary. The cauldron of fire pinned Robertson's men down, and the colonel of his 1st Texas blamed it on "the failure of the troops that were assigned to the position on the left of this (Robertson's) brigade to arrive promptly." General Robertson sent a courier to General Hood (who by this time had been wounded and carried from the field) to complain that "General McLaws' forces were not engaging the enemy to my left (which enabled him to move fresh troops from that part of his line down on me), and that I must have re-enforcements."[10]

In the face of this heavy fire, Robertson's right slowly pressed forward until the terrain finally began to work to their advantage. When Robertson's men reached the stone wall at the base of the so-called "Triangular Field" below Houck's Ridge's western slope, Smith could no longer depress his guns sufficiently to hit the Rebels. Occupying the low ground and using boulders for cover, the Confederates began to pick off Smith's gunners. Smith "saw it would be impossible . . . to hold my position without assistance" and fell back, effectively silencing the four ridge top guns for the remainder of the day. Smith ran "with all the speed in me" back into the Plum Run valley to put his two remaining rear guns into service, but the loss of artillery support was the beginning of the collapse of Sickles' left flank.[11]

The battle for Houck's Ridge dissolved into a series of chaotic attacks and counter-attacks. The 1st Texas regiment advanced toward the center of Ward's line until it was pushed back by a charge from the 124th New York. The Texans reformed and fired a volley into the New Yorkers, "which seemed in an instant to bring down a full quarter" of the regiment. The 44th Alabama from Law's brigade reached the field and helped drive the New Yorkers back up the ridge. In the words of their commander, the Alabamians perceived "that the enemy were giving way [and] sprang forward over the rocks, swept the position, and took possession of the heights" along with Smith's abandoned guns. The 1st Texas charged in their wake and momentarily left the Confederates in command of Houck's Ridge until a Federal counterattack by three of Ward's regiments shoved the Confederates back and briefly recaptured the crest. By this time Smith was working his two remaining guns in the Plum Run valley, "firing obliquely through the gully, doing good execution" against Confederate attempts to work their way into the gorge.[12]

If Longstreet's attack was intended to be a progressive *en echelon* assault, the strategy had thus far served the Confederates poorly. The rough and rocky terrain hampered coordination between Hood's regiments and thrusts had repeatedly stalled as units advanced without support on their flanks. Excluding Gettysburg, Longstreet's offensive record suggests he preferred powerful concentrated attacks. At Second Manassas in August 1862, his massive attack swept everything before it and drove the Union army from the field. Two months after Gettysburg at Chickamauga in September 1863, Longstreet enjoyed perhaps his greatest success when he deployed eight brigades into a deep assault column and attacked a narrow segment of the Union front. By attacking in depth, one brigade behind another, he dented the enemy's line with the first wave and drove through with succeeding waves. Sickles' extended front, however, coupled with the difficult terrain, did not offer an opportunity for Longstreet to stack Hood's and McLaws' eight brigades into a narrow column. Instead, Longstreet settled for an attack depth of just two brigades. At first glance this strategy appears to have worked well at Devil's Den. The successful capture of that rocky eminence by Longstreet's "second line," however, was almost entirely accidental.[13]

Henry Benning's brigade was intended to support Law's brigade during its advance from Warfield Ridge. During the advance Benning could see Robertson's line "about 400 yards in our front" but mistook the men as Law's brigade. If Benning had been behind Law, he would have supported Law's assault on Little Round Top. But Benning could see that the troops ahead of

View of Little Round Top, circa 1890s, looking east across Plum Run Valley from Devil's Den. *Sue Boardman*

him "would not be able alone to carry" Houck's Ridge, "so I advanced without halting." Ward's Federal line had been depleted by the afternoon's hostilities and was stretched dangerously thin, a common side effect of Sickles' extended front. Benning added some 1,400 comparatively fresh Georgians to the Confederate side of the ledger, and his 15th and 20th Georgia united with Robertson's 1st Texas to sweep onto the ridge and finally overwhelm Ward's exhausted brigade. Ward, "with a bullet hole through his hat," withdrew his regiments off Houck's Ridge from right to left. Although there were no substantial reinforcements in sight, some posited that Ward believed he was being officially relieved by men from the Second and Fifth corps, a commonly held misconception in Sickles' Third Corps that afternoon.[14]

General Birney had earlier detached the 6th New Jersey from Burling's brigade and the 40th New York from Regis de Trobriand's brigade into the Plum Run valley "to cover the gorge" against Confederate attempts to flank Devil's Den. The effort is tactically illustrative of Birney's successive attempts to patch up his divisional line. The two regiments fought gamely in support of Smith's two guns in the valley, but Ward's retreat from Houck's Ridge forced the regiments and Captain Smith to also fall back. Although Smith was able to carry his two rear guns off the field, he was bitter about the three that had been captured on Houck's Ridge. Despite the frustration and embarrassment of his battery's capture, Smith still thought Sickles' actions had been for the best. When he published his battery history in 1892, Smith "noticed that those who shed their blood, or who fought in the ranks of this gallant and well-tried old Corps, on the advanced line, have found no fault with their Corps Commander. They know that they were never ordered forward while he remained in the rear."[15]

Sickles had moved his Third Corps forward because he feared that his left would be out-flanked if he remained on Cemetery Ridge. If that was a primary reason for the move, the battle along Houck's Ridge proved that the advance did not cure this defect. Ward's brigade, with modest reinforcements by Birney, had been overrun by portions of three of Hood's brigades. Subtracting for regiments that were detached elsewhere on Sickles' line, Ward began the battle with approximately 1,650 men, while Birney's reinforcements from the 40th New York and 6th New Jersey added another 640 Union troops. The four Confederate regiments from Law and Robertson's brigades that initially hit Ward also totaled about 1,650 men, and Benning added another 1,400 men to the Confederate total. In sum, the Confederate infantry outmanned the Federals defending the Devil's Den area by about 3,000 to 2,300. The Federals, however, had the added weight of Smith's battery and were defending a rugged and elevated position. The Confederates' numeric advantage was real, but it did not exceed the 3:1 odds (or even 2:1 odds) often needed to capture a position during the Civil War. Despite difficult terrain and a stubborn Federal defensive effort, Longstreet's men collapsed Sickles' left flank. Fortunately for the Union cause, by the time Benning commanded Devil's Den it was no longer the left flank of Meade's army. While the Third Corps was defending its line, Union reinforcements were racing to occupy the high rocky hill 500 yards east of Devil's Den, where Meade had intended his left flank to be all along.[16]

To a generation of Gettysburg students who grew up on the novel *The Killer Angels* and the motion picture *Gettysburg*, the Union defense of Gettysburg's second day is the story of Joshua Chamberlain and the 20th Maine saving Little Round Top. Sickles and George Meade, by way of contrast, are mere footnotes to the high drama. Colonel Strong Vincent's Fifth Corps brigade, of which Chamberlain's 20th Maine belonged, performed heroic service for the Union cause that day, but the full story is more complex than the actions of a single brigade or a single regiment from Maine.

Major General George Sykes assumed command of the Fifth Corps when Meade was elevated to army command on June 28, 1863. Sykes arrived at Gettysburg "about 8 a.m." on July 2 and took position in support of Slocum's

Twelfth Corps on the right of the Union line. "While thus situated, I was directed to support the Third Corps, General Sickles commanding, with a brigade, should it be required." Sykes apparently intended to use Brigadier General Stephen Weed's brigade for this purpose. Unfortunately, Sykes' report does not indicate the time he received these directions to support the Third Corps, but his morning deployment near Rock Creek is consistent with the idea that the army's reserve would be needed to support activity on the Union right. Sykes also reported that while he "and other corps commanders were conversing" with Meade at the quickly aborted 3:00 p.m. meeting, "the enemy formed, opened the battle, and developed his attack on our left. I was at once ordered to throw my whole corps to that point and hold it at all hazards." Although Meade ignored the afternoon meeting in his report, he did confirm that upon the Sixth Corps' afternoon arrival, "I immediately directed the Fifth Corps to move over to our extreme left, and the Sixth to occupy its place as a reserve for the right."[17]

David Birney claimed in his report that Sickles had promised Fifth Corps support at the time his division was ordered forward. "He [Sickles] also informed me that a division from the Second and one from the Fifth Corps had been ordered to be in readiness to support me." If this is accurate, then Birney was probably referring to the lone brigade (not division) that Sykes referenced in his report. Birney reported that he was not fully in position until 3:30 p.m. when he "immediately sent an aide to Major-General Sykes asking for the division promised to support my left." Although Birney was not happy with the overall support rendered by the Fifth Corps, he did acknowledge that at least "Major-General Sykes reached my left opportunely, and protected that flank." Sickles' aide Henry Tremain made a similar claim in his memoirs. After the Peach Orchard conference between Sickles and Meade, Sickles sent Captain Moore of his staff to urge the Fifth Corps into position. Tremain commented acidly that "nobody had yet reported their presence in the battle."[18]

Tensions between the Third and Fifth corps had already surfaced by the time Sykes penned his Gettysburg report on the last day of July. Meade's order that the Fifth Corps bolster the Union left, Sykes took pains to note, "of course, relieved my troops from any call from the commander of the Third Corps. En route to the position thus assigned the Fifth Corps, various staff officers from General Sickles met me, and, in the name of that officer, asked for assistance. I explained to them that it was impossible for me to give it; the key-of the battle-field was entrusted to my keeping, and I could not and would not jeopardize it by a division of my forces."[19]

As noted earlier, when Gouverneur Warren reached Little Round Top and spied Longstreet's approaching battle lines, he dispatched two requests for reinforcements. One message was addressed directly to Meade, and the other to Sickles. Lt. Ranald Mackenzie delivered the message to Sickles. Both Mackenzie and Sickles later agreed that Sickles declined Warren's request. "I have none to spare," was how Sickles framed his response, "needing every man, and more, on my front. I advise[d] him to send to the Fifth Corps, already on the march toward us." On at least one occasion, Sickles told a postwar audience that he personally sent Weed's Fifth Corps brigade to Warren on Little Round Top "just in time." Although he had left the hill unoccupied, Sickles' tale rearranged the facts to show that he had somehow managed to save it. The fact that he would often lie following the battle about his role indicates that even he must have realized his blunder in leaving Little Round Top empty.[20]

After Sickles declined Warren's request, Mackenzie rode to locate Sykes near the Wheatfield. Sykes was reconnoitering the terrain while an aide guided his Fifth Corps toward the field. Perhaps Mackenzie sought out Sykes on Sickles' suggestion, as Sickles would have us believe. Regardless, Sykes agreed on the necessity of occupying Little Round Top and sent an aide toward Brigadier General James Barnes, the 61-year-old commander of the First Division of Fifth Corps, with orders to send reinforcements.[21]

Today, Barnes' role at Gettysburg is best remembered through the successful defense of Little Round Top by Barnes' Third Brigade under Colonel Strong Vincent. But the performance of Barnes' other two brigades, Colonel William Tilton's small First Brigade of approximately 655 men and Colonel Jacob Sweitzer's Second Brigade of 1,010 effectives, became lightning rods for some of Gettysburg's (and Sickles') most memorable post-battle criticism. Barnes' division had been moving from Rock Creek toward the "left and front" with Strong Vincent's brigade in the lead. Colonel Vincent had temporarily halted on Cemetery Ridge; theories vary on exactly where, when (as tradition has it) he intercepted the message from Sykes to Barnes. Vincent demanded to know the message's contents and immediately understanding the risks associated with allowing the Confederates to occupy the highest defensible point on the Union left, promised to lead his regiments to "yonder hill." Barnes' report differed considerably with this accepted version. Barnes said that he and Sykes were together reconnoitering the field when Warren personally delivered the request, and it was Barnes himself who detached Vincent. Vincent's standard-bearer, Oliver Wilcox Norton, later wrote a classic history of Little Round Top that perpetuated the Vincent-as-decision-maker scenario.

According to Norton, Barnes' report was "pure fiction." Whether accurate, inaccurate, or something in between, history has preferred Norton's version over Barnes'. However the order was delivered, Strong Vincent, Joshua Chamberlain, and the rest of the brigade marched off to meet their destiny on Little Round Top.[22]

Following the war, Evander Law blamed the Confederate defeat on the notion that General Lee "made his attack precisely where his enemy wanted him to make it and was most fully prepared to receive it." Certainly as far as Little Round Top was concerned, this thesis was entirely inaccurate. Thanks to Sickles' movement, Little Round Top was occupied by Vincent's brigade only minutes before the first Confederate infantry arrived. Vincent posted his line from left to right as follows: 20th Maine, 83rd Pennsylvania, 44th New York, and 16th Michigan along Little Round Top's western and southern slopes and threw out skirmishers. Colonel James Rice of the 44th New York, who later took command of the brigade after Vincent was mortally wounded, reported that the brigade "had scarcely formed line of battle and pushed forward its skirmishers when a division of the enemy's forces, under General Hood, made a desperate attack along the entire line of the brigade." Vincent's successful defense of Little Round Top against portions of Law and Robertson's brigades is best remembered for Chamberlain's face-off with William Oates' 15th Alabama on the far left of the Federal line. Partially due to the collapse of Sickles' line on Houck's Ridge and the retreat of his support in the Plum Run valley, the attacking Confederate left also extended beyond Vincent's right, causing the 16th Michigan's position to collapse and its men began to flee uphill toward the summit. It was while trying to rally his breaking line that Vincent was mortally wounded by a Confederate ball and died a few days later.[23]

Meanwhile, according to Third Corps staff officer Captain Alexander Moore, Sickles ordered him (pursuant to the belief that Sickles was empowered to draw upon the Fifth Corps) to "return to General Sykes and bring up a brigade immediately." Moore reached General Sykes' headquarters but found him absent. Sykes' adjutant had authority to detach a brigade from Brigadier General Romeyn Ayres' Second Division and Moore quickly led Brigadier General Stephen Weed's brigade toward Birney's embattled line. As Weed's brigade marched from its position east of Little Round Top, crossing the Taneytown Road and heading toward the front, Moore and Weed rode ahead to meet with Sickles at the Trostle farm headquarters. What words transpired between Sickles and Weed is unclear, but a signal officer also arrived from Little Round Top and told Sickles (as if he was possibly still unaware of the fact) "that the enemy was advancing in great force, with the evident design of carrying that position, thus flanking General Birney's lines." Sickles directed Moore again "to go for further reenforcements from the Fifth Corps."[24]

While General Weed was meeting with Sickles, his brigade was moving west along the Wheatfield Road just north of Little Round Top. General Warren raced down the hill's north slope and intercepted one of Weed's regiments, the 140th New York led by Colonel Patrick O'Rorke, who told Warren that he was en route to help Sickles. But Warren convinced the colonel that troops were needed immediately on top of the hill. Fortunately O'Rorke consented. As the exhausted Confederates were overwhelming the 16th Michigan's right, O'Rorke and his 140th New York charged toward Vincent's line, slammed into the Confederates, and pushed them back down the hill. For his timely efforts, O'Rorke took a bullet during the charge and was killed instantly. The remainder of Weed's brigade was moved "to the right and front some distance" to support Sickles, but before becoming engaged was somehow ordered (probably by Sykes) back to Little Round Top at the double-quick. The regiments took position on Vincent's right, near the summit, and although General Weed was also killed by a Confederate bullet (thereby preventing him from further illuminating his role in supporting Sickles), they helped discourage further attempts by the Rebels to take the hill. Complicating matters for Longstreet's attack was Hazlett's Battery D, 5th United States Artillery, which reached the summit and began dropping shells into Benning's exhausted Rebels who had conquered Devil's Den.[25]

Not only had Sickles left Little Round Top empty, but both Sykes and Warren also blamed Sickles for nearly diverting Weed's brigade away from the hill. Sykes stated in his report that after posting Tilton and Sweitzer's brigades near the Wheatfield, he rode back toward the Taneytown Road and found Weed's brigade "moving away from the height where it had been stationed, and where its presence was vital." Sykes dispatched a staff officer to determine why Weed was moving and was told, "By order of General Sickles." Sykes claimed he immediately directed Weed to reoccupy it. Later, in 1872, Sykes again complained of "an interference of General Sickles by which General Weed was withdrawn in part from Round Top, and placed en route towards the right, until I met him, and at once returned him to his place."[26]

Warren likewise blamed "earnest appeals for support" that drew the Fifth Corps away from the hill and caused the corps to ultimately reach the position "in such small detachments." Warren thought Sickles' position was "untenable" and it was a "dreadful misfortune of the day that any reinforcements went to that line, for all alike, Third Corps, Second Corps, and Fifth Corps, were driven from it with great loss." Unlike Sickles' left flank at Devil's Den, however, Little Round Top proved impregnable to Southern assault. With Benning's brigade having advanced on Devil's Den (instead of following Law's brigade), Longstreet's attack on Little Round Top lacked the depth necessary to follow up initial repulses. This lack of depth forced regiments such as Oates' 15th Alabama to repeatedly and unsuccessfully attack the same positions. Without reinforcements, the Confederate infantry ultimately fell back, and when the day concluded, the Federals still held the hill.[27]

The successful Fifth Corps defense of Little Round Top yielded Meade at least one clear benefit. The Confederate occupation of Devil's Den was neutralized by the Fifth Corps' higher position only 500 yards to the east. Benning "made my dispositions to hold the ground gained, which was all that I could do" since Little Round Top now appeared "to me almost impregnable to any merely front attack even with fresh men. Indeed, to hold the ground we had appeared a difficult task." Lieutenant Charles Hazlett's battery was throwing shells from the hill "and every head that showed itself was the target for a Minie ball." Longstreet's offensive momentum was stalling. [28]

The military significance of Little Round Top is open for legitimate debate. According to Colonel James Rice, who commanded the brigade after Vincent's fall, "The object of the enemy was evident. If he could gain the vantage ground occupied by this brigade, the left flank of our line must give way, opening to him a vast field for successful operations in the rear of our entire army." Outside of the army, as early as 1866, correspondent William Swinton wrote in *Campaigns of the Army of the Potomac* that Hood's capture of this point "would have taken the entire line in reverse." Had Hood massed his "whole division on the force that had outflanked Sickles' left, pushed boldly for its rocky summit, he would have grasped in his hand the key of the battle-ground, and Gettysburg might have been one of those fields that decide the issues of wars." Numerous later Gettysburg histories, such as Oliver Wilcox Norton's influential *The Attack and Defense of Little Round Top* (1913), echoed this sentiment. Norton wrote that the capture of Little Round Top "would have forced Meade to abandon his strong position in disorderly retreat." While this belief that Little Round Top was the "key" to Meade's line is common throughout Gettysburg historical literature, the novel *The Killer Angels* probably cemented this notion permanently by vividly portraying the 20th Maine's heroic defense of the "end of the line."[29]

Strategically speaking, neither General Lee nor James Longstreet identified Little Round Top as a significant objective in their battle reports. Their objective was to envelop and drive in the Federal left flank, supported by elevated artillery positions along the Emmitsburg Road. Since Lee probably did not believe that the Federal left extended as far south as Little Round Top, there was no need for the hill to be an objective of the attack. However, once Longstreet finally commenced his assault, it became readily apparent that Sickles' line extended farther south than Lee had originally believed. Any attempt to drive the Federal left was going to at least require a successful flanking of Devil's Den, which from a distance mistakenly appeared to numerous Confederate attackers as an extension of Cemetery Ridge itself.

Once the combat moved toward the Southern end of Cemetery Ridge, Little Round Top obviously became the dominant terrain landmark on the left end of Meade's line. As the true left flank of Meade's army, Little Round Top became a critical goal in Longstreet's attack. Meade, Warren, Vincent, and many others equated Little Round Top's defense to the successful outcome of the battle. In order to crush Meade's left, Hood's field commanders saw the obvious need to drive the Fifth Corps reinforcements out of this position. After that, further speculation on what might have happened had the Confederates captured Little Round Top can never be proven, one way or the other. Numerous scenarios could have placed victory in the hands of either side. Claims that Confederate occupation of Little Round Top would have decided "the issues of wars," as Swinton and generations of Gettysburg historians have written, are probably exaggerated. The seminal demonstrable fact is that the Confederates failed to take Little Round Top and drive Meade's army from Cemetery Ridge. When Longstreet failed to drive the Fifth Corps off of Little Round Top, his flank attack increasingly degenerated into a series of frontal assaults farther north on lower Cemetery Ridge. Ignoring the exaggerated postwar claims, the Union defense of Little Round Top remains a pivotal turning point of the fighting on July 2.[30]

In the Dan Sickles story, as the post-battle legend of Little Round Top grew, the fact that this defense was conducted by another corps became a major stumbling block in his efforts to lionize himself as the day's hero. Sickles and his partisans eventually became openly hostile to Sykes' Fifth Corps. The Fifth Corps was being credited with saving the so-called "key" to the battlefield; perhaps saving the battle itself from Third Corps incompetence. Whether or not Little Round Top was the military "key" is somewhat irrelevant, because battle veterans North and South increasingly portrayed it as such at postwar gatherings, and placed an increasing spotlight on Sickles' inability to occupy it. To counter these arguments, the Third Corps party line argued that the Fifth

Corps had been tardy in its arrival, and that two Fifth Corps brigades under William Tilton and Jacob Sweitzer had fought poorly while supporting Sickles.

Tilton and Sweitzer's troubles began when they went to Birney and de Trobriand's support in the Wheatfield. When General Sykes was bringing Barnes' Fifth Corps division onto the field, Sykes claimed that he had told Birney to close to the left and better support Smith's battery at Devil's Den. "I promised to fill the gap he opened," Sykes reported, "which I did with Sweitzer's and Tilton's brigades, of my First Division, posting them myself." This gap ran from the rocky elevation on the Wheatfield's northwest corner (later referred to as Stony Hill) toward the left of Graham's brigade in the Peach Orchard. In reality, Sickles lacked adequate manpower to fill his advanced line, and de Trobriand was unable to connect with Graham's left even before the battle began. As Longstreet's attack rolled along Houck's Ridge, Colonel de Trobriand moved his 17th Maine to bolster his own left, and his 40th New York was detached to support Ward in Plum Run valley. These moves further reduced his ability to cover the gap between the Wheatfield and the Peach Orchard.[31]

When Barnes' division approached the battlefield, Vincent's brigade was in the lead, followed by Sweitzer and Tilton. When Vincent departed for Little Round Top, Sykes and Barnes ordered Sweitzer and Tilton into position near the Stony Hill. Barnes reported that as they moved into position "they passed over a line of troops, understood to be a portion of a brigade of the Third Corps; they were lying down upon the ground."[32]

Like Sykes, Barnes was also worried about that gap between Stony Hill and the Peach Orchard. "Upon the right of our position an open space," Barnes later reported,

> apparently unprotected, extended to some distance. Upon [Barnes] calling the attention of General Sykes to it, he remarked, referring to the part of the Third Corps over which we had passed and then lying down in our rear, that those troops were to be removed. The remaining portion of the Third Corps was understood to be at some distance to the right, and much in advance of what seemed to be their natural and true position. This unguarded space was watched with great anxiety. There was little time, however, for deliberation. General Sykes, called by his duty to the left of the line, went toward that portion of his command. The attack of the enemy commenced almost immediately along my front.[33]

Colonel Sweitzer's brigade largely faced west toward the Emmitsburg Road, except for his 32nd Massachusetts which, exposed on the brigade's left, changed front to the south. Sweitzer had only three of his regiments in line of battle (the 9th Massachusetts was detached on picket duty.) Tilton posted his brigade facing south on Stony Hill's southern slope. Tilton and Sweitzer's reports are confusing because each officer reported that the other was on his left. Tilton, like Sykes and Barnes, was worried that no infantry was on his right. There is some debate regarding the timing of their arrival on Stony Hill, such as whether they arrived before or after G. T. Anderson's first attacks on de Trobriand had already been repulsed. Regardless of the exact time, while Vincent and Weed's brigades were saving Little Round Top, Tilton and Sweitzer went into action awkwardly positioned and with an exposed right flank that worried the Fifth Corps senior officers.[34]

A modern view of Devil's Den and Houck's Ridge taken from the foot of the "Slaughter Pen." (Compare to the early postwar view that appears on page 163.) *Author*

Gross Neglect or Unaccountable Stupidity

T he Federal defense of the Wheatfield was characteristic of Sickles' and Birney's disjointed tactical deployments. Regis de Trobriand was under the impression that his role was to support Birney's other two brigades, so de Trobriand posted his own "in column by regiments, ready to support either of the other two brigades according to circumstances." When it became apparent that Ward would receive the attack first, de Trobriand positioned the 17th Maine behind the stone wall on the Wheatfield's southern end to bolster Ward's right flank. With the 3rd Michigan on the skirmish line and the large 40th New York having earlier been detached into the Plum Run valley, de Trobriand's line was stretched dangerously thin. When the combat eventually swirled into the Wheatfield, Birney sent an aide "through a hail of bullets" to detach still another regiment. "Tell General Birney," Colonel de Trobriand replied, "that I have not a man left who has not upon his hands all that he can do, and tell him that, far from being able to furnish reinforcements to anyone, I shall be in need of them myself in less than a quarter of an hour."

In addition to the brigades of de Trobriand, Tilton, and Sweitzer, the Wheatfield was also supported by two regiments from Burling's brigade (the 8th New Jersey and 115th Pennsylvania). Burling's command, like de Trobriand's, was cannibalized into several pieces, increasing the probability of breakdowns in control as Confederate offensive pressure increased. Birney's presence in this sector might have been intended to mitigate the resulting confusion, but he seems to have personally been responsible for several of the detachments.[1]

In the 17th Maine's rear was Captain George Winslow's New York battery. These guns were posted on an elevation near the Wheatfield's northern end, facing southwest towards Rose's Woods. Once again, Sickles and Birney were unable to "connect" either their infantry or artillery. A 300-yard gap yawned wide between Winslow and John Bigelow's battery on the Wheatfield Road. Private John Haley of the 17th Maine thought that the artillery was "useless as long as the enemy was under cover of good sized trees." Winslow admitted he was unable to effectively hit Longstreet's artillery with counter-battery fire, and the situation barely improved when the Southern infantry commenced its attack. "I was unable from my obscure position to observe the movements of the troops," Winslow wrote, "and was compelled to estimate distances and regulate my fire by the reports of our own and the enemy's musketry."[2]

Whatever the magnitude of Sickles' defensive problems, Longstreet's offensive execution was hardly flawless. G. T. Anderson's Georgia brigade initially deployed in support of Robertson's brigade, but by the time it advanced and struck the Federal lines, the Georgians found themselves on Robertson's left. While Anderson's extreme right helped dislodge Ward from Houck's Ridge, the majority of his men slammed into de Trobriand in the Wheatfield. Like most of Longstreet's July 2 attack, Anderson's first wave was repulsed and his commanders (like Robertson's brigade before them) complained about the lack of support on their left. Captain George Hillyer's 9th Georgia found itself "having for nearly an hour and a half no support on its left, the advance of McLaws' division being for some reason thus long delayed." The delay exposed the 9th's dangling left flank to enfilade fire from McGilvery's Wheatfield Road artillery line. B. H. Gee of the 59th Georgia offered a simpler explanation for Anderson's first repulse. "The men were completely exhausted when they made it," explained Gee, "having double-quicked a distance of some 400 yards, under a severe shelling and a scorching sun."[3]

It is unclear exactly when McLaws attacked, but his division may have waited as long as one hour after Hood's infantry stepped off. The precise reason for the delay has never been clarified, but it has helped fuel theories that Longstreet's attack was intended to be *en echelon*. "I was directed not to assault until General Hood was in position," McLaws wrote his wife on July 7, "Gen H had gone around above me to the right, and found that the enemy were very strongly posted on two rocky hills ... before he could aid me it was necessary to carry one of the hills." In a paper he read in 1878, McLaws claimed he could not attack earlier because "I was waiting General Longstreet's will [sic]. . . ." General Law, who assumed command of Hood's division when the latter was severely wounded by the explosion of an artillery shell during the opening minutes of the attack, believed McLaws was supposed to attack at "the same time" as Hood, a belief that adds doubt to the theory the delay was due to a planned *en echelon* attack.[4]

When the signal was given to move forward, Kershaw's South Carolina brigade, positioned on the right side of McLaws' front line, attacked first. General Kershaw had been directed by Longstreet to attack the Peach Orchard to his left front, "turn his flank, and extend along the cross-road [Millerstown], with my left resting toward the Emmitsburg road." By this time, Kershaw was aware that an attack up the Emmitsburg Road would expose his right flank and rear to the refused portion of Birney's line that stretched from the Peach Orchard to Houck's Ridge. Kershaw had also understood that Hood "was to sweep down the enemy's line in a direction perpendicular to our then line of battle." Because Hood's attack had been underway for some time (and for perhaps as long as one hour), it must have been obvious to many of McLaws' officers that Hood's attack was not going according to plan. Despite all the heavy fighting that had taken place thus far, Sickles' left was not being driven in. By the time McLaws' division was ready to join the fighting, Longstreet's attack was deteriorating into a series of small frontal assaults rather than a turn of the enemy flank. Studying the situation unfolding to his front, Kershaw determined to "move upon" the stony hill beyond the Rose house opposite his center "so as to strike it with my center, and thus attack the orchard on its left rear."[5]

As with each of Longstreet's brigade commanders who had attacked before him, Kershaw expected to connect immediately with William Barksdale's Mississippi brigade, positioned to his left. Both Longstreet and McLaws had previously assured Kershaw "that Barksdale would move with me and conform to my movement; that Semmes would follow me, and Wofford follow Barksdale." But when Kershaw's line was "about the Emmitsburg road, I heard Barksdale's drums beat the assembly, and knew *then* [emphasis in original] that I should have no immediate support on my left, about to be squarely presented to the heavy force of infantry and artillery at and in rear of the Peach Orchard." Given that Kershaw was, by his own admission, in personal contact with both Longstreet and McLaws, this confusion over Barksdale's role seems inexplicable. E. P. Alexander lamented that Barksdale's delay "was especially unfortunate in this case, because advancing Kershaw without advancing Barksdale would expose Kershaw to enfilade by the troops whom Barksdale would easily drive off. Few battlefields can furnish examples of worse tactics." One of the primary weaknesses of Sickles' Peach Orchard salient was its ability

Modern view taken from the "Longstreet Tower" on Warfield Ridge looking east toward the Peach Orchard. Barksdale (left) and Kershaw (right) attacked across the open foreground toward orchard in the center. *Author*

to be attacked on two sides at once; the Confederates continued to oblige him by attacking but one side at a time.[6]

One of the reasons Sickles had occupied the Peach Orchard was because he considered it a strong position for artillery. Confederate brigades under G. T. Anderson, Kershaw, and later Semmes had to cross the low ground south of the elevated orchard to reach the Wheatfield and Stony Hill. Kershaw's problems were compounded by a miscommunication of orders that caused his left regiments to veer to their right and further expose their left flank to fire from McGilvery's Wheatfield Road artillery. "I immediately trained the entire line of our guns upon them, and opened with various kinds of ammunition," reported Colonel McGilvery. When Kershaw's men reached the Rose farm buildings, McGilvery "gave them canister and solid shot with such good effect that I am sure that several hundred were put hors de combat in a short space of time. The column was broken—part fled in the direction from whence it came; part pushed on into the woods on our left; the remainder endeavored to shelter themselves in masses around the house and barn." Ames, Hart, Clark, and Thompson's left sections around the Peach Orchard all pounded away at the South Carolinians. But as John Bigelow noted, they could not completely prevent the Confederates from gaining Rose's woodlot to their front.[7]

About the time of Kershaw's assault, Ames' battery expended its ammunition and received orders to withdraw. Ames reported the time when he retired from the Peach Orchard as 5:30 p.m., "having been engaged for two and a half hours." Ames claimed in his battery's history that "the enemy was advancing a heavy line in front, [when] an order was received from General Sickles to fall back. The enemy was so close that it would have meant the loss of our guns had we attempted to limber up at that time and retreat." As Ames headed back toward Sickles' headquarters at the Trostle farm, there is some debate over whose battery replaced him. Henry Hunt, George Randolph, and Ames reported that his replacement was Malbone Watson's Battery I, Fifth U.S. Artillery, which naturally led to the assumption that Watson moved his guns into the orchard. (Hunt later admitted to John Bachelder that his own report inaccurately placed Watson's battery.) In another scenario, Watson was waiting near the Trostle Farm for orders and was ordered to the front by Sickles (or an aide), but before Watson could reach the orchard the position was collapsing and the other batteries were in retreat. Wherever Watson went, the battery and its crew had a rough afternoon ahead of them.[8]

What is certain about Watson's actions is that his guns were hijacked by Sickles and staff, causing numerous complaints amongst Union commanders.

Watson's battery entered the field sometime between 4:00 p.m. and 5:00 p.m. behind Barnes' division, along with Hazlett and Lt. Aaron Walcott's batteries. While Hazlett was ordered to Little Round Top, Watson and Walcott were left in rear of Barnes with instructions to await orders. Captain Augustus Martin, commanding the Fifth Corps Artillery Brigade, complained in his report, "When positions had been selected and orders sent for the batteries to move to the front, they were not to be found." Walcott was subsequently located "in rear of the Third Corps. The officer commanding reported that he had been ordered there by an officer of General Sickles' staff, who had orders to take any batteries he could find, no matter where they belonged." Watson's battery was "taken in the same way, thus depriving the Fifth Corps of its proper amount of artillery . . . [Watson] was placed in position by some unknown officer of the Third Corps." General Sykes later complained that Watson was "appropriated by Sickles without my knowledge, in consequence of which it was for a time lost." Henry Hunt lodged the same complaint against Sickles' staff officers, saying there was "no necessity" for doing so, as "abundant provision having been made to supply all needs from the Artillery Reserve." Nor did their positioning meet with Hunt's approval. "The batteries were exposed to heavy front and enfilading fires, and suffered terribly." In fact, both Watson and Walcott's batteries would be temporarily captured later in the afternoon.[9]

Artillery alone does not deserve all of the credit for repulsing Kershaw's first attack. As the South Carolinian led his men across the Emmitsburg Road, the 2nd New Hampshire's Colonel Bailey received permission from Graham to "charge" about 150 yards and take up a position along a rail fence at the southern end of the orchard with their right flank on the Emmitsburg Road. From this advanced location, Bailey's men fired on the Confederate infantry advancing to their front and left. The 3rd Maine rushed forward onto Bailey's left, while the 68th Pennsylvania arrived on his right. The three regiments formed a right angle at the Emmitsburg Road, with the 68th facing west while the others fronted to the south. "Many regiments fought in *a* peach orchard at Gettysburg," boasted the 2nd New Hampshire's regimental history, "but the three enumerated above were the only ones who formed a line in '*the*' peach orchard that day [emphasis in original]." The trio of regiments was also joined on the 3rd Maine's left flank by the 141st Pennsylvania and the 3rd Michigan on the far left. These five regiments now formed Sickles' infantry front along the southern edge of the Peach Orchard.[10]

Kershaw was so "roughly handled" that his left regiments took cover to regroup among the available rocks and shrubbery of the Rose farm, where the

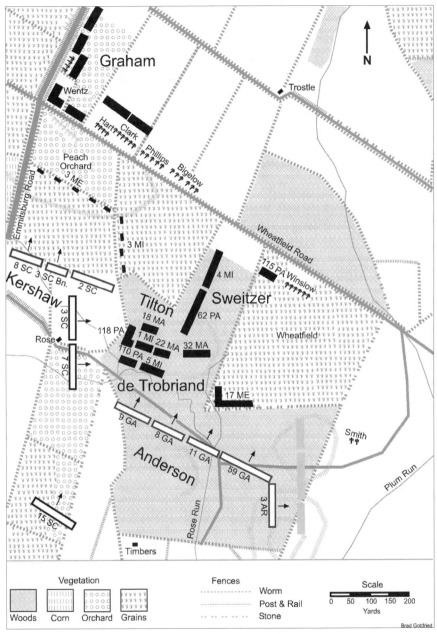

Regis de Trobriand's brigade defends the Wheatfield against attacks from
Anderson's and Kershaw's brigades. Tilton and Sweitzer's Fifth Corps
brigades support de Trobriand and attempt to close the gap with
Graham's brigade in the Peach Orchard before withdrawing
under pressure from Kershaw.

Union batteries continued shelling them. Kershaw's right pair of regiments enjoyed more success. As they approached the Stony Hill, and in what became a hotly debated movement, the awkwardly posted regiments of Tilton and Sweitzer's brigades retreated. Sickles, Birney, de Trobriand, numerous Third Corps veterans, and an anonymous witness dubbed "Historicus" later ridiculed Tilton and Sweitzer for allegedly retreating prematurely and exposing de Trobriand's right flank. As Kershaw's right regiments approached Stony Hill, G. T. Anderson's brigade renewed its attack against Colonel de Trobriand's left. De Trobriand complained in his report that during the "raging" battle "two regiments [sic] from the Fifth Corps, sent there to my support" fell back "without engaging the enemy (by what orders I could never ascertain)."[11]

Colonel de Trobriand described the unfolding chaos more colorfully in his memoirs. An aide approached and "told me that a brigade of the Fifth Corps was lying in two lines behind us, awaiting the time to come into action. This was good news. But, as I went to assure myself of its accuracy, I saw these troops rise up and fall back hurriedly at the command of their officers. I galloped forward towards the nearest of them, and asked them, – 'Where are you going?' – 'We do not know.' – 'Who has given you your orders to retire?' – 'We do not know.' They then filed out of the woods. . . . These regiments belonged to General Barnes' division." Tilton and Sweitzer departed the Stony Hill area and headed toward Trostle's Woods on the north side of the Wheatfield Road.[12]

As usual, everyone had a different story. The most damaging and public criticism of Barnes' brigades would come in March 1864 when an "important communication from an eye-witness" was published in the New York *Herald*. The self-named eyewitness, "Historicus," made several embarrassing accusations against Barnes. According to Historicus, Birney was sent to order Barnes back into line, but Barnes replied, "No. It is too hot. My men cannot stand it." John Bigelow thought that he saw "some Federal troops in good order move out of these very woods the enemy had gained, and marched to the rear, I know not where." According to Robert Carter, who fought in the 22nd Massachusetts, Tilton ordered his brigade to retire only after they were outflanked by Semmes and Kershaw. The veterans of the 118th said the retreat was ordered because "at the same moment the artillery on the right was evidently preparing to withdraw." A captain in Sweitzer's 62nd Pennsylvania remembered that Tilton went first and "left our brigade in a critical condition. We were directed to fall back, which was done deliberately and in good order."[13]

Barnes, Tilton, and Sweitzer emphatically denied the charges. Kershaw's approach, explained Barnes, "had penetrated through the unguarded space" on

Tilton and Sweitzer's right. Barnes was worried that "there were no means of checking his advance toward my rear" and claimed that he only ordered Tilton to change front, which of course was "at once executed, deliberately, yet promptly, and in good order." Barnes claimed that Sweitzer was then "directed to fall back in good order, and to take up a new position a short distance in his rear, for the purpose of co-operating in opposing this heavy attack upon the flank."[14] Colonel Tilton admitted that he too was very worried over his exposed right. He acknowledged more than a "change of front":

> The onslaught was terrible and my losses heavy—so much so that I was somewhat doubtful if our line could withstand it. This fact I communicated to the general commanding division [Barnes], who ordered me to fall back in good order *if unable to hold the position*; [emphasis added] but my men behaved nobly, and twice repulsed the assailants. My colonels wished to advance. Being anxious about my right, however, I reconnoitered in person, and discovered the enemy in large force coming from the direction of Rose's house, with the evident design of outflanking me. *I immediately retired* [emphasis added] and took up a new position (in two lines), at the left and rear of a battery which had been posted about 300 yards to my right and rear. The battery soon commenced to retreat, firing, followed by the rebels, who were now again upon my right flank. To avoid this flank movement, I retired, firing, a short distance in the timber. . . .[15]

Sweitzer, who had the best day of the three officers, addressed the accusations by reporting, "When the attack commenced, word was sent by General Barnes that *when we retired* [emphasis added] we should fall back under cover of the woods." This was only intended to inform the men "how to retire when it became necessary." Sweitzer clearly reported that he did not retreat until after Tilton's brigade had fallen back, and then fell back by Barnes' order. Whether Barnes or Tilton was responsible, each had given Sickles plenty of post-battle opportunity to deflect criticism toward them and away from himself (even though Barnes' problems were at least partially caused by Sickles' over-extended front). [16]

"It was a hard fight," Regis de Trobriand remembered. "The Confederates appeared to have the devil in them." His brigade continued slugging it out as the Confederate infantry advanced on several sides. Private John Haley in the 17th Maine grumbled that while the enemy seemed to be increasing in strength, the

Federals seemed to be fighting without any support of their own, either through "gross neglect on our side or unaccountable stupidity." With ammunition running low, Birney sent an aide to the wall with an order to "fall back immediately!" The breaking of Ward's line on his left, the renewal of G. T. Anderson's attack, Barnes' retreat, and the occupation of Stony Hill by Kershaw finally compelled Colonel de Trobriand to withdraw his own battered brigade.[17]

Even with the combined efforts of both the Third and Fifth corps, Sickles' advanced line was teetering on the edge of destruction. General Birney fully realized the trouble he was in. "As the fight was now furious, and my thin line reached from Sugar Loaf Hill to the Emmitsburg road, fully a mile in length, I was obliged to send for more reenforcements to Major-General Sickles." Sickles apparently requested these reinforcements from Meade, who then sent a courier to Hancock. Meade's courier located Hancock, who sent in Brigadier General John Caldwell's First Division of Hancock's Second Corps, which had been in reserve near the site of the present-day Pennsylvania State Monument. However, the Second Corps reinforcements were not to report to Sickles. According to Hancock, he was "directed by General Meade to send a division to the assistance of the Third Corps, with orders to report to General Sykes, commanding Fifth Corps."[18]

The Second Corps had watched with growing alarm as Longstreet's infantry slammed into Sickles' line. Lieutenant Frank Haskell rhetorically questioned the wisdom of sending more reinforcements to support the position. "To move down and support them there with other troops is out of the question, for this would be, to do as Sickles did, to relinquish a good position, and advance to a bad one. There is no other alternative, – the 3d Corps must fight itself out of its position of destruction! What was it ever put there for?"[19]

General Kershaw later told historian John Bachelder that as Tilton and Sweitzer "seemed to melt away," he spotted a "heavy [Union] column" move "in two lines of battle across the wheat-field" toward Kershaw's right and rear. These approaching troops belonged to General Caldwell, who was rushing forward another 3,200 men to bolster Sickles' crumbling front. Colonel Edward Cross' brigade entered the Wheatfield first, and "steadily drove the enemy back," while Colonel Patrick Kelly's famed Irish Brigade entered the field on Cross' right, hitting Kershaw's right flank.[20]

Caldwell's arrival emboldened Birney and de Trobriand to counter-attack. Lt. Col. Charles Merrill was regrouping his 17th Maine near the Wheatfield

Road when "Major-General Birney rode upon the field and directed our line to advance. With cheers for our gallant commander, the regiment moved quickly forward, and pouring into the enemy volley upon volley, their advance was checked. The contest was now of a most deadly character, almost hand to hand, and our loss was very severe." Colonel de Trobriand, meanwhile, rallied the 5th Michigan and 110th Pennsylvania and "charged through the wheat field, driving the rebels back to the other side of the stone wall." The attack "was also the last effort of my brigade" for de Trobriand received "orders to fall back, and during that movement I understood in what a hazardous position I had been placed without knowing it." Of Birney's three brigades, Ward was in the process of losing Houck's Ridge, and Colonel de Trobriand was leaving the field to reorganize. Only Graham's fate remained undecided.[21]

While these events were unfolding, Sickles had sent Henry Tremain to locate Hancock and confirm that Second Corps help was on the way. As Caldwell's division was moving toward the Wheatfield, Brigadier General Samuel K. Zook's 975-man brigade was bringing up the rear. Tremain ensured they were headed toward Sickles. From that point forward, there are at least two distinct versions of exactly how Tremain appropriated Zook's brigade.[22]

In his memoirs, Tremain wrote that he spotted Caldwell's column moving toward the front and happened on Zook's men in the rear. Realizing that it would take too long to locate either Hancock or Caldwell at the division's head, Tremain asked Zook to detach his brigade immediately. Zook replied "that his orders were to follow the column." But the situation was desperate and both men knew that military protocol had to be followed. According to Tremain, Zook answered, "with a calm, firm look, inspiring me with its significance, 'if you will give me the order of General Sickles I will obey it.'" Tremain responded, "General Sickles' order, general, is that you file your brigade to the right and move into action here." With that understanding, Tremain led Zook and the brigade toward the Wheatfield. Tremain praised Zook's decisiveness. In fact, Zook is one of the few non-Third Corps officers who come off well in Tremain's memoirs. "[H]ad he acted otherwise it might have changed the fate of the day," wrote the aide. "Who knows? It was such acts of sagacity and nobleness that won Gettysburg." The detachment of Zook's brigade was a bold move, but it was also another example of Federal regiments and brigades being scattered all over the field to plug holes in Sickles' line, and being placed under the command of whomever had the greatest momentary emergency.[23]

Josiah Favill, one of Zook's trusted staff officers, told a remarkably different story. Lieutenant Favill was watching the "intensely interesting" opening of Longstreet's attack when Henry Tremain arrived and requested Zook to move to Sickles' assistance. In Favill's version, Zook "instantly put spurs to his horse and galloped directly across the field to Sickles, who, surrounded by a large staff, was in a state of great excitement; the enemy's shot were dropping about him, and he seemed to be very much confused and uncertain in his movements. When Zook approached him, he excitedly asked him to put his command into action on his left, where he admitted Longstreet was steadily driving him back near the two small mountains. Zook declared his willingness to act, and galloped back to his command." When Zook and Favill returned to the brigade, Cross and Kelly "were already on the march toward the threatened left, and we promptly followed."[24]

Tremain and Favill's accounts are so radically different that they are impossible to reconcile. Tremain's memoirs have a tendency to place himself in the middle of momentous occasions, and the Zook episode is no different. If Favill's story is accurate (and Zook had time to ride to Third Corps headquarters and then return to his command), why didn't Zook use that time to try and locate General Caldwell, his own commanding officer? Whichever version is correct, Birney's report confirmed that it was Tremain who guided Zook's brigade into battle. "Major Tremain . . . soon appeared with a brigade of the Second Corps, which behaved most handsomely, and, leading them forward, it soon restored the center of my line, and we drove the enemy from that point."[25]

As Zook's column moved through Trostle's Woods toward the Wheatfield, it passed Tilton and Sweitzer's brigades reforming there after their retreat from Stony Hill. Given the noise, smoke, flying projectiles and general chaos, it would not have been unusual if Barnes' men temporarily slowed Zook's progress. Instead, as will be discussed later, Zook's passage through Trostle's Woods created a memorable post-battle opportunity to heap more insults on Barnes' division. However, the official reports filed from Zook's regiments indicate only that the brigade moved rapidly forward and that nothing unusual occurred.[26]

According to Lieutenant Favill, once the brigade arrived near the Wheatfield it advanced in two lines and, "shortly received a tremendous fire from the front . . . the tumult became deafening . . . no word of command could be heard, and little could be seen but long lines of flame, and smoke and struggling masses of men." The brigade advanced several hundred yards at a run and was in what a New York major called "a deplorable state of confusion; men from every regiment in the division were intermingled with ours in one confused mass." Zook's men may have looked like "one confused mass," but Colonel de Trobriand cheered the brigadier's performance: "*They did not lie down behind us* [emphasis in original]." General Zook fell with a wound in his stomach while leading his men and died on the next afternoon. His death prevented him from answering post-battle questions regarding how his brigade entered the battle, or the behavior of Tilton and Sweitzer's men as he passed them en route to the front.[27]

Colonel John Brooke of Caldwell's Fourth Brigade took over, and with Zook's brigade on his right drove the Confederates out of the Wheatfield. "It was evident to me," Colonel Brooke later wrote, "sometime before our division was sent to that part of the field that the 3d Corps was being worsted in the fight." Brooke's brigade splashed across the western branch of Plum Run, climbed the bluff on the creek's western bank and halted near the Rose woods fronting the Rose farm buildings. Although Brooke's counterattack appeared successful, he had outrun any possible support, and remnants from G. T. Anderson's, Kershaw's, and Paul Semmes' brigades prevented any further movement to his front. The Confederates opened a "withering fire" against Brooke's men, who planted their colors on the crest and returned it. Although it looked for a time as if Zook's and Kelly's brigades were about to secure Stony Hill, Zook's right was unsupported. The Stony Hill position would again become untenable if the Confederates took control of the Wheatfield Road.[28]

After some of the hardest fighting of the war, the Federals held, albeit tenuously, the Wheatfield and Stony Hill. Fewer than 1,300 men from the Third Corps had defended the field. Regis de Trobriand had started with 955 men (excluding the detached 40th New York), and was supported by another 321 from Burling's 8th New Jersey and 115th Pennsylvania. Ignoring the Fifth Corps' minimal assistance, it had taken the addition of Caldwell's 3,200 bodies (a whopping 246% increase in manpower) to clear Anderson, Kershaw, and Semmes. Of the three zones (Devil's Den, the Wheatfield, and the Peach Orchard) occupied by Birney's division of slightly fewer than 5,100 men, the Wheatfield was strategically the least important of the three, yet it took the equivalent of 63% of Birney's total manpower (in the form of Caldwell's division) to temporarily drive the Confederates out of the field. The fighting in the Wheatfield offers additional proof that Sickles lacked adequate strength to defend his position.[29]

For all the faults inherent in Sickles' position, Longstreet had thus far made little progress in driving in the Federal left. His attack was degenerating into a series of uncoordinated frontal assaults across open fields, under both Federal artillery fire and a broiling sun, while many of his subordinate commanders complained about a lack of support. In exchange for heavy casualties in the fighting for Devil's Den and the Wheatfield, Longstreet had captured ground that offered the Confederates little in the way of tactical value. Sickles' line had effectively acted as a "buffer," but Sickles and the reinforcements sent to support him had suffered their own heavy losses in the process. The extended Third Corps line forced Meade to haphazardly juggle troop dispositions, which left holes on Cemetery Ridge when organizations such as Caldwell's division were yanked out of line. Thanks in large part to Sickles, and with help from Longstreet's execution of the attack, the situation was proving to be a bloody mess on both sides.[30]

Although the Federals were in command of the Wheatfield, events unfolding at the Peach Orchard would once again threaten Meade's Cemetery Ridge line.

Chapter 11

The Line Before You Must Be Broken

W est of the Peach Orchard and Sherfy farm, Federal artillery shells continued bursting around Lafayette McLaws' waiting infantry. Being targets of enemy artillery produced a "natural feeling of uneasiness" among the men. An impatient General Barksdale harassed both McLaws and Longstreet, "I wish you would let me go in, General." Longstreet never fully explained how he timed his order for Barksdale's advance, nor did he specify why he allowed Kershaw to attack without Barksdale's support. In his memoirs, Longstreet implied that the delay was due to McLaws' "caution to hold his ranks closed." McLaws, however, claimed the delays were due to the confusion caused by the artillery that Longstreet had placed in his front. Whatever the cause, Colonel Alexander (while neglecting analysis of his own shortcomings) complained about the committing of "four partial attacks of two brigades each [in Hood and McLaws' divisions], requiring at least an hour and a half to be gotten into action; where one advance by the eight brigades would have won a quicker victory with far less loss."[1]

Once Longstreet finally gave the order, Barksdale called his regimental commanders together. "The line before you must be broken—to do so let every officer and man animate his comrades by his personal presence in the front line." It was probably near 6:00 p.m. when the 1,400 Mississippians let loose with the Rebel yell and sprang forward. The brigade formed with the 21st Mississippi on the right, followed by the 17th, 13th, and finally the 18th on the left. Barksdale remained mounted and rode in front of the 13th Mississippi, his hat off and the remnants of his long thin white hair flowing freely. When the brigade front cleared Pitzer's Woods, the order was given "Double-quick, charge!" Heavy Federal artillery fire, admitted a member of the 17th

Mississippi, "knock[ed] great gaps in our line. Then we would fill up the gaps and move on." One witness remembered that Barksdale "threw forward his Mississippians in an unbroken line in the most magnificent charge I witnessed during the war." To Sickles' troops in the Peach Orchard there was little to consider "grand" or "magnificent" about Barksdale's charge. It was simply one more assault against their exposed salient position.[2]

Barksdale advanced along a front approximately 350 yards wide. His three Mississippi regiments on the left moved north of the Wheatfield Road heading toward the Sherfy farm buildings. South of the road, Colonel Benjamin G. Humphreys directed his 21st Mississippi toward the Sherfy Peach Orchard and the 68th Pennsylvania's front. Like Kershaw's South Carolinians before them, the Mississippians rushed forward unsupported on either flank. However, the advanced salient of the Peach Orchard gave Barksdale less ground to cover than Kershaw, leaving the Federal artillery with less time to break up the attacking formations. By essentially hitting the Federal line head-on at the orchard, Barksdale did not present an exposed left flank to the Federal artillery as both G. T. Anderson and Kershaw had done before him. Barksdale's was basically a frontal assault.[3]

The 63rd Pennsylvania in Graham's brigade was probably withdrawn from the Federal skirmish line west of the Peach Orchard during Kershaw's earlier attack. It is not clear which, if any, unit replaced the Pennsylvanians (the 5th New Jersey most likely did so), but the lack of Federal skirmishers must have emboldened Barksdale's Mississippians to think they were truly sweeping everything before them. Lieutenant John Bucklyn's Battery E, 1st Rhode Island Light Artillery, and two guns from Captain James Thompson's Pennsylvania Light Batteries C and F fronted west between the Wheatfield Road and Trostle Lane. With Barksdale's three left regiments approaching them, the artillerymen were getting understandably skittish. Captain Randolph took the liberty of ordering the 114th Pennsylvania to advance and save Bucklyn's battery. The Pennsylvanians charged across the Emmitsburg Road while Bucklyn limbered up and moved to the rear. "My battery is torn and my brave boys have gone, never to return," lamented Bucklyn, who was wounded when case shot sliced through his shoulder during the withdrawal. "Curse the rebels." Bucklyn's battery had the unwelcome distinction of suffering the highest losses out of any Third Corps battery: thirty casualties out of a strength of 108 (27.8%) and forty horses lost.[4]

With Barksdale's Mississippians approaching, Captain Randolph ordered the 57th Pennsylvania, another of Graham's regiments, to also advance across

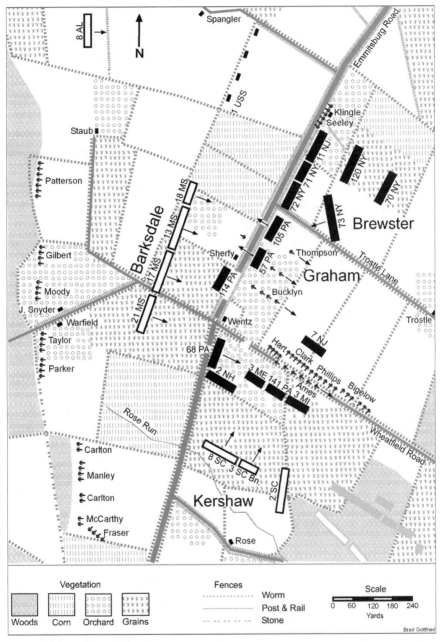

Barksdale's brigade attacks Graham's brigade at the Peach Orchard. The 68th
Pennsylvania withdraws and creates a gap in Graham's line. Third Corps
batteries at the Peach Orchard and along the Emmitsburg Road
begin to fall back under pressure.

the Emmitsburg Road. The 57th did as ordered, taking advantage of the cover afforded by the Sherfy buildings and trees. Once in position, the Pennsylvanians opened fire. A detail of fifteen men from the 57th entered Sherfy's house and fired at Barksdale from its west windows. Captain Edward Bowen remembered "the enemy advancing in force" and ordered the 114th's right wing to advance to the rear of the Sherfy house. Bowen attempted to form a line with the 57th. "I was but partially successful," he recalled, "as the enemy had already advanced so quickly and in such force as to gain the road." A sharp but brief firefight ensued between the Pennsylvania and Mississippi regiments. Barksdale's 13th and 17th Mississippi reached a rail fence about 100 yards away and poured "a murderous fire" against the 114th's flank, throwing "the left wing of the regiment on to the right in much confusion." Seeing their front blocked by the 57th, a third Pennsylvania regiment, the 105th Wild Cats, charged across the road and took position on the 57th's right. "Having gained this position," wrote the 105th's Colonel Calvin Craig, "the fire from the enemy being very severe, we immediately opened fire."[5]

While Barksdale's left faced temporary resistance near the Sherfy buildings, his right regiment, Colonel Humphreys' 21st Mississippi, continued moving toward the Peach Orchard and Colonel Andrew Tippin's waiting 68th Pennsylvania. Tippin's regiment fronted west along the Emmitsburg Road, with the 2nd New Hampshire in its left rear and fronted south. Since these two regiments formed a right angle, they were truly the salient in Sickles' line. Tippin ordered his men to hold their fire until the Mississippians stepped into killing range. When they did, "a destructive fire was opened, the enemy halting and dropping behind a fence." The 21st Mississippi paused at the fence and probably waited for the 17th Mississippi to close up on its left. An alarmed Tippin watched while what looked to him to be "re-enforcements" joined the approaching enemy. "[With] heavy masses of his infantry coming down on our right, I ordered my command to fall back to the position in the rear of the batteries, which was done in good order." Colonel Tippin's decision to fall back not only encouraged the 21st Mississippi (to Colonel Humphreys it appeared he had "broke[en] the first line") but exposed the right flank of the 2nd New Hampshire and the other regiments still holding the Peach Orchard. Tippin's withdrawal had inadvertently opened Sickles' salient. The approach of the strong line of battle (both the 21st and 17th Mississippi) had spooked the colonel; veterans later remembered that heat, fatigue, and the demoralizing impact of enemy artillery also played a factor in his decision.[6]

Whether or not Tippin's retreat was justified, the incredulous men of the 2nd New Hampshire knew their exposed right was now in serious trouble. According to the 2nd's regimental history, the 68th "withdrew up the slope *before the impact came* [emphasis added], and immediately after, the 3rd Maine also fell back." The 3rd Maine was on the 2nd New Hampshire's left, and although there were accusations that the Maine regiment prematurely evacuated, they had already had a particularly long day that began with helping Berdan's sharpshooters flush Cadmus Wilcox's rebels out of Pitzer's Woods. Colonel Moses Lakeman reported that he "saw a large force marching round to cut me off, and ordered my regiment to retire, and while doing so we received a most distressing fire, which threw my command into much confusion, and mixing them up with a portion of the First Brigade, which was also falling back." The 141st Pennsylvania was on the left of the recently departed 3rd Maine. Colonel Henry Madill complained that the regiments on both sides of him, along with the surrounding artillery, abandoned him, and "I found myself alone, with a small regiment of about 180 men." On Madill's left, the 3rd Michigan also found its flanks threatened and joined the mass exodus from the Peach Orchard. With Union infantry support crumbling, Captain James Thompson's artillery also pulled out. If Watson's Battery I, 5th U.S. Artillery ever actually reached the Peach Orchard, then they too probably also retreated at this time. [7]

Earlier, between 5:00 p.m. and 5:30 p.m., General Graham had made an appeal to Sickles for reinforcements. Henry Tremain bore the message to Sickles at his Trostle farm headquarters. (According to Tremain, this occurred prior to his leading Zook's brigade to the Wheatfield.) Sickles directed Tremain to find General Humphreys, with a request to detach one regiment. Things had been relatively quiet along Humphreys' Second Division front. Humphreys had already cannibalized much of Burling's Third Brigade to support Birney, but he apparently had little time to chew on this latest request. At that moment, Humphreys received word that the enemy was driving in his pickets and was advancing in two lines. Despite his pending problems, Humphreys dispatched one of Sickles' former Excelsior regiments, the 73rd New York, to Graham's support. "[A]t the same time" Humphreys ordered an aide to find General Hancock, "with the request that he would send a brigade, if possible, to my support." Around 5:30 p.m., Tremain personally led the 73rd into its new position, placing the regiment "in line of battle facing the highway," near the location of the present-day regimental monument. Unsure whether the regiment should stay there, Tremain rode to find Graham and ask for orders. Graham told Tremain to leave the regiment where it was. As Tremain departed for Sickles' headquarters, Graham shouted to his friend, "We're giving them hell!" Unfortunately for the men of the 73rd, recalled Tremain, "The regiment, it seems, was driven from this position shortly after I had posted it."[8]

The 73rd's Captain Frank Moran wrote that "we were hurried at double-quick to a point directly in rear of the [Sherfy] barn where the 114th Pennsylvania (Collis Zouaves) though fearfully exposed on that deadly crest, were bravely disputing the ground with the Mississippi Brigade." Barksdale's men "came swarming up the slope, yelling like devils." The 73rd apparently took an early volley, but for "a few impatient minutes, our regiments were unable to return a shot." The 114th was unfortunately still in its front west of the Emmitsburg Road, "about forty yards ahead of us, so that it was impossible to fire upon the enemy without shooting our friends in the back altogether, we stood in a shower of bullets from front and a merciless storm of bursting shells from Longstreet's batteries on our left."[9]

While Barksdale's right rolled into the Peach Orchard, his left regiments began driving Federal opposition out of the Sherfy buildings. A "murderous fire" threw the left flank of the 114th Pennsylvania into "much confusion." Captain Bowen noted that the enemy was "already on our left and in our rear" as the Federal regiments on his left had been "swept away." Concerned about being surrounded, Bowen poured one last volley into Barksdale's Mississippians before attempting to rally the 114th across the Emmitsburg Road, "but could not succeed in doing so." Barksdale was "advancing so rapidly and my men falling in such numbers as to prevent my succeeding in doing so. I succeeded, however, in rallying a number around the colors, and brought them off." Of the 114th's numerous wounded who had been left behind on the field, some sought refuge in Sherfy's barn, a decision that was later to have tragic consequences.[10]

The retreat of the 114th exposed the left flank of the 57th Pennsylvania. Sergeant E. C. Strouss, posted near one of Sherfy's large cherry trees on the north side of the house, "learned that the enemy had broken through the angle at the peach orchard, and were swarming up the road in our rear. It was evident that if we remained at the house, we would all be captured, so we were obliged to fall back." A squad from the 57th continued shooting at the Confederates from inside the Sherfy buildings, with some in "an old cellar" that might have been the foundation of an earlier structure. Determined to retrieve the men from inside the Sherfy buildings before the regiment retired, Captain Alanson Nelson and a handful of others raced into the house, where the noise was so deafening that he had to shout directly in the men's ears. "I ran up the stairs and from one room to the other, and started them to the rear as fast as I could get them to understand what I wanted of them. I then started downstairs to notify those in the lower part of the house." Nelson looked out a window toward "the left, where the enemy first broke through our lines" and was horrified to see the Confederates advancing through the yard less than fifty feet away. The Rebels ordered him to surrender, but he outran his would-be captors, jumped the fence surrounding Sherfy's yard, and raced toward the remainder of the regiment. Not everyone was so lucky or fleet-footed. Sergeant Strouss lamented that they could not make many of the men "understand the situation," and more than fifty fell into the hands of Barksdale's Mississippians.[11]

The last regiment of Graham's brigade fighting near the Sherfy house was the 105th Pennsylvania. Colonel Calvin Craig had positioned his Wild Cats on the right of the 57th Pennsylvania, but after only a "short time" he noticed the 114th and 57th regiments "cluster in groups behind the brick house and adjacent out-buildings." A "few moments later" both regiments "fell to the rear . . . leaving my left flank entirely unprotected. The enemy, taking advantage of this, advanced across the Emmitsburg road, in front of the house, and immediately opened fire upon our left flank. Seeing this, I ordered my regiment to retire slowly a short distance." Barksdale poured a "most murderous fire" into the 105th's flank and rear as the regiment retreated. Although men fell like "grass before the scythe," Colonel Craig later wrote that "the boys fought like demons. Their battle-cry was 'Pennsylvania'."[12]

With Graham's line collapsing, the burden of saving Sickles' front along the Emmitsburg Road fell to the 73rd New York. One advantage of the 114th's retreat was that the Excelsiors now had a clear front, and they hit Barksdale with at least one volley that caused the Southerners to fall "in scores among the dead and wounded Pennsylvanians." The Second Fire Zouaves even charged briefly to the west side of the Emmitsburg Road, but since this coincided with the collapse of Graham's Peach Orchard line on their left, the move exposed the 73rd's flank. Captain Moran claimed that "our thin line in the left could be seen melting away through the smoke and our wounded in hundreds went streaming back over the Emmitsburg road, and riderless horses went dashing among them in bewilderment and fright." Realizing that their left was flanked, the New Yorkers quickly fell back, ignoring the pleas of an officer who asked them to save some artillery. "The smoke grew thicker each minute and the sound of exploding shells was deafening. Officers and men were falling every minute and on every side." The men would "fire at the enemy, walk to the rear, loading as they went, take deliberate aim and fire again," remembered one Federal officer, forcing the Confederates to keep a "respectful distance." Captain Moran fell wounded during the retreat. He remained on the field with scores of other injured and killed in the unenviable position "between the fire of friends and foes, the field being open and affording no shelter whatever." Within a few moments, Barksdale's 13th Mississippi "came over me cheering and firing."[13]

Longstreet had stacked his attack against the Peach Orchard with depth, for Brigadier General William Wofford's Georgia brigade advanced behind Barksdale's Mississippians. The sight of Wofford's roughly 1,600 screaming Georgians following several hundred yards behind Barksdale did nothing to strengthen Graham's resolve. Leading Wofford's brigade was none other than General Longstreet himself. In his memoirs, Longstreet explained that his intent was to "urge the troops to their reserve power in the precious moments." Given the lack of coordination between Confederate brigades all afternoon, it is not surprising that there was little apparent cooperation between the attacks delivered by Barksdale and Wofford. Barksdale's three left regiments had wheeled to their left, and although they were not moving up the Emmitsburg Road, they were heading toward General Humphreys at a roughly northeast angle. Instead of moving directly behind the majority of Barksdale's brigade, however, Wofford continued east down the Wheatfield Road. This put his Georgians within supporting distance of only Barksdale's 21st Mississippi regiment. Wofford's (or Longstreet's) decision deprived the majority of Barksdale's brigade of the support they would need for their drive onto lower Cemetery Ridge.[14]

The collapse of the Peach Orchard and Emmitsburg Road line sent the Union artillery scurrying toward the rear. Many retreated past Sickles' headquarters at the Trostle farm, and the fleeing artillery and caissons began to block the entrance into Trostle's farm lane. As the 68th Pennsylvania fell back from the Emmitsburg Road, General Graham halted Colonel Tippin and "ordered me at once to engage the enemy coming down on our right flank, which was promptly done under his directions." The 68th, 2nd New Hampshire, and 3rd Maine temporarily formed a second line near the Wheatfield Road before being pushed back again. Colonel Madill's 141st Pennsylvania claimed to be the last of Graham's regiments to abandon the field. According to Madill, his regiment alone "held [the Confederates] in check for twenty minutes or upward," but when a single Confederate volley took down as many as thirty men, the 141st crumbled. Colonel Madill reported 151 casualties out of 209 engaged. As he trudged to the rear, he was met by Sickles who exclaimed, "Colonel! For God's sake can't you hold on?" A teary-eyed Madill

View of the Trostle farm, circa 1890. Sickles spent much of the battle headquartered under the large tree in the center of the photograph. He was wounded on the west side of the barn, just out of view on the left of the photograph. (See modern photo on page 203.)

Sue Boardman

could only stammer, "Where are my men?" His regiment had suffered the highest casualty rate in Graham's brigade.[15]

While Colonel Tippin and the 68th Pennsylvania were unsuccessfully trying to salvage their last position, General Graham fell wounded. Declining assistance, he directed Tippin to "take command and fight on." Tippin, whose withdrawal of his 68th Pennsylvania from the Emmitsburg Road had helped open the floodgates for Barksdale, was also unable to hold this final position as "the ranks [were] very much decimated by the fire of the enemy, who were pushing forward in heavy masses, I ordered the command to retire in order, which was done." According to John Bigelow, "it does not appear that he (Col. Tippin) took active charge of the brigade at this critical time. . . . None of the reports of the officers commanding the different regiments of the brigade, when they retired, nor of the batteries, make any reference to Col. Tippin, but each seems to have been left to their own resources. . . . There was no commanding officer to collect them and form a second line; nor use them to cover the long gap in the lines, between the Round Tops and the left of the 2nd Corps, which they were leaving open."[16]

While steamrolling through the Peach Orchard, Colonel Benjamin Humphreys' 21st Mississippi captured Charles Graham. General Graham was wounded twice while rallying his brigade, once by a shell fragment in the hip and again by a musket ball that tore through both shoulders. Exhausted by the loss of blood and having his horse shot out from under him, Graham turned command of the brigade over to Tippin and began to walk to the rear. "I supposed him [Graham] able to get to the rear," Tippin reported, "as, after dismounting, he walked with apparently little difficulty."[17]

According to Graham, his brigade had already broken as he was trudging to the rear. Another horse was brought to him, and lifted upon it, he "made an endeavor to collect the remnant of my troops." Graham spotted a regiment approaching, "which I took at first for one of my own but which on approaching within 150 yards of me I discovered to belong to the enemy. As soon as the discovery was made, I turned my horse, drove my spurs into the flanks, at the same time throwing myself forward on his neck to present as little surface as possible." The Confederates called on Graham to surrender, and flight being interpreted as a refusal, they fired at him. Graham's horse was hit by five bullets and, as John McNeily of the 21st Mississippi wrote, "pitched the General over his head, leaving him in a dazed state of mind." The stunned and bloodied Graham was pulled from beneath his horse, officially surrendered, and taken into captivity along with as many as 250 other Union soldiers. One captor recalled that Graham asked who led the charge against his brigade. "Our generals do not do that sort of thing," he scoffed. Graham had followed Sickles from their old days together in New York all the way to the Peach Orchard, and would now spend the next several months in captivity as his reward.[18]

It is unknown if Dan Sickles fully appreciated the full extent of the Peach Orchard collapse. Whether or not George Meade had been too inattentive to affairs on his left flank earlier that morning, responsibility for the advance to the Peach Orchard was Sickles' alone. Much of the Third Corps had fought gamely, thanks to timely support from others, but in the end, his position was crushed because of a combination of factors. The awkward salient is often credited as a primary contributor, but ultimately it fell because Sickles simply did not have enough manpower to plug the numerous holes that routinely formed in his line. Longstreet's assaulting infantry, later supported by Richard H. Anderson's division from A. P. Hill's Third Corps, charged across open fields under Federal artillery and a broiling sun, and fought with their usual spirit and skill. Still, Longstreet had repeatedly sent brigades into action without adequate support on their flanks. In the end, the battle did not reflect well upon the tactical

Modern view of the site of Sickles' wounding. The monument in the foreground marks the general's location at the time he was struck. This view looks east toward the Trostle barn. *Author*

judgment of either Sickles or Longstreet. Such thoughts might have occurred to Sickles during the long postwar years, but in the smoke, chaos, and fading daylight of July 2, Dan Sickles had many other things to worry about.

In stark contrast to General Hancock, who would spend much of this day and the next vigorously riding up and down his lines, Sickles spent the majority of the July 2 battle near his headquarters at the Trostle farm. Numerous accounts placed him there or nearby throughout the day, where he kept aides like Henry Tremain busy running dispatches. Several officers remembered seeing Sickles at headquarters, such as Captain George Winslow who recalled that after being driven out of the Wheatfield, "I reported to Gen. Sickles some two or three minutes before he was wounded and was directed to get my command together and await further orders. The General up to that time supposed that my guns were lost."[19]

Sometime around 6:00 p.m. the Trostle farm became, as Captain Randolph later told historian John Bachelder, "too hot for a corps headquarters; not so much from fire directed at that point as on account of high shots coming over the crest on both sides and centering there. Sickles concluded to move back to the rear of the [Trostle] houses . . . and was hit while on the way, by a round shot just below the knee." A Confederate shot had flown parallel to Sickles' horse and struck the general in the right leg without injuring his mount.[20] Sickles elaborated on his wounding during an 1882 return visit to the Trostle farm:

> A few moments before I was wounded I had, at the suggestion of my staff, passed around the farmhouse yonder. I had been standing upon the brow of the hill just above the barn, when several of my staff insisted that I had better put myself out of range of a heavy fire then concentrated upon us. 'If you will show me a spot on this field where the bullets are not falling thick, I would like to see it,' I replied. A few moments afterwards, I rode around through the low ground below the house and up to this knoll. I had hardly reached it when the shot struck me.[21]

Riding from the Trostle house and farm lane to the knoll where Sickles was wounded, it seems unlikely that Sickles or his staff would have considered the knoll a safe haven from enemy fire. The elevated ridge near the barn, where Sickles was struck, would have offered Sickles a considerably better view of his line than a position in the farm lane, but also would have increased his exposure to Confederate fire. Sickles claimed that he was barely aware of what had transpired:

> I never knew I was hit. I was riding the lines and was tremendously interested in the terrific fighting which was going on along my front. Suddenly I was conscious of dampness along the lower part of my right leg, and I ran my hand down the leg of my high-top boots and pulling it out I was surprised to see it dripping with blood. Soon I noticed the leg would not perform its usual functions. I lifted it carefully over my horse's neck and slid to the ground. Then I was conscious of approaching weakness, and the last thing I remembered was designating the surgeons of my staff who should examine the wound and treat it. They found that the knee had been smashed, probably by a piece of shell, and that the leg had been broken above and also below the knee; but while all this damage had been done I had not been unhorsed, and never knew exactly when the hurt was received.[22]

Confederate artillery shells were continuing to fall as Sickles dismounted. "By this time I was losing blood rapidly. Hurriedly calling to a trooper nearby, I ordered him to bring me a strap from his saddle, and with his aid I bound the leg close up to the body, stationed a guard of twenty men about me and directed that no surgeon be allowed to disturb me until the arrival of Dr. Calhoun." Randolph admitted, "Most of the staff were absent, I do not recollect anyone but myself and a couple of orderlies being with him at the time. We bound his leg first with handkerchiefs and finally with a strap from a saddle, and sent for surgeons and ambulance." The devoted Henry Tremain shortly returned from delivering Zook's brigade to the Wheatfield and wrote, "not an officer was near him; nor was there, as far as I ever could ascertain, when the ball hit him."[23]

Tremain found Sickles "reclining with apparent suffering against the wall of the barn, while a soldier was engaged under the general's direction in buckling a saddle strap, which had been tightly wound around his leg above the knee—thus forming an improvised tourniquet." Sickles ordered in a clear voice, "tell General Birney he must take command." Fearing for the worst, Tremain watched as Sickles "produced the tiniest flask ever carried by a soldier, and wet his lips with its brandy." General Birney reported that it was 6:00 p.m. when he arrived on the scene and took command at Sickles' request. Birney apparently didn't linger for long as he "immediately" went to Humphreys' front.[24] Later histories emphasized Sickles' calm and cool demeanor while he was awaiting his ambulance, but Captain Randolph (who was a Sickles supporter) remembered the scene differently:

> Meanwhile our line had been broken about the Peach Orchard and our infantry and artillery came pouring by in rapid retreat. Sickles' only thought seemed to be fear of being taken prisoner. He repeatedly urged us not to allow him to be taken. It was a very long time (seemingly) before the ambulance and surgeon arrived, but they came in time to save him from the danger he feared most.[25]

"I had no sooner been wounded then the conflict became more terrific than ever," Sickles recalled. About this time, or shortly after, the Third Corps began falling back from the Peach Orchard "toward the spot where I lay. In a moment I was removed from the ground to the field hospital." An ambulance, probably the one that had earlier been summoned by Randolph, finally appeared. The Trostle farm became increasingly dangerous and Tremain thought the ambulance "would be shattered by shot and shell before the patient could be placed in it." Tremain wrote to his family on July 10, "After we had succeeded with much difficulty in getting an ambulance and him into it, I thought he was dying. I was riding with him alone, holding his mangled leg, which was tightly bound by a strap." While still in the ambulance, Tremain was joined by Father Joseph O' Hagan, chaplain of the 74th New York. O'Hagan "also thought the general dying and we administered stimulants by the wholesale. Doubtless this was all that kept him alive." As far as Tremain was concerned, "the end had come."[26]

The wounding of Dan Sickles is one of the most well known aspects of his day at Gettysburg. Legend tells us that in one last act of bravado, Sickles was escorted from the field while theatrically chomping on a cigar and inspiring his men to hold their ground. The most widely read Sickles biography, W. A. Swanberg's *Sickles the Incredible* (1956), is both representative of this image and significantly responsible for perpetuating it. Swanberg told his readers that Sickles "seemed only moderately upset." After coolly directing the placement of an improvised tourniquet, "Sickles was not one to allow this moment to pass without making full use of its dramatic value. Being informed that a rumor had gone around that he was mortally wounded, he requested a stretcher-bearer to remove a cigar from [his inside pocket] and light it for him. He was carried away with the Havan projecting dauntily from his mouth." The moment has become a permanent part of the July 2 imagery. Tellingly, neither Tremain, Randolph, nor even Sickles himself painted such a heroic moment. This raises the question: is the legend accurate? [27]

Contemporary accounts are mixed on the question. Correspondent Whitelaw Reid reported that he passed Sickles along the Baltimore Pike, not on July 2, but on the morning of July 3: "On a stretcher, borne by a couple of stout privates, lay General Sickles—but yesterday leading his corps with all the enthusiasm and dash for which he has been distinguished—today with his right leg amputated and lying there, grim and stoical, with his cap pulled over his eyes, his hands calmly folded across his breast, and a cigar in his mouth!" Reid's account was widely reprinted in various forms during the late 1800s, but sometimes with variations that did not always clarify that his sighting occurred on July 3. Similarly, and perhaps as a result, a reporter for the May 28, 1899, edition of the Philadelphia *Times* "was told on the battlefield . . . that when he was carried from the field he lay on his stretcher smoking a cigar as serenely as if he was still unhurt."[28]

Surgeon Thomas Sim didn't mention cigar-theatrics when he talked to the Washington papers on July 7, but did assure them that Sickles had dismounted from his horse "with utmost coolness." Private John Haley was fighting with his 17th Maine in the Wheatfield. Somewhere between the Trostle barn and the amputating table, Private Haley claimed a glimpse of Sickles. "Our last sight of him in the field is one we shall long remember," wrote the private. "He was sitting in an ambulance smoking and holding his shattered limb and appeared as cool as though nothing had happened. A few minutes later his leg was amputated at or near the knee." Lieutenant Colonel William E. Doster, commander of the 4th Pennsylvania cavalry, wrote in 1915 that while riding from Meade's headquarters, he "noticed Sickles on a stretcher, smoking a cigar. They said his leg had been shot off in the last charge."[29]

Rossiter Johnson's *Campfire and Battlefield* was a popular narrative history of the war published in 1894. Concerning Sickles' wound at Gettysburg, Johnson quoted an observer from Regis de Trobriand's command (possibly staff officer Captain Benjamin Piatt): "I was within a few feet of General Sickles when he received the wound by which he lost his leg." In this version, far from being calmly unaffected, Sickles half-fell to the ground exclaiming excitedly, "'Quick, quick! Get something and tie it up before I bleed to death!' These were his exact words, and I shall never forget the scene as long as I live, for we all loved General Sickles." According to the officer, Sickles was carried to the Trostle house, "coolly smoking a cigar, quietly remarking to a Catholic priest. . . . 'Man proposes and God disposes.' His leg was amputated within less than half an hour after receiving the wound."[30]

What would become one of the most influential primary accounts of Sickles' wounding originated from the pen of Private William H. Bullard, a drummer in the 70th New York. In 1897, Bullard wrote Sickles a letter documenting his memories. The letter resulted from a reunion in Buffalo, New York, where Bullard had apparently promised Sickles to "state as near as I remember my personal experience" concerning the wounding.[31]

During the battle, Bullard was detached along with the other musicians to act as a stretcher-bearer. After carrying several wounded off the field, Bullard was returning to the front "when I noticed a commotion near Gen. Sickles and saw him taken from his horse. I hastened to him thinking I could be of service in some way, the aides on his staff gave way for me." Carrying silk cords and a canteen "filled with stimulants," Bullard examined the wound and bound the leg to stop the blood loss. "I shall never forget how white the Gen. was. I gave him something from my canteen which seemed to revive him. I then placed him on the stretcher and was about to start for the ambulances which were placed behind large rocks." According to Bullard, Sickles asked before they started away, "Won't you be kind enough to light a cigar for me?" Bullard took a small cigar from an inside case in Sickles' pocket, bit the end off, lit the cigar, and placed it in Sickles' mouth. Bullard knew they needed to get Sickles to a surgeon quickly. "I started with him along the line we had to go quite a distance to get to the ambulances."[32] The Third Corps line was breaking, continued Bullard,

> and as we were hastening along the lines the men and officers noticed we had Gen Sickles and the word passed along the line that he was mortally wounded. General Sickles heard them and he raised himself up and said 'No No not so bad as that. I am all right and will be with you in a short time' and in his old Clarion voice the boys knew so well, said 'you must hold your position and win this battle, don't waver, stand firm and you will surely win' or something to that effect.[33]

The sight of their wounded general "seemed to put new life in the men," recalled Bullard, who helped place Dan into the ambulance and was ready to return to the field when Sickles "said it was his wish that I should go with him which I did." Bullard recounted nothing more of the ambulance ride until they "took him to old Penna. Barn or stone barn and Dr. Ash [sic] I think and others amputated his leg."[34]

Another account, which would have a similarly large influence on Sickles' depiction, was the 1902 regimental history of the Excelsiors' 72nd New York: "As he was placed on a stretcher the General was informed that his men thought he was mortally wounded. To correct this report, and cheer up the men, he requested the Drum Major of the First Regiment, who had charge of the brigade stretcher bearers, to take a cigar case from an inside pocket, and light a cigar for him. This having been done, the General was carried along the line, coolly smoking, to a road leading to the rear."[35]

Of all the contemporary accounts, only Tremain and Randolph actually appear to have been on the scene for any length of time. There is no reason to doubt Bullard's assertion that he was also there. Both Tremain and Bullard's recollections were written decades later, however, although Tremain claimed to be relying heavily on correspondence written immediately after the battle. Tremain's Sickles is badly wounded, pale, heavily stimulated, and potentially dying. There is no dramatic encouragement of his men. Perhaps it did indeed occur. But if it did, it was not impressive enough for Tremain to mention. There is also an inconsistency between Tremain and Bullard in that Tremain specifically states that he was riding alone with Sickles until they were joined by O'Hagan.[36]

With this rather inconsistent historical record, twentieth century historians transformed Sickles' wounding into a Gettysburg myth. Sickles' biographers have led the charge, beginning with Edgcumb Pinchon's *Dan Sickles: Hero of Gettysburg and 'Yankee King of Spain'* (1945). "Fearing the effect the news might have upon his men, his orderlies rushed him to the rear. There, stoically smoking a cigar while he waited for the surgeon, he demanded to be kept informed of every development on the battle front." Pinchon's version is relatively understated (which is surprising given the overall tone of his biography), but one wonders if the "stoicism" noted by many was actually a stupor brought on by shock, exhaustion, blood loss, and "stimulants" being pumped into him "by the wholesale."[37]

As noted previously, a decade later Sickles' most widely read biography (Swanberg's *Sickles the Incredible*) took the theme a step further. Swanberg's biography is important in that it has become a standard reference in any study of Dan Sickles. Swanberg's Sickles was "only moderately upset," "cool," and was "carried away with the Havan projecting dauntily from his mouth." Swanberg's sources include Rossiter Johnson's *Campfire and Battlefield*, Tremain's memoirs, William Doster's account, and the 72nd New York regimental history. Swanberg's version was clearly influenced by the 72nd New York's 1902 history, of which Swanberg's description is nearly an abbreviated copy. None of Swanberg's other sources suggested that his cigar was an intentional attempt to rally the troops. Swanberg also relegated to his chapter notes a letter from Private Felix Brannigan of the 73rd New York that called Sickles staff officer Orson Hart "more collected than his superior."[38]

No major Sickles biography appeared for decades after Swanberg, and full-scale treatments of the battle, with Sickles only one among a cast of thousands, generally treated the incident more modestly. Among the major works, Edward Stackpole's *They Met at Gettysburg* (1956) said nothing, and Glenn Tucker's *High Tide at Gettysburg* (1958) touched on the wounding only briefly, recounting how a small detail carried Sickles into the Trostle farmhouse. Edwin Coddington's *The Gettysburg Campaign* (1968) offered no details in his main text, but Coddington had access to John Bachelder's papers and cited George Randolph's rediscovered letter to Bachelder as his primary source. Sickles assumed a more prominent role in Harry Pfanz's *Gettysburg: The Second Day* (1987): "Sickles took it [the cigar] and puffed away. Sickles' condition soon attracted attention. In order to present a brave and calming front, Sickles raised himself on the stretcher so that passers-by could see that he was alive if not well and asked them to stand firm." Pfanz's source was William Bullard's 1897 letter to Sickles.[39]

Pfanz's classic work subsequently became a definitive reference in any post-1987 study on Gettysburg's second day. As a result, William Bullard's letter inadvertently became an authoritative account of Sickles' wounding. A case in point occurs in *I Follow the Course, Come What May*, a 1998 Sickles biography by Jeanne Knoop. "To stop any rumor of his death, which would demoralize his troops," wrote Knoop, "prior to the ambulance's arrival, he kept smoking the cigar and waving to his men." Knoop's source was Pfanz's *Gettysburg: The Second Day*.[40]

In Noah Andre Trudeau's *Gettysburg: A Testing of Courage* (2002), the primary elements of Swanberg and Pfanz's versions were retained. Sickles was transformed from Swanberg's "daunty" to "jaunty." "Before the ambulance appeared to transport him to the Third Corps field hospital, the wounded Sickles had himself propped up with cigar in mouth, jauntily urging the soldiers who passed him to stand firm." In 2003, Stephen Sears' *Gettysburg* was nearly identical: "Game to the end, Sickles puffed jauntily on a cigar as he was carried away."[41]

In 2002, novelist Thomas Keneally graphically described the wounding scene in his Sickles biography, *American Scoundrel*:

Dan was still astride his horse in the Trostle farmyard, an unlit cigar in his mouth, maintaining without apparent effort a deliberate but tautly aware frame of mind . . . a twelve-pound cannonball that had failed to explode came visibly lolloping, far too fast to be avoided by Dan and his mounted staff . . . and shattered and tore to pulp Dan's right leg in its blue fabric . . . Dan was conscious of the damage, yet was not overwhelmed with pain and did not lose consciousness. Already in a heightened, feverish state from the battle he was fighting, perhaps he found it all the easier to marshal the chemicals appropriate to trauma. A captain of the 70th New York, standing nearby, nonetheless feared that the men still fighting on the Third Corps line might be affected if too many of them heard the rumor that their general had been—as it seemed—mortally wounded. The captain formed a detail of a sergeant and six soldiers, who covered Dan with a blanket and carried him to the shade of the Trostle farmhouse. This was, above all, in the hour of his wound, a moment of which the right sort of general could make a myth of his easy gallantry, and Dan managed it, his cigar still stuck between his lips by grimace or by stubbornness.

When he arrived by the wall of the house, he appeared merely moderately upset and told one of the men to buckle a saddle strap tightly over the upper thigh as a tourniquet. . . . A stretcher arrived, Dan had an NCO light his cigar, and that was how he was carried away, cap over his eyes, cigar in mouth, hands folded on chest.[42]

Tremain and Randolph's accounts appear to be the primary sources for Trudeau's version, while Keneally also relied heavily on Tremain. Yet neither Tremain nor Randolph indicated a "jaunty" Sickles; they portrayed a badly wounded and heavily stimulated Sickles who was most worried about being taken prisoner. But as Gettysburg literature entered the twenty-first century, the image of a cigar-chomping Sickles calmly being carried off the field had fully overshadowed primary accounts. This legend may not have been invented by modern historians (we have the likes of Whitelaw Reid, William Bullard, and the 72nd New York regimental historian to thank for that), but it has been significantly perpetuated by historians and biographers who have uncritically accepted the dramatic version as being preferable to more mundane reality.[43]

In the end, an assessment of the "cigar incident" must consider at least one factor. If it occurred, then Sickles' own initial accounts fail to mention it. His battlefield performance became the subject of much scrutiny, and certainly such a self-promoter would have brought attention to the fact that he took time, while badly wounded, to rally and encourage his men. "I was conscious of approaching weakness, and the last thing I remembered was designating the surgeons of my staff who should examine the wound and treat it," Sickles admitted in one interview. Given the shock and blood loss, Sickles may not have even remembered how he acted as he was being carried off the field. In his 1882 on-site interview, before a large crowd and a newspaper reporter, a veteran actually pushed his way through the crowd and gushed, "I want to shake by the hand the man who saved the second day's fight at Gettysburg." Wouldn't such a veteran have wanted to hear how Sickles used his cigar and that moment to encourage and steady his men? Only in later years, after he had time to reconsider things and speak with veterans such as Bullard, did he tell how he "placed a lighted cigar in my mouth and had myself carried down the battle line in order to talk to and encourage my men. They stood firm as a rock, and Longstreet's charge failed."[44]

There is nothing historically remarkable about whether or not Sickles relaxed with a cigar while being led to the field hospital. There are enough accounts to accept that a heavily sedated Sickles smoked a cigar or two before and after his amputation. But besides being a popular Gettysburg image, it also became the heart of his 1897 Medal of Honor citation: that he continued to "encourage his troops after being himself severely wounded," and too many historians have repeated the notion as unchallenged fact. The primary accounts of supporters such as Tremain, Randolph, and Sickles himself question whether he was in any condition to be making "a myth of his easy gallantry." Sickles' own personal history—the Barton Key murder comes immediately to mind—does not suggest that he was one to remain cool under severe trauma. Shock and heavy sedation probably passed for "stoicism" in the heat of battle. Whether he was "stoic," "jaunty," or just heavily sedated, Sickles' ambulance left the field amid the shower of Confederate shot and shell.[45]

Chapter 12

Let Me Die on the Field

Thanks to the collapse of Sickles' front in the Peach Orchard, Wofford's brigade moved down the Wheatfield Road. His thrust flanked Caldwell's right and combined with Kershaw's attack to drive Caldwell's division out of the Wheatfield. In front of Wofford, Colonel Benjamin Humphreys' 21st Mississippi (alone on the far right of Barksdale's line) targeted Phillips and Bigelow's Wheatfield Road batteries. Colonel McGilvery ordered Phillips and then Bigelow to fall back toward the Trostle farm, but as the 21st pursued Bigelow it became further isolated from the remainder of Barksdale's brigade.[1]

While Barksdale's right regiment wiped Federal artillery out of the Wheatfield Road, his three left regiments (the 13th, 17th, and 18th Mississippi) wheeled left and swung toward the last remnants of Graham's brigade and Andrew Humphreys' division. Fortunately for Barksdale, he received support on his own left from Brigadier General Cadmus Wilcox's brigade, part of Richard H. Anderson's division of A.P. Hill's Third Corps. Barksdale and Wilcox provided one of the afternoon's few examples where Confederate infantry managed to successfully hit the Third Corps line simultaneously from two sides. Since Longstreet had failed to significantly drive in the Federal left, Wilcox launched a frontal attack against Humphreys' position. Although this is not what the Confederate leadership had originally hoped for, Wilcox prevented Humphreys from sending more reinforcements toward the collapsing Peach Orchard position. The upshot was that once Barksdale finished disposing of Graham's brigade, his men turned north and together with Wilcox's regiments combined to hit Humphreys on both his left and front.[2]

A short time after detaching the 73rd New York to Graham's support, Humphreys received orders from Birney: "General Sickles having been dangerously wounded and carried from the field." Birney wanted Humphreys to refuse his left, "form a line oblique to and in rear of the one I [Humphreys] then held." Humphreys was informed that Birney would connect with him and "complete the line to the Round Top ridge." The problem, as Humphreys later elaborated—he called Birney's order "bosh"—was that he was unable to comply because Graham and the rest of Birney's troops "passed to the rear and did not wait to swing back with my div." Humphreys did not "see anything more of them that evening." Graham's collapse, coupled with Barksdale's approach, threatened to flank Humphreys' left.[3]

Lt. Francis Seeley, who was wounded while superintending his guns, recalled that "the ground was completely scoured by the projectiles from the Confederate Arty.; shells were screaming through the air and bursting in every direction!" Humphreys was under attack from portions of Wilcox's brigade, as well as General Edward A. Perry's Florida brigade, commanded by Colonel David Lang. The Floridians were moving eastward toward the Emmitsburg Road on Wilcox's left. Humphreys' problems were compounded by the fact that Sickles and Birney had earlier cannibalized Burling's brigade and the 73rd New York away from him. This left Humphreys with perhaps 3,200 effectives. Both his flanks were in the air, and "being the only troops on the field, the enemy's whole attention was directed to my division, which was forced back slowly, firing as they receded." Unfortunately, the official reports penned by the participants are woefully brief on the subject. (Historian Harry Pfanz speculated that Sickles' Excelsiors wrote little because they fought poorly.)[4]

The Excelsiors' final positions are unclear. They probably formed a line fronting south behind the Klingle house, perpendicular to the Emmitsburg Road. Barksdale's three left regiments charged this line, and the 71st and 72nd New York seem to have fled without much of a fight. Putting as good a face on the situation as possible, brigade commander Colonel William Brewster admitted "the enemy advanced upon us in great force, pouring into us a most terrific fire of artillery and musketry, both upon our front and left flank." Brewster's men "returned it with great effect, and for some time held the enemy in check," but without support and "exposed to an enfilading fire" they were "obliged to fall back . . . with a terrible loss of both officers and men." A captain on General Humphreys' staff, however, admitted the 71st and 72nd were routed, in part because Graham's men were fleeing through their lines and encouraging the spread of panic. Another staff officer blamed Birney for

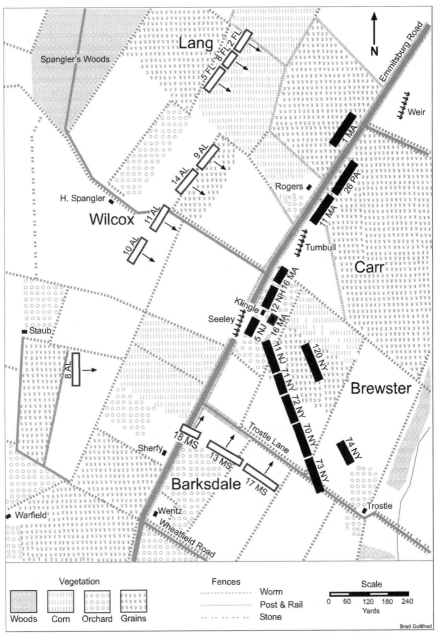

After Graham's brigade retreats, Humphreys' division is left alone to defend
against the attacking brigades of Barksdale, Wilcox, and Lang. Pressed
heavily from the front and on his left, Humphreys is forced to
retreat from the Emmitsburg Road position.

ordering some on Humphreys' left to retreat. As was typical in such cases, the battlefield noise, smoke, and general chaos allowed participants to blame everyone else for their own collapse. As Barksdale's left drove toward the Trostle farm lane, it was temporarily stalled by firing from the 120th New York, which probably gave the Excelsiors' best performance, until it too was overwhelmed on its front and right. The friction of war was beginning to tell on Barksdale's regiments. The distance they had traveled, stout Federal resistance, and the hot July sun all combined to wear down the Mississippi formations. One Mississippi soldier recalled that the men were "faint from exhaustion." In a Jackson-esque performance, Barksdale refused to heed the pleas of his colonels to stop and reform the men. "No! Crowd them—we have them on the run." The combined onslaught from Barksdale, Wilcox, and Lang's brigades finally pried Humphreys' men away from the Emmitsburg Road. Their withdrawal officially ended the Third Corps' occupation of Sickles' advanced line.[5]

As his men were withdrawing, Humphreys finally received orders from Birney to withdraw "to the Round Top ridge." Falling back across open ground, Humphreys and his staff prevented his retreat from turning into an utter rout. "Twenty times did I bring my men to a halt & face about" to return fire on the Confederates, "forcing the men to do it," he wrote. Veterans later debated whether the retreat was a total panic or an orderly withdrawal. Second Corps regiments in Humphreys' right rear remembered fleeing Excelsiors crying out, "Run boys, we're whipped, the day is lost." Nearly everyone agreed that Humphreys was one of the day's great heroes, a man who lived up to the image of the professional who fought for every inch of ground when the amateurs collapsed. One soldier called Humphreys "another man we did not like before the battle, but whom after the battle we were ready to swear by, for he showed himself to be a hero and a leader."[6]

Hero or not, Humphreys was not pleased with the circumstances that conspired to thin his lines before the final combined Confederate attack. "[T]hey had taken away my reserve brigade to support others, and a large part of my second line I had to bring to my front line and part of it went to others. The troops that were to support me were sent to others . . . I have lost very heavily." When he finally reached Cemetery Ridge, Humphreys called his division nothing more than "the fragments of many shattered regiments." Humphreys suffered approximately 2,092 casualties out of 4,924 engaged (42.5%), the third highest numeric total in the Federal army. Birney's division had the fourth highest numeric total (2,011). The heavy losses in both divisions served as testimonials to the inherent weakness of Sickles' advanced position.[7]

After allowing for the passage of Wofford's brigade and believing (or at least so he later wrote) "that the war was nearly over," artillerist Porter Alexander limbered six batteries and "charged in line across the plain and went into action again at the position the enemy had deserted." The gunner could not recall a "more inspiriting moment during the war than that of the charge of these six batteries. An artillerist's heaven is to follow the routed enemy, after a tough resistance, and throw shells and canister into his disorganized and fleeing masses. . . . Now we would have our revenge, and make them sorry they had staid so long." When he reached the Peach Orchard, Alexander quickly became disappointed by what he saw. "We had only a moderately good time with Sickles' retreating corps after all. They fell back upon fresh troops in what seemed a strong position extending along the ridge north of Round Top…Our infantry lines had become disjointed in the advance, and the fighting became a number of isolated combats between brigades." Despite his disappointment, Alexander set up his batteries in the orchard, "firing at everything in sight, and a sort of pell-mell fighting lasted until darkness covered the field and the fuses of the flying shells looked like little meteors in the air."[8]

Historian John Imhof correctly observed that with the occupation of the Peach Orchard by Confederate artillery, "General Sickles' prophecy had been fulfilled." One of Sickles' primary reasons for abandoning Meade's Cemetery Ridge position was his fear that Confederate artillery would occupy the Emmitsburg Road ridge and pummel the Union line into submission. Sickles was right on the first count: Confederate leadership *did* assume that this location would serve as a platform to continue the attack. Sickles' advanced line had, as Alexander noted from his vantage point, successfully caused Longstreet's attacking infantry to suffer heavy casualties and become "disjointed" before ever reaching the heart of Cemetery Ridge. However, events ultimately proved Sickles wrong (along with Lee, Longstreet, and Alexander) when he assumed that the Rebel artillery could *successfully* utilize the Peach Orchard to defeat Meade's army. Meade's own "prophecy" was also proven true: the Peach Orchard was indeed neutral ground, and neither side would use it to advantage.[9]

While Wilcox, Perry, and Barksdale were driving back Humphreys' division from the Emmitsburg Road line, Captain John Bigelow's 9th Massachusetts Battery successfully retreated from the Wheatfield Road line to the Trostle house. The wounded Sickles had already been removed and Third Corps headquarters was now abandoned. For Bigelow, "no friendly supports, of any kind, were in sight; but Johnnie Rebs in great numbers. Bullets were coming into our midst from many directions and a Confederate battery added to our difficulties." The battery was preparing to make a rush "for high ground in the rear" when Colonel Freeman McGilvery arrived with new orders. Not only had Sickles' placement of the Third Corps opened a gap on Cemetery Ridge between the left of Hancock's Second Corps and Little Round Top, but this gap had been widened when Caldwell's division marched to Sickles' support in the Wheatfield. To make matters worse, the retreating Third Corps troops were unable to rally and plug this hole. If something was not done quickly, Barksdale and Wilcox could reach this gap and, possibly, turn Meade's left on Cemetery Ridge. "The crisis of the engagement had now arrived. I gave Captain Bigelow orders to hold his position as long as possible at all hazards, in order to give me time to form a new line of artillery," wrote McGilvery. A "surprised and disappointed" Bigelow ordered his four remaining pieces to fire double canister at the pursuing Confederates, who soon appeared over the crest in their front. Bigelow held off Barksdale's 21st Mississippi and some of Kershaw's South Carolina skirmishers long enough for Colonel McGilvery to form a new artillery line approximately 400 yards in the rear.[10]

Colonel McGilvery formed his new artillery line near the banks of Plum Run "covering the opening which led into the Gettysburg and Taneytown road." This location could have sustained the Third Corps artillery if Sickles had remained in his original position, since McGilvery would manage to successfully use it on both the second and the third days. According to McGilvery's report, his artillery line included Watson's battery, three of Phillips' guns, two guns from Thompson's battery, "a volunteer battery which I have never been able to learn the name of," and Dow's battery. "The rebel batteries had by this time moved up to the Peach Orchard and opened a very heavy fire on us," wrote Phillips. Lieutenant Dow was approaching the front when he met "an ambulance with General Sickles in it, badly wounded." McGilvery told Dow "he [McGilvery] had charge of the artillery of the Third Corps." Dusk was approaching and there was still considerable confusion within the Union lines. Federal troops were racing down the Taneytown Road in McGilvery's rear, while Second Corps reinforcements were arriving on the right. Barksdale's 21st Mississippi pushed through the 9th Massachusetts' now abandoned position. Spotting Watson's battery unlimbering on the left of McGilvery's line, Colonel Humphreys' Mississippians "charged and captured these guns before they fired."[11]

McGilvery's artillery line alone was unlikely to stop Barksdale, Wilcox, and Perry's brigades from reaching Cemetery Ridge. Fortunately for the Union cause, however, the Confederates were approaching General Hancock's

Second Corps front, and it was Hancock who vigorously corrected many of Sickles' mistakes. Hancock wrote in his official report that "about this time" Meade "informed me that General Sickles had been wounded, and directed me to assume command of the Third Corps in addition to that of my own." Hancock "had just before received an order from General Meade to send a brigade to the assistance of General Birney" and Hancock responded by sending in Colonel George Willard's brigade. (Willard's division commander General Alexander Hays sent Willard in with orders to "knock the hell out of the rebs.") Barksdale had successfully helped crush Sickles' line, but he had pushed his men beyond physical endurance and ready support. Willard's New Yorkers slammed into Barksdale's increasingly ragged formations in the low scrub and bushes lining Plum Run, stopping Barksdale just short of Cemetery Ridge. The Southern commander was mortally wounded, later removed to a Union field hospital, and died during the pre-dawn hours of July 3. Colonel Willard was also killed after being struck in the face by an artillery fragment. One of his regiments, the 39th New York, drove ahead and recaptured Watson's battery. Without support, Colonel Humphreys grudgingly ordered his 21st Mississippi to retreat toward the Peach Orchard.[12]

Hancock and staff had raced south along Cemetery Ridge in rear of Willard's brigade, and just before putting them in action, Hancock "encountered General Birney, who informed me that his troops had all been driven to the rear, and had left the position to which I was moving. General Birney proceeded to the rear to collect his command." Hancock later told historian John Bachelder that Birney informed Hancock that the Third Corps "had gone to pieces and fallen to the rear. This was on the spot where I put in Willard's brigade." Hancock could see the fleeing Third Corps soldiers for himself, but had little time to dwell on it since enemy fire was "shortly commencing to fall among us." Hancock admitted that since the Third Corps was "all gone as a force [he] never really exercised any command over any part of the 3d corps in action, save the fragments of General Humphreys' command." The majority of the corps was "scattered, and could not be collected then. That was the end of it as a corps for that day."[13]

Sickles and most of his men were out of the fight, but the ramifications of his movement forward to the Emmitsburg Road were not limited to Meade's left flank. As Hancock continued to close the gaps, he requested more reinforcements. Meade responded by pulling the majority of the Twelfth Corps off Culp's Hill on the far Union right, and by virtue of his interior lines, sent it to reinforce Cemetery Ridge. Corps commander Henry Slocum received the order to send his First Division, temporarily commanded by Brigadier General Thomas Ruger, and two brigades of Brigadier General John Geary's Second Division. Ruger's division arrived on Cemetery Ridge, but Geary's two intended brigades accidentally marched too far south on the Baltimore Pike and out of the fight. Ruger's men (mainly Henry Lockwood's brigade) helped stabilize Hancock and McGilvery's lines, but Ruger's other two brigades largely stood idle. With hindsight, we know that Meade pulled more troops than necessary from Culp's Hill because Longstreet's attacks were eventually repulsed without any help from Geary and most of Ruger's division. The thinning of the Union right left only one Union brigade under General George S. Greene on Culp's Hill. This nearly proved fatal for Meade and the Army of the Potomac later that evening when Richard Ewell launched a heavy infantry attack against the rocky hill. Ironically, Meade had begun the morning focused on his right flank, and by the end of the day he nearly jeopardized his right by sending more troops than necessary to protect gaps on his far left. The after-effects of Sickles' decision were still being felt on Culp's Hill on July 3, as both sides battled for control of the strategic position.[14]

After putting Willard into action, General Hancock moved north on Cemetery Ridge and spotted Wilcox's brigade, advancing on Barksdale's left, making its way toward Cemetery Ridge. The nearest regiment available to him was another in Hancock's own Second Corps, the 1st Minnesota. Colonel William Colvill's regiment had been supporting Evan Thomas' Battery C, 4th Artillery, which was harassing Wilcox's advance. According to Colvill, the 1st Minnesota "arrived at this position just about the time Sickles' troops, broken and disorganized, passed the ridge in retreat, and many of them, to the number of thousands passed between our files." Hancock had earlier ordered Colvill to "stop and put them [Third Corps fugitives] in line; but found it impossible, and demoralizing to my own regiment to do so." Wilcox's Alabama troops arrived almost immediately behind Sickles' fleeing men, but Hancock famously ordered Colvill to "Advance Colonel, and take those colors." The 1st Minnesota charged at the double-quick down the slope into Wilcox's line. The brave sacrifice staggered the Confederate attack, bringing it to a halt. The cost to the Minnesotans, however, was 215 in killed, wounded, and missing.[15]

By this time Wilcox was well beyond any Confederate support, and from the vantage point of the exhausted Alabamians, Cemetery Ridge appeared as a "stronghold of the enemy." Wilcox ordered a withdrawal to "their original position in line;" Lang's Floridians on Wilcox's left followed suit. On Lang's left, another of R. H. Anderson's brigades under Brigadier General Ambrose R.

Wright continued advancing and smashed into the center of Cemetery Ridge in the proximity of the "Copse of Trees" that would come to symbolize "Pickett's Charge" on the following day. Alone and unsupported, Wright was repulsed by more of Hancock's troops, a representative conclusion of how Lee's offensive had gone awry. Having failed to drive the Federal left, Confederate attacks had deteriorated into a series of uncoordinated frontal assaults.[16]

General Meade, meanwhile, had passed an order to Major General John Newton's First Corps (Newton having replaced John Reynolds) to bring two divisions forward. Momentarily alone on Cemetery Ridge with only a few members of his staff, Meade spotted a line of Rebels (probably Wright's Georgians or remnants of Lang's Floridians) heading straight for him. Meade "straightened himself in his stirrups" and braced for impact. In contrast to General Lee's detached command style, Meade was right in the thick of the action. The tension was quickly broken when Newton's two divisions arrived. According to Captain Meade, his father advanced with the First Corps skirmish line, offering the rather unspectacular command, "Come on, gentlemen." In the best spirit of the old army, General Newton offered Meade a flask of whiskey as a Confederate shell dropped in front and showered the two generals with dirt. When an aide remarked that things had seemed pretty desperate, Meade replied "in his hearty way: 'Yes, but it is all right now, it is all right now'"[17]

While Anderson's attack was dying out north of the Wheatfield Road, Longstreet's attack south of the road was reaching its own high water mark. Portions of Benning's, G. T. Anderson's, Semmes', and Kershaw's brigades drove the Federals out of the Wheatfield and into Plum Run valley. Wofford's brigade was on the far left of the ragged Confederate line, and while still primarily driving eastward down the Wheatfield Road, he did manage to capture one prize. His Georgians overran Lieutenant Aaron Walcott's Massachusetts Light, 3d Battery (C) that had been awkwardly posted by one of Sickles' staff officers in Plum Run valley near the John Weikert farm. The earlier confusion over the positioning of Watson's guns, coupled with Walcott's losses, demonstrate that Sickles' staff had a poor day posting Fifth Corps batteries. Wofford had little time to savor his trophies. Brigadier General Samuel L. Crawford, commanding the Third Division of the Fifth Corps, charged across Plum Run valley and, along with Colonel David Nevin's Sixth Corps brigade, drove Wofford back. Union counterattacks were beginning to secure the valley west of Little Round Top's northern slope. With his flank mostly secure, Meade now had reinforcements to spare for fighting off Longstreet's disjointed, and by now largely expended, attack.[18]

After obliterating Sickles' advance line, General Longstreet had watched as Federal reinforcements from other parts of the field arrived to bolster the embattled Union flank. Longstreet's troops had suffered heavy casualties with no hope for further support, while fresh defenders from the Fifth and Sixth corps greeted him in Plum Run valley. "While Meade's lines were growing my men were dropping," Longstreet complained bitterly in his memoir. ["W]e had no others to call to their aid, and the weight against us was too heavy to carry. . . . The sun was down, and with it went down the severe battle. I ordered a recall of the troops to the line of Plum Run and Devil's Den." Longstreet never hesitated to pronounce the Confederate effort that day as "the best three hours' fighting ever done by any troops on any battle field," but agreed that "to urge my men forward under these circumstances would have been madness, and I withdrew them in good order to the peach orchard that we had taken from the Federals early in the afternoon."[19]

With Longstreet's and R. H. Anderson's survivors in full retreat, Hancock's defenders unleashed a counterattack all along their lines, capturing large numbers of Confederate prisoners and rescuing abandoned Federal batteries. Since Sickles and Birney were both out of action, Andrew Humphreys was the last senior Third Corps officer still on the field. "The remnants" of his shattered division rallied with Hancock's help on Cemetery Ridge, near the position Caldwell's division had occupied prior to its charge into the Wheatfield. After rallying whatever able bodies were available, they joined the Union counterattacks and rushed with a yell across the fields they had just abandoned. It was one final measure of revenge for the battered Third Corps, whose survivors nearly reached the Emmitsburg Road before officers called a halt in an attempt to restore the mixed-up regiments. Humphreys bragged that "our troops got back close to the line I had occupied." While his boast was not quite true—Longstreet and Porter Alexander still occupied the Peach Orchard and the Emmitsburg Road ridge south of the Klingle farm— Humphreys' men had ended the day on an uplifting note. With darkness descending quickly on the battlefield, Cemetery Ridge was securely in Federal hands.[20]

Although fighting would continue on the Union right on Culp's Hill and East Cemetery Hill well into the evening, the second day's battle for Meade's left flank was officially over. Sickles' advanced line had disintegrated, and Longstreet retained the Peach Orchard, Devil's Den, and the western side of the Wheatfield. Most importantly, Longstreet failed to drive in Meade's left and Cemetery Ridge was firmly under Union control. "The general line of battle on the left was shortened, strengthened, firm," reported General Sykes, whose

Fifth Corps now anchored the Round Tops. "Now Sickles' blunder is repaired," exclaimed Lieutenant Frank Haskell.[21]

Sickles had departed the battlefield rather ingloriously in an ambulance while Alexander's artillery shells rained down around it. To Tremain, "it seemed to me a long time before a halt was made." According to the New York *Times* on July 18, "He suffered much pain during the ride." When the ambulance finally arrived at a makeshift field hospital, the Third Corps medical staff took charge of the patient. At some point, Chaplain Joe Twichell met and accompanied the ambulance. Twichell remembered a scene that would "never fade from my memory as long as I live. From an ambulance, driven slowly across a green meadow toward the Baltimore Pike, was lifted [Sickles'] "mangled, blood-drenched form." Twichell later described the general as "pale and swooning . . . and he struggled against his deathly faintness to ask intelligence of the battle."[22]

The shattered right leg was examined by the Medical Director of the Third Corps, Surgeon Thomas Sim, who took charge of the case. Sim informed the general that the leg would have to be amputated above the knee. Sickles replied grimly, "Do with me as you please." Sickles later managed to create some confusion over which doctor actually amputated the leg. He told a newspaper in 1882 that Assistant Surgeon J. T. Calhoun "cut off the useless limb." But Tremain, Randolph, Twichell, and Dr. Calhoun himself agreed it was Dr. Sim who performed the operation. Calhoun recorded that "the medical director of the corps, Surgeon Thomas Sim, U.S.V., with my assistance amputated the injured limb." Monument sculptor James Kelly was later fond of repeating a secondhand canard that Sickles' wound was only "slight" but that he ordered a "drunken volunteer surgeon" to amputate the leg and "save him from the mess he got in." This was of course preposterous, but may have been a muddled version of the more common rumor that Sickles' amputation ultimately saved him from a court-martial.[23]

According to Henry Tremain, the amputation was "immediately performed (just at dusk)." The modesty of the era prevented observers from describing the procedure in any detail. "It was fast growing dark, and the scene and actors need not be recalled," Tremain related to his memoir readers. "An improvised operating table, candles in bayonets, lanterns, sponges, the odor of medicines, of chloroform, a few idlers who belonged elsewhere—all are vaguely assembled in uncertain memory." The rattle of musketry could still be heard in the distance when Chaplain Twichell administered the chloroform. "I may not expose too freely," Twichell recalled during an 1888 speech, "even here, the sacred privacy of that scene; and I will not; but we heard him say, over and over . . . again, 'God bless the Third Corps! God bless the Third Corps!'—and saw the smile on his pallid lips with which he said it." His "bearing and words were of the noblest character," muttering comments such as, "If I die, let me die on the field. . . . God bless our noble cause. . . . In a war like this, one man isn't much. . . . My trust is in God." Dr. Sim told the newspapers that before the chloroform rendered him insensible, Sickles "had the whole battlefield before his mind, and gave repeated orders, as if he were hotly engaged with the enemy." However, Sickles eventually faded under the effect of the chloroform, and his right leg was amputated at the lower thigh just above the knee. The fledgling Army Medical Museum in Washington had requested medical officers to forward "all specimens of morbid anatomy . . . which may be regarded as valuable," so someone (perhaps Dr. Sim) saved the severed leg. It was later donated to the museum in a small coffin-like box and accompanied by a visiting card signed, "With the compliments of Major General D.E.S."[24]

The operation was successful, although Tremain recalled that the chloroform "had a very exciting and nervous effect." On waking from the stupor, Sickles complained of feeling weak, and a cup of tea was provided to help his recovery. E. L. Townsend wrote in 1903 that Sickles told the doctor, "if you call this a victory, take the other off." Dr. Sim likewise claimed that the moment his patient awoke, "he inquired anxiously how the fight was going on, and added with great earnestness that he would give the other leg, and his life to boot, to win the battle!" The noise, chaos, and sanitary conditions of a field hospital must have been considered unsuitable, and it was thought best to have the general carried to the rear where he might rest quietly. Sickles requested that Dr. Sim accompany him, leaving the medical care of the corps with Dr. Calhoun. "I immediately selected a new site for the hospital of the corps," wrote Calhoun, since the present location had "been rendered untenable by the fire of the enemy, and had our wounded, over three thousand in number" removed to the new site.[25]

The hospital location where Dan's leg was amputated is another of Gettysburg's uncertainties. This is surprising given Sickles' rank and notoriety, but it is merely an indication of the chaos that transpired within the Union lines, as well as a reflection of the frustratingly imprecise accounts that were later provided. According to Joe Twichell, "the rear was one vast hospital. The wounded were everywhere." W. H. Bullard wrote that the general was taken to an "old Penna. Barn or stone barn and Dr. Ash [sic] I think and others amputated his leg." The New York Monuments Commission history (under

Sickles' supervision) recorded only that "His leg was amputated in the field hospital of the Third Corps." Tom Cook, correspondent for the New York *Herald*, reported on July 6 that it happened in a "wheatfield to the rear." Dr. Sim spoke to newspaper reporters on July 7, but didn't say where the operation occurred. Surgeon George Otis, curator of the Army Medical Museum, said Sickles was removed to "a sheltered ravine a short distance to the rear, where the limb was amputated.... The patient was then sent farther to the rear." E. L. Townsend, a former Third Corps officer, recalled in 1903 that the leg was removed about one-quarter of a mile to the rear. Private Stephen Chase of the 86th New York claimed, "While passing to the [Third Corps] hospital with [a wounded] soldier, we passed the table where General Sickles was having his leg amputated."[26]

Some believe the amputation occurred on a Baltimore Pike farm, but there is good evidence to suggest that it took place in one of the makeshift Third Corps hospitals closer to the Taneytown Road. The chief surgeon of Birney's division, Jonas W. Lyman, initially had difficulty selecting a suitable site along the Taneytown Road to establish his hospital during the early afternoon of July 2 because the Second and Eleventh corps hospitals had already occupied many of the houses. Lyman finally selected an "old barn by the roadside" and moved between 3:00 p.m. and 5:00 p.m. to "a large stone barn." An assistant's account also noted that the initial corps hospital(s) were on the Taneytown Road behind the Round Tops. The Third Corps official U.S. government hospital marker likewise confirmed: "The Division Field Hospitals of the Third Corps were located July 2 in houses and barns along the Taneytown Road from the [Granite] Schoolhouse Road to Mill Road [Blacksmith Shop Road]. During the night they were removed to the south side of White Run three hundred yards from its junction with Rock Creek." Given that the Third Corps hospitals were almost certainly located on the Taneytown Road, it seems likely that the corps surgeon would have also been stationed there, rather than the more distant Baltimore Pike.[27]

On the other hand, Sickles said in 1882 that the operation occurred "on the Baltimore Pike that night." Given the shock of the wounding, the blood loss, and the artificial stimulation, Sickles also admittedly remembered little after being taken off the field. Chaplain Twichell wrote that enemy artillery fire had caused the corps doctors to move farther to the rear at least twice, and recalled that he ultimately met the ambulance (before the amputation) as it approached the Baltimore Pike. This Baltimore Pike amputation site is usually credited as the Daniel Sheaffer farm, located on the western side of the pike a few hundred yards south of White Run. The brick Sheaffer farmhouse dated to about 1780, and the family operated a large sixty-nine acre farm. Given their size and location (on the pike and near White Run), it was an advantageous location for a field hospital, and Sickles spent the night of July 2 in the house. The question remains as to whether the amputation was performed there.[28]

In her postwar damage claim, Mrs. Sheaffer wrote that the farm was used by both the Third and Twelfth corps, and that a number of wounded men were brought to the house. Mrs. Sheaffer stated that "on the second day of July 1863 Maj. Gen. Sickles was carried to the house in consequence of a wound which resulted in the amputation of a leg—he remained over night." Local civilian J. Howard Wert lived on his father's farm approximately three hundred yards from the Sheaffers. Wert wrote in 1886 that he saw "the noble chieftain borne with shattered leg to the somber brick house on the Baltimore pike." The Gettysburg *Star and Sentinel* reported in 1905 that the amputation happened in the Sheaffer house itself, but a sufficient number of post-battle accounts cast doubt on this.[29]

Several contemporary accounts suggest that Sickles was moved to the Sheaffer farm *after* the amputation was performed. As noted previously, Dr. Calhoun wrote that Sickles, accompanied by Dr. Sim, was moved to a new location for post-operative rest. Dr. Calhoun was also forced to select a new hospital site because the location where the leg was amputated had been "rendered untenable by the fire of the enemy." This would again suggest an original location for the surgery closer to the Taneytown Road than to the Baltimore Pike.[30]

Correspondent Tom Cook wrote in the New York *Herald* on July 6 that soon after Sickles' amputation in "a wheatfield," he awoke and addressed Cook: "In this war a man is but a cipher. God rules and directs all for the best." Soon after, the patient was "borne away to a house on the Baltimore turnpike, where he passed the night very comfortably."[31] The New York *Times* of July 18 informed its readers that *after* the amputation:

> It was then thought best to have him carried to the rear to some house, that he might rest quietly. A detail of forty men from the First Excelsior regiment of his old brigade, were sent for to bear the litter. As soon as the brave veterans saw their General lying wounded, they could not control their emotion. . . . Gen. Sickles looked at them, and smilingly said, "Now, boys, take up your poor old General, and be careful not to let him fall, for that would be the last of him."[32]

A modern view of the Daniel Sheaffer farm looking west from the Baltimore Pike. Sickles was taken here after being wounded and might have had his leg amputated at this location. *Author*

Sickles instructed his bearers on how to give the stretcher as little motion as possible, and:

> After being carried a distance of four miles, the General complaining of great exhaustion and fatigue, he was taken to the house of Mr. Shaffer [sic], on the Baltimore road. The family was much alarmed by the fighting in their vicinity, and when a room was asked for the General's accommodation they were in a quandary whether to admit him or refuse him entrance. He was, however, admitted and some tea was given him. He slept little during the night, and said in the morning he felt much better. He appeared in cheerful spirits; talked and laughed with his Staff and remarked he should soon be in the field with a new leg. He got shaved, made his toilette and smoked a cigar. His eyes were as animated as ever, his face was but slightly tinged with paleness. Beyond this there was nothing to indicate that he had passed through any suffering. He was perfectly unconcerned, easy and composed.[33]

According to one of Sickles' own accounts, which must always be taken with a grain of salt, he requested champagne to help fuel his recovery. When a bottle could not be located, wine was used as a substitute. Dan drank a mouthful at a time, finished the bottle during the course of the night, and "thus started on the way to recovery." In truth, the general was still not out of the woods and that first night "was passed in successive watches" by a nervous Tremain, and Captains Alexander Moore and Thomas Fry.[34]

Henry Tremain recalled that "the musketry lingered long beyond the shades of evening" on Gettysburg's second day of battle (the only day Sickles actively participated). By sundown, Sickles' proud Third Corps was shattered. Of the roughly 10,675 troops who followed him off Cemetery Ridge, 4,211 (39.4%) were killed (593), wounded, captured, or missing. Birney's 5,095 men suffered 2,011 casualties (39.5%), and Humphreys' 4,924 soldiers lost 2,092 for a 42.5% rate. Randolph's 596 artillerymen contributed another 106 (a high 17.8% for an artillery brigade). Losses were substantial at every level. The Excelsiors' 73rd New York tied for the fifth highest Federal regiment in number killed (51) and the Excelsior Brigade took 778 casualties overall—42.4% of its 1,837 effectives. These numbers didn't include the troops from the other infantry corps and artillery batteries who helped save the Union left. Sickles never imagined that he would finish the day as a one-legged amputee. As he ended the day in a painful chloroform-induced stupor, he also surely did not realize that he was not finished at Gettysburg. The battle would play a major role in his life for the rest of his days.[35]

While their commander lingered through the night, the day's survivors tried to reassemble the shattered corps and come to grips with what had happened. Lieutenant Colonel Baldwin of the 1st Massachusetts considered the Third Corps "victor of a bloody day. A report was in circulation that General Sickles had been carried from the field severely if not mortally wounded which spread an additional gloom over all, and proved to be nearly true." Officers rounded up stragglers and attempted to bring their regiments back together.[36] "The Third Corps hospital to which nearly all our wounded were taken," a veteran in Ward's brigade later remembered,

> had been established in a grove about half a mile to the left and rear of where we were then lying. . . . The scene at the hospital was one of the most horrid imaginable. During the afternoon and evening nearly 3,000 wounded men had been brought there. . . . The ground of the entire grove . . . several acres in extant [was] . . . literally covered with them; and such

noises filled the air as I never heard before and trust may never reach my ears again . . . away down through the trees flickering lights could be seen, the reflections of which fill with ghastly effect upon the corps of surgeons who, with coats off and sleeves rolled up, were gathered at, or moving rapidly to and fro about the amputating tables.[37]

General Birney's division assembled in the fields near the Taneytown Road. Ammunition wagons were brought up, and refilling the cartridge boxes became first priority. Fires were lit so that the men could get something to eat. "We were still ignorant of the day's results," wrote Regis de Trobriand, "but we well knew what it had cost us. There remained only to find out how many of the missing would rejoin us during the night." Birney, "in a moment of despondency . . . said to me, in a low voice, that he wished he had shared the fate of his horse" that had been killed. "He believed the day lost; he counted up his friends, dead and wounded; he saw his command half destroyed, and, thinking of the Republic, he trembled for it, if the army were beaten. These dark thoughts were dispersed when Birney's young brother, Fitz-Hugh Birney, who was serving on his staff, arrived with news of the last success of Hancock and Crawford."[38]

After the passage of many years, de Trobriand reached the conclusion that the day was strategically indecisive:

All the efforts of the day were concentrated on one object: on one side, to carry the advanced position where Sickles had placed the Third Corps; on the other to hold it. To lose it and retake it twice was well enough while the battle lasted. But to remain there, in order to renew the trial the dangers of which had been demonstrated, would have been a grave fault. Meade did not commit that fault. He brought the army back to the position where he had intended to await the attack of the Confederates, and the morning of the 3d of July found us disposed in regular line on the Cemetery Heights.[39]

As a wounded prisoner behind enemy lines, Captain Frank Moran of the 73rd New York heard a "dozen times" that "Gen'l. Sickles was badly wounded and a prisoner; which was never generally believed among the rebels during the night of the 2nd, but which I was gratified to learn in the morning was contradicted. . . . The fact that our troops still held possession of Round Top and Cemetery Hill, had a marked and depressing influence on the Confederates, who evidently felt that the slight advancement of their line was a beggarly consolation for the serious and almost fatal crippling of Longstreet's fine corps." False rumors were also rampant that Longstreet, too, had been wounded and captured.[40]

That evening, Meade summoned his corps commanders to headquarters at the Leister farmhouse. The meeting was later dubbed a "Council of War." As a corps commander, Meade had complained during the Chancellorsville campaign that Joe Hooker kept his subordinates in the dark about important matters. Meade wished to avoid that mistake, but however laudable his intentions, the post-battle criticism that was heaped upon him must have made him second-guess his decision. David Birney represented the Third Corps; Butterfield and Warren were also there from Meade's staff. There were twelve exhausted attendees in total, all squeezed into a single tiny room.[41]

The conversation began informally. John Gibbon, representing the Second Corps with Hancock, and an old friend of Meade's, later recalled, "It soon became evident that everybody was in favor of remaining where we were and giving battle there. General Meade himself said very little, except now and then to make some comment, but I cannot recall that he expressed any decided opinion upon any point, preferring apparently to listen to the conversation." After some discussion, Butterfield (in his typical administrator mode) proposed that they officially formulate the questions to be asked.[42] Meade agreed, and Butterfield wrote several questions on some notepaper, and then "formally proposed to the council":

> 1. Under existing circumstances, is it advisable for this army to remain in its present position, or to retire to another nearer its base of supplies?

> 2. It being determined to remain in present position, shall the army attack or wait the attack of the enemy?

> 3. If we wait attack, how long?

The attending generals were allowed to weigh in on each question. Although several voted to "correct the position," they agreed (as Henry Slocum famously voted) to "Stay and fight it out." They would not assume the offensive, however, voting instead to await Lee's next move. Birney agreed to stay and await attack, but described the "Third Corps used up, and not in good condition to fight." Meade did not take a prominent part in the discussion, and ended the voting by simply concluding, "Such then is the decision." Hancock, among others, claimed that Meade qualified his view with, "As you wish gentlemen; but Gettysburg is no place to fight a battle in; Lee can turn our flanks." Meade wired Halleck at 11:00 p.m., notifying him that "after one of the severest contests of the war" the enemy had been "repulsed at all points." Sickles was listed among the generals killed or wounded. "I shall remain in my present position to-morrow, but am not prepared to say, until better advised of the condition of the army, whether my operations will be of an offensive or defensive character." The next morning Meade sent a brief note to his wife, "We had a great fight yesterday. . . . Reynolds killed the first day—no other of your friends or acquaintances hurt." He made no mention of Sickles, apparently confirming that he did not qualify as a Meade "friend or acquaintance."[43]

After surviving the night under watch, Sickles' doctors determined that he should be removed from the field to "await the approach of the usual fever." It was eventually decided that he be sent to Washington. Dr. Sim prohibited his removal from a stretcher or transfer to an ambulance, so a detail carried Sickles from Gettysburg on his stretcher, embarking on what Henry Tremain called an "excessively tedious and painful" journey. "We had very hard work getting the general here [Washington]; he was unable to ride in an ambulance, and we had to carry him on a stretcher for many miles." Rumors of roving enemy cavalry forced the party to halt and hide several times. James Rusling, a staff officer who would meet the party in Washington, wrote that during one such stop, a Pennsylvania farmer charged Sickles and his party for their food and drink. In later years, another story arose suggesting that a "thrifty" farmer charged Sickles' attendants $5.00 a piece for cotton sheets to be placed under the stretcher. With their wallets a little lighter, Sickles and his attendants eventually arrived in Littlestown, where Captain Fry had made railroad arrangements for a train to run to Baltimore and then on to Washington.[44]

Although Sickles had departed the field, the influence of his advance to the Peach Orchard continued to be felt on the third day at Gettysburg. Longstreet's occupation of the majority of Sickles' position, along with the occupation of lower Culp's Hill by Richard Ewell's Second Corps (which occurred when Federal troops vacated their positions to reinforce the Union left) convinced General Lee to renew his attack. Lee's January 1864 report elaborated that the Peach Orchard and the Emmitsburg Road ridge would serve as an artillery platform to support another assault by Longstreet on Meade's left. "The general plan was unchanged. Longstreet, re-enforced by Pickett's three brigades . . . was ordered to attack the next morning, and General Ewell was directed to assail the enemy's right at the same time." Longstreet was hesitant to renew the prior day's attack on the Federal left, and Ewell became engaged at Culp's Hill in the early morning hours before Longstreet's dispositions could be completed. Lee's army simply proved unable to coordinate simultaneous flank attacks over such a distance. By noon, Ewell had been completely repulsed at Culp's Hill and Lee devised an alternative plan—the failed afternoon assault on Cemetery Ridge known to history as "Pickett's Charge."[45]

Artillery support was an integral component of Lee's revised plan, first as part of the pre-charge cannonade, and then to advance guns with the infantry. Longstreet's batteries near the Peach Orchard were intended to exploit Lee's exterior lines and combine with Ewell's and A. P. Hill's batteries to strike northern Cemetery Ridge and Cemetery Hill with converging fire from multiple directions. Colonel Edward P. Alexander, again in command of Longstreet's First Corps artillery, posted more than seventy guns in an approximately 1,300 yard long line stretching from the Peach Orchard on the Confederate right to the northeast corner of Spangler's Woods on the left. When the cannonade commenced about 1:00 p.m. with two signal shots from B. F. Eshleman's Washington (Louisiana) Artillery near the Peach Orchard, the Rebel artillery opened a noisy, if ultimately futile, attempt to weaken Meade's defenses.

Unfortunately for Lee's plan, Eshleman's effectiveness was partially diminished because the Federals still occupied Little Round Top and could hit his position with enfilade fire from artillery posted on the high rocky hill. Lee had wanted to use the Peach Orchard as an artillery platform for assaulting Meade's lines—something Sickles had correctly predicted. Unfortunately for the Confederates, dominated as it was by both Little Round Top and Cemetery Hill, the Peach Orchard position simply was not strong enough to accomplish what Lee (and Alexander) hoped. Judged solely on the results, which were admittedly unknown to the participants at the time the decisions were made, both Lee and Sickles overestimated the Peach Orchard's military value. Meade had been correct in preferring to keep his left on Cemetery Ridge.[46]

On the morning of the third, British military observer Arthur Fremantle joined Lee and Longstreet's staff on a reconnaissance in preparation for the attack. An errant Federal shell aimed in their direction ignited the Sherfy barn. Tragically, many of Sickles' wounded, particularly those from the 114th Pennsylvania (and others from the 73rd New York, 57th Pennsylvania, and 68th Pennsylvania) had sought refuge in the barn. Many were too badly wounded to move and so were unable to escape, although accounts from Parker's Virginia battery suggest that they ordered a cease-fire to allow the rescue of as many wounded Yankees as possible. Those unable to escape, wrote Fremantle, "I am afraid, must have perished miserably in the flames." Too badly burned to be identified, some were later recognized only by their distinctive Zouave uniforms. Speaking at the dedication of the 114th regimental monument decades later, Captain A. W. Givin reminded the audience of "that sickening sight that met your gaze as you advanced to where the old barn stood, to find it in ashes, and the charred remains of many of your companions."[47]

What remained of Sickles' Third Corps, back once again under David Birney's command, primarily played the role of observers in the battle's great climax. The corps was posted slightly east of the same position where it had camped on the night of July 1 and the morning of July 2. Second Corps staff officer Frank Haskell noted that the Third Corps was "where, had it stayed, instead of moving out to the front, we should have many more men to-day, and should not have been upon the brink of disaster yesterday." Humphreys occupied a wooded knoll just east of George Weikert's house while Birney's division aligned itself on Humphreys' left. "It is dreadful to look at our brigade this morning," Private Lewis Schaeffer of the 68th Pennsylvania confided in his field diary. Many "happy fellows who were anxious for the fight yesterday are now hushed in death or lay frightfully wounded."[48]

General John Newton recalled that when he asked Birney to more actively support the First Corps, on the right of the Third Corps, Birney replied that "he would rather be excused, as his men had a good deal of hard work and were exhausted . . . so they went into the woods which was rather thick and had coffee." The 68th Pennsylvania's unfortunate Colonel Andrew Tippin, still temporarily commanding Graham's brigade despite his abandonment of the Peach Orchard on the prior day, turned in another poor performance on July 3. Captain Bowen, now in command of the 114th Pennsylvania, complained sarcastically that Tippin was ordered to move the brigade farther to the right, and "whether it was that the brave Colonel didn't know the right from the left, or just which way it was he was ordered to go, or whether it was that his soldierly instinct led him to lead the brigade towards the enemy . . . we were in the midst of a most severe shower of flying missiles of all sorts and kinds." Fortunately for the brigade's survivors, Tippin was removed from command. He was either wounded, or as Private Lewis Schaeffer confided in his diary, "Our colonel was put under arrest [July 3] for being drunk."[49]

Dan Butterfield was slightly wounded in the chest by a piece of spent artillery shrapnel during the cannonade. He claimed that the seriousness of the injury left him barely able to ride, but several veterans later ridiculed the extent of his injury. Washington Roebling echoed these sentiments when he wrote in the margin of his personal copy of Butterfield's *Biographical Memorial*, "The wound was not serious." Butterfield left the army (on what was supposed to be a thirty-day leave) to recuperate on July 5 or 6, "fortunately for him & to the joy of all," wrote General Marsena Patrick. Although it would be months before they realized it, Butterfield's departure banished the Hooker-Sickles-Butterfield trio from the Army of the Potomac forever. George Meade would ensure they never returned as long as he remained in command.[50]

After the ineffective cannonade, the infantry assault against Cemetery Ridge was turned back with heavy losses. Lee had spent his offensive capabilities and no longer had the strength to drive Meade from his position. Longstreet and many of the Confederate commanders worried that Meade might launch a devastating counterattack in the wake of the failed "Pickett's Charge." With years of hindsight, E. P. Alexander wrote in 1877: "I have always believed that the enemy here lost the greatest opportunity they ever had of routing General Lee's army by prompt offensive." Meade did order General Sykes to conduct a reconnaissance in force. Based on the limited information Meade had available to him regarding Lee's condition, the lateness of the day, and a fatigued army of his own, a full-scale counterattack would not have guaranteed Meade success. He had won the battle on the back of his strong defensive position, not because of risky counterattacks. Within the context of his situation Meade's decision was a rational one, but for post-battle critics such as Dan Sickles, his decision to remain in place would become one of but several examples of Meade's apparent inability to finish off Lee's army.[51]

Skirmishing continued until nightfall. When it became apparent that Meade was not going to counterattack, Longstreet issued orders to tighten his lines into a better defensive position and begin withdrawing his corps to the protection of Warfield and Seminary ridges. McLaws' skirmishers retained control of the Peach Orchard through the night of the third, but the balance of Sickles' extended line that had fallen to the Confederates was quietly abandoned. Lee's supply trains began to pull out of Gettysburg early on July 4. That night, A. P. Hill's Third Corps led the infantry retreat. Longstreet followed, and Ewell brought up the rear on the morning of July 5. The battle was over, but Lee's army still had to reach the Potomac River and escape into Virginia. Washington was watching to see if George Meade would prevent that from happening.[52]

Chapter 13

He has Redeemed his Reputation Fully

The New York *Times* of Saturday, July 4, 1863, headlined news of "The Great Battles . . . The Death of Longstreet, and Barksdale of Mississippi . . . Gen. Sickles' Right Leg Shot Off." In recounting the second day's battle, the *Times* claimed that Meade had received "sufficient assurances" that the Rebels were concentrating on his left flank, "which all felt to be secure under the protection of the invincible Third Corps. Our line was immediately strengthened on that flank, Gen. Sickles' corps being sent to its support. . . . The Third Corps received the attack with great coolness." The first accounts of Sickles' wounding were straightforward: "At half-past six Gen. Sickles was struck in the right leg by a piece of shell, and borne from the field. The injury was so great that amputation became necessary, and it was performed successfully—the limb being taken off below the knee." The *Times* report was distributed to papers across the country. Readers in both the North and South read that Sickles' leg was "shot off."[1]

Sickles and his party reached Washington on Sunday morning, July 5. The wounded general settled into a residence at 248 F Street. Dr. Sim believed that Sickles' condition was so unstable that he refused to allow him to be moved, leaving him in his stretcher for several days before being shifted onto a bed. Tremain seems to have agreed with Dr. Sim's prognosis. "Poor Sickles!" he wrote on July 7. "He is not the man he was. Utterly prostrate, weak and feeble as a child, he still lies on his back on the same stretcher on which he was placed after the amputation of his leg."[2]

Lieutenant Colonel James Rusling, Sickles' chief quartermaster, had missed the great battle. When he learned his chief was in town and wounded, perhaps mortally, Rusling raced to the house to see him. He arrived about 3:00 p.m. on

July 5 to find Sickles reclining in his stretcher on the first floor. "I found the General in much pain and distress at times, and weak and enfeebled from loss of blood; but calm and collected, and with the same iron will and clearness of intellect, that always characterized him in those Civil War days, and apparently always will." With Captain Fry being the only other staffer present, Rusling witnessed a most remarkable meeting. History has recorded that this meeting, with the wounded Sickles acting as a calculating and scheming manipulator, had a detrimental impact on the relationship between President Lincoln and General Meade.[3]

According to Rusling, on that first Sunday afternoon (July 5), Sickles, Rusling, and Captain Fry were discussing the battle when an orderly announced that Lincoln and his son Tad had arrived. Lincoln and Sickles exchanged a greeting that "was cordial, though touching and pathetic; and it was easy to see that they held one another in high esteem. They were both American politicians, though of very different schools. . . . Besides, Sickles was a prominent War Democrat, able and astute, and Lincoln was too shrewd to pass by any of these in those perilous war days."[4]

The two "politicians" discussed the battle and Dan's wound. "Sickles was somewhat despondent," but Lincoln replied that he was "something of a prophet that day" and predicted it would not be long before Sickles would be up to visit him at the White House, "where they would always be glad to see him." "Touching and pathetic" it was, but it was the next portion of the conversation that had the most impact on Gettysburg's history. Rusling admitted in 1894 that his accounts did not "give the exact phraseology" of the conversation, but that he had refreshed his memory based on a letter that he had written to his father that same day.[5]

Lincoln asked Sickles "what Meade proposed to do with" the Gettysburg victory. According to Rusling,

> Sickles lay on his stretcher, with a cigar between his fingers, puffing it leisurely, and answered Mr. Lincoln in detail, but warily, as became so astute a man and so good a soldier; discussing the great battle and its probable consequences with a lucidity and ability remarkable for one in his condition—exhausted and enfeebled as he was by the shock of such a wound and amputation. Occasionally he would wince with pain, and call sharply to his valet to wet his fevered wound. But he never dropped his cigar, nor lost the thread of his discourse, nor missed the point of their discussion.[6]

Rusling published at least two versions of this encounter. In 1910, the Third Army Corps Union produced *Lincoln and Sickles*, a pamphlet based on a dinner speech that Rusling delivered at the organization's forty-sixth anniversary in New York. Later, in 1914, he published *Men and Things I Saw in Civil War Days*, an updated series of stories he had earlier published in the magazine *Christian Advocate*. In the latter publication, Rusling included a passage omitted from *Lincoln and Sickles*:

> He [Sickles] certainly got his side of the story of Gettysburg well into the President's mind and heart that Sunday afternoon; and this doubtless stood him in good stead afterward, when Meade proposed to court-martial him for fighting so magnificently, if unskillfully (which remains to be proved), on that bloody and historic July 2d.[7]

"I never saw President Lincoln again," Rusling concluded. "But this conversation made a deep and lasting impression on me. I have told it hundreds of times since, both publicly and privately. . . . General Sickles himself, has also corroborated it substantially, on many occasions, both publicly and privately."[8]

Rusling's story does not specify exactly what Sickles said about Meade. As a result, historians can only surmise the details of what Lincoln learned that day from Sickles. Harry Pfanz wrote: "Sickles told his story, probably a revised version of that told President Lincoln, until his death." Jared Peatman, writing in a monograph for *Gettysburg Magazine* (2003), summarized the historical consensus against Sickles, concluding that the general offered a "slanted view" of the battle, "and his negative assessment of Meade's performance convinced Lincoln that Meade was not the hero of the battle and that he would not vigorously pursue the retreating Confederate army. Sickles was trying to cover up his own mistakes, and was willing to sacrifice Meade's reputation to do so." Peatman admitted that although Rusling did not specify exactly what Sickles said, "it is easy to reconstruct what Sickles said to President Lincoln . . . Sickles' side of the story was that Meade had formed no battle plan and had exhibited no leadership. Rather Sickles portrayed himself as the hero of the battle, saying that had he not advanced Meade would have retreated from Gettysburg and given the field to the Confederates. Sickles argued that his advance had forced Meade to stay and fight it out at Gettysburg."[9]

By July 5 Lincoln had obviously not read Meade's report of the battle, which would not be completed for several months, and was desperate to speak with anyone who had personally participated. At this early date Lincoln was probably unaware of any unauthorized advance on Sickles' part, and was therefore unaware of Sickles' ulterior motives. While a politician as astute as Lincoln may have disregarded some of Sickles' story, Lincoln still seems to have legitimately viewed Sickles as a "fighting general." Conversely, many of the West Point professional soldiers were not viewed as fighters (sometimes for good reason), so Lincoln probably accepted Sickles' view that his aggressive posturing had brought on the battle. We don't know what Sickles told Lincoln, so the specifics are only educated speculation, a point historians sometimes forget.[10]

By July 5, it is arguable whether Sickles had the opportunity to develop a sophisticated counterattack against Meade. His very survival was still in doubt, and that would have been of more immediate concern to him. His later battle against Meade would be primarily fueled by Meade's refusal to return him to command, coupled with critical battle reports penned by Meade and Henry Halleck. However, these events had not occurred yet. Sickles' tactic would center around the supposition that Meade had wanted to retreat from Gettysburg, which Sickles would later claim he learned from Butterfield on the morning of July 2. Since Sickles was grievously wounded and removed from the battlefield only hours later, and Butterfield himself was wounded the following day, it is unlikely the two men had the opportunity by July 5 to develop an extensive assassination of Meade's reputation. Sickles' physical condition, coupled with the amount of time he had spent traveling to Washington, makes this unlikely. Sickles instead probably presented Lincoln with a general portrait that he had fought aggressively and that Meade had paid minimal attention to the critical left flank until it was nearly too late. If so, neither statement was completely inaccurate.

The historical importance of the topic lies in the fact that Sickles has been blamed by some for poisoning the Lincoln-Meade relationship. Some have even written that it was Sickles' "planting the seed" that caused Lincoln to sap Meade's confidence and that, by extension, Sickles adversely affected Meade's performance for the remainder of the campaign. A reading of the historical record indicates that, although Sickles may indeed have "planted the seed" with Lincoln, there were a number of other reasons why Lincoln became dissatisfied with Meade.[11]

On July 4, Meade issued General Order No. 68 congratulating the army on its Gettysburg victory. He added, "Our task is not yet accomplished, and the commanding general looks to the army for greater efforts to drive from our soil every vestige of the presence of the invader." Although Meade had included the qualifier, "Our task is not yet accomplished," when Lincoln read the announcement he famously exclaimed, "Drive the invaders from our soil! My God! Is that all?" and "Will our generals never get that idea out of their heads? The whole country is our soil!" Subsequent dispatches from Generals French and Pleasonton added to Lincoln's impression that the Army of the Potomac was failing to aggressively block Lee's retreat: "These things all appear to me to be connected with a purpose to cover Baltimore and Washington, and to get the enemy across the river again without a further collision, and they do not appear connected with a purpose to prevent his crossing and to destroy him." Whether Lincoln's impression was justified or not, and ironic since he previously considered covering Washington and Baltimore a major priority, the fact is that the army's own actions helped "plant the seed" in Lincoln's mind.[12]

Meade was still unsure of Lee's intentions, and delaying actions by Lee's rearguard slowed Meade's own movements out of Gettysburg. On the night of July 4, Meade called another war council with his generals and, as he had done two days earlier, posed a series of questions, including "Shall we pursue the enemy if he is retreating on his direct line of retreat?" The majority agreed to stay put until Lee's intentions were ascertained, and then to pursue primarily with cavalry. (David Birney represented the Third Corps again and voted against the pursuit question.) Brigadier General Herman Haupt, who had been working on the railroad logistics necessary to supply Meade's army, arrived on July 5. Haupt came away from the visit believing that Meade was unduly resting the army while Lee was being allowed to escape. Haupt wasted little time heading to Washington to tell Lincoln that Meade was moving slowly, and that Lee's army could be damaged if only Meade would act more forcefully.[13]

Sickles' critics have sometimes suggested that proof of his poison can be found in the dispatches that passed between Meade and Washington following Sickles' July 5 meeting with Lincoln. Presumably, the increased pressure that was being placed on Meade to bring Lee to battle north of the Potomac River was at least partially the result of Sickles' criticism of Meade. In fact, despite the Sickles meeting, General Order 68, and General Haupt's worries, surviving correspondence contains the same mixed bag that usually passed between Lincoln/Halleck and the Army of the Potomac's commander. What must be understood is that Lincoln believed there was no better opportunity to destroy Lee's army than to catch it while wounded and still above the Potomac River. Whether this desire was realistic or not was irrelevant, because whoever commanded the army would have had to deal with Lincoln's pressure to bring about a climatic victory on Northern soil—particularly following General

George McClellan's earlier failure to finish the Army of Northern Virginia during the 1862 Maryland campaign. Sickles might have helped reinforce this perception in Lincoln's mind, but to suggest that he created it is an exaggeration.[14]

On July 7, Halleck wired that Meade had been promoted to brigadier general in the Regular Army "to rank from July 3, the date of your brilliant victory at Gettysburg." But later that evening, Washington began to pressure Meade once again. At 8:45 p.m., Halleck told Meade to give the enemy another "stunning blow . . . before he can reach the Potomac. . . . There is strong evidence that he is short of artillery ammunition, and, if vigorously pressed, he must suffer." Halleck passed along a message from Lincoln. Vicksburg had surrendered to General Grant, and "if General Meade can complete his work, so gloriously prosecuted thus far, by the literal or substantial destruction of Lee's army, the rebellion will be over."[15]

The following day, July 8, Meade tried to temper Halleck's expectations. "I expect to find the enemy in a strong position, well covered with artillery, and I do not desire to imitate his example at Gettysburg, and assault a position where the chances were so greatly against success. I wish in advance to moderate the expectations of those who, in ignorance of the difficulties to be encountered, may expect too much." Halleck responded promptly: "The opportunity to attack his divided forces should not be lost. The President is urgent and anxious that your army should move against him by forced marches." Tempers cooled slightly over the next few days. Halleck cautioned, "Do not be influenced by any dispatch from here against your own judgment. Regard them as suggestions only." On July 10, Halleck suggested that Meade withhold from further combat until additional reinforcements reached the army. The communications between July 8 and July 12 are alternatively supportive and critical. If Sickles was sinisterly manipulating events in the background, as some believe, then his influence is not reflected in the official records.[16]

In fact, contrary to popular widespread belief, Meade's army did initiate a pursuit that brought about nearly two dozen skirmishes and small battles in the days following Gettysburg. The action began at Fairfield Gap, Monterey Gap, and Emmitsburg on July 4, and continued through July 12 at Ashby's Gap. The heaviest fighting occurred at Hagerstown on July 6, where the Federals reported 263 casualties and Confederate losses were probably comparable. In total, through the final action at Williamsport on July 14, the Army of the Potomac reported an additional 1,004 casualties. Meade did indeed pursue Lee, but not in enough force or enthusiasm to prevent Lee from reaching the Potomac.[17]

Meade received one piece of good news during this period when Andrew Humphreys agreed on July 8 to replace Butterfield as chief of staff. Humphreys was bitter about the way in which his division was used during the battle. "Had my division been left intact, I should have driven the enemy back, but this *ruinous habit* (it don't deserve the name of system) of putting troops in position and then drawing off its reserves and second line to help others, who if similarly disposed would need no such help, is disgusting." His brief tenure under Sickles had soured the ambitious Humphreys. "[M]y mortification at seeing men over me and commanding me who should have been far below me has destroyed all my enthusiasm and I am indifferent," he continued. "Had I been left alone I should have maintained my position and inflicted severe losses on the enemy. It incenses me to think of it." Still, Humphreys longed for a field command and accepted the position of chief of staff "as temporary, that is until I can get command of a Corps; less than that I cannot stand." Humphreys would never learn to be happy in this new role, but for now Meade had a much closer ally than Butterfield had been. Meade broke the news to Butterfield on July 14, "in view of the suffering you seemed to experience from your wound, and the probability of the length of time you might be kept from the army, together with my knowledge of the fact that the position you occupied was not altogether one of choice, I deemed it proper to appoint a successor."[18]

By July 12, Lee's back was against the flooded Potomac near the town of Williamsport. Lee later asserted that he "would have crossed the Potomac at once," but the river was too swollen to do so. Instead, he constructed a line six to eight miles long with heavy earthworks and inner defenses to protect his army against a vigorous attack. It was a strong position, and many historians have compared it to "Gettysburg in reverse," which is not exactly accurate since Lee's army was weaker and his line longer than what Meade enjoyed on Cemetery Ridge. While Lee did "not stop specially to invite" Meade into an attack, he "would not have been sorry" if Meade had done so.[19]

As the Army of the Potomac lumbered into position east of Lee's line, Meade wrote his wife on the 12th that Lee "appears to be getting into a strong position, where he can act on the defensive. I shall be prudent and not act rashly." That same day, Meade told Halleck that he would attack on the following day "unless something intervenes to prevent it." Lieutenant Ranald Mackenzie of Warren's staff warned that the Potomac was falling and that the fords were now crossable for Lee's infantry. Meade told Humphreys that he intended to order a reconnaissance in force, which would be converted into a real attack should the opportunity offer. In a move that would be heavily criticized, Meade called another council of war on the evening of July 12, ostensibly to give instructions to the corps commanders and also to receive any intelligence that had been collected during the day. Of the seven present corps commanders, only James Wadsworth (representing the First Corps in place of an ill General Newton) and Oliver Howard favored an attack. The other five infantry corps commanders, notably his two most senior commanders— Sedgwick and Slocum—opposed the idea. According to Wadsworth, Meade told the assemblage that he "favored an attack" and did not see any valid reason for not attacking, but "could not take the responsibility of bringing on a general engagement against the advice of his commanders." Meade decided to postpone (or "defer" as Humphreys called it) the attack for another day until a more proper reconnaissance of the enemy lines could be conducted.[20]

Meade and Humphreys reconnoitered the front on July 13. Apparently they learned nothing to dissuade Meade from his original intent, for he ordered Humphreys to draw up plans for a reconnaissance in force again the following day: "[T]he enemy's pickets, supports, and guards will be driven in until a distinct view of his position, defensive works, force, and its arrangements can be had. If it should be necessary to obtain this information, and should be practicable, the enemy should even be made to display his line of battle." Humphreys admitted that this was "similar in most respects" to what Meade had intended for the 13th. Because Meade had reverted back to his original idea, this decision opened him to criticism that he had unnecessarily allowed his corps commanders to delay his attack for one critical day. Lee, meanwhile, notified Longstreet on the 13th that the water had receded sufficiently to allow the Army of Northern Virginia to cross into western Virginia.[21]

Orders were given to move forward "punctually" at 7:00 a.m. on July 14, but before the advance began General Horatio Wright of the Sixth Corps and Oliver Howard of the Eleventh Corps reported that the enemy had withdrawn from their fronts. Wright pushed skirmishers ahead and discovered the enemy entrenchments empty. Meade ordered a general pursuit at 8:30 a.m., but by 11:00 a.m. all of Lee's army except for Heth and Pender's divisions were on the far bank. Although the Federals had some success against Lee's rearguard at Falling Waters, Meade was forced to notify Halleck at 11:00 a.m.: "On advancing my army this morning, with a view of ascertaining the exact position of the enemy and attacking him if the result of the examination should justify me, I found, on reaching his lines, that they were evacuated."[22]

The information angered Washington officials. "I need hardly say to you that the escape of Lee's army without another battle has created great

General Daniel E. Sickles and staff. Henry Tremain is on the far left.
Note Sickles' missing leg. *Library of Congress*

dissatisfaction in the mind of the President," replied Halleck, "and it will require an active and energetic pursuit on your part to remove the impression that it has not been sufficiently active heretofore." Meade was so incensed by this accusation that he offered to resign, but unlike he had with Joe Hooker, Lincoln refused. Anger and frustration at the news of Lee's escape was widespread. Lincoln complained, simplistically and rather unrealistically, "We had them within our grasp. We had only to stretch forth our hands & they were ours."

According to Henry Tremain, Lincoln's visits to Sickles were "frequently repeated" during this period. "At one of them the face of the President was marked with sadness. It was just after Lee's army had crossed the Potomac into Virginia, and the news of it was fresh in all minds." Tremain claimed that an intensely disappointed Lincoln told Sickles that Lee's escape was "the greatest disaster of the war!"[23]

Among all of the post-battle criticism directed at George Meade from enemies such as Dan Sickles, Lee's Williamsport escape might have been the hardest to live down. "I have every reason to believe," Meade concluded, "the attack would have been unsuccessful, and would have resulted disastrously."

Meade formed his opinion after examining Lee's vacated works. Many other Union officers later backed Meade's opinion. Humphreys testified before the Committee on the Conduct of the War that "subsequent information" obtained from inspecting Lee's entrenchments "showed that the enemy had a very strong position, and indicated that had we made an attack we should have suffered very severely."[24]

Meade's supporters have since argued that an attack would have resulted "in the needless sacrifice of soldiers," and that Meade showed moral courage in not ordering a "senseless attack." Meade staffer James Biddle assured *Annals of the War* readers: "Had he assaulted, he would certainly have been defeated." At least one historian has recently written that such an attack "would have replicated the Battle of Gettysburg, but in reverse." Still, Meade and Humphreys had both spent the 13th scouting the lines, and both came to the same conclusion that an advance, or at least a reconnaissance in force, was still justified. Only through information obtained afterward did they convince themselves that the assault would have been a disaster. Ignoring "what if" and speculative scenarios, however, it is simply a matter of history that Lee escaped to fight another day and Meade, rightly or wrongly, was censured by Washington for not preventing it.[25]

Most Gettysburg historians believe that Lincoln was being unrealistic in his expectations of destroying Lee's army, and that Meade performed well in delivering a crucial victory despite having only been on the job for a few short days. Sickles' contribution to Lincoln's expectations needs to be put into context. Blaming Sickles for the criticism that Lincoln heaped on Meade ignores a significant portion of the historical record. Sickles likely did help "plant the seed," as most believe, but it is a stretch to surmise, as at least one author has done, that "Had this idea not been planted, perhaps Lincoln would have given Meade the support he deserved. By extension, Meade would have been a different commander . . . if Lincoln had not treated him so poorly and sapped his confidence." Sickles had more than his share of blame to shoulder as far as Gettysburg was concerned, but enough happened outside of his influence to suggest that he was responsible for Meade's later performance.[26]

Unlike Meade, Sickles was unburdened by public and official disappointment. He could play the roles that politicians play best: critic and second-guesser. He was "the recipient of a great deal of attention" in Washington. Henry Tremain was kept "more than busy replying to letters of sympathy and receiving the visitors who call to enquire." Sickles was under medical orders to "hardly see any one," although the President "frequently" violated this order. Sickles was already concerned with the fate of his beloved corps. As the army was chasing Lee back toward the Potomac, Lincoln assured him, "I understand you are troubled with some report that the 3rd Corps has sustained a disaster, or repulse. I can only say that I have watched closely, and believe I have seen all the despatches [sic] at the Military Telegraph Office . . . and I have heard of no such disaster or repulse."[27]

Tremain told his family that the Third Corps had "as usual, bore the brunt of the fight." There was much worrying about Charles Graham's fate, until they finally confirmed on July 10 that Graham was alive, albeit a wounded prisoner. "This news quite relieves Mrs. Graham," wrote Tremain, adding cryptically, "I could tell you many interesting things about Meade's and Hooker's campaigns until I left, but must postpone it for the present." Like most of Sickles' inner-circle, Tremain was no admirer of George Meade. The aide credited the Union victory to "providence . . . for I saw no evidence of towering military genius displayed by our commanding general." Ironically, Tremain also dismissed most of the accusations directed at Meade. He cautioned his family that another Union victory would not have ended the war.[28]

The national press also began to develop the one-legged war hero image that Dan would spend the next fifty years cultivating. Readers of the New York *Times* awoke on July 6, 1863, to read more news from "the great battlefield of Gettysburgh [sic]" that was "of the most cheering and satisfactory character." Sickles' hometown obviously followed news of his wounding with intense interest, and the *Times* editorialized that the entire country owed Dan a debt of gratitude:

> The misfortune of no one whose lot it has been to be smitten in this war has excited a livelier sympathy than the painful injury sustained in the late battle by Gen. Daniel E. Sickles. . . .
>
> New-York State and City owe a debt of peculiar gratitude to Gen. Sickles. He it is that, in the most signal manner, has proved what militia are capable of, when led by a brave man, even without the advantages of a regular military education. . . .
>
> General Sickles has literally carved his way to fame with his sword. . . . When the roll call of heroes is written for this war, one of the highest on the list will be that of Gen. Daniel E. Sickles, and New York will justly claim him as her own.[29]

While continuing to misspell "Gettysburgh," the *Times* provided more details of Sickles' wounding under a July 14 byline. Prior to being struck, Sickles had supposedly been "riding up and down the field, under a heavy fire of musketry and shell. It seems almost miraculous that he had escaped up to that time, so much had he been previously exposed. He gave his orders in an easy, quiet tone, without any excitement, his eyes constantly scanning his lines to see that no changes should take place without his knowledge." The paper assured New Yorkers, "His absence from his command is severely felt by the army. How much missed is his clear-sighted direction and his all-pervading energy." But, it was suggested, the army should "keep in their memory, as a guiding star, his example of bravery and his words of enthusiastic encouragement. Let his name be to them as Napoleon's to his French soldiers—an impetus to noble deeds." "He has redeemed his reputation fully since this war commenced," concluded another paper.[30]

Dan Sickles' most admirable quality was perhaps his ability to conquer adversity, and the loss of a leg merely became one more career obstacle to overcome. Working with a pair of government-issued crutches, Sickles ignored his doctor's advice and departed for New York during the final days of July. The president extended an invitation for Dan to convalesce at the Lincoln's summer retreat, but Sickles declined, preferring instead to return home. He did pay Lincoln a farewell call at the White House on July 22, and the New York *Times* reported on the 25th that Sickles "endured his journey from Washington to his home here much better than his friends anticipated. He was yesterday comparatively comfortable, and hopes are long to be again in service on the field."[31]

Sickles returned, surprisingly quickly given the circumstances, to his business and social calendar. Having departed New York only two years earlier as a disgraced ex-Congressman, Sickles returned as a genuine war hero. The city Board of Councilmen passed a resolution thanking Dan, "who, leaving his sick bed to take command of his corps, led them to battle and to victory." As his reward, the council authorized presenting Sickles with a gold medal. The *Times* updated readers regularly on "The Movements of Maj. Gen. Sickles." Although Teresa and daughter Laura were noticeably absent from the coverage, his dinner parties once again made news copy. The Gettysburg *Compiler* reported on August 10: "Gen. Dan Sickles has nearly recovered from his wounds, and on Saturday week [sic] gave a dinner party in New York." Even old New York enemies, such as diarist George Templeton Strong, were forcibly converted. "I suppose Sickles," Strong sniffed in his diary, "with his one leg, among our best volunteer officers. His recuperative powers are certainly wonderful. Four years ago he was a ruined man in every sense, a pariah whom to know was discreditable."[32]

Chaplain Twichell visited Dan at the Sickles' fashionable house on Bloomingdale Road in New York. Having apparently overcome his early war aversion, Twichell chatted with both Teresa and her mother. He found Dan "pale and languid, and seemed yet to be suffering, but wonderfully well under the circumstances." Sickles announced that he had been out in a carriage several times and intended to be back in a saddle very soon. On August 11, Dan traveled to Saratoga to continue his recuperation, drawing a large crowd and a brass band serenade. When the crowd called for remarks, Sickles spoke briefly, telling them "that the only way to bring about a peace was to prosecute the war with vigor and send forward reinforcements, and support the Government." While in Saratoga, he immediately began to use his political connections to stimulate his business interests. Apparently overestimating his goodwill at the White House, he asked Lincoln to intercede in the case of a California land grant in which Dan had an interest. Lincoln, the ex-lawyer, curtly rebuffed him: "My Dear Sir, The question presented is a property question, with which I do not think I should meddle as a volunteer. It will save me labor, therefore, if you will first point me to the law which assigns any duty to the President in the case." War Democrats such as Sickles were important to the Administration, but Lincoln still knew where to draw the line.[33]

Sickles was eager to return to command. While in Saratoga, he practiced on a hobby horse in preparation for a return to the saddle.[34] On August 13, the *Times* obtained a letter Sickles had sent to "an officer in the army":

> I shall join the corps the very first day my strength will permit. My stump at present is very painful when a storm approaches, or during its progress. This will not last long. It has not yet shrunk to its natural size, so that I can be measured for an artificial leg; nor has it acquired sufficient hardness to enable me to ride in a carriage faster than a walk over any but a park road. In two weeks all these impediments will be removed, unless some hindrance occurs not now to be foreseen. I expect to be with you, for a trial at least, between the 15th and 20th of August.
>
> You cannot exaggerate my eagerness to be among the noble men who have done so much for the cause, and to whom I am indebted for so much of the military repute and flattering honors I enjoy. I wish to live and die

with them; their fate and mine must always be inseparable; their honor, welfare, pride and pleasures, are part and parcel of my existence.[35]

Sickles missed his self-imposed August deadline to return to the Army of the Potomac. George Templeton Strong was fed "confidential intelligence" that Sickles and Federal troops were instead to be sent to Texas to lead an invasion of Mexico. In fact, Sickles was pestering Secretary of War Stanton for just such an assignment. "It will not be long before I shall be ready to work again—Can you not then give me a command? If you send a column to operate in Texas that is a service I would like very much—Make it a Department & let me take my old Corps with me." His desire to serve in Texas may have also been partially motivated by the now unfriendly confines of the Army of the Potomac's command structure. "Meanwhile please do not permit Gen. Meade to break up my corps—which I hear he contemplates."[36]

Sickles' invasion of Mexico never materialized, but his spirits were boosted in September by news that Charles Graham's release had been arranged via a prisoner exchange. When Graham finally returned to New York, his friends threw a lavish party at Delmonico's. Graham recuperated for several months, but as a Sickles partisan his time with the Army of the Potomac was at an end. He was assigned to command the Naval Brigade with the Army of the James. In November 1864, he was put in charge of the defenses at Bermuda Hundred, and in March 1865 brevetted major general of volunteers.[37]

By late September, Sickles was preparing to finally leave New York and venture toward the army in Virginia. He traveled first to Washington, but stopped en route in Philadelphia to visit an old friend, Daniel Dougherty. It was another opportunity to practice his newest incarnation as wounded war hero. Dougherty arranged a welcome ceremony complete with a band and the requisite speeches. After receiving some praise from Dougherty, Sickles struggled with his new crutches as he rose to speak to the crowd. To "deafening cheers," Sickles thanked the many Pennsylvanians who had fought at Gettysburg, especially his friend David Birney. Missing from his praise was, of course, Philadelphia native George Meade. But what Sickles really focused on was that one theme he would rely on for the rest of his life: he had sacrificed his body and health to save Pennsylvania and the Northern cause. From this time forward, losing a leg became his greatest career move. "Although I am now suffering some little inconvenience, owing to a casualty that occurred in a recent battle, let me tell you and the world that I am proud of that sacrifice."[38]

The origins of the Second Battle of Gettysburg began with a series of events in the fall of 1863. The opening salvo was fired when Meade filed his official report that October. Concerning Sickles' July 2 position, Meade wrote that he had wanted the Third Corps to extend the Second Corps line along Cemetery Ridge, but that Sickles, "not fully apprehending the instructions in regard to the position to be occupied, had advanced, or rather was in the act of advancing, his corps some half a mile or three-quarters of a mile in front of the line of the Second Corps." Meade directed no slights at the Third Corps itself, stressing that they "sustained the shock most heroically." But Meade also made a seemingly innocent statement that later added to Sickles' wrath. "Notwithstanding the stubborn resistance of the Third Corps, *under Major-General Birney (Major-General Sickles having been wounded early in the action)* [emphasis added] the superiority of numbers of the enemy enabling him to outflank the corps in its advanced position, General Birney was compelled to fall back and reform behind the line originally designed to be held." Meade, perhaps unintentionally, implied that the man being toasted as the battle's victor had been wounded early in the action and thus played little part in the outcome. All things considered, Meade's "censure" was fairly moderate. Other generals may have let the matter rest. Sickles, though, was by now too immersed in his new incarnation as one-legged war hero to let accusations of "misapprehension" pass unchallenged.[39]

Sickles' old corps, meanwhile, waited eagerly for his return. His replacement, William H. French, was immensely unpopular with the now battle-hardened veterans. While Third Corps headquarters had gained a reputation earlier that spring for hospitality, the casualties of Chancellorsville and Gettysburg had created a bond that naturally excluded outsiders such as French (who, in any event, did nothing to win over his new corps.) During a meeting of corps officers at Birney's headquarters on September 2, "The Third Army Corps Union" was officially formed to secure funds for embalming and sending home the bodies of officers killed in battle or dying in field hospitals. The organization, the first veteran society formed within the Army of the Potomac, also required corps officers to secure fellow officers' release in the event that they were taken prisoner. The group's most lasting impact was that it doggedly promoted the corps' history, held reunions, and maintained Third Corps pride in the decades after the battle when their Gettysburg record was often under attack. Sickles was elected its first president.[40]

Regis de Trobriand, still hoping for a promotion, noted as early as August that "Sickles will be here before the end of the month and between him and

Birney, they will do me justice, I hope, against the officer Gen. French supports—he is a stranger to our corps and is fond of his favorite 'pets'." When Sickles still had not arrived by late August, de Trobriand wrote, "We are waiting for Gen. Sickles to return next week. The 3rd Corps (the famous 3rd!!!) will offer him a beautiful campaign carriage with a bed and a desk for writing, a superb team, harness etc., etc., to comfort him during the fatigues of war and to express him our feelings for his bravery and his high military capacity." By late September, word finally arrived that Sickles had traveled as far south as Washington.[41]

The wounded war hero departed Washington for the front on October 15. The press thought that Lee and Meade were poised to fight a major battle near the old Manassas field, and that Sickles' return to the army signaled something more significant than it actually was. In New York, the *Times* reported: "The command of the Army of the Potomac is fatal. Gen. Meade in his turn has been compelled to give place to some other man. His removal from command seems to have been determined on. His successor is said to be Major-General Daniel E. Sickles." Another dispatch from Washington that same day was also wide of the mark: "Gen. Sickles and staff left here for the front at 2 o'clock this p.m. In case of a general engagement, he will take command of his old corps." Not everyone was convinced that Sickles was physically ready to return. "General Sickles arrived in the front last night, prepared to take the field if a fight ensue," announced the New York *Tribune* on October 19. "His friends there, however, think his valor carries him too far in his present physical condition."[42]

Sickles arrived that evening at Third Corps headquarters. Joe Twichell met him en route and found him "looking magnificently and showed no signs, save the missing leg, of his misfortune." Sickles entered camp "like an emperor" followed by a cortege of officers. Once his arrival became known to the men, there occurred what Regis de Trobriand described as "grand rejoicing. . . . All the division was lined up on both sides of the road, and when the car where our glorious invalid was, arrived, a storm of hurrahs exploded and continued on all along the journey with an enthusiasm that I never saw in my life." Birney was waiting to meet Sickles in a wagon drawn by four horses. "Their appearance was the signal for a thunder of acclamations, such as I have seldom heard. The wagon passed at a walk, from one end to the other of the line; explosions of hurrahs burst forth on the passage of the carriage, and were kept up long after it was at a distance. Caps were thrown into the air; and the welcome was most enthusiastic." When Sickles climbed out of the carriage at Birney's headquarters and "advanced on his crutch with his leg almost healed, but very healthy and smiling, the din was deafening." Some thought they even saw a tear on Sickles' cheek. After Sickles and the brigade commanders entered Birney's tent, "the men assembled around in throngs, for a long time giving expression to their joy."[43]

De Trobriand "acknowledged that this reception was not only a manifestation in honor of the old corps commander, but also a protest against the successor given to us." General French, a heavy drinker ("addicted to some vulgar vice forbidden amongst themselves"), had done nothing to win the Third Corps' loyalty, "by making of his authority an instrument of intrigues."[44] Sickles' later admission that he believed a battle was imminent helps explain the timing of his return:

> I was convalescent in October—my general health re-established; my wound not yet entirely healed; but anticipating, from the movements of the army, that there would be another engagement—General Lee maneuvering on the right flank of General Meade, and General Meade falling back towards Washington—I came to Washington, en route to the army. Ascertaining from official sources that a battle was expected to be fought by our forces, I went down to the front and reported for duty. I found the headquarters established at Centreville, our army having fallen back and taken position on the Occoquan on the left, and towards Chantilly on the right, resting substantially in the defenses of Washington. . . . I did not expect to meet the army quite as near Washington as that.[45]

Meade admitted to his wife that his "back [was] to Washington," but that he had succeeded in preventing Lee from getting into his rear and was "ready for his [Lee's] attack, if he had chosen to make it." Such was the state of affairs when Sickles finally met with Meade near Fairfax Station on October 18. Sickles must have been uncomfortable asking Meade, of all people, for his corps back. Despite their long and acrimonious history together, Sickles was being hailed throughout the Northeast as a war hero, and the continuation of his new heroic status was now dependent upon Meade.[46]

Sickles described their meeting this way:

> I reported for duty, wishing, as I expressed myself to General Meade, to resume the command of my corps for the coming battle, although not able to report for duty permanently, feeling great doubts as to my ability to hold out for permanent command and active campaigning; but I had a

conviction that my presence with my corps would perhaps be of some advantage to the service, as it would certainly be most gratifying to my own feelings. I therefore solicited leave to take command of my corps, under the existing circumstances, notwithstanding my apparent disability. But General Meade expressed his disinclination, on account of his doubts as to my physical ability to meet the exigencies of the position of a corps commander. He instanced the case of General Ewell, of the rebel army, who had also lost a leg, and who did not resume command for eight or nine months. I very reluctantly yielded assent to this intimation of General Meade, and after reviewing my corps, I left the army.[47]

Since Sickles could not yet support an artificial leg, Regis de Trobriand thought Meade's rejection was "not without reason, that he was not yet able to endure the hardships of service." Still, the "welcome given him by his two old divisions went far to console him for his disappointment." David Birney wrote privately, "Sickles came to take command. Meade preferred that he should not, and kindly resisted that he was not able. We have great faith here in him. His conduct at Gettysburg in firing on the enemy as he was massing in our front was disapproved by Meade's do nothing wait until you can't help it policy but was approved by all of this Corps. Sickles will I think command this army and in time be President. I have great confidence in him and his management."[48]

Within two days of Meade's refusal, Sickles was back in front of Lincoln and Stanton in Washington. As Sickles later admitted, "I could but express my sense of reluctance in again presenting myself to headquarters for assignment to duty without an order from the general-in-chief, which would relieve me from the embarrassment of again tendering my services and exposing myself to the disappointment of having them again declined or again deferred."[49]

Less than charitable modern authors have since declared that it was now "time [for Sickles] to exact retribution" on Meade. Secretary of Navy Gideon Welles witnessed a conversation between Sickles and Abraham Lincoln on October 20. "I met General Sickles at the President's today," Welles recorded in his diary. "When I went in, the President was asking if Hancock did not select the battleground at Gettysburg. Sickles said he did not, but that General Howard and perhaps himself, were more entitled to that credit than any others. He then detailed the particulars, making himself, however, much more conspicuous than Howard."[50]

What Welles overheard was that when Meade arrived at Gettysburg, he was "for abandoning the position and falling back." Meade apparently called a council, at which Sickles was not present, "but [Sickles] wrote Meade his decided opinion in favor of maintaining the position, which was finally agreed to against Meade's judgment." Welles continued:

> Allowance must always be made for Sickles when he is interested, but his representations confirm my impressions of Meade, who means well, and, in his true position, that of a secondary commander, is more of a man than Sickles represents him—can obey orders and carry out orders better than he can originate and give them, hesitates, defers to others, has not strength, will, and self-reliance.[51]

Criticism of Meade's performance, always an occupational hazard for any army's commander, had been appearing in the press throughout the summer and early fall. David Birney complained to a friend, "You are doubtless bewildered at our recent strategic movements! Why should you not be, all of us in the army are." Such criticisms increasingly frustrated Meade, who told Lincoln and Halleck during a September meeting that "if they thought I was too slow or prudent, to put someone else in my place." Meade was summoned to Washington on October 22 (two days after Welles witnessed the meeting between Sickles and Lincoln). He found Lincoln "as he always is, very considerate & kind. He found no fault with my operations although it was very evident he was disappointed that I had not got a battle out of Lee." If not for the need to financially support his family, Meade told his wife, "I would resign today from this army."[52]

The Mine Run campaign late that November did nothing to enhance Meade's public status. Meade was unable to outmaneuver Lee along the Rapidan, and when Meade deemed it inadvisable to attack Lee's entrenched position, the Army of the Potomac withdrew into winter quarters. The failure to once again corner Lee was blamed by some, such as Marsena Patrick, on the poor performance of the Third Corps under General French. Nevertheless, Meade knew where the ultimate blame would settle. "My head is off," he told staff officer James Biddle. "I know that I shall be relieved, but I could not order an assault against my conscience." Meade's friends tried to assure the press that Meade's winter objectives had been achieved, but newspaper rumors were circulating that Meade's days were numbered, undoubtedly giving his enemies the impression that he was an easy target.[53]

The growing tensions escalated when General-in-Chief Henry Halleck filed his report in November. While Halleck based much of his report on input from Meade, he was much more explicit in his criticism of Sickles:

> General Sickles, misinterpreting his orders, instead of placing the Third Corps on the prolongation of the Second, had moved it nearly three-quarters of a mile in advance an error which nearly proved fatal in the battle. The enemy attacked this corps on the 2d with great fury, and it was likely to be utterly annihilated, when the Fifth Corps moved up on the left, and enabled it to reform behind the line it was originally ordered to hold.[54]

As General Halleck saw it, not only was Sickles guilty of "misinterpreting" his orders, but it had been up to another corps to save the Third from likely "annihilation." Halleck mildly censured Meade for allowing Lee's Army of Northern Virginia to cross the Potomac River to safety at Williamsport, but left no doubt as to whom he credited for the victory: "to General Meade belongs the honor of a well-earned victory in one of the greatest and best-fought battles of the war."[55]

"The Gettysburg report falls dead of us," General Birney complained, "tame, lifeless it is a poor tribute. . . . The 3rd Corps is misrepresented, and its gallant conduct under me in the front line on the 3rd ignored although it lost 500 killed and wounded from its decimated ranks. However, we may be partial here, and await with some anxiety Sickles' report which this attack will doubtless elicit." Unfortunately for Gettysburg historiography, Sickles never filed his report on the campaign. He would, however, have plenty to say in other forums.[56]

As the tumultuous year of 1863 drew to a close, Meade anxiously waited for any word from Washington regarding his future. In addition to Williamsport and Mine Run, Gettysburg still remained squarely in the news. "I see the *Herald* is constantly harping on the assertion that Gettysburg was fought by the corps commanders and the common soldiers, and that no generalship was displayed," complained Meade. "I suppose after awhile it will be discovered I was not at Gettysburg at all." The Radical Republicans in Washington began calling for Meade's removal in favor of the reinstatement of Joe Hooker. Although it is not exactly clear when Sickles began working with the Radicals in Congress, by that December he was back in Washington. Sickles, Birney, and Regis de Trobriand traveled to the capital via New York, with Sickles announcing to his companions unexpectedly that a fourth person would join them on the final leg of the train journey: Mary Todd Lincoln. Traveling in a reserved coach, the group arrived in Washington on the evening of December 8. "Sickles wasn't in good health with his crutch," recalled de Trobriand. "He was not able to accompany Madame Lincoln. It was me who took the advantage to offer her my arm when we got out of the car."[57] General Marsena Patrick recorded in his diary entry for December 16:

> Col. [G. H.] Sharpe came down [from Washington] yesterday. . . . He tells me that Sickles openly announces his intention to fight the battle with Halleck, who has made more serious & damaging charges against him than Meade did. He will ask for, either a Court of Inquiry, or a Committee of Investigation in Congress. It is probable he will succeed in flooring both. He is all powerful at the White House & is the Gallant of Mrs. Lincoln, going there at all times, Although the President is sick—too ill to see persons on business, he (Sickles) is said to call on him at any time."[58]

According to Sickles, he felt "keenly of the injustice" done by Halleck and Meade: "I asked President Lincoln to grant me a court of inquiry for the purpose of correcting the serious errors contained in the reports of the battle made by General Halleck and General Meade." Lincoln, however, denied the request, allegedly responding, "Sickles, they say you pushed out your men too near the enemy, and began to fight just as that council of war was about to meet at 2 o'clock in the afternoon of the battle. I am afraid what they say is true and God Bless you for it. Don't ask us to order an inquest to relieve you from bringing on the battle of Gettysburg. History will set you all right and give everybody his just place." When such talk reached the Army of the Potomac, officers such as Frank Haskell were outraged. "It is understood in the Army that the President thanked the slayer of Barton Key, for *saving the day* [emphasis in original] at Gettysburg. Does the country know any better than the President, that Meade, Hancock, and Gibbon, were entitled to some little share of such credit?"[59]

"I furthermore hear that General Sickles asserts that Hancock selected the position," Meade wrote on December 28, "and that he (Sickles), with his corps did all the fighting at Gettysburg. So, I presume, before long it will be clearly proved that my presence on the field was rather an injury than otherwise." Meade's words would prove prophetic. As 1864 dawned, Meade's adversaries within the army and the government escalated their efforts to deny him credit for the Gettysburg victory. Sickles would soon discover that it was unnecessary to call a Court of Inquiry, as there was already an investigative body in place to do the job for him. The politically inexperienced Meade would appear to be no match for the forces arrayed against him.[60]

Chapter 14

Subsequent Events
Proved My Judgment Correct

W hen Congress convened in December 1863, Senator Henry Wilson of Massachusetts, Chairman of the Committee on Military Affairs and a friend of Dan Butterfield, referred a joint resolution thanking and singling out several officers[1] for the victory at Gettysburg:

> A RESOLUTION expressive of the thanks of Congress to Maj. Gen. Joseph Hooker, Maj. Gen. George G. Meade, Maj. Gen. Oliver O. Howard, and the officers and soldiers of the Army of the Potomac.
>
> *Resolved by the Senate and House of Representatives of the United States of America, in Congress assembled,* That the gratitude of the American people, and the thanks of their Representatives in Congress, are due, and are hereby tendered, to Maj. Gen. Joseph Hooker, and the officers and soldiers of the Army of the Potomac, for the skill, energy, and endurance which first covered Washington and Baltimore from the meditated blow of the advancing and powerful army of rebels led by General Robert E. Lee; and to Maj. Gen. George G. Meade, Maj. Gen. Oliver O. Howard, and the officers and soldiers of that army, for the skill and heroic valor which, at Gettysburg, repulsed, defeated, and drove back, broken and dispirited, beyond the Rappahannock, the veteran army of the rebellion.[2]

The resolution was approved January 28, 1864. Meade was "highly honored" to have "my name associated with General Hooker," he wrote sarcastically. "Why they confined the including of my predecessors to Hooker I am at a loss to imagine. He certainly had no more to do with my operations and success at Gettysburg than either Burnside or McClellan." According to John Gibbon, Meade's friends "could see no propriety in connecting, even remotely, Hooker's name with the battle of Gettysburg." Nevertheless, Lincoln approved the resolution and the public record now validated the perception that Hooker shared responsibility for the victory.[3]

It has been suggested that Dan Sickles and his supporters had attempted to replace Meade's name on the resolution with Sickles'. The one-legged general was still a prominent Democrat, however, and the Radical Republicans were only interested in allying themselves with his unsavory reputation up to a certain point. (Some members of the Committee would actually criticize Sickles for irregularities in his quartermaster department.) James Wilson Grimes, a Republican Senator from Iowa, had asked for Howard's inclusion as credit for selecting Cemetery Hill. No direct evidence has yet to confirm that Sickles directly contributed to Howard's inclusion. But as Navy Secretary Gideon Welles witnessed during the previous fall, Sickles claimed that both he and Howard were jointly responsible for the victory. Did such talk indirectly help elevate Howard's contributions? Although Sickles was undoubtedly disappointed to be excluded from the resolution, he certainly must have been pleased to see Hooker elevated over Meade. Perhaps Hooker would be returning to the army after all. If so, Sickles' return to Third Corps command could not be far behind.[4]

Many Gettysburg students presume that Dan Sickles was obsessed with moving the powerful Congressional machinery in order to extract revenge upon George Meade's head. What the actual historical record does clearly show is that Sickles was determined to return to duty. He wanted to contribute to the war effort, and was probably embarrassed when his name was among a lengthy list of generals sent to the Senate who were without commands (and still drawing $445 per month pay along with the services of staffers Tremain and Alexander Moore.) The *Times* called the list "formidable to taxpayers and odious to soldiers who live in the front." Had events transpired more expediently, Sickles might not have even been in Washington while the Second Battle of Gettysburg was fought in the spring of 1864.

In late January, while recuperating in New York, Sickles assured the President that "I have been quite successful" in learning to use an artificial limb. "I can walk without crutches, my health is so far reestablished as to make me anxious for employment." He also told Lincoln:

"The Times" [sic] of today mentions a rumor that I am to be assigned to the Command of the Dep't. of Washington—I hope there is good foundation for the statement—I can be useful in that post. Stationed at Washington, with duties ostensibly Military & appropriate to my rank and in a position where I can Communicate easily with the influential people who will be in Washington this year—I can be most useful in the other aspects about which we have Conversed.

There is another field in which valuable service could be rendered by an officer of rank and ability—occupying half of his time at the Capital & the remainder South. A Military Commissioner, giving his whole attention to the subject, could contribute powerfully to increase and organize the elements of disaffection toward the rebel authorities in North Carolina, Georgia, and elsewhere—and at the same time Contribute largely to the work of reconstruction in Arkansas, Louisiana, Mississippi & Tennessee. The Commissioner should be a man of tact & Address—well acquainted with the Southern people . . . familiar with political movements and the Military situation and the Characters of the Military and political leaders at the South, and the motives which influence them.[5]

Lincoln had another idea. He replied by telegram on January 29, asking if Sickles could "immediately take a trip to Arkansas for me?" An eager Sickles sent a response the same day, "I am ready to go at once." But by February 2, Lincoln had not responded and Sickles was waiting impatiently in New York for word of his diplomatic mission to the Trans-Mississippi Theater. He reminded the President that he was "ready to go" and was "making good use of my time in learning the use of my artificial limb." He also reminded Lincoln of his preferred assignment. "My *first* [emphasis in original] wish is to resume command of my Corps—next to that, the command of Washington—but I shall be entirely satisfied to undertake any duty which you think I can be most useful to the Government."[6]

According to Sickles biographer W. A. Swanberg, "A week later he [Sickles] hurried off to the capital, where he must have explained to the President the importance of his remaining long enough to testify before the Committee on the Conduct of the War." In reality, Lincoln told Sickles on February 10 to "come at your earliest convenience, prepared to make the contemplated trip for me." Sickles replied immediately: "Will go on tomorrow afternoon." The discussed trip west never materialized, because Arkansas officials did not want him there. Both the department commander and the provisional governor urged Lincoln not to send Sickles. "[C]oming here would only be an annoyance and will do no good," Governor Isaac Murphy informed Lincoln.[7]

Instead of Arkansas, the President proposed on February 15 yet another diplomatic mission, a tour "principally for observation and information. . . . You will call at Memphis, Helena, Vicksburg, New-Orleans, Pensacola, Key-West, Charleston-Harbor. . . . Please ascertain at each place what is being done, if anything, for reconstruction. . . . Also learn what you can as to the colored people."[8]

As late as February 25, Lincoln was saying that Sickles "probably will make a tour down the Mississippi." But Sickles didn't depart for his trip. The Joint Congressional Committee on the Conduct of the War was nearly ready to begin calling witnesses on Gettysburg. Presuming that Sickles decided to stay in Washington and willingly testify, which seems a logical assumption, then his decision to remain and cooperate was probably made as late as February 15, when the Arkansas trip was officially killed. Had events moved faster when Lincoln extended the Arkansas invitation on January 29, Sickles might not have even been in Washington to open the Gettysburg portion of the hearings.[9]

The Joint Congressional Committee on the Conduct of the War was a "committee of inquiry into the general conduct of the war," specifically created to investigate the Union's inability to score battlefield victories. The committee consisted of three senators and four representatives, and was controlled by "Radical" Republicans who favored a merciless punishment of the South. Since Southern Democrats had led the charge to secession, the Republicans increasingly linked Union battlefield defeats with the presence of Democrats in the Northern army's leadership and distrusted West Point as a breeding ground of these traitorous Democrat generals.[10]

The committee was chaired by Ohio Republican Senator Benjamin Wade, who proclaimed West Point "the hot-bed from which rebellion was hatched and from thence emanated your principal traitors and conspirators." Senator Wade was a confrontational and fiery opponent of slavery who followed the maxim that the "South has got to be punished and traitors hung." Wade and Michigan Senator Zachariah Chandler dominated the committee. Their self-proclaimed purpose was to "obtain such information . . . as would best enable them to advise what mistakes had been made in the past and the proper course to be pursued in the future." More than a fact-finding body, they also thought it necessary to provide Lincoln "with such recommendations and suggestions as seemed to be most imperatively demanded." Summoned witnesses were allowed no cross-examination and were not allowed to confront their accusers. While Gettysburg students tend to remember the committee for its role in collecting the testimony related to the battle, the body investigated a wide variety of events. But the crushing defeat at Chancellorsville and Meade's widely criticized inability to prevent Lee's escape back to Virginia convinced the committee that Democrat Copperheads still controlled the Army of the Potomac.[11]

In February 1864, the committee began calling witnesses related to the Army of the Potomac's operations under Hooker and Meade. The committee's ultimate and rather ironic objective was to replace Meade (who had won the battle of Gettysburg) with Hooker (who had been defeated at Chancellorsville). The committee's intent demonstrates the extent to which Meade's failure to bring Lee back to battle overshadowed his Gettysburg victory. Politically, Hooker was a Democrat and another untrustworthy West Pointer, but he was deemed more suitable to the Radical agenda since he promoted the image of wanting to conquer the South. Meade's post-Gettysburg performance convinced some members that he was another uncommitted West Point Copperhead Democrat. Meade also had a past history with Chandler. While in Detroit after Fort Sumter, Meade had drawn Chandler's ire by refusing to attend a public rally and renew his loyalty oath to the United States. (Meade objected on the grounds that the attending local authorities had no right to demand such an oath.)[12] What Meade did not yet realize was that the committee was out to prove the following:

1. Meade only followed Hooker's plans at Gettysburg, and did not have any plan of his own. Hooker, and not a confused and indecisive Meade, designed the victory.

2. Meade did not want to fight at Gettysburg, intending instead to retreat to Pipe Creek. Only a collision with Lee's army forced the battle.

3. Meade wanted to retreat on July 2. Only Sickles' battle with Longstreet prevented the Army of the Potomac from abandoning Gettysburg.

4. Meade failed to follow up and finish Lee's army and allowed Lee to escape at Williamsport.[13]

Hooker's return to the Army of the Potomac was not as far-fetched a scenario as it initially appears. Stranger things had happened in that army:

George McClellan had returned for a second stint in command. During late July and early August of 1863, an interesting series of communications passed between Lincoln and Meade regarding Hooker's role with the army. The thrust of the exchange was Lincoln's inquiry as to whether Meade would be agreeable to allowing Hooker to resume command of a corps within the army. Despite Lincoln's assurance that Meade could reply "in perfect freedom," Meade walked a tight diplomatic line when he replied, "I have no hesitation in saying, that if Genl. Hooker is willing to take a command under me, I shall be very glad to have the benefit of his services." In mid-August, Lincoln mentioned the proposal to Hooker, who "seemed gratified" and "would accept the offer if it was still open." Perhaps realizing that it was time to speak or forever hold his peace, Meade sent the following reply to his Commander-in-Chief:

> You seem to think, or rather such is the inference left on my mind, that I
> have made an offer to Genl. Hooker & that I desire his assignment to this
> army. Now in the frankness which has marked your letters, permit me to
> say, this is a mis-apprehension on your part. My position is one of
> acquiescence. I wrote you, that if you desired Genl. Hooker to have a
> command under me I should not object, but you will pardon me, if I call
> to your recollection, that the proposition originated with yourself that the
> offer when made was yours and that I have neither entertained nor
> expressed any desire upon the subject.[14]

Given the committee's agenda, the committee would have pounced on Meade regardless of Sickles' involvement. This fact is sometimes lost on Gettysburg students. Sickles was only a supporting player in a much larger political apparatus. But Dan obviously decided to both cooperate and furnish the committee with fresh ammunition. Meade's report and refusal to allow Sickles' return to the Third Corps may have been the initial stimulus, or perhaps it was Halleck's report that pushed Sickles over the edge. One popular theory is that while recuperating in Washington, Sickles *may* have heard a rumor that only his wound had prevented Meade from court-martialing him. But Meade repeated on several occasions that he believed Sickles had honestly misinterpreted orders. Meade's report, correspondence, and his own Congressional testimony does not suggest that he was considering Sickles a worthy candidate for court martial. Meade might have taken some pre-emptive action if he was aware of Sickles' animosity toward him, but Meade appears to have been relatively unaware until after Sickles had launched his own assault.[15]

It initially seems odd that Sickles, a prominent Democrat, would ally himself with Radical Republicans, but his cooperation would strengthen his image as a "War Democrat"—a far cry from the traitorous Southerners and indifferent Northerners of his party. Sickles had aligned with Republicans before; after all, he was a close friend of Abraham Lincoln. Still, the committee's agenda was more radical and opposed ideologically to Lincoln. In effect, Sickles was spending his nights with the Lincolns (Mary Todd chastised Dan for missing a matinee on February 20 by inviting him to dinner the following evening) while working days with Lincoln's rivals. It was a fine act that only a deft political professional like Sickles could balance. Also working in Sickles' favor with the committee was the fact that he was not a "tainted" West Pointer. For once his status as a military "amateur" would actually benefit him, for he had not been educated in that despised institution.[16]

Sickles had another reason to cooperate with the committee: his participation would put him back in the political and newspaper spotlight. The forced inactivity since Gettysburg must have been unbearable for a man of his energy and ego. More importantly, there was the matter of his fledgling military reputation. Despite the relative brevity of his military career, he had reinvented himself from disgraced politician to war hero. Meade's and Halleck's reports jeopardized that new image. Without his involvement, the committee's proceedings might further incriminate his own July 2 actions, or serve to diminish his role in the battle. Plus, if he wanted his Third Corps command back, getting Meade replaced with Hooker was likely Sickles' last chance. Unfortunately for Meade, Dan had demonstrated during the Key murder trial (when he demolished his wife's reputation) that no price was too high to save his own neck.

Sickles was sworn before the committee on February 25. Since Meade had rejected his attempted return to the army, he explained, "I have been waiting orders . . . meanwhile, giving my best attention to the entire re-establishment of my health and strength for active duty." During his first day's testimony, he answered questions regarding Joe Hooker and the Chancellorsville campaign. Sickles ultimately attributed the campaign's failure "To the giving way of the Eleventh Corps." Prior to Hooker's removal from command (which Dan emphasized was at Hooker's request), "Fighting Joe" had managed to strategically maneuver his army into position between Lee and Washington. "Those movements resulted in compelling General Lee to fight at Gettysburg," Dan testified, "the most advantageous position, I think, that we could have taken for our battle-ground."[17]

The following day, February 26, Sickles became the first witness to present testimony regarding the Gettysburg campaign. His testimony, for whatever character flaws it revealed, demonstrated his skill as an attorney and his comfort level in playing politics. In order to dispel any notions that he had made a near-fatal blunder on July 2, he used the historical record and many of Meade's own communications to spin a complex tale. In this version of Gettysburg, George Meade had intended to retreat, and Sickles' advance to the Peach Orchard had forced Longstreet's attack, thereby preventing Meade from withdrawing. If Sickles had not forced this attack, Gettysburg would not have been fought, and therefore not have been won.[18]

Sickles started his assault by characterizing Meade's Pipe Creek Circular not as a contingency, but rather as an order to "retreat" and "fall back." As Sickles spun it, Meade considered the campaign's objectives to be the protection of Washington, Baltimore, and Pennsylvania—not the destruction of Lee's army. Sickles read the circular to the committee, but only selected those portions that supported his argument. For example, he neglected to read the part where Meade stated: "Developments may cause the commanding general to assume the offensive from his present positions."[19]

Sickles laid the groundwork for the committee's portrayal of a timid and indecisive Meade by pointing out the conflicting orders that Sickles had received while at Emmitsburg on July 1. Oliver Howard had wanted Sickles to come to Gettysburg; Meade had not. Dan criticized Meade's preference for "another line of operations." Despite this apparent reluctance on the part of his commander, "I therefore moved to Gettysburg on my own responsibility." Sickles further misrepresented his July 1, 9:30 p.m. dispatch to Meade as "begging him [Meade] by all means to concentrate his army there and fight a battle, stating that in my judgment it was a good place to fight . . . and that in my judgment it would be most destructive to the morale of the army to fall back, as was apparently contemplated in his order of that morning." In reality, this message to Meade had been nothing of the sort. As discussed earlier, Dan had written the dispatch to defend his decision to leave Emmitsburg without Meade's permission. It is true that Sickles had ended the message with, "This is a good battle-field." But this hardly equated to Sickles "begging" Meade to fight at Gettysburg. Sickles was portraying himself as aggressive, decisive, and competent—exactly the qualities the committee thought Meade lacked. While Sickles did not explicitly tell the committee that he had selected the Gettysburg battlefield, he aggressively implied that he deserved a share of the credit for keeping the army at Gettysburg. In fact, he deserved none.[20]

In order to elevate his own status, Sickles also dispelled the notion that the battle had actually consisted of three days. Although it was "popularly understood" that the battle commenced on July 1, "we in the army do not regard the operations of the two corps under General Reynolds as properly the battle of Gettysburg. We regard the operations of Thursday and Friday [July 2 and 3], when the whole army was concentrated, as the battle of Gettysburg." He later added that July 2 was the "second day of fighting; but, as we in the army consider it, the first day of the battle." This was a popularly reoccurring theme throughout the remainder of his life. Since the Third Corps had not participated on July 1, this day was simply excluded from the battle's history. The second of July, he would repeatedly tell audiences, was the decisive day.[21]

Sickles argued that his advance to the Emmitsburg Road line was necessitated by Meade's lack of attention to the left flank. Dan admitted that he had received orders to relieve Geary's division "at a very early hour," but he was confused over where to go since Geary "was not in position, but was merely massed in my vicinity." Sickles claimed he asked Meade for further orders, received none, and felt his fear over an impending flank attack "was not concurred in at headquarters." Artillery chief Henry Hunt, Sickles explained to the committee, declined to formally approve his advanced line, "although he said it met with the approval of his own judgment; but he said that I would undoubtedly receive such orders as soon as he reported to General Meade."[22]

Sickles seemingly took full responsibility for his Gettysburg actions. Since Meade and Halleck's reports had accused Sickles of "not fully apprehending" and "misinterpreting" his orders, Dan had to choose between portraying himself as either incompetent or as an aggressive fighter who advanced to meet the enemy. Sickles chose the latter. Almost five years earlier, Sickles had publicly accepted blame for reconciling with Teresa with the declaration, "Whatever blame, if any belongs to the step, should fall alone upon me."[23] Now, with the national stakes even higher, he nearly repeated himself:

> I took up that position, which is described in the report of General Halleck . . . which, in his report, he very pointedly disapproves of, and which he further says I took up through a misinterpretation of orders. It was not through any misinterpretation of orders. It was either a good line or a bad one, and, whichever it was, I took it on my own responsibility, except so far as I have already stated, that it was approved of in general terms by General Hunt . . . I took up that line because it enabled me to hold commanding ground, which, if the enemy had been allowed to take-

as they would have taken it if I had not occupied it in force- would have rendered our position on the left untenable; and, in my judgment, would have turned the fortunes of the day hopelessly against us.[24]

Although it was really the only strategy open to him, since Dan would never willingly call himself incompetent, it was still a risky course. If later testimony were to conclusively prove that his advance was a colossal military blunder, then Sickles would have admitted to his own military ineptitude. Sickles attempted to reduce this risk with obviously false testimony, such as, "Fortunately, my left had succeeded in getting into position on Round Top and along the commanding ridge to which I have referred; and those positions were firmly held by the Third Corps." That he was forced into such a lie indicates that even he believed he had blundered by leaving the hill unoccupied. Dan admitted that he had told Meade at the Peach Orchard that "I could not, with one corps, hold so extended a line against the rebel army; but that, if supported, the line could be held; and, in my judgment, it was a strong line, and the best one." Neither Wade nor anyone else on the committee bothered to challenge Sickles on this point. If he knew his line was too extended, and could only be saved by support from others, then why did he advance in the first place? Such lack of scrutiny leads to the suspicion that Wade was treating his "star witness" with kid gloves.[25]

Sickles testified that Meade had promised support from the Fifth and Second corps, as well as "as much artillery as I wanted." He was indebted to Hancock, continued Sickles, but the Fifth Corps "came up, somewhat tardily, to be sure. It was three-quarters of an hour, or an hour I suppose, before it got into position." The enemy's attacks "were successfully repulsed . . . until I was wounded and carried from the field." Sickles lied again by claiming the Third Corps held its advanced position (at least until he was wounded, when it became Birney's problem) and that the Fifth Corps (which defended Little Round Top) had "tardily" offered minimal support. Sickles must have realized that the historical record simply wouldn't support him without these fabrications.[26]

While much of Sickles' testimony was intended to elevate his own part in the Federal victory—and he was far from the only witness to attempt this—his most serious accusation was that Meade had wanted to retreat on July 2. Even if the Pipe Creek order had been proof that Meade did not intend to fight at Gettysburg, Sickles admitted that Meade must have been willing to do so by the evening of July 1, "else he would not have concentrated there." Still, Sickles testified that he had "reason to know that his [Meade's] plan of operations was changed again on Thursday [July 2], and that he resumed, in substance, the plan

. . . to fall back on Pipe creek, or to some place in that neighborhood." Sickles presumably received this "information" from his friend Dan Butterfield during his 11:00 a.m. visit to Meade's headquarters. "I was satisfied, from information which I received [at 11:00], that it was intended to retreat from Gettysburg." This charge painted Meade in the worst possible light, and opened the door for decades of accusations from both camps.[27]

Sickles was questioned rather extensively about troop dispositions around Washington, Baltimore, Harpers Ferry, and the Peninsula both before and after Gettysburg. Since Sickles rejoined the army on June 28 and departed on July 2, he was hardly qualified to address this subject. Nevertheless, he was asked and answered a number of questions concerning Halleck's support of the army. Sickles assumed Meade received more cooperation than Hooker from Halleck because Meade "had the confidence and friendship of General Halleck, while General Hooker had not." Withholding the Harpers Ferry garrison from Hooker, wrote Sickles, "was sacrificing a great end for a minor consideration . . . I cannot conceive of any military reason which explains that extraordinary inconsistency."[28]

Sickles, of course, had not been with the army during Lee's retreat to the Potomac River. But that didn't stop Senator Wade from questioning him on the "propriety" of encountering Lee before he "had an opportunity to recross the river." Sickles' response was direct: Lee "should have been followed up closely, and vigorously attacked before he had opportunity to recross the river. . . . If we could whip them at Gettysburg, as we did, we could much more easily whip a running and demoralized army, seeking a retreat which was cut off by a swollen river; and if they could march after being whipped, we certainly could march after winning a battle."[29]

Whether Meade's decision-making during the retreat was right or wrong, it was perfectly within Sickles' character to opt for the aggressive course. It is also illustrative of the committee's bias that they accepted his opinion on this point. Wade wanted Sickles' opinions as "a military man, and one of a great deal of experience," and Sickles replied "as a military man" that "I do not think there was any military difficulty to prevent a decisive attack upon General Lee, which must have resulted in the destruction of his army." Sickles' very public transformation from disgraced politician-attorney to "military man" continued apace.[30]

In assessing Sickles' testimony before the committee, historians enjoy speculating why Sickles attacked Meade with such relish. Some assume any criticism directed at Sickles' Gettysburg performance was simply unacceptable to a man with his ego and ambition. His public image, however, had survived many career-threatening hits prior to Gettysburg. As a career politician, he was used to harsh criticism. Here, after all, was a man who had once been compared to "fetid gas"; George Meade's Gettysburg report was decidedly mild in comparison. One author deduced that Sickles' "future depended on Meade's destruction." This conclusion surely is an exaggeration, for President Lincoln was almost certainly willing to employ Sickles in some capacity. Whatever his motives, Sickles was not fighting for his "survival." But, he had fallen in love with the trappings of a field command, and more than simply being out for revenge against Meade, Sickles must have hoped that his testimony would buy something practical: the return of both himself and Hooker.[31]

Abner Doubleday appeared before the committee after Sickles. Meade (and many other officers) did not think much of Doubleday's abilities as a commander. In fact, Meade was previously pleased when Doubleday assumed command of Meade's old division because, as Meade put it, the division "will think a great deal more of me than before." The officer assuming the witness chair was justifiably bitter about his treatment at Gettysburg. Doubleday had led the First Corps as well as could be expected following Reynolds' untimely demise on the morning of the battle's first day. But Oliver Howard told Hancock later on July 1 that Doubleday's command "gave way", information Hancock dutifully passed on to Meade. This news played a role in having Doubleday replaced as commander of the First Corps by Major General John Newton—a man David Birney characterized as an "engineer with but little executive capacity, fond of whiskey, and will never distinguish himself although a pet of Meade." The fact that Newton was junior to Doubleday in seniority only added insult to injury. Doubleday's participation, along with his obvious bitterness about the manner in which Meade treated him, has led to suggestions that he coordinated his testimony with Sickles and the committee. When word of Doubleday's testimony reached the Army of the Potomac's camps, First Corps artillery chief Charles Wainwright wondered what Sickles and Doubleday were up to. "A pretty team!—Rascality and Stupidity. I wonder which hatches the most monstrous chicken." It seems that Doubleday's time away had not earned any additional respect from his peers.[32]

Much of Doubleday's testimony defended his own July 1 performance at the expense of Howard's Eleventh Corps. He could barely conceal his anger toward Meade. Doubleday compared the Pipe Creek Circular to giving "us orders after the battle was fought." Meade, he continued, spent July 1 at Taneytown: "It is inexplicable to me that he could hear the thunder of that battle all day without riding up to see something in relation to it." In comparison, "General Sickles did start for that purpose without orders, though too late [on July 1] to be of service." If in fact there was any coordination between the testimony of Sickles and Doubleday, Doubleday did not exaggerate the value of Sickles' arrival on the field.[33]

Meade's only plan, argued Doubleday, was to fight on the "long, feeble line of battle on Pipe Creek" which seemed "to be chosen for defensive purposes, to cover Washington and Baltimore." He contested that if Meade had been allowed to pursue this plan then the Army of Northern Virginia would have "gone on *ad infinitum* plundering the state of Pennsylvania." However, despite several attempts, the committee was unable to get Doubleday to characterize the Pipe Creek Circular as a retreat order. This contradicted Sickles' central premise, and further suggests that Sickles and Doubleday did *not* coordinate their stories.[34]

Doubleday hit a home run when he told the committee that Meade had superseded Howard and himself because Meade "thought a couple of scapegoats were necessary. . . . General Meade is in the habit of violating the organic law of the army to place his personal friends in power. There has always been a great deal of favoritism in the Army of the Potomac. No man who is an anti-slavery man or an anti-McClellan man can expect decent treatment in that army as at present constituted." While not mentioning Meade by name, Doubleday railed against the "pro-slavery cliques controlling that army, composed of men who, in my opinion, would not have been unwilling to make a compromise in favor of slavery." This sort of damning testimony was exactly what the anti-West Point senators and representatives were digging for. The charge painted Meade as another McClellan Democrat who was soft on slavery—a perfect reason to remove him from command. Although Doubleday had not explicitly supported Sickles' most serious charge that Meade planned to retreat, he did provide plenty of anti-Meade ammunition for Wade's committee. Years later Doubleday recanted most of his accusations against Meade. They were based on a belief that Meade was scheming to promote pro-McClellan men, explained Doubleday: "I afterward ascertained that I was mistaken in this respect." But unfortunately for Meade, Doubleday's explanation was well into the future, and did not help the commanding general's status before the committee.[35]

The next witness was a relatively minor figure in Gettysburg's history. Brigadier General Albion Howe commanded the Second Division in Sixth Corps. A West Pointer and career army officer, Howe's pre-Gettysburg resume was most notable for his membership in Robert E. Lee's posse that captured John Brown at Harpers Ferry. In 1865, Howe would serve as part of the honor guard at Lincoln's funeral and as one of nine military officers on the commission that tried the assassination conspirators. Although the presence of the large Sixth Corps provided comforting reassurance for Meade and the rest of the army at Gettysburg, the majority of the corps—including Howe's command—saw little combat. His 3,600 odd-man division suffered fewer than twenty casualties, and his Gettysburg report barely fills three paragraphs. Given the predilections of the committee, Howe's West Point background, minor battle role, and one not directly privy to Meade's strategy makes him an odd choice as a witness. He was primarily called because he was yet another officer disgruntled with Meade. Howe was transferred out of field command to an administrative post on February 29, only two days prior to his testimony. While there is debate as to whether Meade was actually responsible for the transfer, he did not oppose Howe's ouster.[36]

Howe testified that on the evening of July 2, Sixth Corps leader John Sedgwick told him that the army's brain trust was "discussing whether we shall stay here, or move back to Westminster." Howe diminished the impact generalship may have had in bringing about the victory, telling the committee, "Our position mainly did the work for us . . . as a military operation on our side, no particular credit can attach to it. There was no great generalship displayed; there was no maneuvering, no combinations." Following the committee's lead, he added, "I can see no reason why we did not follow them more vigorously" after the battle. When asked if the Williamsport council of war, which delayed Meade's planned assault, "was calculated to weaken the confidence of the army," he replied that he was "decidedly of the opinion that it was."[37]

Following Howe's first day of testimony, Senators Wade and Chandler went to see Lincoln and Edwin Stanton. Due to the "incompetency of the general in command of the army," they demanded Meade's removal. While claiming to not be "advocates of any particular general" the senators "for themselves would be content with General Hooker, believing him to be competent." Although only three witnesses had thus far been called, Wade and Chandler's haste might have been caused by the administration's revival of the rank of lieutenant general on February 26, and Ulysses S. Grant's confirmation on March 2. They may have believed that Grant's pending arrival would reduce their ability to oust Meade in favor of Hooker. Alternatively, Lincoln might have argued that Grant would soon be on the scene to supersede, replace, or prod Meade. Whatever both sides' motives, Lincoln declined their demands.[38]

Undeterred by Lincoln's snub, the committee continued with Howe on March 4. Most of the army's officers, Howe claimed, did not "have full confidence in the ability or state of mind of George Meade" to strike an offensive blow. This may have been fair criticism, but Howe took his testimony one step further. The committee had been tap dancing around the subject of Meade's loyalty, and Howe obliged them much more directly than even Sickles had been willing to state.[39] When questioned on Meade and the corps commanders' inability to "strike an offensive blow," Howe answered:

> I do not know as it would be proper for me to state here the terms we use in the army. However, we say there is too much *copperheadism* [emphasis added] in it . . . with some there is a desire to raise up General McClellan; with others there is a dislike to some of the measures of the government; they do not like the way the Negro question is handled . . . the impression is made upon my mind that there are some who have no faith in this war, who have no heart in it; they will not do anything to commit themselves . . . there is copperheadism at the root of the matter."[40]

Meade and the corps commanders who had won the victory at Gettysburg less than a year earlier were now being characterized as Northern Democrats who opposed the war effort. Lest there be any doubt as to his meaning, Howe added to and clarified his remarks in further questioning, concluding that "there is too much sympathy with men and measures in opposition to the principle measures of the government, and those who are in control of the government." Ironically, one of the reasons Meade had been placed in command of the army was due to a supposed lack of political impulses. Now, due to his alleged politics, he was coming dangerously close to being called a traitor to the Union cause. Sickles had (commendably) not made Howe's outlandish accusations, nor did he suggest that he agreed with the charges during the long years that would follow the close of the committee. Sickles' primary goal had been to convince the committee that Meade was hell-bent upon retreat. He cooperated with the committee, but he did not set its agenda.[41]

On March 3, Sickles' accusations reached the floor of the Senate. Minnesota's Radical Republican Senator Morton Wilkinson, one of Chandler's close friends, told the Senate, "I am told . . . that before the fight commenced at Gettysburg . . . the order went forth from the commander of that army to retreat; and but for the single fact that one of the corps commanders had got into a fight before the dispatch reached him, the whole army would undoubtedly have been retreating." A grim discovery awaited George Meade when he arrived in Washington the following day to conduct business related to the army's reorganization. "When I reached Washington," he later wrote, "I was greatly surprised to find the whole town talking of certain grave charges of Generals Sickles and Doubleday, that had been made against me in their testimony."[42]

The army commander was summoned by the committee, but when he arrived on March 5 he was met by Wade alone, who attempted to hide the committee's real objectives from Meade. "He was very civil," Meade recalled, and "denied there were any charges against me." Wade assured Meade that the committee was only preparing a history of the war. Meade was at a distinct disadvantage because, unlike his opponents, he had had no time (and was probably unaware of the need) to prepare a well-crafted or competently researched defense. His lack of preparation led to some minor errors of details, and in a few instances Meade's testimony distorted truth. For example, Meade testified that when he replaced Hooker on June 28, "I received from him [Hooker] no intimation of any plan, or any views that he may have had up to that moment." Meade was trying to position himself as having received command of the army under the worst possible constraints. In fact he, Hardie, Hooker, and Butterfield met after Meade assumed army command and discussed a variety of matters before Hooker's departure.[43]

Meade assured Wade that it had been his "firm determination, never for an instant deviated from, to give battle wherever and as soon as I could possibly find the enemy, modified, of course, by such general considerations as govern every general officer." Meade dwelled "particularly" upon his decision to concentrate at Gettysburg "in consequence of its having been reported on the floor of the Senate that an order to retreat had been given by me." The Pipe Creek line "I think, was selected; and a preliminary order, notifying the corps commanders that such line might possibly be adopted," but the order was issued "certainly before any positive information" had reached Meade regarding the enemy's location and concentration. Reports from Hancock and others convinced him that the enemy was near Gettysburg. Therefore, the Army of the Potomac was ordered to concentrate there "entirely ignoring the preliminary order, which was a mere contingent one, and intended only to be executed under certain circumstances which had not occurred."[44]

In a rather glaring omission, Meade neglected to mention July 2's aborted 3:00 p.m. meeting with the corps commanders. Meade had already been criticized heavily for Williamsport's council of war and was probably aware that informing the committee of the mid-afternoon council could potentially confirm the accusations that he was an indecisive commander who wanted to retreat. Rather than confronting Sickles at army headquarters, Meade testified, he learned Sickles was out of position when it was "reported to me about two o'clock that the 6th corps had arrived—I proceeded from my headquarters . . . to the extreme left, in order to see as to the posting of the 5th corps, and also to inspect the position of the 3d corps, about which I was in doubt."[45]

Meade told Wade that it was only upon arriving on Sickles' front, shortly before 4:00 p.m., that he "found that General Sickles had taken up a position very much in advance of what it had been my intention that he should take," and too far from support of the rest of the army. Meade told Wade that it was Sykes' Fifth Corps, not Sickles' Third Corps that had successfully manned and saved "Round Top mountain, which was the key-point of my whole position. If they [the enemy] had succeeded in occupying that, it would have prevented me from holding any of the ground which I subsequently held to the last." Although the testimony of previous witnesses had ranged from calling Meade incompetent to an outright traitor, he did not direct any similar charges against Sickles. "It is not my intention in these remarks to cast any censure upon General Sickles. I am of the opinion that General Sickles did what he thought was for the best; but I differed with him in judgment. And I maintain that subsequent events proved that my judgment was correct, and his judgment was wrong."[46]

Historians have wondered why Meade did not criticize Sickles more heavily, particularly in light of the slanderous accusations that were being fired at him. (Meade, rather curiously, told his wife after the session, "I did not spare Genl. S. or D.") One possible scenario is that Meade was simply doing his best to avoid brawling with disgruntled exiles such as Sickles, Doubleday, and Howe. There was, after all, a war still to be fought and won. On the other hand, at face value, the simplest explanation is that Meade's testimony probably reflected his true opinion. Meade simply believed that Sickles' intentions had been for the best, and if he was guilty of anything, it was simply bad judgment. The professional and the amateur military men would never agree on what defined "best judgment." In closing the session, Wade asked, "Is there anything further that you desire to say?" Meade's reply was a fair one: "I would probably have a great deal to say if I knew what other people have said."[47]

When Meade visited Secretary of War Edwin Stanton afterwards, he learned there was "much pressure from a certain party to get Hooker back in command." Apparently the plan included using Sickles and others to bring the matter to a head through the committee. Although Stanton was an old friend of Sickles and had been disappointed by Meade's failure to finish off Lee, the secretary believed Meade's battlefield performance merited his support. Stanton assured a skeptical Meade that the scheme would not work.[48]

Despite Stanton's assurances, Meade left Washington worried about the damage that these "mysterious whisperings" could do to his reputation. He labeled Sickles' charge "absurd, that I had ordered a retreat at Gettysburg, and that the battle was fought in spite of all my efforts to prevent it. It is a melancholy state of affairs, however when persons like Sickles and Doubleday can, by distorting and twisting facts, and giving false coloring . . . take away the character of a man who up to that time had stood high in [public] estimation." Meade hoped that a patient course of action would allow time for the truth to make itself known.[49]

The ambitious cavalry commander Alfred Pleasonton testified on March 7. Pleasonton was outwardly friendly with Sickles, having gushed after Chancellorsville, "[Y]ou will pardon me for expressing to you the admiration excited by the resources with which you met every difficulty on that trying occasion, and I can frankly assure you the courteous politeness and easy composure so conspicuous in all your actions inspired confidence in all around you." But when Pleasonton was once asked privately what he thought of Sickles, he responded: "He is a Tammany Hall politician. If you like that sort of man, you will like Sickles." Pleasonton's cooperation with the committee has puzzled some, including Meade, who thought he had done Pleasonton some favors. However, one of Pleasonton's staff officers was a Lieutenant James Wade—the son of Senator Ben Wade. By Pleasonton's own admission, he became friendly with the elder Wade. Pleasonton continued the testimony against Meade while desperately attempting to inflate his own role. He testified that he had told Meade several times, "there was but one position in which for us to have a fight, and that was at Gettysburg." It seemed that there was no shortage of officers seeking credit for selecting Gettysburg as a battlefield.[50]

David Birney testified that same day. In addition to being a Sickles partisan, Birney's dislike of Meade dated at least as far back as Fredericksburg. Birney's surviving correspondence leaves little doubt that he detested Meade. He wrote that as a brigade and later a division commander, Meade was "always badly beaten, troops flying in disorder." While citizen-soldiers such as Birney and Sickles were (and still are) viewed disparagingly by most professional soldiers, the ridicule appears to have been mutual. In Birney's view, despite the professionals' vaunted education, Meade and his engineer friends were better suited to dig ditches than to exert "power over troops in command." Meade's "only salvation is that he is occasionally led by Warren, otherwise he is a vacillating clever man, who has good defensive qualities but is not aggressive and his campaigns will be voted a failure."[51]

Birney also longed to see Hooker back in command, and so was presumably following the committee's agenda. "We must have Hooker back to this army and I believe he will be sent to us . . . God save us from Engineers." Finally, Birney was proud of the Third Corps record, and told historian John Bachelder as much: "Gettysburg has glory enough for all, and the Third Corps is proud that its 'misapprehension of orders' carried it into and brought on the battle instead of taking its rest." Birney was aware that Meade was contemplating the break-up of the Third Corps, something he considered a "diabolical scheme."[52]

Birney admitted in his testimony that on "the 2d of July I was ordered to relieve Geary's division of the 12th corps, that during the night had bivouacked on my left. I took position with my left at and on Round Top about 9 o'clock in the morning." This contradicted Sickles' claim that Geary had occupied no particular position. Birney also claimed that, after moving forward, Sickles had promised him support from both Sykes and Hancock, but Sykes had responded to Birney's urgent requests by stating that "his men were making coffee and were tired, but that he would come up in time." Although his testimony was not overtly hostile toward Meade (Birney saved that for his private correspondence), he reiterated the committee's view that Meade was hesitant to "hazard a battle" at Gettysburg, and that a Williamsport attack would have resulted in the "utter defeat of the rebel army, I think."[53]

Did Meade retain the army's confidence? "There is no enthusiasm for him. I think he is rather liked by them; but, so far as I know, they have very little confidence in him as a military leader." Although he offered that the "general opinion is that he lacks decision of character," Birney did not follow the committee's lead and blame Meade's indecisiveness on pro-McClellan politics: "I have never known an instance when they have not carried out the orders which they have received." The committee pressed Birney with several follow-up questions along this line of inquiry, but to his credit the Third Corps officer deftly side-stepped the issue. He wouldn't blame Meade's performance on traitorous McClellan sympathies, but he still thought the army was "disheartened. . . . Its history, since the battle of Gettysburg, has been a succession of useless advances and rapid retreats . . . our army has, in every instance, after seeking it, avoided a general engagement."[54]

The day after Pleasonton and Birney testified, Meade complained to his wife on March 8 of "a conspiracy" in which Sickles and Doubleday were the committee's "agents." The timing of these attacks compounded Meade's stress. He was convinced that the imminent arrival of Ulysses S. Grant would shorten his own professional lifespan, for he pragmatically realized that Grant may desire "his own man in command." The March 8 issue of the New York *Tribune* did nothing to assuage Meade's anxiety. The paper repeated the assertion that Meade intended to retreat on both July 1 and July 2, and "that the battle was precipitated by Gen. Sickles." The paper also called Birney and Alfred Pleasonton's testimonies "very damaging."[55]

Meade finally decided to take some action. He contacted Generals Birney and Pleasonton "as your superior officer" and requested a "succinct statement of your evidence." Birney may have realized that since Sickles was no longer serving with the army, it was prudent to mend fences with Meade. His somewhat contrite reply was that newspapers were doing "great injustice to the character of my testimony, and were penned by some person ignorant of it." Birney assured Meade that his testimony was "confined almost entirely to the operations of the division and corps whilst under my command. My opinion as to the movements of the army and its conduct was given only in reply to direct questions. . . . In my opinion, there is nothing in my testimony that should alter the personal and official relations existing between us." Birney went on to decline Meade's request to replay his own testimony, however, explaining that it was under the committee's ownership. "I will with pleasure give you, at any time you may desire," he concluded, "my recollections, reports, and views on the same points." Privately, Birney was considerably less conciliatory toward the commander of the Army of the Potomac. "Meade is a fraud," he told a friend, and an "old granny" who "only claimed to be from Pennsylvania" because "he married the daughter of a Philadelphian."[56]

Pleasonton was even less cooperative. "I desire to inform the major-general commanding that he is mistaken in supposing I have given a succinct statement of my evidence before the war committee to anybody." He admitted that "the evidence was taken down by a stenographer," but he had not since seen it and could not transcribe it from memory. "I am perfectly willing that the major-general commanding should have a copy of my evidence, but as I consider it is now the property of the Government, I will forward a copy of his letter to the chairman of the Committee on the Conduct of the War, with the request that it may be furnished him." Pleasonton forwarded the request on to his friend Chairman Wade, who replied that he saw no reason to depart from the committee's practice of not releasing testimony. Put another way, Meade was officially denied the opportunity to examine the testimony against him.[57]

Gouverneur Warren appeared next as the first pro-Meade witness. Warren, Meade, and Humphreys represented what citizen-soldier David Birney sarcastically called the "engineer clique." Birney thought Warren "ambitious as the devil . . . but he is a very good fellow." Warren told the committee on March 9 that upon taking command Meade kept the army "moving forward as rapidly as possible, for the purpose of hitting Lee's army with something, no matter what it was, so as to bring him into line and bring on a battle." Regarding Sickles' unauthorized advance on July 2, Warren, like Meade, failed to mention the planned 3:00 p.m. meeting of corps commanders. Warren testified that he had fortuitously ridden with "Meade to examine the left of our line, where General Sickles was." Warren firmly disapproved of Sickles' position: "His troops could hardly be said to be in position."[58]

Warren "felt very well satisfied that General Sickles could not hold his position against the force brought against him" and that it had required combined portions of the First, Second, Fifth, Sixth, and Twelfth corps to hold the line. Warren also explicitly contradicted Sickles by stating (correctly) that Little Round Top had been left unoccupied, and that it had been left to Sykes' Fifth Corps, which arrived "barely in time," to save the hill. Although Warren's testimony shed light on Sickles' performance, the committee wasn't interested in that aspect of his appearance. Instead, it steered the questioning to the issue of whether any councils of war were held during the battle. Warren tap danced around the subject: "I do not know that there was; not what I would call a council of war. I think it probable that General Meade asked the opinion of all his officers about what they thought of their position." Warren did admit, however, that the campaign's "lost opportunities" occurred on the evening of July 3 ("we should have advanced") and July 12 at Williamsport.[59]

As a professional soldier, Warren clearly had little respect for Sickles. The engineering officer specifically mentioned Reynolds and Hancock, but not Sickles, among the losses of "a great many of our most spirited officers." When he was asked specifically about Sickles' loss to the army, he replied: "I do not think that General Sickles is as good a soldier as the others; but he did the best he could, and with the corps he had he managed very well. His corps was composed of a little different material from the others."

Question: You considered him a man of resolution and courage, and one that would bring his corps into a fight well?

Answer: Yes, sir, he did very well. I do not think that General Sickles would be a good man to fight an independent battle, which a corps commander would often have to do. I think if he had been educated a soldier he might have stood very high. But when you come down to all the details of a battle, General Sickles has not had the same experience which others have had. The knowledge of those details do not make a soldier, but he should be possessed of them as much as he is of his own language.[60]

Warren's swipe at the entire Third Corps was probably a reflection of the fact that the corps had only one West Pointer (Humphreys) commanding a division or brigade at Gettysburg—the only infantry corps in Meade's army to hold this dubious distinction. Warren's opinion on Sickles accurately reflected the gulf between Sickles and many of his peers. Many considered him a good and aggressive fighter, but his lack of military education precluded his ability to exercise sound military judgment independently. Sickles, of course, was not the only non-professional in the army, but he was the highest ranking non-professional, and as a corps commander he could be required to fight and act without supervision.[61]

Newspaper reports dated March 10 cheered Meade, who observed, "I note the *Tribune* now says that no charges were preferred against me by General Sickles or Doubleday." He had also sent a note to attendees of the July 2 war council, requesting "your recollection of what transpired at the council" and whether he "at any time insisted on the withdrawal of the army from before Gettysburg." Generals Sykes, Newton, Sedgwick, and John Gibbon all replied unequivocally that they had never heard Meade consider a retreat.[62]

Generals Grant and Meade received an invitation to dine with Lincoln in Washington on March 12. Grant was unable to attend, but Meade accepted. The dinner conversation must have been fascinating because (according to the New York *Tribune)* Sickles, Halleck, and Stanton were also in attendance. Knowing that he would be in Washington for the scheduled dinner, Meade took advantage of the opportunity to ask the committee's permission to present more evidence on March 11. Meade may have been a political novice, but he appeared to be learning the game quickly. So it was that a much better prepared Meade appeared again with thirteen orders dated from June 30 and July 1, "a careful perusal of which, I am sure, will satisfy every member of this committee that there was no intention on my part to withdraw my army from the position at Gettysburg." Given his "great exertions" to concentrate the army, Meade testified that "to any intelligent mind . . . it must appear entirely incomprehensible that I should order it to retreat . . . before the enemy had done anything to require me to [retreat]."[63]

More good news rolled in for Meade. He met again with Edwin Stanton, who informed him that Wade was now quite satisfied with Meade's explanations. Meade also learned that several committee members were actually friendly to his cause, and he received favorable newspaper coverage from *The Round Table,* "A Weekly Record of the Notable, the Useful, and the Tasteful."[64] An editorial in the March 12 edition accused Sickles of leading the movement against Meade, "a high-minded gentleman and a thorough soldier":

> Whether General Sickles intentionally disobeyed or unintentionally misinterpreted his orders, was not distinctly stated [in Meade's report]. But one thing is certain, that the fact that General Sickles lost a leg in the engagement saved him from removal from the army. We honor General Sickles for the devotion to the cause of his country; we honor him for the untiring energy and personal bravery he has displayed in its defense; and when the war shall be ended and the roll of honor made out, we shall not be the last to claim for General Sickles no mean place on it. But we cannot blink the fact that General Sickles is quite as much a politician as a soldier. We know that he has accomplished more by personal address, adroitness, and cunning management of newspaper correspondents, than by actual display of military ability.[65]

Unfortunately for Meade, a letter appeared in the same day's New York *Herald* that essentially relegated *The Round Table's* editorial to the scrap heap of forgotten history. The *Herald* published an "important communication from an eye-witness" to Gettysburg as Sickles responded with his most memorable salvo during the Second Battle of Gettysburg.[66]

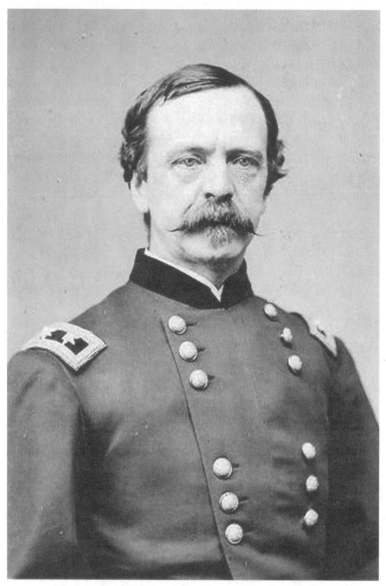

A Matthew Brady photo of Major General Sickles,
taken circa 1864-1865. *Library of Congress*

Chapter 15

My Only Motive is to Vindicate History

THE BATTLE OF GETTYSBURG — IMPORTANT COMMUNICATION
FROM AN EYE-WITNESS—HOW THE VICTORY WAS WON AND HOW
ITS ADVANTAGES WERE LOST — GENERALS HALLECK'S AND
MEADE'S OFFICIAL REPORTS REFUTED, ETC.

To the Editor of the Herald:

> The battle of Gettysburg is the decisive battle of this war. It not only saved the North from invasion, but turned the tide of victory in our favor. The opinion of Europe on the failure of the rebellion dates from this great conflict. How essential, then, that its real history should be known. Up to this moment no clear narrative has appeared. The sketches of the press, the reports of Generals Halleck and Meade, and the oration of Mr. Everett, give only phases of this terrible struggle, and that not very correctly. To supply this hiatus, I send you a connected, and, I hope, lucid review of its main features. I have not ventured to touch on the thrilling incidents and affecting details of such a strife, but have confined myself to a succinct relation of its principal events and the actors therein. My only motive is to vindicate history, do honor to the fallen, and justice to the survivors when unfairly impeached.[1]

The author of this letter, who dubbed himself "Historicus," provided the *Herald's* readers with a point-by-point duplication of Sickles' testimony. According to Historicus, on July 1 Sickles had assumed "the grave responsibility of moving to" the relief of the First and Eleventh corps "without orders." Historicus "saw several copies" of Meade's Pipe Creek Circular "stating that his [Meade's] advance had accomplished all the objects contemplated, namely, the relief of Harrisburg and Philadelphia, and that he would now desist altogether from the offensive." Historicus found it "strange that General Meade should make no mention in his report of this singular and most important fact," that he issued a plan "directing his whole army to retire and take up the defensive on Pipe Creek."[2]

As the narrative progressed to July 2, and quoting from General Lee's battle report, Historicus noted that General Longstreet was ordered to carry a Federal "position from which, if he could be driven, it was thought our army could be used to advantage in assailing the more elevated ground beyond." To Historicus, it was "plain enough that Lee regarded the point where our left was posted as the key to our position. . . . It is not to be supposed that General Meade refused to see this; but as he makes no mention of it in his report, I propose, for the sake of the future historian of the battle, to tell what I know about it."[3] He continued:

> Near this important ground was posted the valiant Third Corps, and its commander, General Sickles, saw at once how necessary it was to occupy the elevated ground in his front toward the Emmitsburg road, and to extend his lines to the commanding eminence known as the Round Top, or Sugar Loaf hill. Unless this were done, the left and rear of our army would be in the greatest danger...Receiving no orders, and filled with anxiety, he reported in person to General Meade, and urged the advance he deemed so essential. "O," said Meade, "generals are all apt to look for the attack to be made where they are." Whether this was a jest or a sneer Sickles did not stop to consider, but begged Meade to go over the ground with him instantly; but the commander-in-chief declined this on account of other duties.[4]

Historicus repeated Sickle's testimony practically verbatim. Artillerist Henry Hunt, he explained, "concurred with Sickles as to the line to be occupied . . . but he declined to give any orders until he had reported to General Meade, remarking, however, that he (General Sickles) would doubtless receive orders immediately." However, Sickles never received such orders: "It has since been stated, upon unquestionable authority, that General Meade had decided upon a retreat, and that an order to withdraw from the position held by our army was penned by his chief of staff, General Butterfield." Meanwhile, as "the enemy's columns were moving rapidly around to our left and rear,"[5] and with no response from headquarters . . .

> The critical moment had now arrived. The enemy's movements indicated their purpose to seize the Round Top hill; and this in their possession,

General Longstreet would have had easy work in cutting up our left wing. To prevent this disaster, Sickles waited no longer for orders from General Meade, but directed General Hobart Ward's brigade and Smith's battery (Fourth New York) to secure that vital position, and at the same time advancing his line of battle about 300 yards, so as to hold the crest in his front, he extended his left to support Ward and cover the threatened rear of the army.[6]

If Historicus was not Sickles, then he was someone intimately familiar with the general's movements on July 2. Historicus' version of the Meade-Sickles Peach Orchard meeting corroborated versions given by both Sickles and Tremain. Meade promised support from the Fifth and Second corps, as well as to "Send to the Artillery Reserve for all you want." After Meade rode away, according to Historicus, "Sickles received no further orders that day."[7]

Historicus did address one common complaint of Sickles' critics: "that Sickles' line was too much extended for the number of troops under his command." He rationalized it by adding: "[B]ut his great aim was to prevent the enemy getting between his flank and the Round Top alluded to. This was worth the risk, in his opinion, of momentarily weakening his lines . . . for the object of Lee, as he states, was 'to carry' the ground which Sickles occupied, and which both generals evidently regarded as of the highest importance."[8]

Regarding the touchy subject of Fifth Corps reinforcements, the Third Corps "fought like lions, against tremendous odds, for nearly an hour before the Fifth Corps" came up and were "immediately put in position by General Sickles." Historicus saved his most memorable passage for the fate of Barnes' Fifth Corps division. As Barnes "suddenly gave way," Birney sent an order to get Barnes back into line. " 'No.' he [Barnes] said; 'impossible. It is too hot. My men cannot stand it.'"[9] Historicus continued:

> Remonstrance was unavailing, and Sickles dispatched his aides to bring up any troops they met to fill this blank. Major [Henry E.] Tremain, of his staff, fell in with General Zook, at the head of his brigade (Second Corps), and this gallant officer instantly volunteered to take Barnes' place. When they reached the ground, Barnes' disordered troops impeded the advance of the brigade. "If you can't get out of the way," cried Zook, "lie down, and I will march over you." Barnes ordered his men to lie down, and the chivalric Zook and his splendid brigade, under the personal direction of General Birney, did march over them and right into the breach. . .[10]

According to Historicus, it was the Third Corps' "good fortune in preserving our position on the left gave us the victory at Gettysburg" and yet Meade "disregarded the repeated warnings of that sagacious officer, General Sickles." After essentially relating the entire battle from only Sickles' perspective, the author relied exclusively on second-hand accounts to criticize Meade's Williamsport performance. It is apparent that Historicus was no longer with the army by the time it reached the swollen Potomac River.[11]

The editorial concluded with the following:

> It is to be hoped that the above narrative will be regarded as dispassionate, as it is meant to be impartial. Some slight errors may have crept in; but this may possibly stimulate others to come forward with a rectification. Had General Meade been more copious in his report and less reserved as to his own important acts, the necessity for this communication would not have existed.
>
> HISTORICUS [12]

An outraged Meade passed the Historicus article to the War Department, asking for action "as may be deemed proper and suitable" particularly since the author was either "present at the battle, or dictated by some one present, and having access not only to official documents but to confidential papers that were never issued to the army, much less made public." Meade had little doubt who was responsible. "I cannot resist the belief that this letter was either written or dictated by Maj. Gen. D. E. Sickles." Meade continued:

> In my official report I deemed it proper to state that this position was a false and untenable one, but I did General Sickles the justice to express the opinion that, although he had committed an error of judgment, it was done through a misapprehension of orders, and not from any intention to act contrary to my wishes. The prominence given to General Sickles' operations in the enclosed communication, the labored argument to prove his good judgment and my failings, all lead me to the conclusion he is directly or indirectly the author.
>
> As the communication contains so many statements prejudicial to my reputation, I feel called upon to ask...that the Department will take steps to ascertain whether Major-General Sickles has authorized or indorses this communication, and, in the event of his replying in the affirmative, I have to request of the President of the United States a court of inquiry,

that the whole subject may be thoroughly investigated and the truth made known...[13]

Privately, Meade complained that the Historicus article was "filled with false and perverted statements, which have astonished even myself." Meade understood that while "my orders were always looking to fighting, I did, at times . . . hold in view the contingency of a reverse and endeavor to be prepared for it. This is the sum and substance of my offense, and I regret to say that, among a certain class of my fellow country men, this will be an offense and indicative of what they call *too much caution* [emphasis in original] . . . proving that I did not have the dash and blundering audacity of others." Not only did Meade have an accurate measure of his critics, but he had also summarized the main difference between himself and Sickles. Meade's critics thought he exuded "too much caution." Sickles, on the other hand, had demonstrated ability in a characteristic that could never be applied to Meade: Sickles was blundering audacity personified. Henry Halleck advised Meade to "ignore" Sickles since "nothing would suit him better than to get you into a personal or newspaper controversy. He would there be perfectly at home, and, with his facilities for controlling or giving color to the New York press, would have greatly the advantage." Lincoln likewise urged Meade to avoid being "diverted" by a court of inquiry."[14]

Was Historicus really Dan Sickles? Historians have been asking the question since 1864. Harry Pfanz summarized the feelings of most when he wrote, "Historicus was Daniel Sickles' alter ego, his partisan, if indeed he was not the general himself." Pfanz also wondered what Henry Tremain "might have had to do" with the article. Four potential suspects have been generally proposed as Historicus: Sickles, Tremain, Dan Butterfield, and historian John Bachelder.[15]

John Bachelder is the easiest suspect to cross off the list. In 1925, Robert Carter told historian W. A. Graham that Sickles probably would have been tried for disobedience "had he not lost a leg. But John B. Bachelder, a loud-mouthed, blatant photographer, and *henchman* [emphasis in original] of Sickles, made the people believe by an avalanche of propaganda that Sickles held back Longstreet, and all *writers began to believe it* [emphasis in original] and praised Sickles' act."[16]

Using Carter as his source, Meade biographer Freeman Cleaves labeled Bachelder as Historicus in his widely reprinted biography entitled *Meade of Gettysburg*. However, historian Richard Sauers observed that no evidence has yet to be uncovered linking Bachelder to Sickles' efforts against Meade. Bachelder was not present during the battle (as Historicus clearly was), and arrived at Gettysburg afterward to begin his studies. Bachelder, with Meade's permission, spent the winter of 1863-1864 with the army interviewing eyewitnesses. Carter may have mistaken John Bachelder for staff officer Lt. Col. R. N. Batchelder. In fact, in the 1890s when John Bachelder, Sickles, and Dan Butterfield were all active in the early memorialization of Gettysburg, Bachelder made it quite clear that he did not support attacks on Meade's reputation.[17]

Regarding Henry Tremain as the sole author, Third Corps historian John Watts de Peyster noted Tremain's "many literary efforts . . . Mr. Tremain has not infrequently been a contributor to the press. During the war he was often a correspondent of the New York *Evening Post*." In 1865, while serving in North Carolina, Tremain also wrote editorials for the Wilmington *Herald*. Tremain's postwar memoirs exhibit an obvious disdain for George Meade, and he remained loyal to the Third Corps cause for the remainder of his life. But Tremain seems unlikely to have acted alone as Historicus. He would have benefited by the return to power of Sickles, Hooker, and Butterfield, but a staff officer working alone to engineer the removal of the commanding general seems improbable. Tremain was also very interested in returning to an assignment following Sickles' wounding. In other words, he had much to risk if he were unmasked as Historicus. Tremain remains a strong potential co-conspirator, however, and he may have physically taken the dictation, placed pen to paper, or helped Historicus craft sentences. But it is doubtful that Historicus originated with Henry Tremain.[18]

In choosing between Tremain, Butterfield, and Sickles as Historicus, the question of Historicus' identity is more easily answered. Historicus is obviously telling Gettysburg from Sickles' point of view. The author arrives on Cemetery Hill on July 1 (with Sickles), and is apparently not present after July 2. Sickles is clearly the battle's hero: "always reliable," "always first" and "making good use" of his time. Historicus follows Sickles all over the battlefield, and is not at headquarters issuing orders with Butterfield or running errands with Tremain. He knows Sickles' actions and even his conversations. Anything that occurred outside of Sickles' sphere is also outside of Historicus' interest. Historicus is not physically at army headquarters with Butterfield drafting the alleged retreat order. This probably rules Butterfield out as the originator, although he obviously provided Historicus with supporting information.

Historicus hit *all* of the themes that Sickles targeted in his congressional testimony and would repeat for decades to come: Howard welcomed Sickles as a savior on Cemetery Hill; Meade had drawn up a retreat order; Hunt agreed with Sickles' position, Meade ignored him, and then promised support; the Fifth Corps was tardy in its assistance; the Third Corps held out alone against Longstreet's overwhelming odds. Dan Sickles spent the next fifty years replaying these themes in newspapers and in speeches. Not only did Historicus have access to official reports, but as he proved when he published a second letter several weeks later, Historicus also had access to private correspondence from Third Corps division commander David Birney. There is nothing in Historicus' account that Dan Sickles would have disagreed with. Sickles may have physically written the letter, or he may have dictated to Henry Tremain or any of his other devoted staff officers. But exactly who physically put the pen to the paper is irrelevant. The Historicus letters relay Sickles' thoughts, motives, and agenda. The letters were written either physically or under the direction of Sickles. There is virtually no doubt that Dan Sickles was Historicus.[19]

Historicus is perhaps best remembered for his criticism of Barnes' division. Earlier that summer, General Barnes had confronted David Birney over "some comments" in Birney's report accusing Barnes of not providing proper support. The survivors of Barnes' division were irate both at the omission of credit to Strong Vincent's brigade on Little Round Top and the severe criticism of the performance of Tilton and Sweitzer's brigades near Stony Hill. Colonel Tilton called the claim that "Barnes' Division broke—a most diabolical lie," and dismissed the idea of "our division lying down to let other troops (tramp) over them to the front!" He thought the entire Historicus manifesto "a slander . . . for the apparent object of praising Maj. Genl. Sickles upon the public as an injured but capable soldier, giving him in fact the whole credit of the victory, which is sickening when we consider how near he came to losing the battle for us. Had Sickles' orders to some of Sykes' Brigade Commanders been obeyed, the rebels would surely have had both Round Tops early in the fight."[20]

In the *Herald's* March 18, 1864, edition, "a staff officer of the Fifth Corps," wished "to correct his [Historicus] misstatements" and refuted seven of Historicus' arguments. General Barnes published a credible reply of his own on March 21. Barnes described the accusation that he had ordered his men to lie down to allow Zook's brigade to pass as "pure invention. No such occurrence as is here related took place. There is not a particle of truth in it." Barnes blamed Tilton and Sweitzer's poor performance on the gaps created by Sickles' overextended line. "The motives and the object of the narrative must be judged by its general tenor," concluded Barnes. "I think it [Historicus] is filled with errors, detracting from the merits of some and exalting the moderate claims of others to a ridiculous excess." Like so many other battlefield controversies, the question of whether Zook's brigade tramped over Barnes' prostrate men was never satisfactorily settled. Since Zook was mortally wounded in battle, he never lived to offer his view, while the veterans (predictably) offered conflicting accounts.[21]

Although Historicus had not disparaged Hancock's Second Corps, a battle Sickles was always careful to avoid, "Another Eye-Witness" appeared to blast Historicus in the *Herald* for omitting Hancock completely from the battle. He also attacked Sickles for advancing unsupported and with flanks exposed. In fact, there was no "just defense for the movements of General Sickles." When Historicus eventually replied again on April 4, he assured the world that "it was far from my intention" to disparage either Hancock or the Second Corps. Historicus admitted that "Another Eye-Witness" was "deeply offended that General Sickles figured so conspicuously in the fight of July 2; but that is no fault of mine. The blame, if any, is to be attributed to the eagerness and activity of General Sickles."[22]

Meade's efforts to solicit friendly sources drew a favorable response from Lieutenant Ranald S. Mackenzie of Gouverneur Warren's staff. As a courier for Warren, Mackenzie had witnessed much of the struggle to place Union bodies on Little Round Top. He assured Meade, "At the opening of the battle of July 2, there were no troops belonging to General Sickles' corps on Round Top ridge. General Sickles, when called upon by General Warren, through me, to furnish troops for the defense of that position, refused to do so, stating that his whole command was necessary to defend his front, or words to that effect."[23]

John Gibbon proved to be one of Meade's strongest allies. The Second Corps division commander told the press that there was "no truth" to published statements that "one of the corps commanders" had a retreat order "in his pocket" on July 2. Gibbon warned Meade privately that Butterfield was willing to swear that he had prepared the retreat at Meade's order. Meade assured Gibbon that it was only intended as a "contingency . . . and I may have told Butterfield to familiarize himself with the roads, etc., so that if it became necessary we would be prepared to do it promptly and in good order. Out of this he has manufactured the lie that I intended *at the time* [emphasis in original] to do so." Meade was "heartsick" that "I am to suffer from the malice of such men as Sickles and Butterfield."[24]

With all of these charges and counter-charges being aired in public, it became easy to lose sight of what, if anything, the Joint Committee was still trying to accomplish. One news report from Washington tried to clarify Sickles' role in the investigation. "The statement that General Sickles had preferred charges against General Meade to the committee on the conduct of the war is erroneous. It appears that the committee, while examining into matters connected with the battle of Gettysburg, were necessarily compelled to notice the reflections of General Halleck and Meade on the conduct of General Sickles, and accordingly he and Generals Pleasonton, Birney, Doubleday, and Howe were summoned to testify."[25]

Andrew Humphreys, another Meade ally, testified before the committee on March 21. Although he led a division in the Third Corps, Humphreys had never joined Sickles' inner circle. Now that he was free of the Third Corps, Humphreys' testimony included (in much detail) Third Corps snafus such as his own circuitous arrival at Gettysburg on July 1, and the collapse of Birney's line on July 2. Humphreys testified that Sickles had erred in moving too far in advance of Meade's battle line. The fact that the Confederates had crushed Sickles' position, but were unable to capture Meade's Cemetery Ridge line on July 3, "undoubtedly" showed that Meade's judgment had been correct. The committee tried to get Humphreys to admit that, having fought a defensive battle, the Army of the Potomac should have been fresher than Lee's army and better equipped to prevent the Confederate escape. Humphreys did believe "we should have attacked them as soon as possible" at Williamsport, but generally thought that the later examination of Lee's line proved that "we should have suffered very severely" had such an attack been launched.[26]

Winfield Scott Hancock was the next witness on March 22. Since Hancock read the newspapers and knew what charges were being directed at Meade, one wonders exactly how friendly he was to his commanding general. Hancock told the committee that Meade had "made up his mind to fight a battle on what was known as Pipe creek." John Reynolds' occupation of Gettysburg "was really a mask" to buy the time needed for the Pipe Creek line to be established in the rear, explained the wounded Second Corps commander. But the Confederates had reached Gettysburg earlier than anticipated, he continued, and Reynolds' First Corps delayed Lee's advance until Meade "should come to some decision." Hancock also appeared to confirm Abner Doubleday's complaint that Meade promoted his friends over superiors. Even though Hancock knew that Meade had received Halleck's permission to promote anyone he chose, Hancock still testified that his own July 1 ascension over his seniors Sickles and Howard was not "legally . . . proper." He further testified that on July 2, Meade thought there would be a "formidable attack by the enemy on the right of our line," leaving the potential interpretation that Meade was ultimately deceived by Lee's attack on the Federal left.[27]

Although Hancock did not score many points on Meade's behalf, he did not take Sickles' side, either. Hancock "could not conceive" the objective of Sickles' July 2 advance and thought "it would be disadvantageous to us." The Confederates had ultimately succeeded in turning Sickles' left flank by passing between the Third Corps and Little Round Top, countering Sickles' claim that his corps had held the mountain. Sickles' move had caused "a vacancy in the original line" which allowed Lee's army to break through "at different places" and required Hancock to "patch up that line all the latter part of the afternoon and evening." All of this was a far cry from Sickles' contention that he had defended Little Round Top. Hancock testified that he knew nothing about Meade's alleged retreat order.[28]

Although he had been desperately wounded in Longstreet's July 3 attack, Hancock was sure Meade would have "won a great victory" had they attacked immediately after Longstreet's repulse. Some historians have called Hancock "a very impressive witness" in Meade's defense, but it is hard to see how he helped Meade significantly. His straight forward delivery could enhance Meade's image as a weak commander who did not want to fight at Gettysburg, a general who violated the army's law of seniority, needed councils of war to strengthen his resolve, and failed to capitalize on his victory. However, Hancock's balanced criticism of both sides also decisively rejected Sickles' July 2 advance and self-proclaimed defense of Little Round Top.[29]

After Sickles, the most noteworthy witness to testify against Meade was Dan Butterfield, who appeared before the committee on March 25. After being replaced as chief of staff with Humphreys, Butterfield had asked Meade if he should report back to the Army of the Potomac, to which Meade replied, "I do not know . . . If you come here I will do the best I can for you but it is impossible to say in advance what that will be." Butterfield instead rejoined Hooker in the Western Theater. In January 1864, Butterfield was offended by a passage in Henry Halleck's report stating that the condition of the Harpers Ferry garrison had been "incorrectly represented" to Meade. Meade admitted that he based his Harpers Ferry decisions upon information obtained from Butterfield, and that this had in fact been incorporated into Halleck's report. Later in February, Butterfield told General William "Baldy" Smith that he possessed a rough draft of the alleged July 2 retreat order.[30]

Butterfield's appearance was one of the few instances where documentary evidence supported Sickles' covert cooperation with the committee. The details are murky, but Butterfield apparently arrived in Washington absent without leave at the end of February. Frustratingly (and conveniently), Butterfield's widow omitted her husband's March 1864 movements from her 1904 *Biographical Memorial* of General Butterfield. Given their stormy personal history, it was not surprising that Butterfield would be hostile to Meade, and this probably explains why Halleck did not want Butterfield in Washington. On February 30, Sickles wrote to Senator Chandler:

(Private) My dear Senator:

Butterfield is at Willards—He has not received permission from Genl. Halleck to come here & apprehends it will be refused—Allow me to suggest that, as in Birneys [sic] Case, he be subpoenaed regularly—He comes now only by *request* from Senator Wade.

It is very important that you have Brig. Genl. S. Williams Ast. Adjt. Genl. Army of the Potomac here *with all orders & Communications* bearing on the Gettysburg Campaign—*original* drafts & Copies as received at Head Quarters—this is *all important* for you to have before you *when Butterfield is Examined*—Then you will get the *real history* of the Campaign.[31]

So summoned, Butterfield requested on March 23 that Meade and Assistant Adjutant General Seth Williams provide the rough minutes of the July 2 war council, as well as "the originals of all dispatches, orders, &c., prepared by me." Williams replied the same day, "As you are not now connected with the Army of the Potomac, the major-general commanding declines furnishing you with the records of said army." After discussing operations under Hooker, Butterfield began his Gettysburg testimony on March 25.

Butterfield claimed that upon assuming command, Meade was indecisive over a course of action and that Meade directed the movement of the army essentially in accordance with Hooker's plans. Butterfield, like Sickles, portrayed the Pipe Creek Circular as proof of Meade's desire to avoid battle. In reading his own copy of the order to the committee, Butterfield emphasized Meade's satisfaction that "the object of the movement of the army in this direction has been accomplished, viz, the relief of Harrisburg, and the prevention of the enemy's intended invasion of Philadelphia, &c., beyond the Susquehanna." Butterfield omitted key passages, including Meade's reasonable disclaimer that "Developments may cause the commanding general to assume the offensive from his present positions." Butterfield testified that he thought such an order was "very bad" for morale and allegedly urged Meade to reconsider.[32]

Surprisingly, Butterfield's version of George Meade was not completely timid. Although he told the committee that Meade did not think the Sixth Corps could arrive before "the matter is pretty well settled" at Gettysburg (implying a pessimistic view of Federal prospects), Butterfield admitted that Meade proposed "making a vigorous attack" early on July 2. Perhaps even more significantly, Butterfield let slip (inadvertently one suspects) that Meade issued orders during Hancock's absence for the other corps "to move towards Gettysburg." If the committee caught this point, then Butterfield was admitting that Meade had ordered the army to Gettysburg without awaiting Hancock's advice. This was a point for Meade that even Hancock's supporters had been unwilling to admit.[33]

However, it was Butterfield's version of July 2 that really gave the committee its money's worth. Butterfield testified that Meade "directed me to prepare an order to withdraw the army from that position." This was potential dynamite, since as author Bill Hyde correctly pointed out, "Whereas Sickles' and others' testimony on this point had been hearsay, Butterfield claimed to have been personally involved in preparing an order to retreat." Butterfield testified that the completed draft met with Meade's approval, and that Meade summoned all of the corps commanders for the intended 3:00 p.m. meeting while the draft was being copied. This conference was aborted, however, by the audible sounds of battle along Sickles' front.[34] When the committee asked if Sickles' "collision" with Longstreet prevented the retreat from being "executed," Butterfield surprisingly stopped short of an all-out indictment on Meade:

> It is impossible for me to state that, because General Meade had not communicated to me his intention to execute that order regardless of the opinions of the corps commanders, or whether he intended to have the order submitted to them. He merely directed me to prepare such an order, which I did. It is for him to say whether he intended to execute it or not. He may have desired it prepared for an emergency, without any view of executing it then, or he may have had it prepared with a full view of its execution.[35]

Since Sickles, Butterfield, and the committee had gone to such great efforts to accuse Meade of planning a retreat, why did Butterfield admit that Meade may not have intended to actually execute the order? Perhaps he truly didn't know, and was unwilling to go on the record if the accusation was later conclusively proven false. Historian Edwin Coddington speculated that Butterfield's "show of restraint" was designed to make his story actually sound more convincing. Or, as Bill Hyde has suggested, Butterfield might have been hedging so that he would not be completely out of favor should Meade not be removed from command. Upon examination, Butterfield admitted that he prepared the retreat order with the understanding that Meade intended to "consult with his corps commanders, and that it was a matter of precaution to have the order in readiness in case it should be decided upon to retreat." Whether Butterfield liked it or not, he was depicting Meade as a general who was planning for multiple contingencies. This was a far cry from a man who was hell-bent on retreat.[36]

Having nearly torpedoed Sickles' retreat accusation, the examination now turned to councils of war and Pipe Creek. Butterfield claimed that Meade had ended the July 2 evening council by pronouncing Gettysburg "no place to fight a battle." He also accused Meade of not making "a vigorous pursuit" on July 3, and of holding another council on July 4 because Meade needed "the earnest assistance and advice of every corps commander." Butterfield initially refused to answer questions regarding the prudence of Pipe Creek, claiming that he did "not like to pass unfavorable criticisms upon a superior officer," but eventually elaborated, "I do not think that circular was a judicious one. I do not think the position designated in that circular was a good one. And I think if we had gone back there it would have resulted in the destruction of our army."[37]

Since Butterfield's testimony regarding the July 2 retreat order was surprisingly weak, it was significant that the committee chose to close his testimony with emphasis on July 1 and Pipe Creek. Perhaps the committee realized by this point that it might have more success trying to prove that Meade never wanted to fight at Gettysburg in the first place. If Sickles was attempting to demonstrate that his July 2 advance had prevented Meade from retreating, then his friend Butterfield had utterly failed to substantiate his case.

General Gibbon, perhaps Meade's friendliest witnesses, appeared on April 1. Meade and Gibbon had known each other since their Old Army service against the Seminoles in Florida. Gibbon told the committee that the Third Corps gave way upon attack, and that he had been forced to send several regiments in support, particularly because Sickles' advance had threatened to cut "him off entirely from our line." Gibbon was asked specifically whether Sickles' line was a "judicious position." Gibbon replied, "I should think it was not." He explained that Sickles had "isolated" himself too far in advance to receive support from the remainder of the army. Contrary to protecting the left flank as intended, Gibbon thought Sickles actually "invited" a flank attack, which was particularly "disastrous" to less disciplined volunteer troops. Gibbon argued that the collapse of the Third Corps supported his argument.[38]

Without being prompted by further questioning, Gibbon elaborated on the charge that Meade planned to retreat. Gibbon admitted that he had been surprised when Butterfield showed him a draft of the order, which Butterfield identified as "an order for the army to retreat." But, he added, Butterfield "did not say that General Meade did intend to leave; he merely said something to the effect that it was necessary to be prepared, in case it should be necessary to leave." Gibbon considered the whole episode to be "remarkable" because he was convinced that Meade "had no idea of falling back from the position there." Upon questioning from moderate Republican Daniel Gooch, Gibbon reiterated that Butterfield had called the retreat order "merely preparatory, in case we might be called upon to retreat." It was the strongest testimony that had yet been placed before the committee in Meade's favor.[39]

Meade knew it was necessary to refute Butterfield's testimony and returned to the stand, wearily one suspects, on April 4. "Now, indulging in the utmost charity towards General Butterfield, and believing that he is sincere in what he says, I want to explain how it is possible that such an extraordinary idea could have got into his head." Invoking "the full solemnity and sanctity of my oath . . . I utterly deny ever having intended or thought, for one instant, to withdraw that army, unless the military contingencies which the future should develop during the course of the day might render it a matter of necessity."[40]

Meade further called the committee's attention to the "absurdity" of a retreat. "Why was the order not issued, or if issued, why was it not executed? There was no obstacle to my withdrawing the army." Meade read dispatches into evidence showing that he intended to attack along his right flank, until dissuaded by Slocum and Warren. Meade decided to await the arrival of the Sixth Corps, which would then permit the Fifth Corps to move to the left and, "if the enemy did not attack me, to make an attack myself from the left." In refuting Butterfield's accusations, Meade gave the committee his first inclination that he had actually considered making *offensive* movements from his *left* (i.e. along Sickles' front.) Meade's final appearance was brief but convincing, and he received favorable coverage in the papers for his effort.[41]

Henry Hunt appeared later that same day. Although Hunt was highly competent as an artillery officer, Meade was playing with potentially dangerous allies, since Hunt was a friend of George McClellan. Around 11:00 a.m. on July 2, Hunt testified, Meade ordered him to accompany Sickles on an examination of "his line, or the line that he wanted to occupy. . . . I think he [Meade] added that General Sickles had no good position for his artillery." This contradicted Meade's claim that he was completely unaware of Sickles' intention to move to a new position. But countering Sickles' testimony that he had advanced with Hunt's approval, Hunt told the committee that he warned Sickles not to move without further orders from Meade. Hunt claimed that he notified Meade that "taken by itself, it was a very good line; but before putting any troops on it, or occupying it, I would advise him to examine it for himself."[42]

On the issue of whether Meade was preparing to retreat, Hunt answered that he did "not think that any order involving the movements of troops could have been given without my knowing it, for the simple reason that the first thing to be provided for in falling back was the movements of heavy trains of ammunition and the reserve artillery." In fact, Meade's ordering of the artillery reserve to Gettysburg seemed to prove that retreating was the last thing on his mind. Congressman Loan cross-examined Hunt extensively on whether he could be sure that he was privy to all orders (even "private orders") issued by Meade, but Hunt held firm. Hunt simply did not accept that such an order could be successfully hidden from the army's chief of artillery. [43] When Hunt was asked whether Sickles' advance was "judicious . . . and did advantage or disadvantage result to us from the adoption of that line by him?", he answered:

> That would depend upon circumstances. If the battle was to have been a purely defensive one, based upon the almost certainty that the enemy must attack us, I suppose our policy would have been to have taken up a strictly defensive line. In that case the line should have been extended, as it was ordered, from Cemetery ridge direct to Round Top, along the crest. If there was fear of our left being turned, our line might have been thrown forward to prevent the attempt, but that should have been done by placing it in *echelon* instead of changing the direction of the line by throwing forward the right flank, as was done of Sickles' corps. I suppose the occupation of that advanced position compelled the enemy to attack us there, even if they had started to turn our left flank. I do not know enough about the numbers of the troops we had there on our left . . . to judge what would have been the result of the enemy turning our position . . . I know it led to a very severe and bloody battle. And it gave great advantages to the enemy on General Sickles' right flank, for they occupied the wood in front, which I said to him must be in our possession, or at least not occupied by the enemy.

On the whole, I cannot say whether it would have been better or not for him to have remained behind. Excepting on that right flank, it was probably as well to fight there as anywhere else. It would have been well, however, if the general commanding had known of it sooner, so as to dispose of troops behind.[44]

Historicus, who had the uncanny habit of appearing whenever George Meade took the stand, reappeared in the *Herald* to answer his critics on April 4. Reminding readers that his "only motive was to aid the future historian," he dredged up the now familiar list of complaints. Meade had "left [Sickles] without orders" because Meade was "entirely engrossed with the plans for a retreat." Claiming that "nothing was easier than to force Lee's whole army to an unconditional surrender at Williamsport," Meade was accused of "inglorious failure . . . to profit by his victory in pursuing and destroying the enemy." Historicus also asserted once again that the Third Corps "was posted on the Little Roundtop. . . . This is a mere quibble and unworthy of the gravity of the subject." As evidence that Zook's brigade had tramped over Tilton and Sweitzer's prone men, Historicus quoted from "a private letter from General Birney, which he will not object I am sure, to my using." More importantly, the access to a private letter from Birney surely seemed strong proof that Sickles was pulling Historicus' strings, and perhaps actually operating his pen. Meade was sure that the recipient of this letter could not have been "anyone but Sickles." Although Meade remained disappointed that Lincoln had "avoided" his request to confront Sickles, he felt confident that his own April 4 testimony proved that he never intended to retreat. Meade also believed that he had a supporter in General Grant, who "talked very freely and properly about my particular friends Hooker, Sickles, and Butterfield."[45]

Despite the committee's best efforts, Meade still had an army to run. What had been rumored for weeks became reality on March 23 when the War Department issued orders formally reorganizing the Army of the Potomac into three infantry corps. Retained were the Second Corps (still under Hancock), the Fifth Corps (now under Gouverneur Warren), and the Sixth Corps (still under Sedgwick). As expected, Sickles' Third Corps, along with the First Corps, was dismantled and rolled into the other surviving corps. (The Eleventh and Twelfth Corps had already been sent to the Western Theater.) David Birney's Third Corps division now became Hancock's Third Division, while Humphreys' former division became Hancock's Fourth Division. Shortly afterward, however, this division was rolled under Birney, to the effect that

David Birney essentially had command of the remainder of the old Third Corps. Meade found personal satisfaction at seeing the demise, in his words, "of the smashed up Third Corps." Sickles and friends had worked overtime in an effort to orchestrate Meade's ouster, but Meade had survived long enough to axe Sickles' beloved corps.[46]

For his part, Birney agreed that the army was now "more compact, fewer poor generals, and now easily handled." Historicus' inclusion of the private Birney letter, however, removed any lingering doubts about Birney's loyalties. Unfortunately for him, Sickles was gone, there would be no return to the Third Corps, Meade was still in command, and Birney now served under one of Meade's allies. For Birney, the situation could not have been more awkward. He accepted service under Hancock, whom he considered a "very great improvement" over French. Hancock tried to smooth things over by sending Birney the Third Corps colors to keep as their "proper custodian." Meade also received word that Barnes had a letter from Birney denying any connection with Historicus. In early April, Birney visited Hancock to disclaim "being a partisan of Sickles." Hancock attempted to intercede with Meade on Birney's behalf, but Meade replied that he had "heard nothing" to justify an explanation "except what I had seen in the papers about his testimony."[47]

Regarding Birney, Meade told his wife, "I don't consider him a reliable man & think the less I have to do with him the better. There is always an issue . . . between us about Fredericksburg." Meade did agree to meet with Birney on April 18. According to Meade, Birney "disclaimed ever having entertained unfriendly feelings towards me, or being a partisan of Sickles, and expressed the hope that he would be permitted to serve under me." Meade "listened to all he had to say, but made no reply, except that I had never heard he had any unfriendly feelings towards me." Afterward, Birney wrote friends, "I am again on very pleasant terms with Gen. Meade." Birney described a "quite pleasant" meeting in which he offered to resign, but Meade "assured me of his high regard" and asked that he remain. Quickly changing his loyalties, Birney now boasted that the Second Corps was "now the handsomest, most completely equipped in the army." It is ironic that Meade had once been viewed as hopelessly outmatched in dealing with Sickles and his political machinery, but now that Dan's hopes for a return had vanished, his supporters were left to grovel for their survival.[48]

The fall of the Third Corps began with the heavy casualties it suffered at Chancellorsville, followed by its decimation at Gettysburg. The corps' death occurred not on a battlefield, but in a series of paper shuffles. "It was a heavy blow to veterans of the old 3rd Corps to sink their identity in another body," one soldier admitted, "but . . . there are no troops in the Army of the Potomac who wouldn't feel proud to fight under Hancock." Hancock seems to have felt somewhat differently. He complained that the old Third Corps performed picket duty very poorly, and at least one Hancock biographer has uncharitably commented, "In truth, the Third Corps under Sickles had become a slipshod outfit."[49]

It is easy for historians to criticize Sickles and the Third Corps, but the organization Hancock inherited was no longer Sickles'. Dan had been gone for nearly nine months. Much of the corps he had led had been killed or maimed on the fields of Chancellorsville and Gettysburg. Major General William H. French had taken the corps after Sickles, and had fattened its roster with garrison troops, unused to the rigors of campaign life. Sickles' former officers detested serving under French and accused him, among other things, of being a chronic drunk. Birney wrote privately that French "is drunk every afternoon, lately screeching drunk, jealous of everyone in his command, conceited easily, is a Marylander without any heart in the cause and is only sustained by the West Point guild. He is hated by the corps." Joseph Carr, a brigade commander under French, claimed that the corps' demise was assured by French berating Meade in a drunken rage during the Mine Run campaign. De Trobriand complained that near French "a glass and a bottle of whiskey appeared to be on the table *en permanence* [emphasis in original]." The manner in which French "exercised his new authority was not calculated to render him popular." Sickles' Third Corps may have been deficient in military training at the top, but despite its lack of battlefield success at Chancellorsville or Gettysburg, Sickles had at least created a fighting spirit among its veterans. To Regis de Trobriand, the replacements in French's tenure never represented the real Third Corps, "the veterans of Sickles." For whatever his battlefield flaws may have been, Sickles was a leader who was beloved by many of his men.[50]

With Grant's arrival, the reorganization, and warmer weather, Historicus and the committee captured a decreasing amount of newspaper coverage and Meade's attention. It was time for another year's campaign. But the committee continued their work and resumed with its final Gettysburg witnesses. After Sixth Corps commander "Uncle John" Sedgwick testified rather uneventfully in Meade's favor (he "never heard of any such" retreat order) on April 8, Brigadier General Seth Williams, Meade's assistant adjutant general, appeared ten days later. Although Williams is not remembered today as one of the battle's leading generals, his testimony was important. Williams' job was to ensure that orders prepared by Butterfield were copied and distributed. He would have been aware of any retreat order if it had existed. In reality, after his first committee appearance, Meade had ordered Williams to search for a copy of Butterfield's retreat order. Williams replied that the order did not exist, and assumed it had been destroyed. Meade eventually told his wife that the headquarter clerks remembered "something of the kind" existing but that it was destroyed as "worthless" since it was never issued. (This passage was omitted from Meade's letters when published by his family.)[51]

Williams told Senator Wade that once Meade had "made up his mind to fight the battle at that place . . . he concentrated the army there with all possible rapidity." Williams provided a detailed and well reasoned response to questions regarding the alleged retreat. To the best of Williams' recollection, Butterfield gave Williams or a clerk "an order looking to a contingency which possibly might happen," but this was never distributed because Butterfield told him not to do so "until I received further instructions from him." Williams could not remember the order's exact terminology, "but to the best of my belief it was an order which, if carried out, would have involved a retrograde movement of the army." Congressman Daniel Gooch asked if Williams had participated in any conference, at any time, in relation to a retreat. "No, sir, none at all. I have very good reason to suppose that General Meade knew nothing of the existence of such an order." Meade's concentration of his army all led to the conclusion that he wanted to fight, not retreat, otherwise "he would have been blocking up the road."[52]

As the spring of 1864 progressed, Meade's correspondence increasingly reflected a pre-occupation with Ulysses Grant's presence and Grant's impact on Meade's future with the Army of the Potomac. While it was still unclear if Meade would survive under Grant, it was becoming increasingly obvious that Sickles was not going to return to field command with the Army of the Potomac.

Dan Sickles in middle-age, still looking formidable in uniform. *GNMP*

Chapter 16

Spoil a Rotten Egg

The 1864 campaign was viewed by both contemporaries and later
historians as Grant's and not Meade's. This took much of the attention
away from attempts to displace Meade. Many of the key players were more
interested in looking for assignments, not wanting to sit on the sidelines as the
war moved into another summer. Brigadier General Samuel Crawford
uneventfully closed the committee's Gettysburg testimony on April 27, and
Wade's committee increasingly lost their ability to influence Meade's fate, if
they ever really possessed that authority to begin with.[1]

Generations of Americans, and Gettysburg visitors, have lived under the
false assumption that Grant "replaced" Meade after Gettysburg. In reality,
Grant may have *saved* Meade. As George Meade Jr. admitted, Grant's
appointment and "continuous presence with the Army of the Potomac, caused
the command of that army to cease to be a position so much to be sought after,
and for a time the labors of the committee [were] diverted to other fields,"
Birney wrote privately that "Grant killed the demonstration for Hooker that
was assuming shape, and would have ended in the decapitation of Meade."
Although Grant's presence dissuaded Meade's enemies from pursuing his head,
Meade had certainly done his part to help his own cause. He hadn't fully
received Congress' "official thanks" for Gettysburg, and he hadn't successfully
refuted the criticism over Lee's escape at Williamsport. But he had convincingly
discredited the alleged Sickles/Butterfield retreat order, even if Wade's
committee would never admit it. A supposed novice at politics and media
manipulation, Meade had essentially beaten Sickles, Wade, and Butterfield.[2]

Much of this activity occurred without Sickles, leaving the full extent of his
involvement with the committee open for question. He had finally departed

Washington in April on Lincoln's diplomatic tour of the South. Accompanied by Henry Tremain, the stops included Nashville, Georgia, Memphis, Arkansas, New Orleans, Pensacola, and Charleston. While in Georgia, he visited Hooker and Butterfield, and could only observe them direct troops at Resaca and the opening of the Atlanta campaign. During a June troop review in Louisiana, one enlisted man noticed that Sickles "rides just as well as if he had both legs. An orderly carried his crutches for him, and a pocket built on the saddle, in which to rest the stump, answered the purpose of a stirrup." But despite his improved equestrian abilities, Sickles returned to Washington in August and then headed home to New York City to await further orders.[3]

In mid-October 1864, Sickles was unexpectedly required in Philadelphia to serve as a pall-bearer at David Birney's funeral. Birney had served with distinction through Grant's 1864 Overland campaign, and was even selected in July to command the Tenth Corps. But the hardships of the fall campaign and the malarial climate had taken their toll on Birney's health. By early October, he had taken ill and (although he refused to leave the army) was forced to return home to Philadelphia. On October 18, he "was attacked by a violent hemorrhage of the bowels" and he died that evening at home, surrounded by his family. Like so many other military men, his delirious mind wandered to the battlefield, his last intelligible words being, "Keep your eyes on that flag, boys!"[4]

In addition to Sickles, the October 21 funeral was attended by Governor Curtin, numerous staff officers, and a long line of dignitaries. One newsman watched Sickles and commented that Dan testified "by his presence with his mutilated body, his sense of the high and soldierly ability that distinguished the lamented deceased, and how profoundly he mourned the loss of a brother-soldier." Birney's favorite horse, which was a gift from Sickles, was led behind the hearse. Birney was buried in full major-general uniform and wore the decoration of the Third Army Corps Union, of which he was then serving vice-president.[5]

"The services of that distinguished officer deserve the signal recognition of his countrymen," Sickles wrote, "and especially do they merit honor at the hands of his fellow-citizens of Pennsylvania." To Regis de Trobriand, Birney "was one of the best friends I had in the army . . . he died, in the midst of his family, still young, without living to see the triumph of the cause to which he had sacrificed his fortune and his life." Perhaps the most surprising tribute came from none other than George Meade. During the 1864 campaign, Birney had earned Meade's professional respect. "This has shocked everyone here . . . General Birney is undoubtedly a loss to the army. He was a very good soldier, and very energetic in the performance of his duties. During the last campaign he had quite distinguished himself. I never liked him personally, because I did not consider him a reliable person," concluded Meade. Given their acrimonious history together, Meade's professional praise was enough.[6]

Sickles made one last futile attempt to re-start the old Third Corps. In the fall, he assured Lincoln that "with proper and sufficient facilities I could reorganize and fill up my old Army Corps with new Regiments. . . ." Although nothing came of the offer, rumors still circulated that Sickles would return once again. Andrew Humphreys wrote privately, "I learn that General Sickles says he expects a command after the election." (Humphreys meanwhile received command of the Second Corps in November 1864.) In 1861, Lincoln had needed War Democrats like Sickles on the battlefield. But the landscape was radically different by late 1864, and Sickles was no longer essential to the cause. Dan had to content himself instead with campaigning for Lincoln during the 1864 presidential re-election. As 1864 drew to a close, and Sickles was still home without an assignment, he made one final plea to the President. "I beg respectfully to remind you that I am still unassigned. Fully restored to health, as competent as ever for active duty, and anxious for employment, I hope to be spared the humiliation of being dropped from the rolls among the list of useless officers. . . ."[7]

Sickles remained on the active rolls, but Lincoln never returned him to that field command which he wanted most. Instead, he was sent on a special diplomatic mission to Columbia and Panama. Riding over mountainous roads on horseback and mules allowed him to make "gratifying progress in the use of my artificial limb. . . . I venture to believe that Gen. Meade even would not now doubt my ability to ride far enough to the front to 'post a battery' or make a reconnaissance. . . ." But it must have been bittersweet when he received word in May of Lee's April surrender while in Bogotá, and more shocking when word of Lincoln's assassination reached him later that month while he was near the Andes. For a man who had been in the thick of American politics since the 1850s, he was more than two thousand miles away in a remote locale as Meade commanded the Army of the Potomac for one final campaign, Grant accepted the surrender, Lincoln was murdered, and Hancock oversaw the execution of the assassination conspirators.[8]

Since the war ended with the Committee on the Conduct of the War having failed to replace Meade, there was little left for Wade's committee to do except to finish their report. The final report was published on May 22, 1865, more than one month after Lee's surrender and Lincoln's assassination. Congress'

Radical Republicans were now re-focusing their efforts on subjugating the conquered South, thus it was simply too late to have any impact on the Union war effort. All they had accomplished was to demoralize and distract Meade and other generals whose efforts would have been better focused on the war. Alfred Pleasonton, of all people, was given primary credit for selecting Gettysburg, although they did accept Meade's claim that he determined to concentrate at Gettysburg before hearing from Hancock.[9] Regarding the July 2 attack:

> General Meade and others criticized General Sickles for the disposition he
> made of his troops before the fighting commenced; claiming that by
> throwing forward his corps from the regular line he exposed himself to
> and invited the attack of the enemy. General Sickles in his testimony gives
> his reason for the course he pursued, and holds that the movement he
> made prevented a disastrous flank attack on our left, which was
> threatened, besides being advantageous in other respects. Some troops of
> the 2d and 5th corps were also engaged in support of the 3d corps.[10]

About the alleged retreat, "There is testimony to show" that Meade "contemplated abandoning his position." The committee admitted "there is some controversy on that point," so it highlighted Butterfield, Williams, Gibbon, Howe, Hunt, Sedgwick, and Meade's testimony to counter-balance both sides of the argument. Sickles was included as believing that the question was to be discussed at the 3:00 meeting, before being broken up by the battle. In reality, the committee telegraphed their bias against Meade since the testimony in Meade's favor, particularly from Hunt and Williams, had been far stronger than Sickles and Butterfield's testimony against him. However, the committee presented the issue as if it were still open for debate. As expected, the report condemned Meade's failure to prevent Lee's escape back to Virginia. An immediate pursuit "would have resulted in a great victory, and the loss of the most, if not the whole" of Lee's artillery. Williamsport, and not the alleged Sickles/Butterfield "retreat," became the one criticism that was hardest for Meade to live down. In summary, Wade's final verdict was: "The battle of Gettysburg, though important in its results, was purely a defensive battle on our part, and was not followed by such active measures as in the opinion of the majority of the witnesses were necessary and practicable to enable us to reap the full fruits of the victory there gained." Viewed by history as a great victory, Gettysburg was officially labeled a disappointment.[11]

At first glance, there were no clear winners in this Second Battle of Gettysburg. Although Meade retained his command, his name and reputation had been dragged through the historical mud. The failure to prevent Lee's escape has dogged Meade in varying degrees since 1863, but after creating the accusation that he planned to retreat on July 2, the committee did at least offer a forum for Meade to successfully defend himself against the charge. The arguments that key officers knew nothing of the order, and that a retreat made no sense given the army's rapid concentration were convincing, even if Wade ultimately did not accept them. Today, few (if any) serious Gettysburg students believe Sickles' accusation that Meade planned to retreat during the afternoon of July 2.

One historian characterized the proceedings as "a battle for the opinion of future generations- a struggle over history and memory." But the participants had actually fought for more immediately practical reasons: notably professional advancement and political agendas. "From the standpoint of military history," historian Bill Hyde analyzed, "Sickles' testimony is so full of misstatements and outright lies as to be of little value. Yet it cannot be disregarded by the serious student of the Civil War or the battle of Gettysburg. Its worth lies in what it represents. Sickles' vendetta against Meade shows the degree and intensity of divisions among members of the officer corps in the Army of the Potomac." Although Sickles is usually singled out for the "lies" in his testimony, nearly everyone (from Doubleday to Butterfield to Meade to Hancock to Warren) were guilty of varying degrees of omissions and "errors." Whether the testimony was accurate or not, the post-battle political posturing within the Army of the Potomac is as much a part of Gettysburg's history as the battlefield tactics and strategies themselves. Sickles was not the only army officer to testify against Meade, nor did he create this environment. But history has generally accepted Meade's version of the "truth" and decided that he was in the right. In that sense, George Meade certainly won the 1864 Gettysburg battle against his more experienced political foes.[12]

From a historical perspective, Sickles' efforts to inflate his own battlefield role and hasten Meade's removal decidedly back-fired against him. Sickles is reviled by many modern Gettysburg students because of these efforts, and he has also helped elevate Meade's historical image as a solid professional officer who was attacked by a den of political vipers. Had Sickles taken a higher road, it is possible that he would be remembered historically in a more positive light. Numerous generals made mistakes on battlefields, at Gettysburg and elsewhere, yet they are not remembered historically as such villains. Ambrose

Burnside's performance at Fredericksburg was arguably more disastrous, yet he is remembered today more as a buffoon than "scoundrel." Sickles' negative image transcends his battlefield performance. What is even worse for Sickles as a historical figure, his political underhandedness has overshadowed the positive services that he later performed in veterans' affairs and the establishment of Gettysburg National Military Park. George Meade beat Dan Sickles in 1864's Second Battle of Gettysburg, and Sickles' historical image remains permanently damaged as a result.

With Gettysburg and the Civil War seemingly behind him, Sickles was assigned to Boston and command of the Second District, Department of the East, in August 1865. He was greeted enthusiastically when he arrived and, noting "the state of his health," he told well-wishers at the Parker House that he hoped his "command would not be a very arduous task." But the country faced the significant challenge of Reconstruction. With the Radical Republicans treating the South like a conquered territory, the former Confederacy was carved into five Military Districts, each under the command of a major general. The general commanding each district was given broad civil and military authority needed to rebuild their destroyed territory, including establishment of voting rights for the freed slaves. Due to his combination of military, political, and diplomatic experience, Sickles received command of the Second Military District. Sickles arrived in Charleston in September 1865, originally tasked with rebuilding South Carolina, but eventually received command of both North and South Carolina. With an initial starting force of about 7,000 troops (many of whom eventually mustered out during Sickles' tenure), Dan was responsible for the order and security of approximately two million people. Although he had missed the end of the war, Sickles was back in the military and political limelight.[13]

Henry Tremain served under Sickles for a time in the Carolinas until he resigned from the army in April 1866 as a brevet Brigadier General. Tremain eventually went onto a successful law career and in 1879 he was elected President of the Third Army Corps Union. Two familiar faces who did not move to Charleston were Teresa and daughter Laura. Both remained, again, in New York. Still married in name, by 1866 the forty-seven year old Sickles was still very much a ladies man, despite his missing leg. But he now managed his private affairs more discreetly than he had in his youth. Reconstruction was difficult, sometimes violent work. Although he played diplomat several times during his long career, he was temperamentally not suited for the tact and diplomacy that was required in the position.[14]

In February 1867, Dan was suddenly called home to New York. Teresa had been ill and died on February 5 at the age of thirty-one. Dan was not there when she died, but he did arrive in time for the funeral on February 9. He attended with Laura (who was now thirteen years old), Teresa's parents, and his own parents. For the first time since 1859, Teresa received recognition as Dan Sickles' wife. But typically, the ceremony was more about Dan the War Hero than Teresa. Among the pallbearers were Dan's new army family of Henry Tremain, Alfred Pleasonton, and Charles Graham. The pastor commented on the "irreparable loss sustained by the sorrowing parents and bereaved husband. He had given up all to go to the aid of his beloved country in the hour of her need." As he and Laura followed the casket from the church, and as reported in the New York *Herald*, his step was "infirm and tottering." Sickles broke down under the "intense feelings" of the occasion and the congregation rushed after him, "testifying in various ways the hold he had upon their hearts. . . ." Dan was, as always, the center of attention, and one more reminder of the Key murder trial was gone.[15]

Laura eventually returned to Charleston with Dan, where (reportedly because of the Key stigma) she had trouble gaining admittance to a good school. Dan had been away for much of her life and as he tried to become a father to a teenage girl, whatever relationship that did exist eventually deteriorated badly. The extent of his guilt over Teresa's isolation and his parental failure has been fodder for Sickles biographers. In the end, we really don't know how Dan felt about Teresa and Laura. For the remainder of his life, when Dan looked back he almost always focused on the war years. Dan was increasingly viewed by himself and the public as a Civil War hero. Teresa, Laura, and the Key murder were not topics that he discussed publicly.[16]

Dan's mourning did not prevent him from lobbying President Johnson on February 26 for a vacant brigadier general position in the Regular Army. "Not desiring civil office, I confess my ambition to deserve and attain a rank in the permanent Military Establishment corresponding to the grade I reached as a Volunteer officer. . . ." Sickles had earlier, and finally, entered the Regular Army in July 1866, to the rank of colonel. In March 1867, he was brevetted brigadier general in the U.S. Army for Fredericksburg (where he saw little action), and then brevetted major general for Gettysburg. The Civil War's most notorious amateur general had finally been recognized as a regular, if not a "professional."[17]

By mid-March, Sickles was back in Charleston. As Sickles later described, part of his duties were to "begin the systematic education of the freed people in these two states" and to direct voter registration. White vigilantes, often ex-Confederates, murdered blacks and occasionally Federal soldiers. As a result, Sickles was called upon to declare martial law and other strict measures in towns where blacks were being terrorized. Complaints of his strict excessiveness frequently reached Washington. Four Carolinians were convicted by a military commission of murdering three of his soldiers, but a federal court issued a writ of habeas corpus in favor of the accused. Sickles refused the court's order, so a federal judge ordered him in contempt and demanded his arrest. When Sickles simply refused this also, President Johnson decided that Sickles had overstepped his boundaries. The President and the Attorney General both agreed that Sickles' authority did not supersede a federal court, so a frustrated Sickles asked to be relieved as he was unable "to protect life, property or the rights of citizens. . . ." Outraged that Sickles would defy a court, Secretary of Navy Welles urged Johnson to "make short work with King Sickles." Johnson finally dismissed Sickles on August 27 using the "alleged harshness and oppression which had characterized the military government of the Carolinas" as his justification.[18]

While the Charleston papers celebrated his departure, Sickles returned to New York, again, as a hero. He was "serenaded into evening . . . by his old comrades of the Excelsior Brigade, the Grand Army of the Republic, and officers and men of the old volunteer army generally." Now motivated by his own dislike of Johnson, Sickles began to campaign for Ulysses Grant's 1868 run for the Presidency. In the process, he temporarily abandoned the Democratic Party in favor of the Republicans. In May 1868, he was chosen chairman of the New York delegation to the Republican National Convention, despite Grant's initial preference that he not attend. When he attended Grant's inauguration in early 1869, Sickles was once again on friendly terms with yet another administration. Yet another remarkable professional turnaround.[19]

When Grant was elected, Sickles felt entitled to some reward for his campaign efforts. In April 1869, Grant rewarded him with a full rank of major general (promoted from his brevet rank) and placed him on the retired list. But politically, Dan was disappointed when his first appointment offer was to the legation in Mexico City, which he declined. Secretary of War John Rawlins suggested, instead, that Sickles be appointed Minister to Spain and Sickles accepted the post in May. The assignment appealed to Sickles, in part, because bringing Cuba into the United States was a favorite topic of his. Newspapers attacked Sickles' character on a level not seen since the Key murder, and certainly not since Gettysburg. The New York *World* commented: "The claim that the man atoned for his hideous offenses against decency and good morals by his service during the war are utterly unfounded." Nevertheless, Charles Graham was among 200 supporters who threw Dan a lavish party on June 30. Although the Senate delayed his confirmation for almost one year, Dan sailed for Spain with Laura and his mother in July. From 1869 to 1873, Sickles was in Spain, which (along with Cuba) dominated his professional attention.[20]

During the late 1860s, the veterans were mostly interested in rebuilding their lives, although the old wartime feuds occasionally flared up. For example, a suspiciously Historicus-like article, signed by "An Officer and Eyewitness" to Chancellorsville appeared in the New York *Times* on June 3, 1867. Obviously intimately familiar with Third Corps movements at Chancellorsville, the author relayed a pro-Third Corps version of the battle. When a Federal counterattack was supposedly proposed following Hooker's wounding, the article depicted a timid Meade who allegedly "sat quietly on his horse outside of Hooker's tent, and declined to fight. . . ." George Meade speculated that Henry Tremain was the author, causing no less a modern historian than Harry Pfanz to connect the dots between Tremain and Historicus.[21]

In 1869, John Watts de Peyster, a former Third Corps officer and fledgling military historian published an article: "The Third Corps at Gettysburg, July 2, 1863. General Sickles Vindicated." De Peyster, primarily using source material favorable to Sickles, concluded that Sickles had acted correctly in advancing. Later in 1869, during a reunion speech in Vermont, Colonel William Grout also supported Sickles, whose corps "became unexpectedly engaged, to the great chagrin of Meade, who was still intent upon falling back to his favorite position near Taneytown." Such statements would contribute later to the battle between Meade and Sickles partisans, but for the time being the debate remained relatively quiet.[22]

The most heated battles fought during this period involved the former Confederate officers. Perhaps no other Gettysburg participant, including Sickles, found himself (and made himself) the target of more heated Gettysburg attacks than Sickles' Peach Orchard opponent, James Longstreet. Longstreet had, through a series of actions, become vilified by many of his former military colleagues. He had allowed some of his comments that were critical of Lee to appear in print and then aligned himself with the hated Republican Party. Longstreet openly supported his close friend Grant's presidential campaign, and embarked on a long career of Republican political appointments. Particularly following Lee's death in 1870, several ex-Confederate generals fiercely attacked his military record. Longstreet, in many ways, became the antithesis of Sickles. Dan had been a professional politician who, despite his controversial battlefield record, had managed to transform himself into a war hero. Longstreet was a professional soldier whose solid war record was muddied by a less than successful transition to politics. Both men had their supporters and detractors, and both men would eventually cross paths in defending their Gettysburg performance.[23]

Unlike Sickles and Longstreet, George Meade had no political ambitions. Following Grant's election, General in Chief William T. Sherman assigned Meade to his Philadelphia hometown where he took command of the Military Division of the Atlantic from Hancock. (Hancock was moved to the Department of the Dakota where he had a singularly unsuccessful stint as an Indian fighter.) Meade and his wife enjoyed being in Philadelphia with family and old friends, but he succumbed to illness and died on November 6, 1872. Significantly, Meade did not live to see the years when Gettysburg became a National Military Park and the veterans returned in large numbers to re-fight the battle. In death, George Meade continued to be attacked by Dan Sickles, and Meade would enjoy the distinct disadvantage of being unable to defend himself.[24]

While veterans such as Sickles were busy getting on with their lives, efforts slowly began to commemorate battlefields such as Gettysburg. Perhaps no one individual deserves more credit for preserving the battlefield for posterity than Gettysburg native David McConaughy, a local attorney and Republican. McConaughy thought "that there would be no more fitting and expressive memorial of the heroic valor and signal triumphs of our army . . . than the battlefield itself. . . ." Within two weeks of the end of the fighting he began purchasing key battlefield locations. On April 30, 1864, the Pennsylvania legislature granted a charter to his Gettysburg Battlefield Memorial Association (GBMA) to "hold, and preserve the battlegrounds of Gettysburg."[25]

Although both McConaughy and Dr. Theodore Dimon (who had arrived in Gettysburg to care for New York's wounded and dead) had earlier proposed similar ideas, it was another local attorney, David Wills, who pushed through the establishment of Gettysburg's Soldiers' National Cemetery. Wills received Governor Curtin's approval to purchase seventeen acres of Cemetery Hill, where internments of 3,512 Union dead began in the fall of 1863. Although President Lincoln's "few appropriate remarks" during the November 19 dedication have been remembered as the "Gettysburg Address," acclaimed orator Edward Everett actually gave the keynote address. In Everett's lengthy oration, Sickles moved forward to "gain a commanding position from which to repel the Rebel attack" and "after a brave resistance on the part of his corps, he was forced back, himself falling severely wounded. This was the critical moment of the second day. . . ." but Everett considered the "most important service" to have been rendered by General Crawford in his counter-attack through the Plum Run valley. It was later within the grounds of the new National Cemetery that the first monuments were placed at Gettysburg. In July 1865, the cornerstone was laid for what would become the Soldiers' National Monument. Then in 1867, veterans of the 1st Minnesota placed a memorial urn in the cemetery to honor their fallen comrades. The precedent was set for placing monuments to commemorate the battle.[26]

A New Hampshire-born artist named John Bachelder had also arrived in Gettysburg shortly after the battle, and would eventually spend the remainder of his life associated with studying and mapping the battlefield. Thus, the GBMA, a National Cemetery, and fledgling historians such as Bachelder formed the groundwork to ensure that the world would, as Lincoln said, "never forget what they did" at Gettysburg. By June 1864, the GBMA owned seventy acres. However, over the next ten to fifteen years, there was a lull in a war-weary population's Civil War interest, and McConaughy's ability to raise funds and preserve land for the GBMA decreased.[27]

Meanwhile, Sickles' work at the legation in Madrid kept him in the news. The question of Cuba's future remained hotly debated, and his political enemies at home watched with interest. Commenting on a March 1871 speech regarding Cuban emancipation, the New York *World* editorialized (under the headline "The Scoundrel Sickles Speaks") that he compared most unfavorably to the other speakers. "There is no reason to suppose that any of them had been a thief, or a forger, or a dependent upon outcast women, or a murderer."[28]

He regained his reputation for entertaining lavishly, well above his estimated $16,800 salary. Dan began a romantic affair with the deposed Queen Isabella II in Paris, and the French press sarcastically dubbed him the "Yankee King of Spain." But in November 1871, he married one of Isabella's twenty-something attendants, Caroline de Creagh. Edgcumb Pinchon's researcher believed that Isabella arranged the marriage, while the widow of New York Governor William Sulzer later insisted that both parties "married in the belief that the other party had plenty of money, or rather, the marriage was arranged. But they were temperamentally unsuited to each other, and never agreed on any subject. . . ." The service was rather small (by Sickles standards) and hastily arranged, although daughter Laura served as a bridesmaid. Dan and the new Mrs. Sickles then boarded a steamer for New York. The New York

Herald was mystified at his reason for coming home, but speculated: "Some of Minister Sickles' friends say he will not return to the Spanish capital."[29]

The newlyweds arrived in New York on December 22, 1871. Sickles insisted that he was only on a three-month vacation, but on behalf of shareholders whom he represented, he directed an overthrow of financier Jay Gould's corrupt management of the Erie Railroad. The episode was very public and he received more newspaper coverage than any time since Gettysburg. Sickles then moved onto Washington, where by February the papers were circulating rumors that there was "pending a serious personal difficulty" between Sickles and Secretary of State Hamilton Fish. There were rumors that one of the two men was about to "retire" from his position. But Sickles instead went to Albany to officially mediate a state political dispute. There were then press hints that Sickles intended to make a run for state governor. When opponents in the New York *World* continued to remind readers of his past indiscretions by calling him a "pimp," Sickles threatened libel, causing diarist George Templeton Strong to famously comment, "One might as well try to spoil a rotten egg as to damage Dan's character."[30]

Sickles finally sailed back for Spain in late April, but as he had in the Carolinas, his lack of tact had worn out its welcome. By late 1872, he was eager to return home, complaining to Secretary Fish, "I confess I'm tired of my useless work here and of these vacillating people." Even worse, his second marriage had not cured his chronic philandering. In May 1873, one anonymous American complained of Sickles to Secretary Fish, "While in Madrid his conduct with women has been simply disgraceful." Caroline was already said to be "heartily sick of her bargain, poor girl." Dan was accused of living in adultery with another woman prior to the marriage and of using "child virgins for the purpose of prostitution. His conduct with lewd women of the town was, and even is, shocking. Are we to have another Philip Barton Key affair in Spain?"[31]

Like most aspects of Sickles' life, what started promisingly ended badly and his diplomatic career reached an ugly conclusion in October 1873. An American blockade runner, the *Virginius*, was captured illegally sneaking arms and men into Cuba to aid insurrectionists. Although the Americans were legally wrong, Secretary Fish had Sickles dutifully remind the Spanish government not to execute the crew without trial. A local official ignored the plea however, and executed fifty-three of the men. An outraged American public called for war with Spain. Fish had Sickles give Madrid a series of demands along with a twelve day deadline, after which Sickles would close the legation and depart Madrid, a clear step toward war. Sickles had an ugly exchange with the foreign minister and after only five days he urged Fish to close the legation. Fish became suspicious that his diplomat seemed too eager for war, and as in past Sickles escapades, Dan's correspondence began to appear anonymously in newspapers. Sickles became exceedingly unpopular in Madrid and rumors of his assassination circulated. Fish and the Spanish government eventually went around him and negotiated a settlement without his knowledge. Sickles was humiliated and became the butt of jokes in Madrid. He resigned in as much disgrace as he was capable of, and as in the Carolinas, his departure was welcomed in all corners. Once again, he had allowed emotions and his temper to overstep his abilities, but had he been more persuasive the United States and Spain could have entered into war two decades before the Spanish-American War. His tenure abroad had not benefited him financially. He had been forced to give up his army salary of $5,625 and later claimed that he spent $30,000 annually from his own pocket to "keep up the dignity of the office."[32]

Now on the outs with Grant's administration, Sickles' career seemed dead once again. With no political or military assignment for the first time in years, Dan moved to Paris with Caroline, Laura, and his aging mother in February 1874. However, relations with Laura broke down permanently, reportedly over her affair with a Spanish military officer. Laura moved back to New York to live with Teresa's mother, and was permanently banished from Dan's life. Dan's mother also died while in Paris. On the positive side, Caroline bore a daughter (Eda) in 1875. The following year, a son (George Stanton) was born. Approaching fifty-seven years old, and with a significant physical disability, Sickles was starting a new family at an age when most men were preparing to retire. But he still found time to return to America. In May 1878, he attended a reunion with Hooker and Joe Twichell of the Third Army Corps Union in Newburgh, New York. Finally, probably unable to miss the excitement of the upcoming 1880 presidential election, Sickles decided in late 1879 to return home to New York permanently. Caroline refused to go, so leaving his new family behind, he set sail for the United States.[33]

If he had planned to immerse himself in battlefield affairs, then Sickles could not have timed his return to the United States more perfectly. By the 1880s, the country was ready to remember the Civil War again. Membership in thousands of Grand Army of the Republic chapters surged across the north. Monument companies flourished. Publishing offered an outlet for participants to write their highly biased reminiscences. In the summer of 1878, during a GAR encampment at Gettysburg, Philadelphia native John M. Vanderslice was disturbed by the "apparent apathy or inactivity" of the GBMA and engineered a buyout of GBMA stock by veterans. They elected a board of directors dominated by GAR members in the GBMA's 1880 election. The veterans now controlled the battlefield, and the 1880s began a surge in monuments and improvements that would ultimately lead to Gettysburg as we know it today.[34]

Major General Dan Sickles and former Third Corps commander Major General Samuel P. Heintzelman. *National Archives*

Chapter 17

Some Strange Perversion of History

The 61-year-old married Dan Sickles returned to New York and set up his bachelor quarters on Fifth Avenue. (There was an impression in the city that Dan was only 57, based upon an assumed birth date of 1823.) As if looking for something to do, Sickles re-started his law practice, which must have seemed less than exciting after decades on the national stage.

Dan had disowned his daughter Laura, who was by then living with her grandmother (Teresa's widowed mother) and sliding into alcoholism after a brief and unhappy marriage. The Philip Barton Key murder was still in the public's subconsciousness. One acquaintance remembered that as late as 1876 children sang, "General Sickles killed a man. Fried him in a frying pan."

Dan still considered himself a soldier, and was moved by the sight of poverty-stricken war veterans begging along the streets. Perhaps his own Gettysburg wound (his missing leg) stirred up some of his sympathy. He reportedly visited his amputated leg frequently at the Army Medical Museum. On what must have been Sickles' first visit, Curator George Otis was supposedly giving him a personal tour of the museum when Sickles finally lost patience, "Oh, yes, yes, but let us come to my leg!" When Otis led him to the limb's exhibit, Sickles questioned Otis harshly: "Where is my foot? What have you done with my foot—that should have been shown too!" When the curator explained that exhibiting the foot really had nothing to do with the wound itself, the former general "became very angry and anathematized [sic] the museum very freely."[1]

Having buried the hatchet over his performance in Madrid, Sickles threw himself into campaigning once again for U. S. Grant. The former Union general in chief had left office in early 1877 following his second term, but was making a

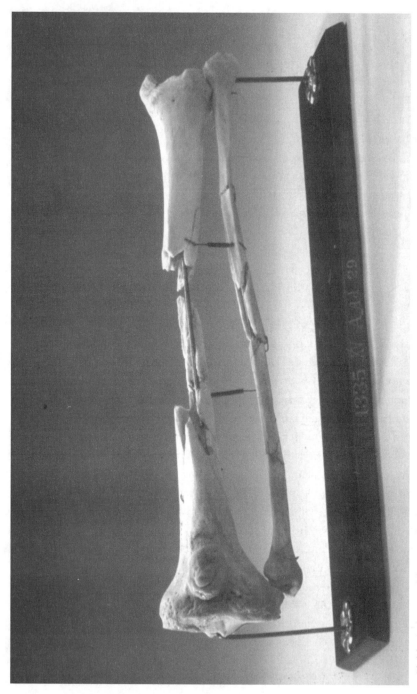

Sickles' shattered leg on display at the Army Medical Museum. *National Museum of Health & Medicine, Armed Forces Institute of Pathology*

run for a third term in the 1880 election. Sickles was still in bed with the Republicans, having declined a Republican Congressional nomination in 1876. On June 1, 1880, Sickles was in Chicago as part of the "National Convention of Republican Soldiers." He was scheduled to make an address, as was his former Gettysburg opponent James Longstreet, who was one of Grant's close friends. When Grant failed to win the Republican nomination, Sickles dismayed his new party members by throwing his support to Democratic candidate and former Second Corps commander Winfield Scott Hancock. Hancock eventually lost the popular vote to James Garfield by a minuscule margin and lost the Electoral College when he failed to carry Sickles' own New York state.[2]

Hancock had managed to briefly attach himself to Gettysburg controversy when, according to artist James Kelly, Hancock told Kelly that Meade "did not care or think it advisable" to remain and fight at Gettysburg on the evening of July 2. (Kelly eventually passed this information on to Abner Doubleday, who used it publicly in his own book.) Hancock was forced to deny these statements during his presidential campaign in order to avoid alienating Meade's friends. When Hancock died in February 1886, he was justifiably praised by many for his Gettysburg performance, which included helping to save the Union left on July 2. This should have triggered Sickles to criticize Hancock, but there was something about Hancock that Sickles had dared never attack. Instead he remembered Hancock favorably. "I never was more surprised in my life," exclaimed Sickles upon learning of Hancock's death. "In all that distinguished array of men on both sides of the great Civil War, none more than Hancock impersonated the best elements of manhood."[3]

Having thrown himself into the camps of two presidential losers (Grant and Hancock) Sickles could expect no immediate favors from James Garfield's White House. Sickles was back in the United States with no official role to channel his considerable energies, still considered himself a soldier, and had the time and financial means to travel. It was natural, then, that when the GAR began leading vast veteran pilgrimages to Gettysburg in the 1880s, Dan Sickles was somehow involved.

Dan's role in Gettysburg's development would evolve over the coming years, but one theme was always constant: he had to address criticism of his July 2 performance. Sickles used this as an opportunity to play offensively, to portray himself as Gettysburg's ultimate hero. In 1882, during one of his earliest returns, he was asked (as he repeatedly would be), "if there was any serious question as to the position you took that day?" "Some critics who knew nothing of the circumstances or needs of the hour," Sickles admitted, "have since indulged in some idle talk about my position, [and] about bringing on the battle too soon." Referring to such talk as "absurdity," he stuck to his guns and declared that if he had "been in the low ground running from Round Top towards Cemetery Hill" then the Third Corps would have "left Round Top entirely uncovered." It was the beginning of a long line of half-truths, misstatements, and contradictions that continue to amuse, annoy, and perplex historians to this day.[4]

When Sickles was asked whether Meade had ever condemned his movements, he replied: "Not that I know of. He certainly never gave me an indication by word or act that he regarded my position at Gettysburg a mistake. Indeed, I do not see how he could have done so for . . . he looked over my position and declined to interfere with it, when I asked if he would suggest any change." Recalling the events of July 2 many times during the 1880s and 1890s, he would repeatedly declare, "I see nothing that I would change either in it or in any of the operations of that day." For better or worse, Dan Sickles would remain forever unrepentant concerning Gettysburg.[5]

Sickles traveled to Gettysburg in June 1882 to "assist in locating" troop positions. "I haven't seen you for nigh twenty years," crowed a one-legged veteran from Maine, "but I love you as well as ever." Sickles and others traversed the field to locate and mark positions from the July 2 fight. The GBMA also hosted a veteran reception in Gettysburg's Town Hall. When Sickles ambled down the aisle, "the crowd arose and accorded him a perfect ovation," remembered one witness. John Bachelder performed as master of ceremonies. There was a call for Sickles to speak, but for once, remembered an eyewitness, he "could not be induced to speak." The ceremonies lasted until after 10:00 p.m., after which the vets pressed forward to shake his hand. "Almost every other man was minus an arm or a leg," observed a newspaper.[6]

Sickles returned to the Trostle farm, the site of his July 2 headquarters and where one of Porter Alexander's artillery projectiles had changed his life. Former Third Corps artillery chief George Randolph accompanied him, as did one of the ubiquitous newspaper reporters who always seemed within shouting distance. Limping to the knoll where he had been wounded almost twenty years earlier, Sickles "seated himself on a great boulder" and vividly recalled that fateful day. A large crowd began to gather, and one veteran pushed his way through the throng saying, "I want to shake by the hand the man who saved the second day's fight at Gettysburg." If Sickles hadn't fully realized it already, it was starting to occur to him that these were the battlefield votes that could be used to re-build his reputation.[7]

As interest in remembering the Civil War expanded, veterans increasingly began to squabble over who held the greatest claims to battlefield glory. These new battles were fought in the sometimes lucrative world of publishing and public speaking. Although General Meade's Gettysburg report had not directed any censure at the fighting men of the Third Corps, the veterans still felt that they had been slighted, and began to speak out about it at various gatherings. During an 1883 address, Lt. Colonel Thomas Rafferty, formerly of the 71st New York, admitted "there were none braver, nobler, more conscientious, nor, as he subsequently proved, more capable of that command than Major-General George G. Meade." Despite this professed admiration, however, Rafferty argued that "it unfortunately falls out that, in attempting to secure justice for my [Third] corps, I am compelled to take issue with him, and endeavor to show that, like all mankind, he was not infallible in his judgment. For General Meade did that corps an injustice, which I doubt not, were he living today, he would be the first to correct." Sickles had moved forward because he feared an attack on his flank. Therefore, Rafferty argued, "Sickles contributed most essentially to the salvation of the army and the subsequent decisive victory." Sickles' actions were ultimately vindicated "in light of the simple fact that his predictions were verified. The enemy's troops were massed and the battle fought out upon his position." Rafferty blamed Meade for not adequately supporting Sickles. "[C]ompelled to make the best disposition he could, [Sickles] fell into the mistake which so many generals both of our own and other wars in world's history committed, viz., in attempting to cover everything he covered nothing."[8]

Rafferty also resurrected the old feud with the Fifth Corps, claiming that Sykes had refused to support Sickles because "his [Sykes'] men had just come off a very long march and were tired, and were then making coffee, but that he would be up in time . . . I submit that, under the circumstances, this would seem to have been an unfortunate time and place to be making coffee." Of course, veterans such as Rafferty would have better served themselves by simply admitting that there was plenty of credit from multiple corps to share for the defense of Cemetery Ridge. Instead speeches like his that credited one corps at the expense of another simply led to further rebuttals and reopened old wounds better left closed (if not fully healed). Rafferty's words demonstrated the loyalty that existed between Sickles and many of his men. For whatever his strategic and tactical faults, Sickles was at least the kind of leader whose men would fight for him twenty years later. Not every Civil War general could make such a claim.[9]

On a more constructive note, while earlier visits had provided opportunity for nostalgia and newspaper coverage, the year 1886 officially changed the nature of Sickles' involvement with the Gettysburg battlefield. His lobbying efforts resulted in the New York State Legislature's passing of an act to establish the New York Monuments Commission for the Battlefield of Gettysburg. Sickles was appointed honorary chairman of the commission, which also eventually included Gettysburg veterans Dan Butterfield, Henry Slocum, and Joseph Carr. For nearly the remainder of his life, Sickles would be consumed by a mission to appropriate and correctly place monuments to all New York regiments, batteries, and ranking commanders on the battlefield. Undertaking much more than the title "honorary chairman" would suggest, he threw himself into the role, despite his advancing age and ever-present wound, with the customary "zeal" he had exhibited in New York politics thirty years earlier. His responsibilities included securing appropriations, charting a battlefield map, overseeing the creation of a detailed history of the battle, and selecting and supervising the creation of new monuments. These new monuments would require dedication speeches, typically in front of enthusiastic veterans. Sickles' new role ensured that he would become a welcome staple at battlefield reunions, re-fighting the action to a wide assortment of aging veterans and an increasing number of attendees who had not been born when he made his controversial move to the Peach Orchard.[10]

The makeup of the monument commission ensured that New York's "history" of the battle would be favorable to the Third Corps. The mission was to "determine such positions and movements" by any means necessary and report to the state legislature "such recommendations as they shall judge proper to secure the permanent marking of the movements and positions of such troops." Funds were appropriated to defray the commissioners' expenses and publish a report of their actions. As chairman, the commission's actions and history were clearly influenced by Sickles himself. He ensured that the New York history and monuments—and as a result a significant portion of Gettysburg's monuments—would have to meet with his approval and tell the story *he* wanted told.[11]

In addition to his new role with the New York Monuments Commission, or probably because of it, the year 1886 witnessed what historian Richard Sauers labeled "a rapid escalation of the controversy" between Meade and Sickles. Dan's increasing popularity as a speaker allowed him to return repeatedly to that favorite topic: that his move to the Peach Orchard had prevented George Meade from retreating at Gettysburg. These speeches frequently received national newspaper coverage, assuring that his message would be spread across the country. Prior to his next Gettysburg visit, he gave two speeches in April 1886 in Boston to a Third Corps reunion that also received wide press coverage. The Boston speeches showcased his unique ability to distort various aspects of the historical record. In addition to the old charge that Meade had wanted to retreat, other favorite themes included an alleged lack of direction from Meade on July 2, that the prominent advance ridge along the Emmitsburg Road actually commanded Little Round Top, an aggressive Sickles had held Longstreet in check, and a valiant defense had been made by an overwhelmed Third Corps until supported by tardy reinforcements.[12]

Sickles admitted that Little Round Top was the "key" to Cemetery Ridge: "You know it was the key of the position. I know it was," he explained before arguing that the Peach Orchard was actually more important tactically because it was the objective that Lee and Longstreet had specifically wanted. "If you discover a piece of commanding ground that the enemy evidently wants, and intends to make effective use of against you . . . don't you think it is pretty good tactics not to let him keep it, but to take it yourself? Now, I do not profess to be a great tactician, but I think there is not a soldier here that is not tactician enough to know that."[13]

To many survivors of the Third Corps, the implication that their chief had nearly lost the battle was a stain on their own record—an implication that they also had nearly lost the battle. Sickles knew this hurt his men's pride, and he used his speeches to paint himself as an aggressive fighter, leading a corps of aggressive fighters. "Now, I know it is said . . . that General Sickles was imprudent in engaging General Longstreet in battle when he had but one corps at his disposal," he exclaimed. "That is true. I acknowledge the truth of that criticism. It may have been imprudent to advance and hold Longstreet at whatever sacrifice but was it not a sacrifice to save the key of the position? . . . I simply advanced out on to the battlefield and seized Longstreet by the throat and held him there. That is to say, you did it." They had been abandoned, he continued, by a commanding general who hadn't given him sufficient support, and then by the other corps who delayed in coming to his aid. "I rode along the lines that afternoon, hour after hour, witnessing the falling, the wounded, and the dying: witnessing the sacrifices—the ghastly sacrifices—you made until supports could come to aid you."[14]

Later that summer Sickles used the battle's twenty-third anniversary to return to Gettysburg; his men couldn't wait to see him. Private Charles Foster, whose 2nd New Hampshire had fought near the Peach Orchard, told John Bachelder:

> I intend if alive to be present at my old 3d Corps reunion to be held at
> Gettysburg July 2, 1886 under the auspices of the old one legged hero of
> that battle Daniel E. Sickles and he was the savior of that battle if anyone
> was not Gen. Hancock, as they wish us to believe at this late day after the
> old ones are all dead[.] They make the next generation believe Hancock
> was the Hero but we don't take any stock now, not but Hancock was a
> good General, but I believe in giving credit where it was due. . . . Everyone
> knows that the 2nd day was the main battle as nearly all the army was
> engaged. . . ."[15]

Sickles joined many of his old friends at Gettysburg, including Henry Tremain, Charles Graham, George Randolph, and Joseph Carr for a battlefield reunion that was described as the largest held up until that time. Colonel Rafferty brought cheers and laughter from the assembled crowd as he introduced Sickles. "As I suppose that none of you know that man that made the victory of Gettysburg possible, I will have to introduce him to you." Sickles frequently manipulated his unavoidably missing leg and set off his own round of cheers by responding, "You will excuse me if I remain seated." When a voice in the crowd shouted, "Where's Longstreet?," Sickles answered with a grim smile, "You ought to have had enough of him on the 2nd of July, 1863."[16]

Ignoring the recent Boston reunion and his testimony before the Committee on the Conduct of the War, Sickles told his audience, "This is the first occasion I have ever taken to make a statement of facts concerning the part borne by the Third Army Corps in the battle of Gettysburg." After reminding the audience of his missing leg for a second time, Sickles stated that he felt "keenly of the injustice" done by Halleck and Meade and told one of his favorite anecdotes. He repeated how he had requested a court of inquiry from Lincoln "for the purpose of correcting the serious errors contained" in Meade and Halleck's reports. He drew loud cheers when he related that Lincoln had replied, "I am afraid what they say is true and God Bless you for it. . . . History will set you all right and give everybody his just place." After lamenting his "twenty three years in unbroken silence," Sickles directed his attention to Longstreet's July 3 assault: "Public attention has always been directed toward Pickett's attack . . . [but] The battle of the second was the battle of Gettysburg, long, stubborn, for hours doubtful, and from the beginning to the end terrible

Generals Joseph Carr (left), Dan Sickles (center), and Charles Graham (right) return to Gettysburg and the Trostle farm, circa 1886. *GNMP*

in the losses suffered by both sides." To Sickles, July 2 alone would always be considered *the* Battle of Gettysburg.[17]

Veterans of the other Union corps were not so accepting. At a tribute to John Reynolds, speaker Colonel A. Wilson Norris took both Howard and Sickles to task (without acknowledging that Sickles had received conflicting orders from Reynolds and Meade) for not arriving earlier in support of the First Corps on July 1. General Carr took great exception to this claim, and remarked that he was "pained" to hear Norris call Sickles "a coward. . . . There was no such order as that described by Colonel Norris issued to General Sickles. He had orders from General Meade to remain at Emmitsburg and reconnoiter for a position. He not only did not receive an order to come to Gettysburg, but his corps started for Gettysburg without his knowledge." Despite such continuing differences of opinion, Sickles enjoyed the activities and renewed limelight. In his closing remarks he "spoke feelingly of the cordial greeting he had received and the many courtesies extended to him since he arrived in Gettysburg."[18]

Sickles' widely publicized 1886 reunion performance triggered an angry response from a former Meade aide named Major James C. Biddle. Writing in the Philadelphia *Weekly Press*, Biddle claimed that Sickles "through ignorance, or from a worse motive, disobeyed the orders of General Meade, his commander, and by that disobedience imperiled the safety of the army, which was saved from serious disaster by the energy of General Meade in sending and bringing reinforcements from other portions of his line."[19]

Sickles' speech even resulted in a public counterattack from the long-dead George Meade. In 1869, prior to Meade's death, G. G. Benedict of Vermont had defended Meade's reputation from Sickles partisans in the Burlington *Free Press*. Those editorial comments had been passed along to Meade, who then corresponded with Benedict in March 1870. Benedict had not made Meade's correspondence public, but decided to do so in August 1886 based on "the recent elaborate attack upon General Meade's military reputation, made by General Sickles in his address at Gettysburg."[20]

Benedict had Meade's correspondence printed in the Philadelphia *Weekly Press* on August 11, 1886. Meade deferred to his testimony before the Committee on the Conduct of the War as his principal statement "against the charges and insinuations of Generals Sickles and Butterfield." Meade continued: "I have avoided any controversy with either of these officers-though both have allowed no opportunity to pass unimproved which permitted them to circulate their ex parte statements, and . . . to distort history for their purposes." In referring to the alleged July 2 retreat order, Meade told Benedict that "both [Sickles and Butterfield] perfectly understand what I meant," and that "I did not retreat when I could have done so with perfect ease at any moment."[21] Meade also denied that Sickles had actually forced Lee and Longstreet to attack:

> As to General Sickles having by his advance brought on the attack, and thus compelled the battle which decided the war . . . it is a very favorite theory with the partisans of this officer. But these gentlemen ignore the fact that of the 18,000 men killed and wounded on the field during the whole battle, more than two-thirds were lost on the second day, and but for the timely advance of the Fifth Corps [onto Little Round Top] . . . where they met the enemy almost on the crest and had a desperate fight to secure the position—I say, but for these circumstances, over which Sickles had neither knowledge nor control, the enemy would have secured Round Top, planted his artillery there, commanding the whole battlefield, and what the result would have been I leave you to judge.[22]

Meade had not severely criticized Sickles in his Gettysburg report because he "honestly believed General Sickles did not know where I wished him to go, and that his error arose from a misapprehension of my orders." After publishing the report, Meade later learned from John Geary, whom Sickles was supposed to relieve on Little Round Top during the morning, that Geary had sent a staff officer to Sickles notifying him of the position and its importance. Geary told Meade that he had waited for some time to be relieved by the Third Corps, but when "his patience was exhausted," he finally withdrew to join the rest of his Twelfth Corps on the Union right flank. Meade considered this "evidence that he [Sickles] knew the position occupied by Geary's division, or could have known, and yet failed to occupy it."[23]

Saving his harshest criticism for last, Meade wrote that "Sickles' movement practically destroyed his own corps, the Third, caused a loss of 50 per cent in the Fifth Corps, and very heavily damaged the Second Corps; as I said before, producing 66 per cent of the loss of the whole battle, and with what result—driving us back to the position he was ordered to hold originally." Meade claimed these crippling losses prevented him "from having the audacity in the offense that I might otherwise have had," laying the blame for Meade's inability to destroy Lee's army right back into Sickles' lap. "If this is an advantage—to be so crippled in battle without attaining an object—I must confess I cannot see it."[24]

Meade's arguments were persuasive, proving once again that Meade could hold his own in any verbal battle with Sickles. But by 1886, Sickles held a distinct advantage over Meade: the army commander was dead and unable to repeatedly present his case to the veterans. Still, since Meade's statement was in the public domain, Sickles was forced to use the New York *Times* to issue "a strong reply" of his own. Sickles always called upon loyal friends when in trouble, and he invited both Tremain and Charles Graham to participate so "that they might correct him if he made any misstatements." Apparently forgetting the recent Gettysburg reunion, and the Boston speeches, Sickles again made the incredulous statement that "I have never spoken of his [Meade's] conduct at Gettysburg except in my own testimony before the Committee on the Conduct of the War."[25]

Sickles called Meade's accusations "altogether mistaken" and argued that Meade "contradicts his own official report of the battle . . . and his testimony before the Committee on the Conduct of the War." Sickles reminded the *Times* that the Committee's final report had "justified me and censured Gen. Meade." He also pointed out that Meade's own testimony had been quite moderate in his criticism of Sickles, thereby implying that Meade must not have felt that Sickles' actions were worthy of censure. Since Meade declined Sickles' offer to pull back from the Peach Orchard and in fact made no "modifications" to the new line, the implication was clear: Meade presumably approved of the new line. These were favorite tactics used by Sickles during the postwar years: he frequently used Meade's lack of direct criticism as apparent proof that Meade had approved of Sickles' Gettysburg actions.[26]

Dan resorted to an outright lie in answering accusations that he was to relieve portions of Geary's Twelfth Corps division on the Union left: "the Twelfth Corps was never at any time, until the very close of the battle on the 2nd of July, in position on the left. The position of the Twelfth Corps during all the day of the 2nd was on the right flank." Sickles attacked Meade's instructions as being "all verbal and extremely vague and indefinite." Since Meade himself had testified that he had provided Sickles some discretion in posting his troops "within the limits of the general instructions I have given you," Sickles implied that if anyone was at fault it was Meade for not directing more specific attention to his left flank.[27]

Saving his favorite accusation for last, Sickles once again credited his advance with preventing Meade from abandoning the field. Again using Meade's own actions against him, Sickles misread a portion of Meade's 3:00 p.m. telegram to Henry Halleck as evidence of Meade's intent to retreat. Sickles claimed that Buford's cavalry had been sent to Westminster as part of this retreat plan, and he also included Pleasonton's claim that the cavalry chief had been busy gathering all cavalry and artillery in the rear "to cover the retreat of the army from Gettysburg." As further evidence, Henry Slocum had also given evidence that Meade considered Gettysburg "no place to fight a battle." As Sickles told it, Meade had a vendetta against any officer who deserved a share of the credit for Gettysburg, and that inaccuracies were standard in Meade's reports, partly because "General Meade knew nothing of Gettysburg." Sickles noted with satisfaction that Congress had officially thanked General Howard for selecting "our position on Cemetery Ridge." Again Sickles claimed that he had advised Meade to concentrate at Gettysburg on the evening of July 1 and that Sickles, too, was a member of this fraternity that had selected the battlefield.[28]

Overall, Sickles' latest attacks offered little new information. But they did document the extent to which he would stretch the truth, and proved that time had not subdued his passion for defending his role at Gettysburg. The battle with Meade was now resurfacing in a very public forum since the New York *Times* had a considerably wider audience than the typical veteran reunion. Twenty-three years after the last shots had been fired at Gettysburg, the

Meade-Sickles battle for Cemetery Ridge was opened once again, with the deceased Meade in no position to mount an effective counterattack.

Other veterans were now free to join in. Not all of the Third Corps survivors were as loyal as Tremain or Graham. The *Pioneer Press* in St. Paul, Minnesota published a rebuttal from the "Chief of Staff for General Humphreys," most probably Captain Carswell McClellan. The writer ridiculed Sickles' claims that he had, on the evening of July 1, possessed sufficient knowledge of the battlefield to make any recommendations whatsoever to Meade. It was based on Sickles' marching orders that Humphreys' division had nearly tramped into Longstreet's camps near the Black Horse Tavern that same evening. "[S]tripped of all mystery, special pleading, and attempted recrimination," McClellan explained, "the story of [July 2] is simply told." Meade's orders to cover Little Round Top were "known at division headquarters" and Sickles had instead chosen to advance into a new position at nearly a "90 degree" angle and with "both flanks in the air." "It requires no abstruse [sic] technical learning to discover the absurd weakness of the disposition." The writer argued that future historians would have no trouble dispelling Sickles' and other malcontents' true motives, and that no damage would be done to "the wreath so honestly won and modestly worn by George G. Meade."[29]

Former Confederate opponents also took up the cudgel against Sickles. Lafayette McLaws, who led a division against the Third Corps line on July 2, rejected Sickles' arguments: "if the public are not satisfied . . . that General Sickles' command was driven back from the position it held on that 2nd of July, and that the Confederates held them until ordered to retire therefrom [sic] on the 3rd . . . [then] the word 'victory' must mean something in the more modern vernacular which is not given to it in the dictionaries." McLaws sarcastically added that the public should remember the true facts surrounding the defense of Little Round Top "before the crown of victory can be accorded to him [Sickles]." McLaws would never share James Longstreet's desire to fall into line with Sickles' arguments.[30]

Although he didn't have a monument of his own at Gettysburg, the year 1887 saw Sickles achieve a certain permanence at the battlefield. In November, the names of Union generals were selected for roads running through the battlefield. The lane stretching from Devil's Den through the Wheatfield was dubbed "Sickles Avenue." It was certainly an appropriate choice, since the July 2 battle may never have occurred there had it not been for Sickles' advance. One wonders about Sickles' reaction to the naming of the road running over Little

Round Top in honor of George Sykes, signifying the Fifth Corps' role in defending what the Third Corps had abandoned.[31]

Sickles returned again to Gettysburg for the twenty-fifth anniversary in July 1888. Although overall Confederate turnout was below expectations, the star attraction was not Sickles or any other Union veteran, but "the man of all others who is never permitted to spend a moment alone is a tall soldierly-looking man with white hair and flowing gray whiskers." Whatever damage the battle had done to his reputation in the South, former Confederate corps commander James Longstreet was the town's biggest celebrity during the summer of 1888. "When it was rumored that Longstreet had arrived at the Springs Hotel hundreds at once began a pilgrimage in that direction." Longstreet attended ceremonies on McPherson's Ridge near John Reynolds' kill site and at one point during the festivities, so many Union veterans swarmed Longstreet that the viewing platform collapsed, sending him tumbling into the arms of his

Postwar image of James Longstreet, circa 1870s.

National Archives

former opponents. Reporters noticed that his health seemed to be failing. Twenty-five years had mellowed Longstreet's views. He accepted the battle's outcome as fate: "there is evidence in its plan and conduct that the hand of God was with the cause of the Federal and against that of the Confederate army."[32]

Sickles and Longstreet met for lunch on June 30. A curious crowd gathered "to see how these old opponents on the battlefield would greet each other." Sickles, after all, "still carried a lively recollection of the unceremonious manner in which he had been handled" by Longstreet on that afternoon so long ago. Anyone expecting a renewal of hostilities was quickly disappointed. "As Sickles entered the dining room Longstreet caught sight of him. Pushing his chair to the rear, the Southerner reached out his right hand. It was quickly grasped by Sickles, around whose shoulder Longstreet threw his disengaged arm. They were friends in a moment, and there was very little eaten at that particular table for 30 minutes as they talked about events a quarter of a century old."[33]

Longstreet later toured Little Round Top with Dan Butterfield. While Butterfield showed Longstreet the site of the proposed 44th New York regimental monument, they were joined by Sickles, Slocum, and Carr, who all arrived from town. The 146th New York's monument was being dedicated nearby, "but as soon as word passed that Longstreet was on the hill one-half of the spectators left their places and scampered to the spot where the famous group was. They found Sickles sitting on a rock at the base of a tree, his leg stump resting on the ground. Gen. Longstreet stood at his right. The crowd rushed forward eagerly to catch Longstreet by the hand" and provided an enthusiastic reception.[34]

While riding down Hancock Avenue, Sickles turned to Longstreet and said, "General, there has been a great deal of controversy about the position I took; its precipitating your attack and causing a great loss of life to the Union army." In view of the fact that Meade had disapproved of the advanced position, Sickles asked Longstreet in "which position would you have preferred to attack me in?" Longstreet took the cue without missing a beat, "Why, on the continuation of Hancock's lines, by all means. It would have enabled me to obtain a much better view of your line and give me more open field in which to work. I was thoroughly acquainted with Hancock's position, but had to go at you in the Peach Orchard without exactly knowing what I was meeting." When the party returned to town, Sickles invited Longstreet to dinner at the Springs Hotel. The carriage was "loudly cheered by Union veterans on the Chambersburg Street, Generals Sickles and Longstreet acknowledging the compliment by lifting their hats."[35]

Even when Sickles did not speak, monument dedications were still a useful tool in promoting his Third Corps agenda. Fortunately for him, there never seemed to be a shortage of contemporaries who admired his military skills. The veterans of his Excelsior Brigade gathered on July 2 for the laying of their monument's cornerstone. Chaplain Joe Twichell gave the oration and credited Sickles with winning the battle. "He was destined to be the master spirit" of the second day "by which we cannot doubt it will be the settled verdict of time, the Battle of Gettysburg was won." Meanwhile, at the dedication of the 86th New York's (Ward's brigade) monument near Devil's Den, another speaker also praised Sickles. When Longstreet launched his July 2 attack squarely on the Third Corps' front, the audience was told that "at such a time, commanded by an inefficient officer, the corps would have been easily destroyed. But General Sickles was equal to the emergency. A braver man never graced a saddle."[36]

Off the field, in a scene that would become increasingly common in the coming decade, April 1889 saw the passing of another old comrade. Charles Graham, who had been with Dan since the old days in New York, and had followed him into Gettysburg's Peach Orchard, died of pneumonia on April 15. Graham had returned to civil engineering projects in New York following the war, and was appointed by President Hayes in 1878 as Surveyor of the Port of New York. Graham had served on the GBMA during the 1870s and in 1886 was appointed engineer of the New York Monuments Commission, a post he held until his death. Both Sickles and Henry Tremain were among the pallbearers at the funeral, which was largely attended by army officers.[37]

*   *   *

As Union monuments began to increase in quantity, so did the squabbles between parties disputing regimental and battery positions. Given his increasing prominence at the battlefield, and his official position with New York's Monument Commission, it was also only natural that Sickles was frequently requested to intervene. At the twenty-fifth anniversary, Henry Hunt chided Sickles over the inaccurate placement of Captain James Smith's New York battery monument at Devil's Den. Major John L. Beveridge asked Sickles to assist in moving the 8th New York Cavalry's monument, which was in the position occupied by Beveridge's 8th Illinois cavalrymen. Captain James Hall asked Sickles for help in placing his 2nd Maine battery's monument. Sickles also asked the GBMA to comply with the veterans' wishes in properly placing the 111th New York's monument. In 1891, when John Bachelder was trying to enlist the New York legislature's help in honoring George Greene's brigade, he learned just how powerful Sickles had become when a veteran admonished, "With General Sickles against you your bill would be likely to fail unless General Slocum aids you," and "if Sickles does not fight it, it will go through."[38]

The GBMA tried to impose some order on monument placement by decreeing that primary regimental monuments be placed "in the position held by the regiment in the line of battle." This caused no major issues in the placement of Union primary monuments. Since Meade's army was primarily on the defensive, Union monuments could meet the GBMA requirements and still be placed in highly visible locations (such as on Little Round Top or where Pickett's Charge was repulsed). But increasingly thorny questions were being asked as to whether Confederate monuments belonged on the field and, if so, where should they be placed. Lieutenant Colonel Byron M. Cutcheon, a Medal of Honor winner who did not fight at Gettysburg, asked, "What positions? The 'Union line' is a fixed quantity. It is where the wall of flesh stood against the wave of steel. But where was the Confederate line?"[39] Many Northerners agreed, but Sickles took a progressive view on the subject, telling John Bachelder:

> I have no hesitation in saying that I see no good reason why the lines of both armies at Gettysburg should not be marked. The Union lines are already shown. Everybody interested in the battlefield would like to know the positions held by both sides in the great conflict. So much has been done already to commemorate the history of Gettysburg, that it would seem to be worthwhile to go on and complete the work. I am sure the survivors of the Third Army Corps would be glad to see the positions held by Longstreet's infantry and artillery plainly marked. The battlefield of Gettysburg should belong to the government. It should be a military post, garrisoned by artillery. With all the monuments prescribed it would be an object lesson of patriotism for mankind through the centuries.[40]

Sickles was popular enough to make yet another Gettysburg visit in 1889 for "Pennsylvania Day." Wet and "miserable" weather dampened the crowds, but the aging Sickles was among the hardy dignitaries who stuck it out. During indoor speeches, the governor of Pennsylvania made a reference to his state's part in Sickles' "gallant forward movement." The Gettysburg *Star and Sentinel* reported, "This reference to Sickles was loudly applauded by the veterans in the auditorium."[41]

Sickles' accusations against Meade, however, left many cold. Speaking at the dedication of the 120th New York (Brewster's brigade) monument in June 1889, Major General George H. Sharpe disagreed with the premise that Meade had planned a retreat, and also told the audience that Sickles' advanced position actually favored the execution of Longstreet's attack. "Longstreet's prescribed order of battle, in which he did not agree, was . . . to sweep up the Emmitsburg Road, under cover of his batteries, and roll up our lines in the direction of Cemetery Hill . . . The Third Corps formation, in its second position, considerably thrown out in advance of the general line from Cemetery Hill to the Round Tops, with an angle at the Peach Orchard, favored the execution of such an order of battle." This was indeed a rare Third Corps monument dedication: Sharpe said nothing complimentary of Sickles, supported Meade, and was generally critical of Birney's performance to boot. Rather than honoring the men who fought, these dedication speeches were frequently degenerating into attacks on each others' records. The squabbling was not lost on the veterans. Captain Charles Hale of the 5th New Hampshire told John Bachelder in 1890, "There has been some strange 'perversion of History' on the field within a year or so."[42]

A planned 1890 visit by the Comte de Paris, a noted Civil War observer who had gotten to know Sickles as a member of George McClellan's staff in 1862, revealed a rift between John Bachelder and the Sickles-Butterfield duo. Bachelder, who could be stubborn and opinionated in his own right, learned that Butterfield desired to exclude him from joining the Comte's party. Bachelder told John Nicholson that Butterfield "knows that I despise his attempt to injure the reputation of General Meade . . . and hence that it would be pleasanter if there was no person present with the Comte to criticize the statements and innuendoes which he and that clique will make." Bachelder referred to the "scandalous attack on General Meade [that] was made in the papers by 'Historicus,' about which I did not hesitate to give my opinion. And General Butterfield knows that I do not sympathize with those who have tried so hard to injure the reputation of the dead Commander-in-chief." To add insult to injury, Bachelder had further drawn Butterfield's ire for omitting Butterfield's July 3 wounding from his popular Isometric Drawing because "I had already found that he lost no blood when he fell from his horse during the cannonade on the 3d day, though he embraced the opportunity to go so far to the rear that he would be in no danger."[43]

Finally, another difference arose over the placement of the planned New York State Monument in the Soldiers' National Cemetery. "The New York

Monument Commission desires to erect a memorial structure on the summit of Cemetery Hill which will overshadow everything on the field—National Monument and all, and I have not acquiesced," explained Bachelder, who wanted to instead place a monument to Meade "on the crowning summit of Cemetery Hill. This as you know would hardly suit the tastes of the man who has never lost the occasion to stab General Meade's reputation under the fifth rib." Sickles had pestered the secretary of war to demand the location, which Bachelder and others hardily resisted. Bachelder did discuss placing monuments to the other Union corps commanders on the field, and the modern editors of Bachelder's Gettysburg papers have speculated that his tensions with Sickles may have resulted, "at least in part," because of Sickles' lack of a Gettysburg statue. It should be noted, however, that as late as 1890, John Reynolds was the only Union corps commander with a statue on the field. Several corps commander statues were placed after the turn of the century—well after Bachelder had passed on—and despite Bachelder's prominence, he did not have the lasting ability to permanently ban a Sickles statue.[44]

The Comte de Paris finally arrived at Gettysburg in October 1890. Although Bachelder was excluded, the menagerie of aging Union generals in attendance included Sickles, Butterfield, Slocum, Doubleday, Howard, and others. The group arrived in town via train, after touring the Antietam battlefield in Maryland, to a large crowd of citizens and cheering college students. They toured nearly every portion of the battlefield and answered questions pertaining to the fighting. Someone questioned Howard when the easiest time would have been for the Confederates to turn Meade's left flank. When Howard replied that the best Confederate opportunity "was just at dawn on the morning of the second," Sickles appeared almost immediately, as if on cue, and "was given a seat in the Count's carriage."[45]

The Comte had, up to this point, prudently and "studiously avoided any comment as to the wisdom of Sickles' forward position." But General Howard walked up to Sickles and stated in a voice "loud enough to be heard by those" nearby, "I am convinced, General, the more I look at the subject that your movement was the proper one with plenty of troops, and saved Little Round Top by gaining time and breaking the rebels." Slocum was more "guarded in his comments, and said he 'didn't know but that the movement was the proper thing.'"[46]

Unable to let the matter rest, Butterfield discussed Meade's "Council of War" on the night of July 2. He recalled that after the vote, Meade had supposedly replied, "Gentlemen, Gettysburg is no place to fight a battle." All of the visiting generals "confirmed" this recollection, although Howard remembered slight differences in the wording. It was nearly three decades since the great battle had been fought, but anti-Meade sentiments still resided with some of the former generals. The group held an impressive dinner that evening with Sickles presiding, and had their portrait taken by local entrepreneur William Tipton in front of the John Reynolds statue in the National Cemetery. The passage of time was aptly captured in a visibly paunchy and balding Sickles seated near white-haired contemporaries Slocum and Butterfield.[47]

Sickles had the visit recorded for posterity in the March 1891 issue of the *North American Review*. The passing decades were not lost on the aging Sickles. "The transition from 1863 to 1890, little more than a quarter of a century, almost confounds the imagination, and makes the reality seem like a dream." Overwhelmed by the reunion of the surviving Union commanders, Sickles believed that "the strongest emotion of the visitor to Gettysburg is the memory of those who here nobly fell in battle." He briefly included Meade among his own roll call of "great leaders," but singled out "Hooker, who reorganized the army and led it almost here, his chosen field, compelling Lee to give battle. . . . The campaigns of Chancellorsville and Gettysburg are monuments of his strategic skill."[48]

Sickles argued, once again, that Meade had wanted to fight on Pipe Creek. Reynolds' battle "was brought on without orders, perhaps against orders," and the "surprise" battle "gave to Howard the choice of position at Gettysburg." Sickles admitted that the Cemetery Ridge position in which Meade intended him to occupy was "perhaps the more desirable tactical position for me to occupy, unless overruled by superior considerations." But he argued that these "superior considerations" included the depression and "swampy character" of the ground before Little Round Top. He admitted that Little Round Top was "obviously the key to our position," but his own force "was insufficient to hold" Meade's intended line. "Impossible to wait longer . . . I advanced my line towards the highest ground in my front, occupying the Emmitsburg Road at the very point where Longstreet hoped to cross it unopposed, covering Round Top and menacing the enemy's flank if he attempted to turn our left." The advanced line of the Third Corps prevented another Chancellorsville, he continued, "every inch of ground was disputed along the whole line, from Round Top to the Peach Orchard."[49]

While active with the veterans, Sickles was not necessarily consumed by all things Gettysburg. The acquitted murderer served a brief stint as sheriff of New

York in 1890, completing a term for a resigned incumbent. Some conjectured that he was appointed in the hopes of strengthening the governor's support from veterans, but there was speculation that Sheriff Sickles had even greater ambitions to be mayor or governor. Not everyone thought Sickles worthy of the office. One report complained that "General Sickles does not represent the grade of soldiers to whom the public feels most grateful." Admitting that Sickles "certainly fought bravely" at Gettysburg, he still "needlessly sacrificed nearly ten thousand men and gave Lee an opportunity to break our line which would have been successful had it not been for the promptness of General Warren." Had Warren not noticed that Little Round Top was unoccupied, "the story of that battle would have been a very different one."[50]

His role as chairman of the New York Monuments Commission extended to fields beyond Gettysburg. During his tenure, the commission would place New York monuments at Vicksburg, Mississippi, Chattanooga, Tennessee, Andersonville, Georgia, Cold Harbor, Virginia, and Antietam, outside Sharpsburg, Maryland. He also oversaw the placing of memorials in New York to Generals John Fremont and Newton Curtis. He continued to remain active with the Third Army Corps Union, whose duties (embalming and sending home Third Corps dead) had ceased with the close of the war. The old soldiers still decided to keep the organization alive and have reunions, often at locations besides Gettysburg. Sickles was an obvious choice as a frequent guest speaker, and as an honored dignitary he was often given amenities, such as private cars and choice accommodations, befitting his always lavish lifestyle.[51]

Sickles did not limit his endless Gettysburg opinions to controversies surrounding the old Third Corps. He was among "400 braves" who represented Tammany Hall at the dedication of the 42nd New York (the "Tammany Regiment") monument on Hancock Avenue in September 1891. The monument features a statue of Indian Chief Tamenend in front of a bronze wigwam, giving generations of Gettysburg visitors the erroneous impression that an Indian regiment fought at the battle. Sculptor James Kelly, who completed Gettysburg's John Buford monument, was approached to do the Tammany monument but declined because he considered the design "ridiculous." He offered the pretense that he could not complete it in the one month that the New York commission was requesting. Upon hearing this, Chairman Sickles berated him: "W-h-a-t! Not do it in a month? W-h-y-! If I were sculptor, I could do it in a month! A-l-l you have to do is get an I-deah – a vivid I-deah!" (When Kelly viewed the final monument on the field he decided, "Sickles m-u-s-t h-a-v-e m-a-d-e it.")[52]

Although the 42nd fought in Hancock's Second Corps, the regiment had been raised by Tammany Hall at the beginning of the war, so it was natural that Tammany's most famous Gettysburg "brave" would speak. Despite the fact that their monument was near the so-called "High Water Mark" where Pickett's assault had been repulsed (a portion of the battle about which Sickles possessed no firsthand knowledge), he was "received with cheers and repeated huzzahs by the old veterans" as he "referred to the pensions now enjoyed by the veterans and said no man could ever be elected chief ruler of this nation who would deprive them of one cent of pension money so justly earned." He combatively offered his opinion of the nearby 72nd Pennsylvania regiment, whose veterans had recently gone to court to have their monument placed farther in advance of the line than they actually occupied on July 3. Pointing toward the Angle, Sickles proclaimed:

> No doubt it has struck many of you with surprise that the [42 NY] monument is not over yonder, and that the Seventy-Second Pennsylvania is not over here or further back beyond the Avenue. You, gentlemen of the Memorial Association, are not responsible for that falsification of history and that grave error. You did all in your power to prevent it, but you were overruled by the judicial authority of your State. Your hands are bound, but no injunction is put on me to prevent me saying what I think. I protest in the name of history, and in the name of the brave men who fell here, against the outrageous position of that Pennsylvania monument.

"I don't know why those men [72nd PA] were so modest that they would not advance when ordered," Sickles rhetorically asked and answered about the 72nd's failure to move forward to the stone wall on July 3. "I don't know why the Forty-second were so immodest as to advance. It must have been because they were Irish-Americans; and saw a head and wanted to hit it." The following speaker, Edward McPherson, diplomatically responded that he hoped for a time when historic truth would outweigh state pride. Sickles may have advanced without orders on July 2, but to a born fighter like himself it was much more preferable than refusing to advance.[53]

Another event revealed Sickles' stubborn character at its worst. He had been estranged from his alcoholic daughter Laura for years, having even declined earlier pleas from his father George to help her. Dan had been warned that it would "make a row" if the newspapers learned that his daughter was penniless while he lived in a $100,000 house. Still, he refused to reconcile. "I have done my whole duty toward the person in whose behalf you write," he answered coldly. "As far as I'm concerned she is dead and buried." When Laura died in Brooklyn from cirrhosis in 1892, Sickles did not attend her funeral. Her death certificate listed her as 39 years old and single. She was interred in a family plot in Brooklyn's Green-Wood Cemetery with Teresa, who had been moved there in 1870. Although Sickles found it within himself to forgive former enemies like General Longstreet, he never forgave Laura for whatever grievance she had caused him.[54]

On a lighter note, Dan's wide-ranging travels carried him to Atlanta in March 1892. Longstreet traveled from his Gainesville home to welcome Sickles to Georgia. On St. Patrick's Day, they both attended a banquet at the "Irish Societies of Atlanta." As Sickles later told it, the 300 attendees burst into "the wildest and loudest 'rebel yell' I had ever heard" when they entered the hall together. Sickles offered a toast to Longstreet's good health and promised the audience that Longstreet would sing the Star-Spangled Banner. "This was, indeed, a risky promise, as I had never heard the General sing," joked Sickles. Longstreet surprised everyone present by singing "admirably," and the crowd joined in with him.[55]

According to Sickles, after consuming large amounts of Irish whiskey the pair left together onto Atlanta's darkened late-night streets. Unable to find a carriage at that hour, the disabled and intoxicated war heroes attempted to walk each other home, but each refused to leave the other so they repeatedly walked back and forth between their respective hotels. "Old fellow," Dan asked on route, "I hope you are sorry for shooting off my leg at Gettysburg. I suppose I will have to forgive you for it some day." A drunken Longstreet exclaimed, "Forgive me? You ought to thank me for leaving you one leg to stand on." The two former enemies increasingly became friends during this period of their long lives. Since both shared the distinction of having their Gettysburg performance assailed by critics on both sides, many historians have assumed they mutually exploited one another in order to defend their war records. At least one author speculated that Sickles was using a politically naive Longstreet to gain favors from Northern Republicans. Although it is a testimonial to both of their postwar reputations that historians will not accept the relationship at face value, each man frequently told anyone who would listen that the other had done right on July 2, 1863.[56]

By the early 1890s, Sickles was not only still active and dangerous (he received a pistol carry permit from New York City) but he was also extremely wealthy. His father, George Sickles, had died in 1887 with an estate full of investments and real estate reportedly valued at a minimum of $4,000,000. George's second wife Mary and three step-daughters received the bulk of the estate (contrary to Dan's claims that he inherited most of it), but Dan was bequeathed several properties. Laura, George Stanton, and Eda were also to share ownership and income on three properties. "The reports of Gen. Sickles' large fortune are not exaggerated," reported the New York *Times* in 1892. He bragged that he owned a large stock and bond portfolio along with a series of rental and commercial properties throughout the city, employing a "clerical force" to collect his rents. His residence on Fifth Avenue was also estimated to be worth several hundred thousand dollars. Dan lived on the first floor and rented out the second and third floors for additional income. The rooms on the house's ground floor were "literally crowded with pictures and relics and statuettes and bric-a brac." Most of the George Sickles properties would be sold at auction in 1895. Dan bought several parcels from the estate himself, notably George's large 100+ acre homestead in New Rochelle, which was purchased jointly with son Stanton and step-sister Alta. He was appointed a trustee for Stanton and Eda's shares of George's estate, and was also named the Executor of his step-mother's estate when she died in 1893. In his mid-seventies, it appeared that Dan would never have to worry financially ever again, but as he demonstrated throughout his life, placing large sums of money in his hands was always a precarious proposition.[57]

Dan had also realigned himself with the Democrats in time for the 1892 presidential election. Democrat Grover Cleveland had spent his time during the war practicing law and politics in Buffalo, New York. Cleveland had already occupied the White House from 1885 to 1889 when, during his first term, he had vetoed several veteran pension bills. Cleveland lost his 1888 re-election bid to Republican challenger Benjamin Harrison. After a four-year hiatus, Cleveland took the unusual step of running again in 1892. Never able to remove himself from a presidential campaign, Sickles received nationwide press coverage when candidate Cleveland's war and veteran records drew his wrath.[58]

Sickles served as a New York delegate to the Democratic National Convention, and announced that 20,000 state Democratic veterans would never vote for Cleveland, whom he ridiculed for furnishing a substitute rather than serving in the army. When Dan received additional coverage for strongly criticizing Cleveland at a Third Corps reunion speech, Democrat leaders quickly began to distance themselves from Sickles. Newspapers asked Sickles if perhaps his criticism had simply been misquoted, but he assured them, "The men heard it, and I meant it, and let us be content. General Sickles can't vote for the coward who hired a substitute; who sneered at the services and sufferings of veterans, and who, often with a scoff, vetoed more than four times as many pension bills as all his predecessors in the Presidential office." Such talk led to rumors that the powerful GAR would support the Republican ticket, and Sickles himself later claimed that the episode caused the Republicans to "seductively beckon" him to their side. But Sickles was outraged at the Republicans when cartoons of himself appeared on the elevated railroads with Sickles reminding riders that "No, no veteran will vote for Cleveland!" The Republican tactics backfired when they convinced Sickles to fall in with the Democrats and soften his rhetoric. The malleable Sickles wore a Cleveland button during a GAR parade, and although he admitted he had opposed Cleveland's initial nomination, he assured the public that he held the "highest regard" for Cleveland. When the voting was tallied, the "coward who hired a substitute" was successfully returned to office.[59]

Like a true politician, Dan had obviously back-peddled to prove his party "loyalty," a fact that did not pass unnoticed. One Democrat paper complained that "1892 will be known as the great Flop campaign. Considering the agile manner in which General Daniel E. Sickles and others of his class have flopped out of the Democratic ranks and then back again, a word of one syllable fails to fully characterize it. Nothing less than the flip-flop campaign will do."[60]

An even more unexpected announcement came on October 17 when Tammany Hall's nomination convention selected their Congressional candidates. After the convention was called to order, Sickles' name was proposed and seconded. The convention announced that he was the Democrats' choice to run in the city's Tenth District. Sickles was not even in the hall when nominated, so it took about ten minutes to retrieve the candidate. The conventioneers arose to cheer him as he entered the hall, where he gave a "short but pointed" acceptance speech, after which he remained to greet well-wishers, including several GAR veterans. Other candidates were announced at the same time, but it was Sickles' return to politics that the *Times* called "the most interesting and significant" choice. The Gettysburg literature frequently portrays Sickles' return to Congress as part of a veritable one-man crusade to create the Gettysburg National Military Park. In fact, Sickles' nomination appears to have been more the result of typical Tammany political maneuvering.[61]

Sickles gave the papers a lengthy explanation for his acceptance, which seems to have been primarily motivated by the Grover Cleveland episode. "I have several times in the past been urged to return to Congress, but I have always refused. This time, however, I felt constrained by the circumstances to accept, because I saw in my nomination the opportunity to quiet once and for all the misrepresentations of the Republicans regarding my alleged opposition to Mr. Cleveland." He accused the Republicans of twisting his words in order to portray him as being opposed to the Democratic National Ticket. "I realized that only the strongest possible action could refute their continued assertions, and I think that I have taken this action in accepting the nomination . . . I am like a soldier. I have enlisted and now go to the front . . . I never do anything by halves, and I will conduct my canvass on such lines as will convince the most skeptical that I am for Cleveland . . . I will give proof of my loyalty." Sickles promptly had Dan Butterfield warn the Republican National Committee "that they refrain hereafter from libeling me."[62]

Everyone in the party seemed happy with the nomination except for General Martin T. McMahon, a former Brevet Major General with the Army of the Potomac, Medal of Honor winner, and Senator. Ironically, McMahon was also a Gettysburg veteran, having served as chief of staff to Sixth Corps commander John Sedgwick during the battle. McMahon had long assumed that the nomination was his, and so was dumbfounded when it fell into Sickles' lap. "I can't understand it. It is the biggest mistake the party could have made. Gen. Sickles has no constituency, no followers at all. He has hurt the national ticket already, and his running for Congress won't help it any." McMahon smelled an opportunity when a candidate in another district, a retired army officer still drawing pay, voluntarily withdrew under the grounds that his army income rendered him ineligible. Sickles was still receiving $5,625 in army pension annually, and McMahon promptly demanded that Sickles withdraw on the constitutional grounds that since he was being paid, he was still in the army, and therefore ineligible to hold public office. Sickles was, McMahon insisted, "a man of vacillating character, and should he at the last moment decide, as I am sure he will, not to go into Congress, he would practically turn over the district to the Republican candidate."[63]

Sickles ridiculed the suggestion that he step aside, noting that he had become well versed with the relevant law when he went to Spain. "You see, in such cases, one should be half a soldier, half a lawyer." He did not think the law applied to him, but if he was proven wrong he would not accept any of his army pension while in Congress (although he would not volunteer to remove himself from the army's retired list). "I am not a poor man. I have my own private fortune, and what is a paltry $5,000 with a few odd hundreds to me? And, anyhow, I get $5,000 as a salary for being in Congress. No, sir, that does not apply to me . . . I hope I shall be elected, and shall certainly not withdraw." It wasn't quite the ardent campaigning of his youth, but he still knew how to play the game.[64]

With little less than a month before the election (there was no lengthy campaign as there is today) there seemed little doubt that Sickles would win. His district was solidly Democrat, and only McMahon had seriously challenged the nomination. Dubbed the "millionaire candidate" by the *Times*, Sickles' return was hailed with delight by Tammany's "boys" of the Tenth District. Some politicians in the district had feared that the campaign would have been a "dry one" if McMahon had run. "Sickles clubs, Sickles guards, and Sickles barbeques are being organized from one end of the district to the other," reported the paper. A canvas suggested that many were willing to vote for Sickles but were simply waiting "for the right sort of substantial persuasiveness to be gathered into the Sickles fold." His residence was being overrun with visitors, and since he was unaccustomed to his renewed popularity, he reportedly took "to his bed for refuge" on more than one occasion. It was also presumed that the "millionaire candidate" would contribute a substantial portion of his own cash to the cause. Veteran affairs were at the top of his agenda. During a speech in Harlem, Sickles announced he was going to Congress "for the very purpose" of "keeping up the pensions system or establishing it on a wider basis." On the eve of election, the *Times* listed Sickles among those candidates "certain of election," and on November 8, more than three decades after his first term had ended, Dan Sickles was once again elected to Congress. The New York *Times* would later marvel that Sickles was returning at "an age when most men are ready to retire."[65]

Congressional duties didn't prevent Dan's attendance at army reunions. In May 1893, the newly elected legislator joined a large group (including Longstreet, Henry Tremain, and Porter Alexander) that again toured Gettysburg. The trip helped further cement the friendship between Sickles and Longstreet. As Sickles later told the story, he assisted Longstreet in climbing Little Round Top. "Sickles, you can well afford to help me up here now," Longstreet joked, "for if you had not kept me away so long from Round Top on the 2d of July, 1863, the war would have lasted longer than it did, and might have had a different ending."[66]

A number of journalists accompanied the party. As reported in the New York *Times*, when Longstreet was asked whether Sickles had advanced too far forward on July 2, Longstreet "sustained Gen. Sickles handsomely." "Old Pete" explained, "Had not Sickles been so far out, we would have taken the Round

Tops without firing a shot, and shelled the Union Army out of its position along Cemetery Hill [sic]. Even had Sickles prolonged the line of the Second Corps, his left flank would not have been heavy enough to resist an attack." Longstreet believed that his attack would have rolled up Sickles' corps "as easily as a cigarette paper. The only thing left for Sickles was to do as he did." Longstreet argued that if the fight began with Sickles covering the Round Tops, "we would have had no problem whatever in working in his rear and outflanking him." Longstreet remained one of Sickles' most valuable allies. Whether he actually believed it to be true or not—and perhaps he really did—Longstreet was always willing to publicly state that he thought Sickles' move had been best for the Union cause.[67]

Sickles' return to Congress came during the era when, as one Pennsylvania congressman put it, Gettysburg "has become a pilgrimage ground for a larger number of citizens and ex-soldiers than any other field of the late strife. A national interest has been awakened in its decoration by monuments contributed by the various states whose soldiers fought and fell on this historic site." His election allowed Sickles, as he had done many times throughout his long career, to take advantage of being in the right place at the right time.[68]

Although veterans were increasing their efforts to memorialize Gettysburg, during the mid 1880s through 1890s large portions of the battlefield were threatened by commercial development. In 1884, the Gettysburg and Harrisburg Railroad ran a line across the fields of Pickett's Charge to a station on the east side of Little Round Top. Thirteen acres were purchased at the end of the track and developed into "Round Top Park." Taking advantage of the increasing commercial potential near Little Round Top and Devil's Den, the local Rosensteel family purchased two acres and eventually established "Rosensteel's Pavilion." That summer, local entrepreneur William H. Tipton also established a photo gallery at Round Top Park. By bits and pieces, the natural landscape of core portions of the battlefield park were being significantly altered.[69]

William "Boss" Tipton was a prominent local photographer, businessman, and politician. He bragged that he had graduated "from the school of Hard Knocks" and was probably similar in temperament to Dan Sickles. In 1892, Tipton incorporated the Gettysburg Electric Railway Company, a commercial venture that threatened to run electric trolley tracks all over the field, including through much of Sickles' advanced battle line. Unable to pry land away from the GBMA's limited holdings, Tipton and principal investor Edward Hoffer negotiated instead with private landowners to gain rights of way across their properties. They successfully obtained a right of way across the Plum Run "Valley of Death" from an elderly General Samuel Crawford for $1.00. Tipton now owned thirteen acres near Devil's Den to commercially rival "Round Top Park." Tipton's workers began heavy blasting and digging that threatened to desecrate what had been Sickles' July 2 left flank. Not surprisingly, public and veteran outcry was immediate and loud. Sickles complained of Tipton's "blasting and leveling rocks and cutting the trees through the Devil's Den region, robbing it of its mystery and jungle wildness. These made the place interesting, independent of its association, and gave a peculiar character to the battle which was fought at and from this point."[70]

With commercialization as the backdrop, the battle's thirtieth anniversary in 1893 probably represented the high water mark of Sickles' involvement in erecting monuments at Gettysburg. The first three days of July were designated "New York Day," capped off by the dedication of Sickles' long hoped-for New York State Monument in the National Cemetery. The New York Monuments Commission was busy throughout the spring, with Sickles and Butterfield issuing a number of circulars as testimony to their active involvement. Sickles was angered when the commission applied for conveyances from the locals and was told the charge would be $25 per day. He successfully threatened local officials that the commissioners would tour the field on foot unless the price was dropped. Rumors also circulated that veteran anger would be directed at Tipton's growing commercial developments.[71] Chairman Sickles issued an appeal to his men:

> Rumors have reached the Commission, apparently well authenticated, indicating the purpose of certain veterans who will visit Gettysburg on 'New York Day' to destroy the trolley railroad now being constructed over the battlefield. The Board, therefore feel constrained by a proper sense of the decorum due to that occasion, to appeal most earnestly to all New York veterans to abstain from any act of violence against property of any description during their visit to Gettysburg, and to refrain from anything like discourtesy toward the persons identified with that undertaking, however obnoxious such persons may have made themselves.
>
> In making this appeal, the Commissioners are by no means insensible to the outrage committed by the vandals, who, for the mere sake of gain are desecrating and destroying the characteristic features of a battlefield which Lincoln said was consecrated ground. . . .

Sickles appealed to his men to punish the commercial ventures financially, not physically. "Veterans! You owe it to your own self-respect to leave the property of the railroad company under the protection of the law, until the proper authorities shall put a stop to the acts which have justly provoked your indignation. . . . *Don't ride in the cars! Advise your friends to keep away from them! Refuse free passes if they are offered to you!* [Emphasis in original]" Did Sickles see any irony in his message? The congressman who had committed murder, and the general who had advanced without orders on this very field, was issuing an appeal for law, order, and non-violence.[72]

New York's National Cemetery monument was dedicated on July 2. The monument consists of a large column topped with a female statue, representing the figure on the state's seal, crying over the battle's dead. As Dan had wanted, not only is the monument visually prominent in the cemetery, but he even managed to incorporate himself on it. The base contains engravings of four key battle scenes, including "The Wounding of General Sickles." As "President of the Day," he gave the address and assimilated many of his favorite Gettysburg themes, including (once again) the accusation that Meade wanted to fight on Pipe Creek.[73]

On a more constructive note, remembering fallen soldiers was also a theme he felt strongly about. "There is no better way, my comrades as you know, to prepare for the next war, than for the people to show their appreciation of their defenders in the last war. [Applause] No nation can long survive the decline of its martial character. When it ceases to honor its soldiers it will have none. [Applause] When it ceases to honor its soldiers, it will deserve none."[74] Sickles called upon the government to stop the destruction of the field:

> The time has come when this battlefield should belong to the government of the United States. [Applause] It should be made a national park, and placed in charge of the War Department. Its topographical features not yet destroyed by the vandals…The monuments erected here must be always guarded and preserved, and an act of Congress for this purpose, which I shall make it my personal duty to frame and advocate [Applause] will contain a clause establishing a military post at Gettysburg, including the battlefield among its dependencies, to be garrisoned by artillery, to the end that the morning and evening sun may forever salute the flag and the Union which were so heroically defended on this historic ground. [Great Applause][75]

"New York Day" also witnessed the dedication of the completed Excelsior Brigade Monument. (The corner stone had been laid in 1888.) Sickles' old brigade was finally receiving its own battlefield recognition, with the monument's base consisting of plaques devoted to each regiment. Five columns support a dome, atop which sits a bronze eagle in a warlike pose. Between the five columns is an empty pedestal. Battlefield lore has long held that this empty pedestal was intended to house a Sickles statue, and the New York *Times* coverage of the ceremonies noted, "Within the inclosure [sic] formed by the five columns it is understood that a bronze bust of Gen. Sickles will be placed when he passes away." A statue was never completed, and today the pedestal remains empty. Although it appears that there was no intention to place a monument there during Sickles' lifetime, probably due to a general restriction prohibiting the honoring of living individuals, one of Gettysburg's oldest battlefield traditions has it that Sickles' expulsion from the monuments commission in 1913 prevented this statue from ever being placed.[76]

Henry Tremain also spoke at the dedication. He proposed that the July 2 battle had been fought for control of the Emmitsburg Road. Without Sickles' actions "yonder Round Top Mountain might have been gained by the enemy without firing a gun." Tremain openly acknowledged that due to Sickles' "persistent efforts are we chiefly indebted for the action of the State of New York in its grand work of monumenting this field, and for projecting and advancing the congressional legislation that will establish here a National Park." After a speech by New York's governor and an oration, Sickles spoke briefly, praising his old brigade's "heroism and never-faltering courage." General Carr presented Sickles with a gold medal as "a testimonial of the affection and loyalty of your comrades of the Third Corps." Sickles was so overcome that he could only briefly promise to "preserve the medal as a priceless treasure and wear it near his heart as long as he lived."[77]

The party continued at Little Round Top on July 3, where the monument to the 44th New York and two companies of the old 12th New York was dedicated. Butterfield, the regiment's one-time commander, designed the monument and was the keynote speaker. He began by warning, "we have acted upon the suggestion that nothing should be said here that would give rise to any comment or controversy." Nevertheless, he felt it necessary to address "certain matters," specifically those who questioned why the hill was "not occupied earlier. I shall only tell you that it was not the fault of General Sickles. He insisted upon its occupancy at the earliest hour in the morning." Butterfield commended Chairman Sickles for his service and introduced him to the crowd.

"General Sickles earned our gratitude and deserves the thanks of the people throughout the United States. Whatever criticism has been made upon his position on this field, was answered by General Longstreet when he said that if Gettysburg was the decisive battle of the war, General Sickles was the man who decided it."[78] Sickles rose to speak. After a few brief anecdotes about his militia service in the 12th, he offered another defense of his July 2 performance:

> General Meade did not expect an attack from the enemy on this part of the field. His attention was then occupied with the contemplated assault that he expected General Slocum to make on our extreme right, Culp's Hill. . . . Later in the day, having discovered that the enemy was massing a very large force to attack this flank of the army, again urgent requests were made by me in person; again and again I sent them over to headquarters calling attention to the fact that double our numbers were already massed for the attack in this direction. Now more than that I do not care to say. I chose to say it here and now because I say it in the presence of Tremain and Moore and Butterfield . . . I quite agree with General Butterfield in his desire to avoid on this occasion any remarks calculated to provoke controversy or ill feeling.[79]

Despite their stated intentions to avoid controversy, "some trouble occurred" following the dedication when William Tipton attempted to photograph the assembled veterans. Noting that Tipton and Sickles "had some disagreements recently . . . over the trolley road," the Gettysburg *Star and Sentinel* reported that Tipton "was not permitted to use his camera. He was told to remove it, but declining to do so, several of the veterans, at the command of Generals Sickles and Butterfield, took it down and laid it on the ground, without breaking it, we believe." The Gettysburg *Compiler* had a slightly different perspective, claiming that "sharp remarks" were exchanged and that Tipton's camera was "pushed down by some one of the veterans and said to be damaged slightly." Tipton returned to town and had a trespassing summons issued against Sickles, who was asleep when the sheriff arrived; Butterfield left town before he could also be summoned. Tipton's attorneys, George Benner and David Wills, filed a claim of $10,000 against Sickles.[80]

"The whole affair is to be deprecated as out of place and uncalled for," scolded the *Compiler*. Overall, the *Compiler* sided with the veterans, noting that Tipton's presence was clearly unwanted. "Mr. Tipton's appearance there at that time, under such circumstances, was an intrusion, and his persistent attempts to photograph the veterans against their will cannot be defended." Sickles was untroubled by the episode. After all, he had been through much worse before and told a reporter, "I think I have a right to determine whom I shall permit to photograph me." He continued to demonstrate his popularity when he also spoke to the survivors of George Greene's Twelfth Corps brigade.[81]

In addition to his congressional duties and his role with the New York Monument Commission, Sickles was elected to the GBMA's Board in June 1891 and served through the organization's final meeting in 1895. He attended the annual meeting in July 1893, in which the two most important issues discussed were the trolley and the potential transfer of the association's land to the United States government. "The effort will be made to have the next Congress act in the matter and the Memorial Association is expecting Grand Army Posts all over the Union to urge their congressmen to vote in favor of the bill when introduced," reported the Gettysburg *Compiler*. As early as his 1890 visit with the Comte de Paris, Sickles had been championing the establishment of "a permanent military post, garrisoned by artillery."[82] Over the years, his view of Gettysburg's future had expanded. "[I]n view of the fact that so many of the old soldiers are approaching the age at which they will be more or less invalid and infirm," he explained,

> a soldier's home should be erected there. The Carlisle Indian School might with propriety be situated at Gettysburg, and perhaps also a GAR museum. . . . Besides this, we want to preserve the natural features and the earth works of Culp's Hill, and also have a law passed marking the lines of the Confederate troops. You can readily see from the improvements already there, the avenues and the many monuments, that we have a splendid foundation on which to build our proposed superstructure.[83]

A news reporter found the new congressman to be "as erect, despite his 60 odd years of life and his crutches, as he was when but a lad of 20. He receives his visitors with a manner that is a mixture of bluff cordiality and the courtesy of the old school. His hand grasp is hearty, and one who is admitted at 33 Fifth Avenue, New York, especially if he be a veteran or a veteran's friend, is made to feel that the house and its belongings are as much his as the general's during the visit." Sickles assured his visitor:

> It is a great comfort to me to meet the boys who fought for the Union, especially if they tell me they fought in my command…Hardly a week of

my life passes that I am not accosted on the street by some man who tells me he fought under me as a private, and in almost all cases he has the bearing and wears the clothes of prosperity. It is true that we who went to the war lost several years' progress in the arts of peace, but the severe discipline that we passed through more than made up, I think, for the time we lost.[84]

Sickles actively championed battlefield and veteran affairs when he reported for the 53rd Congress, which debated several Gettysburg-related resolutions. During the second session, which ran from late 1893 to mid-1894, Sickles supported a resolution to present "medals of honor to the militia and volunteer troops of the several States who volunteered their services for the defense of the States of Maryland and Pennsylvania in the year 1863, prior to and after the battle of Gettysburg." One Congressman drew laughter by ridiculing the idea of giving a debased (silver) medal, and Texas Democrat C. Buckley Kilgore wondered why a distinction was being made for "picnic soldiers" and not those who had served throughout the conflict.[85] "But why," Kilgore wondered, "did they not continue in the service?"

Sickles: Their services were not required.

Kilgore: I suppose they were bankers and other people of that class, and that you had to promise them silver medals in order to get them to go at all. [Laughter] But I understand the gentleman from New York to say that this is a contract entered into by the Government.

Sickles: Yes.

Kilgore: In that case I want to set up the plea of limitations right here and now, because this claim has been running thirty-one years and the statute of limitations bars it.

Sickles: Oh, that statute applies to money obligations, not to obligations of honor. There is no statute of limitations against the recognition of patriotic services in this country, thank God! [Applause]

Kilgore: I understand that; but there were many other people who were engaged in serving their country in a patriotic way and whose claims are equal or greatly superior to these. Beside sir, we have not got the money for this purpose.

Sickles: We are going to tax sugar in a few days, and that will bring us all the money that we want. [Laughter][86]

In August 1890, an attempt was made by Michigan Representative Byron Cutcheon to have the National Government establish a commission to mark the lines of both armies at Gettysburg. In March 1893, a Congressional sundry bill allocated $25,000 for this purpose. A three-man commission was appointed to open or improve avenues along those lines, and also to acquire the land necessary to ensure a "correct understanding" of the battle. By 1894, Sickles wanted at least another 2,500 acres added, thinking that another $100,000 would cover the costs. Before Sickles could begin his self-described "operations," he hoped that the future of Tipton's electric trolley could be settled in court.[87]

The battlefield commission had so far failed to stop Tipton and Hoffer (who was president of the railway company) from blasting Devil's Den apart in the name of the trolley tracks, so in July 1893, concerned local citizens had petitioned the state's Attorney General to intervene and stop further battlefield damage. The United States Government followed suit and notified the railway that it intended to condemn the trolley's land. That August, however, the Pennsylvania Attorney General surprised everyone by announcing that he would not interfere with the railway. On May 15, 1894, the U.S. District Court in Philadelphia ruled in favor of the trolley company, noting that the March 1893 sundry bill did not give Congress the right to acquire land.[88]

Congressman Sickles sprung into action. On May 31, 1894, Sickles requested unanimous consent for the consideration of a joint resolution authorizing the Secretary of War "to acquire by purchase (or by condemnation) . . . such lands, or interests in lands, upon or in the vicinity of said battlefield." Before giving his consent, Texas Democrat J. D. Sayers challenged Sickles on the potential cost. Sickles argued by explaining that "blasting and other work tending to destroy the battlefield will be resumed at once, unless we supplement the act of March 3, 1893, by giving clearly and distinctly the authority" to condemn. Another Texan, Joseph Bailey, also questioned whether or not Congress should even be allowed condemnation authority "for park purposes," and asked for the opinion of the House. Sickles refused any compromises, saying that he was "unwilling to emasculate the resolution," and "if we can not have authority to condemn, then we are at the mercy of a lot of land jobbers, who want to speculate upon this historical ground."[89]

The resolution worked its way through the Senate, with debate over "whether this is one of those public objects which the courts have decided may justify the power of eminent domain." Several proponents noted that the original sundry bill intended to actually cover this, but was omitted and the latest resolution would now close the gap. After eventually passing through both Houses, President Cleveland signed the bill on June 5. The Federal Government apparently now had the power to condemn land at Gettysburg, but the judge in Philadelphia ruled again in favor of the trolley company on April 23, 1895. This time, however, the U.S. Supreme Court overruled the lower court in January 1896. As far as preservation was concerned, it was a landmark ruling confirming the government's right to protect historic land. In reality, however, much of the damage to the battlefield had already been done and the electric trolley actually operated (albeit under different owners) for another twenty years. In the end, the popularity of automobiles killed the trolley more so than did the actions of Sickles and Congress. In 1917, several years after Sickles had died, the government finally appropriated $30,000 to purchase the land and dismantle the line.[90]

Of more lasting effect was Sickles' direct role in establishing Gettysburg National Military Park. Between 1890 and 1899 Congress authorized the establishment of the first four national military parks: Chickamauga and Chattanooga, Shiloh, Gettysburg, and Vicksburg. Despite the great attention paid to it, Gettysburg was not the first Civil War battlefield to be designated a National Military Park. That honor belongs to the Chickamauga and Chattanooga National Military Park, which was so designated in August of 1890—more than four years before a park was established at Gettysburg. And like Gettysburg, the Chickamauga and Chattanooga park was created because of the efforts of veterans alarmed in the late 1880s by their battlefield's rapidly changing landscape. In passing the legislation, Congress recognized "the preservation for national study of the lines of decisive battles . . . as a matter of national importance." It was the first legislation to authorize the preservation of an American battlefield, and laid the foundation for the concept of the national historical park.[91]

The press was reporting that Sickles "has a scheme for the creation of a grand national park, which will include the battlefield and other historic points of interest at Gettysburg." Sickles held onto this notion throughout his last term in Congress, telling a friend in November 1894 (during a break between sessions), "I shall push a Gettysburg Park Bill through at the approaching session if possible." He was also still acutely interested in ensuring that New York received its battlefield due. Noting that Pennsylvania had appropriated funds for Gettysburg statues to Meade, Reynolds, and Hancock, Sickles warned, "We shall not consider our Gettysburg work completed until we have a statue erected on Culp's Hill to Gen. Slocum."[92]

Before tending to any Gettysburg legislation, however, there was the matter of Sickles' re-election. In October 1894, Tammany Hall announced candidates for the upcoming Congressional elections. The Wigwam re-nominated Sickles for another term, the 54th Congress set to begin in March 1895. Different Democratic factions nominated separate candidates in New York and Brooklyn. The state Democratic leaders tried to hammer out a compromise to ensure that the party was united on one candidate in each district. Tammany agreed to withdraw candidates in two districts and all public indications were that Sickles' candidacy in the Tenth District would be pulled. On the surface, Tammany seemed to be abandoning Sickles, but Dan spoke to the press from Tammany headquarters and publicly stated that he was willing to make any personal sacrifice for the good of the party.[93]

In the end, the Democrats ran two candidates in Sickles' Tenth District. Sickles remained Tammany's choice, while George Karsch ran as the "New York State and Empire State Democrat." In the November election, Sickles received 10,925 votes and lost a close race to Republican Andrew J. Campbell's 11,825 votes. Fellow Democrat Karsch received 2,099 votes. Sickles and Karsch had combined to outpoll the Republican, but the two Democrats split the vote and prevented a Sickles re-election. Matters complicated themselves when Congressman-elect Campbell died of Bright's disease just a month later. The immediate presumption was that Sickles' narrow defeat ensured his running again in a special election, to be held in 1895.[94]

It was under this uncertainty (despite Campbell's death Sickles was still officially an outgoing "lame duck") that Dan reported for the 53rd Congress' third and final session in December 1894. Gettysburg historiography frequently tells us that Sickles had gone to Congress for the sole purpose of designating Gettysburg as a national military park. The fact that he waited until the last possible session to do so certainly casts doubt on that theory. That December, he finally introduced a bill "to establish a national military park at Gettysburg, PA." Having already established the precedent at Chickamauga, there seemed little doubt that the bill would pass, and the debate primarily concerned its details.[95]

Sickles' proposal authorized the secretary of war to purchase from the GBMA "a deed of conveyance to the United States of all the lands belonging to said association, embracing about 800 acres, more or less, and being a considerable part of the battlefield of Gettysburg, together with all rights of way over avenues" and that such land, including the National Cemetery, "shall be designated and known as the 'Gettysburg National Military Park.'" The park's commissioners were appointed to superintend the opening of new roads, improve existing ones, and to "properly mark the boundaries of the said park, and to ascertain and definitely mark the lines of battle of all troops engaged in the battle." The secretary of war was also authorized to acquire more land "by purchase, or by condemnation proceedings" and to establish and enforce "proper regulations for the custody, preservation, and care of the monuments." Another section of the proposal authorized the secretary to erect "a suitable bronze tablet" containing President Lincoln's Gettysburg Address and "a medallion likeness of President Lincoln." Always interested in his beloved veterans, Sickles added a provision to establish his long-planned branch of the "National Homes for Disabled Soldiers." To accomplish this ambitious piece of legislation, "the sum of $100,000, or so much thereof as may be necessary, is hereby appropriated. . . ."[96]

As the proposal worked its way through the House, Sickles was forced to modify his bill during meetings with the Committee on Appropriations and the War Department. His pet project Soldiers' Home was dropped, and the appropriation was decreased from $100,000 to $75,000. An addition to Section 4 modified the proposed boundaries as land "not exceeding in area the parcels shown on the map prepared by Maj. Gen. Daniel E. Sickles." In other words, the initial boundaries of Gettysburg National Military Park were accepted based on a map that Dan had drawn up. What would become known as the "Sickles Map" remained in effect until 1974, when a Senate Appropriations Committee accepted a National Park Service recommendation to protect additional acreage and eliminate the map as marking the park's boundary. Not only did Sickles push through the legislation, but for the park's first (nearly) eighty years he determined its boundaries.[97]

Public response to the "Sickles Bill" was generally positive, particularly among veterans. The resolution passed through the House and Senate, and on February 11, 1895, the President officially signed the bill establishing Gettysburg National Military Park. It was the most lasting initiative of Sickles' long career; even if the vast majority of Gettysburg's modern visitors are completely unaware of his involvement.[98]

Gettysburg's population was unsure as to what all this meant for their future, a debate that has not completely abated today. The *Compiler* pondered the long-term result. "All indications point to the conclusion that the Battlefield of Gettysburg will become a National Park and that land all around our town will be purchased for the purpose," explained the paper. "There are many different opinions to the effect which this may have on the business and general welfare of Gettysburg, which time only can decide." The establishment of the park and Federal control of the roads appears to have been treated as two distinct issues and there were concerns in Gettysburg that the park would give the Federal government undue control of the local roads and land.[99]

Gettysburg National Military Park was not the first such park, but Sickles steered it into creation at the right moment in American history. Time had sufficiently cooled the sectional strife to allow the country to do more than just establish national cemeteries and place monuments. The Philadelphia *Record* editorialized that, "by securing and preserving those fields intact, as representative examples of the greatest battles of the rebellion, the Government will be able to perpetuate their history in a concrete physical form for all time to come." Sickles' historical critics often point out that surely someone else would have eventually established Gettysburg National Military Park if Sickles had not done so himself. Perhaps, but no one else bothered to do so in the four intervening years since the designation at Chickamauga, and it is a matter of history that Sickles got the job done. Not only that, but the park accepted his boundary designation well into the 1970s—all of which serves as proof that no other player in the Gettysburg story had the combined battlefield and postwar influence as did Dan Sickles.[100]

With Gettysburg's future attended to, Sickles closed out his final days in Washington. The press acknowledged his long, and sometimes distinguished, service. "The one Democratic Congressman who can look back upon his record in the present House with pride is Gen. Daniel E. Sickles, of New York. He has by his voice and his vote proven that a man may call himself a Democrat and still be a patriotic American in every sense of the word. . . . After the fourth of March he will retire to private life, and he will carry with him the good wishes of all true patriots."[101]

Not surprisingly, he remained busy in "retirement." In May, he attended the last official meeting of the GBMA at the Springs Hotel in Gettysburg. In October 1894, the GBMA board had voted to transfer nearly 600 acres of GBMA land, along with seventeen miles of avenues giving access to 320 monuments, to the United States government, pending official consent of the association's stockholders. Now at the final GBMA meeting in May 1895, resolutions were passed instructing the officers to execute the necessary deeds of conveyance to the government. On motion of Sickles, the vice president and secretary were directed to prepare vouchers for claims outstanding against the GBMA. Sickles made another motion to authorize the compilation, publication, and distribution of the organization's history. Unfortunately many aging contemporaries continued to pass away, and both General Joseph Carr and historian John Bachelder had died since the last GBMA meeting. Sickles and McPherson were appointed to prepare minutes on Carr's death, as well as on the recently deceased Henry Slocum. When the meeting adjourned, dinner was held in the hotel's Ladies Parlor. "At the head [of the banquet table] sat Gen. Daniel E. Sickles, of New York," the *Compiler* reported, "who in his peculiarly happy manner presided." The large dinner broke up at midnight with attendees promising that they would continue to gather socially for as long as they were alive.[102]

The possibility still remained that Sickles would return to his Congressional seat and fill the void created by Andrew Campbell's death. The special election to replace Campbell wasn't held until November 1895, and Tammany didn't convene to nominate their candidate until October. The initial presumption was that Sickles would indeed return, but Charles E. Foote, "said to be Gen. Sickles' secretary," told the assemblage "that he was authorized to state that Gen. Sickles was not a candidate." Foote asked that Sickles' name be withdrawn, but this was unnecessary since Sickles had not been put before the convention as a potential candidate. Tammany instead unanimously chose Congressional veteran Amos J. Cummings, who beat his Republican opponent in November and took Sickles' House seat in December. Sickles' political career was over once again, this time permanently. He was too old to make another comeback in Congress, but he was not finished with public life. In addition to the New York Monuments Commission, Sickles and Butterfield were also members of the Chickamauga Battlefield Committee. Maintaining a vigorous travel schedule of a man half his age, he continued to attend reunions throughout the country.[103]

Cronies such as Henry Tremain also traveled in support of the Third Corps cause. In September 1897, Tremain spoke at the dedication of the Excelsiors' 73rd New York monument (the "Second Fire Zouaves") at Gettysburg. The monument was placed east of the Emmitsburg Road, opposite the Sherfy barnyard, where Tremain had personally led the 73rd into action on July 2, 1863. Tremain returned to his own long-time favorite theme: that the protection of the Emmitsburg Road had led to Sickles' decision to move forward, and "it became essential to decide if the Emmitsburg Road, by which we had marched was to be held or abandoned. . . . In the absence of explicit orders to abandon it, military necessity and good discipline required it should be held." With this statement, the pro-Sickles camp perhaps reached its peak of illogic. Tremain's argument boiled down to this: the absence of Meade's orders actually permitted the Third Corps advance.[104]

Sickles was presented with a Congressional Medal of Honor on October 30, 1897. Critics have scoffed that it took decades for the medal to be awarded, but this was not necessarily an uncommon practice (Joshua Chamberlain of the 20th Maine, for example, waited until 1893 for his medal), particularly in cases where political favors were needed to buttress claims of battlefield gallantry. More difficult to explain was the fact that Sickles became the only corps commander to receive a medal for Gettysburg, and he did so amid accusations that he and Tremain had abused the system to recommend each other. (Accusations of abuse in the award process, it must be pointed out, became increasingly common as the years progressed and were not limited to Sickles by any means.) His decades of portraying himself as the hero of Gettysburg's second day resulted in a citation that read: "Displayed most conspicuous gallantry on the field, vigorously contesting the advance of the enemy and continuing to encourage his troops after being himself severely wounded."[105]

Many survivors were unimpressed with Sickles' attempts to control history. General Alexander Webb was a commissioner on Sickles' New York Monuments Commission. Webb never fell into the Sickles camp, having once told John Bachelder, "I would stop bogus monuments at once. Just [as] I would stop the bogus claims of Sickles, Butterfield & such." On another occasion, Webb told sculptor James Kelly, "I dispute his [Sickles'] claims; have all along. He knows I did. He could fight, yes; as a tactician, no." Kelly once asked Webb, "Why do the officers let Sickles run things?" Webb replied: "They [other officers] have no moral courage. He [Sickles] is a bad man and they are afraid of him, and the reporters like his whiskey and cigars and they all stick to him."[106]

In 1895, New York had allocated $6,000 for Sickles' Monuments Commission to publish a report of its actions, including a "brief history of each New York regiment and battery" that participated in the battle. In November 1898, about a year before the report (authored by Lt. Col. William Fox) appeared, General Webb sent Fox a memo stating that he refused to sign the report as long as a passage existed resurrecting the old allegation that Meade intended to retreat. "I would be condemned by every officer of the Army of the

Potomac who knew General Meade, if I were to sign a report stating that he issued an order for the army to leave Gettysburg." Webb's tactic worked and the final report did not include the damaging passage.[107]

Despite this, the commission's final report as published in 1899 was extremely favorable to Sickles' Gettysburg performance.[108] His stamp of influence on the content was everywhere. Regarding Sickles' advanced position:

> It was a strong tactical position. In its rear lay a wheatfield and other large areas of open ground which, in connection with the roads near by, furnished the necessary ground for maneuvering troops. On the front and south, its elevation, crowned with artillery, commanded the long approaches and open fields over which the enemy must move in attacking either the Round Tops or the position itself.[109]

While Webb had successfully prevented Sickles and Fox from resurfacing the charge that Sickles' move had prevented Meade from retreating, they still accused Meade's "instructions" of being "somewhat indefinite and allowed some latitude, owing to his purpose to attack elsewhere." Sickles thus had to make a decision upon which "the fate of the battle might depend. His corps comprised the only troops on that part of the field, and the enemy was massing on his immediate front and flank. If he occupied the Round Tops he could not hold the ground between him and Hancock. If he remained where he was, the Round Tops would be occupied by the enemy, and his position become immediately untenable."[110]

Fox's contention that Sickles lacked sufficient manpower to hold Meade's line failed to explain, of course, why Sickles then moved into a longer line. Fox explained it this way: Sickles "knew the fighting quality of his corps well enough to feel assured that he could hold such position until the general commanding could bring up the necessary reserves to secure the position and achieve a victory." The new position would be "impregnable [if] held by a proper number of troops, properly supported." In other words, Sickles supposedly moved into his longer line under the presumption that Meade would give him enough support from the other corps.[111]

As has often been noted in the Gettysburg literature, Sickles' decision was strongly influenced by the debacle at Chancellorsville: "Was it to be Chancellorsville again?" The Emmitsburg Road ridge was important, Sickles and Fox argued, because Confederate control would cause Meade's army to "lose communication with the strategic position at Emmitsburg." Rather than blame Sickles' Gettysburg movement on his Chancellorsville withdrawal from Hazel Grove, as Gettysburg authors frequently assume, Sickles and Fox argued that the similarities actually lie in the massing of enemy troops on his flank.[112] Sickles had witnessed firsthand what happened when Stonewall Jackson massed on General Howard's Eleventh Corps flank at Chancellorsville, and was determined (so he wrote) to prevent the same thing from happening again at Gettysburg:

> The movement of the Third Corps is often described as an advance to the Emmitsburg Road, creating thereby an erroneous impression. The real movement was consisted in the left wheel of Birney's Division to the south. . . . Two-thirds of the corps faced southward to meet a flank attack which soon came from that direction. Chancellorsville was lost through a failure to make just such a move in just such a contingency.[113]

Of course, such a "left wheel" by Birney would have been unnecessary had they remained on Cemetery Ridge. Still, when reading Sickles' many and varied excuses for his actions at Gettysburg, it becomes apparent that he was equally (or more) influenced by memories of Jackson's infantry pouncing onto Howard's flank, rather than his forced withdrawal from Hazel Grove. Perhaps had Jackson's flank attack never occurred, Sickles would have spent July 2, 1863 securely in position on Cemetery Ridge.

Sickles, Longstreet, and Dan Butterfield were scheduled to return to Gettysburg once again for a Memorial Day parade and speeches in 1899. The local *Star and Sentinel* commented that the "presence of Sickles and Longstreet is particularly interesting because of the fact that the two Generals were arrayed on opposite sides in the great battle." The paper attempted to summarize the battle "briefly and happily" by noting that "the weakness of [Sickles' advance] position was in the fact that Little Round Top was left unoccupied . . . [But] it should be added that the exhaustion of the Confederates in driving back Sickles from the position which he had assumed had much to do in rendering [the Confederates] unable to drive the Union from its final position." The Philadelphia *Times'* coverage contained a perceptive analysis of the postwar controversies that had entwined both Generals. The "two subordinates who confronted each other on Meade's left and Lee's right were diametrically opposed to those of their respective chiefs." The July 2 battle had put both generals "on the defensive historically, and the Gettysburg battlefield has always had a keener interest than it possesses today for any of the survivors."[114]

Poor health prevented Longstreet from attending in 1899, and he was instead represented by his son, Lieutenant James Longstreet, of the U.S. Army. The younger Longstreet had recently returned from service in Cuba. Sickles attended and spoke of the "good feelings" that now existed between both sides. "I am getting a little mixed with these Memorial Day exercises. Formerly it was the custom to hang Jeff Davis to a sour apple tree; tear the Rebels to pieces and wave the bloody shirt. Now Longstreet is invited to Gettysburg . . . and so many of the boys in gray are now boys in blue we should reverse the exercises on the programme in justice to the new order of things." Sickles admitted, "I get tired of the old story and like the new story better."[115]

"I am sorry that Longstreet is not here," Dan said. "I would have been glad to say something about his assault and the impression he made upon me; things that he would have been glad to hear." Was Sickles willing to admit some regret at his "famous move" toward the Peach Orchard? "I can't come without asking: 'Sickles, suppose the battle of Gettysburg were to be fought tomorrow under circumstances and conditions that existed on July 2, 1863, what would you do?' . . . I would do tomorrow under the conditions and circumstances that then existed exactly what I did on July 2." Reflecting upon almost thirty-six years of controversy, he added, "I have heard all the criticisms and read all the histories and after hearing and reading all I would say to them I would do what I did and accept the verdict of history on my acts. It was a mighty good fight both made and I am satisfied with my part in it."[116]

Chapter 18

The Civil War is Only a Memory

As the twentieth century dawned, Dan Sickles must have reflected on the momentous changes he had witnessed (and had frequently participated in) within American society. "In my time I have seen the birth of railways, steam-ships, telegraphs, telephones, and the applications of steam and electricity to all forms of industries and transportation," he told a rapt Fredericksburg audience in May 1900. The reconciliation of North and South was another frequent theme in his speeches. "It is astonishing how much I like a man after I have fought him," he answered in reference to a question on how he felt about former enemies like James Longstreet. The men who once wore gray were now the "new South, the great South which has risen from the ashes of '61-'65; the progressive South which was born again. . . . Today the South and North know each other better than ever before."[1]

He also continued to use his public platform to lobby for preservation of battlefields besides Gettysburg. "Within a small area near the spot where we are seated, are the great battlefields of Fredericksburg, Chancellorsville, Spotsylvania, and the Wilderness, where more men fought and fell than upon any space of equal dimensions on the face of the earth. These famous battlegrounds should be made a National Military Park. Our battlefield parks are an American institution. . . . They hand down our military traditions to succeeding generations. They keep alive the martial character of our people. They teach the American boy that he belongs to his country and that his country belongs to him."[2]

Although no longer active on a national level, Sickles remained involved in New York politics, running for Alderman in New York's Fifth District and denouncing the current Tammany administration. "There have been times when Tammany Hall was a respectable organization, and I remember such occasions very well, but unfortunately they are long since past." He also served as President of the Board for the Soldiers and Sailors Home in Bath, New York. In an ominous preview of what was to come, the state launched an investigation over allegations of financial misuse by board trustees. The state decided that there was "no supervision" over disposition of funds and the trustees were "lacking in the proper appreciation of the responsibility cast upon them." Sickles and two other board members resigned. The affair was more proof that, despite his many organizational talents, it was not wise to trust Sickles with large sums of money.[3]

Sickles and Dan Butterfield remained closely identified for the remainder of their lives, if not as close in their friendship as they had once been. For his part, Butterfield remained hated by many of his old military comrades. Whatever contempt Alexander Webb felt for Sickles, it seems to have paled against his disgust for the Army of the Potomac's former chief of staff. Webb told James Kelly in 1899 that he considered Butterfield a "lying little knave. He [Butterfield] is one of the most corrupt, scheming, lying scoundrels. . . . He pretends that he was wounded at Gettysburg. And Sickles and I who were writing the official history for the State cross off his claim. He was hit in the throat with the branch of a tree. He tied a handkerchief around it with the bloody side out. Gen. Meade showed him up. . . . Col. Nicholson had to hold me in the streets of Philadelphia to keep me from caning him." Webb also told Kelly that Sickles and Butterfield had some sort of falling out and were "not so much [friends] as they used to be. Sickles does not seem to like having his name coupled with Butterfield so much." Butterfield remained active in the postwar years, and received a Medal of Honor in 1892 for his role at Gaines' Mill. In April 1901, the sixty-nine year old suffered a stroke at his Fifth Avenue home in New York and died on July 17. The business executive turned amateur soldier was buried with full military honors at West Point, an institution he never attended. Sickles memorialized Butterfield as contributing "largely to our success at Gettysburg" due to his "rapid concentration of our widely separated columns." Of the infamous Hooker-Sickles-Butterfield trio, only one remained. And as the last survivor, Dan would lose many more friends during the coming years.[4]

In the fall of 1902, James Longstreet was invited to attend the dedication of Henry Slocum's Gettysburg monument.[5] The aging ex-Confederate declined due to his poor health. Longstreet sent Sickles a letter of regret, in which he formally documented his defense of Sickles' Gettysburg record:

On that field you made your mark that will place you prominently before the world as one of the leading figures of the most important battle of the Civil War. As a Northern veteran once remarked to me, 'General Sickles can well afford to leave a leg on that field.'

I believe it is now conceded that the advanced position at the Peach-Orchard, taken by your corps and under your orders, saved that battle-field to the Union cause. It was the sorest and saddest reflection of my life for many years; but, to-day, I can say, with sincerest emotion, that it was and is the best that could have come to us all, North and South; and I hope that the nation, reunited, may always enjoy the honor and glory brought to it by the grand work.[6]

In early January 1904, Longstreet died in Gainesville, Georgia, just shy of his eighty-third birthday. The nearly forty-one years since Gettysburg had been difficult for Longstreet. Attacks on his war record had overshadowed his active travels and involvement in Republican politics. Controversial in the South, Longstreet had been a popular celebrity in Northern circles. Both Longstreet and Sickles shared the distinction of having to defend their Gettysburg records, but Sickles had been better at it than Longstreet, whose pen often alienated more than he won over. In 1897, Longstreet had married thirty-four year old Helen Dortch. Helen became a celebrity in her own right, and outlived him by fifty-eight years, dying in 1962. She spent much of her remaining life trying to rebuild Longstreet's reputation. In 1904 she published her own defense of Longstreet's war record in *Lee and Longstreet at High Tide*, and asked Sickles to contribute a lengthy introduction.[7]

Sickles began by noting the apparent irony that he might be writing a preface for "a conspicuous adversary." But, he reminded readers, "the Civil War is only a memory, its asperities are forgotten, both armies were American." Sickles thought that Longstreet's war record needed no apology, and clearly believed where the blame for Gettysburg belonged. The failure of the Confederate assaults "must be attributed to the lack of strength in the columns of attack on both days, for which the commanding general alone was responsible."[8] In revisiting the one event that truly brought the two men together, Sickles wrote:

Longstreet was unjustly blamed for not attacking earlier in the day [July 2] at Gettysburg. I can answer that criticism, as I know more about the matter than the critics. If he had attacked in the morning, as it is said he should have done, he would have encountered Buford's division of cavalry, five thousand sabers, on his flank, and my corps would have been in his front, as it was in the afternoon. In a word, all the troops that opposed Longstreet in the afternoon, including the Fifth Army Corps and Caldwell's division of the Second Corps, would have been available on the left flank of the Union army in the morning. Every regiment and every battery that fired a shot in the afternoon was on the field in the morning, and would have resisted an assault in the morning as stubbornly as in the afternoon. Moreover, if the assault had been made in the morning, Law's strong brigade of Alabamians could not have assisted in the attack, as they did not arrive on the field until noon. On the other hand, if Lee had waited an hour later I would have been on Cemetery Ridge, in compliance with General Meade's orders, and Longstreet could have marched, unresisted, from Seminary Ridge to the foot of Round Top, and might, perhaps, have unlimbered his guns on the summit.[9]

Once again, Sickles' interpretation of the historical record was not completely accurate. "Every regiment and every battery" was not simultaneously on the field that morning, and he again made the questionable assumption that had he been in Meade's intended position, Longstreet would have "unlimbered his guns" on Little Round Top. This was also another opportunity to tell an audience that he had prevented Meade from retreating. "Longstreet's attack held the Union army at Gettysburg" and the aborted 3:00 p.m. war council was "broken up by the sound of Longstreet's artillery . . . If Longstreet had waited until a later hour, the Union army might have been moving towards Pipe Creek, the position chosen by General Meade on June 30." By Sickles' reasoning, the nation owed Longstreet a debt of gratitude by timing his attack when he did. Had Longstreet attacked any later, the Federal army would have been gone and no Union victory would come about. Sickles saved an opportunity to give himself credit for disrupting Lee's plan, which "was a repetition of Jackson's attack on the right flank at Chancellorsville."[10]

Sickles was at least satisfied that Longstreet "lived long enough to rejoice with all of us in a reunited nation, and to know that his name was honored wherever the old flag was unfurled. His fame as a soldier belongs to all Americans." Realizing that he was rapidly facing his own mortality, Sickles closed with, "Farewell, Longstreet! I shall follow you very soon. May we meet in the happy realm where strife is unknown and friendship is eternal!" The two men who shared some of Gettysburg's greatest battlefield influence had joined forces for one last time to address their numerous critics and perpetuate their own history of the battle.[11]

Sickles' notoriety and increasing elder-statesman status allowed him to socialize with presidents and other celebrities. Sickles and Oliver Howard escorted President Theodore Roosevelt to Gettysburg for 1904's Memorial Day celebrations. Despite drenching rain, Roosevelt spoke to an estimated 10,000 people from the cemetery's rostrum. The party also spent more than three hours touring the battlefield. Sickles and Howard played guides, with "the entire party listening attentively to the graphic word pictures the two distinguished veterans drew" of the battle. As the newspapers reported, "At the President's request Gen. Sickles pointed out where he received the wound which cost him his right leg. In that connection he said that he did not know precisely when he received the wound, as he did not know that he had been hit until he returned to his headquarters about 6:30 p.m., only discovering the fact then by finding his right hand which had been resting on his leg, covered with blood." A "prolonged stop" was made on Little Round Top, and after hearing a "cross-fire of graphic descriptions" from both Union and Confederate participants, Roosevelt remarked, "This country is all right so long as we can have this kind of talk on Little Round Top."[12]

Former Excelsior chaplain Joe Twichell had become pastor of a fashionable church in Hartford, and had in the process struck up a lifelong friendship with humorist Mark Twain. Twichell always paid a call on both Sickles and Twain when he visited New York. As it turned out, the pair lived across the street from one another, although they never socialized. "He is too old to make visits," Twain wrote, "and I am too lazy." Finally, on a rainy night in January 1906, Twichell managed to get Twain across the street and into Sickles' house.[13] Twain devoted a significant passage in his memoirs to his meeting with Sickles, a testimonial to how famous Sickles had become in his own right. "Sickles," remembered Twain,

> is a genial old fellow; a handsome and stately military figure; talks smoothly, in well-constructed English—I may say perfectly constructed English. His talk is full of interest and bristling with points, but as there are no emphases scattered through it anywhere, and as there is no animation in it, it soon becomes oppressive by its monotony and it makes the listener drowsy. Twichell had to step on my foot once or twice. . . . His talk is much better than it is. . . . His talk does not *sound* [emphasis in original] entertaining, but it *is* [emphasis in original] distinctly entertaining."[14]

Despite the potentially entertaining subject matter, Twain still found it to be a monotonous evening:

> Now when we sat there in the general's presence, listening to his monotonous talk—it was about himself, and is always about himself, and always seems modest and unexasperating, inoffensive—it seemed to me that he was just the kind of man who would risk his salvation in order to do some 'last words' in an attractive way. He murmured and warbled, and warbled, and it was all just as simple and pretty as it could be. And I will also say this: that he never made an ungenerous remark about anybody. He spoke severely of this and that and the other person—officers in the war—but he spoke with dignity and courtesy. There was no malignity in what he said. He merely pronounced what he evidently regarded as just criticisms upon them.[15]

Struggling to stay awake, Twain made a significant observation. "I noticed then . . . that the general valued his lost leg away above the one that is left. I am perfectly sure that if he had to part with either of them he would part with the one that he has got." Twain also observed that Sickles' home was "a curious place" where the floors, walls, and ceilings were literally covered with animal skins, photos, trophy swords, and flags "stuck here and there and yonder."[16] He continued with his description:

> You couldn't walk across that floor anywhere without stumbling over the hard heads of lions and things. You couldn't put out a hand anywhere without laying it upon a velvety, exquisite tiger-skin or leopard skin. . . . Then there was a most decided and rather unpleasant odor, which proceeded from disinfectants and preservatives . . . so it was not altogether a pleasant place, on that account. It was kind of a museum, and yet it was not the sort of museum which seemed dignified enough to be the museum of a great soldier—and so famous a soldier. It was the sort of museum which should delight and entertain little boys and girls. I suppose that that museum reveals a part of the general's character and make. He is sweet and winningly childlike.[17]

There was an effort by friends in 1910 to have Sickles promoted to lieutenant general. Partisans such as Washington's *The National Tribune* thought that Gettysburg "showed, and the testimony of the leading Confederates since fully supports the belief that Gen. Sickles correctly fathomed Gen. Lee's designs, and took the most effective way of frustrating them."[18] The paper continued:

> Gen. Sickles and his friends may well accept Gettysburg as the crown of his military career and a lasting monument to his fame. He rendered services there, as he had before, which under the great Napoleon would have made him a Field Marshal and a Duke of the Empire, and brought him enormous wealth from the National Treasury. In the great battle which was the turning point of the war it was Gen. Sickles who divined the supreme situation involved, who took prompt advantage of it in a most military way, and whose action was approved beyond all question by the battle being fought out there to the ruin of the Confederate army and the success of that of the Union. It will only be a just recognition of this to allow the splendid veteran to end his days as a Lieutenant General of the United States Army. Certainly he deserves this. . . .[19]

There was enough opposition, however, to prevent him from making lieutenant general. Still, he was popular enough with the common men to continue attending reunions and monument dedications. In September 1910, the largest and most expensive of all Gettysburg monuments was dedicated. The Pennsylvania State Memorial, 69 feet tall and costing nearly $200,000, was erected along the southern extension of Cemetery Ridge. The monument's location is near Hancock's July 2 left flank, slightly north of the low ground that Sickles had so strenuously objected to occupying. Organizers wanted the occasion to be "distinctly a Pennsylvania event. There will be no speakers of national prominence. President Taft will not be here." Although the President's attendance was not desired, the non-Pennsylvanian invitees did include Joshua Chamberlain and Dan Sickles. Far from being an outcast, Dan's presence at Gettysburg was considered more desirable than Taft's.[20]

The monument's main design is a large dome topped by a 7,500 pound statue of the "Goddess of Victory and Peace," below which are statues of prominent Pennsylvania generals, President Lincoln, and Governor Andrew Curtin. In addition to Sickles' nemesis George Meade, David Birney was also honored with his own statue, a permanent memorial status that Sickles would never achieve on the field. The base contains ninety bronze tablets intended to honor the approximately 34,000 Pennsylvanians who fought in the battle. The last of these bronze tablets was put in place only hours before the ceremony. In addition to the last-minute efforts to complete the memorial, the Gettysburg *Compiler* complained bitterly about the "bungled" dedication ceremony. "General Daniel E. Sickles, the only surviving corps commander of the Union Army at Gettysburg was one of the invited guests of the Commission, and he was left waiting at the Eagle Hotel for what his hosts were going to do with him." Finally making the discovery that he "had been forgotten, an auto was hired and he took a drive over the battlefield. General Sickles, and General Chamberlain, an ex-Governor of Maine, were scheduled for short speeches but nobody saw to it that they were made and there were many veterans who wanted to see and hear from them."[21]

Increasingly, the veterans were reuniting at funerals instead of monument dedications. Monument sculptor and artist James Kelly spotted Sickles at Alexander Webb's 1911 funeral:

> I looked for Dan Sickles, but strange to say he did not strut down the middle aisle [as was his usual custom]. But as I reached the door on the left of it, there sat Sickles in a chair braced conspicuously against the door jam . . . He was receiving and shaking hands with the mourners as they passed out. It caused a diversion as the poor dead hero's body was in the vestibule on the opposite side and Dan so distracted me that it was only by accident that I saw it. It was the most outrageous piece of impudence I ever saw—I would ever see him do.[22]

When Oliver Howard died in 1909, Sickles achieved venerated status as Gettysburg's last surviving corps commander in either army. Not only had he outlasted his contemporaries, but after General Ward's 1903 death, all of Gettysburg's old Third Corps division and brigade commanders were also gone. Sickles even outlasted Henry Tremain, who despite being twenty-one years younger, died at the age of seventy in 1910. Had the next few years transpired differently, Sickles might truly have closed out his final days doing little more than giving dinner speeches to cheering veterans. (Although "Time is money" was a favorite Sickles-ism, and he reminded favor seekers that he expected to be paid for his talks.) In April of 1911, Sickles was guest of honor at a reunion of veterans of the old 12th New York. So many men turned out that the party filled five banquet rooms. The New York *Times* reported on the festivities: "It was nearly midnight before the dinner was finished. By the time the speaking began Gen. Sickles alone, as he presently announced, had signed no less than 1,861 autographs on as many menu cards handed to him . . . Gen.

Sickles started off the symposium of war-time recollections, and when he asked how long he might talk, the regiment roared 'All night! All night!'"[23]

In order to garner as much attention as possible at such functions, Sickles' repertoire now included some standard tricks to ensure that the spotlight would shine brightly on him. While attending a lecture by Fred Grant in 1911, James Kelly watched in disgust as:

> Just before the lecture, there was a commotion at the door; and Gen. Dan Sickles came in, doing the spectacular—as usual. He puttered laboriously along, a woman supporting him. In his shaky voice he piped up, 'Oh, anywhere,' at the same time heading up the middle aisle for the platform. By this time the whole place was upset.
>
> He stumbled up to the platform, and was boosted into the seat of honor. As he soused down there was a sigh of relief from the people, who were not acquainted with his old-time trick of arriving late and strutting down the middle aisle of the theater or opera, and going out after each act; but his latest pose as "the last survivor" was most effective.[24]

After Grant finished speaking, Sickles was called on to make a few remarks. "Having made allusions to his lost leg at Gettysburg, and told how President Lincoln had often sent for him and profited by his advice, Sickles branched off without any apparent reason to describe with a chuckle the pleasure he took in hugging a pretty girl." Although he was still a chronic attention-getter, Sickles was physically but a shadow of his former self and a far cry from the lady-killer who prowled Washington in the 1850s and Joe Hooker's headquarters in the early 1860s.[25] "Sitting there, with his bald head, around which grew a circle of hair like a tonsure," observed Kelly,

> a friend remarked that even this did not make him look saintly. His bulgy, baggy eyes, his big, straggling mustache, over which hung his bold, aggressive nose, and under which hung his projecting, limp, fleshy, sensual chin, to me—who knew him—was a depressing sight.[26]

Several partisan publications during this period also elevated Sickles' public image. Prior to his death, the devoted Henry Tremain had published his memoirs *Two Days of War* in 1905. Not surprisingly, his recollections were extremely favorable to the Sickles agenda. In 1910, the Third Corps Union published James Rusling's account of the post-battle meetings and friendship between Sickles and Lincoln. Filled with unverifiable anecdotes, it emphasized Lincoln's greatness, and by extension that of the New York Democrat who was worthy of his friendship.[27]

In 1911, Sickles himself published a pamphlet of letters on "the successful movements of the Third Army Corps" on July 2. The pamphlet included Longstreet's 1902 letter, now a prized Sickles possession, which claimed Sickles had "saved that battle-field." The majority of the publication was devoted to several testimonials from acquaintances of Phil Sheridan, including Pennsylvania war-Governor Andrew Curtin, who all testified that Sheridan had heartily approved of Sickles' Gettysburg actions. Of course, Sheridan was not present at the great battle, but in the 1880s he had risen to commanding general of the U.S. Army. Although he had died in 1888, Sheridan's military opinion and name recognition was perhaps second to only Grant and Sherman in the public eye and so still carried considerable weight. Sheridan had reportedly said, "I examined that portion of the battlefield very carefully, and I have no hesitancy whatever in saying that under the circumstances in which General Sickles found himself on that occasion he could have done nothing else but to move out as he did to meet General Longstreet's threatening advance."[28]

General Edward S. Salomon claimed that Sheridan had once told him that "General Sickles is a fighter. He evidently wanted to be aggressive; he assumed the offensive instead of the defensive." Sheridan staffer George A. Forsyth recalled that Sheridan thought, "If it [the move] was a blunder, it was a blunder in the right direction." Sickles also claimed that Ulysses Grant had more than once intimated views in support of his actions. The pamphlet reveals a Sickles who was clearly interested in defending his record for posterity. Perhaps he really thought that such testimonials would be sufficient for history to pass down a favorable judgment.[29]

Other accolades poured in. The aging general joined President Taft at a New York GAR Memorial Day parade in May 1910. In October of that year, Sickles was elected president for life of the Military Medal of Honor Legion in Pittsburgh. By May 1911, he was bragging that he had attended thirty-two fiftieth anniversary celebrations of the war in six weeks. In August 1912, a movement began within the GAR to name Sickles commander-in-chief of the organization. The vets considered it appropriate, given his status as last surviving corps commander. It had been fifty years since the soldiers had gone to war, and the peaks and valleys of Dan's long career were being put in perspective. Lt. Colonel John P. Nicholson, a friend of old Dan's, noted (with great understatement) that "his years have been rich with incident" and given the war's semi-centennial, "Gen. Sickles has been not a little in evidence in the last few months, and his reminiscences have been much sought."[30]

There were still moments of rejection, however, reminders that his status had not erased the old feuds completely from memory. In addition to the failed attempt to elevate him to three-star rank, the New York Commandery of the Loyal Legion, an organization made up of ex-war officers, refused (for the second time) to admit him to membership in 1911. The New York *Times* reported, "Fifty years is not enough to wipe out bitterness engendered in Civil War days." Sickles' membership had been voted down years earlier "because of the strength of certain enmities. His name was brought forward again by admirers who felt that the roll of membership of the Loyal Legion ought to include that of a man whose war record is so distinguished for gallantry. These friends, who are said to have taken the black-balling very much to heart, assumed that the old enmity had died down with the passing of the years." Although the members declined to discuss the vote publicly, it was initially assumed that Sickles' role as chair of the New York Monuments Commission had created some bad blood. But a member of the order said "that the hostility was far older than that, and that to understand it one would have to go back to feelings that were astir long ago."[31]

While Sickles enjoyed his celebrity status, darker clouds were gathering that would attract significant press coverage and severely tarnish his legacy. Throughout this period, there was one constant figure in his life. Sometime during his time in New York, Sickles had become attached to a housekeeper by the name of Eleanor Earle Wilmerding. Eleanor was born in New York in about 1855, and so was a small child when Dan achieved infamy by killing Key in Washington and disobeying Meade at Gettysburg. She appears to have spent much of her life living with her father George and two sisters in New York; there was no mother in the household as early as the 1870 census when Eleanor was just 15 years old. Perhaps the Wilmerdings were family friends, since a William E. Wilmerding attended George Sickles' 1887 funeral. News reports at the time of her death in 1914 suggested that she had then been in Dan's employ for fifteen years. A romantic relationship has been suggested by some (she was extremely possessive and referred to him as "Dear"). Caroline Sickles blamed the breakup of her marriage on "another woman," whom she identified as Wilmerding's cousin. Sickles biographer W. A. Swanberg speculated that Wilmerding was actually the other woman, but this interpretation is dubious, since as late as 1915 (after Wilmerding's death) Dan's son Stanton was considering calling "the prominent society woman" whom he clearly considered to be still alive and responsible for the marriage's breakup to testify in legal action over George Sickles' estate. Dan Sickles also insisted, for whatever his word is worth, that he "was not even acquainted" with Wilmerding when he left Caroline in Europe. The widow of New York Governor William Sulzer, who lived as a tenant in Sickles' house, called Wilmerding "a fine, intelligent, capable and respectable woman." The cause of her devotion "was undoubtedly the hope of securing a goodly share of his worldly goods when he died. So long as he had money, he paid her liberally, and she saved her wages. When his cash was exhausted, he borrowed from her, and her faithful service continued. This went on for years."[32]

Early Sickles biographer Pinchon wrote that Sickles "many, varied—and sometimes scandalous—affairs chagrined and shocked" Wilmerding. Pinchon perpetuated the legend that Dan was still the ladies man at this age, with his dresser drawer containing lady's black stockings and gloves, jewelry, and perfumes. But Mrs. Sulzer had insisted to Pinchon's researcher that "those reports of General Sickles having been a beau and man-about-town up to his last days . . . Mrs. Sulzer declares are positively false." She saw Sickles as "very old, feeble, and infirm," a near-invalid whose "amputation gave him much trouble, and his eyesight was nearly gone. All day long he sat in the Egyptian darkness of an alcove in his big room on the first floor; swathed in blankets, his eyes shielded by an enormous shade. . . . Even his once sonorous voice had become a guttural utterance between a grunt and a cough." The relationship with Wilmerding was probably not romantic, but with his advancing age he had become dependent upon her housekeeping and bookkeeping. Their mutual devotion increased to what has been called a "jealous possessiveness."[33]

Sickles' wife Caroline and now adult-son Stanton had sailed from Europe to New York in 1908. Despite the fact that Dan had now been away from them for nearly three decades, Caroline and Stanton both seemed to genuinely hope for reconciliation. Caroline demanded, however, that in order to reconcile, Sickles was to dismiss Wilmerding from the house. Mrs. Sulzer's recollections suggest that Sickles' family was jealous of Wilmerding's over-protectiveness and likewise assumed that she was stealing from the general. Sickles refused the demand, and Caroline and Stanton were banished to a nearby hotel. Caroline went public and told the press that Wilmerding's presence was preventing reconciliation. Such news would have been very embarrassing publicity for any normal man in those days, but for Dan Sickles it was pretty mild stuff.[34]

Although Mrs. Sulzer recalled that Wilmerding "protected him from the inopportunities of countless panhandlers, including his kin," there is no evidence to suggest that Wilmerding reigned in his extravagant spending. Dan fell for an artist named Princess Lenott Parlaghy, and when she told him she had always wanted a lion cub, he appeared with a litter of six. More significantly, he agreed to guarantee her $5,500 debt to New York's Plaza Hotel. It has also been estimated that in addition to his extravagant spending, he may also have lost as much as four million dollars on Wall Street. As astounding as it sounds, his father's mammoth inheritance was gone; General Sickles was broke.[35]

War hero or not, his creditors began legal actions, including placing his home in foreclosure. In 1912, Caroline learned that an $8,200 judgment had been placed against Dan, and his household goods were to be sold at auction. Despite their continuing estrangement, Caroline was still willing to spare him "the sorrow of parting with his treasures." Accompanied by son Stanton, she pawned her own jewels in a New York pawnshop. "Tears trickled down her cheeks" as she handed over "tokens of the happy days of her youth, when she was a belle at the court of Queen Isabella of Spain." From the pawnshop, they went over to the offices of Lincoln Trust Company, where she "cheerfully" paid the judgment.[36]

Although her sacrifice received extensive press coverage, it did not lead to reconciliation. When Caroline and Stanton journeyed to Dan's home to notify him of the payment, they were refused admittance on orders of Wilmerding. An exasperated Stanton complained, "My father is completely in the clutches of this woman." They were outraged further when Sickles issued a statement openly questioning her motives. He accused Caroline of not actually paying the debt, and she grudgingly admitted that she actually had the judgment transferred to her, although she insisted that she never intended to collect on it. Sickles also argued that many of "her" jewels were actually his in that they originally belonged to his mother and Laura. An angry Caroline denied this. "I will not put up all my money to save his house to have it occupied by him and his housekeeper to the exclusion of me." A few weeks later Sickles was served with yet another judgment. Wilmerding had refused to let the process servers anywhere near the general, so a private detective was sent to the house disguised as a "Special Delivery Messenger." A suspicious Wilmerding initially refused his admittance, but when the detective was finally let in, he handed the papers directly to Sickles. "See that, it's a trick to serve legal papers!" Wilmerding shouted, ordering him out of the house. "I did not wait to hear what the General said," the victorious detective told the *Times*.[37]

Stanton was also alarmed that the children had never received any accounting from their George Sickles inheritance, of which Dan was their trustee, and of his one-third interest in the New Rochelle property that Dan and Stanton had jointly purchased in 1895. When Stanton threatened to make public the name of the mysterious society woman, "for years now the wife of a prominent New York man," whom Stanton believed was somehow mixed up in all of this, he received an anonymous letter "to advise you that if any such action is taken by you to bring disgrace to a woman who is decently living down her past . . . a punishment will be inflicted upon you in a bodily way that will make you regret it as long as you live."

The entire affair only became more sordid. Dan's other child with Caroline, Stanton's sister Mrs. Eda Sickles Crackenthorpe, the wife of a British diplomat who had reunited with her father in 1897, filed suit against Sickles to prevent a disposal of certain properties and to have him removed as trustee. Dan's domestic problems were enthusiastically replayed in the press, just as Teresa's infidelity had been public consumption more than fifty years earlier.[38]

It was against this financial backdrop that the battle's fiftieth anniversary, and the end of Dan Sickles' Gettysburg adventure, arrived in 1913. The general was now in his early nineties, failing mentally, nearly blind, and confined to a wheelchair. It was readily apparent that he was no longer capable of managing his own household affairs, let alone the finances of an organization like the New York State Monuments Commission. Sickles had held the unpaid post as chairman of the commission for twenty-six years. Several months prior to the Gettysburg anniversary, Sickles suffered another public embarrassment. The State Controller had been attempting an accounting of the commission's funds since 1910. When Controller William Sohmer finally saw the books in late 1912, he discovered that chairman Sickles had vouchers for only $417,165 of the $445,641 that had been given the commission for expenditure on state monuments: $28,486 was unaccounted for.[39]

After conferring with the governor and attorney general, Controller Sohmer wrote Sickles on November 21, "under no circumstances will an extension of time for this settlement be granted beyond December 6." Sickles begged for more time, requesting until December 20 "to obtain a loan on my three houses and lots at the corner of Fifth avenue and Ninth street." The extension was granted, although the state's attorney general actually intended to initiate criminal proceedings against the entire eight-man commission. But just as he had refused to consider his Gettysburg performance a "misapprehension" of orders, he once again stubbornly held that, for better or worse, his faults were his own. The chairman accepted responsibility and requested that he be the sole target of the legal proceedings. The state was serious about recouping the

An elderly Sickles enjoying his cigar, circa 1912. *Library of Congress*

money, but ultimately realized that prosecuting a popular ninety-something war-hero was sensitive business. Still, he was embarrassingly deposed as chairman of the commission. For a man who identified himself so strongly with veterans and Gettysburg—and presuming that he was still mentally competent enough to comprehend it all—this may have truly stung him.[40]

The news did not come as a surprise to everyone. "I have traced $60,000 in [New York Monuments money] to Sickles' private account, and I am getting uneasy," monument sculptor James Kelly had cautioned Alexander Webb in 1904. "There is something queer about Sickles, I think." Although Sickles' legions of detractors were, and still are, pre-disposed to believe the worst, a review of Sickles' mental, physical, and financial status at this stage of his life suggests that the shortfall was probably due more to incompetence than malice. According to Horatio King, a member of the commission, "It is most unlikely that the shortage was incurred with dishonorable motives or that there will be any criminal prosecution. General Sickles allowed the shortage to occur through laxness rather than design. He says he will make good on his shortage in about a month."[41]

Caroline and Stanton Sickles intervened once again. Stanton suspected publicly that his father had lost the money on Wall Street, and paid $5,000 out of his own pocket. He arranged for yet another postponement and promised that the state would be reimbursed for the remaining $23,000 and change. Caroline issued a public appeal. "I wish the public would come to the aid of General Sickles. If I can forgive General Sickles, I think the general public can. The thing to do is to save General Sickles." Stanton's son (Dan's grandson) would tell Pinchon's researcher in the 1940s that the funds were missing through Sickles' "carelessness in leaving the accounts to the attention of unscrupulous assistants," specifically naming Wilmerding and Dan's attorney.[42]

Some veterans refused to help him, and the highest ranking GAR official in Missouri claimed that Sickles deserved his troubles. Many, however, wired in their support.[43] Most memorable was the response from Helen Longstreet, who wired Sickles from Gainesville:

> My soul is sorrowed by your troubles. Am wiring the Attorney General of
> New York that I shall raise money among the ragged, destitute, maimed
> veterans who followed Lee to pay the amount demanded if the New York
> officials will allow sufficient time. We are writing into our history the story
> of degenerate descendants of heroic sires. The Republic, whose battles
> you fought, will not permit your degradation.[44]

When word of her offer was made public, Helen told the newspapers, "My husband always spoke of Gen. Sickles as the hero of Gettysburg. General Longstreet, in the last autograph letter he ever wrote . . . to General Sickles told him that the taking of the Peach Orchard by Sickles' corps won the battle for the Union forces. . . . General Longstreet said: 'Sickles can well afford to leave a leg at Gettysburg, for he has made sure his place forever in the hearts of Americans.'" However, Stanton Sickles drew Helen's ire when he said that she owed her position as postmaster in Gainesville to Dan. Nevertheless, she said that she was still willing to help Sickles "if New York pushes the prosecution and none of his Northern friends go to his aid."[45]

The state's attorney general was smart enough to know that he was facing a potential public relations nightmare. "Your sympathetic and patriotic expressions do justice to your heart," he responded to Helen, "but they do violence to the facts in this case." In accusing Sickles of converting public money for "his own use," the attorney noted that "this he has not attempted to justify or defend, admitting that he took the state's money for private use without authority of law, an act which, under our laws and under the laws of all civilized governments, means stealing." The state did not intend to deprecate his public service, but feared that "misdirected sympathy" would turn the accused into a "martyr." "New York State appreciates her heroes and feels humiliated at the spectacle which this case presents."[46]

An order for arrest was issued on Saturday, January 25. News reporters staked out the house and watched as Sickles' valet hung three American flags out the window. New York's Sheriff Julius Harburger did not look forward to the prospect of putting the war hero in jail, and promised that Sickles would have all the comforts of home there. Instead of serving the order over the weekend, the sheriff waited until Sickles' attorney, Daniel P. Hays, had arranged for Sickles' freedom with a $30,000 bond from a surety company. Only then did Hays and Harburger go to Sickles' house on Monday afternoon, followed by a revue of reporters. Sickles and a disdainful Wilmerding were found sitting in a rear room, Sickles attired in an eyeshade and black suit. An apologetic Harburger told Sickles, "You know I have to serve you with these papers. I'm sorry I have to do so, but I have no choice." Sickles tossed the unopened order on his desk. "It is all right. You're one of the best friends I've got, Sheriff." After Sickles signed for the bond, the county charged him a $5.25 serving fee. When he summoned Wilmerding to pay the bill, she replied dutifully, "Yes, dear," but tripped on a carpet and scattered loose change across the floor.[47]

Not only did Sheriff Harburger stall long enough for Sickles to avoid jail time, but he also asked some of New York's richest citizens, including J. P. Morgan, John D. Rockefeller, and Andrew Carnegie to help Sickles out. The sheriff also received a letter from Sickles in which Dan addressed (of all things) criticism of his Gettysburg performance. Sickles included Longstreet's statement that Sickles' advance to the Peach Orchard had helped the Union cause. "You will see from the statement of General Longstreet that I won the great and decisive battle of Gettysburg."[48]

Contrary to popular history, Sickles' troubles did not end with the signing of the bond. Slightly more than a week later, Sheriff Harburger received two more claims against Dan totaling $8,557. These would have to be paid out of the General's property before the Monument Commission's claim could be paid. Sickles' house was set to be sold at foreclosure in March, but once again he received a delay until arrangements could be worked out. It was reported that "sympathy for the aged soldier is said to have been the chief reason for the postponement." It wasn't until early May before Sickles finally dodged the threat of jail time. State Attorney General Carmody issued a statement that despite numerous efforts to recover the remaining $23,000, "not a dollar has yet been turned over to the State authorities for this purpose. If we are satisfied that General Sickles has no assets and that we cannot recover this money, we will not press the body execution the State obtained to satisfy the judgment." Sickles never did "make good" on the full shortage. He had spent the previous fifty years cultivating his war-hero image. In the end, that image combined with his ability to rally supporters saved him from the worst consequences of his chronic financial irresponsibility.[49]

To help relieve the financial pressure, Sickles rented out apartments on the upper floors of his home. Among his tenants was New York Governor William Sulzer, who occupied office for only ten months in 1913 before he ran afoul of his Tammany sponsors and was impeached. Sulzer's wife recalled that Sickles and Governor Sulzer became close friends. As if the preceding months had not been bad enough, a fire erupted in the basement of Sickles' home in late May. Police and firemen burst into his room to inform him that smoke was rapidly filling the house. Showing that he still had some fight, he cried out to the would-be rescuers, "When I see flames I will get up!"[50]

Sickles had transformed from celebrity to what one author has since called a "relic of a bygone era"—and an embarrassing one at that. But if the early months of 1913 represented one of the lowest points of Sickles' public life, the summer still held the promise of Gettysburg's fiftieth anniversary celebrations. His recent legal troubles raised concerns that he would be unable to attend. A GAR committee visited the New York sheriff's office to determine if the authorities would prevent Sickles from leaving New York state. When it was decided that traveling to Pennsylvania would not violate his bond, Sheriff Harburger allowed Sickles to attend the ceremonies.[51]

When July 1913 finally and mercifully arrived, newspapers across the country covered the massive Blue and Gray reunion. Attendance figures have since been debated, but the official count claims that 53,000 Union and 11,000 Confederate veterans attended, along with numerous dignitaries, including a brief appearance by President Woodrow Wilson. A massive encampment was established near the Emmitsburg Road from June 29 through July 6. The celebration was an odd mixture of remembrance and sideshow.

Reports, then and now, gushed when approximately 500 survivors reenacted Pickett's Charge and exchanged handshakes across the stone wall. Even five decades later there was still fight left in some of the veterans. Several men (reports varied between seven and eight) were stabbed in the Gettysburg Hotel's dining room when a fight erupted following verbal abuse of Lincoln. (Despite initial reports that "an old veteran in blue" was responsible, a thirty-something son of an attending veteran was later arrested for the crime.) The July heat was intense, and keeping the old soldiers safe and sober proved a unique challenge. After three veterans were found dead in their tents (conspiracy-minded newspapers believed that the number of veteran deaths was being under-reported), the New York *Times* noted that "the serious conditions among the veterans" had brought an appeal to "close all the saloons and prohibit the sale of liquor in the town." Health authorities even threatened the proposal of "martial law" if their abstinence requests were not granted by the governor. Then, as now, controlling tourist crowds was a concern to the locals. A newsman bemoaned the manner in which visitors "thoughtlessly and recklessly run over" historic properties south of town where the July 2, 1863, combat occurred.[52]

Sickles arrived in Gettysburg in his wheelchair, accompanied by Wilmerding, Joe Twichell, and Sickles' black valet, Frazier Moseley. The event's organizers had solicited Sickles' input for years. In 1910, he had told them that "the most appropriate monument in commemoration of the 50th anniversary would be a monument consecrated to Peace, Liberty, and Patriotism." He had also worried that Confederate veterans would not attend in great numbers, preventing what he hoped would be "a national love feast." By the time he attended, however, he no longer served in any official capacity and was not officially invited to participate in speeches or activities. This may have been simply due to his age and infirmity. Alluding to his recent troubles, Helen Longstreet called him the "tragic figure of this great reunion," and complained publicly. "He was not placed on the program," she grumbled. "He was probably not expected. But he came because he could not help coming. . . . It was his

Dan Sickles, Eleanor Wilmerding, and Union veterans celebrate together one last time at Gettysburg's 50th Anniversary in July 1913. *Library of Congress*

victory. It is his field." Insisting on being "with the boys" one last time, Sickles headquartered himself with the veterans of Carr's brigade at the Rogers house site. At the anniversary twenty-five years earlier, James Longstreet had stolen the show. Now Dan Sickles had returned as the last living corps commander and seems to have been viewed as almost a museum curiosity. He was undeniably a center of attention, and newspaper reports consistently updated readers on his movements. One typical report recorded that he was "the center of attraction of hundreds of men in gray. He sat on the porch of the Rogers House and shook hands with all comers. Before the Southerners left the Rogers House they shouldered the General, carried him out on the battlefield and stood him up before a moving-picture machine." At least a dozen men told him that they remembered seeing him wounded on the field, and at least one man supposedly remembered watching the amputation. An "enthusiastic" woman proclaimed him the "greatest of living Americans." Sickles offered a one word reply: "Correct."[53]

Despite his age and declining health, Sickles served as a news correspondent, writing daily dispatches that were picked up in papers such as the *North American* and *Philadelphia Inquirer*. He rhetorically asked his readers on July 1, "Has it been fifty years ago? I scarcely realize it. . . . The memory of it all comes back to me today." His reports over the next several days provided extremely lucid (one assumes that he at least had a ghost writing assistant) and consistent (despite misspelling the Trostle farm as Brostle) accounts of the great battle. Some things never changed—especially his accounts regarding July 2. "Meade never had been in favor of giving battle at Gettysburg and I knew that he would order me to leave my position and move to Pipe Creek, where he intended to battle." Regarding the reunion, he wrote happily that he was with "my boys" and at Gettysburg for one last time. "I believe I am living right now the happiest days of my life."[54]

At times, Sickles was overwhelmed by the attention. He would eventually slip into what one report called a "coma"-like condition and the hand-shaking sessions would be brought to an abrupt halt. Wilmerding was observed giving him medicine when he grew too weak to continue. One newsman, whose own brother had been a member of Graham's 114th Pennsylvania and was mortally wounded near the Peach Orchard, found Sickles "a wreck mentally and physically." Still, he had to admit that Sickles was also a . . .

> man remarkable for many things, besides being the sole corps commander living on either side . . . first coming into the limelight from his shooting on the streets of Washington . . . he next appears at the beginning of the war as a major general, the commission being tendered him at a time when Lincoln was tactfully endeavoring to placate the Democratic party . . . he seemed to be a failure at Gettysburg, from his disobeying or misunderstanding of orders . . . after his wife died he married again, which was followed by domestic troubles, and this by those of worse than financial ones, which came near getting him in prison; in fact nothing but the action of his deserted wife and the mercy of an outraged law leaves him free.[55]

Sickles was clearly nearing the end of his life, and the reporter found him to be a "pitiable object as he sat on the porch in plain view of where he directed the movements of the Third Corps. . . . Among a host of others I shook hands with him, but with reservations; the greeting being more like that of a corpse, so helpless he seemed as he lay back in his Morris chair trying to smoke. . . . All he said as each one shook his hand, was in a mumbling, low voice: 'Morrow, five o'clock' alluding to a reunion of the Blue and Gray. . . . Poor Old General Sickles! I pitied him as he lay back in his chair in the door yard, a curious throng constantly on the stare around him, a passerby from his old command coming through it now and then to shake his limp, passive hand." The reporter wondered "whether the scenes and sounds of fifty years ago were not breaking through his clouded brain."[56]

Helen Longstreet, the general's widow, arrived on July 1. Dan welcomed her as a crowd of veterans, North and South, immediately gathered to eavesdrop. Helen apparently did not have a place to stay, and a surprised Sickles asked, "Didn't you get that telegram I sent you . . . when I heard that you were coming I wired you that Carr's Brigade would turn over a tent to you." Showing that he still had a little muscle, he added, "I gave the order myself." Like Sickles, Longstreet's widow was doubling as a news correspondent and was a popular attraction herself. She was frequently stopped by old vets who assured her that they "fought under Longstreet." One man even bragged to her that, "Nothing saved us [the South] from utter ruin but the Ku Klux Klan and I am proud to say that I was a member of it." Longstreet's son, Major Robert Lee Longstreet, attended and said that his father and Sickles had predicted this reunion decades earlier.[57]

Before the ceremonies concluded, Sickles managed to create one last sensation when a rumor spread through the camp on July 4 that he had died. The story caused "much excitement among the old soldiers." An aide was sent to the Rogers house site, where he was met by Sickles who proclaimed, "That story, sir, was a damned lie. When I am ready to die you will be informed." But he knew the inevitable truth. He told his readers on July 5: "We don't say it, but 'my boys' know, and I know, that we shall probably never meet again."[58]

As late as 1907, Sickles had still hoped for a monument on the battlefield, telling John Nicholson, "if at some future time it may be the pleasure of the State of New York to place some memorial of myself on that battlefield I should prefer to have it on the high ground at or near the Peach Orchard." Now, as Sickles and Twichell looked out over the field together one last time, Twichell is said to have expressed surprise that there was still no Sickles statue on the field. Battlefield legend tells us that Sickles replied, in essence, that the whole damned battlefield was his monument. The moment symbolically defines Sickles' immense battlefield contributions, as well as his acknowledgment and defiance that he might never receive a statue at Gettysburg. Unfortunately, like so many of the more colorful aspects of the Sickles legend, there is some doubt as to whether he actually spoke those words. Twichell's brief diary entry for June 27 - July 9 makes no mention of it. Sickles' early biographers clouded the issue by treating the conversation differently and not crediting any sources as references. Edgcumb Pinchon claimed that Sickles replied to Twichell, "Never mind Joe—all this is monument enough, isn't it?" W. A. Swanberg did not quote Sickles directly, stating instead, "The general had an answer to that. The whole damned field was his memorial." Whether the quote is accurate or not, like so many other aspects of the Sickles story it seems appropriate to the man and has therefore largely gone unchallenged by subsequent historians.[59]

While we may never see a Sickles statue on the field, his presence is, in fact, nearly everywhere. The lengthy "Sickles Avenue" runs over most of the Third Corps line. From Devil's Den, it passes the Wheatfield and Peach Orchard and ends at the Emmitsburg Road. The Excelsior Brigade monument, even without the legendary missing bust, commemorates both he and the men he raised in New York. In 1901, a marker was placed near the Trostle farm to denote where he was wounded, while the New York Monument in the National Cemetery dramatically depicts the moment. The rear of the Lincoln Speech Memorial, dedicated in 1912, credits Sickles with introducing the legislation that established the park and erected the monument. His name sits at the top of the New York Auxiliary State Monument, dedicated in 1925 (after his death) to the memory of all New York commanders who were not individually honored elsewhere. Under his leadership, New York placed eighty-eight monuments on the battlefield, the state monument in the National Cemetery, statues to two generals (Slocum and Greene), and applications for two more (Wadsworth and Webb). Locales such as Devil's Den, the Wheatfield, and the Peach Orchard might not have any significance today were it not for his July 2 advance. He also established the park's initial boundaries. The "peace memorial" that he supported to commemorate the fiftieth anniversary came to fruition in 1938 as the Peace Light Memorial—an eternal flame to symbolize the nation's unity. Even the fence separating the National Cemetery and the local Evergreen Cemetery was the same that stood in Lafayette Square when Dan killed Barton Key. The whole damn battlefield might not be his monument, but he certainly has his share of it.[60]

* * *

About six months after returning from Gettysburg, Wilmerding took ill and died in February 1914. When her body was carried out of Sickles' home, a rumor started that it was the general who had passed on. With this obstacle removed, Caroline and Stanton finally moved into the house. They opened Wilmerding's safe-deposit box hoping to find some of Dan's lost fortune, but the box was empty. Whatever their relationship had been, Wilmerding had lasted longer than any other woman in his adult life. Several weeks later, rumors spread again that Dan was also near death. On March 29, a reporter for the *Times* telephoned the Sickles house to see if the story was true. The voice on the phone replied, "Yes, this is General Sickles. Am I ill? Nonsense. I was never better in my life. There's nothing to that story. It's all a lie."[61]

Less than a month later, Dan suffered a cerebral hemorrhage on April 24, 1914. Lingering in semi-consciousness, he was surrounded by Caroline, Stanton, an attorney for Mrs. Sickles, and a nurse when he died at his Fifth Avenue home at 9:10 p.m. on May 3. Although his obituary contributed to the confusion over his age by noting that he "lived to be almost 91," he was more likely six months short of his ninety-fifth birthday. Even his age can be debated.[62]

The New York *Times* eulogized "a stirring" career. He was remembered as a "soldier, politician, and diplomat . . . he lost a leg at Gettysburg . . . the last of that galaxy of corps commanders who made possible the achievement of Grant and brought our great civil strife to a triumphant close." Gettysburg was only part of his legacy. The *Times* astutely observed the diversity of his resume as a "Fighter, lawyer, politician, and diplomat, his life was a crowded one." His legacy did not escape one last reminder of the Key murder, which the paper called "the sensation of the day." Regarding Gettysburg, "his courage and activity at Gettysburg are matters of history. All authorities accord him a very important part in that great battle, some contending that his was the master stroke that saved the day." While the *Times* mercifully avoided the Meade-Sickles controversy, it is somewhat surprising that his role in the development of Gettysburg National Military Park was also excluded (although his recent expulsion from the Monuments Commission was mentioned).[63]

The *Times* followed with an editorial on May 5. "Nobody with warm blood flowing through his veins can read the obituary notices of Gen. SICKLES without a certain thrill of admiration. His was truly the adventurous spirit. Under the right inspiration, he might have been an intrepid explorer or a founder of thriving colonies. As it was, he filled many important positions in civil and military life and was always conspicuous in the minds of his contemporaries." After summarizing his resume, the *Times* marveled that he returned for his final stint in Congress at "an age when most men are ready to retire." Noting that his "domestic life was marred by calamities which, unhappily, were always themes of public talk. He never quite lived down the effects of his mad action in 1859. . . . But there was no disposition to withhold frank acknowledgment of his gallantry and military skill in the service of his country, and the loss of one of his legs in battle helped to keep the heroic side of his character in the public mind." Although vilified by many modern Gettysburg students, the contemporary press was able to place his accomplishments in a more appropriately broad perspective. Sickles "certainly had more than one man's share of family troubles," but he "was assuredly a picturesque and interesting character, and his long life was marked by many noteworthy achievements."[64]

Where had Sickles wanted to be buried? In 1905, when his beloved pet spaniel Bo-Bo died, Sickles had him buried in a New Rochelle plot that his father George had purchased for human members of the family. (George was buried there when he died in 1887.) Descendants of George's second wife were outraged when they learned they would be sharing eternity with Dan's dog. There was debate at the time of Bo-Bo's interment over whether Sickles wanted to rest in New Rochelle "beside his faithful dog" or beside the less-faithful Teresa Sickles, who had been moved to an unmarked grave at the Green-Wood Cemetery.[65]

Caroline Sickles touched off a debate (that would resurface nearly eighty years later) when she proposed that the Secretary of War bury Sickles near the New York monument at Gettysburg. "Can not be slightest objection to Sickles' interment," replied John P. Nicholson. The New York *Times* reported on May 5, "This disposed of the idea that the body might be brought to Washington for burial at Arlington."[66] However, this plan was quickly rejected as the *Times* updated readers on May 6:

> Major Gen. Daniel E. Sickles will not be buried at Gettysburg, but in Arlington National Cemetery, according to a statement made yesterday by his attorney, Daniel P. Hays. In April, 1910, Gen. Sickles visited Arlington with the late Major A. J. Zabriskie, at that time Secretary of the New York Monuments Commission, and expressed a desire to be buried there. Major Zabriskie made a note of this and informed his son, who told Mr.

Hays. Confirmation is given in a note which Gen. Sickles left for Mr. Hays, in which he expressed a preference for Arlington.[67]

A memorial service was held at Sickles' home on the evening of May 7. His body lay in a coffin in the back parlor of the house, which was filled with Mrs. Sickles, Stanton, friends, elderly GAR veterans, and flowers. Sickles descendant John Shaud was told by his great-grandmother, Dan's half-sister Roma, that as she and her daughter arrived at the wake, they were "confronted by Stanton who snapped his fingers at them to get their attention and escorted them to the seating in the rear, he seemed to be flaunting the fact that he spoke fluent French as he spoke both in English and French to them in an angry tone. It must have been because he found out that the general left him with no money." A flag was draped across Dan's chest, and at the coffin's foot were his old war cap, sword, and golden epaulettes. A simple silver nameplate bore his name, date of birth (listed as October 20, 1820), and death, and the inscription "Major General of the United States Army." A ritual of the Grand Army was read, reminding the remaining veterans that "soon they, too, would be called to join their late comrade at the Grand Encampment."[68] Gen. George Loud of W. S. Hancock Post 250 delivered the memorial address:

> We stand by this coffin to-night, and think of the heroic achievement of this man in the greatest battle of the world's greatest war, of his heroic courage and sublime patriotism. He was a man of charming cheeriness, the memory of which will long survive in his comrades and friends . . . in the twilight of his life he became in truth a man of sorrows. But the keynote of his career was ever an indomitable courage. He was a faithful friend and a generous foe.[69]

The funeral was held at St. Patrick's Cathedral on Friday morning, May 8. According to Mrs. Sulzer, all agreed that Sickles "would turn in his coffin with unholy indignation at having a Catholic funeral; but he had a most pretentious one" due to the wishes of Caroline Sickles. The coffin was placed upon a caisson and the funeral procession was escorted by the Twelfth Regiment, New York National Guard, the Grand Army Posts, and a battalion of regular troops from Governor's Island. Joe Twichell, one of the last surviving members of Sickles' inner circle, attended and observed the other veterans, "all aged men, including myself—whose hearts were in common stirred with memories of days long past when, in our youth, we followed the Flag together." After mass, a

Dan Sickles' funeral procession, May 8, 1914. *Library of Congress*

train carried the funeral party to Washington for final burial at Arlington National Cemetery, where Sickles was laid to rest on May 9 with full military honors. The procession included the usual military trappings of a rider-less horse. An artillery salute was fired during the procession, while three rifle salvos were fired over the grave. In addition to the Regular Army escort, a number of veterans also turned out to support him one last time.[70]

Sickles was buried as a soldier in a soldier's cemetery. (Ironically, his military ceremony received less resistance than had the funeral of his Gettysburg counterpart and professional soldier James Longstreet.) It was final proof that he was no longer an attorney, politician, or even the murderer of Barton Key. He had long outlived most of his friends and enemies, his first wife and daughter, the Lincolns, Meade, Longstreet, and all of his fellow corps commanders. His uncharacteristically simple Arlington tombstone reads the way he wanted to be remembered:

DANIEL E. SICKLES
Medal of Honor
Maj. Gen.
US Army

Dan Sickles' grave in
Arlington National
Cemetery.

Author

When residents of Gettysburg read of the death, they were reminded that "General Sickles was well known to Gettysburg people and has been a visitor here many times. There is scarcely a citizen of the town who has not at some time attended a camp fire during the re-unions of veterans here, and listened to the thrilling war stories and reminisces of General Sickles." His crutches "alone told a story of valor and suffering, [and] created an impression that will linger long in the memory of those who knew him." The *Star and Sentinel* asked its readers: did Sickles err in advancing to the Peach Orchard on July 2, 1863? The paper supposed that James Longstreet had the answer when he told Sickles in 1902: "I believe that it is now conceded that the advanced position at the Peach Orchard, taken by your corps and under your orders saved that battlefield to the Union cause." But even to the local press, Sickles' controversial Gettysburg performance and ability to spin fascinating anecdotes seems to have overshadowed his role in developing the National Military Park.[71]

After a lifetime of financial excess, it was only fitting that the once wealthy Sickles left an essentially bankrupt estate. Since his Will was dated in August 1912, prior to their reconciliation, Stanton and Caroline were excluded. The only remaining real property was his New York home, which carried two mortgages. Eleanor Wilmerding, since deceased, was left with $5,000 while smaller legacies were left to other servants. The reality was that after the debts were cleared, only $500 of personal property remained in the estate. Perhaps his most prized remaining possessions were three war swords, which were bequeathed to Wilmerding and grandchildren. Even in death, Sickles still managed to garner some news coverage. In 1915, Stanton began action to learn what had become of his grandfather's estate, still threatening to call that same "prominent society woman" he believed had broken up Dan and Caroline's marriage, and Wilmerding's sisters, to testify. Attorney Daniel P. Hays declined to be the estate's executor, saying that he had done his full duty to Dan in life (and neglected to give Stanton that long hoped for accounting of the George Sickles estate), but Hays was "empowered to revise and publish the General's memoirs," which unfortunately have never surfaced. If they had survived, perhaps they might have given some lift to the general's post-burial reputation. They certainly would have been entertaining. In fewer than one hundred years after his death, the man who was buried with full military honors would be cast by many as the villain of Gettysburg.[72]

A modern photo of the Excelsior Brigade monument at Gettysburg. The legendary missing Sickles bust would have been on the inner pedestal between the five columns. This view looks toward the west, with the Excelsiors' 73rd New York regimental monument and Sherfy barn along the Emmitsburg Road in the background. *Author*

That Damn Fool Sickles

I f Dan Sickles went to his grave believing that his long career of "noteworthy achievements" would ensure a favorable posterity, then he most certainly would be disappointed by his image today. J. Howard Wert's published 1886 opinion that Sickles was the "personal ideal of the perfect hero and the fearless soldier" has not been shared by many historians. Today, Sickles is more commonly remembered as "The Congressman Who Got Away With Murder," and even more famously as the amateur general who on July 2 left Little Round Top unoccupied and then spent years attempting to destroy George Meade's career.[1]

From a military viewpoint, an 1893 debate in the pages of *The Nation* symbolized the differing schools of thought on the military value of Sickles' Gettysburg position. Retired General Francis A. Walker dismissed James Longstreet's claim that Sickles' line had delayed him just long enough to prevent the Confederate occupation of Little Round Top by simply pointing out that Sickles would already have been on Little Round Top if he had not advanced to the Peach Orchard. "Gen. Sickles will hardly assert that the splendid brigade of Trobriand [sic] or Ward would not have stood off the Confederate troops just as effectively as Vincent's brigade did."[2]

Not true, replied one H. White. Although he argued inaccurately that Meade did not expect Sickles to hold Little Round Top, he did note that Sickles had acted as a buffer and caused Longstreet's men to waste "all their strength and valor in gaining the Emmitsburg Road, which, after all, was of no particular benefit to them." The merit of this reasoning can never be disproved, but it did reinforce the fact that Longstreet (and A. P. Hill) had expended much of Hood's, McLaws', and R. H. Anderson's divisions overrunning ground at

Devil's Den, the Wheatfield, and the Peach Orchard, which ultimately held no value in driving Meade off Cemetery Ridge.[3]

Although support from other corps had ensured that Sickles' advance to the Peach Orchard would not lose July 2, 1863, for the Union cause, the day's final numbers appeared to prove the error of his ways. Estimates of the second day's Federal casualties approximate 9,000 against 6,000 Confederate losses—a staggering disparity given that the Union spent the afternoon on the defense. Given these results, there is a general presumption by many Gettysburg students that only Sickles' most loyal cronies could possibly have supported his actions. If so, then that list of supporters would actually have been a fairly lengthy one. James Longstreet claimed that Sickles' move had been for the Union's best, but much of Longstreet's postwar commentary is viewed with a healthy dose of skepticism. Phil Sheridan and Ulysses S. Grant reportedly supported Sickles' action. Neither general had fought at Gettysburg, but their military opinions carried no small amount of weight with Americans in the nineteenth century.[4]

Many of the Third Corps survivors, the men who actually fought that day, refused to direct any anger at Sickles. Private John Haley of the 17th Maine admitted that the Third Corps did not hold one "foot of ground" at the day's close, but Haley still considered Sickles "one of the bravest and best fighters of the war. And the curious thing about it all is that he was not a 'West Point Edition.'" Haley acknowledged that Sickles had disobeyed Meade's orders, but Meade had committed the greater sin (in Haley's view) when he "abdicated all generalship . . . what ever of saving grace attached to this days doings here on the left belongs to Gen. Dan E. Sickles . . . 'Old Dan' was a game bird and if he knew the sensation of fear he had a wonderful faculty for concealing it."[5] Private Haley knew that the Third Corps had fought in a poor position, but it still did not diminish his support for Sickles:

> And although it has been claimed by many that Sickles line was exceedingly faulty on that day (which no one denies) still, in my judgment, it was Providential, if there ever was anything of this nature; for he held the rebels in check, and exhausted them, so that when the 6th Corps troops struck them they were checked and hurled back. I believe that if Birney's division had been formed originally as Meade said he intended on the general line or ridge running to Round Top, the rebels would have gone through it like an egg shell, and the troops which relieved us might not have been in position, to fill the gap. . . .[6]

Haley believed that any criticism directed at Sickles occurred because Sickles had not acted "in the regular [army] or West Point way but rather contrary to it." Noting that Meade, not Sickles, "smarted under the sting of presidential criticism after he allowed Lee to recross the Potomac," Haley felt that "to Gen. Dan E. Sickles this country owes a debt of devotion and gratitude only to be gauged by the value of a preserved Union."[7]

Frank Moran of the 73rd New York survived his time in captivity and, like so many others, wrote about his Gettysburg experiences. Moran accused Meade of ignoring Little Round Top's importance by supposedly giving Sickles vague orders to hold the hill "if practicable." Sickles' leaving the hill empty was not only proof that Meade's orders were not practicable, but Meade was at fault again for nearly failing to reinforce it. "Meade left that position without a man or a musket upon it for fully seven hours after Sickles' warning," wrote Moran.[8]

On the other side was Felix Brannigan of the Excelsiors' 73rd New York. Brannigan did not specify Sickles, or any other general, by name when he wrote to his father: "The army it would appear—as a rule—is made subservient to the interests of political schemers, and as a reward for any extraordinary dirty work they may aspire to the most brilliant positions. It makes one's blood boil to think of it. . . . The degradation of being led to slaughter by such infamous scoundrels!" Yet, Brannigan did not favor West Pointers instead of the politicians. He blasted Meade for allowing Lee to retreat to Virginia and even wondered if Lee's escape had been intentional, thinking that it might be a Republican ploy to prolong the war and keep the Democrats out of Washington. "I hope I am wrong in my views, but the fact of Meade being in command still tends to confirm one's suspicions." Brannigan was wrong about Lee's escape, but it remains a fascinating reminder of the political cynicism that existed within the Union Army, even after the Gettysburg victory, and the divided loyalties over who should command.[9]

Andrew Humphreys, who led a Third Corps division that afternoon, never fell into the Sickles camp. He visited the battlefield after the war and firmly decided that Meade's preferred line was the better defensive position, the Peach Orchard salient had been seriously defective, and Sickles had overextended the Third Corps line while being too far from the remainder of the army to be supported. Such differences in assessment highlight the professional chasm that existed between a West Pointer such as Humphreys and the so-called amateurs.[10]

Monument sculptor James Kelly later knew many of Gettysburg's generals, including Sickles, whom he most certainly did not support. Kelly's interview notes suggest that the majority of generals shared his views: "all the officers I interviewed expressed their highest appreciation of Meade's gallantry; all condemned Gen. Sickles and wondered why Gen. Lee did not flank Round Top." During one session, Hancock pointed to a large map and laughed, "There is the peach orchard where Sickles went down and got licked." Alexander Webb thought, "If Sickles had not lost his leg, he would have lost his head." Although not at Gettysburg, Fitz John Porter knew all of the main players. "Gen. Butterfield always did his duty while Gen. Sickles did not do his duty. Sickles is a braggart." Oliver Howard, on the other hand, seemed to defend Sickles: "this action from a military standpoint was to be approved, regardless of our opinion of his private character." Joshua Chamberlain thought he knew why Howard seemed to support Sickles: since both generals "got into trouble at Gettysburg," Sickles defended Howard, who in turn defended Sickles to repay "his debts."[11]

Before the old soldiers passed on, many committed their opinions to paper by publishing memoirs. Regis de Trobriand had been friendly to Sickles, but ultimately didn't buy Sickles' notion that July 2 had been a decisive Third Corps victory. After the day's heavy fighting, Meade had wisely tightened the line on Cemetery Ridge, where he had "intended to await the attack of the Confederates." The "partial engagement of July 1 [resulted] to our disadvantage, continued with desperate fighting on the 2d, without definite result, and finished on the 3d by a decisive victory."[12]

In his 1882 memoirs, Abner Doubleday perceptively thought that it "would seem" that Lee believed the main Federal line ended on the Emmitsburg Road. "McLaws says that Lee thought turning the Peach Orchard was turning the Union left." Regarding the merits of Sickles' position, Doubleday (using a mathematical diagram to illustrate his point) wrote: "The disadvantages of [Sickles'] position are obvious enough. It is impossible for any force to hold its ground when attacked at once on both sides which constitute the right angle." As sometimes happened with controversial individuals of the era, criticism of Sickles could have been muted by the fact that he lived for so long afterward. When an edited version of Frank Haskell's Gettysburg manuscript was published by a Dartmouth classmate in 1898, the editor omitted some of Haskell's criticism of the still-living Sickles.[13]

Henry Tremain published his version of the story, *Two Days of War*, in 1905. Not surprisingly, the work was pro-Sickles. For once, Tremain admitted that July 3 had been important to the battle's outcome, but it had occurred and owed its ultimate success to Sickles' movements on the second. Tremain noted that

Sickles (like Reynolds on July 1) had engaged "in battle at once for the sake of gaining the time necessary for the concentration of the main body of the army, and thus securing it in the final positions carefully selected to resist the final assaults made on the third and last day." The notion that Sickles had advanced to buy time for the rest of the army was ridiculous, and Tremain probably knew it, but it was another example of the devotion that Sickles had created in his men.[14]

Confederate artilleryman Edward Porter Alexander produced no shortage of postwar analysis. Although his artillery had failed to neutralize his Federal counterparts on both the second and third days, he focused much of his written scrutiny on the tactical shortcomings of Generals Lee and Longstreet. Regarding July 2, he was particularly critical of Longstreet's inability to commit all eight of his brigades at one time. In *Military Memoirs of a Confederate* (1907), Alexander presumed that Sickles was influenced by Hazel Grove (and Alexander thereby influenced legions of future historians who rely on his analysis), but he still considered it "bad tactics. It exchanged strong ground for weak, and gave the Confederates an opportunity . . . to crush the isolated 3d corps."[15]

On the other side, Federal artilleryman John Bigelow was not a Third Corps officer, but he still argued for Sickles in his 1910 account *The Peach Orchard*. In referring to Meade's intended position, he wrote, "It is very doubtful whether the small 3rd Corps could have held Gen. Meade's line even until reinforcements arrived, as the ground close in its front was broken by large boulders and a wood, thus offering shelter for attacking infantry; while the Peach Orchard knoll, in its front gave a commanding position for artillery." Bigelow argued that Sickles' "small 3rd Corps could not possibly . . . have occupied the Big and Little Round Tops." Although Bigelow saw artillery value in the Peach Orchard, he had been misled by decades of misinformation into thinking Sickles was required to hold both Round Tops, thus justifying the advance. Bigelow recalled a postwar visit to the Peach Orchard with Henry Hunt, during which Bigelow asked whether Confederate artillery in the orchard would have "swept clean" Meade's intended position. Hunt declined to answer, but did admit, "I will say, that when this advanced position was lost, the opportunity passed away for acting on the offensive after the repulse of Pickett's charge, on July 3rd."[16]

Bigelow also wrote that Sickles' salient position specifically disrupted Lee's offensive strategy. "The advanced position at the Peach Orchard, with the line running back to the Round Tops, seems to have misled Gen. Lee and caused him to insist, against Longstreet's advice to flank the Round Tops, that a direct attack on the supposed exposed flank of Meade's army should be made." The resulting delays in the Confederate attack were understandable and greatly advantageous to Meade—as it allowed time for the Union 5th Corps to "go and hold the Round Tops." The resulting battle was "*in front* [emphasis in original] of this line and thoroughly exhausted both sides. At its conclusion the Confederates had gained nothing of value."[17]

Little Round Top, and not the Peach Orchard, increasingly became the focal point in debates over the merit of Sickles' move. Robert Carter, who fought in Tilton's 22nd Massachusetts, wrote in 1913: "I am more and more firmly convinced, after seven visits to the field, that Sickles' position on July 2 was not only faulty, and should not have been taken, but his losses would not have been so great had he prolonged the line of the Second Corps to the left over Little Round Top." Carter argued that if Vincent's "small" brigade had successfully held the hill from portions of Law and Robertson's brigades, then "it would have been much easier, especially had they [De Trobriand and Ward] been posted early, for these two brigades to have held our extreme left." Sickles could then have been "heavily reinforced by the Fifth and Sixth Corps, and the extreme left well guarded by one or more brigades of the latter in reserve to Ward and de Trobriand." Instead, it became "impossible for the fractions" of the Second and Fifth Corps to "patch up or reinforce a line that was already broken and rushing or breaking to the rear." Admittedly the line proposed by Meade "would seem to be more exposed to an artillery fire, but as the Confederate artillery was used along this line of the Emmitsburg Road, from which the Third Corps had been driven . . . with less loss (statistics show this) to the troops occupying it than actually occurred to the Third Corps at the Peach Orchard—then it is a logical conclusion that the Corps should have prolonged the Second Corps line." Carter somewhat mitigated his criticism against Sickles by calling Meade's orders "not explicit nor sufficiently positive. . . ."[18]

When the last of the battle veterans had passed away, the old Gettysburg debates were taken up by men who had not fought in the great battle. With no friendly partisans alive to protect his memory, Sickles' image began to increasingly suffer, particularly among military professionals. Major E. C. Bertram, the U.S. Army officer in charge of R.O.T.C. at Gettysburg College in the 1930s, thought Sickles committed "a serious error when he took up the position at the Peach Orchard. It is true that the position assigned him by General Meade was not the best terrain for defense, but it was necessary to hold it as a part of a complete defensive position. When a commander plans a defensive, he selects the best terrain available. He cannot take isolated pieces of terrain because of their individual defensive value but must select terrain that will permit a coordinated defense. As a result some poor terrain must often be included in the position. In order to have a coordinated position, General Meade was forced to use the comparatively weak terrain to the right of Little Round Top." Bertram recognized the obvious defects of Sickles' choice and it was only through "Meade's prompt and skillful maneuvers and Confederate blundering that saved the Union position. The only thing to be said in favor of Sickles is that his intentions were good."[19]

Sickles' reputation received a boost in the 1940s and 1950s with two favorable biographies. Edgcumb Pinchon's gushing 1945 work, *Dan Sickles: Hero of Gettysburg and 'Yankee King of Spain,'* referred to Sickles as a "seasoned commander" created by "two years of rigorous campaigning and increasing responsibility." Pinchon attributed Sickles' "confusion" over Meade's orders to the fact that "Geary had left no line . . . and had withdrawn long before the Third Corps began to arrive on the ground. Sickles thus was left in considerable doubt as to the exact location and extent of his sector." After failing to convince Meade that the Confederate attack would land on his left, Sickles' "uncanny prescience" convinced him "that Lee was outsmarting Meade" and that the attack would come "against his own decrepit left." Although Pinchon's published work suggested that he was a vigorous apologist for the general, and time has brought some of his conclusions into question, Pinchon's research benefited from the assistance of a few remaining individuals who had actually known Sickles in life. Stanton's son, and Dan's grandson, Captain Daniel S. Sickles, contributed substantially and financially to the project. (Sickles' image was not always favorably passed down within his own family. Great-grand-nephew John Shaud told this author in 2008 that his first memory of hearing of his famous ancestor was from his grandmother, Dan's niece, who rolled her eyes and said, "Oh, he was a scoundrel and a tyrant.") Pinchon's team even entertained hopes that the book would be made into a film. Whatever his published faults, Pinchon recognized what made Sickles a unique American character: "Ninety-four years of America's turgid adolescence! And some fifty of them spent in the thick of national affairs."[20]

More substantial was W. A. Swanberg's *Sickles the Incredible* (1956), which offered a somewhat more balanced evaluation of Sickles. Swanberg could not deny that Sickles was "a truly adventurous spirit," but regarding July 2, 1863, he wrote:

Without question, General Sickles thought he *was* [emphasis in original] acting for the best, though he was going against Meade's orders. He felt rightly that he knew the ground better than Meade and was apprised of enemy operations that the commander seemed to ignore. He was resentful that Meade was so infernally preoccupied with guarding against an attack on his right that he dismissed the left as of minor consequence. The Third Corps leader- and his trusted General Birney- were both seriously concerned about an enemy maneuver Meade underestimated. Sickles had been guilty of many a foolish impulse in his day, but the change of position was not impulse. It was the fruit of careful deliberation. He had pondered this move for hours. . . .[21]

Despite his best intentions, "Its wisdom was another matter entirely." Swanberg acknowledged the line's many defects: too far in advance from the rest of the army, unsupported flanks, and a longer distance in which Sickles' "lack of depth was greatly magnified." To Swanberg, "Worst of all, Little Round Top, soon to be recognized as the key to the whole Union position, was left without a single fighting man on its rocky height."[22]

No major full-length Sickles biography appeared for decades following Swanberg, leaving Sickles' actions to be covered as part of broader studies of the Gettysburg campaign. Evaluations of the general were mixed. Edward Stackpole's *They Met at Gettysburg* (1956) thought Sickles a "rugged individualist" who "believed strongly in taking the law into his own hands on occasion." Stackpole (who also gave Meade mixed marks) called Meade's orders "oral and not nearly as explicit as they should have been," while Sickles (since he didn't like his assignment) was "purposely slow in assigning troops to the [Meade's] position." Sickles left Little Round Top, Stackpole's "key position" unoccupied, but in evaluating the pros and cons of "The Sickles Controversy," Stackpole wrote that it can "be argued, with considerable plausibility, that Sickles' action strongly influenced the course and possibly the final outcome of the battle." Although Sickles took major casualties and seriously jeopardized Meade's plans, Longstreet ultimately failed to roll up Cemetery Ridge, and with their own heavy casualties Hood and McLaws were "relegated to a minor role for the remainder of the battle. . . ."[23]

Glenn Tucker's *High Tide at Gettysburg* (1958) argued that there was "divided sentiment about the prudence of his move." Although Tucker discredited the accusation that Meade planned a 3:00 p.m. retreat, Meade's orders to Sickles "contained some of the ambiguities that at times ruin battles or empires."

Tucker even thought Meade's intent to occupy Little Round Top was ambiguous. Sickles "implored" Meade to review the ground but was treated "cavalierly, at the very least." Tucker ultimately admitted that Sickles' advance was "unsound, though none can be certain how he would have fared in his old position," and that Longstreet's attack delays were fortuitous for the Confederates, because Sickles moved into the only position that would allow Longstreet to attack up the Emmitsburg Road and turn the Federal left. Conversely, had Sickles defended Little Round Top, Longstreet would have had to change front and attack an "impregnable" position. In the end, Sickles "won handily because he outlived his detractors and went down swinging at the age of ninety-five. He got fifty years of argument, political appointment, and glory out of one afternoon of fighting, but never a monument—like the other corps commanders—on the battlefield."[24]

In *The Gettysburg Campaign: A Study in Command* (1968), Edwin Coddington recognized that Sickles' forward move had nearly negated Meade's advantages of position. But the strength of Meade's interior lines had combined with the faulty Confederate tactics to allow Meade to throw reinforcements into holes created by Sickles. Coddington thought "Longstreet could not have hit the Union left flank at a more inopportune moment for Meade. The timing of Sickles' move to a new position compounded the inherent defects in the line Sickles had chosen for his Third Corps. Before his men could dig in and Meade could shift the Fifth Corps from right to left, Longstreet opened his attack." Rather than the capture of ground that ultimately held no value, Coddington considered "temporarily knocking out thirteen of Meade's brigades" to be Longstreet's greatest accomplishment. While true, the losses in both armies were nearly proportional as a percentage of available strength, and Lee could not afford to suffer large casualties as could his Union counterparts. Hood and McLaws had also been badly mauled and their unavailability on July 3 contributed to the Pickett's Charge debacle. Coddington rejected the argument that Sickles acted as a buffer or "breakwater," arguing instead that Sickles was more like "an empty harbor"—with nothing to protect behind him. Coddington accurately noted that the Union Third and Fifth corps could have defended Cemetery Ridge much easier had Sickles been in line. But Coddington also supported the debatable assumption that if Sickles had remained on Cemetery Ridge, Longstreet's Confederate divisions would have blindly attacked northward up the Emmitsburg Road in a vain attempt to locate Meade's left, and that Sickles would have simply raked Longstreet's exposed right flank and rear.[25]

No work has had a greater influence on public perceptions of Gettysburg than Michael Shaara's Pulitzer Prize-winning novel *The Killer Angels* (1974) and Ronald Maxwell's motion picture *Gettysburg* (1993), which was based upon Shaara's novel. Shaara's readers and Maxwell's viewers will forever consider July 2, 1863, as the story of Joshua Chamberlain's defense of Little Round Top. In the novel, an "amazed" Strong Vincent told Chamberlain, "That damn fool Sickles, you know him? . . . The Bully Boy. You know the one. The politician from New York. Fella shot his wife's lover. The Barton Key affair . . . Well, the damn fool was supposed to fall in on the left of Hancock. . . . But he didn't like the ground." In the film, Sickles and any such references are omitted entirely, leaving viewers without an accurate understanding of why the 20th Maine was raced into position in the first place. Meade hardly fares better. When he does make cameo appearances, he is cantankerous and (in the novel) his "damn fool orders" are scoffed at by the virtuous Chamberlain. In fact, it is easy to walk away from the novel and/or film with the inescapable conclusion that Winfield Hancock ran the Army of the Potomac. Until something more popular comes along, Shaara and Maxwell have cemented the notion that Little Round Top was the key to the second day, and although Sickles is mostly absent, the implication is clear: only a "damn fool" would leave the hill unoccupied.[26]

Harry Pfanz, in his *Gettysburg: The Second Day* (1987), considered Sickles "not quite the peer of either John F. Reynolds or Hancock . . . but he was competent, and his aggressive spirit, like theirs, was sadly lacking among the corps commanders of the Army of the Potomac in the closing half of the campaign."[27] Still, Pfanz could not escape the conclusion:

> General Sickles increased the odds of Confederate success when he advanced his Third Corps from its important and relatively secure position on Cemetery Ridge. In doing so he abandoned vital terrain, isolated his corps, and put the entire army at special risk. It was a grievous error mitigated only by the hard and costly fighting of his corps and the assistance given it by the corps of Hancock and Sykes.[28]

James M. McPherson, in his best-selling *Battle Cry of Freedom* (1988), thought that "Sickles' unwise move may have unwittingly foiled Lee's hopes." McPherson believed that upon finding the Union left in an unexpected position, Longstreet did not, and "probably should" have, notified Lee. Scouts reported the Round Tops "unoccupied, opening the way for a flanking move around to the rear," but Longstreet, having already failed to dissuade Lee from attacking, refused to change his plans as he "did not want to risk another rebuff. Lee had repeatedly ordered him to attack here, and here he meant to attack." Little Round Top remained in Union hands, thanks largely in McPherson's narrative to Joshua Chamberlain, and the left was secure. July 2, 1863, was a Union victory because "Confederate assaults were uncoordinated and disjointed" while Union "officers from Meade down to regimental colonels acted with initiative and coolness."[29]

In a 1993 essay, "The Peach Orchard Revisited: Daniel E. Sickles and the Third Corps on July 2, 1863," William Glenn Robertson pointed out that both Sickles and Meade "carried mental baggage to Gettysburg that hampered their smooth cooperation in the crisis." Robertson posited: "From the perspective of the Third Corps, Sickles' advance to the Peach Orchard ridge made sense." A move that was coordinated with Meade might have worked well, but given his unilateral execution without Meade, "Sickles' movement was decidedly improper" and placed the army in jeopardy. Robertson believed Sickles lacked the manpower to occupy Little Round Top in force, and that his actions might have fortuitously caused Meade to reinforce his left flank at a crucial moment. While admitting to the hypothetical nature, Robertson thought that if Longstreet had gained his ground uncontested, it was "quite possible" that Meade "might have lost the Round Tops and the southern end of Cemetery Ridge." While Robertson criticized Sickles for acting without orders, "Dan Sickles was not perfect on July 2, 1863, but neither was he the military buffoon so often portrayed."[30]

The popular explosion of Civil War and Gettysburg studies in the 1990s was reflected in the creation of Internet message boards and publications such as *Gettysburg Magazine*. Whatever the media format, Sickles has been regularly pummeled by Gettysburg enthusiasts. Among notable examples, in "Deception and the Citizen-General," K. Paul Raver focused thorough detail on Sickles' "unequaled ability to spin particulars into seemingly plausible, yet deceiving, pretenses." In "George Gordon Meade and the Defense of Cemetery Ridge," Richard Rollins wrote: "Dan Sickles and his friends indulged in lies, deceit, and innuendo and political machinations to publicly assassinate Meade's character." Jared Peatman, writing in "General Sickles, President Lincoln, and the Aftermath of the Battle of Gettysburg," blamed Sickles as a "large factor" in Lincoln's dissatisfaction with Meade. Without Sickles, Lincoln would have supported Meade differently and "By extension, Meade would have been a different commander" following the battle had Lincoln not "sapped his confidence."[31]

To many students, particularly those with military backgrounds, Sickles represents the ultimate amateur in a war filled with them. That Sickles' lack of training achieved prominence on Gettysburg's large stage ensures that his military abilities will be debated long after many of his "amateur" contemporaries have been forgotten. "Throughout the history of the U.S. Army," wrote retired Colonel Kavin Coughenour, "regular officers have always accepted the precept that professionals are predictable, but the world is full of amateurs." In referring to both Sickles and Butterfield, he observed, "Meade had to endure dealing with some very difficult subordinate amateur generals." Referring specifically to the high Third Corps casualties, Coughenour thought that "Generals who are aggressive, show initiative, and use good judgment on a battlefield are showing the qualities of great captains. While Sickles was aggressive and showed initiative, he was clearly guilty of stupendously poor judgment at Gettysburg."[32]

The enmity heaped on Sickles today has as much, if not more, to do with his post-battle campaign against Meade than with his battlefield performance. Many generals made blunders at Gettysburg, with Robert E. Lee jumping readily to mind. But Sickles chose to conduct a "despicable mud-slinging campaign to justify his misconduct on the battlefield and to discredit the man who won the Battle of Gettysburg—George G. Meade." It is Sickles the unscrupulous politician, not the questionable general, who has primarily tarnished his historical legacy. Had he taken the high road after the extremely moderate treatment he received in Meade's report, he might be better remembered today as another of the Civil War's great eccentrics. But the commander of the Army of the Potomac always wore a perpetual target on his back and Sickles was "despicable" in many of the methods that he used to exploit this situation. Dan Sickles the historical figure has paid a permanent price for this, overshadowing the laudable work he did as an early force in establishing Gettysburg National Military Park.[33]

The increased popularity of Gettysburg-related topics, along with the increased availability of publishing outlets, saw the number of available Sickles biographies double. Jeanne Knoop, a "distant relative" of the general, produced *I Follow the Course, Come What May* in 1998. Self-described as an "interpretation from a woman's point of view," the book's strength rests in some interesting nuggets of information regarding the family and pre-war years, rather than in any new analysis of Dan's role at Gettysburg.

In 2002, novelist Thomas Keneally (author of *Schindler's List*) produced the brilliantly-titled *American Scoundrel*. Keneally's work was entertaining, but at least as far as Gettysburg is concerned, occasionally suffers for accuracy. While Gettysburg enthusiasts can admittedly be frustratingly devoted to the most arcane minutiae, Keneally produces several misstatements of some basic facts, such as an inability to place the battle on the correct days of the week. (Keneally places July 2, 1863, on a Sunday.) The book's strengths lie in its focus on Dan and Teresa's marriage. Teresa comes off favorably, and Keneally admitted in closing that he would be "happy" if the book succeeds in invoking the "gentler and pleasant spirit" of "this beautiful, pleasant, and intelligent girl." Readers obtained a fuller appreciation of Dan and Teresa as a couple, but by adding nothing to the Gettysburg story, it is arguable whether Dan's target market will ever read it.[34]

Sickles returned in a major Gettysburg study, and his historical image probably reached its nadir, in Noah Andre Trudeau's *Gettysburg: A Testing of Courage* (2002). Sickles, wrote Trudeau,

> . . . gambled with the fate of an army with no more concern than he would exhibit while squandering several fortunes over a colorful lifetime. . . . Whether one of his possible prizes might be a place in the White House would depend to a great extent on how well his luck held today. If he could maintain his position even to a tactical draw, his cunning and connections would let him weave his tale of near disaster into a glowing paean of victory.[35]

Although there is no contemporary evidence to prove that Sickles moved to the Peach Orchard with an eye on the White House, and nothing in his character to suggest that he was willing to sacrifice his Third Corps for a "tactical draw," it was a significant indicator of how far the general's stock had fallen. Less than ninety years after his death, Sickles had been transformed from an aggressive blunderer to a conniving schemer willing to destroy the army in order to satiate his political ambitions. If Longstreet had been Gettysburg's Southern villain during the early postwar years, by the 21st century Sickles had replaced him as the most despicable scoundrel on the battlefield.

In studying the Joint Committee on the Conduct of the War, Bill Hyde's *The Union Generals Speak* (2003) admitted that Sickles was "probably the most interesting, and certainly the most controversial, character to testify before the committee." To Hyde, Sickles "matured (the term 'grew up' is not quite accurate) into an overindulged playboy." Despite his numerous personal faults, Hyde considered Sickles a "good" attorney and politician, and "for a person with little military experience, Sickles proved to be a good officer." Still, Hyde sharply criticized Sickles' performance before the committee, describing it as a combination of ego and opportunity to remove his nemesis Meade from command.[36]

Historian Richard Sauers has authored the best full-scale treatments of the so-called "Meade-Sickles Controversy," with *A Caspian Sea of Ink* and *Gettysburg: The Meade-Sickles Controversy.* "I had few preconceptions about where my research would take me," Sauers admitted. "By the time I was finished with my work, what I found had made me very biased in favor of General Meade's point of view." The argument against defending Sickles was "too strong." Sauers analyzed each of Sickles' self-proclaimed defenses in detail and found Sickles lacking on all counts. There was certainly enough evidence to prove that Sickles had received orders from George Meade on the morning of July 2. Sickles "failed to utilize properly either the ground or his men" by moving into a longer line. Sauers also dismissed Sickles' rationale that he advanced after his skirmishers had discovered the Confederate flanking movements by pointing out that Longstreet was not yet in position. While this was true as far as Longstreet was concerned, it doesn't necessarily explain the apparent confirmation of Confederate movements from the Berdan-Wilcox fight in Pitzer's Woods. Regarding Sickles' claim that the higher ground of the Peach Orchard would have made his Cemetery Ridge position "untenable," Sauers stressed that of such "what if" scenarios, the "result will never be known." Finally, Sauers disproved that Meade had ever intended to retreat during the afternoon of July 2, 1863. Sickles, concluded Sauers, had clearly disobeyed Meade's orders and had "jeopardized the entire Federal line." Not only were his post-battle attacks on Meade "dirty politics," but Sickles had "effectively damaged Gettysburg historiography."[37]

Prolific Civil War historian Stephen Sears produced a full-length study entitled *Gettysburg* in 2003. Sears repeatedly emphasized Sickles' status as an "amateur," "cocksure, decidedly untrained," and a "political general" pitted against the "professional soldier" Meade. When Sears wrote *Chancellorsville* in 1996, he admitted that "Sickles made up for his lack of military training by acting on the battlefield with reckless courage, and was much admired for it by his men." In *Gettysburg,* Sickles had been castrated to "all noise and notoriety . . . at Chancellorsville he blundered pugnaciously about the battlefield . . . Sickles was operating at a level far beyond his talents, and most everyone recognized it but Dan Sickles." Sears described Sickles' advance to the Peach Orchard as "folly."[38]

Sickles' lack of popularity might explain the surprising lack of coverage that he receives in histories of the National Military Park. His critics sometimes argue that the park would have developed just fine without him. Dr. David Martin, writing a modern introduction to a reprint of John Vanderslice's *Gettysburg: Then and Now*, seemed almost startled that the proposal to publish the Gettysburg Battlefield Memorial Association's history "was made early in 1895 by *none other than Daniel E. Sickles, the notorious general* [emphasis added] who had lost his leg at Gettysburg." In Barbara Platt's excellent *This is Holy Ground: A History of the Gettysburg Battlefield* (2001), Dan's involvement in the establishment of the GNMP was limited to the "Sickles Map," which served as a "de facto map of the park limits" until 1974. The "Sickles Bill" was likewise given only brief notice in Jim Weeks' *Gettysburg: Memory, Market, and American Shrine* (2003).[39]

Sickles was remembered, however, during non-historic tree removal as part of the National Park Service's comprehensive and controversial plan to return the battlefield, as closely as possible, to its 1863 appearance. Some of the earliest non-historic cuts occurred on a small hillock just north of Little Round Top on property owned in 1863 by John Munshower. (The area has since been dubbed "Munshower Field.") Park Ranger and historian Eric Campbell wrote in early 2005 that prior to the cuts he had "always attempted to give Gen. Sickles the benefit of the doubt." But Campbell noted that after the Munshower cuts, "the distance between certain points (say from the [George] Weikert farm to Little Round Top) was much closer than I had earlier imagined, thus changing my perspective of these features and their relationships with each other. Little Round Top literally *looms* [emphasis in original] over the entire Third Corps' original position. It is now hard to understand how Sickles *could not* [emphasis in original] have seen the importance of the hill." Or, as this author overheard another prominent local historian say, Campbell's logic "proved that Sickles was an idiot." On a note that Sickles would probably be happier with, the Park's rehabilitation plans also included the replanting of Sherfy's peach orchard, as well as orchards at the Wentz and Trostle farms.[40]

Dan Sickles was in the headlines, and almost returned to Gettysburg, once again in early 1993. Noted Gettysburg historian Lt. Col. Jacob M. Sheads uncovered Caroline Sickles' unsuccessful attempt to have Sickles buried at Gettysburg. Sheads was joined by Dr. William H. Ridinger, and Richard "Red" Davis, a Civil War enthusiast who had taken to reenacting Sickles, in lobbying for Sickles to be exhumed from Arlington and re-buried at Gettysburg's National Cemetery. "I can't imagine any circumstances in which Sickles . . .

would want to be buried in Virginia," claimed Davis. "It's Southern soil." They were then supported by John Shaud, Sickles' great grandnephew, who also favored the efforts based on the wishes of "the General's wife, my great grand aunt. . . . Yes, Arlington is a national treasure [but] so is Gettysburg—a National Park brought forth by Dan Sickles, shedding his blood and awarded the Medal of Honor." Despite the fact that both the cemetery's original semi-circle and the added-on section for Civil War and Spanish American War veterans had long since been closed for burials, they wanted Sickles reinterred on July 2, 1993— the 100th anniversary of the New York State Monument's dedication.[41]

The question centered on whether or not Sickles had wanted Gettysburg to be his final resting place, and whether the burden of evidence was sufficient enough for a court to support exhuming him from Arlington. Sickles sparked a spirited debate within forums such as the Gettysburg *Times* (which supported Sickles' reburial "if that was his wish"). Sheads and Dr. Ridinger noted Lincoln's appreciation for Sickles as a fighting general, Longstreet's support, the affection of his Third Corps survivors, and his introduction of the bill establishing the National Military Park. "Why isn't this accomplishment enough for him to be rightly referred to as 'The Father of The Gettysburg National Military Park?'" Sheads and Ridinger continued: "The issue of Sickles' reinterment at Gettysburg is not, and should not be, about his personal life, character, or generalship. Nor should it be about his postwar years, good or bad, beneficial to Gettysburg or not." They argued that Sickles' choice was Gettysburg and that his presence would make Gettysburg "more attractive" to "thousands of Civil War 'buffs.'"[42]

One retired military officer, a profession that will always remain among Sickles' harshest critics, dismissed Sheads and Ridinger's rationale. He acknowledged that the Third Corps veterans "bought Sickles a buggy-bully for them. . . . Private soldiers seldom see the big picture in any battle. They follow orders and just hope the guy in charge knows what he is doing." Admittedly, Abraham Lincoln found value in Sickles, but "he is the same commander-in-chief who gave his volunteers McDowell, McClellan, Pope, Burnside, and Hooker. . . ."[43]

"As far as we're concerned, he was the patron saint of the Park," then-battlefield superintendent Jose Cisneros said. Cisneros offered to allow Sickles' interment in the Cemetery Annex, but wondered, "If he really wanted to be buried at Gettysburg, he would have made arrangements to do that." Davis would argue that a 1904 Pennsylvania Supreme Court case, Pettigrew v. Pettigrew, had given the "paramount right" of disposition to the surviving spouse. Future superintendent John Latschar disagreed. "There's not a chance in hell General Sickles is going to be disinterred," Latschar exclaimed. "It would take a court order to get him out of Arlington. I'm certainly not going to support that." Dr. Latschar later explained that there was "extremely sparse" evidence that Sickles ever intended to be buried at Gettysburg, and that it simply did not meet the burden of proof necessary to have him moved from Arlington.[44]

Historian and Licensed Battlefield Guide Tim Smith was also skeptical that Sickles wanted to be buried at Gettysburg. Smith located the May 6, 1914, edition of the New York *Times*, which stated that Sickles had expressed a desire to be buried at Arlington. Smith passed this information along to park officials. Given that this was the best available indicator of the general's wishes, they used it to help deny the reburial effort. Davis continued to press his case in subsequent years, arguing that the 1914 *Times* article was only circumstantial proof of Sickles' intentions (since it was primarily based on the word of Sickles' attorney Hays) and not sufficient to ignore Pettigrew v. Pettigrew. Dr. Latschar continued to disagree, countering that the "deceased's written wishes always trump a surviving spouse's." Until any contrary evidence surfaces that is accepted by a court, as of this writing it appears that efforts to rebury Sickles at Gettysburg have been rebuffed by the National Park Service.[45]

*   *   *

Given his role in establishing New York's Central Park, two tenures in Congress, diplomatic service abroad, his successful use of the temporary insanity defense, his rise to major general in the Army of the Potomac, and his part in creating Gettysburg National Military Park, Daniel E. Sickles' career remains noteworthy for the sheer volume of his accomplishments. But he will always be most associated with that single afternoon at Gettysburg in July 1863 when, without orders, he marched his Third Corps toward the Emmitsburg Road and Joseph Sherfy's peach orchard. The battlefield results of that decision, his efforts to remove Meade from command, the fact that he had once murdered a man, was a dreaded "political general," and was expelled from the New York Monuments Commission have virtually guaranteed that posterity will remember him unfavorably. The passage of time has erased some of the favorable qualities that many of his contemporaries were able to accept in him. Still, he would probably at least enjoy the fact that his name still provokes strong emotions and arguments nearly a century after his death. While the general public may be oblivious to him, Gettysburg has given him immortality among those same battle students who often so enthusiastically hate him.

Ultimately, continuing debate over the merits of Sickles vs. Meade's position may be pointless. The historian of the 141st Pennsylvania regiment might have achieved the closest level of historical accuracy when he wrote in 1885: "It is the easiest thing to see a mistake after it has been committed, and to speculate as to what other combinations would have been more successful after a battle has been fought. This, however, may be said of the battle of Gettysburg, that the success of the Union arms was due very much more to the intelligent patriotism and invincible courage and determination of the rank and file, than upon the plans or efforts of Generals. The men felt they were on the sacred soil of the dear old Commonwealth, and there they would conquer or die." While Sickles and Meade partisans have battled for decades over who deserved credit for the victory, perhaps it belonged with the enlisted men all along.

Although Daniel E. Sickles failed to convince history that he won the battle of Gettysburg, there were few other generals who crowded as many accomplishments (good and bad) into their lives. Occasionally some Civil War students are able to see past the negatives. Michael S. Bennett, Commander of Sickles Camp 3, SUVCW observed:

> With Sickles, it's all out there in the open for everyone to see. He was as imperfect as any of us—perhaps a little less perfect than we would like to be, but he was a real person with real problems and real struggles that we can all identify with. . . . Where some leaders of the Civil War era seem larger than life and their exploits seem far beyond what we might hope to ever achieve ourselves, Sickles remains one of us. He is relatable. . . . He made mistakes. He had failings and flaws; and he had moments of genius and greatness.[46]

Whether a Gettysburg scholar agrees, disagrees, or has even heard of Dan Sickles and his performance on July 2, 1863, it is indisputable that the National Military Park and some of the battle's most colorful history exist as we know them today in large part due to his efforts. For that, Daniel E. Sickles deserves to be remembered.

Notes

Preface

1. *New York at Gettysburg*, 1:5.

Chapter 1: Murder!

1. For another discussion of Sickles' varying birth year, see Brandt, *The Congressman Who Got Away with Murder*, 217-218. Sickles' first major biographer, Edgcumb Pinchon (*Dan Sickles: Hero of Gettysburg and 'Yankee King of Spain,'* published in 1945) based much of his research on the recollections of Sickles' grandson Captain Daniel S. Sickles. Pinchon struggled with the correct birth year and Captain Sickles was "positive" in 1942 that Dan Sickles "tried to be younger than he really was" and that "1819 (or 1820) was the year of his birth." (See William Hobart Royce to Edgcumb Pinchon, July 16, 1942, and Edgcumb Pinchon to William Hobart Royce, December 5, 1941, William Hobart Royce Papers, MSS. & Archives Section, NYPL.) Pinchon thus accepted 1819 due to uncredited "family archives." Captain Sickles, who funded much of Pinchon's work, was clearly relying upon his memory for many dates and other family information. Two of Sickles' contemporaries also stated or implied an 1819 birth, and several news accounts later said that he was thirty-two at the time of his marriage. Sickles' most widely circulated biography, W.A. Swanberg's *Sickles the Incredible* stated, without comment, that the date was October 20, 1819. Apparently Swanberg's source was Pinchon. See Swanberg, 77, 396 (n. 1). Jeanne Knoop (*I Follow the Course, Come What May*) acknowledged the dispute, but again cited unspecified "family papers attest to the 1819 date." See Knoop, 11. Sickles descendant John Shaud told this author that he is not aware of any such family papers. (Email to author, August 15, 2008.) Thomas Keneally's *American Scoundrel* (6) also accepted 1819 without comment. But for examples of other potential dates see: Daniel E. Sickles Military Records, copy at GNMP, Box B-36; Department of Commerce and Labor Bureau of the Census, 1910 U.S. Federal census; "Gen. Daniel E. Sickles," New York *Times*, February 6, 1898; New York *Times,* May 4, 1914; *Dedication of the New York Auxiliary State Monument*, 107. The 1820 Federal census has a George G. Sickles in New York's 5th Ward with no male dependants under the age of ten. There are four household members, including one male between ten and sixteen, which would probably exclude this from being Dan's household. See the 1820 Federal Census. The New York Auxiliary history (107) stated, however, that Sickles was born "in Hudson Street" which seemed to be included in the 5th Ward.

2. Edgcumb Pinchon to William Hobart Royce, December 5, 1941, William Hobart Royce Papers, MSS.& Archives Section, NYPL.; "Gen. Daniel E. Sickles," New York *Times,* February 6, 1898; Brandt, *The Congressman Who Got Away With Murder*, 17-19; Swanberg, *Sickles the Incredible*, 77-80; *Dedication of the New York Auxiliary State Monument*, 107; Byrne and Weaver, *Haskell of Gettysburg*, 84-85; "Antonio Bagioli," New York *Times*, February 12, 1871.

3. Brandt, *The Congressman Who Got Away With Murder*, 19-20; Swanberg, *Sickles the Incredible*, 81.

4. Brandt, *The Congressman Who Got Away With Murder,* 20-21, 25; "Gen. Daniel E. Sickles," New York *Times,* February 6, 1898; Swanberg, *Sickles the Incredible,* 81-82; *Dedication of the New York Auxiliary State Monument,* 107; George Sickles Law License, November 19, 1845, Daniel E. Sickles Papers, LOC. When did Sickles pass the bar? As is often the case with his early career, one finds potentially conflicting dates. Swanberg (81) says Dan passed the bar in 1843. The New York State Auxiliary Monument dedication biography (107) says Dan was "called to the bar when twenty-three years of age." But since this same biography lists his date of birth as 1825, this would imply 1848 as the year Dan obtained his law license. George Sickles' law license was dated 1845, and in it he stated that he studied in his son's law office since September 1842. See Brandt, 223 (n. 40).The 1848 estimate seems too late, but whatever the exact year, Dan was clearly a practicing lawyer by the early 1840s.

5. Brandt, *The Congressman Who Got Away With Murder,* 22-25; "Gen. Daniel E. Sickles," New York *Times,* February 6, 1898; *Dedication of the New York Auxiliary State Monument,* 107; *New York at Gettysburg,* 1:341.

6. *Dedication of the New York Auxiliary State Monument,* 107; "Gen. Daniel E. Sickles," New York *Times,* February 6, 1898; Brandt, *The Congressman Who Got Away With Murder,* 22-23; *Life and Death of Fanny White,* 7; Swanberg, *Sickles the Incredible,* 83.

7. *Life and Death of Fanny White,* 8; New York *Times,* March 15, 1859; Brandt, *The Congressman Who Got Away With Murder,* 25-26; Swanberg, *Sickles the Incredible,* 86; "Says He's Sickles' Son," New York *Times,* August 31, 1913; "Sickles' Son?," Adams County *News,* September 6, 1913. The James Gordon Bennett Jr. rumor is in William Hobart Royce to Edgcumb Pinchon, December 6, 1941, William Hobart Royce Papers, MSS. & Archives Section, NYPL. The Sickles' marriage license (which erroneously lists Dan's middle name as Egbert) is dated March 2, 1853, representing the second ceremony. The Sickles biography in the *Dedication of the New York Auxiliary State Monument* (116) says that they married in 1853 and Laura was born in 1854 "at the old Sickles estate in Bloomingdale" while Sickles was abroad in London.

8. William Hobart Royce to Edgcumb Pinchon, August 31, 1942, William Hobart Royce Papers, MSS.& Archives Section, NYPL; Brandt, *The Congressman Who Got Away With Murder,* 26-28, 224 (n. 63).

9. Pinchon's researcher thought Sickles quickly realized that that he had married into a "rather low, common Italian family," see William Hobart Royce to Edgcumb Pinchon, August 31, 1942, William Hobart Royce Papers, MSS.& Archives Section, NYPL; "Gen. Daniel E. Sickles," New York *Times,* February 6, 1898; Brandt, *The Congressman Who Got Away With Murder,* 26-28; Swanberg, *Sickles the Incredible,* 90-91; Klein, *President James Buchanan,* 226-227; *Dedication of the New York Auxiliary State Monument,* 107.

10. Edgcumb Pinchon to William Hobart Royce, October 22, 1941, also Royce to Pinchon, August 31 and September 3, 1942, William Hobart Royce Papers, MSS.& Archives Section, NYPL; Klein, *President James Buchanan,* 236, 238, 242, 453 (n.4); Brandt, *The Congressman Who Got Away With Murder,* 30-31; *Life and Death of Fanny White,* 8; Swanberg, *Sickles the Incredible,* 91-96, 397 (n.14). Sickles said that his militia rank was captain at the time he went to London. See *New York at Gettysburg,* 1: 341.

11. "The Founder of Central Park, in New York," Daniel E. Sickles Papers, LOC; "Gen. Daniel E. Sickles," New York *Times,* February 6, 1898; National Register of Historic Places Inventory Nomination Form: Central Park, NPS; Brandt, *The Congressman Who Got Away With Murder,* 31-33; Swanberg, *Sickles the Incredible,* 99-100; *Dedication of the New York Auxiliary State Monument,* 107; Warner, *Generals in Blue,* 179.

12. Swanberg, *Sickles the Incredible,* 5; Brandt, *The Congressman Who Got Away with Murder,* 34-36; *Dedication of the New York Auxiliary State Monument,* 107; "Buchanan and Breckinridge Meeting," New York *Times,* July 9, 1856.

13. Brandt, *The Congressman Who Got Away With Murder,* 53-54; Tagg, *The Generals of Gettysburg,* 67-68; Swanberg, *Sickles the Incredible,* 10-13; "Application for a warrant for Libel against the Editor of the Herald," New York *Times,* October 14, 1857.

14. Brandt, *The Congressman Who Got Away With Murder,* 59-68; "Entertainment to Hon. Daniel E. Sickles," New York *Times,* December 3, 1858.

15. New York *Times*, March 15 and April 13, 1859; Brandt, *The Congressman Who Got Away With Murder*, 13-17; Swanberg, *Sickles the Incredible*, 3-17.

16. Swanberg, *Sickles the Incredible*, 20-32, 34-36, 39-40; New York *Times*, April 13 and April 19, 1859; Brandt, *The Congressman Who Got Away With Murder*, 76; *Dedication of the New York Auxiliary State Monument*, 107. See Desjardin, *These Honored Dead*, 62, for an excellent example of the sentiment against Sickles in Gettysburg literature. When Sickles eventually killed Key: "He [Sickles] murdered, in cold blood. . . . Finding his ego too traumatized to ignore the affair and his courage insufficient to settle the matter in the proper manner of the day—a duel—Sickles simply walked up to Key and fired three times. . . ." While entertaining, it ignores the fact that Sickles had given Key the opportunity to confess, and it was Key who lacked the courage to admit it.

17. Swanberg, *Sickles the Incredible*, 41-43.

18. *Ibid.*, 44-49.

19. *Ibid.*, 49-51.

20. Edgcumb Pinchon to William Hobart Royce, October 22, 1941, William Hobart Royce Papers, MSS.& Archives Section, NYPL; Brandt, *The Congressman Who Got Away with Murder*, 113-118; Swanberg, *Sickles the Incredible*, 52-53.

21. Brandt, *The Congressman Who Got Away With Murder*, 118-119, 121; New York *Times*, April 9, 1859; Keneally, *American Scoundrel*, 126.

22. New York *Times*, April 9, 1859; Brandt, *The Congressman Who Got Away With Murder*, 121-122; Swanberg, *Sickles the Incredible*, 1 54-55.

23. New York *Times*, April 9, 1859; Brandt, *The Congressman Who Got Away With Murder*, 122-124, 131; Swanberg, *Sickles the Incredible*, 55-58; Keneally, *American Scoundrel*, 129.

24. New York *Times*, March 5, 1859; Gettysburg *Compiler*, March 7, March 28, and May 2, 1859; Brandt, *The Congressman Who Got Away With Murder*, 126.

25. New York *Times*, March 15 and April 5, 1859; Swanberg, *Sickles the Incredible*, 55-58.

26. *The United States vs. Daniel E. Sickles;* New York *Times*, April 5, 1859; Swanberg, *Sickles the Incredible*, 62-63; Brandt, *The Congressman Who Got Away With Murder*, 165; Keneally, *American Scoundrel*, 78, 150-151; Woodward, *Mary Chesnut's Civil War*, 92 (n.7); Rezneck, "It Didn't Start With O.J.," Washington *Post*, July 24, 1994.

27. *The United States vs. Daniel E. Sickles;* New York *Times*, April 5, 1859; Brandt, *The Congressman Who Got Away With Murder,* 168.

28. *Ibid.*, 164-165, 169-171.

29. *The United States vs. Daniel E. Sickles;* Brandt, *The Congressman Who Got Away With Murder*, 170-173; New York *Times*, April 12, 1859; Fleming, "A Husband's Revenge," in *American Heritage*, 69. The insanity defense had increasingly gained American acceptance following the British establishment in 1843 of the M'Naghten Rule. The rule held that persons could not be convicted if they were laboring under such a defect of reason that they did not know what they were doing. In other words, that they could not tell right from wrong. But this was the first time that someone had raised the notion of a defendant being only temporarily mad. See Brandt. 170-172.

30. New York *Times*, April 13 through April 19, 1859; Brandt, *The Congressman Who Got Away With Murder*, 174-176.

31. New York *Times*, April 16 and April 18, 1859; Brandt, *The Congressman Who Got Away With Murder*, 176-177; Swanberg, *Sickles the Incredible*, 59-62.

32. Brandt, *The Congressman Who Got Away With Murder*, 176-177; New York *Times*, April 18, 1859; *The United States vs. Daniel E. Sickles*.

33. Brandt, *The Congressman Who Got Away With Murder*, 177-180; *The United States vs. Daniel E. Sickles.*

34. Brandt, *The Congressman Who Got Away With Murder*, 181-182; *The United States vs. Daniel E. Sickles.*)

35. New York *Times*, April 27, 1859; Gettysburg *Compiler*, May 2, 1859; Brandt, *The Congressman Who Got Away With Murder,* 182-187; *The United States vs. Daniel E. Sickles*; Woodward, *Mary Chesnut's Civil War*, 186. Fifty-two years later, Sickles' friend John Nicholson credited the acquittal to "the unwritten law [which] was summoned to his defense." It seems that few

considered the temporary insanity defense to be significant, even half a century later. See "Loyal Legion Bars Gen. Sickles Again," New York *Times*, November 2, 1911.

36. Brandt, *The Congressman Who Got Away With Murder*, 188-189, 240 (n. 80); Swanberg, *Sickles the Incredible*, 67; "In Lafayette Square," New York *Times*, May 18, 1884.

37. Gettysburg *Compiler,* June 27, 1859.

38. *Ibid.,* June 27 and July 18, 1859; New York *Times*, July 21, 1859; Brandt, *The Congressman Who Got Away With Murder*, 190-191; Swanberg, *Sickles the Incredible*, 70-72.

39. New York *Times*, July 21, 1859; Gettysburg *Compiler,* July 18, 1859; Brandt, *The Congressman Who Got Away With Murder*, 190-193.

40. *Ibid.*, 194-195; Gettysburg *Compiler,* July 25, 1859.

41. Gettysburg *Compiler,* July 25, 1859; Brandt, *The Congressman Who Got Away With Murder*, 195-197.

42. *Ibid.*, 198-199; Swanberg, *Sickles the Incredible*, 107; Woodward, *Mary Chesnut's Civil War*, 379-380.

Chapter 2: The Making of a First Class Soldier

1. De Trobriand, *Four Years With the Army of the Potomac*, 134; *Sickles, Oration Delivered . . . At Fredericksburg,* 23; Swanberg, *Sickles the Incredible*, 19, 36; Keneally, *American Scoundrel*, 252-253; Gettysburg *Star and Sentinel*, March 18, 1888.

2. Swanberg, *Sickles the Incredible*, 109-116; De Trobriand, *Four Years With the Army of the Potomac*, 427; *Dedication of the New York Auxiliary State Monument*, 107; Keneally, *American Scoundrel*, 214-215.

3. Sickles, "Leaves From My Diary," 1-4, NYPL; *Dedication of the New York Auxiliary State Monument*, 107-108; The National *Tribune*, March 31, 1910; Swanberg, *Sickles the Incredible*, 114-117; Strong, *Diary of the War*, 122, 135; Styple, *Generals in Bronze*, 100; McPherson, *Battle Cry of Freedom*, 266, 324; De Trobriand, *Four Years With the Army of the Potomac*, 147.

4. Stevenson, *History of the Excelsior or Sickles' Brigade*, 5, 7; Dedication of New York State Auxiliary Monument, 108; Oates, "Excelsior!," *America's Civil War*, 42-45.

5. Stevenson, *History of the Excelsior or Sickles' Brigade*, 8.

6. *Ibid.*, 7-9; Sickles, "Leaves From My Diary," 3, NYPL; Swanberg, *Sickles the Incredible*, 114-117; Warner, *Generals in Blue*, 179; *Dedication of the New York Auxiliary State Monument*, 108; *New York at Gettysburg*, 2: 600; Messent and Courtney, *Civil War Letters of Joseph Hopkins Twichell*, 1, 2, 10, 20.

7. Messent and Courtney, *Civil War Letters of Joseph Hopkins Twichell*, 23. The widow of New York Governor William Sulzer said Sickles and Nelson Miles were "among the founders of a violent anti-Catholic organization called the American Protective Association." See William Hobart Royce to Edgcumb Pinchon, December 25, 1941, William Hobart Royce Papers, MSS.& Archives Section, NYPL.

8. *Ibid.*, 23-24.

9. "The Old Excelsior Brigade," Daniel E. Sickles Papers, LOC; Sickles, "Leaves From My Diary," 4-5, NYPL; Swanberg, *Sickles the Incredible*, 116-119; Messent and Courtney, *Civil War Letters of Joseph Hopkins Twichell*, 25-26. Swanberg (117) wrote that this was the first meeting between Sickles and Lincoln, but Sickles stated that he had first met Lincoln during his last few weeks in Congress.

10. "The Sickles Brigade—Another Disaffected Company," New York *Times*, July 1, 1861; Messent and Courtney, *Civil War Letters of Joseph Hopkins Twichell*, 25-26, 38-39, 54; Sickles, "Leaves From My Diary," 7-8, 10-11; Swanberg, *Sickles the Incredible*, 119-123; Stevenson, *History of the Excelsior or Sickles' Brigade*, 8-9.

11. United States War Department, *The War of the Rebellion: A Compilation of the Official Records of the Union and Confederate Armies*, series 1, vol. 2, 745. (Hereafter cited as OR (all subsequent citations are from Series 1 unless otherwise noted); Daniel E. Sickles Military Records, copy at GNMP, Box B-36; "The Old Excelsior Brigade." Daniel E. Sickles Papers, LOC; Swanberg,

Sickles the Incredible, 119-123; Stevenson, *History of the Excelsior or Sickles' Brigade*, 8-9; Dedication of the New York Auxiliary State Monument, 108; Messent and Courtney, *Civil War Letters of Joseph Hopkins Twichell*, 20-26, 54-55; Oates, "Excelsior!," *America's Civil War*, 47.

12. Swanberg, *Sickles the Incredible*, 124-125; Sickles, "Leaves From My Diary," 10; "Gen. Sickles Sued for Money Advanced in 1861," New York *Times*, February 9, 1877.

13. McPherson, *Battle Cry of Freedom*, 328-329; Warner, *Generals in Blue*, 35-37, 60-61, 281-283, 293-294, 317-318, 426-428, 447-448.

14. De Trobriand, *Four Years With the Army of the Potomac*, 89; Warner, *Generals in Blue*, 121-122.

15. OR 5: 372-374, 387-388, 609-610; *Dedication of the New York Auxiliary State Monument*, 108-109; Swanberg, *Sickles the Incredible*, 134-137; Keneally, *American Scoundrel*, 254-257.

16. Warner, *Generals in Blue*, 227-228, 233-235; Swanberg, *Sickles the Incredible*, 126-131, 135; *Dedication of the New York Auxiliary State Monument*, 108; Messent and Courtney, *Civil War Letters of Joseph Hopkins Twichell*, 102-106; Styple, *Generals in Bronze*, 41.

17. General Order No. 6, April 6, 1862, Daniel E. Sickles Papers, LOC; Swanberg, *Sickles the Incredible*, 139-141; Messent and Courtney, *Civil War Letters of Joseph Hopkins Twichell*, 99-100; *Dedication of the New York Auxiliary State Monument*, 109; Stevenson, *History of the Excelsior or Sickles' Brigade*, 16-17.

18. *Dedication of the New York Auxiliary State Monument*, 109; "Gen. Sickles Makes a Reconnoissance [sic] to Stafford Court House," Bangor *Daily Whig and Courier,* April 7, 1862.

19. General Order No. 6, April 6, 1862, Daniel E. Sickles Papers, LOC; OR 11/1: 450, 467, 480; Messent and Courtney, *Civil War Letters of Joseph Hopkins Twichell*, 108-109, 111, 123-124; *Dedication of the New York Auxiliary State Monument*, 109; Swanberg, *Sickles the Incredible*, 140-141.

20. OR 11/3: 190-191; Swanberg, *Sickles the Incredible*, 135, 142-146; Messent and Courtney, *Civil War Letters of Joseph Hopkins Twichell*, 120-121, 128-130; Stevenson, *History of the Excelsior or Sickles' Brigade*, 22-24.

21. OR 11/1: 749, 759, 817, 820, 822-823; Messent and Courtney, *Civil War Letters of Joseph Hopkins Twichell,* 131; Swanberg, *Sickles the Incredible*, 149; *Dedication of the New York Auxiliary State Monument*, 110-111.

22. OR 11/2: 26, 109-110, 117, 134-136; *Dedication of the New York Auxiliary State Monument* 110; Messent and Courtney, *Civil War Letters of Joseph Hopkins Twichell*, 145, 149.

23. Sickles, *Oration Delivered . . . . At Fredericksburg,* 9-11.

24. *Dedication of the New York Auxiliary State Monument*, 110; OR 11/3: 325, 19/1: 170, 215-216, 270-271; Messent and Courtney, *Civil War Letters of Joseph Hopkins Twichell*, 167, 169, 182-183; Swanberg, *Sickles the Incredible*, 156-157, 160; Warner, *Generals in Blue*, 234; Sears, *Landscape Turned Red*, 23, 215, 359. For examples of Sickles' recruiting ads, see the New York *Times* of August 18, 22, 25, 26, 27, 28, and 29, 1862. Warner, *Generals in Blue*, (446) erroneously states that Sickles fought at Antietam. This error has been repeated elsewhere.

25. Oates, "Excelsior!," *America's Civil War*, 47; OR 21/1:1, 53-54, 354; Swinton, *Campaigns of the Army of the Potomac*, 231-32; Stackpole, *The Fredericksburg Campaign*, 75; Warner, *Generals in Blue*, 57, 481.

26. Swanberg, *Sickles the Incredible*, 162-163; *Dedication of the New York Auxiliary State Monument*, 110; Keneally, *American Scoundrel*, 253; Messent and Courtney, *Civil War Letters of Joseph Hopkins Twichell*, 147.

27. De Trobriand, *Four Years With the Army of the Potomac*, 426-427.

28. Styple, *Generals in Bronze*, 177-178; Twain, *Mark Twain's Autobiography*, 1:337-338; W.H. Bullard to Dan Sickles, September 13, 1897, Misc. Mss. Daniel Sickles, courtesy of New York Historical Society.

29. Styple, *Generals in Bronze*, 99, 177-178.

30. McPherson, *Battle Cry of Freedom*, 328-332; Warner, *Generals in Blue*, 290-292, 322-323; Stackpole, *The Fredericksburg Campaign*, 57.

31. OR 21/1: 53-54; Stackpole, *The Fredericksburg Campaign*, 279; Davis, *Life of David Bell Birney*, 1-11, 13, 16, 18, 25, 27, 30-31, 44-45, 73; Warner, *Generals in Blue*, 34-35, 554.

32. Davis, *Life of David Bell Birney*, 28-29; Pfanz, *Gettysburg: The Second Day*, 84-85; Tagg, *The Generals of Gettysburg*, 65; Styple, *Generals in Bronze*, 88; De Trobriand, *Four Years With the Army of the Potomac*, 316-317.

33. De Peyster, *Gen. H. Edwin Tremain*, 1-3; OR 21/1: 824.

34. OR 21/1: 47, 66-67, 355, 358, 377-378; Longstreet, "The Battle of Fredericksburg," in *Battles and Leaders*, 3:70; Rable, *Fredericksburg! Fredericksburg!*, 58-60, 86-90, 132-133, 157, 168-170; *Sickles, Oration Delivered . . . At Fredericksburg*, 1.

35. OR 21/1: 378; Rable, *Fredericksburg! Fredericksburg!*, 174-176, 184, 190.

36. OR 21/1: 450, 480, 510; Meade, *Life and Letters*, 1:337; Stackpole, *The Fredericksburg Campaign*, 180-186; Rable, *Fredericksburg! Fredericksburg!*, 194-195.

37. OR 21/1: 480, 511-512; George Meade to Margaret Meade, December 16, 1862, George Meade Collection, HSP; Meade, *Life and Letters*, 1:337; Stackpole, *The Fredericksburg Campaign*, 183-184, 188-190, 192; De Trobriand, *Four Years With the Army of the Potomac*, 367; Rable, *Fredericksburg! Fredericksburg!*, 211-213.

38. OR 21/1: 358-360, 362, 454, 511-512; Biddle, "General Meade at Gettysburg," in *The Annals of the War*, 205; Rable, *Fredericksburg! Fredericksburg!*, 215-216. Meade claimed he sent three messages to Birney; who admitted receiving one. See Rable, 513, n. 38. Hooker complained in his report that "during the attack of General Franklin, without any knowledge or information on my part, these two divisions [Birney and Sickles] were ordered forward with Franklin." See OR 21/1: 355-356.

39. OR 21/1: 360-361, 378-379, 455; Messent and Courtney, *Civil War Letters of Joseph Hopkins Twichell*, 200-201; Stackpole, *The Fredericksburg Campaign*, 183-184, 188-190, 192, 279; Davis, *Life of David Bell Birney*, 87-99. Edward Stackpole wrote that Birney's "brigades fought magnificently. . . . Had it not been for Birney, there is no telling what might have happened."

40. OR 21/1: 450, 511-512; George Meade to Margaret Meade, December 16, December 20, December 30, 1862 and April 11, 1864, George Meade Collection, HSP; Meade, *Life and Letters*, 1:338; Davis, *Life of David Bell Birney*, 87-99; Rable, *Fredericksburg! Fredericksburg!*, 513, n. 38-40. Bill Hyde in *The Union Generals Speak* (147), wrote: "Although Meade had quickly forgotten the incident, Birney harbored ill feelings for what he believed to be unfounded charges. . . ." Meade's April 1864 correspondence strongly suggests he had *not* "quickly forgotten" Fredericksburg.

41. David B. Birney to George Gross, December 28, 1862 and April 13, 1863, David B. Birney Papers, USAMHI.

42. Davis, *Life of David Bell Birney*, 102; Pfanz, *Gettysburg: The Second Day*, 3. For examples of the historical treatment Birney's Fredericksburg performance has received, Larry Tagg wrote in *The Generals of Gettysburg* (66) that Birney "again got into some trouble, this time for allegedly balking when asked to support General Meade's division. . . . Oddly, he was complimented in General George Stoneman's official report . . . ." Bill Hyde, in *The Union Generals Speak* (147): "Although Meade had quickly forgotten the incident, Birney continued to harbor ill feelings for what he believed to be unfounded charges. . . ." Ezra Warner portrayed Birney more positively in *Generals in Blue*, noting the "charge was not substantiated and Birney was, in fact, highly praised by General George Stoneman." See Warner, 34. Edward Stackpole praised Birney, and while George Rable blamed Franklin for much of the fiasco, he still found Birney "hapless" and his excuses "lame." See Rable, 215-216.

43. OR 25/2: 3-4; George Meade to Margaret Meade, December 16, 1862, George Meade Collections, HSP; Meade, *Life and Letters* 1:338; Basler, *The Collected Works of Abraham Lincoln*, 6: 78-79; Benjamin, "Hooker's Appointment and Removal," in *Battles and Leaders*, 3:239-240; De Trobriand, *Four Years With the Army of the Potomac*, 413-414; Swanberg, *Sickles the Incredible*, 169 Although Meade frequently disavowed ambitious thoughts, Stanton's letter of 11/29/62 did cause him to rhetorically ask his wife, "Do you think major general sounds any better than brigadier?" See Meade, *Life and Letters*, 1: 338.

44. OR 25/2:6; Couch, "The Chancellorsville Campaign," in *Battles and Leaders*, 3:154; Butterfield, *A Biographical Memorial*, 4-10; *Dedication of the New York Auxiliary State Monument*, 116-118; Warner, *Generals in Blue*, 62-63; Hyde, *The Union Generals Speak*, 238-239; Cleaves, *Meade of Gettysburg*, 95-96; Sears, *Chancellorsville*, 63; Styple, *Generals in Bronze*, 223.

45. OR 25/2:6; Couch, "The Chancellorsville Campaign," in *Battles and Leaders,* 3:154; Butterfield, *A Biographical Memorial,* 111-112; *Dedication of the New York Auxiliary State Monument,* 116-118; George Meade to Margaret Meade, December 17, 1862, George Meade Collection, HSP; Hyde, *The Union Generals Speak,* 238-239; Cleaves, *Meade of Gettysburg,* 95-96.

46. OR 25/2: 15-29, 51, 180; Swanberg, *Sickles the Incredible,* 168; De Trobriand, *Four Years With the Army of the Potomac,* 420-421; Messent and Courtney, *Civil War Letters of Joseph Hopkins Twichell,* 220; Daniel E. Sickles Military Records, copy at GNMP, Box B-36.

47. De Trobriand, *Four Years With the Army of the Potomac,* 416-417; Byrne and Weaver, *Haskell of Gettysburg,* 84-85; Swanberg, *Sickles the Incredible,* 168. Haskell's allegation that Sickles had "criminal intercourse" with his mother-in-law for years is, of course, an interesting accusation.

48. OR 25/2: 15-29, 48, 51; Meade, *Life and Letters,* 1:353.

49. OR 25/2: 52; Davis, *Life of David Bell Birney,* 108-110; De Trobriand, *Four Years With the Army of the Potomac,* 420-422; David Birney to George Gross, March 16, 1863, David B. Birney Papers, USAMHI; Warner, *Generals in Blue,* 31-32.

50. Messent and Courtney, *The Civil War Letters of Joseph Hopkins Twichell,* 208; Williams, *Lincoln and His Generals,* 211; De Trobriand, *Four Years With the Army of the Potomac,* 398; Swanberg, *Sickles the Incredible,* 166; Cleaves, *Meade of Gettysburg,* 100; Sears, *Chancellorsville,* 55.

51. De Trobriand, *Four Years With the Army of the Potomac,* 413; Meade, *Life and Letters,* 1:365; Sears, *Chancellorsville,* 60. Biographer Edgcumb Pinchon struggled with conflicting reports over the extent of Sickles' drinking; see Edgcumb Pinchon to William Hobart Royce, October 22, 1941, and Royce to Pinchon, December 25, 1941, William Hobart Royce Papers, MSS. & Archives Section, NYPL.

52. Roebling's quote regarding Butterfield's arson was from a handwritten note on the flyleaf of Roebling's copy of *A Biographical Memorial of General Daniel Butterfield,* edited by Julia Butterfield. Roebling further wrote: "This incident is not mentioned in this book nor are some others." Roebling's copy is #177 of only 400 printed and is currently [2008] in the Special Collections of Gettysburg College. Adams was quoted in Swanberg, *Sickles the Incredible,* 173-174 and Lash, "The Congressional Resolution of Thanks for The Federal Victory at Gettysburg," *Gettysburg Magazine* 12, 87.

53. Coughenour, "Assessing the Generalship of George G. Meade During the Gettysburg Campaign," *Gettysburg Magazine* 28, 28-30; Styple, *Generals in Bronze,* 156; George Meade to Margaret Meade, January 26, 1863, George Meade Collection, HSP; Meade, *Life and Letters,* 1: 351.

54. Meade, *Life and Letters,* 1: 357-358.

55. Coughenour, "Assessing the Generalship of George G. Meade During the Gettysburg Campaign," *Gettysburg Magazine* 28, 29.

56. Meade, *Life and Letters,* 1: 360; Styple, *Generals in Bronze,* 149; Coughenour, "Assessing the Generalship of George G. Meade During the Gettysburg Campaign," *Gettysburg Magazine* 28, 34; Williams, *Lincoln and His Generals,* 260.

57. Meade, *Life and Letters,* 1:354, 357; De Trobriand, *Four Years With the Army of the Potomac,* 425-426; Messent and Courtney, *Civil War Letters of Joseph Hopkins Twichell,* 219-220.

58. Favill, *Diary of a Young Army Officer,* 225; Davis, *Life of David Bell Birney,* 118-130; De Trobriand, *Four Years With the Army of the Potomac,* 427-428; Sears, *Chancellorsville,* 78; Tagg, *The Generals of Gettysburg,* 65.

59. David Birney to George Gross, April 7, 1863, David B. Birney Papers, USAMHI ; Meade, *Life and Letters,* 1: 363-366, 368; De Trobriand, *Four Years With the Army of the Potomac,* 428; *Sickles, Oration Delivered...At Fredericksburg,* 18-19; Butterfield, *A Biographical Memorial,* 159-161.

60. OR 25/2: 152; Davis, *Life of David Bell Birney,* 30-31, 73; Butterfield, *A Biographical Memorial,* 116-117; Sears, *Chancellorsville,* 72, 80-81; Scott, *History of the One Hundred and Fifth Regiment of Pennsylvania Volunteers,* 22, 70-71.

61. Report of the Joint Committee on the Conduct of the War, 3. (Hereafter cited as CCW.); Swanberg, *Sickles the Incredible,* 176; Favill, *Diary of a Young Officer,* 228; Meade, *Life and Letters,* 1: 366-367.

Chapter 3: I Think it is a Retreat

1. OR 25/1: 171; Couch, "The Chancellorsville Campaign," in *Battles and Leaders*, 3:156; Swinton, *Campaigns of the Army of the Potomac*, 271-273; Doubleday, *Chancellorsville and Gettysburg*, 2-3; Dodge, *The Campaign of Chancellorsville*, 26-27.

2. OR 25/1: 171, 796; Meade, *Life and Letters*, 1: 370-371; Dodge, *The Campaign of Chancellorsville*, 34-37; Alexander, *Military Memoirs*, 323-325; Swinton, *Campaigns of the Army of the Potomac*, 227-273, 277; Sears, *The Chancellorsville Campaign*, 97-100; Couch, "The Chancellorsville Campaign," in *Battles and Leaders*, 3:156-157; Doubleday, *Chancellorsville and Gettysburg*, 8; Krick, "Lee at Chancellorsville," in *Lee: The Soldier*, 362.

3. OR 25/1: 384-385; CCW, 4; Acken, *Inside the Army of the Potomac*, 234-235; Dodge, *The Campaign of Chancellorsville*, 37-38.

4. Swinton, *Campaigns of the Army of the Potomac*, 277-281; OR 25/1: 507; Sears, *Chancellorsville*, 200-201, 208-212, 223-224, 226; Couch, "The Chancellorsville Campaign," in *Battles and Leaders*, 3:159; Meade, *Life and Letters*, 1: 370-371; Doubleday, *Chancellorsville and Gettysburg*, 11-14; Dodge, *The Campaign of Chancellorsville*, 44-45, 56-57; Krick, "Lee at Chancellorsville," in *Lee: The Soldier*, 364; Alexander, *Military Memoirs*, 327.

5. Sears, *Chancellorsville*, 224, 231-234, 239-241, 243; Allan, "Memoranda of Conversations with General Robert E. Lee," in *Lee the Soldier*, 9; Dodge, *The Campaign of Chancellorsville*, 62-66; Krick, "Lee at Chancellorsville," in *Lee: The Soldier*, 365; Doubleday, *Chancellorsville and Gettysburg*, 20-21; Alexander, *Military Memoirs*, 329-330; Pleasonton, "The Successes and Failures of Chancellorsville," in *Battles and Leaders*, 3:177; Happel, *The Last Days of Stonewall Jackson*, 21.

6. OR 25/1:385; CCW, 4-5, 34-35; Sears, *Chancellorsville*, 235-237, 246; Swinton, *Campaigns of the Army of the Potomac*, 282; De Trobriand, *Four Years With the Army of the Potomac*, 439-440; Dodge, *The Campaign of Chancellorsville*, 66.

7. OR 25/1: 385; CCW, 4-5; Howard, "The Eleventh Corps at Chancellorsville," *Battles and Leaders*, 3:194-195; Doubleday, *Chancellorsville and Gettysburg*, 20-21; Sears, *Chancellorsville*, 237-238.

8. CCW, 4-5, 34-35; Doubleday, *Chancellorsville and Gettysburg*, 22; Dodge, *The Campaign of Chancellorsville*, 66-67; Sears, *Chancellorsville*, 244-247; Alexander, *Military Memoirs*, 331.

9. CCW, 4-5, 34-35; OR 25/1: 404, 408; Doubleday, *Chancellorsville and Gettysburg*, 23; Dodge, *The Campaign of Chancellorsville*, 66-67; Sears, *Chancellorsville*, 244-247; Bohannon, "Disgraced and Ruined by the Decision of the Court. . . ." in *Chancellorsville: The Battle and its Aftermath*, 205.

10. OR 25/1: 386, 449, 459; Sears, *Chancellorsville*, 245, 248.

11. OR 25/1: 386; CCW, 5; Doubleday, *Chancellorsville and Gettysburg*, 25-27; Dodge, *The Campaign of Chancellorsville*, 67-68; Sears, *Chancellorsville*, 254-255.

12. OR 25/1: 386, 491; CCW, 5, 34-35; Dodge, *The Campaign of Chancellorsville*, 68; De Trobriand, *Four Years With the Army of the Potomac*, 439; Collins, "When Stonewall Jackson Turned Our Right," in *Battles and Leaders*, 3: 183; Bohannon, "Disgraced and Ruined by the Decision of the Court. . . ," in *Chancellorsville: The Battle and its Aftermath*, 205-209; Sears, *Chancellorsville*, 254-257.

13. OR 25/1: 386; CCW, 4-5; Dodge, *The Campaign of Chancellorsville*, 69; Sears, *Chancellorsville*, 255-256.

14. OR 25/1: 386; Dodge, *The Campaign of Chancellorsville*, 70; Alexander, *Military Memoirs*, 332; Howard, "The Eleventh Corps at Chancellorsville," in *Battles and Leaders*, 3:196-197; De Trobriand, *Four Years With the Army of the Potomac*, 440; Pleasonton, "The Successes and Failures of Chancellorsville," in *Battles and Leaders*, 3:177; Sears, *Chancellorsville*, 256, 262, 264, 269. Stephen Sears, critical of Sickles' inability to mount an earlier attack against Jackson commented: "With his quarry gone, Sickles seemed to be fighting just for the sake of fighting." While later events ultimately proved that Sickles, Hooker, Slocum, and Howard erred in not acting earlier against Jackson's column, there is no reason to suppose that Sickles was fighting only "for the sake of fighting." He may have thought, as he later claimed, that he could do some legitimate damage to the retreating column. As often happens in warfare, both sides also appeared willing to respond to the enemy's resistance by committing more troops. See Sears, 256.

15. OR 25/1: 386-387, 25/2: 370; Howard, "The Eleventh Corps at Chancellorsville," in *Battles and Leaders*, 3:196-197; Dodge, *The Campaign of Chancellorsville*, 68; Sears, *Chancellorsville*, 262-263, 269.

16. OR 25/1: 387; CCW, 5-6; Sears, *Chancellorsville*, 268; Pleasonton, "The Successes and Failures of Chancellorsville," in *Battles and Leaders*, 3:177; Styple, *Generals in Bronze*, 122.

17. CCW, 5-6; OR 25/1: 387; Sears, *Chancellorsville*, 257-258, 261-262; Dodge, *The Campaign of Chancellorsville*, 90-91.

18. OR 25/1: 387-388; CCW, 6, 34-35; De Trobriand, *Four Years With the Army of the Potomac*, 441-442; Dodge, *The Campaign of Chancellorsville*, 97-98; Pleasonton, "The Successes and Failures of Chancellorsville," in *Battles and Leaders*, 3:180-181; Styple, *Generals in Bronze*, 123; Doubleday, *Chancellorsville and Gettysburg*, 36; Huntington, "The Artillery at Hazel Grove," in *Battles and Leaders*, 3: 188. Stephen Sears (290) wrote that Sickles and Pleasonton had succeeded only in stopping about 200 of Doles' men, who, in fact had stopped on their own orders. Dodge (111) similarly wrote that Sickles and Pleasonton overstated the importance of the episode. Captain Huntington resented Pleasonton's failure to give him credit for holding his battery in position.

19. CCW, 4, 35; Meade, *Life and Letters*, 1: 370-371; Favill, *Diary of a Young Army Officer*, 233; Dodge, *The Campaign of Chancellorsville*, 98-99.

20. Alexander, *Military Memoirs*, 337; De Trobriand, *Four Years With the Army of the Potomac*, 444; Doubleday, *Chancellorsville and Gettysburg*, 35, 39; Sears, *Chancellorsville*, 284-294; CCW, 6; OR 25/1:449; Favill. *Diary of a Young Army Officer*, 233; Dodge, *The Campaign of Chancellorsville*, 108-111; Krick, "The Smoothbore Volley...," in *Chancellorsville: The Battle and its Aftermath*, 109, 112, 119-121, 127, 129, 133.

21. Sears, *Chancellorsville*, 290, 300; OR 25/1: 389; De Trobriand, *Four Years With the Army of the Potomac*, 446; CCW, 35; Dodge, *The Campaign of Chancellorsville*, 114-115; Doubleday, *Chancellorsville and Gettysburg*, 41.

22. De Trobriand, *Four Years With the Army of the Potomac*, 446-450, 452; Dodge, *The Campaign of Chancellorsville*, 114-115; Doubleday, *Chancellorsville and Gettysburg*, 41-42; Sears, *Chancellorsville*, 300-301.

23. OR 25/1: 390; CCW, 35; De Trobriand, *Four Years With the Army of the Potomac*, 457; Racine, *Unspoiled Heart*, 13; Sears, *Chancellorsville*, 302.

24. OR 25/1: 390; CCW, 8; Doubleday, *Chancellorsville and Gettysburg*, 43-44; Dodge, *The Campaign of Chancellorsville*, 126-128; Alexander, *Military Memoirs*, 342; Sears, *Chancellorsville*, 193, 286, 312-313. Stephen Sears, critical of Sickles' overall Chancellorsville performance, admitted that there was danger at Hazel Grove, but thought that Sickles might have been capable of holding the position with seven brigades and 38 artillery guns. Sears wrote: "And whatever Dan Sickles might have lacked in military judgment he could make up for with military pugnaciousness." See Sears, 313.

25. CCW, 8; De Trobriand, *Four Years With the Army of the Potomac*, 457; Doubleday, *Chancellorsville and Gettysburg*, 46; Dodge, *The Campaign of Chancellorsville*, 128; Sears, *Chancellorsville*, 316-320.

26. OR 25/1: 391; Sears, *Chancellorsville*, 314, 321-324; De Trobriand, *Four Years With the Army of the Potomac*, 457-458; Warner, *Generals in Blue*, 32.

27. OR 25/1: 392, 460, 463; Dodge, *The Campaign of Chancellorsville*, 137; Sears, *Chancellorsville*, 325-326.

28. De Trobriand, *Four Years With the Army of the Potomac*, 458; Sears, *Chancellorsville*, 334-336; Scott, *History of the One Hundred and Fifth Regiment of Pennsylvania Volunteers*, 73-74; OR 25/1: 421.

29. De Trobriand, *Four Years With the Army of the Potomac*, 460-461; Sears, *Chancellorsville*, 336-337, 342-343; Favill, *Diary of a Young Army Officer*, 234-235.

30. CCW, 8, 15; De Peyster, *Gen. H. Edwin Tremain*, 4; Doubleday, *Chancellorsville and Gettysburg*, 53; Styple, *Generals in Bronze*, 42; Sears, *Chancellorsville*, 336-337, 357-358.

31. CCW, 8-9; Dodge, *The Campaign of Chancellorsville*, 144-145; Couch, "The Chancellorsville Campaign," in *Battles and Leaders*, 3: 169-170; Swinton, *Campaigns of the Army of the Potomac*, 294-295, 298-299; Sears, *Chancellorsville*, 364-365, 372-374; Reardon, "The Valiant Rearguard...," in *Chancellorsville: The Battle and its Aftermath*, 163-166.

32. Swinton, *Campaigns of the Army of the Potomac*, 299-301; Sears, *Chancellorsville*, 393-394, 403; Couch, "The Chancellorsville Campaign," in *Battles and Leaders*, 3:170; OR 25/1: 394.

33. Couch, "The Chancellorsville Campaign," in *Battle and Leaders*, 3: 171; OR 25/1: 512; Dodge, *The Campaign of Chancellorsville*, 226-227; Sears, *Chancellorsville*, 420-421.

34. Couch, "The Chancellorsville Campaign," in *Battle and Leaders*, 3: 171; OR 25/1: 512; Dodge, *The Campaign of Chancellorsville*, 227; Sears, *Chancellorsville*, 421-422; Hyde, *The Union Generals Speak*, 170-171.

35. Couch, "The Chancellorsville Campaign," in *Battle and Leaders*, 3: 171; Sears, *Chancellorsville*, 421-422; Gibbon, *An Address on the Unveiling of the Statue of Major General George G. Meade. . .* , 12.

36. Couch, "The Chancellorsville Campaign," in *Battle and Leaders*, 3: 171; Meade, *Life and Letters*, 1:380; *Dedication of New York Auxiliary State Monument*, 111; Sears, *Chancellorsville*, 421-422.

37. OR 25/1: 178-180; Messent and Courtney, *Civil War Letters of Joseph Hopkins Twichell*, 234; Doubleday, *Chancellorsville and Gettysburg*, 71; David Birney to George Gross, May 15, 1863, David B. Birney Papers, USAMHI; Sears, *Chancellorsville*, 441. Birney and Graham directed much criticism at Col. Charles Collis, a Medal of Honor winner for Fredericksburg who later made his retirement home in Gettysburg and is buried in Gettysburg's National Cemetery. In forwarding Collis' report, Graham cautioned: "In forwarding this report, which I do merely as a matter of duty, it is incumbent upon me to say that it is a complete fraud from beginning to end. Collis has had his attention called to these errors, but he has refused to correct them." Birney forwarded, adding: "The officer is under arrest on charges of misbehavior before the enemy." See Dodge, *The Campaign of Chancellorsville*, 117. Birney wrote to friends privately: "Collis is a gross fraud and is now under arrest for his behavior at the last battle. General Graham during the attack [could] not make him leave a tree for shelter, and before the fight was concluded he went to the rear to find hospital sick." Birney to Gross, May 15, 1863, USAMHI. Captain Francis Donaldson of the 118th Pennsylvania encountered Collis being carried to the rear on a stretcher, "his whole appearance and manner . . . denoted fear of the most abject kind. The men smiled contemptuously as they passed him by . . . they had been a witness to the humiliating loss of honor and self-respect of a man so widely known." Acken, *Inside the Army of the Potomac*, 244-245.

38. Sears, *Chancellorsville*, 437. Stephen Sears listed Sickles among Chancellorsville's failures for failing to "organize a determined assault on Jackson's flanking column, and in the bargain misread what he saw and made the fateful announcement that Lee was giving up the field in retreating." But Sears also rightly labeled almost everyone in authority including Hooker, George Stoneman, Howard, and Sedgwick as failures.

39. Meade, *Life and Letters*, 1: 372-376; Sears, *Chancellorsville,* 432, 436.

40. Meade, *Life and Letters*, 1: 377.

41. *Ibid.*, 1: 381; OR 25/1: 510-511.

42. Sears, *Gettysburg*, 25; OR 25/1: 511.

43. OR 25/1: 511.

44. Peatman, "General Sickles, President Lincoln, and the Aftermath of the Battle of Gettysburg," *Gettysburg Magazine* 28, 118; Swanberg, *Sickles the Incredible*, 196; Lash, "The Congressional Resolution of Thanks for The Federal Victory at Gettysburg," *Gettysburg Magazine* 12, 88.

45. Swanberg, *Sickles the Incredible*, 191-192; The Hornellsville *Tribune*, May 21, 1863; Strong, *Diary of the Civil War*, 323; Peatman, "General Sickles, President Lincoln, and the Aftermath of the Battle of Gettysburg," *Gettysburg Magazine* 28, 118.

Chapter 4: No One Ever Received a More Important Command

1. Swanberg, *Sickles the Incredible*, 193; Favill, *Diary of a Young Army Officer*, 235-236; Davis, *Life of David Bell Birney*, 157; Warner, *Generals in Blue*, 34; Scott, *History of the One Hundred and Fifth Regiment of Pennsylvania Volunteers,* 76-77; De Trobriand, *Four Years With the Army of the Potomac*, 474.

2. Humphreys, *Andrew Atkinson Humphreys*, 25, 30-45, 156-177, 183-185, 194, 197; Stackpole, *The Fredericksburg Campaign*, 217-218; Tagg, *The Generals of Gettysburg*, 73.

3. Humphreys, *Andrew Atkinson Humphreys: A Biography*, 183-184, 194, 197; David Birney to George Gross, October 28, 1863, *David B. Birney Papers*, USAMHI; Meade, *Life and Letters*, 1:378; Tagg, *The Generals of Gettysburg*, 73.

4. Scott, *History of the One Hundred and Fifth Regiment of Pennsylvania Volunteers,* 76-77; Styple, *Our Noble Blood*, 103-104.

5. Styple, *Our Noble Blood, 105-106;* Scott, *History of the One Hundred and Fifth Regiment of Pennsylvania Volunteers,* 77; Conklin, *Women at Gettysburg*, 97, 107; Frassanito, *Early Photography at Gettysburg*, 140.

6. Styple, *Our Noble Blood*, 105-106; CCW, 13.

7. Keneally, *American Scoundrel*, 273-274.

8. Longstreet, "Lee's Invasion of Pennsylvania," in *Battles and Leaders*, 3:245-249; Jones, *Life and Letters of Robert E. Lee*, 247; Freeman, *Lee's Lieutenants*, 3:41-46; Coddington, *The Gettysburg Campaign*, 5-9; Brown*, Retreat from Gettysburg*, 12-15; Allan, "Memoranda of Conversations with General Robert E. Lee," in *Lee the Soldier*, 11-17; Lee, "Letter from General Fitzhugh Lee, March 5, 1877," in *Southern Historical Society Papers*, 4: 69-72. (Hereafter cited as *SHSP*); Pfanz, *Gettysburg: The First Day*, 2-3.

9. OR 27/1: 29-32; 27/2: 293; Humphreys, *Andrew Atkinson Humphreys*, 185.; Smith, A Famous Battery and Its Campaigns, 97-98; Coddington, *The Gettysburg Campaign*, 74; Oeffinger, *A Soldier's General*, 189-190.

10. Meade, *Life and Letters*, 1:382-383, 385-386.

11. Adams quoted in Swanberg, *Sickles the Incredible*, 196-197; George Meade to Margaret Meade, June 25, 1863, George Meade Collection, HSP; Meade, *Life and Letters*, 1: 385, 388-389. For examples of General and Mrs. Meade's resentment over Reynolds, see George Meade to Margaret Meade: December 2, 16, 21, and 30, 1862, George Meade Collection, HSP. Such talk was not included in Meade's published *Life and Letters*.

12. OR 27/1: 60; Meade, *Life and Letters*, 1: 387; Coddington, *The Gettysburg Campaign*, 130.

13. New York *Times,* June 17, 1863; Sickles, "Further Recollections of Gettysburg," in *North American Review*, 259; Smith, *A Famous Battery and Its Campaigns*, 97-98.; Styple, *Our Noble Blood,* 110-111.

14. CCW, 13; Sickles, "Further Recollections of Gettysburg," in North *American Review*, 259.

15. OR 27/1:61.

16. Benjamin, "Hooker's Appointment and Removal," in *Battles and Leaders*, 3:242-243; Meade, *Life and Letters*, 2: 2-4, 11-12; OR 27/1: 61-62.

17. Meade, *Life and Letters*, 1: 389; Benjamin, "Hooker's Appointment and Removal," in *Battles and Leaders*, 3:243; Coughenour, "Assessing the Generalship of George G. Meade During the Gettysburg Campaign," *Gettysburg Magazine* 28, 31.

18. Meade, *Life and Letters*, 2:33; Benjamin, "Hooker's Appointment and Removal," in *Battles and Leaders*, 3:243; Byrne and Weaver, *Haskell of Gettysburg*, 93; Acken, *Inside the Army of the Potomac*, 289.

19. CCW, 14; Hyde, *The Union Generals Speak*, 32; Sickles, "Further Recollections of Gettysburg," in *North American Review*, 259.

20. OR 27/1: 482; Styple, *Our Noble Blood,* 110-111.

21. Hyde, *The Union Generals Speak,* 239; *Dedication of the New York Auxiliary State Monument*, 118; Coughenour, "Assessing the Generalship of George G. Meade During the Gettysburg Campaign," *Gettysburg Magazine* 28, 33.

22. Humphreys, *Andrew Atkinson Humphreys*, 186-187; Hyde, The Union Generals Speak, 183-184; Coughenour, "Assessing the Generalship of George G. Meade During the Gettysburg Campaign," *Gettysburg Magazine* 28, 33.

23. Hyde, *The Union Generals Speak*, 246-247; Lash, "The Congressional Resolution of Thanks for The Federal Victory at Gettysburg," *Gettysburg Magazine* 12, 88; Pfanz, *Gettysburg: The First Day*, 31.

24. OR 27/1: 61-62, 114; 27/3: 398; CCW, 329-330; Hyde, *The Union Generals Speak*, 103; Meade, *Life and Letters*, 2:3,8,11; Callihan, "Passing the Test...," *Gettysburg Magazine* 30, 32; Pfanz, *Gettysburg: The First Day*, 32; Smith, *A Famous Battery and Its Campaigns,* 98-100; Scott, *History of the One Hundred and Fifth Regiment of Pennsylvania Volunteers,* 81; Craft, *History of the 141st Regiment Pennsylvania Volunteers*, 111.

25. OR 27/2: 307, 317, 358; 27/3: 933-934; Longstreet, *From Manassas to Appomattox*, 333, 346-348; Longstreet, "Lee's Invasion of Pennsylvania," in *Battles and Leaders*, 3: 249-250; Lee, "Letter from General Fitzhugh Lee, March 5, 1877," in *SHSP*, 4:74; Freeman, *Lee's Lieutenants*, 3: 35, 49. There is some debate over whether the spy Harrison arrived on the 27th or 28th. Lee and Longstreet both said that Harrison reached camp with this intelligence on the evening of the 28th, and most historians have followed suit. However, Lee's orders to Ewell at 7:30 a.m. on June 28 began with: "I wrote you *last night*, [emphasis added] stating that General Hooker was reported to have crossed the Potomac, and is advancing by way of Middletown, the head of his column being at that point in Frederick County." See *OR* 27/3: 933-934. It is possible that Lee's note was misdated, and was actually sent the morning of the 29th, since both Ewell (See *OR* 27/2: 443) and Jubal Early (See *OR* 27/2: 467) reported receiving their orders to move toward South Mountain on the 29th. See Brown, *Retreat From Gettysburg*, 20, 422 (n.32) for a recent discussion on whether Lee decided to concentrate on the 27th or 28th.

26. OR 27/3: 395-396, 398.

27. Messent and Courtney, *Civil War Letters of Joseph Hopkins Twichell*, 247; OR 27/3: 399; Meade, *Life and Letters*, 2:12.

28. OR 27/3: 420.

29. OR 27/3: 415, 421; Meade, *Life and Letters*, 2: 15-16; Lash, "Congressional Resolution," *Gettysburg Magazine* 12, 89.

30. OR 27/1: 922-923; 27/2: 317, 358, 607, 637; 27/3: 400, 402, 414-415.

31. OR 27/3: 414-416, 418; Meade, *Life and Letters*, 2: 15-16. Howard appears to have been confused by Reynolds' lack of precise directions, telling Reynolds: "I have received both your notes. One division occupies the place you did last night, and is ordered to be held in readiness to move at short notice. Another occupies a position near the Gettysburg road, on the right of the town. Would you wish me to join you along the Gettysburg road?... Please send me word as to where you want support, in case you do. I think it important to hold these roads toward Chambersburg, do you not? I want a map of Adams County, if possible. I have nothing." See *OR* 27/3: 419.

32. OR 27/3: 407-408, 414-417, 419-420; Meade, *Life and Letters*, 2: 14-16; Coddington, *The Gettysburg Campaign*, 200-201.

33. OR 27/3: 407-408, 414-416, 419, 422; Meade, *Life and Letters*, 2: 15-16; Coddington, The Gettysburg Campaign, 231.

34. OR 27/3: 422.

35. *Ibid.*, 27/3: 424.

36. Hyde, *The Union Generals Speak*, 184.

37. OR 27/3: 424-425; Brown, *History of the Third Regiment, Excelsior Brigade*, 104; Racine, *Unspoiled Heart*, 46; Email from John Miller to author, February 9, 2008. According to Mr. Miller, the locals of the area believe that Sickles stayed at the farmhouse on MD-140 and Bull Frog Road. Miller also "used to know people who metal detected the fields and found all sorts of Union items." Although the historical marker is clearly visible along MD-140 and opposite the farm, moving traffic does not easily facilitate stopping to read it. The marker was placed by the Maryland Civil War Centennial Commision and reads: "Bridgeport. As part of General Meade's screen for Washington as the Confederates invaded Maryland and Pensylvania, the Third Corps, Army of the Potomac, arrived here June 30, 1863 from Taneytown. Next day General Daniel E. Sickles marched this corps to Emmitsburg."

38. OR 27/1: 924. At one point during the day, Reynolds thought, "if the enemy advances in force from Gettysburg, and we are to fight a defensive battle in this vicinity, that the position to be occupied is just north of the town of Emmitsburg, covering the Plank road to Taneytown. He

will undoubtedly endeavor to turn our left by way of Fairfield and the mountain roads leading down into the Frederick and Emmittsburg pike, near Mount Saint Mary's College. The above is mere surmise on my part." See OR 27/3: 417-418.

Chapter 5: The Third Corps Marches in the Right Direction

1. OR 27/1: 61-62; 27/3: 416; Ladd, *John Bachelder's History of the Battle of Gettysburg*, 196; Callihan, "Passing the Test. . . ," *Gettysburg Magazine* 30, 32; Grimsley and Simpson, *Gettysburg: A Battlefield Guide*, 12-13.

2. CCW, 330; Callihan, "Passing the Test," *Gettysburg Magazine* 30, 32.

3. OR 27/3: 458-459.

4. CCW, 295, 329-330; Hyde, *The Union Generals Speak*, 33, 105.

5. OR 27/3: 460; *Meade, Life and Letters*, 2:34; Pfanz, *Gettysburg: The First Day*, 49.

6. Tremain, *Two Days of War*, 3-8, 10-12; Brown, *History of the Third Regiment, Excelsior Brigade*, 104. General Wadsworth, commanding Reynolds' First Division, said that Reynolds was usually "very particular in communicating his orders to his division commanders," but on July 1 "he communicated none, if he had any." See Hyde, The Union Generals Speak, 229.

7. Tremain, *Two Days of War*, 12-14, 18.

8. CCW, 388-389; Hyde, *The Union Generals Speak*, 184; Craft, *History of the 141st Regiment Pennsylvania Volunteers*, 112.

9. Meade, *Life and Letters*, 2: 35-36; Hancock, *Reminiscences of Winfield S. Hancock*, 186-187; CCW, 403-404.

10. Meade, *Life and Letters*, 2: 35-36; CCW, 404; Hyde, *The Union Generals Speak*, 208.

11. OR 27/3: 461; Meade, *Life and Letters*, 2:36-37. As will be discussed later, there would be a disagreement over the wording of this order. At the Joint Committee hearings in 1864, Meade submitted a version of this order that read: "If you think the ground and position there a (better) suitable one to fight a battle. . . ." Hancock's widow and others later asserted that "better" indicated that Hancock had been given responsibility for choosing Gettysburg, while the insertion of "suitable" was afterwards designed to downplay the impression that Meade had not wanted to fight at Gettysburg and also intended to minimize Hancock's part in choosing Gettysburg. See Hancock, *Reminiscences of Winfield S. Hancock*, 186-187 and Hyde, *The Union Generals Speak*, 209.

12. OR 27/3: 461, CCW, 330, 377; Hyde, *The Union Generals Speak*, 104, 166-167.

13. OR 27/1: 61; CCW, 404-405; Hancock, *Reminiscences of Winfield S. Hancock*, 187-189; Hyde, *The Union Generals Speak*, 208-209; Tagg, *The Generals of Gettysburg*, 34, 62; Coddington, *The Gettysburg Campaign*, 284-285. Hancock, Howard, and Sickles were all promoted to major general dated 11/29/62, but Hancock was junior due to date of brigadier promotion. See Pfanz, *Gettysburg: The First Day*, 337 and Hyde, *The Union Generals Speak*, 209.

14. OR 27/1: 696, 702-703; 27/3: 463; Pfanz, *Gettysburg: The First Day*, 137.

15. Tremain, *Two Days of War*, 18; CCW, 296-297; Raver, "Deception and the Citizen-General," *Gettysburg Magazine* 31, 62. Tremain's arrival time is based on an assumption that he departed Gettysburg around 10:00 a.m. and that it took between 90 minutes and two hours to reach Emmittsburg. See Raver, reach.

16. OR 51/1: 200; Tremain, *Two Days of War*, 18; Raver, "Deception and the Citizen-General," *Gettysburg Magazine* 31, 62. Sickles' response to Howard's order is timed at 3:15 m. See OR 27/3: 463-464. Howard stated in his OR that Sickles received the message around 3:30. See OR 27/1: 703.

17. CCW, p 296-297. One presumes that Sickles' testimony should read, "My preliminary orders in going to *Emmitsburg* were to go there and hold that position with my corps." Emmitsburg was regarded as both an important flanking position to cover the rear and communications.

18. OR 27/3: 463; Tremain, *Two Days* of War, 18.

19. *Ibid.*, 27/3: 464.

20. *Ibid.*, 27/1: 482, 519, 531; 27/3: 464-465; CCW, 296-297; Smith, *A Famous Battery and Its Campaigns*, 100; Meade, *Life and Letters*, 2: 56; Hyde, *The Union Generals Speak*, 36.

21. OR 27/1: 530; 27/3: 465; CCW, 388-389; Hyde, *The Union Generals Speak,* 184-185; Humphreys, *Andrew Atkinson Humphreys*, 187-188.

22. Sickles, "Further Recollections of Gettysburg," *North American Review*, 262.

23. Rafferty, "Gettysburg," in *Personal Recollections of the War of the Rebellion*, 10; Sears, *Gettysburg*, 190-191.

24. Raver, "Deception and the Citizen-General," *Gettysburg Magazine* 31, 62-63; OR 27/1: 482, 703.

25. Hyde, *The Union Generals Speak*, 35-36.

26. OR 27/3: 466.

27. A. Wilson Greene, "Howard and Eleventh Corps Leadership," in *The First Day at Gettysburg*, 78-79, 85-86; Hunt, "The First Day at Gettysburg," in *Battles and Leaders*, 3:281; Meade, *Life and Letters*, 2:53-54; CCW, 404-405; OR 27/1: 696-697, 704; Pfanz, *Gettysburg: The First Day*, 338; Hancock, *Reminiscences of Winfield S. Hancock*, 189-190.

28. Meade, *Life and Letters*, 2: 54; OR 27/1: 252; 27/2: 307-308; Hunt, "The First Day at Gettysburg," in *Battles and Leaders*, 3:283-284; Hancock, *Reminiscences of Winfield S. Hancock*, 189-190; Pfanz, *Gettysburg: The First Day*, 333-335, 344-345; Longstreet, *From Manassas to Appomattox*, 359; Freeman, *Lee's Lieutenants*, 3: 90-99, 171-172.

29. Longstreet, "Lee's Right Wing at Gettysburg," in *Battles and Leaders*, 3: 339; OR 27/2: 308; Fremantle, *Three Months in the Southern States*, p 255-256. As a general rule, the later Longstreet's account was written, the generally more agitated was his portrayal of Lee's decision making. For a discussion of Longstreet's varying accounts of this conversation, see Freeman, *Lee's Lieutenants*, 3: 108-109. Also compare *Battles and Leaders* 3: 339 with *From Manassas to Appomattox*, 357-359.

30. OR 27/1: 696-697, 704. Howard stated that Slocum arrived around 7:00, but Hancock wrote at 5:25 that "Slocum is now coming on the ground. . . ." See OR 27/1: 366.

31. *Ibid.*, 27/1: 825; CCW, 405.

32. OR 27/1: 71-72, 366; Hancock, *Reminiscences of Winfield Scott Hancock*, 191-193; Hyde, *The Union Generals Speak*, 105, 124, 212-213; Meade, *Life and Letters*, 2: 37-39; Biddle, "General Meade at Gettysburg," in *The Annals of the War*, 210-211. There was some debate later as to whether Meade decided to concentrate at Gettysburg before or after receiving Hancock's endorsement of the Cemetery Hill position. There were conflicting accounts as to whether Meade sent his 6:00 dispatches before or after hearing the verbal report of Hancock's aide. In one version, Meade responded to the 4:00 report by stating, "I will bring up the troops." See Hancock, *Reminiscences of Winfield Scott Hancock*, 191-193, and Hyde, *The Union Generals Speak*, 105, 124. Meade's staffer James Biddle emphasized in *The Annals of the War* (210-211) that Meade concentrated the army "without waiting to hear from Hancock" and that the first message from Hancock did not arrive until 6:30.

33. OR 27/3: 467-468; Meade, *Life and Letters*, 2: 40.

34. OR 51/1: 200-201.

35. Tremain, *Two Days of War*, 22-23, 27-28, 30-31.

36. CCW, 297; OR 27/1: 482; Meade, *Life and Letters*, 2:56; Tremain, *Two Days of War*, 31-32; Craft, *History of the 141st Regiment Pennsylvania Volunteers*, 117. Birney reported that he arrived at 5:30; but Hancock wrote at 5:25 that the Third Corps had not yet arrived, and both Howard and Meade reported that Sickles arrived about 7:00. See OR 27/1: 704.

37. CCW, 297; Hyde, *The Union Generals Speak*, 37, 211.

38. OR 27/3: 468.

39. Sickles, "Further Recollections of Gettysburg," in *North American Review*, 262-263.

40. CCW, 297.

41. OR 27/3: 464; Charles Graham account, February 16, 1865, Participant Accounts File 5, GNMP.

42. Frassanito, *Early Photography at Gettysburg*, 151-152.

43. CCW, 405; Hyde, *The Union Generals Speak,* 213; Byrne and Weaver, *Haskell of Gettysburg,* 102. Once again there is an inference from Hancock and supporters that Meade had chosen Gettysburg based upon Hancock's advice. But for an opposing viewpoint, Henry Hunt, who had a significant personality clash with Hancock, stressed that Hancock's reports were "not very encouraging" and that Meade's decision was based on information received from "others." Historical accuracy is often dependent on which version one chooses to believe. See Hunt, "The Second Day at Gettysburg," in *Battles and Leaders,* 3: 291-292.

44. Meade, *Life and Letters,* 2:41, Hunt, "The Second Day at Gettysburg," in *Battles and Leaders,* 3: 291-292; Pfanz, *Gettysburg: The Second Day,* 42; Rollins, "George Gordon Meade and the Defense of Cemetery Ridge," *Gettysburg Magazine* 19, 73; Byrne and Weaver, *Haskell of Gettysburg,* 103; Styple, *Generals in Bronze,* 177.

45. Meade, *Life and Letters,* 2:41, 62-63, Hunt, "The Second Day at Gettysburg," in *Battles and Leaders,* 3: 291-292; Pfanz, *Gettysburg: The Second Day,* 58-59; Rollins, "George Gordon Meade and the Defense of Cemetery Ridge," *Gettysburg Magazine* 19, 73-75; Coddington, *The Gettysburg Campaign,* 330, 716 (n..34); Styple, *Generals in Bronze,* 177.

46. Carter, *Four Brothers in Blue,* 317-319. Sickles is frequently taken to task for claiming ignorance of Geary's July 1st position and for not utilizing the Paine map to place his corps on the morning of July 2nd. But the Paine map copy that is often reprinted, which may not even be the same map that Paine actually prepared that morning, does not place Sickles, Geary, or any other troops on Little Round Top. If Sickles was told to replace Geary's position on July 2nd, then there is actually evidence to suggest that the Paine map would have offered him no clarity. See Rollins, "George Gordon Meade and the Defense of Cemetery Ridge," *Gettysburg Magazine* 19, 74-75, including n. 100 on 74.

47. CCW, 389; Hyde, *The Union Generals Speak,* 184-185; Meade, *Life and Letters,* 2: 59-60; Humphreys, *Andrew Atkinson Humphreys,* 188. The doctor was probably either Andrew or Robert Anan of Emmitsburg. See Pfanz, *Gettysburg: The Second Day,* 44, 474 (n.44) and Humphreys, 190.

48. CCW, 389; Hyde, *The Union Generals Speak,* 185-186; OR 27/1: 531.

49. OR 27/1: 543; Humphreys, *Andrew Atkinson Humphreys,* 188, 190; Rafferty, "Gettysburg," in *Personal Recollections of the War of the Rebellion,* 5.

50. CCW, 389-390; Hyde, *The Union Generals Speak,* 185-186; OR 27/1: 531; Humphreys, *Andrew Atkinson Humphreys,* 191-192; Meade, *Life and Letters,* 2: 56; Rafferty, "Gettysburg," in *Personal Recollections of the War of the Rebellion,* 5. Humphreys later replayed this story in some detail for the Congressional Committee on the Conduct of the War because, he said, "to explain why it was that I was so late in getting upon the field." Humphreys may also have blamed his division's July 2nd performance on its exhausted condition, and he also probably enjoyed highlighting the breakdown in Sickles' communication chain.

Chapter 6: In Some Doubt as to Where He Should Go

1. OR 27/1: 519 ; Styple, *Our Noble Blood,* 116; Haynes, *A History of the Second Regiment, New Hampshire Volunteer Infantry,* 166-167; Smith, *A Famous Battery and Its Campaigns,* 100; Toombs, *New Jersey Troops,* 180. Historian Edwin Coddington took Graham, de Trobriand, and Burling to task for not departing Emmitsburg immediately upon receiving their orders. He noted that Meade's orders did not allow for any delay in departure. See Coddington, *The Gettysburg Campaign,* 335. But the participant accounts do not indicate that there was any intentional delay; simply that in the darkness it took some time to bring the scattered command back together. Graham said the "troops were immediately withdrawn and took up their march." See Charles Graham account, *February* 16, 1865, Participant Accounts File 5, GNMP.

2. OR 27/1: 914-915, 927-928, 939, 1032 ; R.L. Murray, *E.P Alexander and the Artillery Action in the Peach Orchard,* 45; Pfanz, *Gettysburg: The Second Day,* 86, 88-89, 97, 105, 131, 485 (n. 53); Petruzzi, "John Buford at Gettysburg," in *America's Civil War,* 37.

3. Tremain, *Two Days of War,* 36-40 ; Craft, *History of the 141st Regiment Pennsylvania Volunteers,* 117-118; Scott, *History of the One Hundred and Fifth Regiment of Pennsylvania Volunteers,* 82.

4. Tremain, *Two Days of War*, 36-40; *OR* 27/1: 498, 500; *Pennsylvania at Gettysburg*, 1: 387, 393; Scott, *History of the One Hundred and Fifth Regiment of Pennsylvania Volunteers,* 82; Georg, "The Sherfy Farm and the Battle of Gettysburg," 8; Fasnacht, *Historical Sketch 99th Pennsylvania*, 8-9.

5. Georg, *The Sherfy Farm and the Battle of Gettysburg*, .2-6 ; Lossing, *Pictorial History of the Civil War*, 3:65; Imhof, *Gettysburg Day Two*, 8; Coco, *A Strange and Blighted Land,* 38.

6. Georg, "The Sherfy Farm and the Battle of Gettysburg," 6; Imhof, *Gettysburg Day Two: A Study in Maps*, 10; *Survey Report for Restoration and Rehabilitation of Historic Structures: Wentz Buildings*, GNMP, January 31, 1957; Haynes, *A History of the Second Regiment, New Hampshire Volunteer Infantry*, 170-171.

7. Georg, "The Sherfy Farm and the Battle of Gettysburg," 8-9; Imhof, *Gettysburg Day Two*, 5-8.

8. Tremain, *Two Days of War,* 40-42. Tremain's memoirs are obviously biased towards Sickles and against Meade. Upon receipt of Birney's report, Tremain wrote that he then reported to Meade, who told him that cavalry would be placed as a screen on Sickles' left. This is a questionable recollection since Buford's cavalry had already been placed on the Union left flank on the evening of July 1.

9. Meade, *Life and Letters*, 2: 63-64; Coddington, *The Gettysburg Campaign*, 333; Byrne and Weaver, *Haskell of Gettysburg*, 103.

10. *OR* 27/1: 592-593, 600; Hunt, "The Second Day at Gettysburg," in *Battles and Leaders of the Civil War*, 3:296; Meade, *Life and Letters*, 2: 63-64. The accounts of both Hunt and Captain George Meade confirm that the Fifth Corps was originally placed in reserve near Rock Creek and the Baltimore Pike to support Twelfth Corps.

11. Bigelow, *The Peach Orchard*, 51; Coddington, *The Gettysburg Campaign*, 332-333.

12. Tremain, *Two Days of War*, 42-43.

13. Hyde, *The Union Generals Speak*, 106, 167; Hunt, "The Second Day at Gettysburg," in *Battles and Leaders of the Civil War*, 3:297.

14. Hyde, *The Union Generals Speak*, 232-23.

15. *OR* 27/1: 825, 839. The regimental history of the 141st Pennsylvania regiment also states that the 5th Ohio and 147th Pennsylvania occupied Little Round Top during the morning of the 2nd. See Craft, *History of the 141st Regiment Pennsylvania Volunteers*, 118.

16. *OR* 27/1: 115-116.

17. CCW, 297.

18. *OR* 27/1: 482.

19. Meade, *Life and Letters*, 2: 73; George Meade Jr. to Alexander Webb, December 2, 1885, Alexander Webb Papers, Manuscripts and Archives, Yale University Library. There must be some license in Captain Meade's claim that he considered the Third Corps "posted comfortably" at 7:00 AM, since nearly two hours later Captain Meade would be claiming that he had no knowledge of the position that his father intended Sickles to be in.

20. CCW, 331.

21. Craft, *History of the 141st Regiment Pennsylvania Volunteers*, 118; Hyde, *The Union Generals Speak*, 38, 107; Meade, *Life and Letters*, 2: 354; Carter, *Four Brothers in Blue*, 317-319. Private (later Captain) Carter, of the 22nd Massachusetts (Tilton's brigade), specifically stated in his memoirs that Sickles did not receive written orders. Carter's account, published in 1913, was presumably based on second-hand information, perhaps Meade's own account.

22. Rafferty, in *Personal Recollections of the War of the Rebellion*, 6-8; Fasnacht, *Historical Sketch 99th Pennsylvania*, 8.

23. *New York at Gettysburg*, 1: 342-343; Sears, *Chancellorsville*, 235-237.

24. Meade, *Life and Letters*, 2:66.

25. *Ibid.*, 2: 66-67.

26. *Ibid.*, 2: 67.

27. *Ibid.*

28. *CCW*, 297; Charles Graham account, February 16, 1865, Participants File 5, GNMP; *OR* 27/1: 519-520, 522; Haynes, *A History of the Second Regiment, New Hampshire Volunteer Infantry*,

167-168; Smith, *A Famous Battery and Its Campaigns,* 101; Rafferty, in *Personal Recollections of the War of the Rebellion,* 6-8; Humphreys, *Andrew Atkinson Humphreys,* 192; Coddington, *The Gettysburg Campaign,* 335-336; Styple, *Our Noble Blood,* 116 . Several accounts, such as Captain Smith's and the 141st Pennsylvania's regimental history, timed their arrival around 9:00 a.m. See Craft, *History of the 141st Regiment Pennsylvania Volunteers,* 118.

29. Rafferty, "Gettysburg," in *Personal Recollections of the War of the Rebellion,* 7; OR 27/1: 511; Humphreys, *Andrew Atkinson Humphreys: A Biography,* 192; *Pennsylvania at Gettysburg,* 2:606; Hyde, *The Union Generals Speak,* 187-188. Historian Bill Hyde thought it "curious that Sickles felt it necessary to issue such a direction to Humphreys, a professional military man. There is no record that Sickles issued a similar order to Birney, a political general. . . . Birney did not remove the fences in his front, and his negligence created problems for the artillery in the battle, resulting in costly delays." However, Colonel Benjamin L. Higgins, of the 86th New York in Ward's brigade (Birney's division) clearly reported that at 10:00 "I was ordered by General Ward to send forward a sufficient body of men . . . to demolish all stone walls and fences in our front to the Emmitsburg road."

30. OR 27/1: 585; Pfanz, *Gettysburg: The Second Day,* 133; Murray, *E. Alexander and the Artillery Action in the Peach Orchard,* 45. Pfanz assumes that someone in authority such as Birney perceived a special threat along the Emmitsburg Road at this early hour. Murray seems to suggest that Clark was positioned to support Berdan's mid-afternoon reconnaissance. Unfortunately Clark specifically reported the move as occurring about 9:30 A.M., at least ninety minutes earlier than Berdan's afternoon mission. If this scenario is accurate, then Clark reported the time inaccurately, which unfortunately for historians was not an uncommon practice.

31. CCW, 297-298; Meade, *Life and Letters,* 2:70-71; Johnson, *Campfire and Battlefield,* 263. Sickles' claim to "not receive any orders" is often misinterpreted as a contention by Sickles that he never received any orders from Meade at any time during the morning. Since there is ample evidence to the contrary, this would be clear proof that much of Sickles' Congressional testimony was an outright lie. But Sickles' own earlier testimony clearly admitted that he received orders to relieve Geary earlier that morning, and that he "did not receive any [further] orders" when he expressed confusion over Geary's position. Sickles may ultimately still have been lying over this latter point, but that fabrication is not nearly as conclusive as it would have been if Sickles claimed to receive no orders of any kind from Meade at any time during the morning. See Hyde, *The Union Generals Speak,* 38-39; Downs, "His Left Was Worth a Glance," in *Gettysburg Magazine* 7, 39; "Gen. Sickles Speaks Out," New York *Times,* August 14, 1886.

32. Meade, *Life and Letters,* 2:70-71; CCW, 298; Hyde, The Union Generals Speak, 41, 107.

33. Hunt, "The Second Day at Gettysburg," in *Battles and Leaders,* 3: 301; OR 27/1: 232.

34. Meade, *Life and Letters,* 2:70-71; Hunt, "The Second Day at Gettysburg," in *Battles and Leaders,* 3: 301; CCW, 298; Hyde, *The Union Generals Speak,* 40-41. Hyde believed that Henry Hunt did not support Sickles' claim that they were to examine "the best line for us to occupy." This author disagrees with Hyde's conclusion, since Hunt clearly wrote that Meade told Hunt, in Sickles' presence, that he "wished me to examine a new line."

35. Meade, *Life and Letters,* 2:73-74; CCW, 298; Hunt, "The Second Day at Gettysburg," in *Battles and Leaders,* 3: 301. Note that Hunt omits references to this meeting in his Official Report.

36. Quoted in Sauers, *Gettysburg: The Meade-Sickles Controversy,* 157.

37. Hunt," The Second Day at Gettysburg," in *Battles and Leaders of the Civil War,* 3:301; Meade, *Life and Letters,* 2: 74; Powell, "Advance to Disaster," *Gettysburg Magazine* 28, 40 ; Busey and Martin, *Regimental Strengths and Losses,* 245; Adelman and Smith, *Devil's Den,* 5-6.

38. Hunt, "The Second Day at Gettysburg," in *Battles and Leaders,* 3: 301-302; Powell, "Advance to Disaster," *Gettysburg Magazine* 28, 40.

39. Hunt, "The Second Day at Gettysburg," in *Battles and Leaders,* 3: 301-302.

40. Meade, *Life and Letters,* 2:73-74; Hunt, "The Second Day at Gettysburg," in *Battles and Leaders,* 3: 301-302; Powell, "Advance to Disaster," in *Gettysburg Magazine* 28, 40.

41. Meade, *Life and Letters,* 2: 73-74; Hunt, "The Second Day at Gettysburg," in *Battles and Leaders,* 3: 301-302; CCW, 298.

42. Meade, *Life and Letters*, 2: 73-74; Hunt, "The Second Day at Gettysburg," in *Battles and Leaders*, 3: 301-302.

43. Hunt, "The Second Day at Gettysburg," in *Battles and Leaders*, 3: 302.

44. *Ibid.*, 3: 302-303.

45. *Ibid.*, 3: 302-303; Meade, *Life and Letters*, 2:73-74.

46. Hunt, "The Second Day at Gettysburg," in *Battles and Leaders,* 3: 303; Meade, *Life and Letters*, 2: 74-75.

47. Tremain, *Two Days of War*, 44-45; Ladd, *The Bachelder Papers*, 1:192.

Chapter 7: No Relation to the General Line of Battle

1. OR 27/2: 446; Early, "Reply To General Longstreet," in *SHSP*, 4: 285-286; Taylor, "Second Paper By Colonel Walter H. Taylor," in *SHSP*, 4: 129; Allan, "Memoranda of Conversations With Lee," in *Lee the Soldier*, 14; Freeman, *Lee's Lieutenants*, 3: 100-105; Pfanz, *Culp's Hill and Cemetery Hill*, 82-87.

2. Longstreet, *From Manassas to Appomattox*, 362; Fremantle, *Three Months in the Southern States*, 257; John B. Hood to James Longstreet, June 28, 1875, reprinted in SHSP, 4:147-148; Samuel Johnston to Fitzhugh Lee, February 11, 1878; Johnston to Lafayette McLaws, June 27, 1892. Copies of both letters are on file at GNMP; Hyde, "Did You Get There?," *Gettysburg Magazine* 29, 86-88. Other reconnaissances were done that morning by Armistead Long and William N. Pendleton. All of these would contribute toward Lee's decision to attack Meade's left. See Pfanz, *Gettysburg: The Second Day*, 105-107.

3. McLaws, "Gettysburg," in *SHSP*, 4: 68-69; Sorrel, *At the Right Hand of Longstreet,* 167.

4. Samuel Johnston to Fitzhugh Lee, February 11, 1878; Johnston to Lafayette McLaws, June 27, 1892, both copies on file at GNMP.

5. Longstreet, "Lee's Right Wing at Gettysburg," in *Battles and Leaders*, 3: 340; Longstreet, *From Manassas to Appomattox*, 363-365; Freeman, *Lee's Lieutenants*, 3: 114-115; Sorrel, *At the Right Hand of Longstreet*, 167; Pfanz, *Gettysburg: The Second Day*, 111-113; Hyde, "Did You get There?," *Gettysburg Magazine* 29, 86-91. Hyde speculated that Johnston reached Big Round Top (this author agrees that Big Round Top is a more likely scenario than Little Round Top) around 5:30 a.m., and given the time of his trip, it was actually not so mysterious that Johnston missed seeing or hearing Federal troops in that locale. Hyde also believed that Johnston could have easily slipped through Buford's cavalry line, which might have stretched 2800-2900 exhausted men for as long as nine miles.

6. Alexander, "The Great Charge and Artillery Fighting at Gettysburg," in *Battles and Leaders*, 3:359; Alexander, "Letter From General E. P. Alexander," in *SHSP*, 4: 101-102; Alexander, *Military Memoirs*, 392; McLaws, "Gettysburg," in *SHSP*, 7:69; Kershaw, "Kershaw's Brigade at Gettysburg," in *Battles and Leaders*, 3:331; Longstreet, "Lee's Right Wing at Gettysburg," in *Battles and Leaders*, 3:340; Longstreet, *From Manassas to Appomattox*, 366; Johnston to Lafayette McLaws, June 27, 1892, copy on file at GNMP; Freeman, *Lee's Lieutenants*, 3: 116; Pfanz, *Gettysburg: The Second Day*, 118-119. Taking a route today from the intersection of Black Horse Tavern and Fairfield Roads to Willoughby Run Road, and then following the road past Pitzer's Schoolhouse to the Millerstown Road, and then onto Seminary Ridge covers 2.3 miles.

7. Meade, *Life and Letters*, 2: 73-74; Hunt, "The Second Day at Gettysburg," in *Battles and Leaders*, 3: 301-302; Tremain, *Two Days of War*, 45-48 ; OR 27/1: 482, 515-516; OR 25/1: 386; Marcot, "Berdan Sharpshooters at Gettysburg," *Gettysburg Magazine* 1, 39.

8. OR 27/1: 482, 516-517; Murray, *Letters from Gettysburg*, 82; Pfanz, *Gettysburg: The Second Day*, 98-99; Marcot, "Berdan Sharpshooters at Gettysburg," *Gettysburg Magazine* 1, 37-39.

9. Tremain, *Two Days of War*, 49-50; OR 27/3: 1086. Writing his memoirs over forty years later, Tremain claimed that he had several meetings with Meade that afternoon. In Tremain's narrative, additional artillery support was discussed at a meeting after Berdan's reconnaissance, and it is plausible that the above referenced order was issued at that time. However, based on the time of this message, and for reasons that will be discussed later, I question whether the later

meetings actually occurred as he described. See Tremain, *Two Days of War*, 54-61 and Pfanz, *Gettysburg: The Second Day*, 138-139.

10. OR 27/1: 482, 507, 515-517; 27/2: 613, 617; Marcot, "Berdan Sharpshooters at Gettysburg," *Gettysburg Magazine* 1, 37; Pfanz, *Gettysburg: The Second Day*, 98-101; Murray, *Letters from Gettysburg*, 82.

11. OR 27/3: 487-488.

12. *Ibid.*, 27/1: 914-915, 927-928, 939, 1032; 27/3: 1086; Meade, *Life and Letters*, 2:71; Wittenberg, "The Truth About the Withdrawal of Brig. Gen. John Buford's Cavalry," *Gettysburg Magazine* 37, 71-77; Petruzzi, "John Buford at Gettysburg," *America's Civil War*, 37; Pfanz, *Gettysburg: The Second Day*, 86, 97, 105, 131, 485 (n. 53). Buford's division suffered approximately 176 total casualties out of 4,073 engaged, for a less than 5% casualty rate, but that included forty-nine casualties of Wesley Merritt's 1,321-man brigade. The epilogue of the motion picture *Gettysburg* has helped popularize the notion that Buford suffered significant casualties on July 1. In the film, his "shattered" division is withdrawn to guard the supply trains.

13. OR 27/1: 914-915, 927-928, 939, 1032; 27/3: 490; Meade, *Life and Letters* 2:71; Pfanz, *Gettysburg: The Second Day*, 86, 97, 105, 131, 485 (n. 53).

14. OR 27/3: 487-488.

15. *Ibid.*, 27/1: 116; Hyde, *The Union Generals Speak*, 253-254.

16. OR 27/1: 482-483, 515 – 516; Marcot, "Berdan Sharpshooters at Gettysburg," *Gettysburg Magazine* 1, 37.

17. Marcot, "Berdan Sharpshooters at Gettysburg," *Gettysburg Magazine* 1, 39; Pfanz, *Gettysburg: The Second Day*, 101.

18. See Pfanz, *Gettysburg: The Second Day*, 101-102. Harry Pfanz argued that the morning skirmishing should have left "no doubt that there were Confederates in Spangler's Woods . . . Thus the only new information that Berdan's men could have provided was that the Confederates in some force were moving into the north end of Pitzer's Woods. Berdan might have assumed more and told a greater tale, but that is all his expedition uncovered and all he could rightly report. He could have seen nothing of Longstreet's corps, for it was out of his sight. His force might have delayed Wilcox's brigade in occupying its position on Anderson's right, but this was a meaningless achievement. . . ." The point is that the entire Third Corps leadership "*assumed more*"—they assumed that the discovery confirmed Confederate movements toward their left. Ironically, although Sickles assumption was based on a discovery of Wilcox instead of Longstreet, the conclusion reached was essentially correct. Confederates were planning an attack on his left.

19. Sickles, "Introduction," in *Lee and Longstreet at High Tide*, 23-24.

20. *Ibid.* Longstreet later that he abandoned secrecy because he believed he may have been seen near Black Horse Tavern by the Union signal station on Little Round Top. "It seemed to me useless, therefore, to delay the troops any longer with the idea of concealing the movement, and the two divisions advanced." If true, why did Longstreet countermarch his column?. Longstreet, "Lee's Right Wing at Gettysburg," *Battles and Leaders*, 3: 340.

21. OR 27/1: 483, 486.

22. Hyde, *The Union Generals Speak*, 187-188; OR 27/1: 531-532, 558-559; Humphreys, *Andrew Atkinson Humphreys*, 192.

23. OR 27/1: 533; Imhof, *Gettysburg Day Two*, 10-15.

24. OR 27/1: 483, 531, Hyde, *The Union Generals Speak*, 187-189.

25. Ladd, *The Bachelder Papers*, 2: 1194; Hyde, *The Union Generals Speak*, 214; Byrne and Weaver, *Haskell of Gettysburg*, 117; Favill, *Diary of a Young Army Officer*, 245.

26. Ladd, *The Bachelder Papers*, 3: 1354.

27. Byrne and Weaver, *Haskell of Gettysburg*, 117. It must be said, that despite Haskell's posturing against non-professional political soldiers, Haskell was an "amateur" himself. Prior to the war, Haskell had been an attorney and fledgling local political candidate in Wisconsin. Perhaps Haskell's resentment against politicals such as Sickles resulted from the differences in rank. See Byrne and Weaver, 2-16.

28. Rafferty, "Gettysburg," in *Personal Recollections of the War of the Rebellion*, 7-8.

29. OR 27/1: 581-582.

30. Tremain, *Two Days of War*, 104.

31. OR 27/1: 483; Smith, *A Famous Battery and Its Campaigns*, 101-102; Imhof, *Gettysburg Day Two*, 10-15.

32. OR 27/1: 520, 582; Styple, *Our Noble Blood*, 116; Imhof, *Gettysburg Day Two*, 10-15; Jorgensen, *The Wheatfield at Gettysburg: A Walking Tour*, 30-31.

33. Haynes, *A History of the Second Regiment, New Hampshire Volunteer Infantry in the War of the Rebellion*, 169-170; Craft, *History of the 141st Regiment Pennsylvania Volunteers*, 119; Scott, *History of the One Hundred and Fifth Regiment of Pennsylvania Volunteers,* 82; Imhof, *Gettysburg Day Two*, 10-15.

34. Imhof, *Gettysburg Day* Two, 12-17; Scott, *History of the One Hundred and Fifth Regiment of Pennsylvania Volunteers,* 82; Ladd, *The Bachelder Papers*, 1: 193.

35. Rafferty, "Gettysburg," in *Personal Recollections of the War of the Rebellion*, 6-8, 10-11.

36. McLaws, "Gettysburg," in SHSP, 7:69-71.

37. OR 27/2: 298-299, 308-309.

38. *Ibid.*, 27/2: 318-319.

39. *Ibid.*, 27/2: 358-359. Calef's battery had been stationed near the Peach Orchard in the morning, and Judson Clark's battery had also been placed in advance of Cemetery Ridge. It's plausible that either battery could have been referred to by Lee.

40. *Ibid.*, 27/2: 318-319.

41. *Ibid.*, 27/2: 358-359; Cooksey, "Up The Emmitsburg Road," *Gettysburg Magazine* 26, 50-52. Cooksey notes that too many historians make the mistake of using information that was unavailable to Lee to decipher his plans. The question is less a matter of where the Union line actually was, and more a question of where Lee *thought* the line was. Anyone who has ever stood in front of the present-day North Carolina monument can see the increasingly deceptive terrain as the Emmitsburg Road winds south. While apparent to modern students, who spend countless hours walking the field and debating the battle, we need to remember that Lee and Longstreet had been on the ground for less than 24 hours when they formulated their July 2 attack.

42. Oeffinger, *A Soldier's General,* 195-196.

43. OR 27/2: 367-368.

44. *Ibid.*, 27/2: 367-368.

45. *Ibid.*, 27/2: 367-368; Oeffinger, *A Soldier's General,* 195-196; Freeman, *Lee's Lieutenants*, 3:118.

46. OR 27/2: 375, 429.

47. *Ibid.*, 27/2: 380.

48. *Ibid.*, 27/2: 358-359; Cooksey, "Up The Emmitsburg Road," *Gettysburg Magazine* 26, 45-48. Cooksey proposed that the Confederates probably believed that the Union line ended along the Emmitsburg Road somewhere between the Rogers and Codori houses. In this scenario, the original plan called for McLaws to deploy in the low ground just south of the Peach Orchard before sweeping up the Emmitsburg Road.

49. OR 27/2: 308-309, 318-320, 359.

50. Hunt, "The Second Day at Gettysburg," in *Battles and Leaders*, 3:300.

51. Sauers, *Gettysburg: The Meade-Sickles Controversy*, 155-156. Sauers seems to have accepted the premise that Lee believed Meade's line ended on Cemetery Ridge, not on the Emmitsburg Road.

52. Cooksey, "Up The Emmitsburg Road," *Gettysburg Magazine* 26, 49; Imhof, *Gettysburg: Day Two*, 17.

53. Longstreet, "Lee's Right Wing at Gettysburg," in *Battles and Leaders,* 3:340-341.

54. McLaws, "Gettysburg," in SHSP, 7:72; Oeffinger, *A Soldier's General,* 195-196; Pfanz, *Gettysburg: The Second Day*, 152-153; Longstreet, *From Manassas to Appomattox*, 366-367.

55. OR 27/2: 367-368, 372. The report of Major R. C. Maffett of Kershaw's 3rd South Carolina further confirmed Kershaw's "swing toward the Peach Orchard" objective.

Chapter 8: Isn't Your Line Too Much Extended?

1. *OR* 27/3: 1086; Meade, *Life and Letters*, 2: 71-72.

2. *OR* 27/1: 72.

3. *Ibid.*, 27/1: 467-468; Hyde, *The Union Generals Speak*, 253-255; Meade, *Life and Letters*, 2: 181-183; Coughenour, "Assessing the Generalship of George G. Meade During the Gettysburg Campaign," *Gettysburg Magazine* 28, 34.

4. *OR* 27/1: 467-468; Hyde, *The Union Generals Speak*, 253-254.

5. Hunt, "The Second Day at Gettysburg," in *Battles and Leaders*, 3: 297-301.

6. Sickles, "Further Recollections of Gettysburg," in *North American Review*, 265.

7. Meade, *Life and Letters*, 2: 72-73; Hyde, *The Union Generals Speak*, 168; Toombs, *New Jersey Troops*, 199; Biddle, "General Meade at Gettysburg," in *The Annals of the War*, 211.

8. Hyde, *The Union Generals Speak*, 44. Henry Tremain also contributed to the confusion over the chain of events that led up to Sickles being summoned to headquarters at 3:00 p.m. Tremain said that, following Berdan's reconnaissance, Tremain had been sent to headquarters for yet another status report. In this meeting, Tremain said that the conversation primarily centered on the need for more artillery in the new position. If Tremain is to be believed, then Meade authorized the drawing of artillery from the Artillery Reserve, but incredibly there was no further discussion on why this was needed. Tremain returned to the Peach Orchard, where he now discovered Hood's division crossing the Emmitsburg Road to the south! Sickles supposedly sent Tremain to headquarters once again, and this time Meade responded by summoning Sickles to headquarters. Tremain returned to Sickles, but to Tremain, Meade's invitation did not seem urgent, so Sickles declined the request! It was not until two more couriers arrived from Meade that Sickles finally realized that he must report to headquarters. While Harry Pfanz admits that Tremain is unfortunately the only available source for this remarkable chain of meetings, he seems to have accepted it as the correct series of events. See Tremain, *Two Days of War*, 54-61 and Pfanz, *Gettysburg: The Second Day*, 138-139. In contrast, Edwin Coddington has Sickles completely skipping the 3:00 p.m. meeting. In Coddington's version, Meade visited the left flank shortly before 4:00 m. to supervise posting of the Fifth Corps and, finally, to inspect Sickles' position. Meade was stunned to see where Sickles was posted, and summoned him directly on the field. Coddington, *The Gettysburg Campaign*, 344-345. The version supported by Coddington is consistent with Meade's Congressional testimony and Meade's report. Author Bill Hyde, in examining the Congressional testimony, speculates that Meade omitted the particulars of the 3:00 p.m. meeting either because he knew it could be used to portray him as timid and indecisive, or he may have simply forgotten the incident. See Hyde, *The Union Generals Speak*, 107-109. Captain George Meade admitted the meeting in *Life and Letters*. See Meade, *Life and Letters*, 2: 72-73.

9. Hyde, *The Union Generals Speak*, 44; Meade, *Life and Letters*, 2:72-73; Tremain, *Two Days of War*, 60-61; Sickles, "Further Recollections of Gettysburg," in *North American Review*, 265-266.

10. Hyde, *The Union Generals Speak*, 44; Tremain, *Two Days of War*, 62; Toombs, *New Jersey Troops*, 195.

11. Meade, *Life and Letters*, 2: 72-73; Trudeau, *Gettysburg: A Testing of Courage*, 320; Coddington, *The Gettysburg Campaign*, 388.

12. Meade, *Life and Letters*, 2: 72-73; *OR* 27/1: 116.

13. Hyde, *The Union Generals Speak*, 108.

14. Meade, *Life and Letters*, 2:78-79. In James Biddle's version, Sickles offered to withdraw and Meade replied that the enemy would not allow it. Before he finished the sentence, Longstreet's artillery opened. See Biddle, "General Meade at Gettysburg," in *The Annals of the War*, 211.

15. Hyde, *The Union Generals Speak*, 44-45.

16. *Ibid.* 45.

17. Undated Newspaper Clipping, J. Howard Wert Scrapbook, *Battle of Gettysburg*, Vol. 3, #34, 7, ACHS; Sickles, "Further Recollections of Gettysburg," in *North American Review*, 266; Tremain, *Two Days of War*, 62-63, 104.

18. Meade, *Life and Letters*, 2:68.

19. Rafferty, "Gettysburg," in *Personal Recollections of the War of the Rebellion*, 12. For a thorough defense of Meade's role, see Downs, "His Left Was Worth a Glance," in *Gettysburg Magazine* 7, 29-40.

20. Hyde, *The Union Generals Speak*, 168; Norton, *Attack and Defense of Little Round Top*, 308-311; Coddington, *The Gettysburg Campaign*, 388, 740 (n. 206); Desjardins, *Stand Firm Ye Boys From Maine*, 36.

21. Humphreys, *Andrew Atkinson Humphreys*, 193; Meade, *Life and Letters*, 2: 82-83; Woods, "Humphreys' Division's Flank March To Little Round Top," *Gettysburg Magazine* 6, 59.

22. Humphreys, *Andrew Atkinson Humphreys*, 193-194; Woods, "Humphreys' Division's Flank March To Little Round Top," *Gettysburg Magazine* 6, 60. Humphreys later told an acquaintance that "My official report is of course a lifeless affair, an exact statement of facts which have a certain value, but that which makes the thrilling interest of a battle is the personal incident, and of that I could, if I had leisure, tell a good deal. . . ." See Humphreys, 194.

23. Alexander, "The Great Charge and Artillery Fighting at Gettysburg," in *Battles and Leaders*, 3: 359-360; Pfanz, *Gettysburg: The Second Day*, 303; Murray, *E.Alexander and the Artillery Action in the Peach Orchard*, 72-73, 81.

24. Alexander, "The Great Charge and Artillery Fighting at Gettysburg," in *Battles and Leaders*, 3: 359; Alexander, *Military Memoirs*, 395.

25. Alexander, *Military Memoirs*, 395; Murray, *E.Alexander and the Artillery Action in the Peach Orchard*, 41-44; Pfanz, *Gettysburg: The Second Day*, 160; Coco, *A Concise Guide to the Artillery at Gettysburg*, 55. Murray's excellent study of the Peach Orchard artillery fight concludes that Alexander began with only eleven of Henry's guns and fourteen of Cabell's deployed. Murray assumes Alexander had a total of fifty-nine at his disposal, a minor discrepancy from Alexander's own estimate of fifty-four. Given the amount of attention, or lack of, devoted to the July 2 artillery battle, there is frequently a discrepancy in the number of guns that Alexander actually deployed. Alexander wrote in *Military Memoirs* (395) that he opened with thirty-six guns against the Peach Orchard and ten additional guns "against the enemy's left." Several modern studies, such as Greg Coco's *A Concise Guide to the Artillery at Gettysburg* (55-56), follow the lead and have Alexander initiate the assault with thirty-six guns (from Cabell's and his own battalion) and accepts Alexander's total of fifty-four. The Federal and Confederate primary accounts confirm that there was no, or minimal, Confederate artillery on Barksdale's front west of the Peach Orchard when the action began. But regardless of the exact numbers, it seems apparent that at no point did Alexander have all of his guns in play.

26. OR 27/1: 504, 581-582, 586-587; Murray, *E.Alexander and the Artillery Action in the Peach Orchard*, 46, 48; Toombs, *New Jersey Troops*, 201; Ladd, *The Bachelder Papers*, 2:843; Smith, *A Famous Battery and Its Campaigns*, 101-102.

27. OR 27/1: 234-235; Hunt, "The Second Day at Gettysburg," in *Battles and Leaders*, 3: 303-304; Murray, *E.Alexander and the Artillery Action in the Peach Orchard*, 50.

28. OR 27/1: 900; Ames, *History of Battery G*, 62-63; Murray, *E.Alexander and the Artillery Action in the Peach Orchard*, 51; Coco, *A Concise Guide to the Artillery at Gettysburg*, 26.

29. Ames, *History of Battery G*, 64-67; Murray, *E.Alexander and the Artillery Action in the Peach Orchard*, 52-53.

30. Messent and Courtney, *Civil War Letters of Joseph Hopkins Twichell*, 248.

31. Bigelow, *The Peach Orchard*, 11.

32. *Ibid.*, 52; Murray, *E.Alexander and the Artillery Action in the Peach Orchard*, 58-60.

33. Ladd, *The Bachelder Papers*, 1: 167; Murray, *E.Alexander and the Artillery Action in the Peach Orchard*, 65-71.

34. OR 27/1: 235, 887; Ladd, *The Bachelder Papers*, 3: 1788; Murray, *E.Alexander and the Artillery Action in the Peach Orchard*, 66-67.

35. Ladd, *The Bachelder Papers*, 3: 1788.

36. Haynes, *A History of the Second Regiment, New Hampshire Volunteer Infantry*, 169-170; Toombs, *New Jersey Troops*, 205-206; Woods, "Humphreys' Division's Flank March to Little Round Top," *Gettysburg Magazine* 6, 60.

37. OR 27/1: 582, 589-590, 900; Alexander, "The Great Charge and Artillery Fighting at Gettysburg," in *Battles and Leaders*, 3:359; Murray, *E.Alexander and the Artillery Action in the Peach Orchard*, 50, 54-55, 57; Pfanz, *Gettysburg: The Second Day*, 133, 154.

38. Murray, *E.Alexander and the Artillery Action in the Peach Orchard*, 55; Alexander, "The Great Charge and Artillery Fighting at Gettysburg," in *Battles and Leaders,* 3:359.

39. OR 27/1: 235, 582, 887, 900; Ladd, *The Bachelder Papers*, 1: 167, 2: 844; Murray, *E.Alexander and the Artillery Action in the Peach Orchard*, 65-67.

40. OR 27/1: 498-499, 500, 502, 504, 901; 27/2: 432; Murray, *E.Alexander and the Artillery Action in the Peach Orchard*, 55-56; Haynes, *A History of the Second Regiment, New Hampshire Volunteer Infantry*, 170-174; Charles Graham account, February 16, 1865, Participants File 5, GNMP; *Pennsylvania at Gettysburg*, 1: 356; Craft, *History of the 141st Regiment Pennsylvania Volunteers*, 121; Scott, *History of the One Hundred and Fifth Regiment of Pennsylvania Volunteers,* 82.

41. Brown, *History of the Third Regiment, Excelsior Brigade*, 104; Rafferty, "Gettysburg," in *Personal Recollections of the War of the Rebellion*, 23; Campbell, "Remember Harper's Ferry," *Gettysburg Magazine* 7, 63.

42. OR 27/1: 235, 532, 590, 881, 890; 27/2: 636; *Pennsylvania at Gettysburg*, 2:910; Ladd, *The Bachelder Papers*, 1: 607; Toombs, *New Jersey Troops,* 202; Murray, *E.Alexander and the Artillery Action in the Peach Orchard*, 67-71. Captain Thompson said at the battery's monument dedication that he actually relieved Ames' battery, and took the position that Ames had formerly occupied. See *Pennsylvania at Gettysburg*, 2:910.

43. Alexander, "The Great Charge and Artillery Fighting at Gettysburg," *Battles and Leader*, 3: 359-360; OR 27/2: 375; Murray, *E.Alexander and the Artillery Action in the Peach Orchard*, 72-77, 81-88. Murray's study assumes the following Confederate guns were not deployed during the assault itself: McCarthy (two guns), Bachman (four guns), Garden (four guns), Woolfolk (four guns), and Jordan (four guns). Woolfolk and Jordan were, however, later called out of reserve. The Federal totals assume deployments for: Turnbull (six guns), Seeley (six guns), Thompson (six guns), Bucklyn (six guns), Ames (six guns), Hart (four guns), Clark (six guns), Phillips (six guns), Bigelow (six guns), and Smith (four guns).

44. OR 27/1: 242; Murray, *E.Alexander and the Artillery Action in the Peach Orchard*, 88-89. Alexander thought Hood attacked "perhaps" thirty minutes after the artillery began; i.e. about 4:15. See Alexander, *Military Memoirs*, 395.

Chapter 9: The "Key" of the Battleground

1. New York at Gettysburg, 1:42; Sickles, in "Further Recollections of Gettysburg," *North American Review*.

2. From Oates' "The War Between the Union and the Confederacy," quoted in Norton, *Attack and Defense of Little Round Top*, 80; *New York at Gettysburg*, 2:868; Jorgensen, "John Haley's Personal Recollections of the Battle of the Wheatfield," *The Gettysburg Magazine* 27, 69-70.

3. OR 27/1: 202.

4. Hood to Longstreet, June 28, 1875, in *SHSP*, 4: 148-150; Meade, *Life and Letters* 2:80. Longstreet's motives in continuing the attack can be interpreted in a number of ways. His persistence with both Hood and McLaws may have simply been a case of his realizing that the afternoon was slipping away. Historian Robert K. Krick, a known Longstreet detractor, attaches more sinister motives to Longstreet's actions. "To alter it would be to impair the lesson Lee needed to learn." See Krick, "James Longstreet and the Second Day," in *The Second Day at Gettysburg*, 75. Porter Alexander wrote that it was unlikely that Hood's proposal "would have accomplished much." Noting that Lee's exterior line was being stretched beyond its limits, "Had our army been more united and able to follow up the move in force, it might have proved a successful one." See Alexander, *Military Memoirs*, 394.

5. Fox, *New York at Gettysburg*, 1:44-45; Trudeau, *Gettysburg: A Testing of Courage*, 332; Toombs, *New Jersey Troops*, 202.

6. OR 27/2: 367-368, 404, 614, 618; Alexander, *Military Memoirs*, 393-394; Coddington, *The Gettysburg Campaign*, 384; Cooksey, "Around the Flank: Longstreet's July 2 Attack at Gettysburg," *Gettysburg Magazine* 29, 104-105.

7. OR 27/2: 358, 372; Longstreet, "Lee's Right Wing at Gettysburg," in *Battles and Leaders*, 3: 341; Longstreet, *From Manassas to Appomattox*, 369.

8. Law, "The Struggle for 'Round Top', in Battles and Leaders, 3:323; *New York at Gettysburg*, 1:45, 2:868; Norton, *Attack and Defense*, 255-256; OR 27/1: 493, 515-516; Ladd, *The Bachelder Papers*, 2: 767; Adelman and Smith, *Devil's Den*, 23-24; Coddington, *The Gettysburg Campaign*, 386.

9. OR 27/1: 493, 588; 27/2: 392, 404; Norton, *Attack and Defense*, 256-257; Desjardin, *Stand Firm Ye Boys From Maine*, 41; Ladd, *The Bachelder Papers*, 1: 36-37, 498; Hunt, "The Second Day at Gettysburg," in *Battles and Leaders*, 3:305; Adelman and Smith, *Devil's Den*, 22, 135-137; Smith, *A Famous Battery and Its Campaigns*, 102-103, 136; Fox, *New York at Gettysburg*, 1:46. Both Hunt and Captain Smith agreed later that Smith's current battery monument is inaccurately placed. Some historians have traditionally placed Smith between modern-day Sickles Avenue and the so-called "Triangular Field," but historians Tim Smith and Gary Adelman make a convincing case that Smith's four guns were actually on the ridge's crest near the present-day 99th Pennsylvania monument. In a historical sketch of the 99th Pennsylvania, C. H. Fasnacht said that Smith's battery was to the *right* of the monument. See Fasnacht, *Historical Sketch 99th Pennsylvania*, 10.

10. OR 27/1: 493, 511, 522, 589; 27/2: 404-405, 407-408; Adelman and Smith, *Devil's Den*, 26-32; Smith, *A Famous Battery and Its Campaigns*, 102-103; De Trobriand, *Four Years With the Army of the Potomac*, 496; Ladd, *The Bachelder Papers*, 1:36-37.

11. Smith, *A Famous Battery and Its Campaigns*, 104, 139; Adelman and Smith, *Devil's Den*, 31; OR 27/1: 588-589; Ladd, *The Bachelder Papers*, 1:36-37.

12. OR 27/1: 493, 513, 588-589; 27/2: 393-396; Adelman and Smith, *Devil's Den*, 32-35, 38-42; Fasnacht, *Historical Sketch 99th Pennsylvania*, 10; Smith, *A Famous Battery and Its Campaigns*, 105; *Pennsylvania at Gettysburg*, 1:538; Murray, *Letters from Gettysburg*, 86. Smith was able to remove one piece from Houck's Ridge to prevent its capture.

13. DiNardo, "James Longstreet, the Modern Soldier," in *James Longstreet: The Man, The Soldier, The Controversy*, 38; Alexander, *Military Memoirs*, 395; Wert, *General James Longstreet*, 311.

14. OR 27/1: 493, 513, 526-527, 570-571, 577-578; 27/2: 408-409, 414-415, 422; Ladd, *The Bachelder Papers*, 1: 117, 374, 498; Adelman and Smith, *Devil's Den*, 43-52; Imhof, *Gettysburg Day Two*, 68-69, 85; Busey and Martin, *Regimental Strengths and Losses*, 245, 281; *Pennsylvania at Gettysburg*, 1:538; Smith, *A Famous Battery and Its Campaigns*, 104-105; Toombs, *New Jersey Troops*, 213-215; Fasnacht, *Historical Sketch 99th Pennsylvania*, 11; Law, "The Struggle for 'Round Top', in *Battles and Leaders*, 3:324. Evander Law thought in his *Battles and Leaders* account that it had only taken slightly less than one hour for Devil's Den to fall.

15. Smith, *A Famous Battery and Its Campaigns*, 106-108, 154-155; OR 27/1: 526-527, 577-578, 589; 27/2: 416, 424-425; Adelman and Smith, *Devil's Den*, 51; Ladd, *The Bachelder Papers*, 1:36-37; Toombs, *New Jersey Troops*, 215.

16. Busey and Martin, *Regimental Strengths and Losses*, 245, 280-281; Adelman and Smith, *Devil's Den*, 24. The 3,000 to 2,300 differential does not include any participation by G.T. Anderson's brigade, which was comparatively minimal. Nor does it include the flank fire of the 17th Maine in the Wheatfield.

17. OR 27/1: 116, 592.

18. *Ibid.*, 27/1: 483; Tremain, *Two Days of War*, 67.

19. OR 27/1: 592.

20. Sickles, "Further Recollections of Gettysburg," in *North American Review*, 266; Ranald Mackenzie to George Meade, March 22, 1864, quoted in Norton, *Attack and Defense*, 292. The fact that Sickles played into his critics' hands and was forced to address criticism of his inability to occupy Little Round Top is more proof that he realized it was an important position. Mackenzie, for his part, would achieve post-war renown as an Indian fighter in the 4th U.S. Cavalry.

21. Sickles, "Further Recollections of Gettysburg," in *North American Review*, 266; OR 27/1:600-601; Norton, *Attack and Defense*, 263-264; Pfanz, *Gettysburg: The Second Day*, 207-208;

Woods, "Humphreys' Division's Flank March To Little Round Top," *Gettysburg Magazine* 6, 60-61; Trudeau, *Gettysburg: A Testing of Courage*, 326.

22. Busey and Martin, *Regimental Strengths and Losses*, 59-60; Norton, *Attack and Defense*, 296; OR 27/1: 600-601; Desjardins, *Stand Firm Ye Boys From Maine*, 34-36; Imhof, *Gettysburg Day Two: A Study in Maps*, 39-41; Pfanz, *Gettysburg: The Second Day*, 207-208; Gottfried, *Brigades of Gettysburg*, 235-241; Raver, "An Investigation Into the Route Taken From Rock Creek to Little Round Top," *Gettysburg Magazine* 27, 52-64. Sweitzer had an estimated 1423 in his brigade on July 2, but that included approximately 412 men of the 9th Massachusetts infantry, who were on picket duty on the Union right. See Busey and Martin, 60.

23. Law, "The Struggle for 'Round Top', in *Battles and Leaders*, 3: 322; Ladd, *The Bachelder Papers*, 1: 243-244, 465, 3:1928; OR 27/1: 617, 623-624; Norton, *Attack and Defense*, 258-260; Vanderslice, *Gettysburg: Then and Now*, 152-156; Fox, *New York at Gettysburg*, 1:45; Fletcher, *Rebel Private: Front and Rear*, 79; Imhof, *Gettysburg Day Two*, 117-118, 120-121; Desjardin, *Stand Firm Ye Boys From Maine*, 42.

24. OR 51/1: 201; Tremain, *Two Days of War*, 76-77.

25. Norton, *Attack and Defense*, 259-260, 310-311; Ladd, *The Bachelder Papers*, 1: 243-244, 465, 2: 894-897, 3:1928; OR 27/1: 623-624, 651-652; Fox, *New York at Gettysburg*, 1:45; Vanderslice, *Gettysburg: Then and Now*, 152-156; Fletcher, *Rebel Private: Front and Rear*, 79. Col. Kenner Garrard, filing the report for Weed's brigade, wrote that the brigade (minus the 140th New York) "were led to the right and front some distance, and formed in line in a narrow valley to support a portion of the Third Corps and Watson's battery, then severely pressed by the enemy. Before becoming engaged, however, orders were received for these regiments to return at double-quick to Round Top ridge, and secure and hold that position." See OR 27/1: 651-652.

26. OR 27/1: 593; Sykes statement to Porter Farley, quoted in Norton, *Attack and Defense*, 294-295.

27. Warren to Porter Farley, July 13, 1872, quoted in Norton, *Attack and Defense*, 310-311; Fletcher, *Rebel Private: Front and Rear*, 80; Vanderslice, *Gettysburg: Then and Now*, 152-156; OR 27/2: 415 .

28. OR 27/2: 424-425, 462; Adelman and Smith, *Devil's Den*, 54.

29. Swinton, *Campaigns of the Army of the Potomac*, 346; Norton, *Attack and Defense*, 13; OR 27/1: 617.

30. Norton, *Attack and Defense*, 295. It is not this author's intention to debate whether or not Little Round Top was the "key" to the Union cause, as many have written. There were many pivotal moments in this battle. But the actions of many Union and Confederate participants confirm that those present at the battle considered Little Round Top to be a critical position, certainly one worth attacking and defending. See Gary Adelman's *The Myth of Little Round Top* for a full discussion on historically changing interpretations of Little Round Top's importance.

31. OR 27/1: 592-593. While Sykes said in his report that Birney did close to the left as requested, Sykes later said that his report was in error and "Birney did not close the gap I asked him to, near the battery on the left of his line." See Norton, *Attack and Defense*, 293-295.

32. OR 27/1: 601.

33. *Ibid.*

34. *Ibid.*, 27/1: 593, 607, 610-611; Imhof, *Gettysburg Day Two*, 74-75; Jorgensen, *Gettysburg's Bloody Wheatfield*, 64-69; Meade, *Life and Letters*, 2:332-335; Ladd, *The Bachelder Papers*, 3: 1672; Imhof, *Gettysburg Day Two*, 61-64; Pfanz, *Gettysburg: The Second Day*, 246. Jorgensen's conclusion was that Barnes was on Stony Hill in time for Anderson's initial assault. For an opposing interpretation, Imhof concludes, using Tilton's account, that they clearly did not participate in Anderson's first assault.

Chapter 10: Gross Neglect or Unaccountable Stupidity

1. OR 27/1: 519-520, 524, 571; De Trobriand, *Four Years With the Army of the Potomac*, 497; Imhof, *Gettysburg Day Two*, 53, 65, 69; Pfanz, *Gettysburg: The First Day*, 140.

2. Jorgensen, "John Haley's Personal Recollections of the Battle of the Wheatfield," *Gettysburg Magazine* 27, 71; OR 27/1: 587; Jorgensen, *Gettysburg's Bloody Wheatfield*, 37.

3. OR 27/2: 396-397, 399, 403; 27/1: 522, 881; Jorgensen, *The Wheatfield at Gettysburg: A Walking Tour*, 7-8; Imhof, *Gettysburg Day Two*, 69.

4. Oeffinger, *A Soldier's General*, 196; McLaws, "Gettysburg," in *SHSP*, 7:73; Alexander, *Military Memoirs*, 395; Law, "The Struggle for 'Round Top', in *Battles and Leaders*, 3: 325; Longstreet, *From Manassas to Appomattox*, 370; Coddington, *The Gettysburg Campaign*, 403, 749 (n.104). Coddington thought that a one hour estimate seemed "excessive," but given the amount of time needed for Law, Robertson, Benning, and Anderson to advance and in some cases make repeated attacks, one hour is probably not too far off of the mark.

5. OR 27/2: 367-368, 372; Kershaw, "Kershaw's Brigade at Gettysburg," in *Battles and Leaders*, 3:332-334; Cooksey, "Around the Flank: Longstreet's July 2 Attack at Gettysburg," *Gettysburg Magazine* 29, 100-102.

6. OR 27/2: 367; Kershaw, "Kershaw's Brigade at Gettysburg," in *Battles and Leaders*, 3:333-334; Alexander, *Military Memoirs*, 397.

7. OR 27/1: 881-882, 887, 901; 27/2: 368, 372; Alexander, *Military Memoirs*, 397; Ames, *History of Battery G*, 66-67; Kershaw, "Kershaw's Brigade at Gettysburg," in *Battles and Leaders*, 3:334-336; Ladd, *The Bachelder Papers*, 1:167, 172; Pfanz, *Gettysburg: The Second Day*, 315-316.

8. OR 27/1: 236, 583-584, 660, 901; Ames, History of Battery G, 73-74; 120th New York file, Robert Brake Collection, USAMHI; Hunt to Bachelder, January 6, 1866, in Ladd, *Bachelder Papers*, 1:228; Imhof, *Gettysburg: Day Two*, 147; Pfanz, *Gettysburg: The Second Day*, 317. Watson's battlefield tablet (which is incorrectly located due to the postwar development of modern United States Avenue) states that the battery arrived on the field about 4:30 p.m. and first took position north of Little Round Top: "[At] 5:30 moved to the front at the Peach Orchard." Thompson's battery is sometimes cited as Ames' actual replacement (see Georg, *The Sherfy Farm and the Battle of Gettysburg*, 14 as an example.) Thompson ended up in the Peach Orchard and appears to have been in position for at least an hour before the position collapsed. If Ames' reported 5:30 p.m. departure time is accurate, his replacement would have been in position for less than one hour when the orchard fell, making Thompson problematic as the replacement. On the other hand, reported times during the Civil War were frequently unreliable. See Murray, *E. P. Alexander and the Artillery Action in the Peach Orchard*, 97-98, for a discussion on Thompson. Ultimately, Pfanz (317) placed Watson in the orchard; Imhof (147) did not. Thanks to Licensed Battlefield Guide George Newton for alerting this author to the existence of Hunt's 1866 letter to Bachelder in which Hunt admitted "the error in the position of Watson's Battery" in Hunt's report.

9. OR 27/1: 236, 659-660; Sykes to Porter Farley, quoted in Norton, *Attack and Defense*, 294-295.

10. Haynes, *A History of the Second Regiment, New Hampshire Volunteer Infantry*, 170-171, 177-178; Craft, *History of the 141st Regiment Pennsylvania Volunteers*, 120; OR 27/1: 504-505, 508; Imhof, *Gettysburg Day Two*, 110.

11. OR 27/1: 483, 520-521; 27/2: 368; Haynes, *A History of the Second Regiment, New Hampshire Volunteer Infantry*, 178; Imhof, *Gettysburg Day Two*, 101-102.

12. De Trobriand, *Four Years with the Army of the Potomac*, 497-498; Imhof, *Gettysburg Day Two*, 101. Not that de Trobriand's versions are above scrutiny. Robert Carter, who fought in the 22nd Massachusetts, later wrote that de Trobriand's accounts were "calculative without further explanation, to mislead any reader of the history of the battle unacquainted with the true facts." See Ladd, *The Bachelder Papers*, 3: 1671-1672.

13. OR 27/1: 132-133; Ladd, *The Bachelder Papers*, 1: 172, 3: 1671-1672; *Pennsylvania at Gettysburg*, 1: 383, 2: 634; Parker, *History of the Twenty-Second Massachusetts*, 334-335.

14. OR 27/1: 601.

15. *Ibid.*, 27/1: 607-608. Historians have generally laid the blame completely on Barnes. See Imhof, *Gettysburg Day Two*, 102 for example. "Tilton asked General Barnes for permission to withdraw—permission that was immediately granted." But Tilton's own report indicates that he was given discretion to determine when best to retreat and that he executed this discretion.

16. *Ibid.*, 27/1: 611.

17. De Trobriand, *Four Years With the Army of the Potomac*, 498-500; Jorgensen, "John Haley's Personal Recollections of the Battle of the Wheatfield," *Gettysburg Magazine* 27, 71; OR 27/1: 520, 522-523; Ladd, *The Bachelder Papers*, 2:849; Imhof, *Gettysburg Day Two*, 104.

18. OR 27/1: 369, 483; Ladd, *The Bachelder Papers*, 2: 1195; Hartwig, " No Troops on the Field Had Done Better," in *The Second Day at Gettysburg*, 146.

19. Byrne and Weaver, *Haskell of Gettysburg*, 120

20. Kershaw, "Kershaw's Brigade at Gettysburg," in *Battles and Leaders*, 3: 335-336; Ladd, Bachelder Papers, 1:472, 2: 1195; Hartwig, " No Troops on the Field Had Done Better," in *The Second Day at Gettysburg*, 137-141; Busey and Martin, *Regimental Strengths and Losses*, 241-242; Vanderslice, *Gettysburg Then and Now*, 159-160.

21. De Trobriand, *Four Years with the Army of the Potomac*, 500-501; OR 27/1: 522-523; Imhof, *Gettysburg Day Two*, 109; Ladd, *The Bachelder Papers*, 2: 1059; Styple, *Our Noble Blood*, 116-117.

22. OR 27/1: 483; Rafferty, "Gettysburg," in *Personal Recollections of the War of the Rebellion*, 22-23; Imhof, *Gettysburg Day Two*, 97; Gottfried, *Brigades of Gettysburg*, 121-123; Hartwig, "No Troops on the Field Had Done Better," in *The Second Day at Gettysburg*, 155-156; Busey and Martin, *Regimental Strengths and Losses*, 241-242; Tagg, *The Generals of Gettysburg*, 41-42.

23. Tremain, *Two Days of War*, 81-84; Hartwig, "No Troops on the Field Had Done Better," *The Second Day at Gettysburg*, 155-156. Hartwig noted that "such acts can just as well lose battles."

24. Favill, *Diary of a Young Army Officer*, 245.

25. OR 27/1: 483.

26. *Ibid.*, 27/1: 394, 396-397; Imhof, *Gettysburg Day Two*, 115.

27. Favill, *Diary of a Young Army Officer*, 245-248; De Trobriand, *Four Years with the Army of the Potomac*, 500; OR 27/1: 398; Coco, *A Strange and Blighted Land*, 199; Gottfried, *Brigades of Gettysburg*, 133, 63n.

28. OR 27/1: 400-401; Kershaw, "Kershaw's Brigade at Gettysburg," in *Battles and Leaders*, 3: 335-337; Hartwig, " No Troops on the Field Had Done Better," in *The Second Day at Gettysburg*, 159-163; Ladd, *The Bachelder Papers*, 2:1141-1143; Imhof, *Gettysburg Day Two*, 132, 141, 150-151, 154-155, 159-160; Jorgensen, *Gettysburg's Bloody Wheatfield*, 104-105.

29. Troop totals are taken from Jorgensen, *Gettysburg's Bloody Wheatfield*, 136-142 and Busey and Martin, *Regimental Strengths and Losses*, 241-242, 245.

30. Casualty totals are taken from Jorgensen, *Gettysburg's Bloody Wheatfield*, 136-137 and Busey and Martin, *Regimental Strengths and Losses*, 280-282. Kershaw's totals include some regiments who faced Federal troops in and around the Peach Orchard. Anderson's totals do not include the 7th Georgia which was detached and suffered only twenty-one casualties out of 377 available for a 5.6% casualty rate. See OR 27/2: 396.

Chapter 11: The Line Before You Must Be Broken

1. McLaws, "Gettysburg," in SHSP, 7: 72-73; OR 27/2: 430; Longstreet, *From Manassas to Appomattox*, 370; Winschel, "Their Supreme Moment: Barksdale's Brigade at Gettysburg," *Gettysburg Magazine* 1, 74; Gottfried, *Brigades of Gettysburg*, 411-412; Ladd, *The Bachelder Papers*, 2: 902; Alexander, "The Great Charge and Artillery Fighting at Gettysburg," in *Battles and Leaders*, 3:359-360; Alexander, *Military Memoirs*, 395, 399; Imhof, Gettysburg Day Two, 126.

2. McLaws, "Gettysburg," in SHSP, 7: 72-74; Winschel, "Their Supreme Moment: Barksdale's Brigade at Gettysburg," *Gettysburg Magazine* 1, 74; Gottfried, *Brigades of Gettysburg*, 412; OR 27/1: 499, 500, 503, 586, 887; *Pennsylvania at Gettysburg*, 1:394, 2:606; Ladd, The Bachelder Papers, 1: 480; Haynes, *History of the Second Regiment, New Hampshire*, 179.

3. Ladd, *The Bachelder Papers*, 1: 480; Imhof, *Gettysburg Day Two*, 143; Winschel, "Their Supreme Moment: Barksdale's Brigade at Gettysburg," *Gettysburg Magazine* 1, 74; Gottfried, *Brigades of Gettysburg*, 412.

4. OR 27/1: 498, 502-503, 584,590; *Pennsylvania at Gettysburg*, 1: 387, 2: 610-611 ; Toombs, *New Jersey Troops*, 206-208, 228; Imhof, *Gettysburg Day Two*, 99-101, 136-137; Ladd, *The Bachelder*

Papers, 1:72-73; Pfanz, *Gettysburg The Second Day*, 322-323; Busey and Martin, *Regimental Strengths and Losses*, 247; Georg, "The Sherfy Farm and the Battle of Gettysburg," 14. Kathleen Georg wrote that the 63rd retired "before overwhelming numbers," which isn't clear from either their OR or their monument dedication speech. Perhaps the sight of several waves of approaching infantry contributed to their withdrawal. Humphreys said in his report that the 5th New Jersey relieved some of Graham's pickets who overlapped a portion of Humphreys' line. It is possible that the 5th's left took up where the right of the 63rd had ended. But none of this is clear from the 5th New Jersey's own report. See OR 27/1: 533, 575; Imhof, 47, 139, 141. New Jersey historian Samuel Toombs wrote (1888) that the 5th reported to Humphreys and "was ordered to relieve the Sixty-third Pennsylvania, on picket duty on the Emmetsburg [sic] road." Toombs recorded that the 5th was subjected to artillery fire for one hour when Barksdale appeared to their left and front. See Toombs, 206-208, 228.

5. OR 27/1: 497, 500, 503; *Pennsylvania at Gettysburg*, 1:356, 2:607; Georg, "The Sherfy Farm and the Battle of Gettysburg," 19; Gottfried, *Brigades at Gettysburg*, 192.

6. OR 27/1: 498-499; 504-505, 508; Haynes, *A History of the Second Regiment, New Hampshire Volunteer Infantry*, 170-171, 177-178; Craft, *History of the 141st Regiment Pennsylvania Volunteers*, 120; Imhof, *Gettysburg Day Two*, 110, 143; Bigelow, *The Peach Orchard*, 11-12; Ladd, *Bachelder Papers*, 1: 480-481; *Pennsylvania at Gettysburg*, 1:394.

7. OR 27/1: 505, 508, 524, 889; Craft, *History of the 141st Regiment Pennsylvania Volunteers*, 121-122; Haynes, *A History of the Second Regiment, New Hampshire Volunteer Infantry*, 179-180; Ladd, *Bachelder Papers*, 1: 480, 2: 846-847; *Pennsylvania at Gettysburg*, 2: 910; Georg, "The Sherfy Farm and the Battle of Gettysburg," 17; Pfanz, *Gettysburg: The Second Day*, 339. The question remains as to whether or not Thompson's battery had replaced Ames. Thompson later said that he did. See Murray, *E. P. Alexander and the Artillery Action in the Peach Orchard*, 98, for a discussion. Kathleen Georg seemed to accept that Thompson had replaced Ames, and Watson then came up to support Thompson. See Georg, 17.

8. OR 27/1: 532-533, 559; Tremain, *Two Days of War*, 79-81; Imhof, *Gettysburg Day Two*, 141-142; *New York at Gettysburg*, 2:605-606; Hawthorne, *Gettysburg: Stories of Men and Monuments*, 77.

9. Ladd, *The Bachelder Papers*, 1:225, 2:773, Gottfried, *Brigades of Gettysburg*, 220-221.

10. OR 27/1: 503; *Pennsylvania at Gettysburg*, 2: 605-606, 612; Imhof, *Gettysburg Day Two*, 143, 146; Gottfried, *Brigades of Gettysburg*, 192; Georg, "The Sherfy Farm and the Battle of Gettysburg," 22. The rules governing monument placement dictated that statues must face the enemy. Dedicating the regiment's monument in 1888, Sergeant (later Captain) A.W. Givin noted that the lone Zouave statue atop the monument faces to the left (roughly south rather than to the west) "looking to our left which is being driven back.... Men of the One hundred and fourteenth stood as this man stands, contesting the ground inch by inch."

11. OR 27/1: 497; *Pennsylvania at Gettysburg*, 1:356; Georg, "The Sherfy Farm and the Battle of Gettysburg," 19-22; Gottfried, *Brigades of Gettysburg*, 192-193. Of the fifty-five members of the 57th Pennsylvania who were captured at Gettysburg, forty-four reportedly died in southern prisons. See *Pennsylvania at Gettysburg*, 2; 357.

12. OR 27/1: 500-501; Scott, *History of the One Hundred and Fifth Regiment of Pennsylvania Volunteers*, 83.

13. *The Bachelder Papers*, 1:225, 2:773; Georg, "The Sherfy Farm and the Battle of Gettysburg," 24; Imhof, *Gettysburg Day Two*, 148-151; Gottfried, *Brigades of Gettysburg*, 220-221.

14. Longstreet, *From Manassas to Appomattox*, 372; Alexander, *Military Memoirs*, 399; Fremantle, *Three Months in the Southern States*, 261; Wert, *General James Longstreet*, 275-76. John Imhof, 150, considered "one of the most important, yet least discussed controversies" of the battle to be: "why did Longstreet divert Wofford's men from their role as support for Barksdale?" Longstreet claimed he wanted to strike Federal forces in the Wheatfield and Plum Run Valley in the right flank and "lift our desperate fighters to the summit" of Little Round Top.

15. OR 27/1: 58, 498-499, 505, 887; Ladd, The Bachelder Papers, 2: 846-847, 3:1797; Imhof, *Gettysburg Day Two*, 151, 155-156; Pfanz, *Gettysburg: The Second Day*, 338-339; Toombs, *New Jersey*

Troops, 253-254; Busey and Martin, *Regimental Strengths and Losses*, 247; Haynes, *A History of the Second Regiment, New Hampshire Volunteer Infantry*, 180-182; Craft, *History of the 141st Regiment Pennsylvania Volunteers*, 122-123. Busey and Martin estimated the 141st's casualties at 149 out of 209 total men (71.3%), including twenty-five killed, 103 wounded, and twenty-one MIA. Although the 68th and 114th had higher numeric casualties, the 141st had the highest rate in Graham's brigade. The 68th suffered 152 casualties out of 320 engaged (47.5%), while the 114th's totals were 155 out of 259 (59.8%). See Busey and Martin, *Regimental Strengths and Losses*, 245.

16. OR 27/1: 498-499; Bigelow, *The Peach Orchard*, 12.

17. OR 27/1: 498-499; Charles Graham account, February 16, 1865, Participants Accounts File 5, GNMP; Craft, *History of the 141st Regiment Pennsylvania Volunteers*, 137; Ladd, *The Bachelder Papers*, 1: 480-481.

18. Charles Graham account, February 16, 1865, Gettysburg Participants Accounts File 5, GNMP; OR 27/1: 498-499; Craft, *History of the 141st Regiment Pennsylvania Volunteers*, 137; Tucker, *High Tide at Gettysburg*, 278-279; Gottfried, *Brigades of Gettysburg*, 412-413; Trudeau, *Gettysburg: A Testing of Courage*, 380; *Dedication of the New York Auxiliary State Monument*, 146-147. Among the Federal infantry, estimated missing/captured in Graham's brigade alone was 165. Among other nearby regiments, the 3rd Maine's estimate was forty-five, the 3rd Michigan was seven, and the 2nd New Hampshire was thirty-six. See Busey and Martin, 245-247.

19. Ladd, *The Bachelder Papers*, 1:591.

20. *Ibid.*, 1: 239-240. The horse was evidently later hit by a bullet. See Tremain, *Two Days of War*, 88. As usual, there was some discrepancy on the precise time that the wound occurred. Randolph told John Bachelder in 1886 that it was "towards 5 or 6 o'clock." David Birney reported that it occurred "at 6 o'clock." See OR 27/1. The New York *Times* reported under a July 14 byline that Sickles wound occurred "about" 6 o'clock. See "Affairs at Gettysburgh," New York *Times*, July 18, 1863. Sickles said in 1884 that the incident occurred between 5:30 and 6:00, as "the last memorandum in my field book was made at 5:38 p.m." See "Seventy Five Years Ago," news clipping, Box B-36, Misc. Info—Gen. Daniel Sickles, GNMP.

21. 1882 Sickles interview, undated newspaper, J. Howard Wert Scrapbook, #34, Vol. 3, 4-5, ACHS.

22. *Dedication of the New York Auxiliary State Monument*, 112-113; 1882 Sickles interview, undated newspaper, J. Howard Wert Scrapbook, #34, Vol. 3, 4-5, ACHS.

23. 1882 Sickles interview, undated newspaper, J. Howard Wert Scrapbook, #34, Vol. 3, 4-5, ACHS; Ladd, *The Bachelder Papers*, 1: 239-240; Tremain, *Two Days of War*, 88-89.

24. Tremain, *Two Days of War*, 88-89; OR 27/1: 483, 494.

25. Ladd, *The Bachelder Papers*, 1:239-240.

26. 1882 Sickles interview, undated newspaper, J. Howard Wert Scrapbook, #34, Vol. 3, 4-5, ACHS; Tremain, *Two Days of War*, 89-90, 105.

27. Swanberg, *Sickles the Incredible*, 216-217.

28. The Reid passage was quoted in Trimble, "Agate: Whitelaw Reid Reports From Gettysburg," *Gettysburg Magazine* 7, 27; Andrews, The North Reports the Civil War, 422; Brown, *History of the Third Regiment, Excelsior Brigade*, 105; "Longstreet and Sickles to Meet at Gettysburg," Philadelphia *Times*, May 28, 1899, copy in GNMP files 11-60. For examples of Reid's reprinted account, see: Davis, *Life of David Bell Birney*, 184-185 and Scott, *History of the One Hundred and Fifth Regiment of Pennsylvania Volunteers*, 84-85.

29. Jorgensen, "John Haley's Personal Recollections of the Battle of the Wheatfield," *Gettysburg Magazine* 27, 73; Ladd, *The Bachelder Papers*, 2: 768; Doster, *Lincoln and Episodes of the Civil War*, 217. Sim spoke to the Washington *Republican* on July 7 and was re-printed in the Detroit *Free Press*, July 10, 1863, Robert L. Brake Collection, USAMHI.

30. Johnson, *Campfire and Battlefield*, 265-266. The quotation used by Johnson is sometimes mis-credited to Captain Don Piatt, an Ohio officer who was not at Gettysburg. But Regis de Trobriand did have a Captain Benjamin Piatt on his staff. See de Trobriand's OR 27/1: 521.

31. W.H. Bullard to Dan Sickles, September 13, 1897, Misc. Mss. Daniel Sickles, courtesy of New York Historical Society.

32. *Ibid.*

33. *Ibid.*

34. *Ibid.*

35. Brown, *History of the Third Regiment, Excelsior Brigade*, 105.

36. Tremain, *Two Days of War*, 105.

37. Pinchon, *Dan Sickles*, 201-202.

38. Swanberg, *Sickles the Incredible*, 216-217, 404 (n. 10-14); Brown, *History of the Third Regiment, Excelsior Brigade*, 105; Letter from Felix Brannigan to Father, original in Library of Congress, copy on file GNMP.

39. Stackpole, *They Met at Gettysburg*, 215; Tucker, *High Tide at Gettysburg*, 272; Coddington, *The Gettysburg Campaign: A Study in Command*, 414, 755 (n. 27); Pfanz, *Gettysburg: The Second Day*, 334-335, 534 (n. 131).

40. Knoop, *I Follow The Course, Come What May*, 1-2, 169 (n. 2).

41. Trudeau, *Gettysburg: A Testing of Courage*, 377, 628; Sears, *Gettysburg*, 301.

42. Keneally, *American Scoundrel*, 287-289.

43. Trudeau, *Gettysburg: A Testing of Courage*, 377, 628; Keneally, *American Scoundrel*, 287-289, 369-370 (n. 29-30).

44. 1882 Sickles interview, undated newspaper, J. Howard Wert Scrapbook, #34, Vol. 3, 4-5, ACHS; "The Medal of Honor," Box B-36, Misc. Info-Gen. Daniel Sickles, GNMP.

45. *Dedication of the New York Auxiliary State Monument*, 112-113.

Chapter 12: Let Me Die on the Field

1. Kershaw, "Kershaw's Brigade at Gettysburg," in *Battles and Leaders*, 3: 336-337; OR 27/1: 386, 400-401, 394; Ladd, *The Bachelder Papers*, 1: 167-168, 480-481, 2:1141; Hartwig, "Caldwell's Division in the Wheatfield," in *The Second Day at Gettysburg*, 162-163; Jorgensen, *Gettysburg's Bloody Wheatfield*, 108-112; Imhof, *Gettysburg Day Two*, 169-73.

2. OR 27/2: 608, 614, 618; Winschel, "Their Supreme Moment," *Gettysburg Magazine* 1, 74. The reports of Generals Hill, Anderson, and Wilcox appear to agree on the role of Anderson's division in Longstreet's attack. Hill wrote that he was to cooperate "with such of my brigades from the right as could join in," and unlike Longstreet's commanders, Hill specifically referred to their attack as being "en echelon." Longstreet's post-battle writing implies that a contributing factor to the attack's failure was Wilcox's alleged inability to cover McLaws' left flank. This caused Wilcox to join the legion of postwar Longstreet detractors. An indignant Wilcox wrote to Jubal Early's *Southern Historical Society* in 1878, "the orders given me during the day were to advance when the troops on my right moved forward; and I may add now that these orders were repeated three times during the day. Nothing was ever said or ordered of an echelon movement of which my brigade was to be the directing brigade, or that I was to guard McLaws' flank." See OR 27/2: 359; Wilcox, "General C. M. Wilcox on the Battle of Gettysburg," in *SHSP*, 6:98.

3. OR 27/1: 533; Ladd, The *Bachelder Papers*, 1:225-226; De Trobriand, *Four Years With The Army of the Potomac*, 503; Pfanz, *Gettysburg: The Second Day*, 365.

4. OR 27/1: 533; Ladd, *The Bachelder Papers*, 1: 607-608; Gottfried, *Brigades of Gettysburg*, 221; Pfanz, *Gettysburg: The Second Day*, 347-348.

5. OR 27/1: 559, 566; Toombs, *New Jersey Troops*, 237-240; Gottfried, *Brigades of Gettysburg*, 221-222; Pfanz, *Gettysburg: The Second Day*, 347-348; Imhof, *Gettysburg Day Two*, 161; Winschel, "Their Supreme Moment," *Gettysburg Magazine* 1, 74. The 120th reported practically as many casualties, 203 total (53.0% casualty rate), as the 71st and the 72nd regiments combined. Although historians have been quick to assail the Excelsiors' performance, the 70th did manage 117 casualties (40.6%), including only four M/C, while the 71st (91 K/W/C) and 72nd (114 K/W/C) both estimated 37.4%. The 72nd had the highest number of M/C in Brewster's brigade at twenty-eight. See Busey and Martin, 246.

6. OR 27/1: 422, 533, 27/2: 618, 631; Wilcox, "General C.M. Wilcox on the Battle of Gettysburg," in *SHSP*, 6:99; *Imhof, Gettysburg Day Two*, 157, 166, 171-179; Pfanz, *Gettysburg: The*

Second Day, 348-349; Meade, *Life and Letters,* 2:88-89; Humphreys, *Andrew Atkinson Humphreys,* 198-199; Gottfried, *Brigades of Gettysburg,* 212, 221; Coddington, *The Gettysburg Campaign,* 413-414, 755 n.22; Hyde, *The Union Generals Speak,* 191; Ladd, *The Bachelder Papers,* 1:193-194; Felix Brannigan to father, undated, original in Library of Congress, copy in ALBG files, GNMP; Brown, *History of the Third Regiment, Excelsior Brigade,* 104; Rafferty, "Gettysburg," in *Personal Recollections of the War of the Rebellion,* 26-27.

7. Humphreys, *Andrew Atkinson Humphreys,* 198-199; OR 27/1: 422, 533; Busey and Martin, *Regimental Strengths and Losses,* 246, 272; Gottfried, *Brigades of Gettysburg,* 221; Coddington, *The Gettysburg Campaign,* 413-414, 755 (n. 22); Hyde, *The Union Generals Speak,* 191; Imhof, *Gettysburg Day Two,* 157, 179. Based on Busey and Martin's estimates, only Wadsworth and Rowley's First Corps divisions suffered higher numeric losses. See Busey and Martin, 272.

8. Alexander, "The Great Charge and Artillery Fighting at Gettysburg," in *Battles and Leaders,* 3:360.

9. Imhof, *Gettysburg Day Two: A Study in Maps,* 166; Hartwig, "Was Dan Sickles the Savior of the Union Left on July 2?," *North & South,* Vol. 8, Number 4, 59.

10. Bigelow, *The Peach Orchard,* 16-19, 22, 55-58, 60; Ladd, *The Bachelder Papers,* 1:168; OR 27/1: 882, 897.

11. Bigelow, *The Peach Orchard,* 22-26; Ladd, *The Bachelder Papers,* 1:168-169; OR 27/1: 882-883, 897; Winschel, "Their Supreme Moment," *Gettysburg Magazine* 1, 76; Campbell, "Remember Harper's Ferry," *Gettysburg Magazine* 7, 70.

12. OR 27/1: 370, 472, 660; Winschel, "Their Supreme Moment," *Gettysburg Magazine* 1, 76; Pfanz, *Gettysburg: The Second Day,* 349, 404, 408-409; Bigelow, *The Peach Orchard,* 22-26; *Dedication of the New York State Auxiliary Monument,* 138-139; Campbell, "Remember Harper's Ferry," *Gettysburg Magazine* 7, 51-59, 62-65, 70; Gottfried, *Brigades of Gettysburg,* 175-176; Ladd, *The Bachelder Papers,* 1:481, 3: 1868-1869.

13. OR 27/1: 370; Ladd, *The Bachelder Papers,* 2: 1134, 3:1356; Hancock, *Reminiscences of Winfield S. Hancock,* 196; Campbell, "Remember Harper's Ferry," *Gettysburg Magazine* 7, 64-65; Hyde, *The Union Generals Speak,* 216.

14. OR 27/1: 371, 759, 770, 778, 804; Cleaves, *Meade of Gettysburg,* 154; Pfanz, *Culp's Hill and Cemetery Hill,* 194-197; Ladd, *The Bachelder Papers,* 2:1135; Imhof, *Gettysburg Day Two,* 190-193, 206, 224. For a discussion on exactly how many men Meade intended to detach from Culp's Hill, see Pfanz, *Culp's Hill and Cemetery Hill,* 194-195.

15. OR 27/1:371, 425; Meade, *Life and Letters,* 2:88; Hancock, *Reminisces of Winfield S. Hancock,* 199-200; Ladd, *The Bachelder Papers,* 1, 256-257, 2: 1135; Imhof, *Gettysburg Day Two,* 193, 197; Hill, Throll, and Johnson, "On This Spot. . . ," *Gettysburg Magazine 32,* 96-97; Pfanz, *Gettysburg: The Second Day,* 374.

16. OR 27/2: 608, 614, 619, 621, 623-624, 631-633; 27/1: 422; Wilcox, "General C.M. Wilcox on the Battle of Gettysburg," in *SHSP,* 6:103; Swinton, *Campaigns of the Army of the Potomac,* 352; Imhof, *Gettysburg Day Two,* 197-198, 201-203.

17. Meade, *Life and Letters,* 2:88-89; Cleaves, *Meade of Gettysburg,* 152-154.

18. Jorgensen, *Gettysburg's Bloody Wheatfield,* 124-125, 129; OR 27/1: 593, 654, 657, 662, 685; Meade, Life and Letters, 2:87-88; *Pennsylvania at Gettysburg,* 1: 224-226; Ladd, *The Bachelder Papers,* 2: 1198; Styple, *Generals in Bronze,* 84. Many of the Sixth Corps men were resting and making coffee when they were called into action. Sedgwick's chief of staff Martin McMahon later wondered if this was the cause of the rumors that Sykes' Fifth Corps delayed their support of Sickles in order to make coffee. See Styple, 84.

19. OR 27/2: 358-359; Longstreet, "Lee's Right Wing at Gettysburg," in *Battles and Leaders,* 3:341; Longstreet, *From Manassas to Appomattox,* 373; Longstreet, "General Longstreet's Second Paper On Gettysburg," in SHSP, 5:258. Of course Longstreet's claims that he was facing the entire Federal army was an exaggeration, but as he once explained, "It has never been claimed that we met this immense force of 65,000 men at one time; nor has it been claimed that each and every one of them burnt powder in our faces. But they were drawn off from other parts of the field to meet us, and were hurried to our front and massed there, meaning to do all the mischief

they could." See Longstreet, "General Longstreet's Second Paper On Gettysburg," in SHSP, 5:261.

20. *OR* 27/1: 371, 422, 434, 501,534, 804-806; *New York at Gettysburg*, 2: 606-607; Humphreys, *Andrew Atkinson Humphreys*, 198-199; Brown, *History of the Third Regiment, Excelsior Brigade*, 105; Busey and Martin, *Regimental Strengths and Losses*, 246; Coddington, *The Gettysburg Campaign*, 423-424; Imhof, *Gettysburg Day Two*, 213.

21. *OR* 27/1: 593; Byrne and Weaver, *Haskell of Gettysburg*, 123; Cleaves, *Meade of Gettysburg*, 153.

22. "Affairs at Gettysburgh," New York *Times*, July 18, 1863; Tremain, *Two Days of War*, 90, 103-105; *New York at Gettysburg*, 2: 579. In a letter written to his sister on July 5, Twichell said, "I met the ambulance in which he had been placed, accompanied it, helped lift him out. . . ." Thus it is plausible that Twichell accompanied the ambulance for all or some portion of its ride to the hospital. But taken within the context of Twichell's entire letter, it appears that Twichell was at the hospital, and not on the front line, when he met the ambulance. Perhaps he accompanied the ambulance some short distance to the amputating table. See Jos. Hopkins Twichell to Sister, July 5, 1863, Yale University Library, quoted in Messent and Courtney, *Civil War Letters of Joseph Hopkins Twichell*, 249.

23. "Affairs at Gettysburgh," New York *Times*, July 18, 1863; 1882 Sickles interview, undated newspaper, J. Howard Wert Scrapbook, #34, Vol. 3, 4-5, ACHS; Ladd, *The Bachelder Papers*, 1:239.240; *The Medical and Surgical History of the Civil War*, 2:142, 11:254; Coco, *A Strange and Blighted Land*, 197; Styple, *Generals in Bronze*, 152-153; 225; Detroit *Free Press*, July 10, 1863, Robert L. Brake Collection, USAMHI. Some historians have mistakenly followed Sickles' lead: Knoop in *I Follow the Course, Come What May* (1-2) chooses Calhoun over Sim.

24. Tremain, *Two Days of War*, 90, 105; Ladd, *The Bachelder Papers*, 1:239-240; "Affairs at Gettysburgh," New York *Times*, July 18, 1863; *New York at Gettysburg*, 2: 579-580; Coco, *A Strange and Blighted Land*, 197; *The Medical and Surgical History of the Civil War*, 11: 242; Messent and Courtney, *Civil War Letters of Joseph Hopkins Twichell*, 249; Detroit *Free Press*, July 10, 1863; Henry, *Armed Forces Institute of Pathology*, 11, 29-30.

25. Tremain, *Two Days of War*, 105; "Affairs at Gettysburgh," New York *Times*, July 18, 1863; *The Medical and Surgical History of the Civil War*, 2:143; Detroit *Free Press*, July 10, 1863; "Second Day at Gettysburg," Industrial School *News*, August 13, 1903, copy in Box B-36, GNMP; Pfanz, *Gettysburg: The Second Day*, 334-335.

26. Messent and Courtney, *Civil War Letters of Joseph Hopkins Twichell*, 249; "Affairs at Gettysburgh," New York *Times*, July 18, 1863; W.H. Bullard to Dan Sickles, September 13, 1897, Misc. Mss. Daniel Sickles, New York Historical Society; *The Medical and Surgical History of the Civil War*, 11: 242; Coco, *A Strange and Blighted Land*, 197-200; *Dedication of the New York Auxiliary State Monument*, 112-113; Detroit *Free Press*, July 10, 1863; Coco, *A Vast Sea of Misery*, 80-81; Accounts of S.Chase, E.L. Townsend, and New York *Herald*, July 6, 1863 in Box B-36, GNMP; Andrews, *The North Reports the Civil War*, 422.

27. Coco, *A Strange and Blighted Land*, 197-203; Conklin, *Women at Gettysburg*, 107. Sickles biographers W.A. Swanberg and Thomas Keneally accepted the hospital site as a "ghastly huddle of tents near Taneytown Road." See *Sickles the Incredible*, 217 and *American Scoundrel*, 287-289.

28. 1882 Sickles interview, undated newspaper, J. Howard Wert Scrapbook, #34, Vol. 3, 4-5, ACHS; Coco, *A Vast Sea of Misery*, 80-81; *New York at Gettysburg*, 2: 579; Messent and Courtney, *Civil War Letters of Joseph Hopkins Twichell*, 248-249.

29. For a vast list of potential sites, see Coco, *A Vast Sea of Misery*, 80-81 and *A Strange and Blighted Land*, 199-200; "Interesting Note on Amputation of Sickles' Leg," Gettysburg *Star and Sentinel*, April 19, 1905, Gregory A. Coco Collection, Box B-36, GNMP; Wert, *A Complete Hand-Book*, 121.

30. "Affairs at Gettysburgh," New York *Times*, July 18, 1863; The *Medical and Surgical History of the Civil War*, 2:143.

31. Andrews, *The North Reports the Civil War*, 422; New York *Herald*, July 6, 1863, copy in Box B-36, GNMP.

32. "Affairs at Gettysburgh," New York *Times*, July 18, 1863.

33. *Ibid.*

34. Coco, *A Vast Sea of Misery*, 81; Tremain, *Two Days of War*, 92-93.

35. Tremain, *Two Days of War*, 90-91, 105; Busey and Martin, *Regimental Strengths and Losses*, 245-246, 262, 265. Although the Third Corps' heavy casualties are usually blamed on Sickle's poor positioning, his corps did not suffer the highest Union casualties during the battle. That honor belonged to John Reynolds' First Corps which suffered 6,059 casualties for a 49.6% loss. See Busey and Martin, 270.

36. Ladd, *The Bachelder Papers*, 1:194; Haynes, *A History of the Second Regiment, New Hampshire Volunteer* Infantry, 184; Craft, *History of the 141st Regiment Pennsylvania Volunteers*, 125.

37. *New York at Gettysburg*, 2:873-874.

38. De Trobriand, *Four Years with the Army of the Potomac*, 505-506; OR 27/1: 484-485.

39. De Trobriand, *Four Years with the Army of the Potomac*, 507.

40. Ladd, *The Bachelder Papers*, 2:775; Law, "The Struggle for 'Round Top', in *Battles and Leaders*, 3: 326. The story that Longstreet had been captured, or worse, was replayed in several Northern newspapers following the battle

41. Gibbon, "The Council of War on the Second Day," in *Battles and Leaders*, 3: 313; OR 27/1: 73; Styple, *Generals in Bronze*, 66, 116.

42. Gibbon, "The Council of War on the Second Day," in *Battles and Leaders*, 3: 313-314; OR 27/1:73.

43. Meade, *Life and Letters*, 2: 95-96; OR 27/1: 73-74; Gibbon, "The Council of War on the Second Day," in *Battles and Leaders*, 3: 313-314; Doubleday, *Chancellorsville and Gettysburg*, 184-185; Styple, *Generals in Bronze*, 66; George Meade to Margaret Meade, July 3, 1863, George Meade Collection, HSP. Hancock's allegation that Meade did not like his Gettysburg position was related to sculptor James Kelly in 1880. As William Styple noted, "General Hancock had always been cited by Meade's friends as a supporter of their claim, but his statements to Kelly suggest otherwise." See Styple, 66-67. As will be noted later, the same can also be said of Hancock's Committee on the Conduct of the War testimony.

44. Tremain, *Two Days of War*, 93, 103-105; Brown, *History of the Third Regiment, Excelsior Brigade*, 105; "Affairs at Gettysburgh," New York *Times*, July 18, 1863; Detroit *Free Press*, July 10, 1863; Account of James Rusling, "Misc. Info—Gen. Daniel Sickles," Box B-36, GNMP; "Sued by a Snap-Shot Man," New York *Times*, July 4, 1893.

45. OR 27/2:308, 320, 359, 447; Longstreet, "Lee's Right Wing at Gettysburg," in *Battles and Leaders*, 3: 341-343.

46. OR 27/2: 434; Alexander, "Letter From General E. P. Alexander, March 17th 1877," in *SHSP*, 4: 103-104; Harman, *Cemetery Hill*, 44, 107, 150-151; Hartwig, "Was Dan Sickles the Savior of the Union Left on July 2," in *North & South*, 59; Georg, "The Sherfy Farm and the Battle of Gettysburg," 26. Harman argued persuasively that not only did Sickles prevent Lee from enfilading Cemetery Hill on July 2, but his move also allowed Cemetery Hill artillery to concentrate on destroying Latimer's Battalion on Benner's Hill. See Harman, p 151.

47. Fremantle, *Three Months in the Southern States*, 262; *Pennsylvania at Gettysburg*, 2; 606-607, 612; Georg, "The Sherfy Farm and the Battle of Gettysburg," 25.

48. Craft, *History of the 141st Regiment Pennsylvania Volunteers*, 125; Scott, *History of the One Hundred and Fifth Regiment of Pennsylvania Volunteers*, 83; Diary of Lewis Schaeffer, July 4, 1863 entry, West Virginia University Libraries; Byrne and Weaver, *Haskell of Gettysburg*, 140.

49. Craft, *History of 141st PA*, pg 125; Scott, *History of the One Hundred and Fifth Regiment of Pennsylvania Volunteers*, 83; Styple, *Generals in Bronze*, 77-78; Gottfried, *Brigades of Gettysburg*, 193; Diary of Lewis Schaeffer, July 4, 1863 entry, West Virginia University Libraries. Tippin, in his report, wrote only that in the evening "I was relieved of the command." See OR 27/1: 499.

50. Butterfield, *A Biographical Memorial*, 116, 125-126; *Dedication of the New York Auxiliary State Monument*, 118; Hyde, *The Union Generals Speak*, 239, 258-259; Robert L. Brake Collection, Northern Commanders and Staff Officers Box 4, USAMHI. Washington Roebling's hand-written note is in the margin of 126 of his personal copy of Butterfield's *Biographical Memorial*, housed in the Special Collections of Gettysburg College.

51. OR 27/1: 654, 943; 27/2:360; "Letter From General E. P. Alexander, March 17th 1877," in *SHSP*, 4:109; Longstreet, "Lee's Right Wing at Gettysburg," in *Battles and Leaders*, 3:347; Biddle, "General Meade at Gettysburg," in *The Annals of the War*, 215; Coddington, *The Gettysburg Campaign*, 532-534; Wert, *Gettysburg: Day Three*, 253-254; Brown, *Retreat From Gettysburg*, 10.

52. OR 27/2: 309, 360-361, 370, 373, 376, 430, 448, 608-609; Longstreet, "Lee's Right Wing at Gettysburg," in *Battles and Leaders*, 3:349; Georg, "The Sherfy Farm and the Battle of Gettysburg," 26-27; Brown, *Retreat From Gettysburg*, 73, 75, 93; George Meade to Margaret Meade, July 5, 1863, George Meade Collection, HSP.

Chapter 13: He has Redeemed his Reputation Fully

1. "The Great Battles," The New York *Times*, July 4, 1863; "Latest News From the North," *Weekly Standard* (Raleigh N.C.), July 15, 1863.

2. Tremain, *Two Days of War*, 99-100, 103-104; Rusling, *Lincoln and Sickles;* Swanberg, *Sickles the Incredible*, 221.

3. Rusling, *Lincoln and Sickles*, Daniel E. Sickles Papers, LOC. Pages are not numbered.

4. *Ibid.* Both Lincoln and Fry were deceased when Rusling reprinted the story.

5. *Ibid.;* Peatman, "General Sickles, President Lincoln, and the Aftermath of the Battle of Gettysburg," *Gettysburg Magazine* 28, 117.

6. Rusling, *Lincoln and Sickles.*

7. Quoted in Pfanz, Gettysburg: *The Second Day*, 437; Peatman, "General Sickles, President Lincoln, and the Aftermath of the Battle of Gettysburg," *Gettysburg Magazine* 28, 117.

8. Rusling, *Lincoln and Sickles.*

9. Pfanz, *Gettysburg: The Second Day*, 437; Peatman, "General Sickles, President Lincoln, and the Aftermath of the Battle of Gettysburg," *Gettysburg Magazine* 28, 117-120.

10. Peatman, "General Sickles, President Lincoln, and the Aftermath of the Battle of Gettysburg," *Gettysburg Magazine* 28, 120. Dr. Richard Sauers correctly wrote: "The extant references . . . do not mention exactly what Sickles told Lincoln or any of his other visitors about Meade." See Sauers, *Meade-Sickles Controversy*, 49.

11. Peatman, "General Sickles, President Lincoln, and the Aftermath of the Battle of Gettysburg," *Gettysburg Magazine* 28, 122-123.

12. OR 27/3: 519, Basler, *The Collected Works of Abraham Lincoln*, 6:318; Peatman, "General Sickles, President Lincoln, and the Aftermath of the Battle of Gettysburg," *Gettysburg Magazine* 28, 121; Williams, *Lincoln and His Generals*, 265-266; Goodwin, *Team of Rivals*, 533-536.

13. Hyde, *The Union Generals Speak*, 259-260; Brown, *Retreat from Gettysburg*, 262; Coddington, *Gettysburg Campaign*, 540, 544, 812, (n. 56, n. 60); OR 27/3: 532-533; Peatman, "General Sickles, President Lincoln, and the Aftermath of the Battle of Gettysburg," *Gettysburg Magazine* 28, 120.

14. Peatman, "General Sickles, President Lincoln, and the Aftermath of the Battle of Gettysburg," *Gettysburg Magazine* 28, 120-122.

15. OR 27/1:82-83; Meade, *Life and Letters*, 2:307.

16. OR 27/1:83-85, 88-89.

17. *Ibid.*, 27/1: 193.

18. Humphreys, *Andrew Atkinson Humphreys,* 198-202; Butterfield, *A Biographical Memorial,* 125-126. Less than one year later, in the spring of 1864, Humphreys wrote, "I made a mistake in accepting this position of Chief of Staff and I am vexed at myself for doing it. I have not had a cheerful professional feeling since, except when the Army got into tight places. It has been almost unendurable to me at times." Humphreys' field ambitions were finally realized in 1864 when he received command of the Second Corps. See Humphreys, 218.

19. Coddington, *The Gettysburg Campaign*, 565-566; Allan, "Memoranda of Conversations with Lee," in *Lee the Soldier*, 14; Trudeau, *Gettysburg: A Testing of Courage*, 549.

20. George Meade to Margaret Meade, July 12, 1863, George Meade Collection, HSP; OR 27/3: 669; Brown, *Retreat from Gettysburg*, 318-319, 326; Coddington, *The Gettysburg Campaign*, 567-568; Hyde, *The Union Generals Speak*, 175, 199-200, 234 .

21. OR 27/3: 675, 27/2: 323; Coddington, *The Gettysburg Campaign*, 567-570; Longstreet, "Lee in Pennsylvania," in *Lee the Soldier*, 410; Hyde, *The Union Generals Speak*, 200.

22. OR 27/1: 93, 27/3: 675, 683-684; Coddington, *The Gettysburg Campaign*, 568-570; Brown, *Retreat from Gettysburg*, 353.

23. OR 27/1: 93-94; Meade, *Life and Letters*, 2:312, Cleaves, *Meade of Gettysburg*, 178, 184; Tremain, *Two Days of War*, 100-102; Williams, *Lincoln and His Generals*, 268; Trudeau, *Gettysburg: A Testing of Courage*, 549. Simon Cameron had visited Meade's army and wired Lincoln on the 14th "that the decision of General Meade's council of war on Saturday night, not to attack the rebels, would allow them to escape. His army is in fine spirits and eager for battle. They will win, if they get a chance." Lincoln wanted, in reply, "much to be relieved of the impression that Meade, Couch, Smith, and all, since the battle of Gettysburg, have striven only to get Lee over the river, without another fight." See OR 27/3: 700, 703.

24. OR 27/1:106-110; Hyde, *The Union Generals Speak,* 200-201; Coddington, *The Gettysburg Campaign*, 568-569.

25. OR 27/1: 106-110; Coughenour, "Assessing the Generalship of George G. Meade During the Gettysburg Campaign," *Gettysburg Magazine* 28, 37; Biddle, "General Meade at Gettysburg," in *The Annals of the War*, 216; Trudeau, *Gettysburg: A Testing of Courage*, 549; Hyde, *The Union Generals Speak,* 200-201. As an additional example, Peatman wrote: "Attacking Lee's entrenched army was a move that a general like Dan Sickles might have advocated, and no doubt did advocate to Lincoln on July 5, but was not one that a trained soldier like George Meade would be so foolish as to undertake." See Peatman, "General Sickles, President Lincoln, and the Aftermath of the Battle of Gettysburg," *Gettysburg Magazine* 28, 122-123. This rationale ignores the fact that Meade delayed his attack because he was essentially talked out of it, not because he believed it the correct course of action, and that "trained soldiers" Meade and Humphreys still intended to proceed with the plan after spending the 13th reconnoitering. The only accomplishment that we can ultimately be certain of is that the extra day bought Lee time to escape without another battle.

26. Peatman, "General Sickles, President Lincoln, and the Aftermath of the Battle of Gettysburg," *Gettysburg Magazine* 28, 122-123.

27. Tremain, *Two Days of War*, 100, 104; Basler, *The Collected Works of Abraham Lincoln*, 6:322.

28. Tremain, *Two Days of War*, 105-107.

29. New York *Times*, July 6, 1863.

30. "Affairs at Gettysburgh," New York *Times*, July 18, 1863; War Brevities," The Hornellsville *Tribune*, July 23, 1863. Even long-time detractor George Templeton Strong restrained himself from criticism in his diary, recording simply on July 4, "It would seem that General Daniel Sickles has lost a leg." See Strong, *Diary of the Civil War*, 328.

31. Swanberg, *Sickles the Incredible*, 225; "The Health of Gen. Sickles," New York *Times*, July 25, 1863.

32. "Board of Councilmen," New York *Times,* July 29, 1863; "Movements of Maj. Gen. Sickles," New York *Times*, August 12 and August 16, 1863; The Gettysburg *Compiler,* August 10, 1863; Strong, *Diary of the Civil War,* 350-351, 353.

33. Messent and Courtney, *Civil War Letters of Joseph Hopkins Twichell*, 257-258; "Movements of Maj. Gen. Sickles," New York *Times*, August 12 and 16, 1863; Basler, *The Collected Works of Abraham Lincoln*, 6: 402.

34. Army Navy *Journal*, August 29, 1863.

35. "A Letter from Gen. Sickles," New York *Times*, August 13, 1863.

36. Strong, Diary of the Civil War, 350-351; Swanberg, *Sickles the Incredible*, 225-226.

37. Charles Graham account, February 16, 1865, Participant Accounts File 5, GNMP; *Dedication of the New York Auxiliary State Monument*, 146-147; Swanberg, *Sickles the Incredible*, 230, 405 (n. 31); Warner, *Generals in Blue*, 179; Tagg, *The Generals of Gettysburg*, 69.

38. Swanberg, *Sickles the Incredible*, 231; Lash, "The Congressional Resolution of Thanks for the Federal Victory at Gettysburg," *Gettysburg Magazine* 12, 90.

39. OR 27/1: 116.

40. Miller, *Photographic History of the Civil War*, 10:290; Davis, *Life of David Bell Birney*, 111-112; "The Third Army Corps Union," New York *Times*, May 4, 1890; *Dedication of the New York Auxiliary State Monument*, 109.

41. Styple, Our *Noble Blood,* 130-132, 136.

42. "Another Battle on the Bull Run Battle Ground—Gen. Meade succeeded Gen. Sickles," *Burlington Weekly Hawkeye,* October 17, 1863; Swanberg, *Sickles the Incredible*, 405 (n. 38).

43. Styple, *Our Noble Blood*, 140; De Trobriand, *Four Years With the Army of the Potomac*, 545-546; Messent and Courtney, Civil War Letters of Joseph Hopkins Twichell, 269-270.

44. Styple, *Our Noble Blood*, 140; De Trobriand, *Four Years With the Army of the Potomac*, 545-546.

45. CCW, 303.

46. George Meade to Margaret Meade, October 17, 1863, George Meade Collection, HSP; Swanberg, *Sickles the Incredible*, 232; De Trobriand, *Four Years With the Army of the Potomac*, 545.

47. *CCW*, 304.

48. De Trobriand, *Four Years With the Army of the Potomac*, 545; David Birney to George Gross, October 28, 1863, David B. Birney Papers, USAMHI.

49. CCW, 304.

50. Lash, "The Congressional Resolution of Thanks for the Federal Victory at Gettysburg," Gettysburg *Magazine* 12, 91; Swanberg, *Sickles the Incredible*, 236; *Desjardin, These Honored Dead*, 66.

51. Quoted in Swanberg, *Sickles the Incredible*, 236; Desjardin, *These Honored Dead*, 66; Lash, "The Congressional Resolution of Thanks for the Federal Victory at Gettysburg," *Gettysburg Magazine* 12, p 91.

52. Meade*, Life and Letters*, 2: 147, 150, 316; David Birney to George Gross, November 5, 1863, David B. Birney Papers, USAMHI; George Meade to Margaret Meade, October 21 and 23, 1863, George Meade Collection, HSP.

53. Lash, "The Congressional Resolution of Thanks for the Federal Victory at Gettysburg." *Gettysburg Magazine* 12, p 92; CCW, 474; Biddle, *George Gordon Meade: An Address,* 8; "Rumored Removal of Gen. Meade, The Adams *Sentinel,* December 8, 1863.

54. *OR* 27/1: 16.

55. *Ibid.,* 27/1: 16-17.

56. David Birney to George Gross, November 16, 1863, David B. Birney Papers, USAMHI.

57. Meade, *Life and Letters*, 2: 147, 159-160, 318-319; Styple, *Our Noble Blood*, 149-150; Lash, "The Congressional Resolution of Thanks for the Federal Victory at Gettysburg," *Gettysburg Magazine* 12, p 92.

58. Quoted in Swanberg, *Sickles the Incredible*, 238; Desjardin, *These Honored Dead*, 67.

59. "Third Corps Reunion," Undated newspaper clipping, GNMP Vertical File 4-10K; Byrne and Weaver, *Haskell of Gettysburg*, 188.

60. Meade, *Life and Letters* 2:164; Swanberg, *Sickles the Incredible*, 238; Desjardin, *These Honored Dead,* 67; Lash, "The Congressional Resolution of Thanks for the Federal Victory at Gettysburg," *Gettysburg Magazine* 12, p 92.

Chapter 14: Subsequent Events Proved My Judgment Correct

1. Meade, *Life and Letters*, 2: 161; Lash, "The Congressional Resolution of Thanks for the Federal Victory at Gettysburg," *Gettysburg Magazine* 12, 92. Butterfield had written to Wilson as his "friend" in December 1862 when Meade replaced him as commander of Fifth Corps. See Butterfield, *A Biographical Memorial,* 112.

2. OR 27/1: 140.

3. Meade, *Life and Letters*, 2: 161; Lash, "The Congressional Resolution of Thanks for the Federal Victory at Gettysburg," *Gettysburg Magazine* 12, 92, 94-95; Jordan, *Winfield Scott Hancock*, 105-107. On February 20, a letter signed "Truth" appeared in the Army and Navy *Journal* wondering "by what strange process or reasoning or distortion of facts is the name of Major General Howard placed in this resolution?" It stated, probably accurately, that Hancock was

(after Meade) the most prominent Union general at Gettysburg. Howard wrote Hancock assuring him that he did not "want to enter into a newspaper controversy" and that Hancock also deserved the thanks of Congress. Hancock replied, "I do consider that an act of injustice was done by Congress, in singling out any corps commander at Gettysburg for his services there. . ." See Jordan, 105-106. Further proof that newspaper, ego, and battles for recognition within the Army of the Potomac were not limited to Dan Sickles.

4. Lash, "The Congressional Resolution of Thanks for the Federal Victory at Gettysburg," *Gettysburg Magazine* 12, 93-94.

5. "List of General Officers Without Commands," New York *Times*, January 15,1864; Swanberg, *Sickles the Incredible*, 243-244; Basler, *The Collected Works of Abraham Lincoln*, 7:160.

6. Basler, *The Collected Works of Abraham Lincoln,* 7:160.

7. Swanberg, *Sickles the Incredible*, 245; Basler, *The Collected Works of Abraham Lincoln*, 7:176, 180, 185, 204-205.

8. Basler, *The Collected Works of Abraham Lincoln*, 7:185.

9. *Ibid.*, 7: 204-205.

10. Tap, *Over Lincoln's Shoulder*, 18, 21, 22-24; Hyde, *The Union Generals Speak*, X, 2-5; Sauers, *Gettysburg: The Meade-Sickles Controversy*, 50; Byrne and Weaver, *Haskell of Gettysburg*, 84.

11. Tap, *Over Lincoln's Shoulder*, 25-30, 167, 176-177; Hyde, *The Union Generals Speak*, 6-15, 18-19; Sauers, *Gettysburg: The Meade-Sickles Controversy*, 50.

12. Tap, *Over Lincoln's Shoulder*, 177-180; Sauers, *Gettysburg: The Meade-Sickles Controversy*, 50-51.

13. Sauers, *Gettysburg: The Meade-Sickles Controversy*, 50-51.

14. Basler, *The Collected Works of Abraham Lincoln*, 6: 350, 381.

15. Sauers, *Gettysburg: The Meade-Sickles Controversy*, 50, 170-171, n. 3; Swanberg, *Sickles the Incredible*, 240. Bruce Tap, in his study of the committee, wrote: "W.A. Swanberg states that Sickles met privately with Wade and Chandler to discuss strategy, which suggests not an impartial investigation but one instituted to prove a foregone conclusion." Tap references Swanberg 232-240 as the source of this statement. See Tap, 178, 288 (n. 25). However, what Swanberg actually says in that passage is considerably less certain. "*Undoubtedly* [emphasis added], during that fall and winter he had a few private tête-à-têtes with Senators Wade and Chandler." See Swanberg, 240. Swanberg provides no sources for this statement.

16. Hyde, *The Union Generals Speak*, 31; Swanberg, *Sickles the Incredible*, 245; Tap, *Over Lincoln's Shoulder*, 178.

17. CCW, 3-4, 14, 304.

18. CCW, 295-296; Hyde, *The Union Generals Speak*, 32.

19. CCW, 296-297; Hyde, *The Union Generals Speak*, 33-34, 53.

20. CCW, 297; Hyde, *The Union Generals Speak*, 37; OR 27/3: 468.

21. Hyde, *The Union Generals Speak*, 32-33, 46.

22. *CCW*, 298; Hyde, *The Union Generals Speak*, 38-42.

23. OR 27/1: 16-17, 116; Brandt, *The Congressman Who Got Away With Murder*, 194-195; Gettysburg *Compiler,* July 25, 1859.

24. CCW, 298; Hyde, *The Union Generals Speak*, 42-43.

25. Hyde, *The Union Generals Speak*, 44-45.

26. Hyde, *The Union Generals Speak*, 44-45; *CCW*, 298-299.

27. *CCW*, 299-300; Hyde, *The Union Generals Speak*, 38-39, 46.

28. CCW, 300-301; Hyde, *The Union Generals Speak*, 48-49, 53-54.

29. CCW, 302; Hyde, *The Union Generals Speak*, 46-50.

30. CCW, 302-303; Hyde, *The Union Generals Speak*, 46-50.

31. Hyde, *The Union Generals Speak*, 31.

32. *Ibid.*, 58-64; David Birney to George Gross, October 28, 1863, David B. Birney Papers, USAMHI; Tagg, *The Generals of Gettysburg*, 26; Desjardin, *These Honored Dead*, 71, 213, n. 23;CCW, 15.

33. Hyde, *The Union Generals Speak*, 58-60, 67.

34. *Ibid.*, 68-73.

35. *Ibid.*, 73-77.

36. Tagg, *The Generals of Gettysburg*, 111-112; Hyde, *The Union Generals Speak*, 79-80; Kauffman, *American Brutus*, 337; *OR* 27/1: 675. Howe also blamed Sedgwick, not Hooker, for the Chancellorsville defeat, further suggesting that he was in bed with the Republicans. See Tap, *Over Lincoln's Shoulder*, 179-180.

37. Hyde, *The Union Generals Speak*, 82-86, 93.

38. Meade, *Life and Letters*, 2: 172-173; Hyde, *The Union Generals Speak*, 81 Sauers, *Gettysburg: The Meade-Sickles Controversy*, 53-54; Tap, *Over Lincoln's Shoulder*, 182; Desjardin, *These Honored Dead*, 70.

39. Hyde, *The Union Generals Speak*, 94-95.

40. *Ibid.*, 95.

41. *Ibid.*, 96.

42. *Ibid.*, 100-101, 105-106, 293; Meade *Life and Letters*, 2: 171-175; George Meade to Margaret Meade, March 6, 1863, George Meade Collection, HSP; Sauers, *Gettysburg: The Meade-Sickles Controversy*, 54.

43. George Meade to Margaret Meade, March 6, 1863, George Meade Collection, HSP; Meade, *Life and Letters*, 2: 171-175; CCW, 329; Tap, *Over Lincoln's Shoulder*, 183; Hyde, *The Union Generals Speak*, 102.

44. CCW, 330-331; Hyde, *The Union Generals Speak*, 103-105.

45. CCW, 331; Hyde, *The Union Generals Speak*, 106-107.

46. CCW, 332-333; Hyde, *The Union Generals Speak*, 108-109.

47. George Meade to Margaret Meade, March 6, 1863, George Meade Collection, HSP.

48. CCW, 342-343, 347; Meade, *Life and Letters*, 2:171, 175; Hyde, *The Union Generals Speak*, 100-101, 121, 293; Sauers, *Gettysburg: The Meade-Sickles Controversy*, 53-54, 56; Desjardin, *These Honored Dead*, 71. Stanton's support of Meade is surprising. In addition to his relationship with Sickles, Stanton had supported the committee's efforts from the beginning and believed that West Pointers were too soft on slavery. Ironically, despite his long Sickles relationship, Stanton derided military officers who exposed themselves to politics. The administration also realized that a public feud between two high-ranking generals would do the war effort no good. Stanton eventually sent Meade word that a court of inquiry was unnecessary and would play into Sickles' hand. See Hyde 100, 292.

49. George Meade to Margaret Meade, March 6, 1863, George Meade Collection, HSP; Meade, *Life and Letters*, 2:169-170.

50. *OR* 25/1: 773-774, Styple, *Generals in Bronze*, 121-122, 132; Hyde, *The Union Generals Speak,* 139-140, 143; Swanberg, *Sickles the Incredible*, 194.

51. David Birney to George Gross, October 28, 1863, and March 16, 1864, David B. Birney Papers, USAMHI.

52. Ladd, *The Bachelder Papers*, 1:100; David Birney to George Gross, September 25, 1863 and March 16, 1864, David B. Birney Papers, USAMHI.

53. CCW, 367-368; Hyde, *The Union Generals Speak*, 149-159. Author Bill Hyde, in his modern study of the committee, thought that Birney's testimony about relieving Geary's division and putting his line "on Round Top" was "at odds with Birney's battle report." On this point, this author disagrees with Hyde's assessment. Birney states in his report that his left was "on the Sugar Loaf Mountain"; this is materially close enough to Birney's testimony in this author's opinion. There is a discrepancy in timing, his report states 7:00, while his testimony said it occurred about 9:00; but timing differences were common. Hyde also believes that Birney omitted "receiving orders from Sickles" in order to not undermine Sickles' claim to have no orders. But Birney's testimony clearly states that he received orders from someone—it seems logical that those orders would be received from Sickles (his commanding officer). See *OR* 27/1:482.

54. CCW, 375; Hyde, *The Union Generals Speak*, 159-162.

55. Meade, *Life and Letters*, 2: 176-177, 320-321.

56. *OR* 27/1: 122; David Birney to George Gross, March 16, 1864, David B. Birney Papers, USAMHI.

57. *OR* 27/1: 125-126, 136-137.

58. CCW, 377; David Birney to George Gross, October 28, 1863 and April 5, 1864, David B. Birney Papers, USAMHI; Hyde, *The Union Generals Speak*, 166-168.

59. CCW, 377-381; Hyde, *The Union Generals Speak*, 168-169, 172-173, 179.

60. CCW, 384-385; Hyde, *The Union Generals Speak*, 170, 178.

61. Hyde, *The Union Generals Speak*, 179-181.

62. Meade, *Life and Letters*, 2: 176-177; *OR* 27/1: 123-127.

63. Sauers, *Gettysburg: The Meade-Sickles Controversy*, 56-57; Basler, *The Collected Works of Abraham Lincoln*, 7: 235; CCW, 347-349; Hyde, *The Union Generals Speak*, 122-123. General Meade also revised his earlier (March 5) appearance and now stated that he "did not wait for the report from General Hancock, as I can prove from staff officers who took my orders" before concentrating at Gettysburg. Meade submitted his July 1 (1:10 m.) order to General Winfield Hancock as Exhibit 'H'. It reads: "If you think the ground and position there a (better) suitable one to fight a battle under existing circumstances, you will so advise the general, and he will order all the troops up." See CCW, 356. But when Hancock testified on March 22, 1864, he submitted his copy of the order, which only stated, "If you think the ground and position there a better one to fight. . . ." In Hancock's copy, the word "suitable" was omitted. See CCW, 412. It is interesting to note that General Daniel Butterfield's copy also did not include the word "suitable." See CCW, 423.

At question is whether Meade waited for Hancock's messages before deciding to concentrate at Gettysburg, and whether Hancock was supposed to compare the ground at Gettysburg as "better" than Pipe Creek. Given the committee's agenda, it was to Meade's obvious benefit to prove that he decided, on his own, to advance on Gettysburg without awaiting the counsel of any of his subordinates. In Meade's favor, Meade had wired Halleck at 6:00 p.m. on July 1, 1863, indicating that all corps except the Sixth (Sedgwick) were now marching to the field, and "I see no other course than to hazard a general battle." Meade said that he was not influenced by the report of Major William Mitchell (which Hancock had sent from Gettysburg around 4:00 m.). However, Hancock's widow later wrote that Meade's second version was "in error." She argued that it would "seem quite improbable" that Meade would order up the army without hearing from Hancock. She also accused Meade of doctoring the order to Hancock which was deposited with the War Department, specifically changing the word "better" in his original order to "suitable" to de-emphasize Meade's desire for Hancock to compare Gettysburg and Pipe Creek. Mrs. Hancock also believed that the marching orders for the Fifth and Sixth Corps were not timed until 7:00 and 7:30 m., proving that Meade did not order these corps forward until he had heard from Hancock. But George Sykes said that he left Hanover *at* 7:00, implying that he must have received the order earlier. In sorting through the matter, esteemed historian Edwin Coddington decided that Mitchell's report "probably" arrived just after Meade sent the 6:00 message. See *OR* 27/1: 71-72; 27/3: 483; Hyde, *The Union Generals Speak*, 124-125; Hancock, *Reminiscences of Winfield Scott Hancock*, 191-193. Coddington, *The Gettysburg Campaign*, 324.

64. Sauers, *Gettysburg: The Meade-Sickles Controversy*, 56-57; Tap, *Over Lincoln's Shoulder*, 185.

65. Meade, *Life and Letters*, 2: 321-323.

66. *Ibid.*, 2: 180, 323-331.

Chapter 15: My Only Motive is to Vindicate History

1. *OR* 27/1: 128.

2. *Ibid.*, 27/1: 129-130.

3. *Ibid.*, 27/1: 130.

4. *Ibid.*, 27/1: 130-131.

5. *Ibid.*

6. *Ibid.*, 27/1: 131.

7. *Ibid.*, 27/1: 131-132.

8. *Ibid.*, 27/1: 132.

9. *Ibid.*

10. *Ibid.*, 27/1: 132-133.

11. *Ibid.*, 27/1: 133-134.

12. *Ibid.*, 27/1: 135-136.

13. *Ibid.*, 27/1: 127-128.

14. Meade, *Life and Letters*, 2: 178-180; *OR* 27/1: 137-139.

15. Pfanz, *Gettysburg: The Second Day*, 143, 484 (n.30).

16. Graham, *The Custer Myth*, 318.

17. Cleaves, *Meade of Gettysburg*, 229-230; Sauers, *Gettysburg: The Meade-Sickles Controversy*, 172 (n.30); Ladd, *The Bachelder Papers*, 1:9-10; Hyde, *The Union Generals Speak*, 291; Desjardin, *These Honored Dead*, 84-85. Since Bachelder had Meade's permission to remain with the army through the winter, then it seems unlikely that Bachelder would have risked Meade's wrath by becoming Historicus. Meade's relations with his critics were never cordial, and if discovered as Historicus then Bachelder's fledgling research risked being decapitated before it had barely begun. Bachelder's 1890s correspondence on the Sickles/Butterfield/Meade debate will be discussed later in this narrative. See Ladd, *The Bachelder Papers*, 3: 1904-1907.

18. De Peyster, *Gen. H. Edwin Tremain*, 8.

19. Meade, *Life and Letters*, 2:339.

20. James Barnes to David Birney, August 22, 1863, copy Robert Brake Collection, USAMHI; William Tilton to James Barnes, March 14, 1864, copy on file GNMP.

21. Meade, *Life and Letters*, 2:331-335. For different veterans' versions of the encounter between Zook and Barnes' troops, see *Pennsylvania at Gettysburg*, 2:683-684; Parker, *History of the Twenty-Second Massachusetts*, 335; Pfanz, *Gettysburg: The Second Day*, 275.

22. Meade, *Life and Letters*, 2:338; Sauers, *Gettysburg: The Meade-Sickles Controversy*, 59.

23. *OR* 27/1: 138. Mackenzie's letter was in response to a request from Meade. See Norton, *Attack and Defense*, 292.

24. Meade, *Life and Letters*, 2: 181-183.

25. "General Meade and the Army of the Potomac," The Adams *Sentinel*, March 15, 1864.

26. CCW, 388-389, 393-395, 397-398; Hyde, *The Union Generals Speak*, 182-193, 195-202.

27. Jordan, *Winfield Scott Hancock, A Soldier's Life*, 107; CCW, 403-405; Hyde, *The Union Generals Speak*, 207-208, 211-212, 214.

28. CCW, 407; Hyde, *The Union Generals Speak*, 214-216.

29. CCW, 407-408, 410, 412; Hyde, *The Union Generals Speak*, 216, 218-220, 223, 225-226.

30. CCW, 429-431; Butterfield, *A Biographical Memorial*, 126-127, 135; Warner, *Generals in Blue*, 62; Hyde, *The Union Generals Speak*, 238-241, 264-267; Tap, *Over Lincoln's Shoulder*, 185-186.

31. Quoted in Swanberg, *Sickles the Incredible*, 253; Hyde, *The Union Generals Speak*, 240; Sauers, *Gettysburg: The Meade-Sickles Controversy*, p 62; Tap, *Over Lincoln's Shoulder*, 185-186. For the gap in Butterfield's movements for March 1864, see Butterfield, *A Biographical Memorial*, 142-143.

32. *OR* 27/1: 138-139; 27/3: 458-459; CCW, 417-419, 422; Hyde, *The Union Generals Speak*, 241-246, 250-251, 269, 271.

33. CCW, 422-423; Hyde, *The Union Generals Speak*, 251-253.

34. CCW, 424; Hyde, *The Union Generals Speak*, 254-256.

35. CCW, 425; Hyde, *The Union Generals Speak*, 256.

36. CCW, 433; Hyde, *The Union Generals Speak*, 256, 270-272; Coddington, *The Gettysburg Campaign*, 340.

37. CCW, 439-441; Hyde, *The Union Generals Speak*, 257-259, 268, 272-275.

38. CCW, 439-441; Hyde, *The Union Generals Speak*, 278-280; Gibbon, *An Address on the Unveiling of the Statue of Major General George G. Meade*, 3.

39. CCW, 441-442; Hyde, *The Union Generals Speak*, 282-283.

40. CCW, 435-436; Hyde, *The Union Generals Speak*, 293-295; Sauers, *Gettysburg: The Meade-Sickles Controversy*, 63.

41. CCW, 436-438; Hyde, *The Union Generals Speak*, 296-299; "The Battle of Gettysburg, Statement by Major General Meade," The Adams *Sentinel*, April 12, 1864. Meade read his 3:00 p.m. July 2 message to Halleck into evidence, which does not indicate any specifics of a potential attack from his left.

42. CCW, 449-451; Hyde, *The Union Generals Speak*, 304-307.

43. CCW, 452; Hyde, *The Union Generals Speak*, 310-311, 317-320.

44. CCW, 453-454; Hyde, *The Union Generals Speak*, 312-313.

45. Meade, *Life and Letters*, 2:186-190, 337-340; Sauers, *Gettysburg: The Meade-Sickles Controversy*, 61-62; Jacob Sweitzer to James Barnes, April 8, 1864, copy on file GNMP.

46. Jordan, *Winfield Scott Hancock*, 107-108; *Meade Life and Letters*, 2: 189-190; Davis, *Life of David Bell Birney*, 211; De Trobriand, *Four Years With The Army of the Potomac*, 564, 567; OR 27/1:104-105.

47. David Birney to George Gross, April 5 and April 18, 1864, David B. Birney Papers, USAMHI; Meade, *Life and Letters*, 2: 189-190; George Meade to Margaret Meade, April 11, 1864, George Meade Collection, HSP; Jordan, *Winfield Scott Hancock*, 108.

48. George Meade to Margaret Meade, April 11 and 18, 1864, George Meade Collection, HSP; David Birney to George Gross, April 5 and April 18, 1864, David B. Birney Papers, USAMHI; Meade, *Life and Letters*, 2: 189-190; Jordan, *Winfield Scott Hancock*, 108.

49. Jordan, *Winfield Scott Hancock*, 108.

50. David Birney to George Gross, October 28, 1863, David B. Birney Papers, USAMHI; De Trobriand, *Four Years with the Army of the Potomac*, 517-518, 530; Styple, *Generals in Bronze*, 96-97; Coddington, *The Gettysburg Campaign*, 559-560.

51. Hyde, *The Union Generals Speak*, 299-300, 324-328; CCW, 464; Coddington, *The Gettysburg Campaign*, 340, 719 (n. 68); Meade *Life and Letters*, 2: 182. Although Sedgwick testified that he had never heard any retreat talk, Martin T. McMahon, who served as Sedgwick's chief of staff during the battle, later claimed that Sedgwick had told him prior to the council that Meade "was thinking of a retreat." See Styple, *General in Bronze,* 84.

52. CCW, 464-468; Hyde, *The Union Generals Speak*, 333-339; Sauers*, Gettysburg: The Meade-Sickles Controversy*, 65.

Chapter 16: Spoil a Rotten Egg

1. CCW, 468-473; Hyde, *The Union Generals Speak*, 340-351; Meade, *Life and Letters*, 2: 186-188; Tap, *Over Lincoln's Shoulder*, 187-192. After Crawford, the committee took additional testimony relative to Meade's tenure in command. Provost Marshal General Marsena Patrick testified on February 1, 1865 regarding the Mine Run campaign, whose failure he primarily blamed on the performance of the Third Corps under French. See CCW, 474. Meade (May 16, 1865) and Ulysses Grant (May 18, 1865) were also called to offer their opinions regarding Edwin Stanton's management of the War Department. See CCW, 523-524.

2. Meade*, Life and Letters*, 2: 175; David Birney to George Gross, April 5, 1864, David B. Birney Papers, USAMHI.; Meade, *Life and Letters*, 2: 203-205 .

3. *Dedication of the New York Auxiliary State Monument*, 113; De Peyster, *Gen. H. Edwin Tremain*, 5; Butterfield, *A Biographical Memorial*, 246-247; Swanberg, *Sickles the Incredible*, 260-265; Van Alstyne, *Diary of an Enlisted Man*, 341.

4. Davis*, Life of David Bell Birney*, 274-279; De Trobriand, *Four Years With The Army of the Potomac*, 654; Warner, *Generals in Blue*, 34-35.

5. Davis*, Life of David Bell Birney*, 283, 292, 301, 305, 307; Philadelphia Newspaper clipping, July 17, 1914, David B. Birney Papers, USAMHI.

6. Davis*, Life of David Bell Birney*, 327; De Trobriand, *Four Years With The Army of the Potomac*, 654; George Meade to Margaret Meade, October 19, 1864, George Meade Collection, HSP; Meade, Life and Letters, 2: 235. Meade's quote that "I never liked him personally. . . ." was stricken from the published *Life and Letters*.

7. Swanberg, *Sickles the Incredible*, 266-268; Humphreys, *Andrew Atkinson Humphreys*, 256-257; *Dedication of the New York Auxiliary State Monument*, 113; Jordan, *Winfield Scott Hancock*, 171-175.

8. Sickles, "Leaves From My Diary," 18-19; Swanberg, *Sickles the Incredible*, 269, 272-273; *Dedication of the New York Auxiliary State Monument*, 113; Daniel E. Sickles Military Records, copy in Box B-36, GNMP. In January 1865, Sickles wrote a testimonial praising "The Palmer [Artificial] Leg." Sickles wrote, "I have great pleasure in bearing testimony to the excellence of the artificial leg you made for me. I have used it long enough to convince me of the superior mechanical construction of the limbs you make." See Box B-36, Misc. Info—Gen. Daniel Sickles, GNMP.

9. CCW, LV; Hyde, *The Union Generals Speak*, 352-354; Tap, *Over Lincoln's Shoulder*, 192.

10. CCCW, LXI; Hyde, *The Union Generals Speak*, 361.

11. CCW, LXI-LXVI, LXXV; Hyde, *The Union Generals Speak*, 361-370, 372-373, 378-379.

12. Desjardin, *These Honored Dead*, 76; Hyde, *The Union Generals Speak*, 55-56, 380-381; Sauers, *Gettysburg: The Meade-Sickles Controversy*, 66.

13. Daniel E. Sickles Military Records, copy in Box B-36, GNMP; "Major-Gen. Daniel E. Sickles in Boston," New York *Times*, August 20, 1865; *Dedication of the New York Auxiliary State Monument*, 113; Sickles, *Oration Delivered . . . At Fredericksburg*, 15; Swanberg, *Sickles the Incredible*, 275-280; O'Connor, *Sheridan*, 286-287. The other Military Districts were: First (Virginia) under John Schofield, Third (Georgia, Alabama, and Florida) under John Pope, Fourth (Arkansas, Mississippi) under Edward Ord, and Fifth (Louisiana, Texas) under Phil Sheridan.

14. De Peyster, *Gen. H. Edwin Tremain*, 6-8; Swanberg, *Sickles the Incredible*, 275, 282-283; Keneally, *American Scoundrel*, 324: Knoop, *I Follow the Course*, 117.

15. Brandt, *The Congressman Who Got Away With Murder*, 207-209, Pinchon, *Dan Sickles*, 224-225; Swanberg, *Sickles the Incredible*, 284-286; Keneally, *American Scoundrel*, 327-329; Knoop, *I Follow the Course*, 118.

16. Brandt, *The Congressman Who Got Away With Murder*, 207-209, Pinchon, *Dan Sickles*, 224-225; Swanberg, *Sickles the Incredible*, 284-286; Keneally, *American Scoundrel*, 327-329; Knoop, *I Follow the Course*, 118. As an example of biographer treatment, Edgcumb Pinchon speculated in 1945 that "in his heart he doubted if she [Laura] ever would cease to blame him for her mother's desolation, her own blighted childhood." See Pinchon, 224-225. More recently, biographer Jeanne Knoop may have come closer to the mark when she speculated that Dan had neither the time nor experience to adjust as a father: "Dan was not used to dealing with an adolescent and the time it would take away from his busy schedule. . . ." See Knoop, 120.

17. *Dedication of the New York Auxiliary State Monument*, 113; Daniel E. Sickles Military Record, Box B-36, GNMP; Swanberg, *Sickles the Incredible*, 286.

18. Sickles, *Oration Delivered . . . At Fredericksburg, VA*, 15; *Dedication of the New York Auxiliary State Monument*, 113; Sickles, "Leaves From My Diary," 22-24, NYPL; Swanberg, *Sickles the Incredible*, 278-281, 287-292; "Progress of Reconstruction in South Carolina," New York *Times*, September 24, 1867; "The Conflict Between the Civil and Military Powers. Gen. Sickles' Defence of His Administration," New York *Times*, September 6, 1867; "Removal of Gen. Sickles," New York *Times*, September 2, 1867. Not that Sickles was an enlightened crusader for racial equality by modern standards. During a 1900 speech in Fredericksburg, Sickles frequently referred to blacks as "Sambo," and mimicked speech patterns that would be considered insensitive to modern ears. Sickles was a product of the time he lived in and such talk was, nevertheless, perfectly acceptable to 1900 audiences. See *Sickles, Oration Delivered . . . At Fredericksburg*, 5-6.

19. Swanberg, *Sickles the Incredible*, 296, 298, 302-306; *Dedication of the New York Auxiliary State Monument*, 113-114; "Serenade to Gen. Sickles," New York *Times*, September 14, 1867.

20. Swanberg, *Sickles the Incredible*, 306-312; *Dedication of the New York Auxiliary State Monument*, 114; General Orders # 54, June 18, 1869, Sickles Papers, LOC. A significant portion of Sickles' Library of Congress papers consist of correspondence concerning Spain and Cuba. See Daniel E. Sickles Papers, Container 2.

21. "Chancellorsville," New York *Times*, June 3, 1867. For Meade and Pfanz's thoughts on the Tremain-Historicus connections, see Pfanz, *Gettysburg: The Second Day*, 143, 484 (n.30).

22. Sauers, *Gettysburg: The Meade-Sickles Controversy*, 67-69.

23. Swinton, *Campaigns of the Army of the Potomac*, 340-341; Piston, *Lee's Tarnished Lieutenant*, 96, 104-105, Wert, *General James Longstreet*, 413, 422. A full accounting of Longstreet's postwar

controversies is beyond the scope of this work. Much of Longstreet's battles were fought in the pages of the Southern Historical Society Papers. See "Causes Of The Defeat Of General Lee's Army At The Battle Of Gettysburg — Opinions Of Leading Confederate Soldiers," in SHSP Vol. IV, No. 2-6, August through December 1877 for examples.

24. Meade, *Life and Letters*, 2: 300-306; Cleaves, *Meade of Gettysburg*, 340, 346-351; Jordan, *Winfield Scott Hancock*, 229.

25. Hempel, "Gone and Nearly Forgotten," *Gettysburg Magazine* 34, 86-89, 92; Platt, *This is Holy Ground*, 3,5; Harrison, "A Fitting and Expressive Memorial," 1-2; Smith and Adelman, *Devil's Den*, 73-74.

26. Cole and Frampton, *Lincoln and the Human Interest Stories of the Gettysburg National Cemetery*, 7-9, 14-16; Georg, "This Grand National Enterprise," GNMP, 1-10; Hempel, "Gone and Nearly Forgotten," *Gettysburg Magazine* 34, 89-91; Everett's speech quoted from http://douglassarchives.org/ever_b21.htm; Hawthorne, *Gettysburg: Stories of Men and Monuments*, 7, 131.

27. Ladd, *The Bachelder Papers*, 1:9-10; Platt, *This is Holy Ground*, 5-6; Platt, *This is Holy Ground*, 5; Vanderslice, *Gettysburg: Then and Now*, 360; Smith and Adelman, *Devil's Den*, 73-74; Cole and Frampton, *Lincoln and the Human Interest Stories*, 17.

28. Swanberg, *Sickles the Incredible*, 326.

29. *Ibid.*, 320-321, 325, 328, 331; William Hobart Royce to Edgcumb Pinchon, December 25, 1941 and July 26, 1942, William Hobart Royce Papers, MSS. & Archives Section, NYPL; "Minister Sickles' Marriage and Trip to New York," New York *Herald*, November 28, 1871; "Minister Sickles' Marriage and Tour from Madrid," New York *Herald*, November 30, 1871; *Dedication of the New York Auxiliary State Monument*, 114; Keneally, *American Scoundrel*, 335. Swanberg placed his salary at $16,800 but Sickles later said that his pay was only $12,000. See Swanberg, 325 and "Gen. Sickles' Latchstring," New York *Times*, October 28, 1892.

30. Swanberg, *Sickles the Incredible*, 333-338, 340-341; "Alleged Difficulty Between General Sickles and Secretary Fish," New York *Herald*, February 6, 1872; "General Sickles as a Mediator," New York *Herald*, February 14, 1872; Keneally, *American Scoundrel*, 337.

31. Swanberg, *Sickles the Incredible*, 341, 343-345; Keneally, *American Scoundrel*, 335-337.

32. Swanberg, *Sickles the Incredible*, 345-351; Gettysburg *Compiler*, December 21, 1873; The Dixon *Telegraph*, December 3, 1873; "Gen. Sickles' Latchstring," New York *Times*, October 28, 1892.

33. Swanberg, *Sickles the Incredible*, 323, 351-358; Keneally, *American Scoundrel*, 338-339.

34. Vanderslice, *Gettysburg: Then and Now*, 363-364, 367; Hempel, "Gone and Nearly Forgotten," *Gettysburg Magazine* 34, 96; Platt, *This is Holy Ground*, 7; Smith and Adelman, *Devil's Den*, 74; Weeks, *Gettysburg*, 59.

Chapter 17: Some Strange Perversion of History

1. Pinchon, *Dan Sickles*, 263-264; Swanberg, *Sickles the Incredible*, 358-359; William Hobart Royce to Edgcumb Pinchon, December 6, 1941, William Hobart Royce Papers, MSS. & Archives Section, NYPL; Sauers, *Gettysburg: The Meade-Sickles Controversy*, 69; GAR Citizens Auxiliary Committee telegram to Sickles, May 31, 1882, Daniel E. Sickles Papers, LOC (copy in Reel #1 USAMHI); Crecy, "Personal Recollections of Old Medical Officers.," in Military Surgeon 60, 73-74. Special thanks to Michael Rhode, Otis Historical Archives, National Museum of Health and Medicine, Armed Forces Institute of Pathology, for directing the author to the Sickles/Otis story.

2. Swanberg, *Sickles the Incredible*, 359; "Congressional Nominations," New York *Times*, October 26, 1876; "A Grand Grant Meeting," New York *Times*, June 1, 1880; The Mountain *Democrat*, October 9, 1880; The Helena *Independent*, October 29, 1880; Jordan, *Winfield Scott Hancock*, 280, 283, 306, 313-315.

3. Jordan, *Winfield Scott Hancock*, 283, 306, 313-315; Styple, *Generals in Bronze*, 68-70; Hancock, *Reminiscences of Winfield Scott Hancock*, 250-251; "Tributes From Two Comrades," New

York *Times*, February 10, 1886. Although Hancock had publicly repudiated his claims that Meade wanted to retreat, Kelly claimed that Hancock admitted that the statement was true during a meeting in April 1885, only a few months before Hancock's death. Regarding the July 2 War Council, Doubleday wrote in his book that Meade was "displeased with the result . . . and said angrily, 'Have it your own way, gentlemen, but Gettysburg is no place to fight a battle in.' Although Doubleday offered a number of reasons why a retreat was justified, he added that there was "no question in my mind" that Meade "did desire to retreat." See Doubleday, *Chancellorsville and Gettysburg*, 184-185.

4. Wert Scrapbook, Volume 3, #34, 7-8, ACHS.

5. *Ibid.*

6. "At Gettysburg," Chester *Times*, June 8, 1882.

7. Wert Scrapbook, Volume 3, #34, 4-5, ACHS.

8. Rafferty, "Gettysburg," In *Personal Recollections of the War of the Rebellion*, 1:16-19, 23-24, 28-29, 31-32. Rafferty blamed Meade's staff, not Meade himself, for deceiving the new commander into thinking an attack would hit the Federal right.

9. *Ibid.*, 1:20-21. Rafferty also claimed, inaccurately, "The fact remains that the Fifth Corps did not move till Hood's flank attack had broken and rolled up Sickles' line."

10. *New York at Gettysburg*, 1: 1-6; Pinchon, *Dan Sickles*, 263-264.

11. *New York at Gettysburg*, 1: 1-6, 32-68. New York's sacrifice was certainly worthy of commemoration. Approximately 23,105 New York soldiers served at Gettysburg and sustained total casualties of 6,700 (29%). New York suffered the highest numeric casualties of any state at Gettysburg. See Busey and Martin*, Regimental Strengths and Losses at Gettysburg*, 275.

12. Sauers, *Gettysburg: The Meade-Sickles Controversy*, 70.

13. *Ibid.*; "Sickles at Gettysburg," press clipping, June 29, 1886, GNMP.

14. "Sickles at Gettysburg," press clipping, June 29, 1886, GNMP.

15. Foster to Bachelder, March 5, 1886, in Ladd, *The Bachelder Papers*, 3: 1951-1952.

16. "Third Corps Reunion," Undated newspaper clipping, GNMP Vertical File 4-10K.

17. *Ibid.*

18. *Ibid.*; Washington *Post*, July 3, 1886.

19. Sauers, *Gettysburg: The Meade-Sickles Controversy*, 72-73.

20. Meade, Life *and Letters*, 2: 350-351.

21. *Ibid.*, 2: 352. Meade wrote that he actually agreed with James Longstreet's criticism of Lee's battle plan. "Longstreet's advice to Lee was sound military sense; it was the step I feared Lee would take, and to meet which, and be prepared for which was the object of my instructions to Butterfield, which he so misrepresented." In referring to the Pipe Creek order, Meade correctly called it for what is was: a contingency that supposed "a part of my army, overwhelmed by superior numbers, compelled to fall back." See *Life and Letters*, 2: 352-353.

22. *Ibid.*, 2: 353.

23. *Ibid*, 2: 354.

24. *Ibid.* The National Park Service quotes from this letter in its existing Peach Orchard wayside exhibit, ensuring that modern visitors will be swayed to Meade's version of the controversy.

25. "Gen Sickles Speaks Out," New York *Times,* August 14, 1886.

26. *Ibid.*

27. *Ibid.*

28. *Ibid.* For the *Times* interview, Sickles read Meade's 3:00 Halleck telegram as: "If satisfied the enemy is endeavoring to move to my rear I shall fall back to my supplies at Westminster." Meade's actual wording was: "If not attacked, and I can get any positive information of the position of the enemy which will justify me in so doing, I shall attack. If I find it hazardous to do so, or am satisfied the enemy is endeavoring to move to my rear and interpose between me and Washington, I shall fall back to my supplies at Westminster." See OR 27/1: 72.

29. "Sickles at Gettysburg," reprinted in Philadelphia *Weekly Times*, August 16, 1886. Copy on file at GNMP; Sauers, *Gettysburg: The Meade-Sickles Controversy*, 174 (n. 15). Sauers notes that

McClellan was living in Minnesota at that time. Humphreys refers to Captain McClellan specifically in his report as "my special aide." See OR 27/1: 535.

30. McLaws, "The Federal Disaster on the Left," Philadelphia *Weekly Press*, August 4, 1886. Copy on file GNMP vertical files, *Gettysburg Newspaper Clippings*, 6: 117-119.

31. Vanderslice, *Gettysburg: Then and Now*, 379-380.

32. "It's Again a Tented Field," New York *Times*, July 1, 1888; Undated newspaper article, Folder #190, Battle of Gettysburg: 25th Anniversary, ACHS; Wert Scrapbook, #34, Vol. 3, 146; Gettysburg *Star and Sentinel*, July 17, 1888.

33. "It's Again a Tented Field," New York *Times*, July 1, 1888.

34. New York *World*, July 4, 1888. Copy in ACHS, Folder #190, Battle of Gettysburg 25th Anniversary.

35. *Ibid.*; Wert, Gettysburg Battlefield Scrap Book, ACHS, #34, Vol. 3, 149.

36. *New York at Gettysburg*, 2: 575, 698.

37. *Dedication of the New York Auxiliary State Monument,* 147; Tagg, *The Generals of Gettysburg*, 69; "Funeral of Gen. Charles K. Graham," New York *Times*, April 20, 1889; Vanderslice, *Gettysburg: Then and Now*, 392; Warner, *Generals in Blue*, 180.

38. Smith, *A Famous Battery and Its Campaigns*, 14 9; Ladd, *The Bachelder Papers*, 3: 1600, 1756, 1766-1767, 1793, 1803; Hawthorne, *Gettysburg: Stories of Men and Monuments*, 12.

39. Vanderslice, *Gettysburg: Then and Now*, 376; Ladd, *The Bachelder Papers*, 3: 1601, 1673.

40. Ladd, *The Bachelder Papers*, 3: 1961-1962.

41. "Pennsylvania Day," Gettysburg *Star and Sentinel*, September 17, 1889.

42. *New York at Gettysburg*, 2: 814-820; Ladd, *The Bachelder Papers*, 3: 1757.

43. Ladd, *The Bachelder Papers*, 3: 1905-1907. Bachelder's comments would seem to prove that he had no involvement with Historicus.

44. Ladd, *The Bachelder Papers*, 3: 1905-1907. Lt. Col Richard N. Batchelder (Quartermaster General's Office) also wrote to Bachelder on September 29, 1890: "I directed Col. Hudington to write you about Gen. Sickles attempt to get the high point in the Cem. as a site for the N.Y. Monument. Gov. Beaver has since filed a protest with the Sec. and I think the New Yorkers will have to seek a new location." See Ladd, *The Bachelder Papers*, 3:1964. For speculation on Bachelder's influence on Sickles' lack of statue, see Ladd, *The Bachelder Papers*, 3:1837 (n. 73). The dates of monuments to other Union Corps commanders are: Hancock (1896), Howard (1932), Reynolds (1871 and 1899), Sedgwick (1913), and Slocum (1902). Meade's was erected in 1896. A few statues, Buford and Warren, do pre-date these. See Harrison, *The Location of the Monuments, Markers, and Tablets on Gettysburg Battlefield*, 41-42.

45. "Visit of the Count of Paris," Gettysburg *Star and Sentinel*, October 21, 1890. Copy in ACHS.

46. *Ibid.*

47. *Ibid.*

48. Sickles, "Further Recollections of Gettysburg," in *North American Review*, 258-259.

49. *Ibid.*, 260-267.

50. Swanberg, *Sickles the Incredible*, 364; *Dedication of the New York Auxiliary Monument*, 114; Colorado Spring *Gazette*, April 3, 1890; *Morning Oregonian*, April 6, 1890; *Freeborn County Standard*, April 10, 1890.

51. *Dedication of the New York Auxiliary State Monument*, 114; "The Third Army Corps Union," New York *Times*, May 4, 1890.

52. Hawthorne, *Gettysburg: Stories of Men and Monuments*, 113-114; Styple, *Generals in Bronze*, 99.

53. Gettysburg *Star and Sentinel*, September 29, 1891; Wert Scrapbook, #33, Vol. 2, 203-204, ACHS. The GBMA had ruled that monuments were to be placed where regiments had formed in a line of battle. This would have placed the 72nd's monument near present Hancock Avenue, where several monuments such as the 42nd New York are located. During the battle, the men of the 72nd had hesitated to advance from this line to the stone wall when ordered to do so by their new brigade commander, Alexander Webb. However, as "Pickett's Charge" increased in

post-war popularity, the men of the 72nd insisted on placing their monument near the stone wall. They were ultimately allowed to place their monument in this position after carrying their case to the Pennsylvania Supreme Court. See Hawthorne, *Gettysburg: Stories of Men and Monuments*, 119.

54. Sickles Correspondence, November 22, 1883, Daniel E. Sickles Papers, LOC (copy in Reel #1 of Sickles Papers, USAMHI). When did Laura Sickles die? Swanberg (365), Keneally (343), and Brandt (209) all say 1891, and Brandt provides a date of December 10. The Green-Wood Cemetery records indicate, however, that she died May 23, 1892 and was buried on May 26. Thanks to Jane Cuccurullo at The Green-Wood Cemetery and Licensed Battlefield Guide Ellen Pratt for providing this information. William Hobart Royce was also told by a Sickles acquaintance (admittedly many years after the fact) that it occurred in 1892, although December 10, 1891 would be close enough. See Royce to Edgcumb Pinchon, December 6, 1941, William Hobart Royce Papers, MSS. & Archives Section, NYPL.

55. Sickles, "Introduction," in *Lee and Longstreet at High Tide*, 18-19; "Ninth's Veterans Swap War Yarns," New York *Times*, May 28, 1911.

56. Sickles, "Introduction," *Lee and Longstreet at High Tide*, 18-19; "Ninth's Veterans Swap War Yarns," New York *Times*, May 28, 1911; Sawyer, *Before Manassas & After Appomattox,* 104.

57. Last Will and Testament of George Sickles, Anthony Jerome Griffin Papers, Manuscripts and Archives Division, NYPL; "General Sickles' Latchstring," New York *Times*, October 28, 1892; "Sale of the Sickles Property at Auction Yesterday," New York *Times*, October 9, 1895; "The Sickles Estate Sold at New Rochelle Yesterday," New York *Times*, October 15, 1895; "Mrs. Mary S. Sickles' Will," New York *Times*, July 16, 1893; NYC Police Department to Sickles, December 17, 1884; "The Veteran Congressman Sickles," The Marion *Daily Star*, June 14, 1894. Robert L. Wensley to Dan Sickles, July 16, 1898, Sickles Papers, LOC, shows that Dan was receiving money as trustee for Stanton and as General Guardian of Eda. Thanks to John Shaud for providing access to George Sickles' will.

58. "Veterans, How Can You Vote For Cleveland or McKaig?," *The Herald and Torchlight*, October 6, 1892; "Sickles on His Talks," The Trenton *Times*, October 22, 1892; www.whitehouse.gov.

59. "Veterans, How Can You Vote For Cleveland or McKaig?," *The Herald and Torchlight,* October 6, 1892; "Sickles on His Talks," The Trenton *Times*, October 22, 1892; "Veterans Favor Mr. Cleveland," Gettysburg *Compiler*, October 18, 1892; "Sickles for Cleveland," Gettysburg *Compiler*, October 25, 1892.

60. The Salem *Daily News*, November 1, 1892.

61. "Sickles Up For Congress," New York *Times*, October 18, 1892. As a typical example of how Sickles' return to Congress has been treated by authors, Pinchon (264) stated that Sickles really had only one goal, to rescue the Gettysburg battlefield from commercialization, souvenir hunters, and vandals via government intervention. While this was undoubtedly one of Sickles' personal pet goals, it was an unlikely motivation for New York's Tammany Hall to offer his nomination, and an equally unlikely reason for New Yorkers to vote for him.

62. *Ibid.*; "Sickles for Cleveland," Gettysburg *Compiler*, October 25, 1892. Sickles' "loyalty" to Cleveland did not apparently extend beyond Sickles' election. In June 1893, shortly after taking office, Sickles told the newspapers: "Everybody knows that I have not the utmost confidence in Mr. Cleveland's political capacity or statesman like quality." See "The Financial Situation," Decatur (Ill) *Daily Republican*, June 1, 1893.

63. "Gen McMahon Protests," New York *Times*, October 18, 1892; "McMahon Will Fight Sickles," The Trenton *Times*, October 20, 1892; "Sickles Means to Stick," New York *Times*, October 20, 1892; Styple, *Generals in Bronze*, 83.

64. "Sickles Means to Stick," New York *Times*, October 20, 1892. The decision over whether Sickles was entitled to receive his retired army pay continued even after he took office. See "Gen. Sickles' Case Undecided," *The Herald and Torchlight* (Hagerstown, MD), December 14, 1893.

65. "Sickles on His Talks," The Trenton *Times*, October 22, 1892; "Gen. Sickles' Latchstring.," New York *Times*, October 28, 1892; "New York," New York *Times*, November 7, 1892; The Trenton *Times*, November 9, 1892; New York *Times*, May 5, 1914.

66. "Hooker's Old Guard," The Trenton *Times*, April 6, 1893; Sickles, Introduction, *Lee and Longstreet at High Tide*, 20; "On Gettysburg Field Again," New York *Times*, May 1, 1893; Swanberg, *Sickles the Incredible*, 367; Sawyer, *James Longstreet: Before Manassas & After Appomattox*, 121.

67. "On Gettysburg Field Again," New York *Times*, May 1, 1893.

68. Record of 51st Congress 1st Session, House of Representatives Report #2069.

69. Smith and Adelman, *Devil's Den*, 78-81.

70. *Ibid.*, *Devil's Den*, 83-86.

71. *New York at Gettysburg*, 1: 195-209; "Sued by a Snap-Shot Man," New York *Times*, July 4, 1893.

72. *New York at Gettysburg*, 1: 204.

73. *Ibid.*, 1: 235; Hawthorne, *Stories of Men and Monuments*, 134-135.

74. *New York at Gettysburg*, 1: 236-240.

75. *Ibid.*, 1: 238.

76. "At Their Memorial Temple," New York *Times*, July 3, 1893; Hawthorne, *Gettysburg: Stories of Men and Monument*, 76; Email from Fred Hawthorne to author, March 18, 2009; *New York at Gettysburg*, 2:574.

77. *New York at Gettysburg*, 2:584-586, 596-597; "At Their Memorial Temple," New York *Times*, July 3, 1893.

78. Hawthorne, *Gettysburg: Stories of Men and Monument*, 54; *New York at Gettysburg*, 1: 340.

79 *New York at Gettysburg*, 1: 342-343.

80. Gettysburg *Star and Sentinel*, July 11, 1893; Gettysburg *Compiler*, July 11, 1893; Gettysburg *Compiler*, October 3, 1893; "Sued by a Snap-Shot Man," New York *Times*, July 4, 1893; Adelman and Smith, *Devil's Den: A History and Guide*, 86.

81. Gettysburg *Compiler*, July 11, 1893; "Sued by a Snap-Shot Man," New York *Times*, July 4, 1893; *New York at Gettysburg*, 1:266.

82. Vanderslice, *Gettysburg: Then and Now*, 396; "Election of Officers," Gettysburg *Star and Sentinel*, June 2, 1891; "Memorial Association Meeting," Gettysburg *Compiler*, July 11, 1893; Sickles, "Further Recollections of Gettysburg," in *North American Review*, 270-271.

83. Gettysburg *Compiler*, August 28, 1894.

84. "The Veteran Congressman Sickles," The Marion *Daily Star*, June 14, 1894.

85. Record of 53rd Congress, 2nd Session, HR #205, 190, 192.

86. Record of 53rd Congress, 2nd Session, 7657-7658.

87. Smith and Adelman, *Devil's Den*, 87; Harrison, "A Fitting and Expressive Memorial," 3; Platt, *This is Holy Ground*, 7-8; "Improvements at Gettysburg," Gettysburg *Compiler*, August 28, 1894.

88. Smith and Adelman, *Devil's Den*, 87; Platt,, *This is Holy Ground*, 7.

89. Record of 53rd Congress, House of Representatives, 2nd Session, 5535-5537. Copy in ALBG files.

90. Record of 53rd Congress, Senate, 2nd Session, 5630-5631, 5925. Copy in ALBG files; Smith and Adelman, *Devil's Den*, 87, 90; Platt, *This is Holy Ground*, 7; "The Gettysburg Trolley," Washington *Post*, June 1, 1894.

91. Paige and Greene, Administrative History of Chickamauga and Chattanooga National Military Park, http://www.nps.gov/chch/adhi/adhi.htm.

92. "Battle Lines at Gettysburgh," House of Representatives, 51st Congress, 1st Session, 1-6; Lee, *Origin & Evolution of the National Military Park*; "Sickles Wants a Park," *Evening Times*, August 27, 1894; Sickles Correspondence, November 20, 1894. Original in Library of Congress, copy on file at GNMP.

93. "Tammany Hall Nominations," Bangor *Daily Whig and Courier*, October 12, 1894; "Healing Democratic Differences," Middletown *Daily Argus*, October 24, 1894; The Hornellsville *Weekly Tribune*, October 26, 1894.

94. "Vote for Congressman," New York *Times*, November 8, 1894; "Congressman Elect Dead," The Trenton *Times*, December 7, 1894; Gettysburg *Compiler*, December 11, 1894; "Died of Bright's Disease," Bangor *Daily Whig and Courier*, December 7, 1894.

95. Record of 53rd Congress, House of Representatives, 105. Copy in ALBG files.

96. Record of 53rd Congress, House of Representatives, 3rd Session, 1038-1039. Copy in ALBG files.

97. *Ibid.*, 1226-1227. Copy in ALBG files; Platt, *This is Holy Ground*, 37-38.

98. Record of 53rd Congress, Senate, 3rd Session, 577, 1278, 1715, 1815, 2010, 2109; House Record 1227.

99. Gettysburg *Compiler*, January 29, 1895; "The Part Which Gettysburg Has in the Two Bills," Gettysburg *Compiler*, June 4, 1895; "Gettysburg's Opposition to the Park," Philadelphia *Inquirer* editorial reprinted in Gettysburg *Compiler*, June 4, 1895.

100. "National Parks," Gettysburg *Compiler*, May 7, 1895.

101. "Forget They Were Foes," Fort Wayne *Weekly Gazette*, February 7, 1895; Indiana *Weekly Messenger*, March 6, 1895.

102. "The Battlefield Memorial Association," Gettysburg *Compiler*, May 28, 1895; Vanderslice, *Gettysburg: Then and Now*, 388-391; Platt, *This is Holy Ground*, 8.

103. "Amos J. Cummings Nominated," New York *Times*, October 6, 1895; "The Choice for Congress," New York *Times*, October 14, 1896; "Parade of the Army and Naval Veterans Yesterday at Pittsburg." Hamilton *Daily Republican*, September 12, 1894; "To Settle the Monument Site," New York *Times*, October 3, 1895; "Fairfield Items," Gettysburg *Compiler*, November 1, 1898; "New Sachems of Tammany," *Evening Times* (Cumberland MD), April 16, 1895; "Dead on Both Sides Remembered," *Evening Times*, May 31, 1895.

104. Hawthorne, *Gettysburg: Stories of Men and Monuments*, 77; *New York at Gettysburg*, 2: 599, 605.

105. Arrington, *The Medal of Honor at Gettysburg*, 23; www.medalofhonor.com.

106. Ladd, *The Bachelder Papers*, 3: 1504; Styple, *Generals in Bronze*, 148-149, 161.

107. *New York at Gettysburg*, 1: 1-6; Coddington, The Gettysburg Campaign, 340-341.

108. *New York at Gettysburg*, 1: 1-6, 32-68.

109. *Ibid.*, 1:37.

110. *Ibid.*, 1:38.

111. *Ibid.*, 1: 38-39.

112. *Ibid.*

113. *Ibid.*

114. Gettysburg *Star and Sentinel*, May 30, 1899; "Longstreet and Sickles to Meet at Gettysburg," Philadelphia *Times*, May 28, 1899; GNMP copy.

115. Gettysburg *Compiler*, June 6, 1899. Lieutenant Longstreet told the crowd: "My father is both a good speaker and a good fighter. I am not a good speaker but want to be a good fighter but have not had a good chance . . . I have never worn the gray but I have worn the blue and I know that my southern people are proud of me for it." It was less than forty years since the battle and the son of the Confederacy's supposed "outcast" was speaking to a Northern audience while wearing a US Army uniform.

116. Gettysburg *Compiler*, June 6, 1899.

Chapter 18: The Civil War is Only a Memory

1. *Sickles, Oration Delivered . . . . At Fredericksburg*, 2, 4, 17-18, 20.

2. *Ibid.*, 24.

3. "Gen. Sickles Lauds Low," New York *Times*, October 25, 1903; W.M. Stewart to Governor Roosevelt, March 13, 1900, Daniel E. Sickles Papers, LOC (copy in reel #1, Sickles Papers, USAMHI).

4. Styple, *Generals in Bronze*, 72, 148-149; Butterfield, *A Biographical Memorial*, 76, 220-221, 245; "Gen Butterfield Suddenly Stricken," New York *Times*, April 14, 1901; Gettysburg *Compiler*, July 9, 1901; "Gen. Butterfield Dead," New York *Times*, July 18, 1901; Atlanta *Constitution*, July 18, 1901. Sickles is largely absent from Julia Butterfield's *Biographical Memorial*, adding to the possibility of a late-life rift between the two men.

5. Pinchon, *Dan Sickles*, 266-267; Longstreet, *Lee and Longstreet at High Tide*, 15. The Henry Slocum equestrian monument was dedicated on September 19, 1902. See Harrison, *The Location of Monuments, Markers and Tablets*, 41.

6. Longstreet, *Lee and Longstreet at High Tide*, 15-16.

7. *Ibid.*, 7-17; Wert, *General James Longstreet*, 425-426; Connelly, *The Marble Man*, 90. Author Thomas Connelly's description of Longstreet's death is stereotypical of much of the Gettysburg literature. "In 1904, deaf, pain-ridden by his Wilderness wound, and half blind from cancer, the outcast Longstreet died in Georgia." Although his health was indeed poor, Longstreet's final years had not been as empty as the "outcast" label implies. The Southern Historical Society attacks on his war record had created much anger and bitterness, but they had not dominated the final decades of his life. Longstreet was surrounded throughout this period by his large family, traveled when his health permitted, was active in politics, and was a popular speaker throughout the North.

8. Sickles, "Introduction," in *Lee and Longstreet at High Tide*, 17-18, 30.

9. *Ibid.*, 21-22.

10. *Ibid.* 22-25. In further defending Longstreet's decision not to attack earlier on July 2, Sickles noted that Lee's report *had* implied some censure towards Longstreet's actions on July 3, when Lee stated that "Longstreet's dispositions were not completed as early as expected." Therefore, Sickles pointed out, "If General Lee did not hesitate to point out unlooked for delay on July 3, why was he silent about delay on July 2? His silence about delay on July 2 implies that there was none on July 2." See 22-23.

11. *Ibid.*, 30; Pinchon, *Dan Sickles*, 267-268.

12. "On Historic Spot," Washington *Post*, May 31, 1904; "Roosevelt Visits Gettysburg Field," New York *Times*, May 31, 1904.

13. Kaplan, *Mr. Clemens and Mark Twain*, 82; Twain, *Mark Twain's Autobiography*, 1:337. There are numerous references to Twichell in Twain's memoirs. See *Mark Twain's Autobiography* 2:5-6, 21-26, 204-212. Twain related how twenty-five years earlier in Hartford, on a Sunday morning as he was getting ready to preach, Twichell received a false report that Sickles had died. Twichell's mind became "far away. All his affection and homage and worship of his general had come to the fore. His heart was full of these emotions. He hardly knew where he was." The congregation was amazed as he began his sermon "in this broken voice and with occasional tears trickling down his face . . . half crying—his voice continually breaking." The congregation had never seen him like that and the episode had evidently aroused Twain's curiosity about a man who could arouse such devotion. See Twain 1-341-342.

14. Twain, *Mark Twain's Autobiography*, 1:337-338.

15. *Ibid.*, 1:339.

16. *Ibid.*, 1:339-340.

17. *Ibid.*, 1:340-341.

18. The National *Tribune,* March 31, 1910.

19. *Ibid.*

20. Hawthorne, *Gettysburg: Stories of Men and Monuments*, 82-83; Gettysburg *Compiler*, August 3, 1910; Gettysburg *Compiler,* September 14, 1910, Gettysburg *Compiler*, September 28, 1910.

21. Hawthorne, *Gettysburg: Stories of Men and Monuments*, 82-83; Gettysburg *Compiler*, October 5, 1910.

22. Styple, *Generals in Bronze*, p 162.

23. "Sickles Guest of the 12th," New York *Times*, April 22, 1911; "For General Sickles' Book – Personal Research," William Hobart Royce Papers, MSS. & Archives Section, NYPL. See Tagg, *The Generals of Gettysburg* for a quick reference on the dates of death of the other corps commanders. Of the old Third Corps, Birney died in 1864 (67), Graham in 1889 (69), Ward in 1903 (71), Regis de Trobriand 1897 (72), Humphreys in 1883 (75), Joseph Carr in 1895 (77), Brewster in 1869 (79) and George Burling died in 1885 (80).

24. Styple, *Generals in Bronze*, 100.

25. *Ibid.*

26. *Ibid.*

27. *Lincoln and Sickles,* and *Letters on the Successful Movements of the 3rd Army Corps* are both in Daniel E. Sickles Papers, LOC.

28. Affidavit of L. Edward Jenkins, formerly a sergeant in the 1st Mass. Infantry, April 28, 1911. Included in *Letters on the Successful Movements of the 3rd Army Corps,* Daniel E. Sickles Papers, LOC; "Gen Sickles Dead," Gettysburg *Star and Sentinel,* May 5, 1914. Included in the correspondence between Sickles and Curtin was a letter from Sickles dated October 23, 1889. This has since been reprinted in Ladd, *The Bachelder Papers,* 3: 1653-1654.

29. Brig. General Edward S. Salomon to Sickles, January 8, 1911; George A. Forsyth to Gen. Goodale, January 28, 1911. Included in *Letters on the Successful Movements of the 3rd Army Corps,* Daniel E. Sickles Papers, LOC.

30. Adams County *News,* October 15, 1910; Gettysburg *Times,* May 31, 1910, "Ninth's Veterans Swap War Tales," New York *Times,* May 28, 1911; Gettysburg *Compiler,* August 14, 1912; "Loyal Legion Bars Gen. Sickles Again," New York *Times,* November 2, 1911.

31. "Loyal Legion Bars Gen. Sickles Again," New York *Times,* November 2, 1911; New York *Times,* May 4, 1914.

32. United States Federal Census for 1870, 1880, and 1900; William Hobart Royce to Edgcumb Pinchon, December 25, 1941, William Hobart Royce Papers, MSS. & Archives Section, NYPL.; Swanberg, *Sickles the Incredible,* 417 (n.16); "Miss Wilmerding Dead," New York *Times,* February 11, 1914; "George G. Sickles Buried," New York *Times,* March 21, 1887; "Sickles Bitterly Assails His Wife," Gettysburg *Times,* September 27, 1912; "Gen. Sickles' Son Seeks Lost Million," New York *Times,* September 4, 1915. Stanton's 1915 interview clearly indicates that he considered the other woman to still be alive.

George Wilmerding's household of daughters Joanna, Julia, and Eleanor are on the 1870 Federal Census in New York's 15th Ward. Eleanor's birth is "about 1855." In the 1880 census, the family has moved to Suffolk, New York. George's occupation is farmer. "Ella" is 24 and still at home. By the 1900 census, the three sisters are still together (all single) in Suffolk, with the oldest sister Joanna (48 years old) as the head of household. Eleanor is 44 years old on the 1900 census, with a birth date of "June 1855." Stanton confirmed in his 1915 interview that Eleanor had two sisters named Johanna [sic] and Julia, both of whom were still living.

33. William Hobart Royce to Edgcumb Pinchon, December 25, 1941, William Hobart Royce Papers, MSS. & Archives Section, NYPL; Pinchon, *Dan Sickles,* 268-269, 271; Keneally, *American Scoundrel,* 346-347. In approaching Sickles' romantic liaisons, Pinchon admitted that Sickles "seems to have been notorious for his amours.... But in all this I have not a single fact to quote. I have rumors only." Pinchon received much assistance from Sickles' grandson who "explicitly . . . does not wish this side of his grandfather's character glossed over . . ." See Pinchon to Royce, October 22, 1941, Royce Papers, NYPL.

34. William Hobart Royce to Edgcumb Pinchon, December 25, 1941, William Hobart Royce Papers, MSS. & Archives Section, NYPL; Swanberg, *Sickles the Incredible,* 380; Pinchon, *Dan Sickles,* 268-269, 271; Keneally, *American Scoundrel,* 348-349. Based on contemporary accounts, it is assumed that Wilmerding lived with Dan. However, the 1910 U.S. census only has Sickles residing with servants Frazier and Sarah Mosley. The census also confirms the confusion over Dan's birth year, which is listed as "about 1826." See Department of Commerce and Labor Bureau of the Census, 1910 U.S. Federal census.

35. William Hobart Royce to Edgcumb Pinchon, December 18 and December 25, 1941, William Hobart Royce Papers, MSS. & Archives Section, NYPL; Pinchon, *Dan Sickles,* 268-269, 271; Keneally, *American Scoundrel,* 348-349; New York *Times,* May 14, 1914.

36. "Sickles' Goods Saved by Wife," Adams County *News,* September 14, 1912; New York *Times,* May 4, 1914; Keneally, *American Scoundrel,* 350; Swanberg, *Sickles the Incredible,* 382.

37. "Sickles Will Not See Wife," Adams County *News,* September 21, 1912; "Sickles Bitterly Assails Wife," Gettysburg *Times,* September 27, 1912; "Poses as Messenger to Serve Sickles," New York *Times,* October 4, 1912; "Mrs. Sickles Saves Husband's Home Again," Adams County *News,* October 26, 1912; New York *Times,* May 4, 1914.

38. New York *Times*, May 4, 1914; "Sickles Will Not See Wife," Adams *County News*, September 21, 1912; "Son Gets Threatening Note," New York *Times*, October 4, 1912; "Daughter Sues Sickles," Adams County *News*, December 14, 1912; "Gen. Sickles' Son Seeks Lost Million," New York *Times*, September 4, 1915.

39. Swanberg, *Sickles the Incredible*, 384; "Sickles in More Trouble," Adams County *News*, December 14, 1912; Pinchon, *Dan Sickles*, 208-209.

40. Swanberg, *Sickles the Incredible*, 384-385; "Sickles in More Trouble," Adams County *News*, December 14, 1912; Pinchon, *Dan Sickles*, 208-209.

41. "Sickles in More Trouble," Adams County *News*, December 14, 1912; Styple, *Generals in Bronze*, 153.

42. "To Pay Big Debt," Adams County *News*, December 28, 1912; "Wife Makes Appeal," Adams County *News*, February 8, 1913; William Hobart Royce to Edgcumb Pinchon, December 18, 1941, William Hobart Royce Papers, MSS. & Archives Section, NYPL; Swanberg, *Sickles the Incredible*, 384.

43. "Missouri Won't Aid Sickles," New York *Times*, January 30, 1913.

44. "Helen Longstreet's Offer," New York *Times*, January 28, 1913; Swanberg, *Sickles the Incredible*, 385.

45. "Mrs. Longstreet to Aid Sickles," Adams County *News*, February 1, 1913; "Denies Sickles Aided Her," New York *Times*, January 29, 1913.

46. "Must Ignore Sickles' Work," Adams Country *News*, February 1, 1913.

47. "Sickles to Prison To-day, But Gently," New York *Times*, January 27, 1913; "Sickles in Custody for a Minute Only," New York *Times*, January 28, 1913; "Mrs. Longstreet to Aid Sickles," Adams County *News*, February 1, 1913; Swanberg, *Sickles the Incredible*, 386-387.

48. "Mrs. Longstreet to Aid Sickles," Adams County *News*, February 1, 1913; Swanberg, Sickles the Incredible, 387.

49. "More Executions," Adams County *News*, February 8, 1913; "Sickles Saved Again, Adams County *News*, March 15, 1913; "Sickles Safe," Adams County *News*, May 3, 1913.

50. William Hobart Royce to Edgcumb Pinchon, December 25, 1941, and "Personal Research," William Hobart Royce Papers, MSS. & Archives Section, NYPL; "Sickles Not Scared," Adams County *News*, May 31, 1913.

51. Warner, Generals in Blue, 447; Gettysburg *Compiler*, January 5, 1910; "Sickles May Come," Adams County *News*, June 21, 1913.

52. "Old Soldiers Defy Heat at Gettysburg," New York *Times*, July 2, 1913; *The Public Ledger*, July 7, 1913; Reardon, *Pickett's Charge in History and Memory*, 192-195; "Lincoln Abused; 7 Men Are Stabbed," Raleigh *News and Observer*, July 3, 1913; The Philadelphia *Inquirer*, July 4 and July 5, 1913; "Gettysburg to Honor Girls of 63," New York *Times*, July 1, 1913; Cohen, *Hands Across the Wall*, 13; "After 50 Years," Untitled newspaper clipping, July 19, 1913, GNMP 11-61.

53. Sickles to General Louis Wagner, November 10 and 23, 1910, PA State Archives; Sickles again mentioned a memorial to the 50th anniversary in the Philadelphia *Inquirer*, July 5, 1913; The Baltimore *Sun*, July 2, 1913; "Gettysburg To Honor Girls of 63," New York *Times*, July 1, 1913; "Will Dedicate New Monument," Gettysburg *Times*, June 28, 1913; Philadelphia *Record*, July 1, 1913; *The North American*, July 3, 1913; Pinchon, *Dan Sickles*, 270. Although Sickles was unique as the last surviving corps commander, he was not the oldest vet in attendance, as one man reportedly topped out at 112. The senior surviving Confederate general, Evander Law, was also in attendance at the relatively young age of seventy-seven. See Cohen, *Hands Across the Wall*, 13.

54. *The North American*, July 1, 1913; The Philadelphia *Inquirer*, July 2 and 3, 1913. Sickles' accounts from the 50th Anniversary can be found in the large scrapbooks on file at the Pennsylvania State Archives (Harrisburg, PA).

55. *The Public Ledger*, July 1, 1913; "After 50 Years," Untitled newspaper clipping, July 19, 1913, GNMP 11-61.

56. *Ibid.*

57. "Old Soldiers Defy Heat," New York *Times*, July 2, 1913, GNMP 11-61; The Baltimore *Sun*, July 2, 1913; "Son and Grandsons of Gen. Longstreet," Atlanta *Constitution*, June 30, 1913; Cohen, *Hands Across the Wall*, 13, 36; Pinchon, *Dan Sickles*, 271.

58. "Sickles Denies Death," *The Public Ledger*, July 5, 1913; "Will Never Meet Again," The Baltimore *American*, July 5, 1913.

59. Journal of Joseph Hopkins Twichell, June 27 – July 9, 1913, Yale Collection of American Literature, Beinecke Rare Book and Manuscript Library; *Dedication of the New York Auxiliary State Monument*, 4, 114-115; Pinchon, *Dan Sickles*, 271; Swanberg, *Sickles the Incredible*, 390. Swanberg's end notes (418, n. 23-24) suggest that he used Twichell's diary as a source. For another example of how the "battlefield is my monument" quote is treated, Knoop (151) paraphrased Swanberg, "Sickles replied that the whole damned battlefield was his memorial, and so it is."

60. It should be noted that New York actually dedicated few individual commander monuments during Sickles' lifetime. Gouverneur Warren's 1888 monument was the first, but was erected without state aid. Slocum's monument followed in 1902, and then George Greene's in 1907. The pace accelerated after Sickles' death: James Wadsworth in 1914, Alexander Webb in 1915, Doubleday and John Robinson in 1917, and Francis Barlow in 1922. In 1923, the New York Monument Commission, which continued after Sickles' death, requested an appropriation for the Auxiliary State Monument "for the purpose of erecting a memorial at Gettysburg to the corps, division or brigade commanders from this state engaged in the battle or who were in charge of New York troops there to whose memory no individual memorial on the field had been provided." Given Sickles' expulsion from the commission, and his inclusion on the Auxiliary monument, it seems unlikely that serious thought was given to him after the Auxiliary dedication in 1925. See *Dedication of the New York Auxiliary State Monument*, 2-4, 114 and Harrison, *The Location of the Monuments, Markers, and Tablets*, 40-42.

61. "Miss Wilmerding Dead," New York *Times*, February 11, 1914; New York *Times*, May 4, 1914; William Hobart Royce to Edgcumb Pinchon, December 25, 1941, William Hobart Royce Papers, MSS. & Archives Section, NYPL. There were conflicting reports over the location of Wilmerding's death and the length of her illness. The *Times* said that she had been ill about three weeks and died at Dan's home. The Reno *Evening Gazette* of February 11 passed along a New York wire report: "Miss Eleanor Earl Wilmerding, for many years the housekeeper for Gen. Daniel Sickles, died yesterday at the home of her sister, with whom she lived. She had been ill about three months."

62. New York *Times*, May 4, 1914; *Swanberg, Sickles the Incredible, 390;* Brandt, *The Congressman Who Got Away With Murder*, 17.

63. New York *Times,* May 4, 1914.

64. New York *Times*, May 5, 1914.

65. "Objection to Bo-Bo's Grave," New York *Times*, August 27, 1905; "George G. Sickles Buried," New York *Times*, March 21, 1887.

66. "Mrs. Sickles Wins Plea," New York *Times*, May 5, 1914. Thanks to Richard "Red" Davis for providing this author with a copy of Nicholson's May 4, 1914 response to the burial request.

67. "Bury Sickles at Arlington," New York *Times*, May 6, 1914.

68. "Comrades in Arms Mourn Gen. Sickles," New York *Times*, May 8, 1914; Email from John Shaud to author, August 22, 2008.

69. *Ibid.*

70. *Ibid.*; William Hobart Royce to Edgcumb Pinchon, December 25, 1941, William Hobart Royce Papers, MSS. & Archives Section, NYPL; "Bury Sickles at Arlington," New York *Times*, May 10, 1914; Journal of Joseph Hopkins Twichell, May 8, 1914 entry, Yale Collection of American Literature, Beinecke Rare Book and Manuscript Library.

71. "Gen. Sickles Dead," Gettysburg *Star and Sentinel*, May 5, 1914.

72. "Gen. Sickles' Will Filed," New York *Times*, November 8, 1914; "Sickles Left Only $500," New York *Times*, November 10, 1914; "Gen. Sickles' Son Seeks Lost Million," New York *Times*, September 4, 1915.

Epilogue: That Damn Fool Sickles

1. New York *Times*, May 5, 1914; Wert, *A Complete Hand-Book*, 121.

2. "Sickles at Gettysburg," *The Nation*, May 1893, copy in Robert L. Brake Collection, USAMHI.

3. *Ibid.*

4. Pfanz, *Gettysburg: The Second Day*, 431; Coddington, *The Gettysburg Campaign*, 442; *Letters on the Successful Movements of the 3rd Army Corps*, Daniel E. Sickles Papers, LOC.

5. Jorgensen, "John Haley's Personal Recollections . . . ," *Gettysburg Magazine* 27, 73.

6. Ladd, *The Bachelder Papers*, 2:995.

7. Jorgensen, "John Haley's Personal Recollections . . . ," *Gettysburg Magazine* 27, 75-77.

8. Moran, "About Gettysburg," National *Tribune*, November 12, 1891. Moran argued that Warren was the day's true hero for having the foresight to occupy Little Round Top.

9. Undated letter from Felix Brannigan to father, copy on file ALBG, original in Library of Congress.

10. As retired U.S. Army officer and Licensed Battlefield Guide Kavin Coughenour wrote: "These divergent opinions represent the gulf in understanding the proper use of terrain in battle between the amateur citizen-soldier [Birney] and the professional, West Point trained Regular Army officer." Coughenour, "Assessing the Generalship of George G. Meade During the Gettysburg Campaign," *Gettysburg Magazine* 28, 35.

11. Styple, *Generals in Bronze*, 90, 98, 99, 177, 194, 215, 225-226.

12. De Trobriand, *Four Years with the Army of the Potomac*, 507, 510.

13. Doubleday, *Chancellorsville and Gettysburg*, 163-164, 167; Byrne and Weaver, *Haskell of Gettysburg*, 245, 248. Sanitizing documents for posterity was a relatively common practice. George Meade's *Life and Letters* as edited for publication omitted criticism of contemporaries such as John Reynolds and even David Birney. For a full summary of mixed accounts that appeared between the 1860s and early 1900s, see Sauers, *Gettysburg: The Meade-Sickles Controversy*, 85-94.

14. Tremain, *Two Days of War*, 12.

15. Alexander, *Military Memoirs*, 392-393.

16. Bigelow, *The Peach Orchard*, 36-37.

17. *Ibid.*

18. Carter, *Four Brothers in Blue*, 318-319.

19. "Sickles Line," undated statement, GNMP Vertical Files 4-10K.

20. Pinchon, *Dan Sickles*, 3, 187-202; Edgcumb Pinchon to William Hobart Royce, October 22, 1941, and Royce to Pinchon, July 16, 1942, William Hobart Royce Papers, MSS. & Archives Section, NYPL; Email from John Shaud to author, August 17, 2008.

21. Swanberg, Sickles the Incredible, 210-211, 390.

22. *Ibid.*, 211.

23. Stackpole, *They Met at Gettysburg*, 190, 192-199, 216, 219-220.

24. Tucker, *High Tide at Gettysburg*, 236-237, 238, 240, 242, 244, 245.

25. Coddington, The Gettysburg Campaign, 445-447.

26. See Shaara, *The Killer Angels*, 175, 208-209.

27. Pfanz, *Gettysburg, The Second Day*, 431.

28. *Ibid.*, 425.

29. McPherson, *Battle Cry of Freedom*, 657-660.

30. Robertson, "The Peach Orchard Revisited," in *The Second Day at Gettysburg*, 53-56.

31. Raver, "Deception and the Citizen-General," in *Gettysburg Magazine* 31, 59; Rollins, "George Gordon Meade and the Defense of Cemetery Ridge," in *Gettysburg Magazine* 19, 59; Peatman, "General Sickles, President Lincoln, and the Aftermath . . . ," in *Gettysburg Magazine* 28, 120,123.

32. Coughenour, "Assessing the Generalship of George G. Meade During the Gettysburg Campaign," *Gettysburg Magazine* 28, 34.

33. *Ibid.*

34. Keneally, *American Scoundrel*, 277, 356.

35. Trudeau, *Gettysburg: A Testing of Courage*, 367.

36. Hyde, *The Union Generals Speak*, 28-31.

37. Sauers, *Gettysburg: The Meade-Sickles Controversy*, xi, 153-159.

38. Sears, *Chancellorsville*, 65; Sears, *Gettysburg*, 35, 146, 190, 250-251, 269, 301.

39. Platt, *This is Holy Ground*, 38; Weeks, *Gettysburg*, 60-61; Martin, Introduction to Vanderslice, *Gettysburg Then and Now*, II.

40. Campbell, "An Interpreter's View of Munshower Field," The Gettysburg *Quarterly*, Spring 2005, 1,3; "Replanting Gettysburg's Historic Orchards," The Gettysburg *Quarterly*, Fall 2004, 1.

41. "Will Sickles Return to Gettysburg?," Gettysburg *Times*, January 16, 1993; "Sickles' descendant would like to see 'Uncle Dan' transferred to Gettysburg," Gettysburg *Times*, January 23, 1993; "National cemetery historic section is closed to Sickles," Gettysburg *Times*, March 12, 1993; "Park: Why Sickles won't be re-buried with his men," Gettysburg *Times*, March 20, 1993; Email from John Shaud to author, August 15, 2008. In addition to the cemetery being closed, the desire to re-bury Sickles with his men was further complicated by the fact that the original semi-circle was intended for those who had fallen in battle.

42. "If he wished it, allow Sickles to return to Gettysburg," Gettysburg *Times*, January 27, 1993; "Sickles should be buried at Gettysburg," Gettysburg *Times*, February 26, 1993.

43. "Gen. Sickles: Gettysburg or Arlington?," Gettysburg *Times*, March 9, 1993.

44. "Local Park officials think not," Gettysburg *Times*, January 16, 1993; Dr. John Latschar to Richard H. Davis, March 8, 1995; "It's Official and Final: Sickles Won't Be Moved," *Civil War News*, February/ March 2007; www.arlingtoncemetery.net/dsickles.htm. Thanks to Richard Davis for providing copies of his personal correspondence and background on Pettigrew v. Pettigrew.

45. Emails from Tim Smith to author, February 10 and 14, 2008; "Bury Sickles at Arlington," New York *Times*, May 6, 1914; "The Sickles Burial Dispute Solved . . . By The General Himself," The Battlefield *Dispatch*, April 1993; "NPS says Gen. Sickles favored Virginia burial," Gettysburg *Times*, April 8, 1993; "Would like Sickles' to be buried here," Gettysburg *Times*, February 13, 2001; "It's Official and Final: Sickles Won't Be Moved," *Civil War News*, February/ March 2007. The author would like to thank Tim Smith, Red Davis, and John Shaud for providing their viewpoints on this episode. Although the Pettigrew case gives preference to the spouse's wishes, it is not definitive, and each case is weighed on its own merits. There is also a heavier burden of proof when someone wants to "undo" something, such as reinterring a corpse. Thanks to Marianne Drummond for providing Legal perspective on Pettigrew v. Pettigrew.

46. Email from Michael Bennett to author, August 10, 2008.

Bibliography

Abbreviations

ACHS   Adams County Historical Society
ALBG   Association of Licensed Battlefield Guides
CCW   Congressional Committee on the Conduct of the War
GNMP   Gettysburg National Military Park
HSP   Historical Society of Pennsylvania
NYHS   New York Historical Society
NYPL   New York Public Library: Astor, Lenox and Tilden Foundations
OR   Official Records
SHSP   Southern Historical Society Papers
USAMHI   United States Army Military History Institute (Carlisle, PA)

Archival Sources

Adams County Historical Society
Gettysburg College Musselman Library Special Collections
Gettysburg National Military Park
Historical Society of Pennsylvania
    George Gordon Meade Collection
Library of Congress, Manuscripts Division
    Daniel E. Sickles Papers
New York Historical Society
    Misc. Mss. Sickles, Daniel
New York Public Library: Astor, Lenox and Tilden Foundations
    Ezra A. Carman Papers, Manuscripts and Archives Division
    Anthony Jerome Griffin Papers, Manuscripts and Archives Division
    William Hobart Royce Papers, Manuscripts and Archives Division
    Daniel Edgar Sickles Papers, Manuscripts and Archives Division
Pennsylvania State Archives (Harrisburg, PA)
    Fiftieth Anniversary of the Battle of Gettysburg Collection
    Gettysburg Scrapbooks (6 Volumes)
United States Army Military History Institute (Carlisle, PA)
    David B. Birney Papers
    Robert L. Brake Collection
    Daniel E. Sickles Papers
University of North Carolina at Chapel Hill, Southern Historical Collection, Wilson Library
    James Longstreet Papers
    Lafayette McLaws Papers

West Virginia University
   Diary of Lewis Schaeffer
Yale Collection of American Literature, Beinecke Rare Book and Manuscript Library
   Journal of Joseph Hopkins Twichell
Yale University Library, Manuscripts and Archives
   Alexander Stewart Webb Papers

Newspapers

Adams County News
The Adams Sentinel and General Advertiser
Army Navy Journal
Atlanta Constitution
Baltimore American
Baltimore Sun
Burlington Weekly Hawkeye
The Chester (PA) *Times*
Civil War News
Colorado Spring Gazette
Detroit Free Press
The Dixon (IL.) *Telegraph*
Evening Times (Cumberland, MD)
Freeborn County Standard (Albert Lea, MN)
Gettysburg Compiler
Gettysburg Star and Sentinel
Gettysburg Times
The Helena (MT) *Independent*
Herald and Torch Light (Hagerstown, MD)
Hornellsville Tribune
The Marion (OH) *Daily Star*
Morning Oregonian (Portland, OR)
The Mountain Democrat (Placerville, CA)
The National Tribune
Newark (OH) *Daily Advocate*
New York *Herald*
New York *Times*
New York *World*
The North American
Philadelphia Weekly Times
The Public Ledger
Raleigh News and Observer
Salem (OH) *Daily News*
Trenton (NJ) *Times*
Waikesha (WI) *Freeman*
Washington Post
Weekly Standard (Raleigh N.C.)
Undated Newspaper Clipping, "Third Corps Re-Union," GNMP Vertical File 4-10K (Coverage of 23rd Anniversary).
   Newspaper Clipping, "After Fifty Years," July 19, 1913, GNMP Vertical File 11-61.
   Newspaper Clipping, "Sickles at Gettysburg"; Gettysburg PA; June 29, 1886, GNMP Vertical File 4-10K (Coverage of Boston Veterans Speech).

Official Documents, Reports, and Government Papers

Annual Reports of the Gettysburg National Military Park Commission 1893-1904, Washington: Government Printing Office, 1905.

Congressional Records
>	51st Congress-1st Session ("Battle Lines at Gettysburg")
>	53rd Congress-2nd Session
>	53rd Congress-3rd Session

Report of the Joint Committee on the Conduct of the War, Washington: Government Printing Office, 1865.

United States Census, for the Years: 1820, 1870, 1880, 1900, 1910.

The War of the Rebellion: A Compilation of the Official Records of the Union and Confederate Armies. Washington: Government Printing Office, 1880-1901.

Campbell, Eric. "An Interpreter's View of Munshower Field." *The Gettysburg Quarterly* (Spring 2005):1,3.

Georg, Kathleen. "The Origins of Gettysburg's Soldiers' National Cemetery & Gettysburg Battlefield Memorial Association." GNMP, May 1982.

———. "The Sherfy Farm and the Battle of Gettysburg." National Park Service Environmental & Interpretive Planning, Research & Curatorial Division, January 1977.

Harrison, Kathleen Georg. "A Fitting and Expressive Memorial: The Development of Gettysburg National Military Park." GNMP, January 1988.

Henry, Robert S. *The Armed Forces Institute of Pathology: Its First Century, 1862-1962.* Washington: Office of the Surgeon General, Department of the Army, 1964.

Lee, Ronald F. *The Origin & Evolution of the National Military Park Idea.* National Park Service, 1973.

National Register of Historic Places Inventory Nomination Form: Central Park, National Park Service.

Paige, John C. and Jerome A. Greene. *Administrative History of Chickamauga and Chattanooga National Military Park.* National Park Service, February 1983.

"Replanting Gettysburg's Historic Orchards." *The Gettysburg Quarterly* (Fall 2004):1-2.

Survey Report for Restoration and Rehabilitation of Historic Structures, Gettysburg National Military Park: Wentz Buildings, January 31, 1957.

The United States vs. Daniel E. Sickles. Circuit Court of the District of Columbia, County of Washington.

Books, Magazines, Maps, and Pamphlets

Acken, J. Gregory, editor. *Inside the Army of the Potomac: The Civil War Experiences of Captain Francis Adams Donaldson.* Mechanicsburg, PA: Stackpole Books, 1998.

Adelman, Gary. *The Myth of Little Round Top.* Gettysburg: Thomas Publications, 2003.

Adelman, Gary E. and Timothy H. Smith. *Devil's Den: A History and Guide.* Gettysburg: Thomas Publications, 1997.

Allan, William. "Memoranda of Conversations with General Robert E. Lee." *Lee the Soldier,* edited by Gary Gallagher, 7-24.

Alexander, Bevin. *Robert E. Lee's Civil War.* Holbrook, MA: Adams Media Cor, 1998.

Alexander, E. Porter. "The Great Charge and Artillery Fighting at Gettysburg." *Battles and Leaders,* 3: 357-368.

———. "Letter From General E. P. Alexander, March 17th, 1877." *Southern Historical Society Papers,* 4: 97-110.

———. *Military Memoirs of a Confederate.* Harrisburg, PA: The Archive Society, 1995. Reprint of the 1907 edition.

Ames, Nelson. *History of Battery G, First Regiment N.Y. Light Artillery.* Wolcott, NY: Benedum Books, 2000. Reprint of the 1900 edition.

Andrews, J. Cutler. *The North Reports the Civil War.* Pittsburgh: University of Pittsburgh Press, 1955.

Arrington, B.T. *The Medal of Honor at Gettysburg.* Gettysburg: Thomas Publications, 1996.

Bachelder, John B. *Position of Troops, Second Day's Battle.* New York: Office of the Chief of Engineers, U.S. Army, 1876.

Basler, Roy, editor. *The Collected Works of Abraham Lincoln.* New Brunswick, NJ: Rutgers University Press, 1953.

Benjamin, Charles F. "Hooker's Appointment and Removal." *Battles and Leaders of the Civil War,* edited by Robert U. Johnson and Clarence C. Buel, 3:239-243.

Biddle, James C. *George Gordon Meade: An Address Delivered by Colonel James C. Biddle at Gen. Meade's Statue, Fairmount Park, Philadelphia on Memorial Day, May 30, 1888.* Philadelphia: 1888.

———. "General Meade at Gettysburg." *The Annals of the War Written by Leading Participants North and South,* Morningside House reprint, 205-219.

Bigelow, John. *The Peach Orchard.* Baltimore: Butternut & Blue, 1984. Reprint of the 1910 edition.

Bohannon, Keith S. "Disgraced and Ruined by the Decision of the Court: The Court-Martial of Emory F. Best, C.S.A." *Chancellorsville: The Battle and Its Aftermath,* edited by Gary Gallagher, 200-218.

Brandt, Nat. *The Congressman Who Got Away With Murder.* New York: Syracuse University Press, 1991.

Brown, Henri Le Favre. *History of the Third Regiment, Excelsior Brigade, 72d New York Volunteer Infantry.* Jamestown, NY: 1902.

Brown, Kent Masterson. *Retreat from Gettysburg: Lee, Logistics, and the Pennsylvania Campaign.* Chapel Hill: The University of North Carolina Press, 2005.

Busey, John W. and David G. Martin. *Regimental Strengths and Losses at Gettysburg.* Hightstown, NJ: Longstreet House, 1994. Reprint of the 1982 edition.

Butterfield, Julia Lorillard, editor. *A Biographical Memorial of General Daniel Butterfield.* New York: The Grafton Press, 1904.

Byrne, Frank L. and Andrew T. Weaver, editors. *Haskell of Gettysburg: His Life and Civil War Papers.* Kent, OH: The Kent State University Press, 1989.

Callihan, David L. "Passing the Test: George G. Meade's Initiation as Army Commander." *Gettysburg Magazine* 30 (January 2004): 30-48.

Campbell, Eric. "'Remember Harper's Ferry': The Degradation, Humiliation, and Redemption of Col. George L. Willard's Brigade." *Gettysburg Magazine* 7 (July 1992); 51-74.

Carter, Robert. *Four Brothers in Blue.* Washington, D.C.: Gibson Bros., 1913.

Cleaves, Freeman. *Meade of Gettysburg.* Norman: University of Oklahoma Press, 1960.

Coco, Gregory A. *A Concise Guide to the Artillery at Gettysburg.* Gettysburg: Thomas Publications, 1998.

———. *A Strange and Blighted Land.* Gettysburg: Thomas Publications, 1995.

———. *A Vast Sea of Misery.* Gettysburg: Thomas Publications, 1988.

———. *On the Bloodstained Field: 130 Human Interest Stories of the Campaign and Battle of Gettysburg.* Gettysburg: Thomas Publications, 1987.

Coddington, Edwin B. *The Gettysburg Campaign: A Study in Command.* Dayton: Morningside Bookshop, 1979.

Cohen, Stan. *Hands Across the Wall.* Missoula, MT: Pictorial Histories Publishing Co., 1982.

Cole, James M. and Roy Frampton. *Lincoln and the Human Interest Stories of the Gettysburg National Cemetery.* Hanover, PA: The Sheridan Press, 1995.

Collins, John L. "When Stonewall Jackson Turned Our Right." *Battles and Leaders of the Civil War,* edited by Robert U. Johnson and Clarence C. Buel, 3:183-186.

Conklin, Eileen F. *Women at Gettysburg.* Gettysburg: Thomas Publications, 1993.

Connelly, Thomas L. *The Marble Man: Robert E. Lee and His Image in American Society.* Baton Rouge: Louisiana State University Press, 1978.

Cooksey, Paul Clark. "Up The Emmitsburg Road: Gen. Robert E. Lee's Plan for the Attack on July 2nd on the Union Left Flank." *Gettysburg Magazine* 26 (January 2002): 45-52.

————. "Around the Flank: Longstreet's July 2 Attack at Gettysburg." *Gettysburg Magazine* 29 (July 2003): 94-105.

Couch, Darius N. "The Chancellorsville Campaign." *Battles and Leaders of the Civil War*, edited by Robert U. Johnson and Clarence C. Buel, 3:154-171.

Coughenour, Kavin. "Assessing the Generalship of George G. Meade During the Gettysburg Campaign." *Gettysburg Magazine* 28 (January 2003): 27-39.

Craft, David. *History of the 141st Regiment Pennsylvania Volunteers.* Salem, MA: Higginson Book Co, 1998. Reprint of the 1885 edition.

Cutrer, Thomas W., editor. *Longstreet's Aide: The Civil War Letters of Major Thomas J. Goree.* Charlottesville: University Press of Virginia, 1995.

Dalessandro, Paul and Scott Hartwig. "Was Dan Sickles the Savior of the Union Left on July 2?" *North & South*, Vol.8, Number 4 (June 2005): 52-60.

Davis, Oliver Wilson. *Life of David Bell Birney: Major-General United States Volunteers.* Gaithersburg MD: Ron R. Van Sickle Military Books, 1987. Reprint of the 1867 edition.

Desjardin, Thomas. *Stand Firm Ye Boys From Maine: The 20th Maine and the Gettysburg Campaign.* Gettysburg: Thomas Publications, 1995.

————. *These Honored Dead: How the Story of Gettysburg Shaped American Memory.* Cambridge: Da Capo Press, 2003.

De Peyster, John Watts. *Gen. H. Edwin Tremain, President Third Army Corps Union.* New York: C.G. Burgoyne, 1880.

De Trobriand, Regis. *Four Years with the Army of the Potomac.* Gaithersburg, MD: Ron R. Van Sickle Military Books, 1988. Reprint of the 1889 edition.

DiNardo, R.L. and Albert Nofi, editors. *James Longstreet: The Man, the Soldier, the Controversy.* Conshohocken, PA: Combined Publishing, 1998.

Dodge, Theodore Ayrault. *The Campaign of Chancellorsville.* New York: Da Capo Press, 1999. Reprint of the 1886 edition.

Doster, William E. *Lincoln and Episodes of the Civil War.* New York: G.Putnam's Sons, 1915.

Downs, David B. "'His Left Was Worth a Glance': Meade and the Union Left on July 2, 1863." *Gettysburg Magazine* 7 (July 1992): 29-40.

Doubleday, Abner. *Chancellorsville and Gettysburg.* Stamford, CT: Longmeadow Press, 1996. Reprint of the 1882 edition.

Early, Jubal. "Reply To General Longstreet." *Southern Historical Society Papers*, 4: 282-302.

Fasnacht, C.H. and E.K. Martin. *Historical Sketch and Oration Delivered at Dedication of 99th Pennsylvania Monument.* Lancaster, PA: Examiner Steam Book and Job Print, 1886.

Favill, Josiah Marshall. *Diary of a Young Army Officer.* Baltimore: Butternut & Blue, 2000. Reprint of the 1909 edition.

Fleming, Thomas J. "A Husband's Revenge." *American Heritage* (April 1967): 65-75.

Fletcher, William A. *Rebel Private: Front and Rear.* New York: Meridian, 1997. Reprint of the 1908 edition.

Frassanito, William A. *Early Photography at Gettysburg.* Gettysburg: Thomas Publications, 1995.

Freeman, Douglas Southall. *Lee's Lieutenants.* New York: Charles Scribner's Sons, 1944.

Fremantle, Arthur J.L. *Three Months in the Southern States.* Lincoln, NE: University of Nebraska Press, 1991. Reprint of the 1864 edition.

Furgurson, Ernest B. "The 4 Fatal Actions of Stonewall Jackson." *America's Civil War* (May 2008): 26-33.

Gallagher, Gary, editor. *Chancellorsville: The Battle and Its Aftermath.* Chapel Hill: The University of North Carolina Press, 1996.

————. *Lee: The Soldier.* Lincoln: University of Nebraska Press, 1996.

————. *The First Day at Gettysburg: Essays on Confederate and Union Leadership.* Kent, OH: The Kent State University Press, 1992.

————. *The Second Day at Gettysburg: Essays on Confederate and Union Leadership.* Kent, OH: The Kent State University Press, 1993.

Gibbon, John. *An Address on the Unveiling of the Statue of Major-General George G. Meade in Philadelphia, October 18th, 1887.* Philadelphia: Allen, Lane, & Scott's Printing House, 1887.

Goodwin, Doris Kearns. *Team of Rivals: The Political Genius of Abraham Lincoln.* New York: Simon & Schuster, 2005.

Gottfried, Bradley M. *Brigades of Gettysburg.* Cambridge: Da Capo Press, 2002.

Graham, W.A. *The Custer Myth.* Mechanicsburg, PA: Stackpole Books, 1995. Reprint of the 1953 edition.

Greene, A. Wilson. "From Chancellorsville to Cemetery Hill: O.O. Howard and Eleventh Corps Leadership." *The First Day at Gettysburg: Essays on Confederate and Union Leadership*, edited by Gary W. Gallagher, 57-91.

Grimsley, Mark and Brooks D. Simpson. *Gettysburg: A Battlefield Guide.* Lincoln, Nebraska: University of Nebraska Press, 1999.

Hancock, Almira. *Reminiscences of Winfield Scott Hancock.* Gaithersburg, MD: Olde Soldier Books. Reprint of the 1887 edition.

Happel, Ralph. *The Last Days of Stonewall Jackson.* Fort Washington, PA: Eastern National, 2003. Reprint of the 1976 edition.

Harman, Troy D. *Cemetery Hill: The General Plan Was Unchanged.* Baltimore: Butternut & Blue, 2001.

Harrison, Kathleen Georg. *The Location of the Monuments, Markers, and Tablets on Gettysburg Battlefield.* Gettysburg National Military Park.

Hartwig, D. Scott. " 'No Troops on the Field Had Done Better': John C. Caldwell's Division in the Wheatfield, July 2, 1863." *The Second Day at Gettysburg*, edited by Gary Gallagher, 136-171.

Hawthorne, Frederick. *Gettysburg: Stories of Men and Monuments.* Gettysburg: Association of Licensed Battlefield Guides, 1988.

Haynes, Martin A. *A History of the Second Regiment, New Hampshire Volunteer Infantry in the War of the Rebellion.* Salem, Mass: Higginson Book Company, 1998. Reprint of the 1896 edition.

Hempel, Kathrine. "Gone and Nearly Forgotten: David McConaughy, The Man Behind the Soldiers' National Cemetery and the Gettysburg National Military Park." *Gettysburg Magazine* 34 (January 2006): 86-97.

Hessler, Jim and Jack Drummond. "Sickles Returns." *Gettysburg Magazine* 34 (January 2006): 64-85.

Hill, Patrick, Perry Tholl and Greg Johnson. "'On This Spot . . .' Locating the 1st Minnesota Monument at Gettysburg." *Gettysburg Magazine* 32 (January 2005): 96-114.

Hood, John B. "Letter From General John B. Hood." *Southern Historical Society Papers*, 4:145-150.

Howard, Oliver O. "The Eleventh Corps at Chancellorsville." *Battles and Leaders of the Civil War*, edited by Robert U. Johnson and Clarence C. Buel, 3:189-202.

Humphreys, Henry H. *Andrew Atkinson Humphreys: A Biography.* Gaithersburg, MD: Ron R. Van Sickle Military Books, 1988. Reprint of the 1924 edition.

Huntington, James. "The Artillery at Hazel Grove." *Battles and Leaders of the Civil War*, edited by Robert U. Johnson and Clarence C. Buel, 3:188.

Hyde, Bill, editor. *The Union Generals Speak: The Meade Hearings on the Battle of Gettysburg.* Baton Rouge: Louisiana State University Press, 2003.

————. "Did You Get There? Capt. Samuel Johnston's Reconnaissance at Gettysburg." *Gettysburg Magazine* 29 (July 2003): 86-93

Imhof, John D. *Gettysburg Day Two: A Study in Maps.* Baltimore: Butternut & Blue, 1999.

Johnson, Robert U., and Clarence C. Buel, editors. *Battles and Leaders of the Civil War.* Harrisburg: Archive Society, 1991. Reprint of the 1887-1888 edition.

Johnson, Rossiter. *Campfire and Battlefield.* Slovenia: Trident Press International, 1999. Reprint of the 1894 edition.

Jones, J. William. *Life and Letters of Robert E. Lee.* Harrisonburg, VA: Sprinkle Publications, 1978. Reprint of the 1906 edition.

Jordan, David M. *Winfield Scott Hancock: A Soldier's Life.* Indianapolis: Indiana University Press, 1988.

Jorgensen, Jay. *Gettysburg's Bloody Wheatfield.* Shippensburg: White Mane Books, 2002.

———. "John Haley's Personal Recollections of the Battle of the Wheatfield." *Gettysburg Magazine* 27 (July 2002): 65-77

———. *The Wheatfield at Gettysburg: A Walking Tour.* Gettysburg: Thomas Publications, 2002.

Kaplan, Justin. *Mr. Clemens and Mark Twain.* New York: Simon and Schuster, 1966.

Keneally, Thomas. *American Scoundrel: The Life of the Notorious Civil War General Dan Sickles.* New York: Nan A. Talese, 2002.

Klein, Philip S. *President James Buchanan: A Biography.* University Park, PA: Pennsylvania State University Press, 1962.

Knoop, Jeanne W. I *Follow the Course, Come What May: Major General Dan Sickles, USA.* New York: Vantage Press, 1998.

Krick, Robert K. " 'If Longstreet . . . Says So, It Is Most Likely Not True': James Longstreet and the Second Day at Gettysburg." *The Second Day at Gettysburg,* edited by Gary Gallagher, 57-86.

———. "Lee at Chancellorsville." *Lee: The Soldier,* edited by Gary Gallagher, 357-380.

———. "The Smoothbore Volley That Doomed the Confederacy." *Chancellorsville: The Battle and Its Aftermath,* edited by Gary Gallagher, 107-142.

Ladd, David and Audrey, editors. *The Bachelder Papers: Gettysburg in their Own Words.* Dayton, OH: Morningside House, 1994.

———. *John Bachelder's History of the Battle of Gettysburg.* Dayton, OH: Morningside House, 1997.

Lash, Gary. "The Congressional Resolution of Thanks for the Federal Victory at Gettysburg." *Gettysburg Magazine* 12 (January 1995): 85-96.

Lee, Fitzhugh. "Letter from General Fitzhugh Lee, March 5, 1877," *SHSP,* 4:69-76.

The Life and Death of Fanny White: Being a Complete and Interesting History of the Career of That Notorious Lady. New York: 1860.

Lincoln and Sickles. The Third Army Corps Union, 1910.

Longstreet, Helen D. *Lee and Longstreet at High Tide.* Gainesville: 1905.

Longstreet, James. *From Manassas to Appomattox.* Cambridge, MA: Da Capo Press, 1992. Reprint of the 1895 edition.

———. "The Battle of Fredericksburg." *Battles and Leaders of the Civil War,* edited by Robert U. Johnson and Clarence C. Buel, 3:70-85.

———. "Lee's Invasion of Pennsylvania." *Battles and Leaders of the Civil War,* edited by Robert U. Johnson and Clarence C. Buel, 3:244-251.

———. "Lee's Right Wing at Gettysburg." *Battles and Leaders of the Civil War,* edited by Robert U. Johnson and Clarence C. Buel, 3:339-354.

———. "General James Longstreet's Account Of The Campaign And Battle." *SHSP,* 5: 54-86.

———. "General Longstreet's Second Paper On Gettysburg." *SHSP,* 5: 257-269.

Lossing, Benson J. *Pictorial History of the Civil War in the United States of America.* Hartford: T. Belknap, 1868.

Marcot, Roy. "Berdan Sharpshooters at Gettysburg." *Gettysburg Magazine* 1 (January 1989): 35-40.

Meade, George. *The Life and Letters of George Gordon Meade.* New York: Charles Scribner's Sons, 1913.

The Medical and Surgical History of the Civil War. Wilmington, North Carolina: Broadfoot Publishing Company, 1990. Reprint of the 1870 edition.

McLaws, Lafayette. "Gettysburg." *SHSP,* 7: 64-90.

McPherson, James M. *Battle Cry of Freedom.* New York: Ballantine Books, 1988.

Messent, Peter and Steve Courtney, editors. *The Civil War Letters of Joseph Hopkins Twichell: A Chaplain's Story*. Athens, GA: The University of Georgia Press, 2006.

Miller, Francis Trevelyan, editor. *Photographic History of the Civil War*. New York: The Review of Reviews Co., 1911.

Moe, Richard. *The Last Full Measure: The Life and Death of the First Minnesota Volunteers*. New York: Avon Books, 1993.

Murray, R.L. *E. P. Alexander and the Artillery Action in the Peach Orchard*. Wolcott, NY: Benedum Books, 2000.

———. *Letters from Gettysburg: New York Soldiers' Correspondences from the Battlefield*. Wolcott, NY: Benedum Books, 2000.

New York Monuments Commission for the Battlefields of Gettysburg and Chattanooga. *Final Report on the Battle of Gettysburg*. Albany, NY: J.B. Lyon Company, 1902.

New York Monuments Commission for the Battlefields of Gettysburg, Chattanooga, and Antietam. *Dedication of the New York Auxiliary State Monument on the Battlefield of Gettysburg*. Albany, NY: J.B. Lyon Company, 1926.

Nicholson, John, editor. *Pennsylvania at Gettysburg*. Harrisburg: W.M Stanley Ray, 1904.

Norton, Oliver Wilcox. *The Attack and Defense of Little Round Top*. Gettysburg: Stan Clark Military Books, 1992. Reprint of the 1913 edition.

Oates, Christopher Ryan. "Excelsior!" *America's Civil War* (March 2008): 39-47.

O'Connor, Richard. *Sheridan: The Inevitable*. New York: Smithmark Publishers, 1995. Reprint of the 1953 edition.

Oeffinger, John C., editor. *A Soldier's General: The Civil War Letters of Major General Lafayette McLaws*. Chapel Hill: The University of North Carolina Press, 2002.

Parker, John L. *History of the Twenty-Second Massachusetts Infantry, the Second Company Sharpshooters, and the Third Light Battery in the War of the Rebellion*. Boston: 1887.

Peatman, Jared. "General Sickles, President Lincoln, and the Aftermath of the Battle of Gettysburg." *Gettysburg Magazine* 28 (January 2003): 117-123.

Petruzzi, J. David. "John Buford at Gettysburg: A Study in Maps." *America's Civil War* (July 2008): 33-37.

Pfanz, Harry W. *Gettysburg: Culp's Hill and Cemetery Hill*. Chapel Hill: The University of North Carolina Press, 1993.

———. *Gettysburg: The First Day*. Chapel Hill: The University of North Carolina Press, 2001.

———. *Gettysburg: The Second Day*. Chapel Hill: The University of North Carolina Press, 1987.

Pinchon, Edgcumb. *Dan Sickles: Hero of Gettysburg and 'Yankee King of Spain'*. Garden City, NY: Doubleday, Doran and Company, 1945.

Piston, William Garrett. *Lee's Tarnished Lieutenant: James Longstreet and His Place in Southern History*. Athens, GA: University of Georgia Press, 1987.

Platt, Barbara. *This is Holy Ground: A History of the Gettysburg Battlefield*. Self Published, 2001.

Pleasonton, Alfred. "The Successes and Failures of Chancellorsville." *Battles and Leaders of the Civil War*, edited by Robert U. Johnson and Clarence C. Buel, 3:172-182.

Powell, David. "Advance to Disaster: Sickles, Longstreet, and July 2nd, 1863." *Gettysburg Magazine* 28 (January 2003): 40-48.

Rable, George C. *Fredericksburg! Fredericksburg!* Chapel Hill: The University of North Carolina Press, 2002.

Racine, Philip N., editor. *"Unspoiled Heart": The Journal of Charles Mattocks of the 17th Maine*. Knoxville: University of Tennessee Press, 1994.

Rafferty, Thomas. "Gettysburg." *Personal Recollections of the War of the Rebellion*, edited by James Grant Wilson and Titus Munson Coan, 1: 1-32.

Raver, K. Paul. "An Investigation Into the Route Taken from Rock Creek to Little Round Top by the Third Brigade, First Division, Fifth Corps on July 2, 1863." *Gettysburg Magazine* 27 (July 2002): 52-64.

————. "Deception and the Citizen-General: The Sickles Faction at Gettysburg." *Gettysburg Magazine* 31 (July 2004): 59-78.

Reardon, Carol. "From 'King of Spades' to 'First Captain of the Confederacy': R. E. Lee's First Six Weeks with the Army of Northern Virginia." *Lee: The Soldier*, edited by Gary Gallagher, 309-330.

————. *Pickett's Charge in History and Memory.* Chapel Hill: The University of North Carolina Press, 1997.

————. "The Valiant Rearguard: Hancock's Division at Chancellorsville." *Chancellorsville: The Battle and Its Aftermath*, edited by Gary Gallagher, 143-175.

Robertson William Glenn. "The Peach Orchard Revisited: Daniel E. Sickles and the Third Corps on July 2, 1863." *The Second Day at Gettysburg*, edited by Gary Gallagher, 33-56.

Rollins, Richard. "George Gordon Meade and the Defense of Cemetery Ridge." *Gettysburg Magazine* 19 (July 1998): 57-83.

Sauers, Richard. *Gettysburg: The Meade-Sickles Controversy.* Dulles, VA: Brassey's, 2003.

Sawyer, Gordon. *James Longstreet: Before Manassas & After Appomattox.* Gainesville: Sawyer House Publishing, 2005.

Scott, Kate M. *History of the One Hundred and Fifth Regiment of Pennsylvania Volunteers.* Baltimore: Butternut and Blue, 1993. Reprint of the 1877 edition.

Sears, Stephen W. *Chancellorsville.* New York: Houghton Mifflin Company, 1996.

————. *Gettysburg.* New York: Houghton Mifflin Company, 2003.

Shaara, Michael. *The Killer Angels.* New York: Ballantine Books edition, 1974.

Sickles, Daniel E. "Further Recollections of Gettysburg." *North American Review* (March 1891): 257-271.

————. "Leaves From My Diary." Reprinted from the *Journal of the Military Service Institution of the United States* (Vol. 6, No. 22 -23): 1-30. New York Public Library, Astor, Lenox and Tilden Foundations.

————. *Oration Delivered by Maj-Gen. D.E. Sickles, USA Before the Society of the Army of the Potomac at Fredericksburg, VA, May 25, 1900.* Society of the Army of the Potomac: 1900.

Smith, James E. *A Famous Battery and Its Campaigns, 1861-'64.* Wolcott, NY: Benedum Books, 1999. Reprint of the 1892 edition.

Sorrel, Moxley. *At the Right Hand of Longstreet.* Lincoln: University of Nebraska Press, 1999. Reprint of the 1905 edition, *Recollections of a Confederate Staff Officer.*

Stackpole, Edward J. *The Fredericksburg Campaign.* Mechanicsburg, PA: Stackpole Books, 1991. Reprint of the 1957 edition.

Stevenson, Jas. *History of the Excelsior or Sickles' Brigade.* Paterson, NJ: Van Der Hoven & Holms, 1863.

Strong, George Templeton. *Diary of the Civil War.* Edited by Allan Nevins. New York: The Macmillan Company, 1952.

Styple, William B., editor. *Generals in Bronze: Interviewing the Commanders of the Civil War.* Kearny, NJ: Belle Grove Publishing Co., 2005.

————. *Our Noble Blood: The Civil War Letters of Major-General Regis de Trobriand.* Translated by Nathalie Chartrain. Kearny, NJ: Belle Grove Publishing Co., 1997.

Swanberg, W.A. *Sickles the Incredible.* Gettysburg: Stan Clark Military Books, 1991. Reprint of the 1956 edition.

Swinton, William. *Campaigns of the Army of the Potomac.* Secaucus, NJ: The Blue & Grey Press, 1988. Reprint of the 1866 edition.

Tagg, Larry. *The Generals of Gettysburg.* Cambridge, MA: Da Capo Press, 2003.

Tap, Bruce. *Over Lincoln's Shoulder: The Committee on the Conduct of the War.* Lawrence: University Press of Kansas, 1998.

Taylor, Walter H. "Second Paper By Colonel Walter H. Taylor, Of General Lee's Staff." *SHSP*, 4: 124-139.

Toombs, Samuel. *New Jersey Troops in the Gettysburg Campaign.* Orange, NJ: The Evening Mail Publishing House, 1888.

Tremain, Henry Edward. *Two Days of War—A Gettysburg Narrative and Other Excursions.* New York: Bonnell, Silver, and Bowers, 1905.

Trimble, Tony L. "Agate: Whitelaw Reid Reports From Gettysburg." *Gettysburg Magazine* 7 (July 1992): 23-28.

Trudeau, Noah Andre. *Gettysburg: A Testing of Courage.* New York: HarperCollins, 2002.

Tucker, Glenn. *High Tide at Gettysburg.* Gettysburg: Stan Clark Military Books, 1995. Reprint of the 1958 edition.

Twain, Mark. *Mark Twain's Autobiography.* New York: Harper and Brothers, 1924.

United States Christian Commission. *Second Report of the Committee of Maryland.* Baltimore: Sherwood & Co, 1863.

Van Alstyne, Lawrence. *Diary of an Enlisted Man.* New Haven: Tuttle, Morehouse, & Taylor, 1910.

Vanderslice, John M. *Gettysburg: Then and Now.* Dayton: Morningside House, 1983. Reprint of the 1899 edition.

Warner, Ezra J. *Generals in Blue: Lives of the Union Commanders.* Baton Rouge: Louisiana State University Press, 1964.

Weeks, Jim. *Gettysburg: Memory, Market, and an American Shrine.* Princeton, NJ: Princeton University Press, 2003.

Wert, J. Howard. *A Complete Hand-Book of the Monuments and Indications and Guide to the Positions on the Gettysburg Battle-Field.* Harrisburg, PA: R.M. Sturgeon & Co, 1886.

Wert, Jeffry D. *General James Longstreet: The Confederacy's Most Controversial Soldier.* New York: Simon & Schuster, 1993.

———. *Gettysburg: Day Three.* New York: Simon & Schuster, 2001.

Wilcox, Cadmus M. "General C.M. Wilcox on the Battle of Gettysburg." *SHSP*, 6: 97-124.

Williams, T. Harry. *Lincoln and His Generals.* New York: Grosset & Dunlap, 1952.

Wilson, James Grant and Titus Munson, editors. *Personal Recollections of the War of the Rebellion.* Wilmington, NC: Broadfoot Publishing, 1992. Reprint of the 1891 edition.

Winschel, Terrence J. "Their Supreme Moment: Barksdale's Brigade at Gettysburg." *Gettysburg Magazine* 1 (July 1989): 70-77.

Wittenberg, Eric J. "The Truth About the Withdrawal of Brig. Gen. John Buford's Cavalry, July 2, 1863." *Gettysburg Magazine* 37 (July 2007): 71-82.

Woods, James A. "Humphreys' Division's Flank March to Little Round Top," *Gettysburg Magazine* 6 (January 1992): 59-61.

Woodward, C. Vann, editor. *Mary Chesnut's Civil War.* New Haven: Yale University Press, 1981.

Yarrow, Henry Crecy. "Personal Recollections of Old Medical Officers." *Military Surgeon* 60 (1927): 73-76, 171-75, 449-55, 588-93.

Electronic Sources: Internet

www.douglassarchives.org/ever_b21.tm (Edward Everett speech)

www.arlingtoncemetery.net/dsickles.htm (Burial information)

www.medalofhonor.com. (Congressional Medal of Honor information)

www.nps.gov/chch/adhi/adhi.htm (Administrative History of Chickamauga and Chattanooga National Military Park)

www.nps.gov/frsp/fredhist.htm (Fredericksburg information)

www.nps.gov/history/history/online_books/history_military/ (Lee's Origin & Evolution of the National Military Park)

www.whitehouse.gov (Historical information on Presidential elections)

Index

Adams, Capt. Charles Francis, 44, 69, 73

Alabama Military Units; 8th Infantry, 125; 10th Infantry, 125; 11th Infantry, 125; 15th Infantry, 172, 174; 44th Infantry, 167

Alexander, Col. Edward Porter, 60, 62, 139, 152-153, 156-159, 163, 181, 193, 217, 222-223, 232, 234, 318, 341, 393, 428(n)

American Express Company, the, 41

American Protective Association, the, 410(n)

American Scoundrel, 210, 400

Ames, Capt. Nelson, 154, 157-158, 183, 434(n)

Anderson, Gen. George T., 177, 180, 183, 185-186, 188, 191, 194, 221, 433(n)

Anderson, Gen. Richard H., 125, 142, 147, 163, 202, 213, 220-222, 389, 436(n)

Andersonville, GA, 335

Angle, the, 336

Annals of the War, 244

Antietam, battle of, 32-33, 152, 333, 335

Archer, Gen. James, 60

Arlington National Cemetery, 383-386, 403-405, *photo*, 386

Army Medical Museum, the, 224-225, 315-316

Army of Northern Virginia, the, 33, 49, 72, 77, 240, 242, 254, 269

Army of Northern Virginia Military Units; First Corps, 49, 72, 122-123, 128, 232; Second Corps, 60-61, 72, 88; Third Corps, 72, 213, 234;

Army of the James, the, 248

Army of the Potomac, the, 21, 40, 42-44, 55, 65, 68, 72-74, 82-83, 120, 145, 152, 220, 234, 239-241, 247, 249- 250, 253, 255, 257, 261, 268-269, 272, 276, 289-291, 296, 301, 303, 305-306, 340, 355-356, 360, 398, 400, 405, 418(n), 443(n)

Army of the Potomac Military Units; 4th United States Artillery, 430(n); 5th United States Artillery, 173, 183, 197; First Corps, 33, 38, 44, 59, 76, 78, 80-81, 85-87, 92-94, 104, 221, 233, 242, 268, 277, 281, 289, 296, 323, 437(n), 439(n); Second Corps, 46, 78-79, 84, 86, 88, 97, 105, 146-147, 158, 168, 174, 201-202, 216, 249, 266, 277, 283, 288-289, 303-304, 317, 325, 336, 342, 362, 394, 398, 440(n); at Chancellorsville, 50, 52, 58, 62; Hancock takes command, 69, 78; Cemetery Ridge position, 107-110, 117, 146, 254; Caldwell's division, 130-131, 188-189; consolidated with Third Corps, 296-297; Third Corps, 46-47, 74, 76,